A Companion to the Horror Film

A Companion to the Horror Film

Edited by

Harry M. Benshoff

WILEY Blackwell

Registered Office
John Wiley & Sons Ltd, The Atrium, Southern Gate, Chichester, West Sussex, PO19 8SQ, UK

Editorial Offices
350 Main Street, Malden, MA 02148-5020, USA
9600 Garsington Road, Oxford, OX4 2DQ, UK
The Atrium, Southern Gate, Chichester, West Sussex, PO19 8SQ, UK

For details of our global editorial offices, for customer services, and for information about how to apply for permission to reuse the copyright material in this book please see our website at www.wiley.com/wiley-blackwell.

Library of Congress Cataloging-in-Publication Data
A companion to the horror film / edited by Harry M. Benshoff.
    pages cm
  Includes bibliographical references and index.
  ISBN 978-0-470-67260-0 (cloth) ISBN 978-1-119-33501-6 (paper)
  1. Horror films—History and criticism. I. Benshoff, Harry M., editor of compilation.
  PN1995.9.H6C65 2014
  791.43′6164—dc23

                                                                2014007067

A catalogue record for this book is available from the British Library.

Cover image: *Evil Dead*, 2013, directed by Fede Alvarez. Filmdistrict / The Kobal Collection

Typeset in 10.5/13pt, MinionPro by SPi Global, Chennai, India.

Printed in Singapore by C.O.S. Printers Pte Ltd

10 9 8 7 6 5 4 3 2 1

Contents

Notes on Contributors

Harry M. Benshoff is Professor of Media Arts at the University of North Texas, USA. He is the author of several books on cinema, including *Monsters in the Closet: Homosexuality and the Horror Film* (1997) and co-author of *Queer Images: A History of Gay and Lesbian Film in America* (2006), and *America on Film: Representing Race, Class, Gender, and Sexuality at the Movies, Second edition* (Wiley Blackwell, 2009).

John Edgar Browning is a Marion L. Brittain Postdoctoral Fellow in the Writing and Communication Program at the Georgia Institute of Technology. He is a Ph.D. from the Department of Transnational Studies at the University at Buffalo (SUNY), where he was an Arthur A. Schomburg Fellow in the American Studies Program. Browning has contracted, co-/edited, or co-/written 12 academic and popular trade books and 40 articles, book chapters, and reviews on subjects that cluster around Cultural Studies, horror, the un-dead, Bram Stoker, and the Gothic. His books include *Speaking of Monsters: A Teratological Anthology*, with Caroline J. S. Picart (Palgrave Macmillan, 2012), *The Forgotten Writings of Bram Stoker* (Palgrave Macmillan, 2012), and two forthcoming volumes, *The Palgrave Literary Dictionary of Bram Stoker* and a book on Dracula for Cornell University Press.

Chris Dumas is the author of *Un-American Psycho: Brian De Palma and the Political Invisible*. His work has appeared in *Critical Inquiry*, *Cinema Journal*, and *Camera Obscura*.

Steffen Hantke is author of *Conspiracy and Paranoia in Contemporary Literature* (1994) and editor of *Caligari's Heirs: The German Cinema of Fear after 1945* (2007) and *American Horror Film: The Genre at the Turn of the Millennium* (2010). He teaches at Sogang University in Seoul.

Adam Charles Hart received his PhD from the University of Chicago, where his dissertation was titled *A Cinema of Wounded Bodies: Spectacular Abjection and the Spaces of Modern Horror.*

Joan Hawkins is an Associate Professor in the Department of Communication and Culture at Indiana University Bloomington. She is the author of *Cutting Edge: Art-Horror and the Horrific Avant-garde* (2000; University of Minnesota Press) and numerous articles on horror, experimental, and independent cinema.

Kevin Heffernan is Associate Professor in the Division of Film and Media Arts at Southern Methodist University. He is currently writing a book on contemporary East Asian cinema tentatively titled *A Wind From the East* and another book tentatively titled *Porn in the USA: Hidden Empires of American Popular Culture.*

Matt Hills is Professor of Film and TV studies at Aberystwyth University. He is the author of five books, including *Fan Cultures* (Routledge 2002), *The Pleasures of Horror* (Continuum 2005), and *Triumph of a Time Lord* (IB Tauris 2010). He is also the editor of *New Dimensions of Doctor Who* (IB Tauris, 2013). Matt has published widely on cult media and fandom, and his recent horror-related work includes contributions to the edited volumes *Horror Zone* (2010), and *Horror After 9/11* (2012).

Dale Hudson teaches at New York University Abu Dhabi, specializing in transnational and postcolonial frameworks for understanding contemporary media. His work has appeared in *Afterimage*, *American Studies*, *Cinema Journal*, *French Cultural Studies*, *Screen*, and other journals and anthologies. With Patricia R. Zimmermann, he is coauthor of *Thinking through Digital Media: Transnational Environments and Locative Places* (Palgrave, forthcoming in 2015).

Daniel Humphrey is Associate Professor of Film Studies and Women's and Gender Studies at Texas A&M University. He is the author of the book *Queer Bergman: Sexuality, Gender, and the European Art Cinema* and articles published in *Screen*, *GLQ*, *Post Script*, and *Criticism*.

I.Q. Hunter is Professor of Film Studies at De Montfort University, Leicester. His publications include *British Trash Cinema* (BFI/Palgrave, 2013) and *Cult Film as a Guide to Life: Fandom, Adaptation and Identity* (Bloomsbury, 2016).

Peter Hutchings is Professor of Film Studies at Northumbria University. He is the author of *Hammer and Beyond: The British Horror Film*, *Terence Fisher*, *The British Film Guide to Dracula*, *The Horror Film*, and *The Historical Dictionary of Horror Cinema*.

Mark Jancovich is Professor of Film and Television Studies at the University of East Anglia, UK. His books include *Rational Fears: American Horror in the 1950s* (MUP, 1996) and *Horror, The Film Reader* (Routledge, 2001). He is currently writing a history of horror in the 1940s.

James Kendrick is an associate professor of Film & Digital Media at Baylor University. He is the author of *Darkness in the Bliss-Out: A Reconsideration of the Films of Steven Spielberg, Hollywood Bloodshed: Screen Violence and 1980s American Cinema*, and *Film Violence: History, Ideology, Genre*. He is also the film and video critic for the website Qnetwork.com.

Adam Lowenstein is Associate Professor of English and Film Studies at the University of Pittsburgh, where he also directs the Film Studies Program. He is the author of *Shocking Representation: Historical Trauma, National Cinema, and the Modern Horror Film* (Columbia University Press, 2005) and *Dreaming of Cinema: Spectatorship, Surrealism, and the Age of Digital Media* (Columbia University Press, 2015).

Daniel Martin is Assistant Professor of Film Studies in the Department of Humanities and Social Sciences at the Korea Advanced Institute of Science and Technology (KAIST) and Honorary Researcher in the Institute of Contemporary Arts at Lancaster University. He is the co-editor of *Korean Horror Cinema* (Edinburgh University Press, 2013).

Jay McRoy is Associate Professor of English and Cinema Studies at the University of Wisconsin — Parkside. He is the author of *Nightmare Japan: Contemporary Japanese Horror Cinema* (Rodopi, 2008), the editor of *Japanese Horror Cinema* (Edinburgh University Press, 2005), and the co-editor, with Richard Hand, of *Monstrous Adaptations: Generic and Thematic Mutations in Horror Cinema* (Manchester University Press, 2007).

Xavier Mendik is Director of the Cine-Excess International Film Festival and DVD label at Brighton University. He has written extensively on cult and horror traditions, and his publications include the books *Peep Shows: Cult Film and the Cine-Erotic* (2012), *100 Cult Films* (with Ernest Mathijs, 2011), *The Cult Film Reader* (2008), *Alternative Europe: Eurotrash and Exploitation Cinema Since 1945* (2004), *Underground USA: Filmmaking Beyond the Hollywood Canon* (2002), *Shocking Cinema of the Seventies* (2002) and *Dario Argento's Tenebrae* (2000). Beyond his academic writing, Xavier Mendik also has an established profile as a documentary filmmaker and is currently developing a feature film remake of *The House on the Edge of the Park* with director Ruggero Deodato.

Andrew Hock Soon Ng is Senior Lecturer in Literary Studies at Monash University Malaysia. He is the author of *Dimensions of Monstrosity in Contemporary Narratives* (2004), *Interrogating Interstices* (2008) and *Intimating the Sacred* (2011).

Ian Olney is an Associate Professor of English at York College of Pennsylvania, where he teaches film studies. He is the author of *Euro Horror*: *Classic European Horror Cinema in Contemporary American Culture* (Indiana University Press, 2013), as well as several articles on European cinema and the horror film.

Julian Petley is the co-editor (with Steve Chibnall) of *British Horror Cinema*, and the author of *Censorship*: *a Beginner's Guide*, and *Film and Video Censorship in Modern Britain*. He is the chair of the Campaign for Press and Broadcasting Freedom, a member of the advisory board of Index on Censorship, and of the editorial board of *Porn Studies*. He is Professor of Screen Media at Brunel University.

Caroline Joan "Kay" S. Picart is a scholar and attorney at law practicing in federal and state appellate criminal law, and publishes peer-reviewed journal articles and books principally on law, criminology, sociology and film. A former tenured professor, she has authored 18 books and numerous articles and book chapters nationally and internationally, and is the Series Editor of the Fairleigh Dickinson University Press Series on Law, Culture and the Humanities. Her books on film include: *Cinematic Rebirths of Frankenstein*; *Remaking the Frankenstein Myth on Film: Between Laughter and Horror*; with David Frank, *Frames of Evil: Holocaust as Horror in American Film*; with Cecil Greek, *Monsters In and Among Us: Towards a Gothic Criminology*; with John Browning, *Speaking of Monsters* and *Dracula in Visual Media*; and with Michael Hviid Jacobsen and Cecil Greek, *Framing Law and Crime: An Interdisciplinary Anthology*.

Isabel C. Pinedo is Associate Professor of Film and Media Studies at Hunter College, CUNY. She is the author of *Recreational Terror*: *Women and the Pleasures of Horror Film Viewing* (SUNY Press, 1997). Other publications address the fallout of 9/11 in relation to blowback, torture, and affective strategies in commemoration programming.

Christopher Sharrett is Professor of Communication and Film at Seton Hall University. He has published several books on film, including *The Rifleman* and *Mythologies of Violence in Postmodern Media*. He is co-editor with Barry Keith Grant of *Planks of Reason*: *Essays on the Horror Film*, the first critical anthology in English on the horror film. His essay "The Horror Film in Neoconservative Culture" appears in Grant's pivotal collection *The Dread of Difference*: *Gender and the Horror Film*. His work has appeared in numerous critical compendia. He writes regularly for *Film International* and *Cineaste*.

Aaron Smuts is Assistant Professor of Philosophy at Rhode Island College. His interests range across a wide variety of topics in ethics and the philosophy of art. Currently he is working on two projects. The first is on the nature and value of well-being. The other project concerns the normative assessment of emotions.

Robert Spadoni is associate professor at Case Western Reserve University, where he teaches film studies. Publications include *Uncanny Bodies: The Coming of Sound Film and the Origins of the Horror Genre* (University of California Press, 2007) and essays on the horror genre. He is writing a book on film atmosphere.

Travis Sutton teaches film classes at Blinn College in Bryan, Texas and is currently working on his PhD in English at Texas A&M University. His research interests include popular films, queer theory, and American literature. Travis completed the Media Arts program at Brigham Young University in 2004 and received his MA in Film Studies at the University of North Texas in 2009. He co-authored an essay on Mormonism and *Twilight* in the recent anthology *Horror After 9/11*.

Joe Tompkins is an assistant professor of communication arts at Allegheny College, where he teaches critical media studies. He has articles either published or forthcoming in *Cinema Journal, Television & New Media, Post-Script,* and *Popular Communication.*

William Whittington is the Assistant Chair of Critical Studies at the University of Southern California, where he teaches and conducts research in film and television, genre, audio and digital culture, adaptation, and gender and sexuality. He is the author of *Sound Design and Science Fiction* (University of Texas Press, 2007).

Rick Worland received his Ph.D. in Motion Picture/Television Critical Studies from UCLA. He is a Professor in the Division of Film & Media Arts at Southern Methodist University where his teaching includes Film History, Documentary, popular genres including the Western and the horror film, and the films of Alfred Hitchcock. His work has been published in *Cinema Journal, The Journal of Film & Video,* and *The Journal of Popular Film & Television* among others. His first book, *The Horror Film: An Introduction* appeared in 2007 from Wiley-Blackwell Publishing. He is currently working on a new book for Wiley-Blackwell, *Ultimate Trips: Hollywood Films in the Vietnam Era, 1960–1979.*

Preface

Monsters are everywhere these days. They are on movie screens certainly, although oddly enough, not always in horror films. As Adam Charles Hart's chapter in this volume demonstrates, today monsters are at the very heart of Hollywood blockbuster action films and CGI spectacles, in franchises such as *The Hobbit* and *Pirates of the Caribbean*, films that few critics or scholars would likely classify as horror films *per se*. Monsters are also ubiquitous in animated kids films [*ParaNorman* (2012), *Frankenweenie* (2012)], television programming, video games, pornography ("dinosaur porn," anyone?), advertising, music, and cultural happenings such as "zombie runs" and "Thriller" flash mobs. This reflects, I think, the fact that monsters are and always have been potent metaphors for just about any and all aspects of human experience. In the twenty-first century alone, they have been used—so far—to speak of teenage romance (the *Twilight* franchise), extreme rendition and enhanced interrogation techniques (torture porn), our ever-increasing surveillance culture (found footage horror films), and survival itself in a world whose infrastructure is crumbling—or at least appears to be (the proliferation of zombie apocalypse texts across all aspects of the media landscape). In its current form, the horror film itself may still be somewhat ghettoized in popular culture as a critic-proof, low-class, low-budget exploitation genre aimed at thrill-seeking teenagers, but the monsters the genre contains continue to fascinate. Putting it another way, monsters are not just for horror films anymore.

It goes without saying that the contributors to this volume understand horror films to be definitely more than low-class, low-budget exploitation flicks aimed at "impressionable" young people and/or moral degenerates. That had been (and may still be) the view of the genre held by many critics and other social reformers supposedly concerned with the genre's allegedly negative effects on public health. As the chapters in this volume by Matt Hills, Kevin Heffernan, and Julian Petley explore, horror films have often been the instigator of "moral panics," especially as each new generation of filmmakers seeks to outdo their predecessors in terms of gore, shock, provocation, and politically incorrect titillation. But those factors are themselves the building blocks of the genre, the blood-soaked façade that allows horror films to tackle social issues in ways no other genre can. A mainstream Oscar-winning film such as *Driving Miss Daisy* (1989) may take on racism in its own soft-pedaled, golden-hour kind of way, but the blood, guts, and smarts of a film such as *Tales from the Hood* (1995) arguably explores the topic in far more complex and nuanced ways. Horror films can say what other socially sanctioned genres often cannot.

My own personal history with the horror film began when I was a child, fascinated with their images of Otherness, images that I found both frightening and alluring. Many of the authors represented in this volume speak of similar attractions to the genre. Indeed, the genre is designed to arouse intense personal responses in its audiences, and people are known to be passionate about horror, loving it as life-long fans, or hating it just as much. And while much criticism has been heaped on the genre for its alleged appeal to audiences' sadistic impulses, that argument has also been countered by others that assert that the genre affords primarily masochistic pleasures. I do not think one simple explanatory paradigm can fully explain *anything* in popular culture, and as such, remind my readers that whether one loves or hates the genre (or is simply neutral toward it), it probably means different things to different people. Readers familiar with my work will discern that my predominant interests lie more in gothic horror than in slasher or gore-hound horror, but I try not to privilege one form over the other (though it is sometimes hard not to) given the status of *all* horror as low or disreputable culture.

As is probably obvious by now, my interests in the horror film today relate to what has been broadly called the *reflective* nature of film genres, and especially the horror film. That is to say, film genres do not arise or exist *de novo*: they are made by and consumed by people within specific historical and sociocultural contexts, and as such they "speak" to those same people about the issues of the day. The insights offered by Robin Wood (1979) (among others) in the 1970s — on how the genre functions as a sort of collective nightmare, figuring any given culture's repressed and oppressed Others as monstrous — still permeate much horror film scholarship today, including this volume. But even if we discount psychoanalysis — as some contemporary cultural critics would have us do — we may still invoke Stuart Hall's (1980) "Encoding and Decoding" model: contemporary cultural studies approaches to film genre emphasize the semiotic and discursive relationship between texts, those who produce and consume them, and the larger spheres of culture and ideology. Cultural texts such as horror films tell us facts about the cultures in which they reside: details about gender, about sex, about race and class, about the body, about death, about pain, about being human, ultimately. Whether or not they speak to our repressed desires (and I think they do, whatever we understand repression to be), horror films nonetheless comment on and/or negotiate with multifarious cultural anxieties and fears, whatever they may be.

This volume contains 30 new chapters on various aspects of the horror film, many written by some of the most well-known and well-respected scholars on the subject. It was designed to provide an introduction to (or overview of) various concepts in horror film scholarship, as well as explore older and newer films within different theoretical paradigms and/or sociohistorical contexts, drawing on primary resources and offering original scholarship on the subject. Although some of the chapters tend to gravitate toward one pole over the other, it was my consistent aim that all of these chapters be helpful and informative to novices, fans, and scholars alike. Thus, some chapters may read a bit like a primer, while others more closely resemble content in scholarly journals. All readers will hopefully encounter familiar faces, figures, and subgenres, as well as — to borrow the title of one infamous horror movie musical from 1964 — an ever-expanding genre universe filled with "incredibly strange creatures who stopped living and became mixed up zombies." A full chapter-by chapter-breakdown of the *Companion* follows, but a brief sampling of its somewhat unusual contents would have to include chainsaws mutating out of Japanese schoolgirls' butts, the rarely seen American Sign Language horror film *Deafula* (1975), Ken Russell's foray into the nunsploitation genre, "hopping vampire" action movies from Hong Kong, the cult fandom surrounding the so-bad-it's-brilliant *Troll 2* (1990), the potential camp appeal of *The Exorcist* (1973), and extreme niche horror films such as *Slaughtered Vomit Dolls* (2006). For the traditionalist, the volume also contains thoughtful explorations of *Dracula* (1931), *The Curse of Frankenstein* (1957), *Peeping Tom* (1960), *The Haunting* (1963), and *Rosemary's Baby* (1968), among many others. In short, this volume demonstrates one of the most exciting things about the horror film genre: it is an ever-changing and ever-expanding repertoire of the perverse and the abject. If one has the guts for it (if I can be pardoned the pun), I think it has much to tell us about the human condition.

Part I: Approaches and Contexts, explores some of the more important ways the horror film has been studied by scholars. It begins with a chapter by Aaron Smuts; it explores some of the cognitive and philosophical issues that the horror film raises, such as "Why do we like to be frightened?" Are the fears felt in horror films "real," as compared to the fears felt in relation to events such as global warming, disease and death, or terrorist attacks? Perhaps unexpectedly, Smuts notes the difficulty in answering many of these sorts of questions, even as they continue to inspire thought and scholarship within those contexts. The next several chapters (by Chris Dumas, Daniel Humphrey, Christopher Sharrett, and Travis Sutton) explore in greater detail various psychoanalytic approaches to the genre, and comment on how it is used — following Robin Wood — to shape and delimit such "real life" discourses as gender, sexuality, race, class, and dis/ability. The final three chapters in this section turn to the contexts of horror film reception (Matt Hills), distribution and exhibition (Kevin Heffernan), and censorship (Julian Petley). These chapters are meant to ground and reply to (if not actually answer) some of the questions explored in previous chapters: just how do actual audiences interact with horror films? What pleasures do audiences find within them? How might their popularity be dependent on the historical and industrial processes of distribution and exhibition, rather than (or in addition to) what they might be saying in some coded psychoanalytic way? Julian Petley's chapter surveys a century of British and American censorship related to the horror film, noting how various waves of "moral panics" have contributed to the horror film's status as a "bad object." (I. Q. Hunter's chapter in Part V, "Trash Horror and the Cult of the Bad Film," engages with many of these same issues and can be productively read in conjunction with the final three chapters of Part I).

Part II: The Form of Horror, features three chapters that explore the stylistic dimensions of cinematic horror. Robert Spadoni's chapter, which surveys decades of critical reaction to the genre, attempts to explore what we really mean by mood and/or atmosphere, especially in relation to horror film narrative and mise-en-scene. In his discussion, Spadoni also draws on recent cognitive and philosophical work on emotions such as fear and dread, teasing out their implications for viewing audiences. Next, William Whittington's chapter on sound design in horror films draws on his similar work on science fiction sound; the chapter is both theoretical and grounded in the industrial practices and discourses of those who actually create sound for horror films. Invoking a basic distinction between "raw" and "refined" sounds, Whittington explores the many different ways that sound design can be used to startle, terrify, unsettle, and/or create related experiences of cognitive dissonance. Part II concludes with "Mellifluous Terror: The Discourse of Music and Horror Films" by Joe Tompkins. Engaging with some of the same ideas explored by Whittington in the preceding chapter, Tompkins surveys the history of horror film music and the different ways it can be used; he also considers how the musical avant-garde has been incorporated into the sound of horror.

Part III: A History of the (Western) Horror Film, sketches out the various twists and turns of the English-language horror film. Despite this, and as many of the chapters in this volume note, the Western horror film has always been international in its development, reach, and influence. It has roots in Eastern European folklore, gothic literature, and German expressionist cinema; by the twenty-first century, one strand of the English-language horror film seems devoted solely to remaking horror film hits from Spain, Japan, and Korea (among other nations). My own chapter begins this section by exploring some of those roots just mentioned, as well as the films of Lon Chaney and the "old dark house" melodramas of stage and screen that predate the release of *Dracula* (1931), the film that most scholars agree "created" this thing we now speak of as "the horror film." John Edgar Browning then offers an overview of the rise and fall of classical Hollywood horror films, exploring how *Dracula* (the film) was drawn from *Dracula* (the play), and some of the ways that era's cultural critics tried to make sense of this new and disturbing phenomenon in their midst. Mark Jancovich's chapter on horror in the 1940s argues (as much of his recent work does) that 1940s horror was understood by its audiences and critics in much broader terms than it is today. The term *horror* was used to describe (what other critics have subsequently classified as) mysteries, thrillers, films *noir*, women's pictures, and even social problem films. Jancovich rightly shows there is far more to 1940s horror than Val Lewton's moody RKO films and Universal's "omnibus" monster rallies such as *Frankenstein Meets the Wolfman* (1943). Next, Steffen Hantke explores the postwar context that gave rise to the science fiction horror film hybrids of the 1950s, seeing in their evolution an increasing self-reflexivity that finds its apex in horror movies such as *The Blob* (1958) and *The Tingler* (1959).

Part III continues with Rick Worland's chapter on what he terms "The Gothic Revival" *(1957–1974)*. His chapter, like the one following it by Peter Hutchings, emphasizes the increasingly global nature of the genre, and traces the gothic revival from the United States [*The Black Sleep* (1956)] to the United Kingdom [Hammer's *The Curse of Frankenstein* (1957)], to Italy [with films such as *The Horrible Dr. Hichcock* (1962)], and back again to America via American International Pictures and Roger Corman's much vaunted Edgar Allan Poe adaptations starring Vincent Price. Similarly, Hutchings examines the somewhat opposing critical constructions of 1970s horror, and in so doing explores both the "modern" or "realist" American horror of the era (associated with leftist horror auteurs such as Wes Craven, George Romeo, Tobe Hooper, *et al.* who were praised by Robin Wood), and the rise of what has been subsequently labeled "Eurohorror" or "Eurocult" horror (associated with filmmakers such as Mario Bava, Dario Argento, Jess Franco, and Jean Rollin). Then, James Kendrick explores how new technologies in make-up design and special effects changed the look of 1980s horror; Kendrick then focuses on a genealogy of that era's most prolific horror subgenre, the slasher film. Adam Charles Hart had the unenviable task of trying to encapsulate the last 20 years or so of the English-language horror film, a genre that Hart sees as more international than ever before, as well as more diffuse and diverse due to the innovations of new media technologies and distribution systems. Finally, Part III concludes with Isabel C. Pinedo's consideration of several of the films that were (in)famously described as "torture porn" in the mid-2000s, creating yet another media panic over the cultural status of the genre.

Part IV: Selected International Horror Cinemas, can only begin to hint at the rich and diverse traditions that delineate horror cinemas outside of English-speaking contexts. Ian Olney offers a fairly comprehensive look at Spanish horror cinema, while Xavier Mendik offers a more specific analysis of what he calls the Mezzogiorno Giallo film, and how it draws upon and expresses discourses related to assumptions about Italy's rural south versus its more industrialized north. James McRoy, a scholar well-known for his work on Japanese horror cinema, offers an overview of several recent trends in that tradition, including the outrageous postmodern body horror of films such as *Tokyo Gore Police* (2008), *Vampire Girl versus Frankenstein Girl* (2009), and *Mutant Girl Squad* (2010). Next, Daniel Martin examines Korean horror cinema and how it relates to the family melodrama, or more specifically, that culture's *shinpa* film—narratives of exaggerated emotion, tragic romance, and female suffering. Andrew Hock Soon Ng's chapter closes this part of the *Companion*, and traces how a similar folkloric character type—the spirit or ghost of a woman who has died during childbirth—has been adapted in different ways according to the national cultures of three Southeast Asian nations: Thailand, Indonesia, and Malaysia. The chapter explores how the specific parameters of religion, gender, and politics (in each of the three cultures) inflect and delineate this centuries-old archetype in distinctly national ways.

Dale Hudson's chapter on how the archetype of the vampire has been adapted across the globe could easily have ended Part IV, but herein it leads off Part V: Selected Archetypes, Hybrids, and Crossovers. Hudson's chapter explores how the vampire is today and always has been a transnational figure who raises issues about foreigners and borders, but the vampire as protean character type has also allowed for some of the most fascinating cross-cultural pollinations, appearing in Indian *masala* films and Hong Kong action-comedy films. Next, I. Q. Hunter explores how "bad," "trashy," and now "extreme" horror films have, in recent decades, become cult objects, adored by fans of what Jeffrey Sconce (2010) has dubbed "paracinema." Joan Hawkins's entry examines the films of Ken Russell—and particularly *The Devils* (1971)—in relation to discourses of art cinema and horror. [Ian Olney's chapter on Spanish Horror Cinema (in Part IV) provides a similar interrogation of Spanish-language art-horror filmmakers including Luis Bunuel, Pedro Almodovar, and Guillermo del Toro.] Next, Adam Lowenstein explores horror in relationship to what anthropologist James Clifford (1988) has called *ethnographic surrealism*, using Jerzy Skolimowski's *The Shout* (1978) as a case study. Part V concludes with a study by Caroline Joan S. Picart, who argues that Steven Spielberg's *Schindler's List* (1993) and *Munich* (2005), which purport to be objective docu-dramas, nonetheless contain stylistic traces associated with the horror film genre.

No single volume, not even one of this length, can hope to cover the entire scope of this fascinating and ever-morphing genre. One glaring omission could be a chapter on the ultra-violent films of the "New French Extremity"—films such as *Haute Tension* (2003), *Inside* (2007), and *Martyrs* (2008). (In truth, I did contract such a chapter although it failed to materialize at the last moment.) That said, I would like to close this brief introduction by thanking my horror film colleagues who contributed to this volume (and even those who did not). While this project has been a massive undertaking (with concomitantly massive frustrations, at times) it has also been a pleasure to work in this capacity with some of the most renowned horror scholars from around the globe. I have learned much from them in compiling this volume, as I hope its readers will. I also hope it will serve as a reference to and a beacon for horror film scholarship for many years to come.

References

Clifford, J. (1988) On ethnographic surrealism, in *The Predicament of Culture: Twentieth-Century Ethnography, Literature, and Art* (ed J. Clifford), Harvard University Press, Cambridge, MA, pp. 117–151.

Hall, S. (1980) Encoding/decoding, in *Culture, Media, Language* (eds S. Hall *et al.*), Hutchinson, London, pp. 128–139.

Sconce, J. (2010) 'Trashing' the academy: Taste, excess and an emerging politics of cinematic style. *Screen*, **36** (4), 371–93.

Wood, R. (1979) An introduction to the American horror film, in *The American Nightmare* (eds R. Wood and R. Lippe), Festival of Festivals Publications, Toronto, pp. 7–33.

Part I

Approaches and Contexts

1

Cognitive and Philosophical Approaches to Horror

Aaron Smuts

Philosophical work on horror has been predominantly focused on the horror film, though little of what has been written on horror is medium specific. It is just that the overwhelming majority of examples in the literature are movies (Schneider and Shaw, 2003). Here, I continue the trend. This entry concerns a relatively small topic in a sub-area of film theory that is often called the *analytic-cognitivist tradition*. This tradition has no clear unifying, positive doctrine (contra Sinnerbrink, 2011: 4–5). Instead, the tradition is best described negatively. Two aversions are important: first, film theorists of the analytic-cognitive stripe exhibit a pronounced suspicion of psychoanalytic accounts of mental activity, preferring instead explanations from contemporary cognitive psychology. Second, analytic-cognitivist film theorists tend to have a strong antipathy to much of what is called *continental philosophy*, whatever that might be. They align with the dominant approach in the English-speaking world, that of analytic philosophy (Carroll, 1996).

Although these labels are much maligned, there are important differences between analytic and continental philosophical practice. This is not a mere sociological divide (Leiter, 2013). Analytic philosophy is primarily problem driven, rather than book or figure focused. One does not do philosophy in the analytic style through another philosopher. No, one simply does philosophy. Similarly, analytic philosophy emphasizes work on live problems, not on what others have had to say about the issues. Analytic philosophers tend to address small problems rather than aim for systematicity, though there are lots of exceptions. The analytic tradition emphasizes clarity of thought and rigorous argumentation, not textual interpretation. Stylistically, the traditions differ greatly, though there is a lot of bad writing on both sides of the divide. These are crude, but characteristic differences between the two schools. At its worst, analytic philosophy is logic-chopping legalistic philosophy of no clear relevance to

A Companion to the Horror Film, First Edition. Edited by Harry M. Benshoff.
© 2014 John Wiley & Sons, Inc. Published 2017 by John Wiley & Sons, Inc.

larger human concerns. But work in the tradition need not be so uninspiring. The
caricature is undermined by some of the work we find on horror.

The Main Issues

Four main issues have occupied center stage in the analytic-cognitivist work on horror: (i) What is horror? (ii) What is the appeal of horror? (iii) How does it frighten
audiences? (iv) Is it irrational to be scared of horror fiction?

The first question asks for a definition. This is clearly the driest question in the
bunch. But it has important implications for how we answer the others, particularly
the second question. The appeal of supernatural horror and slasher movies might be
very different. There might be no common source of appeal between the two. If so,
only a definition that excludes slasher movies would allow for a general account of
horrific appeal. We will look at just such a definition in the next section.

The second question is closely related to the general problem in the philosophy of
art, a problem that is sometimes called the *paradox of tragedy* or, as I prefer, the *paradox of painful art*. Why do people seek out horror films, melodramas, sad songs, bleak
conspiratorial thrillers, and works in other genres that arouse unpleasant emotions?
It is puzzling that people so readily subject themselves to horror films that arouse
fear and disgust. How can we account for this?

The first question also has important implications for the third and fourth. These
both concern, what has become known as, the *paradox of fiction*. We can state it as a
question for now: If audiences know that no one is really threatened by the monster
in *Jeepers Creepers* (2001), can they, nevertheless, feel genuine, rational fear? Surely,
it must be irrational to fear a monster that one knows is merely fictional! The rest of
this chapter is structured around these four questions.

Issue 1. What is Horror?

Years ago, before Netflix and Amazon streaming, there were these curious places
called *video stores*. They were for-profit lending libraries holding movies. Most video
stores were arranged in a predictable manner. Numerous copies of new releases were
grouped in one area, but most of the rest of the store was arranged by genre: comedy,
drama, action, horror. When we ask, "What is horror?" we are trying to determine
the features a work should have in order to be properly classified under the horror section. We might say that we are looking for the essence of horror. We want a
definition of horror.

If you asked a video store clerk, "What is a horror movie?" you would have likely
received a snide answer: "Look over there. See that movie: *Suspiria* (1977) is a horror movie." The irritated clerk would have offered you an ostensive definition—a
definition by pointing. But that is not what we are looking for. We are not looking for instances of horror; rather, we are wondering what makes it appropriate to

classify all those instances under the same category. We want a real definition. A real definition tells us the properties that an object must have in order to be a work of horror. More precisely, a real definition lists the necessary and jointly sufficient conditions an object must have in order for the concept to apply. It tells us both what properties are required and what properties in combination are enough.

In the philosophy of horror, we find very few definitions of horror. The most well-developed definition is one proposed by Noël Carroll (1990). According to Carroll, a work of horror must include, or at least suggest the presence of, a monster. This is key. By "monster" he has something very specific in mind: a monster is a fearsome creature whose existence is not acknowledged by current science (presumably in the world of the fiction). A silly, harmless ghost is not a monster on this conception. It is not a monster because it is not fearsome (Carroll, 1999). Typically, monsters are also categorically interstitial. They do not fit into our conceptual scheme cleanly, occupying something between categories—human and wolf, or animal and vegetable as in *The Thing from Another World* (1951).

Horror films not only include monsters, they are designed to arouse fear and disgust directed at a monster. The fearsomeness of the monster arouses fear. The categorical interstitiality arouses disgust. This combination of reactions directed at a monster is what distinguishes horror from all other genres. Thrillers evoke fear and sometimes disgust, but not at a monster. Gross-out comedy might arouse disgust and sometimes fear, but, again, not at a monster. Science fiction may include creatures that are not acknowledged to exist by current science, but they are not monsters in the fiction. In the world of *Star Wars* (Lucas, 1977), Chewbacca is acknowledged to exist by the leading scientific authorities (though not in our world). And he is not fearsome. Hence, he is not a monster. No, he is just the furry pal of Han Solo. That is why *Star Wars* is not a horror movie. But *Alien* (Scott, 1979) is. The face-huggers are fearsome! Their mother, more so. Monsters make horror.

Carroll's definition properly excludes comedies, thrillers, fantasy, and science fiction, and it accurately includes a wide array of what we classify as horror fiction. Any number of classic examples fit the theory perfectly. For Carroll, it is fair to say that the paradigm of a horror movie is something akin to *Bride of Frankenstein* (1935). This is indeed a good model. But many worry that his definition is under-inclusive.

As Carroll notes, his definition excludes movies such as *Psycho* (1960), *Silence of the Lambs* (1991), *Halloween* (1978), and maybe *Jaws* (1975). Norman Bates is not something unaccounted for by contemporary science. Nor are Hannibal Lecter, Buffalo Bill, and Michael Myers. They are all species of psychopaths. Our prisons are full of them. In reply to this worry, Carroll argues that his theory can account for why we are tempted to classify these kinds of films as works of horror. They arouse fear and disgust directed at something that is monster-like. Norman Bates is "nor man, nor woman." He is categorically interstitial and disgusting when dressed as mother or carrying around her skeleton. So, Carroll concludes, his definition is not uninformative. It tells us why these are edge cases. But these edge cases are just that, edge cases. They do not technically fall under the category when we draw a clear border. So be it.

But few have found this reply palatable. The titles above are probably some of the first that we would list if asked to name some key horror movies. Carroll's definition appears to exclude too many central cases. *Silence of the Lambs*, or better, *Manhunter* (1986) is not an edge case. It is a paradigm of the genre. But it does not include a supernatural monster. It does not even suggest one. The problem is that a successful definition must account for the paradigm cases. Carroll's does not.

If we accept the force of this objection, there are roughly two options available: (i) reject the requirement that horror films must feature a monster or (ii) reject the supernatural conception of what it is to be a monster. Since it is hard to imagine a horror movie without at least a suggested monster, the second option seems more promising. There do indeed appear to be more kinds of monsters than just the supernatural type. Slasher movies, such as *Halloween*, feature naturalistic, or realistic, monsters. Michael Myers, for instance, is not supernatural. He's mean, creepy, and very hard to kill, but not supernatural. Nor are the hillbillies in *The Texas Chain Saw Massacre* (1974). Looked at this way, horror appears to be a genre with two main sub-types, supernatural horror and realist horror.

Unfortunately, I know of no plausible way to precisely characterize realist horror monsters. That's not to say it can't be done, but I don't know how to do it. They are evil, but this isn't sufficient. The presence of the evil Darth Vader doesn't make *Star Wars* a horror movie. Nor does Amon Goeth (Ralph Fiennes' evil Nazi character) make *Schindler's List* (1993) a horror movie. Evil is not sufficient, nor does it seem necessary. The monsters in *Alien* are not evil. The chief monster is simply a mother defending her offspring. They are parasitic, ugly, and very dangerous. But I'm reluctant to call them evil. Are birds of prey evil or simply dangerous to little lambs?

There are few competing accounts of what it is to be a monster in the literature. They are all failures. For instance, consider the idea that a monster is something that has failed to achieve its natural end, that has in some way subverted its nature (Yanal, 2003). This won't do. The monster in *Jeepers Creepers* is doing exactly what a creature of its kind does. It realizes its nature effectively. The same holds for the face-huggers in *Alien*.

Since the prospect of a formal definition rides on our ability to define what it is to be a monster, we are left at this point without a workable real definition. We are not in a much better position than the irritated video store clerk who flippantly offered an ostensive definition. But we have come to an important insight: the contemporary horror genre, as popularly understood, has both supernatural and realist traditions. This will complicate things as we proceed.

Issue 2. What is the Appeal of Horror?

Much like the genres of comedy and suspense, horror is named after the characteristic response it engenders in audiences. Accordingly, we might say that horror horrifies, or at least tries to (though some deny that this is the case: Solomon, 2003). This seems right, but it depends on what it is to be horrified. As we saw in the previous section, a plausible characterization of what it is to be horrified is to experience fear and disgust. Both fear and disgust are often called *negative emotions* (with the qualification that disgust might not be an emotion proper), or, better, species of negative affect. But, once again, it is not entirely clear what this means. Affects are feelings. That is clear. But just what makes a feeling warrant the label "negative" is ambiguous. There are two ways in which one might characterize an experience as negative: (i) by its typical action tendency and (ii) by its felt quality. We might say that an affect is negative if it is avoided, or if subjects typically avoid objects that elicit such feelings. Alternatively, we might say that an affect is negative because it feels bad. It has a negative hedonic tone. This is likely the more important meaning.

Regardless of how we characterize negative affect, if fear and disgust are indeed negative, we have a puzzle on our hands: people go to horror movies knowing full well they will experience fear and disgust. We do not have to be tricked into buying tickets to a comedy to sit through a horror movie. Here is the problem: if fear and disgust are the kinds of feelings that people typically avoid, or, if they feel bad, then why in the world do people go to horror movies? This problem is known as the *paradox of horror*. It is a species of the *paradox of tragedy*.

The more general paradox of tragedy concerns the question of why people pursue works that they know are likely to arouse negative emotions. In some cases, such as those of profound sadness, we would go so far as to say that the emotions aroused are painful. Hence, the general issue under consideration could be called the *paradox of painful art*. The problem encompasses far more than mere tragedy. In fact, the breadth of negative emotional experiences to which audiences willingly submit themselves is incredible. For example, the religious bio-pic *The Passion of the Christ* (2004), designed specifically to disgust and outrage viewers, became a box-office hit. This is not a rare case. A tremendous amount of religious-themed art in the Western tradition seeks to provoke painful emotional reactions via depictions of the suffering of Christ and the martyrdom of saints.

The paradox of painful art can be stated as follows:

1. People voluntarily avoid things that provide painful experiences and only pursue things that provide pleasurable experiences.
2. Audiences routinely have net painful experiences in response to putatively painful art (PPA), such as tragedies, melodramas, religious works, sad songs, and horror films.
3. People expect to have net painful experiences in response to PPA.
4. People voluntarily pursue works that they know to be PPA.

The paradox boils down to a simple question: if people avoid pain then why do people want to experience art that is painful?

Most of the literature on the paradox of tragedy has been concerned with a motivational question: what motivates audiences to pursue artworks that arouse negative emotional responses? The problem is that the motivational question is seldom stated in the same way, and it is rarely shown to be a formal paradox. And depending on how one asks the question, different solutions drop out. As it is typically stated, the paradox of tragedy asks how it is possible for audiences to feel pleasure in response to the fictional portrayal of events in a tragedy. But this formulation of the issue begs a central question, namely, whether or not tragedies afford pleasurable experiences. And even if they do, there are certainly works in other genres, such as melodrama, that are not clear sources of audience pleasure. Surely, the lovelorn do not always, or even typically, listen to sad songs to feel better!

There are a variety of answers to the paradox in the philosophical literature (Smuts, 2009). *Control* theorists argue that the putative painfulness of some artworks is mitigated by our ability to stop experiencing them at will (Morreall, 1985). *Compensation* theorists typically argue that any painful reactions must be compensated for by other pleasures, either in the craft of the narrative or in the awareness that we are sympathetic creatures responsive to the suffering of others (Feagin, 1983). *Conversion* theorists argue that the overall experience of painful artworks is not one of pain but of pleasure, as the pain is converted into a larger, more pleasurable experience (Hume, 1985). *Power* theorists argue that we enjoy the feeling of power that arises from either the realization of the endurance of humanity, or through the overcoming of our fear (Price, 1998; Shaw, 2001). *Rich experience* theorists argue that there are many reasons why people do things other than to feel pleasure. The overall experience of painful art may be one of pain, but the experience can still be seen as valuable, and, as such, motivating (Smuts, 2007).

The most popular style of solution to the paradox of horror, and to the paradox of tragedy in general, is the *hedonic compensatory solution*. This solution holds that the negative affect, the fear and disgust, is compensated hedonically. That is, the bad feelings are overshadowed by the good. We get more pleasure than displeasure, or pain, from watching horror movies. The pleasure compensates for the pain.

Hedonic compensatory theories differ in what they indicate as the source of the pleasure. Carroll, for instance, defends a hedonic compensatory solution to the paradox of horror (Carroll, 1990: 158–214). He argues that fear and disgust are "the price we are willing to pay" for the cognitive pleasures we take from watching horror movies. On his account, the cognitive pleasures come from thinking about how one might go about responding to the threat of a monster. (Recall that his theory is specific to supernatural monster horror.) The pleasures derived from such curiosity would be impossible if there were no monsters. And if there is a monster, there will be fear and disgust. Hence, the pleasures and displeasures are linked. You need a monster for the curiosity and the accompanying pleasure, but the monster also gets you fear and disgust. You cannot have one without the other. But it is ultimately the pleasure that we are after. Fear and disgust are necessary evils for the cognitive pleasures that works of horror afford.

There is certainly something plausible about this solution, but it should raise a few eyebrows. Although there are some pleasures to be had from thinking about how one would confront a monster, it is not clear that they compensate for the displeasure of fear and disgust. At least, that is not how people talk about horror movies. Think about what makes a good horror movie. If someone has seen the latest release, our first question is this: was it scary? There are some good horror movies that are more funny than scary, but an excellent horror movie is one that makes you afraid to turn out the lights before going to bed. Rather than the pleasures of curiosity, it certainly seems that we want to be scared.

Hedonic compensatory solutions assume that we must be looking for some source of pleasure. They assume that the pleasure is what motivates horror audiences to see the latest release (or, at least, to torrent a copy). If this is right, we would expect that people would praise and criticize works of horror based on what it is that brings them pleasure. But few praise horror movies by saying something such as: "It was so interesting thinking about how one might go about confronting such a monster." No, they praise films in reference to how much fear they elicit. Hence, it does not seem that fear is the price to be paid for what we are really after. To the contrary, it appears that fear is precisely what we seek from a good horror movie. It is not the price, but the reward.

This suggests that one of two assumptions is wrong. Either (i) people are not principally after pleasure when they go to horror movies. Or (ii) the fear and disgust we experience in response to horror is not painful or unpleasant. To take the first option is to reject the general hedonic compensatory model. One might be tempted to reject this model for good reasons. It seems to assume a wildly implausible theory of motivation, namely psychological hedonism (or egoism)—the theory that the ultimate source of all human motivation is to seek pleasure and avoid pain. Few take this theory seriously. The proverbial soldier in a foxhole who throws himself on a grenade to save his comrades is a clear counterexample. Sometimes psychological hedonists will try to account for apparently altruistic behavior by arguing that people only help others to avoid feeling bad. But this reply does not help the theory. We only feel bad when someone suffers if we care about them. We would not feel bad otherwise (Butler, 1726). And there is no reason to think that we cannot be motivated by care. Psychological hedonism is a nonstarter.

For those of us not blinkered by a benighted theory of human motivation, when we consider painful art in general, it seems highly plausible to suggest that people are sometimes motivated by more than pleasure. Once again, think of sad songs. Although they may eventually help us work through our emotions, I doubt that this plays any motivational role whatsoever for the lovelorn. Rather, those suffering from heartache seem to want to intensify the pain (Smuts, 2011). The unintentional effects are one thing; the motives another. And here we are interested in the motives. Our apparently self-punishing behavior might be somewhat puzzling, but this does not give us reason to think that there must be some source of hidden pleasure behind it all.

Although rejecting the first assumption is compelling when it comes to some genres, it is far from clear that it applies to horror. I cannot for the life of me figure out why someone would seek out painful fear and disgust for the sake of painful fear and disgust. It does not seem intrinsically valuable. It is not clear that the fear and disgust are instrumental to some kind of cognitive insight or to any kind of value. Nor is it clearly constitutive of any kind of value. Hence, we should take a look at the second assumption, that the fear and disgust felt in response to horror are unpleasant. This is questionable. On reflection, it seems that the fear and disgust involved in attending to horror fictions are not typically painful (or unpleasant). Rather, they seem enjoyable (Neill, 1992). Of course, there are limits. Many of us do not like to watch horror alone. We become too frightened in the house alone, too frightened to sleep. That is no fun. But we do seem to enjoy a good scare.

Consider disgust: the disgust we feel in response to horror movies is peculiar. To see why, it helps to draw a distinction between two different kinds, or sources, of disgust. Few people would want to attend a horror happening, where the audience was confronted with putrefying flesh, feces, and vermin. Seasonal haunted houses staffed with antisocial criminals do not even go that far. No one wants to have to smell the stuff of horror fiction. Smell-O-Rama is not a technology well-suited to the genre. When David Cromer piped the smell of bacon into the theater during his production of *Our Town* (2013), it might have induced tear-jerking nostalgia. But if we piped the smell of a rotting corpse into a theater showing *Jeeper's Creepers* (2001), everyone would leave. Disgusting images that arouse disgusting imaginings are not typically as unpleasant as disgusting smells. Images do not threaten to taint our orifices with impurities. Typically, but not always, the disgust we experience in watching horror movies is attenuated, or of a different kind. The smell of putrefying flesh is unpleasant; similar images can be exciting in some contexts. Something similar can be said of fear.

If it is true that fear and disgust are sometimes enjoyable, this does not so much as provide a comprehensive account of the appeal of horror as it provides a solution to the paradox. It shows that there is no paradox, not even if we assume psychological hedonism. But it does not tell us why people choose horror movies over thrillers. An account of the appeal of horror should probably be able to tell us what is particularly appealing about the genre. It should tell us why some love it and why others hate it. Once again, this will likely require developing different stories for supernatural horror and realist horror. Although this is not the place to delve further into the issue, before we turn to the next topic, it would pay to briefly mention one account of the appeal of a subtype of realist horror.

Recently, a violent sub genre of horror has become popular. Movies like *Saw* (2004) and *Hostel* (2005) are often called *torture porn*. Although I am a huge horror fan, I do not like watching torture porn. And I am not alone here. But many do enjoy the subgenre. I assume that the source of the appeal must differ greatly from that of my favorite works of horror. But what could it be? A common psychoanalytic explanation for the appeal of torture porn goes like this: we have powerful desires to do violence to others. In order to live in civilization, these desires must be repressed. Sometimes these desires are interjected, turned upon ourselves in the form of guilt. But some horror movies give us a chance to see our violent impulses realized. By identifying with the killers and monsters in horror fiction, we are able to vicariously satisfy our desire to do harm to others. The movies also give us a way to hide this fact from ourselves. We are able to vicariously satisfy desires that we can happily deny having.

This is a simplified account. Even in a more developed form it would suffer from an array of serious problems (including a suspect psychological theory and a bogus notion of identification). But one problem is most glaring. The problem shows that we do not need to make recourse to psychoanalysis to explain the appeal of torture porn. The problem is this: torture porn audiences do not seem to be in denial. They go to the theater to see fictional torture. There is no disguised wish fulfillment here. It is out in the open. If sadism is indeed involved, it is flagrant.

Issue 3. How does Horror Frighten Audiences?

The question "How does horror frighten audiences?" is not a philosophical problem as stated. It is largely an empirical question best answered by film scholars and psychologists. A comprehensive answer would require a long, psychological detour. I will not take that route. An alternate approach to the question is available. Although this issue is largely an empirical matter, there are important conceptual controversies concerning the nature of the emotions. The most important is whether audiences feel genuine fear in response to horror fictions. An answer to this question depends on the correct characterization of the nature of the emotions.

One of the leading theories of the emotions is called the *cognitive theory*. The cognitive theory of the emotions holds that emotions are object-directed attitudes that essentially involve evaluations. On this view, emotions are not mere feelings or physiological reactions (Prinz, 2004). No, emotions require a cognitive evaluation of a situation, whether the evaluation is a judgment or a way of seeing, a construal (Solomon, 1980; Roberts, 1988). The object-directed character of standard emotions is apparent in that it always makes sense to say "I am [pick your emotion] that." I am *afraid that* late blight will kill my tomato plants (Roberts, 1988: 195; Helm, 2009: 2). Emotions are directed at objects.

Defenders of the cognitive theory typically distinguish between emotions and mere moods, such as being grumpy or being cheerful, or simply being in a good mood. Some terms, such as "happy," seem to cover both emotions and moods. One might be happy that something is the case. And one might just be happy. The term is very ambiguous. But, properly construed, moods do not take objects, at least not specific objects. Perhaps moods take everything as their objects. This would account for how they color the way we see the world. But taking everything as the object of an attitude is akin to taking nothing. Consider a simple mood: one is not grumpy that such and such. No, one is just grumpy. One might be grumpy *because* of a hangover. But one is not grumpy *at* the hangover. Nor is one grumpy that one is hung over. Although someone might be ashamed that he was once again unable to resist the siren call of bourbon, this is not the object of his grumpiness. At most, it is the mere cause. Shame is an emotion; grumpiness is a mere mood.

The cognitive theory of the emotions is readily supported by our everyday practice of justifying our emotions. We assume that emotions involve evaluations or something much like evaluations. That is precisely why we try to convince those angry with us that we did nothing wrong, that a perceived insult, for instance, was merely an accident. If emotions lacked an evaluative component, our everyday practice would be senseless. But it is not. Hence, the cognitive theory appears well supported.

Based on the cognitive theory of the emotions, some deny that we have genuine emotional reactions in response to fiction. Genuine fear requires a belief that we or someone we care about is in danger. But horror audiences, as with children playing cops and robbers, lack such a belief. A child playing a robber does not run away in fear. She does not believe that the "cop" is a genuine threat. She does not believe that she is in danger of having to do serious jail time if arrested. Nor do horror audiences believe that they are or anyone else is in danger. Instead, they make believe that they are in danger (Walton, 1978). And make-believe fear (or quasi-fear) is not real fear. No, real fear requires a genuine belief that one is in danger.

Thus, to the opening question "How does horror horrify?" this account answers: it does not. Horror fiction, much like other props in games of make believe, is simply used by audiences playing along. Horror does not horrify. No, it helps audiences play games where they make-believedly fear monsters. Audiences do not feel genuine sadness, genuine fear, genuine anger, or any other genuine emotion in response to fiction.

But who, apart from a few philosophers, could believe this? This absurd implication only follows if we grant a highly controversial assumption, namely, that real fear requires a belief in the reality of its object. But, we might ask, why should we grant this assumption? The argument merely asserts that real fear requires a genuine belief that one is in danger. But this is widely contradicted by the evidence at hand. People talk about the emotional responses they have in response to art as if they were genuine, not some diminished quasi versions. It simply defies credibility to say that a theater full of weeping audience members does not feel genuine sadness in response to melodramas. Similarly, it is preposterous to say that terrified viewers who sleep with the lights on after watching a scary movie did not experience genuine fear (Smuts, 2003).

Hence, something must go. (i) Either genuine emotions do not require a belief in the reality of their objects, or (ii) audiences must really believe in the reality of fictions. The second suggestion is as absurd as denying that people feel genuine fear in response to movies. The problem stems from a problematic theory of fictional engagement, the *illusion theory* (Schaper, 1978; Carroll, 1990: 63–68; Radford, 1975: 71–72; Walton, 1978: 7). In a popular guise, it holds that audiences "suspend disbelief" when they are engaged with works of fiction. This sounds nice, but it is as suspect as it is vague. Not only is it highly implausible that people can suspend disbelief, it is even less likely that anything of the sort is needed to engage with fiction.

The notion that we suspend disbelief is lacking in phenomenological support. I cannot recall ever actively doing anything of the sort. And I do not see any reason to think that I do so unconsciously. I simply do not experience movies as if they are real. To suggest otherwise fails to accord with our experiences of engaging with fiction. And it fails to explain audience behavior. No one calls the FBI when the aliens land in a science fiction film, nor do we call the police when Michael Myers follows his prey in *Halloween* (1984). However, if we even partially believed that Freddy Kruger was alive, we would likely wet our pants and hide under the seat. While watching a movie, we may yell "Look out!" or "Behind you!" in frustration, but no sane person thinks that she can communicate with the characters on the screen, or that she is threatened by the monsters on the page. There is no belief in the reality of the characters; there is no illusion. No one ran from the Lumière brother's *L'arrivée d'un Train* in 1895. Nor do contemporary audiences typically believe that fictions are real. Watching movies is not a form of temporary insanity or pronounced irrationality (contra Radford, 1975; see Joyce, 2000 and Matravers, 2005).

Shakespeare reduced the illusion theory of fictional engagement to absurdity via the Rude Mechanicals in *A Midsummer Night's Dream*. Worried that the play might scare the women in the audience, Bottom decides that he will remind everyone that what they are about to see is merely fiction:

> I have a device to make all well. Write me a prologue, and let the prologue seem to say we will do no harm with our swords, and that Pyramus is not killed indeed. And, for the better assurance, tell them that I, Pyramus, am not Pyramus, but Bottom the weaver. This will put them out of fear. (III.1:15–20)

Of course, no such clarification is necessary. Bottom's well-meaning prolog is funny precisely because the illusion theory is wrong: audiences do not confuse fiction and reality, not even a little. They do not need to be told that Pyramus is Bottom the weaver, or that the lion is Snug the joiner.

If audiences do not believe in the reality of fictional characters and events, and if audiences have genuine emotions in response to fictions, then genuine emotions must not require a belief in the reality of their objects. One prominent suggestion, the thought theory, holds that emotions only require that we entertain, or suppositionally imagine, that the events are taking place (Carroll, 1990; Lamarque, 1981). On this suggestion, we need not believe that anyone is in danger. No, we need only imagine that it is the case. Works of fiction are guides to the imagination. They provide the bulk of the content of the thoughts we are to entertain. Some of these arouse fear and disgust. Why? That is just how we are. We are capable of responding emotionally to merely imagined scenarios. Very roughly, the thought theory answers, that is how horror does it.

Issue 4. Is it Irrational to be Scared of a Fictional Monster?

Assuming that we do indeed feel genuine fear in response to horror fiction, we can ask a further question: "Is it rational?" Consider what the thought theory seems to imply: we are scared of our thoughts. But how could it be rational to be scared of our thoughts? That sounds downright loony. Thoughts are not dangerous. In comparison with the literature on the "how" question, the literature on the "rationality" question is sparse and often confused. Too often the interlocutors simply talk past one another. This is due to the lack of clarity around the concept of rationality that gets employed.

One of the issues that interests philosophers of emotion is whether standard emotions admit of rational justification. This issue is often said to concern the rationality of the emotions. But what people mean by this varies radically (Jones, 2004: 333–336). In the literature on the emotions, there is a wide variety of different standards for evaluating the rationality of emotions. We can discern at least five: (i) reasonableness, (ii) aptness, (iii) proportionality, (iv) self-interest, and (v) intelligibility. We might wonder if an emotion is reasonable given the evidence. Alternatively, we might wonder if it fits the situation, if the emotion is apt. For standard emotions, this would require showing that their evaluations are correct. Or we might wonder whether the intensity of an emotion is proportional to its object. Or we might ask if the emotion was in one's long-term best interest. Or we might try to understand why someone would respond that way. If we can understand why they reacted as they did, the emotion is intelligible.

All of these standards are interesting, but only one concerns us here, that of aptness — whether the emotion is appropriate to the features of its object. And, here, it seems that emotional reactions to fiction might be inappropriate. For nearly 30 years, Colin Radford claimed that our reactions to fiction were irrational (Radford, 1975). He argues "that we are irrational, inconsistent, and incoherent in being moved to pity for fictional characters [. . .] and we are nonetheless moved" (1995: 75) (Figure 1.1).

Radford thinks that emotions directed at fictions are irrational because they occur in absence of a corresponding belief in their objects. In this way they are similar to

Figure 1.1 Is it irrational to fear outright fictions, like mind-controlling worms from outer space, as in *Slither* (2006)? Directed by James Gunn. Produced by Gold Circle Films, Strike Entertainment, Brightlight Pictures, and Slither Productions.

phobias and to sadness felt after one learns that someone was pulling your leg via a tale of woe. Phobias are irrational because the phobic purports to believe that the object is harmless. Our reactions to fiction are similar. We know that the worms in *Slither* (2006) are harmless. They are harmless because they do not exist. No one is threatened. No one except some fictional characters. We feel fear when entertaining thoughts of the mind-controlling little phalluses asserting themselves down our throats, but we lack any corresponding belief in their existence. We are like arachnophobes who are afraid of imaginary spiders. That is beyond silly.

One might object to Radford's claim by noting that there are other instances of perfectly rational emotional responses that occur in the absence of belief. Radford considers such a reply. He asks us to imagine a mother who hears about a bus crash in a distant city. Although she does not think that her own children are in danger, she clutches them in relief when they arrive home from school. The mother is not irrational; she is perfectly normal. If we should not think that she is irrational, then we should not think that we are irrational in responding to fictional characters and events that we do not believe are real. The absence of a belief in the reality of the threat is not sufficient to make the emotion irrational.

This may seem plausible, but Radford replies that there is an important difference between the mother and someone watching a movie. The mother thinks that it is likely that her children could be injured. Hearing about the crash made their vulnerability clear. However, the reader of a novel does not think it is likely that a fictional character could be injured. Fictional characters do not exist! In contrast, Radford argues that feeling bad for a fictional character is akin to feeling bad for your sister who has two children, because had she not had children she would have been miserable. But that would be silly. Why would anyone feel bad for someone over something that did not happen? The object of such sadness is not probable. Not in the least. Sadness at a such a thought would be very odd. So, too, are our reactions to fiction. We are frightened by events that are not likely, events we know are not real.

In response to Radford's charge, Carroll replies that fearing fictions is perfectly normal. We all have the capacity to respond to fictional characters and events. It is probably adaptive, as it helps us understand stories about potential dangers. Hence, it is rational to fear imagined scenarios. But this reply does not meet the challenge. It operates on a different notion of rationality. Whether the capacity to feel genuine emotions in response to merely imagined scenarios has adaptive value is one thing; whether our particular reactions are fitting is another. Further, Radford would be right to reply that what is normal is not necessarily rational. We are normally subject to all manner of irrationalities, such as the gambler's fallacy. In fact, Radford admits that it is perfectly normal to fear fictions. There is no dispute here. What he denies is that it is rational.

Before we accept the claim that our emotional reactions to fiction are all irrational, we should consider another example. Imagine someone who is afraid of the victim in a horror move, say Laurie Strode (Jamie Lee Curtis' character) in *Halloween*. Or imagine something even more ridiculous: someone scared of the (fake) leaves on the ground in *Halloween*. This would be the height of irrationality. Fearing Michael

Myers and fearing Laurie Strode are very different things. If we want to be able to acknowledge the difference, as we should, we must resist Radford's charge that all fictional emotions are irrational (Gaut, 2007: 216–227).

Up to this point, I have been talking as if people are scared of horror monsters. But this leaves an ambiguity. It is doubtful that people are typically frightened for themselves. That is, they do not fear that the monster will get them. No, audiences fear for the characters. They fear for others. We might be startled and disgusted by horror, but that is different than fear. Neither startles nor disgust are emotions proper. Neither essentially involves an evaluation that can be assessed in terms of evaluative correctness, that is, appropriateness. Startles and disgust are primitive. But when it comes to fear, we are dealing with an emotion proper. It would be the height of irrationality to fear for oneself when watching a horror movie. I would have to be insane to think that one of Herbert West's reanimated bodies in *Reanimator* (1985) is a threat to me. Likewise, it would be ludicrous for me to fear that rapist demon in *The Entity* (1982) might come after me next.

Although self-directed fear in response to fictions would be irrational, other-directed fear might not be. Although we know that the teenagers in *Return of the Living Dead* (1985) do not really exist, in the world of the fiction they are threatened by Tarman (Figure 1.2). When we engage with works of fiction, we imagine other possible worlds where the events take place (Neill, 1993). We can even come to care about characters that we imagine to exist in other worlds. Though we do not believe that we are threatened, we do believe that the characters we care about are in danger in their worlds. No one in the world of *The Cure* (1997) should look into the hypnotist's flame. Although it would be irrational to fear the leaves or to fear Laurie Strode in *Halloween*, it is not irrational to fear *for* Laurie while she

Figure 1.2   Other-directed fear in *Return of the Living Dead* (1985), as fictional teenagers are menaced by Tarman. Directed by Dan O'Bannon. Produced by Hemdale Film, Fox Films Ltd., and Cinema 84.

Figure 1.3 Do horror movies make us fear for ourselves, or for the characters they depict? "Bughuul" on the prowl in *Sinister* (2012). Directed by Scott Derrickson. Produced by Alliance Films, IM Global, Blumhouse Productions, Automatik Entertainment, and Possessed Pictures.

is stalked by Michael Myers. Hence, we can account for the difference between the normal film viewer and the fool who fears the leaves by distinguishing between fear for others and fear for oneself.

This account is compelling, but it rests on two controversial premises. First, that horror audiences do not fear for themselves. And, second, that it is rational to care about and feel for characters who inhabit merely imagined worlds. These are both problematic. Consider the first: is it clear that audiences do not fear for themselves? If so, why is it that people are scared to turn out the lights after watching a horror movie? Why are people scared to look out the window at night after watching Bughuul in the bushes in *Sinister* (2012)? They surely are not scared for the characters hours or days after watching the movie. No, they seem to be scared for themselves. I confess, Mr. Boogie scares me. Perhaps the movie just induces a persistent, jumpy mood, but I have my doubts (Figure 1.3).

The second assumption seems to deny the charge of irrationality without any argument. The rationality of fearing for the inhabitants of merely imagined worlds is precisely what is at issue. Noting that the characters inhabit an imagined world does not make them any more real. Accordingly, it is unclear how this refinement makes it any more rational to fear for their safety. Of course, this is not the end of the story. But we have yet another unsolved problem on our hands.

Concluding Remarks

In this chapter I evaluated some of the leading answers to four questions that occupy center stage in the analytic-cognitivist literature on horror: (i) What is horror? (ii) What is the appeal of horror? (iii) How does it frighten audiences? (iv) Is it irrational to be scared of horror fiction?

The first question, What is horror? is hard to tackle. The central difficulty here is in accounting for both supernatural and realist horror. The multi-faceted genre eludes our attempts to pin it down in a classical definition. But this should not be too surprising. Genres are the products of our messy efforts at categorizing works of art. We should not expect to find a neat and tidy arrangement. Genres are not natural kinds. No periodic table of genres is likely to be forthcoming.

As for the second question, we left the appeal of horror unexplained. But what we did discover is that we will likely need separate accounts for the various types of horror movies. Supernatural horror and realist horror have different charms. As do the films in the same broad category. Simply consider the differences between the work of David Cronenberg and Dario Argento. We are likely dealing with a genre too diverse to canvas in a single account. But we were able to develop a plausible solvent for the paradox of horror: It is unlikely that the fear and disgust felt in response to most horror fiction is indeed painful, or unpleasant. It is typically fun to be scared by a horror movie.

The third and fourth questions concern the two faces of the paradox of fiction: How is it that we fear fictions? And is it rational? I dismissed accounts that suggest we only feel quasi-emotions in response to fiction. When we cry at a melodrama, we do not shed mere crocodile tears. No, we are genuinely sad. Likewise, when we are terrified by a horror movie, we feel genuine fear. The fact that we do not run and hide is easily explained: we are watching a movie. The object of our fear is a mere representation. There is no reason to hide.

Although it seems clear that we feel genuine fear in response to horror movies, it is less clear that it is rational. How could it be rational to fear a fictional monster? In attempting to answer this question, I drew a distinction between fear for self and fear for others. When watching horror movies, we fear for characters, not for ourselves, or so it seems. Yes, it would be irrational to fear for our own safety, but not so irrational to fear for the safety of the characters in the fiction. This is helpful, but the distinction does not resolve the problem. It still seems suspect to fear for the safety of characters that do not exist. And, besides, it is unclear that horror audiences do not also fear for themselves.

These are the central problems in the analytic-cognitivist literature on horror. They all await answers.

References

Butler, J. (1726) *Fifteen Sermons Preached at the Rolls Chapel*. J. and J. Knapton, London.

Carroll, N. (1990) *The Philosophy of Horror; or, Paradoxes of the Heart*, Routledge, New York.

Carroll, N. (1996) Prospects for film theory: a personal assessment, in *Post-Theory: Reconstructing Film Studies* (eds N. Carroll and D. Bordwell), University of Wisconsin Press, Madison.

Carroll, N. (1999) Horror and humor. *The Journal of Aesthetics and Art Criticism*, **57** (2), 145–160.

Feagin, S. (1983) The pleasures of tragedy. *American Philosophical Quarterly*, **20** (1), 95–104.

Gaut, B. (2007) *Art, Emotion, and Ethics*, Oxford University Press, New York.

Helm, B. (2009) Emotions as evaluative feelings. *Emotion Review*, **1**, 1–12.

Hume, D. (1985) Of tragedy, in *Essays Moral, Political, and Literary*, Liberty Fund, Indianapolis.

Jones, K. (2004) Emotional rationality as practical rationality, in *Setting the Moral Compass: Essays by Women Philosophers* (ed. C. Calhoun), Oxford University Press, New York.

Joyce, R. (2000) Rational fear of monsters. *British Journal of Aesthetics*, **40** (2), 209–224.

Lamarque, P. (1981) How can we fear and pity fictions? *British Journal of Aesthetics*, **21** (4), 291–304.

Leiter, B. (2013) "Analytic" and "Continental" Philosophy, http://www.philosophicalgourmet .com/analytic.asp (accessed 19 February 2014).

Matravers, D. (2005) The challenge of irrationalism, and how not to meet it, in *Contemporary Debates in Aesthetics and the Philosophy of Art* (ed. M. Kieran), Blackwell, New York.

Morreall, J. (1985) Enjoying negative emotions in fictions. *Philosophy and Literature*, **9** (1), 95–103.

Neill, A. (1992) On a paradox of the heart. *Philosophical Studies*, **65**, 53–65.

Neill, A. (1993) Fiction and the emotions. *American Philosophical Quarterly*, **30** (1), 1–13.

Price, A. (1998) Nietzsche and the paradox of tragedy. *British Journal of Aesthetics*, **38** (4), 384–393.

Prinz, J. (2004) *Gut Reactions: A Perceptual Theory of Emotion*, Oxford University Press, New York.

Radford, C. (1975) How can we be moved by the fate of Anna Karenina? *Proceedings of the Aristotelian Society*, **69**, 67–80.

Radford, C. (1995) Fiction, pity, fear, and jealousy. *Journal of Aesthetics and Art Criticism*, **53**, 71–75.

Roberts, R.C. (1988) What and emotion is: a sketch. *The Philosophical Review*, **XCVII.2**, 183–209.

Schaper, E. (1978) Fiction and the suspension of disbelief. *The British Journal of Aesthetics*, **18** (1), 31–4.

Schneider, S.J. and Shaw, D. (eds) (2003) *Dark Thoughts: Philosophical Reflections on Cinematic Horror*, Scarecrow press, Lanham, MD.

Shaw, D. (2001) Power, horror, and ambivalence, in *Horror, Special Issue of Film and Philosophy*, 1–12.

Sinnerbrink, R. (2011) *New Philosophies of Film: Thinking Images*, Continuum, New York.

Smuts, A. (2003) Haunting the house from within: disbelief mitigation and spatial experience, in *Dark Thoughts: Philosophic Reflections on Cinematic Horror* (eds S.J. Schneider and D. Shaw), Scarecrow.

Smuts, A. (2007) The paradox of painful art. *Journal of Aesthetic Education*, **41** (3), 59–77.

Smuts, A. (2009) Art and negative affect. *Philosophy Compass*, **4** (1), 39–55.

Smuts, A. (2011) Rubber ring: why do we listen to sad songs?, in *Narrative, Emotion, and Insight* (eds J. Gibson and N. Carroll), University Park, Penn State UP.

Solomon, R. (1980) Emotions and choice, in *Explaining Emotions* (ed. A.O. Rorty), University of California Press, Los Angeles.

Solomon, R. (2003) Real horror, in *Dark Thoughts: Philosophic Reflections on Cinematic Horror* (eds S.J. Schneider and D. Shaw), Scarecrow.

Walton, K. (1978) Fearing fictions. *Journal of Philosophy*, **75** (1), 5–27.

Yanal, R. (2003) Two Monsters in Search of a Concept. *Contemporary Aesthetics*, 1, http://www.contempaesthetics.org/newvolume/pages/article.php?articleID=201 (accessed 19 February 2014).

2

Horror and Psychoanalysis
An Introductory Primer

Chris Dumas

Something is terribly wrong. People are not themselves: they seem to have changed, to be controlled by mysterious forces. Who is killing everybody? What do these weird runes mean? What happened to the original governess? Why is that pale little girl standing at the end of the hallway, and what's that dark liquid dripping off her? A man in a mask is stalking teenagers, mostly the sexually active ones; some say that there's something dark in his past, maybe an incident (a neighborhood legend) involving a babysitter and a knife. Someone is hung on a hook while still alive; the freezer is stuffed with bodies, and the sausages at the local barbecue joint have a familiar, uncomfortably *intimate* taste. There is something creepy and disturbing about these old family photographs — and why does this long-dead little boy look just like your son? The locals say that something horrible happened in the old mental hospital, up there on the hill; I don't remember exactly what, but maybe you should check the old newspapers in the library. (Don't worry, they're all on microfilm.) I apologize for our children's behavior; they don't normally behave so strangely, but things have been different around here since the priest died — and in such a horrible fashion! I wouldn't open that old wooden box if I were you: there's something, how you say, *ancient* about it. What's this weird mucosal goo all over the banister? Wait a minute, are those *eggs*? Mother — oh, God, Mother! Blood! Blood!

Please forgive this burst of clichés; I have chosen to begin this way in order to point out that horror films seem to be built on a set of recurring themes: parents and children, sex and blood, secrets from the past, loss, repetition, trauma, death. Unlike other genres built on recurring cataclysms of violence — the action thriller, say, or the combat movie — horror films may perhaps be typified by the idea that their violence is motivated by sexual aberrations with roots in the past. Perhaps this is too obvious a way to put it; maybe we should just say that horror films break down doors that

A Companion to the Horror Film, First Edition. Edited by Harry M. Benshoff.
© 2014 John Wiley & Sons, Inc. Published 2017 by John Wiley & Sons, Inc.

Figure 2.1 A family portrait. *Halloween* (1978). Directed by John Carpenter. Produced by Compass International Pictures and Falcon International Productions.

are chained shut, disclose secrets that were thought permanently forgotten, open up containers that are meant to keep their contents forever hidden. What escapes from its confines is, of course, the Monster—whatever that word means. And it is not just the body that is in danger in horror films: it is the *sexual* body, the pubescent body, the all-too-mortal body with a vulnerable personality inside it. If horror films resemble nightmares, it is not just because they generate (or, mostly, just *try* to generate) fear, repulsion, panic, and other feelings remembered from childhood. Whether you are watching a film about human monsters or non-human ones, about vengeful spirits from the past or psychotic madness in the present, horror cinema *always* trades on irrationality, and irrationality, in psychoanalytic terms, is always sexual in origin.

It may simply be an effect of history, but horror cinema—from its very earliest moments, more than a century ago, to the latest made-for-cable slasher flick—is soaked in ideas that came to it from the work of Sigmund Freud, the inventor of psychoanalysis. The historical claim is generally justified by the fact that Freud's theories and the cinema appeared at more or less the same time: Edison premiered the Kinetoscope in 1893, right around the time that Freud, along with his early colleague Wilhelm Fleiss, made a crucial breakthrough in the diagnostic etiology of hysteria. Freud's subject was human behavior, and in contradistinction to previous theories of mind, Freud essentially postulated that human rationality is an illusion, that every person is "civilized" only insofar as they have managed to *repress*, or censor, their worst impulses, and that most mental illness—previously imagined to be biological in origin—was, in fact, the result of traumatic disturbances in childhood. For a world torn apart by the First World War, Freud's theories made a new kind of sense: surely a race of creatures capable of such awful violence was not truly rational or in control of itself. Freud's influence on American popular culture, in particular, was strongest in the 1940s and 1950s (during the years of Hiroshima, Auschwitz, McCarthyism, atomic weaponry, Benjamin Spock's *Baby and Child Care*, and the Kinsey reports). Its direct influence has waned over the years, but its ideas and vocabulary linger, even today, in the basic assumptions we make about ourselves, other people, and human motivations in general.

The film scholar Noël Carroll has called *psychoanalysis* a "cultural myth, like Christianity," which "pervades the thinking of literate Westerners (and many non-literate ones as well)"; he notes that "we can see its concepts, scenarios, and imagery in the work of filmmakers and authors with no express commitment to psychoanalysis." (2004: 258). When he calls it a "cultural myth," Carroll is addressing the pervasive discourse about the logical system called *psychoanalysis*, not the truth-value of that system; its basic ideas and its vocabulary are omnipresent in our lives, so much so that its influence is, in many ways, invisible. Whether or not one "believes in" Freud's theories, one cannot ignore the ways in which his system of thought impacted the cinema during the twentieth century, or the ways in which the cinema, in turn, impacted the development of psychoanalysis during Freud's lifetime and afterwards. (It is widely reported that Freud himself disliked movies, but—anecdotally speaking—it seems that most psychoanalysts in his wake have been positively obsessed with them.) You can see the influence of Freud's thinking, for example, in the *mise-en-scène* of the classics of German expressionism, in the onscreen behavior of nearly every character in American *films noir*, in melodramas of the 1950s, in "new wave" films from most of the countries where those waves occurred, and even—if you look closely enough—in the last few winners of the best picture Oscar.

In reference to horror film, psychoanalysis is as close to essential as any conceptual model can get. You may or may not be convinced of the veracity of Freud's theories, but when you talk about horror cinema, you really cannot avoid them—and if you try, you miss the very heart of the genre itself. Perhaps one reason for this is that when you invoke ideas like "anxiety" or "desire," you are already in the realm of the psychoanalytic, and horror cinema is all about anxiety and desire—indeed, these are the bases of the entire genre. When you watch a horror film, part of you fears the destruction that you know is coming, while another part of you wishes to participate in that destruction: in the slasher film, for example, you want the breasts, and *then* the blood. Other genres may be predicated on suspense, but *defilement* is the province of the horror film. One asks: Why is that so? Where do these images of violence and sexuality come from, and what makes us, as viewers, react to them so deeply?

Freud: Trauma, Memory, Violence

Sigmund Freud was born (in 1856) into a world divided between the modern physical sciences and a pre-modern morality. Trained as a physician, Freud was interested in the science of the brain, and initially studied organic brain disorders such as cerebral palsy. After a period in training with the French neurologist Jean-Martin Charcot, Freud became fascinated by hysteria, a nervous disorder that mainly affected women. At this historical moment, persons suffering from hysteria (a disorder that affected the body but seemed to have no biological origin), were thought either to be malingerers, or afflicted by some mysterious innate female madness. Freud, working with his colleague Josef Breuer, found his way to a new understanding of the disorder by simply *listening* to the patients and paying close attention to their speech—not only their memories, their descriptions of their dreams, and the odd mistakes and slippages in the way they organized their thoughts, but in their words themselves. He found that engaging the patients at the level of language allowed him access to parts of their personalities that *they themselves could not see*, and this very fact—that people were split against themselves—led him to reconceptualize subjectivity in a radical new way. When personality disturbances do not have a biological origin, where exactly do they come from? Freud's major discovery was that they come *from the past*. As he put it, persons with emotional disturbances "suffer from *reminiscences*" (1919: 16; italics mine).

To describe Freud's discoveries as briefly as possible, one must resort to gross oversimplification—the advanced student might scoff at how reductively I sketch these theories, and rightfully so. Freud's writings can be a tough slog for the beginner (I would recommend that the *completely* uninitiated start with *Five Lectures on Psycho-Analysis*, a short book comprised of talks that Freud gave at Clark University in Massachusetts in 1909), but they can perhaps be generalized into a set of very simple ideas and observations about human behavior. First: sexuality pervades every aspect of human life and behavior. Second: sexuality is not just sex (i.e., heterosexual coitus, committed in marriage with an aim toward procreation, is not the *definition* of sexuality, but merely an *instance* of it). Third: sexuality arises within, and can only be understood in reference to, the experiences of childhood and the family. Fourth: where sexuality is concerned, there is no "normality"—only varying degrees of social acceptability.

Freud's masterstroke was opening up the idea of sexuality to include nearly any behavior that works toward achieving some kind of pleasure (or even displeasure). Indeed, sexuality is involved in nearly the entire range of human behavior, from the bedroom to the town hall, and it begins with the infant's feelings of satisfaction and need at the mother's breast. In the first part of the twentieth century, Freud scandalized the West by insisting that children do, indeed, have sexual feelings, although it is not until late childhood that eroticism becomes localized in the genitals (or, in the case of perversion, elsewhere in and on the body). What we understand as adult sexuality—both "normal" and "abnormal"—therefore has its behavioral roots in the fulfilled and unfulfilled desires of childhood. Of course the very young child has no understanding of sexual difference, of what makes men and women themselves and not each other; they do not understand their own bodies or the bodies of their parents or caregivers. At the very beginning, the child does not even distinguish between itself and the mother's body. But as the child grows and enters language (and therefore society), it also enters a phase of negotiation, a kind of research into the nature of the closed world it inhabits—a phase in which it must come to terms with the fact that it cannot be at its mother's breast forever. Something must tear the child away from the mother, and that something—usually the father—therefore becomes a kind of primitive rival. This phase is Freud's notorious *Oedipus complex*, and all children pass through it—most of them successfully, but some not. The passage through this phase optimally results in the child giving up part of him- or herself, some part of his or her desire for satisfaction in the mother, in exchange for a satisfaction that will arrive sometime in the future ("when you are an adult, you can have a family of your own"); when this phase is not completed successfully, emotional turbulence in adulthood is virtually guaranteed. The Oedipus complex is what gives horror cinema its particularly familial cast: the traumatic knot of children's relationship to their parents, in horror, unleashes a violence that can only be understood as an archaic response to a primal dissatisfaction. (The Oedipus complex is one of the most counter-intuitive of Freud's ideas, and students often have a lot of trouble with it, especially when it is understood too literally: "you mean that when I was a kid, I wanted to murder my father and marry my mother? That's disgusting!" In such an instance, the easiest beginner's guide to the notion of the Oedipus complex is found in Nasio, *Oedipus: The Most Crucial Concept in Psychoanalysis*.)

As a person, your earliest experiences shape you irrevocably; you may not remember them, but all your memories live inside you, not exactly *forgotten* but, rather, shoved aside. Your parents are objects of fear and love, of hatred and desire—of all emotions, of all affects—and all the other persons you encounter in your life will (to varying degrees) activate, or be framed by, the emotional residue of those earliest experiences of your parents and the rest of your family. What is difficult to grasp is the extent to which these experiences have effects on the body and, therefore, on sexuality. For example, you might or might not have a penis; perhaps it makes no *actual* difference whether or not you have one, but the ways in which the people *around* you (such as your parents) think about the issue of having or not-having a penis will affect the way that *you* think about it. Children are curious about their bodies, and as they think about other people, they also question the impact that other people will have on their bodies, and that their bodies will have upon other people. Since we live in a culture in which certain parts of the body are supposed to be covered and certain bodily functions are supposed to be hidden, the way in which children learn these rules (rules about hidden vs public, clean vs dirty, and so on) will influence the way that they behave for the rest of their lives.

The most scandalous aspect of Freud's discoveries was the way that he began to think of childhood development, which he saw as necessarily traumatic. At the beginning of his search, Freud heard so many patients tell stories about being sexually abused by their parents that he thought that there was an epidemic of molestation in Vienna; later, he realized that many (but not all) of these stories were *fantasies*, retroactively constituted in order to make sense of the trauma of attaining consciousness. He came to the conclusion that whether or not an individual narrative of abuse was true (and of course sexual abuse does occur, far more often than most people would like to admit), that fact is, for diagnostic purposes, immaterial: what matters is the *fantasy* that each person constructs around his or her experiences of early sexuality (and around his or her theories about the sexuality of adults), a fantasy that will determine their entire personality structure. Note that the term *fantasy*, when used by Freud, is not the opposite of *fact*: it refers not to the *truthfulness* of a storyline, but the mere fact that a narrative has been constructed, a narrative that undergirds a person's entire self-conception and unconsciously determines the way that they understand reality itself.

Freud concludes that the results of the child's negotiations with meaning (especially sexual difference) are the basis for all adult behavior. Most adults manage to acquire a more or less stable concept of sexual difference, and they are therefore afflicted with the ordinary disorders of personality that typify life in an industrial age. These are the *neurotics* (you are probably one of them), and while neurosis comes in many flavors, it only registers as a condition to be treated when it makes daily life unbearable. (Obsessive-compulsive persons—you probably know a few—fall into this category.) Other persons, however, do not achieve this level of stability: this is where madness occurs. And madness—what Freud, like other physicians of his time, called *psychosis*—is always typified by disturbances in meaning (especially around the concept of gender) and can generate violence. Horror cinema, of course, is also typified by disturbances in meaning, especially around issues of gender; and of its violence, one might perhaps assert that it is the symptom that gives the genre its meaning.

For students of horror cinema, one of the central Freudian ideas is the concept of *castration*. Yes, this means exactly what it sounds like—and yet it does not. Castration can be understood literally (and in horror cinema, it often is), but it is usually a metaphor for some kind of *loss*, an absence that each one of us must undergo in order to be accepted into society. Perhaps it is less common today than it was a century ago for parents (or teachers or guardians) to react to a male child's transgressions by threatening to cut off his penis; in Freud's time, masturbation was understood to be a terrible sin (and a primary cause of adult sickness), and very young children were prevented, in any way possible, from being too curious about their genitals. Maybe parents are more enlightened today, and maybe they are not. But given that the penis is invariably invested (by parents, by culture and society) as a symbol of power, tensions in the child's own sense of power and potency will always register within the child's sense of his or her body. The way that Freud applied this line of thinking to girls and women—who, after all, already do not have a penis—remains controversial today, and indeed the most significant weakness in Freud's model of personality development is centered on the way he thought of women and female sexuality. (His idea of "penis envy" is very difficult to accept for a number of reasons.) All the same, there is something about the ubiquity of phallic symbols in our culture that must have an effect on any woman who grows up in it. Certainly it has an effect on men: one does not need to look very far (in horror films, or in culture in general) to see evidence of male fears of the female body, which is seen to be already castrated and, therefore, potentially castrating to men who encounter it. Indeed, one might say that *all* violence in horror films is always about castration and punishment, and therefore always about gender.

How is it that such strange and violent fantasies can operate in each of us without our being aware of it? If this model of development applies to each of us, then how can we possibly function normally? Freud speaks of the mind operating in several

Figure 2.2 The son inside the mother; the mother inside the son; the maternal remnant. *Psycho* (1960). Directed by Alfred Hitchcock. Produced by Shamley Productions.

different registers at once—that is, that in any person, there is always and inevitably a permanent split between one's self and one's real motivations. There is the *conscious* mind, where your everyday thoughts occur: this is that part of you which you perceive as "yourself," that is, your everyday thoughts and reveries, the part of you that speaks (or so you think). Behind (under? within? against?) the conscious is the *unconscious*, where your desires live and where your dustiest memories are stored. The conscious speaks (it calls itself "I"), but the unconscious speaks too—in mistakes, in dreams, in fantasies and little everyday delusions. As for memories, Freud postulates that the mind does not forget *anything*; everything is recorded, and while some things are edited out or partially forgotten, they cannot be erased. (Neurology seems to support this idea.) Early traumas, and other bad feelings and memories, undergo a process that Freud called *repression*: they may be shoved aside (out of sight, out of mind), but it takes constant energy to keep these things hidden, and this energy, while expended within the unconscious, has ripple effects in the conscious.

Like an old sandwich in the refrigerator (or a corpse buried in a backyard garden), repressed feelings or memories will eventually cause unusual occurrences in other places, and the more extreme the memory or trauma, the more noticeable the effects. Freud calls this set of effects the *symptom*: the marker of sickness. Eruptions of irrationality into everyday behavior can signal that something repressed has returned, or is threatening to return, to consciousness. This is what Freud means when he writes about the *compulsion to repeat*: traumas return in the form of symptoms, which is why some people get locked into patterns of incomprehensible behavior—or why killers return to the scene of the crime. What makes the repetition compulsion so strong is the fact that *enjoyment* is tied up in the symptom; the neurotic, like the killer, takes a kind of pleasure (conscious or unconscious) from this repetition—it is one way for the libido to express itself, even if it is a strangled kind of expression, dependent on certain forces *not* achieving their goal. Why do smart people repeat stupid behaviors? Why do some nice persons always choose to get involved with abusers? What keeps us trapped in cyclical patterns? The answer, for Freud, has to do with the way each of us, as a child, learns to handle pleasure and pain, satisfaction and disappointment: as children, we teach ourselves to repeat behaviors for reasons that later, as adults, will remain opaque to us. What else is the typical slasher film about, after all, but the fact that its central scenario must happen over and over and over?

Later in his life, Freud moved away from the consciousness/unconsciousness model (one area of the mind *behind* or *under* another one, with a sort of gatekeeper or doorway between them) and toward an understanding of the self as a set of forces and resistances. In this second model, he postulated three entities within the self: the *id* contains all the desires, all the rage, all the frustration and the need, while the *superego* is the set of restrictions imposed upon, and *internalized* by, each of us—behavioral chains which can be both practical ("do not kill people") and irrational ("do not ever look anyone in the eye"). The third entity is the *ego*, the self, the stage upon which this central opposition plays out; often the self has no knowledge of the nature or purpose of this drama, even as it affects everything it does, sometimes to the point of illness or incapacitation. The id, of course, is central to the entire horror genre: awful pleasures that must be locked away (sometimes literally, as in the puzzle-box at the heart of the *Hellraiser* series begun in 1987) erupt through the barriers that keep ordinary folks, like you and me, safe from the awful things that lurk outside (and within) us. Since the id is within us, how does it appear outside us? Freud suggests that all of us, to varying degrees, project our fears *outside* ourselves, as if our worst impulses are not ours, but instead belong to others. This is what the scholar Margaret Tarratt postulated in her germinal article about science-fiction cinema, "Monsters from the Id": conflicts within the protagonist are externalized as battles with "sinister monsters," reflecting "the individual's anxiety about his or her own repressed sexual desires, which are incompatible with the morals of civilized life" (1970: 38). This obviously relates to the common horror trope of people encountering their doubles (a theme Freud explored in his famous essay, "The Uncanny"), and the genre's common body-snatcher theme is also an expression of this idea.

One line of film theory notes the resemblance between films and dreams: essentially, you relax and they happen to you. Since your conscious mind does not control what you experience when you watch a film, spectatorship also resembles an encounter with the unconscious itself. In this regard, the terminology that Freud introduces in *The Interpretation of Dreams* is useful. For Freud, all dreams are expressions of repressed wishes, and bits of memories and old feelings always wash up inside them; these are the *dream thoughts*, and the process by which wishes are expressed and memories knotted together—that is, the way that potentially dangerous unconscious material is *censored* for the conscious mind—is called *dream work*. One component of this is *condensation* (in which two or more ideas are represented by an image) and another is *displacement* or *substitution*, whereby one thing stands in for another. These are metaphorical operations: in a dream, a spider could represent a smashing-together of multiple ideas, or it could be an image covering over, and substituting for, another image—it depends on the person dreaming. (A spider will signify differently for one dreamer than it will for another.) Freud cites these two operations, condensation and displacement, as being typical of the unconscious in general: symptoms, being a sort of coded message from the unconscious, are always metaphors. Freud further concluded that what matters in dreaming is not the specific content, but the way that the various images relate to one another, that is, the specific narrative that the dream constructs out of the elements within it. The single most useful term in all of Freud's writing on dreams—at least for the student of horror cinema—is *overdetermination*: if an object or image (or motion, or sound, or color) comes to symbolize multiple themes, then its meaning cannot be unpacked without reference to multiple sources—that is, many determinations. Think of the penis-like, turd-like "monsters from the id" that plague the apartment complex in Cronenberg's *They Came From Within* (1975) or the crashed spaceship in the original *Alien* (1979) with its vaginal openings, and you can see how overdetermination is part and parcel of how horror often achieves its effects. In fact, one might suggest that the whole process of dream work—the displacement and condensation of dangerous ideas, and the revision that makes them intelligible—has a certain resemblance to the process of creating a horror film.

Psychoanalysis and Horror

Freud's model of normal human consciousness connects to horror cinema through his vision of abnormality: the origin and effects of the monstrous, the disgusting, the hidden, the murderous, the perverse. Why are so many horror films about children? Why is there such turbulence around issues of sexuality? Why do so many horror films present the return of some kind of trauma from the past, and why would something from the past be the cause of so much fear? (And what *is* fear, anyway?) To choose an example: rationally, we know that zombies do not actually exist, so if we are afraid of zombies, we must be afraid of something *else*, something that zombies *represent*. What would that be? Logically, you might assert: "I'm not afraid of zombies *per se*, but I *am* afraid of being bitten, and I'm *definitely* afraid of dying"—to which the proper response would be, "So why are you afraid of being bitten?—and if you're afraid of dying, then why are you particularly afraid that it might come from being bitten? What is it about the mouth, the teeth, that is particularly frightening? Is it a fear of being eaten, consumed by another person? Why is that such a powerful fear?" It does not take much imagination to extend this kind of inquiry in all directions.

Since horror cinema and psychoanalysis have more or less grown up together, it seems natural to apply them to one another. Siegfried Kracauer wrote the first convincing use of Freud, applying psychoanalytic categories to the Weimar silent cinema [*The Cabinet of Dr. Caligari* (1920) for example]. For film students of my own generation, the classic scholarly work in this vein was done by Robin Wood, a British film scholar who wrote some of the earliest and best English-language treatments of Alfred Hitchcock and who later turned his considerable intelligence to the matter of zombies and vampires. The central plank in Wood's reputation, and perhaps his single most powerful gesture as a film scholar, is a set of essays that he wrote for various publications in the late 1970s and early 1980s, including "An Introduction to the American Horror Film" (later republished as "The American Nightmare"), "Neglected Nightmares," and "Return of the Repressed." (These essays later appeared, enlarged and refined, in his classic book *Hollywood from Vietnam to Reagan*, and many of the other chapters in that book are extensions of its basic inquiry.) Wood's point, in all of these essays, is that horror films necessarily operate on principles described by Freud (and, for Wood, developed further by Herbert Marcuse in the 1960s): sexuality is pervasive, and is especially subject to traumatic punishment; objects of fear arise out of the unconscious, and obey rules antithetical to rationality; forms of desire that run counter to the "normal," masculinist rules of Western society—homosexuality, for instance, or feminism—are always identified with the monstrous; and so on. Wood frames these ideas with a larger political idea, that is, that civilization (specifically, Western capitalism) must punish certain human energies in order to protect itself and its values, and that this punishment—this *repression*—has powerful repercussions on individual lives. Thus, for Wood, what happens to the characters in horror films is always metaphorical for what happens to persons living within capitalism, and what happens in (for example) American horror films has to do with what is happening, at any given moment, in America itself. Therefore, there is a potentially (and paradoxically) revolutionary component to any horror film, since that which erupts is always that which has been repressed. This juxtaposition of aesthetics, politics, and psychoanalysis was not new to Wood, but his inventiveness—and his willingness to watch the most extreme cinema for the sake of scholarship—was unprecedented, and his methodology is still highly influential.

Wood distilled his interpretive methodology into a wonderfully suggestive six-word rule, with which he defined the entire horror genre: "Normality is threatened by the Monster" (1986: 78). This is a powerful claim (all the more for its extreme simplicity), and Wood applies its logic rigorously. Normality is repression, personal and social; the monster is what *returns*, that is, what is created by normality and that which seeks to shatter it. Perhaps, reading "The American Nightmare," the advanced student will notice the ways in which Wood's understanding of Freud might be said to be limited (or simply dated); she may also disagree with his conclusions—for example, many scholars are dissatisfied with Wood's reading of the films of David Cronenberg (myself included). And other scholars have since offered subtler readings of many of these same films, using a more nuanced methodology. However, Wood's work remains, for me, the best starting point for the film student interested in psychoanalysis and its relationship to horror; if you read him with some imagination, you can see that most (if not all) of his basic principles and methods are still valid, even thirty years after he first published them.

In lieu of simply inserting 20 paragraphs' worth of Wood's writing, I will use his methodology to offer a brief sketch of some of the ways in which psychoanalytic questions may be useful in the study of horror films. I will concentrate on four particular American movies, all chosen because they were enormous popular successes: *Psycho* (1960), *The Exorcist* (1973), *Halloween* (1978), and the American version of *The Ring* (2002). *Psycho* is probably the paradigmatic work of horror cinema, at least in regard to the amount of scholarly attention it has received, and each of the other three has inspired more than its fair share of academic writing. Each one also begat an entire subgenre (sicko loner movies, demonic possession movies, slasher films, J-horror remakes), and you could reasonably apply the discussion below to any film made in the shadow of these classics.

First, let us consider the way that each film constructs a monster, and how that monster is gendered. *Psycho* plays the game of allowing the first-time viewer to think that Norman Bates's vengeful, jealous mother is the murderer; when it is revealed that Mrs. Bates died long ago, the viewer is cued to wonder: if she is dead, then who is killing on her behalf? The answer, of course, is Norman himself, whose fragile ego was shattered long ago and who has since internalized the voice of his mother—in a way, he has become his own mother. (A forensic psychiatrist makes an appearance at the end, explaining that Norman is not *exactly* a transvestite, even though he sometimes wears his mother's clothes.) The monster of *The Exorcist* is a young girl on the verge of womanhood who begins acting strangely; by the film's climax, she is seen to spray a priest with green vomit, speak in the voices of dead persons, and turn her head completely around on her shoulders. It turns out that she is possessed by an ancient demon; she is only saved when said priest sacrifices himself for her—it is his way of atoning for the sin of abandoning his elderly mother, who dies midway through the film (of natural causes, one assumes). *Halloween* presents a little Midwestern boy who murders his promiscuous older sister with an enormous carving knife; years later, he escapes from a mental hospital and returns home on Halloween night, butchering all the sexually active teenagers he can find. (Only the virgin survives, with the help of the boy's gun-toting former psychiatrist.) And in *The Ring*, a monstrous little girl with potent supernatural powers, abandoned to die in a well by superstitious adults, avenges herself against the living through the medium of a VHS tape; the clues to the nature of her trauma are encoded in the images on the tape—clues that, when unraveled, reveal a story of parental abandonment and pure, murderous otherness. Note that in each of these instances, the monster is created in the home; something happens there, something in the past, that creates and/or unleashes a rage against (as Wood would say) normality itself.

The most common route of psychoanalytic inquiry into horror cinema is through considerations of the monster's gender and sexuality. The canonical trio of articles on this theme—"canonical" not only in the sense of definitiveness, but also because they are so commonly anthologized and read together—are Linda Williams's "When the Woman Looks," Barbara Creed's "Horror and the Monstrous-Feminine: An Imaginary Abjection," and Carol Clover's "Her Body, Himself: Gender in the Slasher Film." All three of these articles concern the gender of the monster, and all three use psychoanalytic interpretive methods, although to three very different ends. (Note that these articles all first appeared in the mid-1980s, during what some would call the Golden Age of psychoanalytic film criticism; this was the era of Reagan, when a backlash against the feminism of the 1970s made the study of horror—especially misogynist horror of the slasher variety—particularly urgent.) What is central to all three is the place of *woman* in the horror film—as object of the camera's gaze, as monster, and as victim. Williams writes of the use of woman as victim (and as object, and occasionally subject, of the gaze) in the genre, while Creed and Clover discuss opposite manifestations of the monster/victim binary: Clover discusses the figure of the "final girl" in the slasher film, who survives the attack of the (male) monster by becoming male in some way, while Creed observes the ways in which woman becomes monstrous and disgusting, that is, the barely-human (or too-human) object that produces horror.

Creed uses the ideas of the post-Freudian psychoanalyst Julia Kristeva, who writes about *abjection*—the process by which a person can come to identify with blood, excrement, and other forms of waste and filth. To this end, consider *The Exorcist*, which gives the clearest example of woman-as-abject-monster in all of horror cinema: the possessed girl vomits, bleeds, masturbates, and blasphemes, and her victims—a friend of the family and two priests—are all men, destroyed by the uncontainable power that is feminine sexuality. Similarly, *The Ring* is built around the image of a drowned woman, her face covered by a curtain of slimy black hair, who crawls out of a TV set, dripping with water, to annihilate her victims—a vision that depends on a sense of woman as pure otherness and pure, inexorable, murderous desire. On the other hand, *Halloween* contains the paradigmatic instance of the "final girl" discussed by Clover: the virginal girl, shrieking and bruised, can only survive the unmistakably phallic attack of the monster because she has not yet acquired sexual knowledge. And in *Psycho*, naturally, the character of Marion Crane is set up to be sacrificed because she is seen, in the movie's first moments, to be an adult, sexual being—albeit unmarried and, therefore, outside the bounds of proper sexual propriety. Note that all four of these films can easily be read as conservative visions of sexual roles—women who have sex outside of marriage, who have desires of their own, who express sexuality in any form, are either victims or monsters—and Robin Wood, indeed, questions whether all of horror cinema is, by its very nature, conservative. (If there is a liberatory or anti-repressive impulse in horror, it is paradoxically embodied in the monster: thus the difficulty in assigning cut-and-dried political positions to these films.)

What creates these monsters? *Psycho* assigns blame purely to familial trauma, while *Halloween* obscures the childhood origins of Michael Myers's psychosis and, at the very end, raises the specter of some kind of supernatural interference. (Rob Zombie's symptomatic remake, released in 2007, dives into the childhood-trauma theme with remarkable abandon; you may judge for yourself whether this explicitness results in a better, or truer, film.) *The Exorcist* gets God and Satan involved, but the local, familial themes are still there: the possessed girl's father is absent from the scene, for example, and—given that this is the early 1970s, during the first large-scale hangover from the sexual revolution of the 1960s—we, as viewers, are cued to assign significance to his absence. (On his daughter's birthday, he is vacationing in Rome and out of contact; the girl witnesses her mother's expletive-laced tirade upon being unable to reach him by telephone. The visible signs of possession begin in the very next scene: a single mother is not powerful enough to protect her family from such pressures.) And *The Ring* works hard to make it impossible to tell where parental failures end and supernatural evil begins. In each of these films, something malign passes from an older generation to a newer one; children are destroyed, and in turn, children destroy. Priests are flung from windows and policemen down staircases; naked women are stabbed to death; teenagers in the bloom of their youth are found rotted away from the inside, their faces locked in an awful scream. At the center of the film, the monster: a lonely, smiling psychotic in a gingham housedress and white wig; a girl with a pasty, lacerated face and orange eyes; a man in a mask; a wet, slithering female form with syrupy black hair. Each one has a causal relationship to some kind of long-ago violence against (and within) the family that has been purposefully hidden or forgotten, a repressed trauma that returns, erupting like a cyst into the midst of normality. (Even the monster in *The Exorcist*—supposedly thousands of years old—speaks to the priest in the voice of the priest's dead mother.)

In keeping with Freud's theories about childhood sexuality—or, to be slightly more precise, regarding the impact of infantile desires upon early consciousness, and therefore upon adult behavior — the trauma, whether it is revealed or kept hidden, always expresses itself *sexually*, that is, in a certain kind of highly charged, very *private* violence. (Without this element of violence, most horror films would simply be family melodramas.) Norman Bates — or the Mother inside him — kills women, specifically the women that he finds attractive (and which therefore arouses the jealousy of the Mother within him); he/she famously kills Marion Crane in the shower, the most private of private spaces. Michael Myers, reenacting the murder of his sexually active sister, kills only those with raging hormones: he leaves the young children, those in their latency period, quite alone. The demonic presence in *The Exorcist* (a horrible old man living inside a girl's body) urges the priests to bugger each other, and — most memorably — forces her mother's face into her bleeding crotch. (She/he has just masturbated, violently, with a crucifix.) And the undead woman-thing of *The Ring* comes at her victims inexorably, like a repressed memory (or like a rapist), leaving only a broken shell of a person behind. Of these films, only *The Exorcist* allows the erupting trauma to be solved (or re-repressed); once it is all over, the girl, true to form, remembers nothing of her possession. The other films suggest the ultimate powerlessness of normality to contain the monster (the monster escapes, or goes into hiding, or survives imprisoned). But, of course, all four films have sequels.

There are other psychoanalytic inquiries one could pursue with these films. There is the God problem, for example. Freud, an atheist, considered all religious feeling (and especially religious activity) as essentially delusional, that is, entirely built on fantasies of security and punishment with roots in earliest childhood. Therefore psychoanalysis, at its deepest levels, is profoundly anti-spiritual: God is *literally* understood to be the father. In other words, theories about the Creator (or angels, or demons, or ghosts) are nothing more than childish theorizing about the role of parents — and mankind, being resolutely irrational, will always be plagued by this delusion. (See Freud's monograph *The Future of an Illusion*.) Attention to the supernatural aspects of any of these films, then, requires an inquiry into these remnants of childhood; the moment that any horror film passes into the supernatural, one may be sure that fantasies about parents and origins are being invoked — *The Exorcist* is most explicit in this regard. Hitchcock's *Psycho*, on the other hand, is a purely psychoanalytic movie: it takes place in a Godless world, in which any person's behavior is no more meaningful or productive, in the long run, than the squirming of an insect on a pin. (The advanced student could use *Psycho* to understand the affinity between psychoanalysis and existentialism: watch it and then read *Civilization and its Discontents*.)

Additionally, there are many subgenres of horror, each with its own set of common preoccupations (and mutual differences). Consider the haunted-house film. What is the relationship between domestic architecture — bedrooms, bathrooms, hallways, staircases — and the nightmares of childhood? It is a complex one, no doubt, and films like *The Shining* (1980) or *The Woman in Black* (2012), given their insistence on the fear of being indoors (and on the distinction between inside and outside, public and private), take place on the borderline between childhood

Figure 2.3 Abjection, or how Child becomes Woman. *The Exorcist* (1973). Directed by William Friedkin. Produced by Warner Bros and Hoya Productions.

fantasy and the incomprehensible, cadaverous sexuality of adult life. Somehow, the darkest childhood traumas linger on, inhabiting these houses, hotels, abandoned hospitals; that is why so many of them are haunted by children. There is also the rural family-of-monsters subgenre, epitomized by Tobe Hooper's original *The Texas Chain Saw Massacre* (1974); what is this subgenre about, if not the determining effects of familial trauma? (Note that monster-family movies seem to be a staple in every film-producing country in which there is a severe divide between the wealthy cities and the impoverished rural countryside, guaranteeing an economic/political subtext as well.) And what about the problem of ex-human monsters, or non-human ones? Vampires, werewolves, zombies are all ex-human, while flesh-eating blobs and mutant plants are not human; in all instances, the earliest childhood questions are being invoked: What has a mind, and what does not? What wants to hurt me, and why? The paradoxical bodies of ex-humans reflect questions about the body, especially the strange changes that befall each of us: transitions between childhood and adulthood, between sickness and death, between ignorance and knowledge (of sexuality, for instance). The bodies of the elderly, the bodies of siblings who died too young, the bodies of parents laid out in coffins: these reappear in movies, thirsty for blood, reflecting again the infant's confusion about the borders between the animate and the inanimate.

Finally, there is a lot of scholarship that uses psychoanalysis to address the idea of the audience for horror films: What is it in people that makes them *want to watch* these movies? Are horror spectators *sadistic*, or *masochistic*? What is their relationship (social or personal) to this sort of material? This kind of scholarship often (but by no means always) has a faintly judgmental tone to it, a tone that does not appear in regard to most other genres: no one assumes that fans of musicals or romantic comedies are pathological, and yet of course they could be. (See, e.g., the first four essays in Schneider, ed, *Horror Film and Psychoanalysis: Freud's Worst Nightmare.*) Leaving aside the judgment factor, one runs up against the fact that each person is a different kind of spectator; filmgoers (and neurotics) are like snowflakes, all alike and yet each one different. A personal anecdote: years ago, a good friend of mine—an adult in his late thirties, and by no means an immature or emotionally unhealthy person—was so unsettled by a horror film that he had nightmares for weeks. That film was *The Ring*, which I saw with him; I enjoyed the film and was on edge while watching it in the theater, but I was amused that he was so deeply and atypically affected by it—until, just a month or two later, I watched Brad Anderson's *Session 9* (2001), which truly *freaked me the hell out*. (I heard those warbly, tape-scrubbed voices in my dreams for nearly a year.) The two films resemble each other in some ways—analog recording devices, family trauma, certain stylistic gestures, and so on—and yet they worked differently on my friend and myself, since after all we are different persons and have different fears. I offer this mundane observation in order to advise you to take seriously your own reactions—indeed, *anyone's* reactions—to any horror film. Even if you are the kind of devoted horror fan who will watch *any-thing* and does not scare easily, you should still ask what any run-of-the-mill horror film is *trying* to accomplish inside your head and why; and on the rare occasion that one genuinely gets to you, you should pay very, very close attention. If anything, psychoanalysis demands attention to the details. Anyway, in an essay this short, I can only scratch the surface of what Freud's system offers the film student—and I have not even mentioned the other psychoanalysts working in Freud's wake, whose own ideas have relevance for horror film, such as Jacques Lacan or Melanie Klein. Further research is up to you.

Acknowledgments and Dedications

Thanks to Tabitha Lahr for processing the frame grabs. This essay is dedicated with gratitude to Pat Day, Susan Fischman, and Dan Goulding.

References

Carroll, N. (2004) Afterword: psychoanalysis and the horror film, in *Horror Film and Psychoanalysis: Freud's Worst Nightmare* (ed. S.J. Schneider), Cambridge University Press, New York.

Creed, B. (1986) Horror and the monstrous-feminine: an imaginary abjection, reprinted in *The Dread of Difference: Gender and the Horror Film* (ed. B.K. Grant), University of Texas Press, Austin, 1996.

Clover, C. (1987) Her body, himself: gender in the slasher film, reprinted in *The Dread of Difference: Gender and the Horror Film* (ed. B.K. Grant), University of Texas Press, Austin, 1996.

Freud, S. (1900) *The Interpretation of Dreams*, Bard/Avon, New York.

Freud, S. (1910) *Five Lectures on Psycho-Analysis*, W.W. Norton & Co, New York, 1977.

Freud, S. (1919) The uncanny, reprinted in *The Uncanny*, Penguin, New York, 2003.

Freud, S. (1930) *Civilization and Its Discontents*, Norton, New York, 1989.

Gay, P. (ed.) (1989) *The Freud Reader*, Norton, New York.

Hobson, J.A. (2005) *Dreaming: A Very Short Introduction*, Oxford University Press, New York.

Nasio, J.-D. (2011) *Oedipus: The Most Crucial Concept in Psychoanalysis*, SUNY Press, Albany, NY.

Tarratt, M. (1970) Monsters from the Id. *Films and Filming*, **17** (3), 38–42.

Williams, L. (1983) When the woman looks, reprinted in *The Dread of Difference: Gender and the Horror Film* (ed. B.K. Grant), University of Texas Press, Austin 1996.

Wood, R. (1986) *Hollywood from Vietnam to Reagan*, Columbia University Press, New York.

3

Gender and Sexuality Haunt the Horror Film

Daniel Humphrey

It almost seems unnecessary to state the importance of an approach to the horror genre that focuses on—or at least takes into account the issues raised *by*—human sexuality and gendered human subjectivity. Nevertheless, there was a time in the not-so-distant past when such a focus would have seemed pertinent only among those focused on feminist film studies and hardly central to broader studies of the operations of the genre itself. While one can point to the influence of the "body horror" subgenre exemplified by David Lynch's *Eraserhead* (1977) and the work of David Cronenberg, as well as the lasting impact of films like *Rosemary's Baby* (1967) and *Carrie* (1976), the quality of the compelling arguments made by the first feminist and queer scholars to venture into the debate are what made it seem essential to regard horror films according to considerations of sex and gender. This chapter will adumbrate some of the most influential work in this specific sub-field of criticism, while offering its own modest contribution to the discussion with another look at one of the key texts at issue in the field, the 1973 blockbuster *The Exorcist*.

Thinking about Gender and Sex: Feminism and Queer Theory Goes to the (Horror) Movies

Carol J. Clover's *Men, Women, and Chainsaws: Gender in the Modern Horror Film* and Barbara Creed's *The Monstrous-Feminine: Film, Feminism, Psychoanalysis*—both published in paperback in 1993—are often considered the first two major books to explore horror cinema in terms of gender and sexuality. This exciting sub-specialty in the study of the field has been sustained ever since. Film Studies was hardly a long-established scholarly discourse by the early 1990s, and yet the fact that Creed

A Companion to the Horror Film, First Edition. Edited by Harry M. Benshoff.
© 2014 John Wiley & Sons, Inc. Published 2017 by John Wiley & Sons, Inc.

could justifiably complain about the dearth of previously published scholarship on the role of women in the horror genre does come as something of a surprise. As Creed points out, however, a lot of work had been done on the horror film, just not much involving gender and sexuality. When it could be found at all, the topic of gender and sexuality was discussed in passing, at best, or, at the worst, in language betraying the (usually male) authors' sexism and myopia. There were a few exceptions, of course. Creed notes Stephen Neale's argument in his 1980 book *Genre*, developed out of psychoanalytic theory, that "most monsters tend … to be defined as 'male'" and represent the anxiety of castration that male spectators bring with them to the theater (61). Neale's almost throwaway comments on the topic, in retrospect, might be seen as having inspired Creed's own project. He remarks, "it could well be maintained that it is woman's sexuality, that which renders them desirable—but also threatening—to men, which constitutes the real problem that the horror cinema exists to explore" (61). As Creed put it, "Neale argues that man's fascination with and fear of female sexuality is endlessly reworked within the signifying practices of the horror film" (5).

Creed's study is indebted to the psychoanalytic work of French-Bulgarian scholar Julia Kristeva, particularly Kristeva's (non film related) book, *Powers of Horror* (Kristeva, 1982), which, as Chris Dumas reminds us in his essay for this collection, focuses on the concept of "abjection" (2014). As Creed puts it, Kristeva's work "suggests a way of situating the monstrous-feminine [basically the horrific female monster] in the horror film in relation to the maternal figure and what Kristeva terms 'abjection,' that which does not 'respect borders, positions, rules,' that which 'disturbs identity, system, order'" (8). For Creed, simply put, in the horror film, abject elements include things like blood, excrement, and other forms of waste and filth. Since the abject, in both Kristeva's and Creed's arguments, is most profoundly tied to the female body through the fact of menstrual bleeding, *The Monstrous-Feminine* analyzes a wide variety of female-centered horror films in terms of how on-screen women are connected to "biological bodily functions" in excess or distress (9). Creed's project would be little more than a catalogue of disgusting images related to women in horror cinema, and thus simply one arguing that the genre is misogynistic, were it not for the complex way in which abjection functions for Kristeva and, subsequently, for Creed. "The abject must … be tolerated," Creed writes, "for that which threatens to destroy life also helps to define life" (9). In other words, women's abject status in the male imagination (and the horror films that come out of it) is necessary for men to see themselves as human. With the stakes set that high, *The Monstrous-Feminine's* survey of movies from *Psycho* (1960) to *Basic Instinct* (1992) is fecund and provocative, decisively shifting the debate from a near-constant focus on horrifying male creatures (the Wolf-Man, King Kong, Frankenstein's monster, etc.) to female monsters (Regan in *The Exorcist*, *Carrie* etc.).

Like Creed's, Carol Clover's study is largely focused on the cinema of the 1970s and early 1980s, and together both are largely responsible for that era's films being so central to the academic film-studies canon (1992). But where Creed focuses on often-grotesque images of woman-as-monster served up for the horrified male's contemplation, Clover's book is at once more simple and complex, focusing on film *plots* instead of cinematic *images,* and hero or heroines more often than monsters or villains. Rather than chart the repulsion of spectators taking in traumatic images on the screen, Clover's work concerns itself with narrative engagement and the spectator's identification with a film's characters—engagement and identification that she argues crosses biological sex and allows young male viewers to engage in (unrecognized) transgender experiences through the particularities of the genre. As Clover puts it, film theory needs to entertain "the possibility that male viewers are quite prepared to identify not just with screen females, but the screen females in the horror-film world, screen females in fear and pain. That identification, that official denial of that identification, and the larger implications of both these things are what [*Men, Women, and Chain Saws*] is about" (5).

Clover's wording ("not just") suggests male viewers are willing to identify with female characters outside of the horror genre. Her book, however, leaves open the possibility that horror-film spectatorship is conducive of a kind of cross-sex iden-tification young males can only process if and when they are able to also feel hor-rified. Outright horror distracts from the misogyny and homophobia that might otherwise destroy the emotional engagement necessary for males to fully enjoy other female-centered genres, such as romantic comedies. (And, after all, there is little evidence young men regularly and passionately consume other genres that focus primarily on female protagonists.) To make her argument, Clover had to upend the conventional wisdom of psychoanalytic feminist film theory of the time, inspired by Laura Mulvey's landmark essay "Visual Pleasure and Narrative Cinema" (Mul-vey, 1975), that suggests that sadism is the dominant dynamic among men watch-ing (horror) films. Against that, Clover posits male *masochism* at work when men identify with women protagonists under siege (the so-called "Final Girl"). Although Clover acknowledges that "middle-aged, middle-class people of both sexes … have 'come out' to [her] about their secret appetite for so-called exploitation horror" (the sub-genre upon which she largely focuses), she restricts herself to exploring "the relationship of the 'majority viewer' (the younger male) to the female victim-heroes who have become such a conspicuous screen presence in certain sections of horror" (7). This restriction likely exasperated some feminist readers impatient with scholars, in this case a feminist scholar, who still focused on young males. Nevertheless, this focus allowed Clover to identify and explore previously unacknowledged dynamics of transgender and homoerotic engagements within a film genre ostensibly favored by those least likely to admit to such an inconvenient concept.

One earlier, briefer study—Linda Williams's "When the Woman Looks" (Williams, 1983)—is problematic for both Creed and Clover. It is problematic to Creed for its avoidance of what she feels is the core issue of female monstrosity (6), and to Clover for its focus being maintained on sadism rather than masochism as the spectator's entry point into cinematic engagement (47–48: n36). Nevertheless, by focusing on the unlikely rapport between the female spectator and the on-screen male monster, Williams pointed the way toward more diverse spectator reading positions *vis-à-vis* the horror film that resulted in some of the most interesting post-Clover/Creed work on the topic. Rhona J. Berenstein's *Attack of the Leading Ladies: Gender, Sexuality and Spectatorship in Classic Horror Cinema* (Berenstein, 1996) serves as a refreshingly non-schematic study that contests various binary distinctions that had already begun to creep into the literature. For one thing, as she puts it, "to claim that the genre is either politically progressive [as Robin Wood (1979) claimed] or conservative [as Bruce Kawin (1981) has argued] oversimplifies one of its most important qualities; namely, its function as a site of ideological contradiction and negation" (10). More provocatively Berenstein suggests that, "in the [horror film's] figure of the monster … presumptions of sexual difference on the basis of biology are as fraught with ambiguities and are as historically constructed as those based on gender attributes" (29). Indeed, Berenstein claims that, "the genre is so troubling to conventional assumptions regarding gender … because its terrors cannot be reduced to one prima facie theme or generative cause" and that "its terrors and fascinations are grounded, in large part in its celebration of multiple and shifting forbidden themes" (18). Perhaps most importantly, Berenstein employs the theory of "gender performativity" developed by Judith Butler (1990) and previously alluded to only briefly in Clover's work (159) to "offer a theory of classic horror spectatorship as a form of performance"—female viewers acting scared along with the films' heroines while male viewers attempt to act as tough as their on-screen counterparts. Berenstein calls this "spectatorship-as-drag" (30).

Harry M. Benshoff continued to complicate and add nuance to the discussion with *Monsters in the Closet: Homosexuality and the Horror Film* (Benshoff, 1997), which focuses on both male and female homosexuality at multiple points across the cinematic apparatus: in the production of films, in characters and *mise-en-scene*, in narrative patterns, and in the viewer in the audience. Taking an approach less beholden to Freudian psychoanalysis than his predecessors, Benshoff lightly grounds his work on the theories of French historian Michel Foucault, who charts the ways in which societal discourses construct cultural meaning and indeed what we finally understand sexuality and sexual identity to be, often in complex and counter-intuitive ways. Like Williams in her essay, Benshoff accepts the theory, going back to Mulvey's "Visual Pleasure" essay, that cinema's default position is to assume and engage with the spectator as if he is a heterosexual male. Also like Williams, however, he concerns himself with another type of viewer, essentially asking what happens when the homosexual looks. Earlier historical studies of homosexuality and film, such as Vito Russo's *The Celluloid Closet* (Russo, 1987) waxed indignant at the homophobia present in classical Hollywood cinema, assuming the gay or lesbian spectator's only valid choice was, essentially, to reject it for its insulting images. Benshoff, however, brought forward more ambivalent, queer forms of identification that non-normative gay, lesbian, or bisexual spectators can have with the classical horror genre, much of which actually had been crafted by queer artists exercising a good deal of radical agency [for instance James Whale, director of *Frankenstein* (1931), *The Old Dark House* (1932), *The Invisible Man* (1933), and *Bride of Frankenstein* (1935)].

Such radical forms of cinematic engagement by minority filmgoers would continue to be studied by scholars focusing on the horror film and its connected genres and subgenres. Although not focused exclusively on horror films, Patricia White's *Uninvited* (White, 1999) examines lesbian spectatorship during the era of heightened self-censorship in the American film industry (1933–1967) and finds queer specters haunting classical Hollywood ghost stories such as *The Uninvited* (1944) and *The Haunting* (1963). Inspired by Terry Castle's *The Apparitional Lesbian* (Castle, 1995), which argues in White's summary that "the ghostly is one of the primary tropes of lesbian (in)visibility" (xxi), *Uninvited* offers an exemplary assessment of how various conventions of film genres both illuminate and obfuscate "unacceptable" minorities in censorious eras. [Space constraints prohibit me from offering more than a tip of the hat to Barry Keith Grant's invaluable anthology *The Dread of Difference: Gender and the Horror Film* (Grant, 1996) which excerpts chapters from Creed's, Clover's, and Berenstein's landmark books, and reprints Williams's "When the Woman Looks," among many other fine essays on the subject.]

The twenty-first century has seen the study of gender and sexuality as reflected in horror cinema effectively incorporated into differently focused studies, such as Joan Hawkins's *Cutting Edge* (2000). That work delineates the high-brow/low-brow divide in horror, and uses feminist film theory to better tease out the ways in which gendered and sexual meanings are molded by aesthetic regimes beholden to ideas about, and reactions to, "good" and "bad" taste. Adam Lowenstein's *Shocking Representation* (2005) also makes judicious use of the insights of feminist critics, including Clover and Creed, to incorporate issues of gender into a compelling account of the ways in which horror films function to allegorize historical trauma. Finally, Sue Short's (Short, 2006) monograph *Misfit Sisters: Screen Horror as Female Rites of Passage* brings us to the realm of the female centered horror film as regarded by female spectators. Selecting a handful of recent films and television series focusing on young women and the supernatural, Short productively reads them as the contemporary equivalent of classic fairy tales, to articulate the "range of meanings, and possible pleasures the narratives … might have to offer a female audience" (3). This is a particularly important avenue of study, as recent data from Hollywood has finally been able to prove that women actually make up the majority of ticket buyers for theatrical horror films in the United States, from more psychologically nuanced features like "2002's *The Ring* (60% female), 2004's *The Grudge* (65% female), and 2005's *The Exorcism of Emily Rose* (51% female)" to the "slice-and-dice remakes and sequels" previously considered the cultural property of, largely, adolescent males (Spines, 2009: 31–33).

Five *Exorcists*, More or Less Queer

If there is one important thing this author feels has not been fully explored in relation to gender and sexuality in the horror film, it is the relationship of queer American culture and its love of "camp aesthetics" to the horror genre. Another missing element in this author's estimation, is a fully queer survey of what are now five feature-length films inspired by William Peter Blatty's 1971 novel *The Exorcist*. The remainder of this chapter will address both. Despite the volumes of discussion devoted to the film *The Exorcist*, not to mention its two sequels and two prequels, it is perhaps surprising that the subject of homosexuality, as a theme woven into and identifiable within the work(s), has only occasionally been raised. *The Exorcist* is generally described, somewhat misleadingly, as a film about a pubescent American girl who has become possessed by a demon. However, *The Exorcist* also chronicles an attempt to cast that spirit out of the girl's body by two priests, an older man with experience in such remarkable supernatural events, who is joined by a younger, more progressive priest who is suffering an intense crisis of faith. In an intriguingly ambivalent way, the film's director, William Friedkin, recalls a queer interpretation of the film he happened to read:

> One guy wrote a piece saying that what the film was really about was a kind of a homosexual wet dream about the two priests both being lovers, and having to destroy the female, in this case the little girl, in order to consummate their love ... It was *great*! It has *nothing* whatever to do with what I intended but I guess it's a totally valid analysis. (Quoted in (Kermode, 1997): 35; emphasis in the original)

As far-fetched as such an interpretation sounds, at least in Friedkin's canny summary (his acknowledgment of it serves to prove Friedkin's open mindedness even as he frames any queer reading of the film as nothing more than overactive ingenuity), a palpable and largely compelling queer specter *does* haunt *The Exorcist*. Indeed, it haunts the franchise as a whole, which, as of this writing, includes William Peter Blatty's original 1971 novel, its 1983 sequel, *Legion*, and five feature films: *The Exorcist*, *Exorcist II: The Heretic* (1977), *The Exorcist III* (1990), *Exorcist: The Beginning* (2004), and *Dominion: Prequel to the Exorcist* (2005). This queerness is arguably responsible for at least some of the vexations the series has suffered, including what seems to be a remarkable first in film history: the temporary scuttling of an expensive, full-length film after principle photography had been completed. The much-maligned *Dominion* only appeared on home video as an alternative to its willfully more heterosexual "replacement," *Exorcist: The Beginning*. Sadly, the financial and critical success of only the first of these five films offers even more evidence, if we needed any, that a homophobic dynamic existed in 1970s mainstream film spectatorship and the critical discourses surrounding it. Ultimately, *The Exorcist*'s success in *avoiding* a kind of "hysterical camp" reading and the cultural critiques that would have emerged with it, a fate many films of the era could not avoid—think *Boom!* (1968), *Myra Breckinridge* (1970), *Performance* (1970), and others, as read by Harry M. Benshoff (2008)—arguably made a potentially queer friendly film into a homophobic one. At the very least it resulted in one that sees gender and issues of sexuality in convincingly absolute, and moralistic, terms.

The Exorcist's popularity, despite its unprecedented catalogue of shocking images and its purported harrowing, even traumatizing, effects on audiences, is especially remarkable. [Adjusted for inflation, *The Exorcist* stands as the ninth most financially successful motion pictures of all time (*Box Office Mojo*, 2013).] The fact that the four subsequent attempts to recreate that success have yielded a rather disparate succession of fascinatingly botched (and unprofitable) results is also at least somewhat surprising. (Safe, profitable sequels, regardless of their artistic merit, is one thing Hollywood generally seems to know how to do pretty well, especially within the horror genre.) Another noteworthy element of the original film, both obvious and ignored (pointing to yet another blind spot in *Exorcist* reception studies) is the way in which it, and, in various ways, its sequels and prequels, offers pleasures associated with the international prestige cinemas of the post-war years in concert with those pleasures associated with the so-called "camp" vernacular.

The late 1960s and early 1970s was a period in which big-budget Hollywood films routinely adopted art film styles and concerns to impressive effect, from *Bonnie and Clyde* (1967) to *The Godfather* (1972). [The former famously channeled the French New Wave while the latter borrowed from a number of Luchino Visconti films including *Rocco and His Brothers* (1960) and *The Leopard* (1963) to effect its aura of operatic profundity.] The appearance of *The Exorcist* in that period as a major Warner Bros. studio release and as part of what was acclaimed at the time as the New Hollywood Cinema guaranteed that it would be judged as a sophisticated work. The fact that it approaches its subject with a strong focus on big themes *as* big themes—not buried in the subtext but right on the surface—themes like "good versus evil" and/or "guilt and redemption" also suggests the art cinema mode. Finally, the casting of Max Von Sydow in the titular role is perhaps the clearest sign that *The Exorcist* is attempting, at least in part, to present itself as "art cinema." Von Sydow was best known by the early 1970s as the star of many of Ingmar Bergman's acclaimed Swedish films, such as *The Seventh Seal* (1957), *Through a Glass Darkly* (1961), and *The Passion of Anna* (1969); as those titles suggest, many of the Bergman/Von Sydow collaborations focused on religious, specifically Christian, themes. Others, such as *The Magician* (1958) and *Hour of the Wolf* (1968) can, for their parts, be considered art-horror films specifically. As such, Von Sydow was very nearly the perfect choice to give *The Exorcist* a sense of cultural respectability as a serious (if also horrifying) film on theological issues. [The fact that Von Sydow had also played Jesus Christ in *The Greatest Story Ever Told* (1965) and a Protestant missionary in *Hawaii* (1966) further adds to the serious religious tone *The Exorcist* attempts to sound.]

Until the late 1960s, imported art films also had been among the only motion pictures released in the United States to deal, however subtly, with homosexuality. Federico Fellini's *I Vitelloni* (1953) had a gay subplot that resulted in censorship problems, while *The Silence* (1963) was just one of many Ingmar Bergman films to deal with homosexuality. Furthermore, Von Sydow's character in *Hour of the Wolf* is easily readable as a conflicted gay or bisexual man (Humphrey, 2013). Indeed, the first major English-language movie to feature the word "homosexual" in its dialog was the British feature *Victim* (1961), about a gay blackmailing ring, which was released in art-film theaters in North America. As a result of all of this, a film with an art-house sensibility would have seemed the natural place for homosexual elements to emerge by the early 1970s. Finally, the fact that one of William Friedkin's earlier films, *The Boys in the Band* (1970), was one of the few Hollywood films to focus on gay characters might well have also primed *The Exorcist*'s audiences to notice the subtle homosexual references or inferences it contains.

Throughout the film, various signs appear in both the imagery and dialogue that raise the specter of homosexuality. In one early scene, the soon-to-be-possessed young girl, Regan, is reading a Hollywood gossip magazine. As the daughter of well-known actress Chris MacNeil, Regan seems to be doing so to learn about her own parent's separation in a story illustrated by a photograph of her mother and herself. As spectators reflect on the unique phenomenon of reading about one's own family problems in a national publication, one notices a headline on the magazine's cover for another story: "Rock Hudson in Head-On Crash! His Story from the Hospital!" As a celebrity whose homosexuality was something of an open secret even in the early 1970s, the reference to Hudson is perhaps the first evidence of queerness to appear in the film, and by being juxtaposed with gossip about the MacNeils, it suggests a commonality, a common queerness involving both these Hollywood stars, the fictitious Chris MacNeil and the very real Rock Hudson.

Somewhat later in the film, police detective William Kinderman pursues a curious, homosocial relationship with Father Karras (the younger, more doubting of the film's two exorcists). Kinderman tries to sweet talk his new priestly acquaintance into going to the movies with him — he's not gay; it's just that his wife "gets tired … never likes to go" to the cinema. In a flirtatious line of dialogue from the novel that is carried over into the film, he asks: "'Do people ever tell you look like Paul Newman?'" Even more remarkably, when spurned by Karras at the end of the conversation, he says "I lied! . . . . You look like Sal Mineo" [Blatty, 2013 (1971): 181, 183]. This reflects a typical "pick up" mentality in which a heterosexually identified man attempts to win over the object of his homosexual desire through a masculine form of camaraderie: he belittles his own wife, asks the man if he would like to hang out, and compliments the man's looks by comparing him to an attractive, masculine, also heterosexually defined public figure (in this case, Paul Newman.) When rebuffed, in a predictable act of projection, Kinderman attempts to turn the tables by quickly asserting his own heterosexuality through an inference comparing the person who has rejected him to a homosexual, in this case Sal Mineo, whose homosexuality was, like Hudson's, an open secret, but whose gender affect was far less manly, arguably more effeminate than Hudson's *or* Newman's.

Father Karras will die a spectacular death before Kinderman gets another chance to ask him to the movies, but in the final pages of the novel (and in the extended version of the film released in 2000) he approaches Karras's good friend in the priesthood, Father Dyer, with a slightly amended line: "You know, you *look* a little bit like [Humphrey] Bogart" (Blatty: 385; emphasis in the original). With more of a heterosexual affect than even Paul Newman, the comparison of Dyer to Bogart is faintly absurd. In the book, Dyer is described as "pink faced" and "diminutive, with fey eyes" (Blatty: 69). As played by William O'Malley in the film, Father Dyer — first seen as a piano-playing lover of show tunes at a party at the MacNeil's — offers even stronger affective signifiers of gayness. He claims "my idea of heaven is a solid white nightclub with me as a headliner for all eternity and they *love* me!" In the book, referring to a party conversation he is eager to resume in another corner of the room, Dyer's curious formulation is: "I think I've got something going on over there with the astronaut" (74).

Carol Clover, in her analysis of *The Exorcist* in *Men, Women, and Chain Saws* points to another sequence from the book in which "Karras is interrupted in his research on possession by a visit from the flirtatious Father Dyer" (89):

> "She [Mrs. MacNeil] can help us with our plan for when we both quit the priesthood."
> "Who's quitting the priesthood?"
> "Faggots. In droves. Basic black has gone out. Now I — "
> "Joe, I've got a lecture to prepare for tomorrow," said Karras as he set down the books on his desk (Blatty: 248).

Father Dyer is hardly the only priest who comes to Karras with queerly mixed signals. In an earlier passage in the book, another young Jesuit knocks on Karras's door and asks if he might come in to talk:

> The young priest fumbled; faltered; seemed shy.... Of all the anxieties that Karras encountered among the community, this one had lately become the most prevalent. Cut off from their families, as well as from women, many of the Jesuits were also fearful of expressing affection for fellow priests; of forming deep and loving friendships.

> "Like I'd like to put my arm around another guy's shoulder," [the young priest tells Karras], "but right away I'm scared he's going to think I'm queer. I mean you hear all these theories about so many latents attracted to the priesthood." (Blatty: 99)

Indeed. And if accounts of widespread homosexuality in the priesthood were not as prevalent in early-1970s as they are today, Blatty explicitly spells this out for his reader with this passage, just as surely as Friedkin suggests it with the performance he elicits from O'Malley as Father Dyer in the film adaptation.

If queerness in the case of Father Dyer is transferred from the novel to the film through casting and/or performance, as well as a couple of lines of dialogue (the screenplay was written by Blatty himself, who also produced), it seems a complete addition to the movie in the case of the character of Burke Dennings, the director of the film-within-the-film that Chris MacNeil is shooting. Although supposedly based upon director J. Lee Thompson, known for three heterosexual marriages across a long career in many genres, Jack MacGowran's performance as Dennings suggests nothing so much as the kind of gay show-business personage often described as a "fierce old queen," replete with an Oscar Wildean hauteur and a rapier wit. Understandably, Chris is spending a lot of time with her director; presumably not only for professional reasons but also for the emotional support he can offer as she contemplates what looks to be a bitter, upcoming divorce from a husband whom we never see. Still, the naive 12-year-old Regan sees him as a threat to her parents' marriage, something which serves as a motive for what Chris fears is Regan's murder of Dennings later in the film. On the other hand, the fact that Chris seems so sincere in claiming that nothing has been going on between her and Dennings when Regan first asks, further suggests the character's homosexuality.

However, it is the character's ultimate fate that provides the strongest evidence of his queer nature, one supplied by the demon actually responsible for the murder. In both the *Exorcist* novel and film, the body of Dennings, who we are led to believe was pushed out the window by the possessed Regan, is found at the bottom of a long flight of steps next to the MacNeil house with its head turned 180 degrees around on its neck. This is the original act of bodily contortion that leads to the later, famous scene when the taunting demon inside of Regan turns her head around 180 degrees — an event not present in the book — to speak to Chris in Dennings's voice and accuse her daughter of the murder: "Do you know what she did, your cunting daughter?" (Figure 3.1) But what is the logic of the sequence? What does it mean for a head to be turned around so that its owner is looking directly behind him or her? As a number of critics have pointed out, it seems to have been an element in black masses. As Noel Carroll (1990: 232, n7) further explains, "[r]otating the head 180 degrees is a feature of orgies of the sort associated with black sabbaths; it is a practice Satan putatively indulges [in] when sodomizing witches." With that in mind, by leaving Dennings's dead body in such a way as to suggest he had been sodomized by Satan before his death, with his head positioned so he could look directly into the eyes of his devil-lover, *The Exorcist* offers up the possibility of an appalling horror that few have recognized, and one that ultimately begs a key question: is *The Exorcist* haunted by a queer spirit or a homosexual demon? If the first is the case, if a puckish queer spirit inhabits the film [in the way one can say that *The Wizard of Oz* (1939) has a

Figure 3.1   Regan MacNeil (in the form of a special effect dummy) supernaturally misbehaving in *The Exorcist* (1973). Directed by William Friedkin. Produced by Warner Bros and Hoya Productions.

certain queer or gay spirit to it] an argument can be made that *The Exorcist* has the power to subvert and undermine the cultural values standing behind mainstream assertions of heterosexual normalcy. If the latter is the case, however, and the demon possessing the young Regan in the film might be thought of as homosexual—in the same way that the transgender Buffalo Bill in *The Silence of the Lambs* (1991) gives that film its trans-phobic quality—*The Exorcist* ultimately must be considered for its potentially reactionary or homophobic inferences.

To entertain the idea that *The Exorcist* (and now, for clarity's sake, I focus on the film only) is positively haunted by or, perhaps more fittingly, *possessed by* a queer spirit raises the specter (so to speak) of camp. Critic Susan Sontag has been credited with bringing mainstream attention to the concept in her 1964 essay "Notes on 'Camp,'" in which she defined camp as a certain "sensibility," the essence of which is a "love of the unnatural: of artifice and exaggeration" (275). Sontag and the many critics and scholars who have followed after her in the study of camp maintain that "a peculiar affinity and overlap" exists between a gay sensibility and a camp sensibility and that, "homosexuals, by and large, constitute the vanguard—and are the most articulate audience—of camp" (290). Perhaps the most controversial claim in Sontag's formative essay is that the camp sensibility is apolitical, something many feminist and queer theorists have strongly disputed. For example, Brett Farmer holds that camp is at least "potentially" subversive "because its central re-presentation of gender as theatrical role-playing" makes it "a form of anti-essentialist feminism *avant la lettre,* a coded theory of gender as performative masquerade" (2000: 122). In other words, the camp habit of embracing what seems like a failure to behave, or to be in good taste, or to be real, sometimes knowingly and other times unknowingly, forces one to question behavior, taste, and what it actually means to be real. Realizing that historically homosexuals have been oppressed by social conventions demanding they behave according to heterosexual notions of good taste (simply put: be heterosexual or vanish) brings the subversive possibilities of camp into focus.

With queer fans of camp cinema known for lovingly laughing at batty monster movies like *Bride of Frankenstein* (1935), the over-the-top histrionics of Hollywood melodramas such as *Mildred Pierce* (1945), and Grand Guignol thrillers like *What Ever Happened to Baby Jane?* (1962), one might have expected some public evidence of *The Exorcist* falling victim to the gleefully respectful disrespect of a camp reaction from queer audiences. After all, it involves a cute, pubescent girl possessed by a demon who then, horrifyingly enough, swears like a foul-mouthed truck driver; pees on a carpet in front of her mother's friends at a cocktail party; levitates three feet above a bed like a magician's assistant; and, perhaps most famously, projectile vomits onto a priest who, with old-world decorum, gently wipes the bile off of his glasses with a handkerchief. Surely one would expect that all of this would result in some level of puckish tittering from devotees of camp. Perhaps there have been camp screenings of *The Exorcist* at private parties in various enclaves of the gay subculture. Still, it never seems to have been *publically recognized* as part of the official camp canon: as, for instance, a "special event" screening at San Francisco's Castro Theater, in which filmgoers are invited to dress up as a character from the film; in the form of an off-Broadway production by camp auteurs such as Charles Busch; or discussed as an example of camp by queer theorists or GLBT cultural critics in any of the major go-to texts (Farmer, 2000; Gerstner, 2006; Halperin, 2012). In other words, its successful seriousness seems to have helped it to dodge the bullet of camp appropriation. Seemingly having feared the fate of camp disrespect from the beginning, William Peter Blatty admitted that *The Exorcist* "could have easily descended into an unintentionally hilarious comedy," crediting Friedkin's "driving, intense, narrative pace" as decisive in avoiding such a result [quoted in Baer, 2011 (Baer, 2008): 60, 45].

A key term in Sontag's argument about camp is that it involves a "failed seriousness" (287), and had *The Exorcist* failed in its serious attempt to dramatize what its director calls "the mystery of faith" [quoted in Crouch, 2011 (1974): 73] it most likely would have become a camp classic. But while Blatty's explanation for the film's success seems cogent, one might remember that any number of motion pictures accused of descending into unintentionally hilarious comedy—such as *Showgirls* (1995), the remake of *The Wicker Man* (2006), and even *Exorcist II: The Heretic*—also maintained a "driving … narrative pace." (Indeed, fast pacing can be credited with adding to the zany sense of irreverence many camp films inadvertently evoke in their spectators.)

Crucial, perhaps, to the film's unlikely triumph, is the fact that the demonic voice emanating from the young Regan, meant to be that of a minor male, Babylonian deity, Pazuzu, comes, in fact, from a deep-voiced female actor, Mercedes McCambridge. McCambridge, whose career includes work in such classic Hollywood films like *All the King's Men* (1949) and *Johnny Guitar* (1954), is best known today for two small roles in which she initially was not even accorded screen credit: *The Exorcist* and Orson Welles's *Touch of Evil* (1958), in which she played a butch lesbian bike-gang member. The queer affect she expressed throughout her career was hardly a result of the Welles film alone. "Known for strong roles," as her *New York Times* obituary put it, McCambridge had "a reputation as a strong-willed, outspoken woman on and off the screen," although her appearances in movies were "sporadic" because "she did not fit the glamour-girl image that was prevalent in post-war films" (*The New York Times*, 18 March, 2004: B10). Instead, McCambridge thrived due to her "radio-trained voice," which made her "an ideal portrayer of hard-driving women." Reasonably enough, the *Times* credited her "great vocal skills" for having been cast as Pazuzu. The casting of a mannish woman to play the male voice of the demon in *The Exorcist*, seems, in retrospect, to have been a canny decision on the part of the filmmakers. The male demon's masculine personality is well represented by the depth and rough tenor of McCambridge's voice, while young Regan's vocal chords, through which the demon was, of course, obliged to speak, is realistically represented by the voice actresses' noticeably feminine modulations. Had Friedkin simply cast a man as Pazuzu's voice, *The Exorcist* could have seemed a campy cousin to John Walters's cult classic *Female Trouble* (1974).

Released just months after *The Exorcist*, *Female Trouble* is profoundly evocative of a camp sensibility for, among other things, its casting of obese male drag artist

Figure 3.2   Dawn Davenport (Divine) as John Waters's ultimate bad girl in *Female Trouble* (1974). Directed by John Waters. Produced by Dreamland.

Divine in the central role of Dawn Davenport, a character who evolves on screen from a female juvenile delinquent to a death-row mass murderer. The scene in which the teenaged Dawn goes berserk after not getting the Christmas gift she wanted from her parents, stomping on her family's wrapped presents and then pushing her frail mother into the decorated tree, is the film's most famous scene and one that compares to some of Regan's over-the-top misbehavior in *The Exorcist*. Considering *Female Trouble* would have been in production just as *The Exorcist* was becoming a global phenomenon, it may not have been sheer happenstance that Dawn's father calls his girl a "devil" as she performs acts of mayhem on Christmas morning. ("Not on Christmas, not on Christmas!" Dawn's mother moans, on the floor under the tree, noting the desecration inherent in the timing of rampage.) By the end of Waters's film, with Dawn's transmogrification into a deformed, maniacal mass murderer, the resemblance to Regan in *The Exorcist* is particularly strong (Figure 3.2, compare to Figure 3.1). Many gay men schooled in the fine art of camp spectatorship tend to find Waters's film hysterical—its on-screen rapes, murders, and other carnage notwithstanding—but, interestingly, there was simply not a similar, measurable reaction to the equally over-the-top behavior on screen in *The Exorcist*.

If *Female Trouble* gives us the campy image of a gay man in the garb of a female character, *The Exorcist* suggests a less conventionally comedic and arguably more homophobic image of a homosexual woman taking over the body of a pubescent girl, positing lesbianism as a possible allegorical referent behind the film's sharp good versus evil plot: a possession made all the more verisimilar by the voice of a biological female (McCambridge) in the body of what people in the transgender community call a cisgender girl (Linda Blair, the young actress who effectively portrays Regan). Had a male voice been used, and even subconsciously recognized as such, a failure of verisimilitude might well have resulted, and a failure of seriousness would have been reflected in a breaking down of the belief that gender is always essentially immutable. In a sense, then, *The Exorcist*'s unlikely success in avoiding the pitfalls of camp can be said to have kept the film away from the potentially subversive and liberating effect that would have resulted in using the metaphor of demonic possession to allegorize bad gender performance, bad sex-role behavior and, by extension, to unmask gender and sexuality as, at best, merely "good" performance. It could have helped shift, as Brett Farmer (114) suggests in his definition of camp, "the emphasis from seeing gender as an essentalized ontology, a fixed expression of an inner truth to seeing it as a performative production." In other words, had *The Exorcist* failed as a horror film and succeeded as camp, it would have been readable as a vision of gender *ine*ssentialism, in which a man's (or a male demon's) possession of a young girl comes across as socially constructed dramatics, rather than a metaphysical horror.

In that way, *The Exorcist*'s success at avoiding "failed seriousness" results in a potentially queer-friendly film becoming, arguably, a successfully homophobic one, at least one that sees gender and sexuality in convincingly absolute terms. For its part, *Exorcist II: The Heretic* would seem a far more likely candidate for horror film camp classic, since it is almost universally regarded as a failed film, one with the ambitiousness necessary to define its failure as a spectacular one. Its attempt to replace the first film's rather simple good-versus-evil, literalist theology with a more complex, progressive, almost "new age" theology inspired by the heretical writings of French Jesuit Pierre Teilhard de Chardin, results in a number of risible moments — the film is worth sitting through just to see James Earl Jones wearing a traditional African locust costume, something that resembles the Orientalist camp costumes in "exotic" musicals of the 1940s. Indeed critic Pauline Kael used the word camp twice to describe the film in her single-paragraph review [collected in Kael, 1980 (1978): 429]. The fact that the film has such an enormously complex story, however, keeps it from functioning as the sort of simple camp allegory the first film could have possibly become. Still, if a gay audience never quite embraced this film either, a number of reviews of the film by (presumably heterosexual) critics like Kael suggests that the negative reactions to the film resulted, at least in part, from critics incorrectly thinking the film was actually functioning as some sort of gay camp, camp they suspected was there, but that they were not about to appreciate.

The Exorcist III, for its part, directed by William Peter Blatty himself and based upon his novel *Legion*, picks up on the friendship between Lt. Kinderman and Father Dyer that began to develop at the end of the first film. However, as if he was made uncomfortable by the pronounced gay affect that William O'Malley brought to the role in *The Exorcist*, Blatty recast the role for the newer film. In it, Ed Flanders as Dyer comes across so completely heterosexualized, that even a throwaway line of dialogue in which he says he enjoys reading women's magazines for the fashion news does not serve to raise suspicions regarding his sexuality. In the book, the same disavowal is achieved in a passage in which Kinderman and Dyer, movie buddies after all these years, go to a theater to watch matinee of a campy old film. A man sitting to the other side of Kinderman placed his "hand on Kinderman's thigh, at which point Kinderman turned to him, incredulous, breathing out, 'Honest to God, I don't believe you,' while snapping a handcuff around the man's wrist" (Blatty, 1983: 36). By identifying homosexuality squarely in the personage of a stereotypical movie theater pervert, one forgets the possibility of same-sex desire emerging between Kinderman and Dyer, even if Blatty continues to characterize the latter by "his fey blue eyes" (1983: 35). Perhaps having learned from working as a producer beside Friedkin on the original film, Blatty manages to stage a number of risky scenes, including one in which a possessed senior citizen crawls across the ceiling of a hospital room like a cockroach, without quite falling into the territory of camp. Still, the film is hardly traditionally "good" either; Batty seems hamstrung by the fear that his film might veer into *Exorcist II*-like craziness to the point that it comes across as the opposite of good camp, as sodden and dull.

It was only with the unprecedented fact that a long-awaited prequel to *The Exorcist* was almost completely finished by one director according to one script, only to be scuttled and filmed again with a revised script by a different director, that one was able to compare an almost purely art-film *Exorcist* (Paul Schrader's *Dominion: Prequel to the Exorcist*) with an utterly campy one (Renny Harlin's *Exorcist: The Beginning*). Veteran filmmaker Paul Schrader has long worked in a hybrid Hollywood/art-cinema mode while also teasing out homoerotic/homophobic elements in a number of his projects, including *American Gigolo* (1980), *Mishima: A Life in Four Chapters* (1985), *The Comfort of Strangers* (1990), and *The Canyons* (2013). He completed principle photography on his version in 2003, only to have the studio behind it force him to resign from the project so a new filmmaker could be hired to craft a more commercial version. As James Kloda put it, "Schrader had made 'un film de Paul Schrader,' a sober character study of existential crisis" (Kloda, 2011: 462). In other words, he made an art film for a company that only belatedly decided they wanted a sensationalistic horror film. Perhaps more distressingly for the financiers of this prequel, however, Schrader's take on the material comes disturbingly close to fully outing the potentially homoerotic sensibilities inherent in scenarios of same-sex demonic possession and exorcism as developed in what one might call the Christian imagination.

A back-story to the original *Exorcist* (both the novel and film), *Dominion* tells of a long-ago exorcism performed on a boy in Africa by Father Merrin. An account of this had been presented briefly in flashback sequences in *Exorcist II* (thus the opportunity to put James Earl Jones in a locust outfit), but the prequel, as scripted by novelist Caleb Carr, meant to tell the tale more fully. According to Schrader, the idea was to turn the premise of the original *Exorcist* "on its head and [have] a boy glorified, an afflicted boy glorified, rather than a girl tormented" (quoted in Myers, 2005: 484). In other words, the demon would take a crippled boy and, in the act of possession, make him strong, healthy, and beautiful in appearance for the young, disillusioned priest, Father Merrin, who is faced with rejecting and then exorcizing (or perhaps, falling prey to) this "glorified" male being. As filmed — with attractive Filipino pop music performer Billy Crawford nearly naked in a loincloth as the possessed pubescent African boy — the series' homoerotic, if also troublingly homophobic subtexts emerge stronger than ever. Although queasy mixtures of homophobia and homoeroticism can be found in a number of highly successful films, one suspects that this, more than simply the art-film style Schrader brought to the project, was what scared the studio into ultimately spending an additional 50 million dollars to rewrite and re-film the prequel, which now bears little resemblance to the account of an exorcism in Africa alluded to by Blatty, by Friedkin's film, and by *Exorcist II.*

In Renny Harlin's do-over prequel, *Exorcist: The Beginning*, the African boy is reduced to little more than a cameo, and an attractive *female* character becomes possessed in his place to heterosexualize the narrative. Ironically, however, the replacement director's version lacks the tastefulness of Friedkin (not to mention the uncanniness of Mercedes McCambridge's voice), the surreal complexity seen in John Boorman's original sequel, or the timid professionalism of Blatty-as-director on display in the third film, which together now stand as something of an *Exorcist* trilogy. Finally, with Stellan Skarsgård's Father Merrin forced into the un-priestly persona of an Indiana Jones-like character in Harlin's redux, as Schrader not unfairly describes it [quoted in Myers, 2011 (2005): 494], and a fully grown woman acting like the teenage brat Linda Blair's Regan almost but never quite became decades before, a subversively camp (un-homoerotic) *Exorcist* finally does exist. As it stands, particularly in relation to the other films in the series, *Exorcist: The Beginning* seems like the modern day equivalent of the great Hollywood camp classics; instead of *Cobra Woman* (1944) or *Devil Goddess* (1955), we finally have "Pazuzu Woman," a film that almost serves to desecrate the seriousness of the entire *Exorcist* enterprise. As such, the pretenses of masculinity, Christian metaphysics, and feminine grace are all queerly, if inadvertently, deconstructed. Nothing finally could be campier, or queerer.

Conclusion

Future work on horror cinema as it relates to human sexuality and socially constructed gender roles will likely always be indebted to the work adumbrated at the beginning of this chapter, but it will also need to consider radical leaps beyond psychoanalytic paradigms into largely ignored territory for women's and gender studies scholars studying film, including the philosophical perspectives opened up by the work of Gilles Deleuze (Deleuze, 1986; Deleuze, 1989) and, perhaps, the neo-formalist approach advocated by David Bordwell (1985). The data now made available by the recently introduced practice of studio exit polling, which allowed *Entertainment Weekly* to state, unequivocally, that women attend horror films more than men—at least in the theaters and at least on opening weekends (Spines, 2009: 31–33)—may well inspire potentially revelatory sociological studies into the genre from a women's and gender studies perspective. One promising avenue, already pursued largely outside of gender studies considerations by William Paul in his study comparing and contrasting horror films with gross-out comedies (1994), has recently been shown by Sarah Arnold to yield interesting results for the horror/gender studies scholar. Her *Maternal Horror Film: Melodrama and Motherhood* (2013) has a twin focus on horror and melodrama, and like William

Paul's critical convergence of horror and comedy, it suggests that in an era in which genres are combining rather than bifurcating, the study of one genre in relation to another has a great deal to tell us about merging gender roles and relational, or even reactionary, forms of sexuality. Despite the impressive body of work already found in studies of the horror genre from a woman's and gender studies/queer studies perspective, it is clear that a potentially endless number of sequels, prequels, reboots, and remakes of those theoretical and critical bodies of work will emerge to accompany us to and from the theaters, giving us thrills and chills throughout the night.

References

Arnold, S. (2013) *Maternal Horror Film: Melodrama and Motherhood*, Palgrave Macmillan, New York.

Baer, W. (2008) A Conversation with William Peter Blatty. Olson, D. 35–60.

Benshoff, H.M. (2008) Beyond the valley of the classical hollywood cinema: rethinking the 'Loathsome Film' of 1970, in *The Shifting Definitions of Genre: Essays on Labeling Films, Television Shows, and Media* (eds L. Geraghty and M. Jancovich), McFarland, Jefferson, NC, pp. 92–109.

Benshoff, H.M. (1997) *Monsters in the Closet: Homosexuality and the Horror Film*, Manchester UP, Manchester, UK.

Berenstein, R.J. (1996) *Attack of the Leading Ladies: Gender, Sexuality, and Spectatorship in Classic Horror Cinema*, Columbia UP, New York.

Blatty, W.P. (1971) *The Exorcist*, Harper, New York, p. 2013.

Blatty, W.P. (1983) *Legion*, Simon and Schuster, New York.

Bordwell, D. (1985) *Narration in the Fiction Film*, U of Wisconsin P, Madison, WI.

Box Office Mojo (2013) An IMDB Company. Web. 26 October,.

Carroll, N. (1990) *The Philosophy of Horror: or, Paradoxes of the Heart*, Routledge, New York.

Castle, T. (1995) *The Apparitional Lesbian: Female Homosexuality and Modern Culture*, Columbia UP, New York.

Clover, C.J. (1992) *Men, Women, and Chain Saws: Gender in the Modern Horror Film*, Princeton UP, Princeton, NJ.

Creed, B. (1993) *The Monstrous-Feminine: Film, Feminism, Psychoanalysis*, Routledge, New York.

Crouch, W. (1974) Interview with William Friedkin. Olson, D. 61–82.

Deleuze, G. (1986) *Cinema 1: The Movement-Image*, U of Minnesota P, Minneapolis, MN.

Deleuze, G. (1989) *Cinema 2: The Time-Image*, U of Minnesota P, Minneapolis, MN.

Dumas, C. (2014) Horror and psychoanalysis: an introductory primer, in *A Companion to the Horror Film* (ed. H.M. Benshoff), Wiley-Blackwell, Malden, MA.

Farmer, B. (2000) *Spectacular Passions: Cinema, Fantasy, Gay Male Spectatorships*, Duke University Press, Durham, NC.

Gerstner, D.A. (ed.) (2006) *Routledge International Encyclopedia of Queer Culture*, Routledge, New York.

Grant, B.K. (1996) *The Dread of Difference: Gender and the Horror Film*, U of Texas P, Austin, TX.

Halperin, D.M. (2012) *How to be Gay*, Belknap/Harvard University Press, Cambridge, MA.

Humphrey, D. (2013) *Queer Bergman: Sex, Gender, and The European Art Cinema*, U of Texas P, Austin, TX.

Kael, P. (1980) Fear of movies 1978, in *When the Lights Go Down: Film Writings, 1975–1980*, Holt, Rinehart and Winston, New York, pp. 427–440.

Kawin, B. (1981) The mummy's pool. *Dreamworks*, **1** (4), 291–301.

Kermode, M. (1997) *The Exorcist*. BFI Modern Classics, British Film Institute, London.

Kloda, J. (2011) In the beginning there was *Dominion*: a duel for the soul of *The Exorcist* prequel, in *The Exorcist: Studies in the Horror Film* (ed. D. Olson), Centipede Press, Lakewood, CO, pp. 458–481.

Kristeva, J. (1982) *Powers of Horror: An Essay on Abjection* Trans. Leon S. Roudiez, Columbia UP, New York.

Lowenstein, A. (2005) *Shocking Representation: Historical Trauma, National Cinema, and The Modern Horror Film*, Columbia UP, New York.

Mercedes McCambridge, 87, (2004) Actress Known for Strong Roles. *New York Times* (Mar 18), p. B10.

Mulvey, L. (1975) Visual pleasure and narrative cinema. *Screen*, **16**, 6–18.

Myers, E.K. (2005). Interview with Paul Schrader. Olson, D. 482–506.

Neale, S. (1980) *Genre*, British Film Institute, London.

Olson, D. (ed.) (2012) *The Exorcist: Studies in the Horror Film*, Centipede, Lakewood, CO.

Paul, W. (1994) *Laughing Screaming: Modern Hollywood Horror and Comedy*, Columbia UP, New York.

Russo, V. (1987) *The Celluloid Closet: Homosexuality in the Movies*, Rev. edn, Harper & Row, New York.

Short, S. (2006) *Misfit Sisters: Screen Horror as Female Rites of Passage*, Palgrave Macmillan, New York.

Sontag, S. (1964) Notes on 'Camp.', in *Against Interpretation: and Other Essays*, Picador, New York, 2001, pp. 275–292.

Spines, C. (2009) Horror Films … and the Women Who Love Them!. *Entertainment Weekly* (Jul 31), pp. 31–33.

White, P. (1999) *Uninvited: Classical Hollywood Cinema and Lesbian Representability*, Indiana UP, Bloomington, IN.

Williams, L. (1983) When the woman looks, in *Re-Vision: Essays in Feminist Film Criticism* (eds M.A. Doane, P. Mellencamp, and L. Williams), University Publications/American Film Institute, Frederick, MD, pp. 83–99.

Wood, R. (1979) An introduction to the American horror film, in *The American Nightmare* (eds R. Wood and R. Lippe), Festival of Festivals Publications, Toronto, pp. 7–28.

4

The Horror Film as Social Allegory (And How it Comes Undone)

Christopher Sharrett

There is no film genre more subversive, more innately critical of the values of white bourgeois patriarchal society, than the horror film. There is no need to recapitulate the arguments for the horror film's inherent radicalism; this has been well accomplished by Robin Wood (1979) in a crucial essay and by others with a concern for the politics of the genre [Grant and Sharrett, 2004 (1984)]. With the powerful influences of Expressionism and Surrealism, modernist art movements concerned with both psychological turbulence under the repression of patriarchal capitalism and the agony of a civilization plunged into two world wars as a consequence of capitalist inter-imperial rivalry, the horror film is the most honest and forthright art form in discussing the relationship of the Other to the heteronormative, the bourgeois family, "normal" community life, and/or "functional" society under capital. And yet the genre always contains intimations of the reinstatement of repression, with the knowledge that Eros and the death wish remain in close competition so long as patriarchal capitalism rules. In the period of profound reaction that began in the United States, and throughout the world, with the post-Vietnam/Watergate backlash, the assault on civil rights and feminism, and the return of unfettered capitalism with Reagan–Thatcher–Kohl, the horror genre's attempt to retain its radical impulses has been difficult, as art itself tends to embody and enforce death over life, the nullification of the erotic and the creative.

The horror cinema of the Weimar era offered films, as Robin Wood noted, "made in the very shadow of Freud," involved explicitly in problematizing the idea of the monstrous (2004: xv). One can pick a film almost at random, but Murnau's *Nosferatu* (1922) is perhaps the most instructive. Count Orlock is a symbol of desire that the heterosexual bourgeois world cannot resist; he is vanquished not by the efforts of the citizens but by his own uncontrollable desires. Yet the film is deeply

A Companion to the Horror Film, First Edition. Edited by Harry M. Benshoff.
© 2014 John Wiley & Sons, Inc. Published 2017 by John Wiley & Sons, Inc.

disturbing in its portrayal of Orlock as a grotesque, perhaps the most repulsive of all vampires in film history. He is portrayed as an enormous rat and, not incidentally, as an Eastern European Jew, with caricatured bald head, hooked nose, and wringing hands with long, talon-like fingers. What is going on here? Desire is portrayed as an insurmountable force, yet the monster embodying it is unremittingly predatory and physically horrible. Murnau could not, in his day, shake off the burdens of Christian civilization (although his interest in the occult suggests he tried mightily), and as a homosexual in the Germany of the early twentieth century without any of the supports of the modern era, Orlock may suggest Murnau's self-hatred, his vampire lacking even the touch of charm supplied to the superannuated Dracula by his Victorian anti-Semitic creator Bram Stoker. But Murnau was well aware of the dangerous assumptions about self and other, about "evil" and the norm, fostered by western culture, as he supplied part of the template for what was to come. He recognized that even as the unconscious prevails, even as the Other wreaks havoc on society, the monster remains monstrous. The revolution has not yet occurred that is truly liberatory. And *Nosferatu* reminds us how the horror film, like all art, is subject to the forces of reaction, as indeed it was with the bourgeois retrenchment of the late twentieth century. But before the reaction to the progressive activity of the Sixties, the horror film was distinctive in its remarks about the actual horrors of the bourgeois world.

Horror and the Coming of Feminism

Nosferatu points us to the tensions within the genre, the attempt by the forbidden to burst free while still being shackled, and often destroyed, by bourgeois society. Desire emerges, but it is constructed as repulsive (the view of it demanded by the order of things); it "triumphs" to the extent that it points to basic contradictions within civilization, but then is cut down. Still, the monster is often resurrected (if not in sequels then by the suggestion, in the best films, that the other cannot be fully vanquished). The monster is often constituted as a force *in opposition to* liberation, as the Terrible Father enacting his law with a vengeance. For example, in Edgar G. Ulmer's *The Black Cat* (1934) and Jacques Tourneur's *Night of the Demon* (1957), two works where devil-worshippers are closely associated with the ruling class (in *Night of the Demon*, a key theme is the ability of the ruling class to impose its will on the impressionable and defenseless, usually portrayed as people of a lesser class) are explicitly about the struggle against repression/oppression. In Michael Reeves's *Witchfinder General* (1968), the supporters of the church impose terror and murder, the "righteous" ultimately bringing on an apocalypse that is an expression of the ruling class's basic nihilism, ideas also basic to Ulmer and Tourneur.

Two films of the 1960s suggest similar dynamics of patriarchal civilization, and of the challenges on the horizon brought by the arrival of feminism, with Betty Friedan's *The Feminine Mystique* appearing in 1963. In them, the demonic and the supernatural are tools marshaled by patriarchy. Robert Wise's accomplished *The Haunting* (1963), and Roman Polanski's masterpiece *Rosemary's Baby* (1968) examine the threats posed to patriarchy by the potentially liberated woman, the residual effects of the notion of woman as monster [see, e.g., the City Woman in *Sunrise* (1927)]. Both films share in common a degree of nihilism; they suggest that the female has no way out. Where they differ is in their analysis. While *The Haunting* shows sympathy for Eleanor, it offers nothing but despair, while *Rosemary's Baby*'s radical concept satirizes all patriarchal institutions.

The Haunting is in the tradition of Terrible House narratives, the trouble within such houses flowing from family history and the patriarchal legacy, with ghosts and the like "haunting" the building in the sense that the assumptions of the past live on in the present. In *The Haunting*, Eleanor is suddenly freed, with the death of her mean demanding mother, from years of caregiving, only to be trapped in her sister's stifling nuclear family. Her escape comes via her recruitment, due to her psychic skills, by paranormal researcher Dr. Markway, as a participant in a group investigation of the supposedly haunted Hill House. What is in fact haunted seems less about ghosts than the will of the man who lived there, and the ongoing effects of patriarchal civilization in the supposedly modern present. Eleanor is the archetypal "old maid" whose thoughts, as she drives to Hill House (after a nasty family squabble) are about a home of her own, one with middle-class respectability. It also becomes clear that she hopes Markway will have some sexual interest in her. Eleanor's sexual options appear to widen when she meets the beautiful Theo, another psychic who is coded as a lesbian; the coding is hardly subtle when she winks at the idea of she and Eleanor living in Hill House "like sisters," and most especially when Eleanor angrily turns on her, calling her a "monster" and, like the strange house, "one of nature's mistakes." Theo must "pull back" her lesbianism, hiding it under her *haute couture* as if she is merely a sophisticate rather than a debauched homosexual—but unlike the Wolfman, she is comfortable in her own skin, not desiring death in order to stifle desires that keep emerging against her will.

Markway, although benevolent enough, is quickly associated with Hugh Crain, the tyrannical, ultra-religious builder of Hill House, whose two wives died under strange circumstances (Figure 4.1). This Terrible House's "legacy of evil" is located specifically in the actions of its builder. Further, Hugh Crain's actions are centered on marriage and sexual activity, as are those of subsequent residents of the house (the companion of Abigail particularly). Although Eleanor is a very neurotic woman (screenwriter Nelson Gidding intended for the film to be about her nervous breakdown, but the term, meaningless from any psychiatric standpoint, needs to be understood within the context of the film's examination of repression, and its devastating effects on the female), she carries on an internal monologue that is the film's voiceover, frequently commenting on "what the house wants," which must be read as what Crain/Markway/patriarchy want. Crain's daughter Abigail self-infantilized by living her entire life in her nursery—after her father damaged her with fire-and-brimstone biblical admonitions. Abigail hired a young female companion in her last years (a parallel to the Theo-Eleanor pairing), who left her one evening to have a sexual tryst with a lover; Abigail's pounding with her cane therefore went

Figure 4.1 The tyrannical, ultra-religious patriarch of Hill House, Hugh Crain, whose terrible presence and vile deeds constitute the core of *The Haunting* (1963). Directed by Robert Wise. Produced by Argyle Enterprises.

unnoticed by the caregiver. The associations with Eleanor's life are made obvious. Like Abigail, Eleanor was infantilized by a cruel old woman who used a cane to get her attention. Eleanor was herself mentally damaged by a parent. Like Abigail's companion in the backstory, Eleanor becomes a sexual woman wishing to discover a new life.

The connections between Hugh Crain and the paranormal "family" become most evident when the group discovers the sculptures in the arboretum entitled "St. Francis Curing the Lepers." The wisecracking Luke notes that the group could be Hugh Crain and his family. Theo pushes the analogy, suggesting that the statues could be Markway, Eleanor, Theo, and Luke. The ills of patriarchy are passed down through the ages, an idea amplified when Theo rebuffs the advances of Luke, thus making evident (to the group) her lesbianism, suggesting for a passing moment (especially with Luke's snide retort "more than meets the eye") that she is the "monster" in their midst (this disturbing point is the extent to which the film both endorses and criticizes the notion of Theo-as-monster). Theo sees Eleanor's attraction to Markway, and enrages Eleanor by making a point of the new hairstyle and wish-fantasies of her roommate, the film hinting at sexual competition and jealousy poisoning even the alternative sexuality that dethrones patriarchy. Eleanor's hope for a relationship with Markway is crushed when his wife arrives to check up on her errant husband. The disheartened Eleanor overlooks the fact that Markway's marriage is a disaster—he is unconcerned, it seems, even when his wife disappears within Hill House, to be found only in the final act. The film's most intelligent point is that the paranormal group (that is, a group of supposedly unusually perceptive intellects) cannot see the sexual impulses that are glaringly obvious.

Eleanor's extreme neurosis (centered in her sexual wish-dreams) make Markway send her home. As she starts to drive away, Theo runs to the car, saying an affectionate farewell ("Nelly, my Nell") suggesting that Eleanor's sexual needs remain both unrecognized and unresolved, her frustration greater than ever, as she continues to think of dying and joining the rest of the terrible, repressed ghosts of Hill House. Her car hits a tree as she is distracted by Markway's wife dashing across the drive. As the group look at the dead Eleanor, Markway says that the house "got what it wanted." The film seems to recognize, in 1963, the frustrations of women under bourgeois patriarchal society, while also arguing that there is no way out. Even while offering the option of same-sex relations, the male and his property interests (symbolized by the immense Hill House) ultimately triumph. In this view, the film takes back what it offers. *The Haunting* is nihilist and defeatist in outlook, but understanding of the struggles to come.

Roman Polanski's masterpiece *Rosemary's Baby* might be said to be as nihilist as *The Haunting*, but it is saved by its sardonic vision, its satire of marriage, the family, organized religion, and capitalism. The film shows a clear understanding of the institutions undergirding patriarchy, responsible for the oppression of women. The film's appearance in an apocalyptic year, 1968, seems not incidental; Robin Wood (1986: 84) has noted that during this period, many genre films entered an "apocalypse phase," with *The Wild Bunch* appearing the following year. Rosemary and Guy Woodhouse are a young married couple setting up housekeeping in New York City at the mammoth, ancient Bramford apartment building (actually the Dakota, most famous today as the site of John Lennon's murder, which provides a resonance no doubt producing upset to at least one generation of viewers). Guy is an aspiring actor, full of frustration and nervous energy—as played by legendary actor/director John Cassavetes, Guy's very facial appearance takes on a demonic aspect. Guy makes a Faustian deal with the devil-worshipping Minnie and Roman Castavet to allow Rosemary to be impregnated by Satan (Guy after taking a potion) so that Guy's career success will be guaranteed. The devil narrative is made so ludicrous (Minnie is a nosy, grating *yenta*, Roman a paragon of bad taste), it is little more than a dramatic device; not that the film is not unnerving, but its sense of dread flows from its constant emphasis on the female's entrapment.

From early in the film there is a strong sense of the husband as manipulator, rooted in Guy's desire for public approval and professional success. Rosemary watches him on a television commercial for Yamaha—a smarmy pitchman asks him to "join the swingin' world of Yamaha," to which Guy quickly responds "OK." The notion of the banality of evil is entirely appropriate here. As Guy positions Rosemary to be the mother of the devil, he coerces her into eating a drugged dessert; he later berates her for a then-fashionable Vidal Sassoon haircut (one that coded Mia Farrow as waif). Guy censors Rosemary, throwing in the garbage the book on witchcraft given her by her old friend Hutch. The monstrous Dr. Sapirstein, who attends to Rosemary, tells her "don't read books!" when she complains of pains and mentions information from a self-help medical text. The control of the female's mind and body is constantly in the foreground. The tendency of the female to study, and therefore gain wider understanding of herself and the world, is a taboo of patriarchy that the film insists remains in the present—Polanski makes a point of showcasing the trappings of modernity, including the new furniture purchased by Guy and Rosemary (Minnie asks what they cost). The price of upward mobility becomes literally the loss of soul, but with the female as key sacrificial victim.

The film's most dreadful moment is the marital rape, especially as we see Rosemary's after-the-fact acquiescence, knowing that the wife must surrender herself to the husband as an expectation of the marital contract. Rosemary notes the scratches on her body as she awakens from a drugged sleep into which she fell as she was impregnated by Satan/Guy at the behest of the evil cult. Guy quickly notices Rosemary examining her body and says he has just "filed 'em down" (his fingernails). He further states that he did not want to "miss baby night" just because Rosemary was drunk (as he explains to her). The couple had an opulent meal in preparation for the sex act that they hoped would result in her pregnancy, which Guy had already arranged to be the conception of the devil's child. The horror of the moment again flows from the normal, from what the female must expect under current gender assumptions.

A key point is that Rosemary is oppressed as much by the patriarchal world that she has internalized as by the actions of Guy. In one of two pivotal dream sequences, Rosemary, drifting into dream sleep, sees a shriveled old nun berating her in parochial school. The nun's voice is actually that of Minnie, brow-beating her husband for the suicide of a young woman who was being groomed for the role finally forced on Rosemary. The voice, heard through the partition, is typically fused in Rosemary's anxious dream state with bad memories. In so doing, oppressions past and present become one. Both the "good" and the "evil" patriarchal institutions are made synonymous. Later, when Rosemary is impregnated by Guy-turned-devil in a satanic orgy, Rosemary dreams of being on a yacht piloted by President Kennedy. When Rosemary asks Kennedy if her atheist friend Hutch can come aboard, he says that he is "sorry about these prejudices," but refuses to let him aboard. We see Hutch on the beach, warning of a typhoon as winds almost knock him down—Hutch is cast as a prophet warning of Armageddon. In the same dream, as a costumed Roman paints Rosemary's nude body with blood, the Pope comes forward, offering his ring for Rosemary to kiss—the jewel of the ring consists of the odd, smelly amulet given to Rosemary by Minnie. JFK, the Pope, and the Satanists are one and the same, the alternatives to patriarchy no more than the silly, empty dichotomy offered by liberalism and conservatism.

The film's most remarkable moment is Rosemary's panicked visit to Dr. Hill, a young, kindly physician whom Rosemary believes will help her flee Guy and his horrid friends. Hill seems sympathetic, stating that while he does not believe in witches, he knows that "there are a lot of crazy people in the city," and offers to place her in a hospital. Rosemary's mention of Dr. Sapirstein gives Hill momentary pause. When Rosemary awakens from a brief nap in Hill's pleasant office, Hill has returned with Guy and Sapirstein. It seems doubtful that Hill is part of the conspiracy; he is simply unwilling to challenge an older, highly respected member of his profession, figuring Rosemary to indeed be another hysterical woman.

The film's final scene is a parody of the Nativity, with the baby devil, "the only son" of Satan, in a cradle draped in black, approached by "wise men" from around the world bearing gifts. Rosemary enters the room unseen by the others (who still want to keep the truth from her). She is horrified by the site of her offspring, but soon acquiesces and agrees to rock his cradle. The scene is handled with a tone both highly satiric [the broad, smiling faces of the cultists—some of them recognizable actors (like Hope Summers) from 1960s TV programs such as *The Andy Griffith Show*—make the film's acid commentary most emphatic] and oppressively disturbing. The female has lost, perhaps for all time. But one leaves the film with a sense that it understands clearly the nature of gender and the oppression/repression surrounding us under patriarchal arrangements.

The Obsolescence of the Zombie

In 1968, George Romero released one of the pivotal horror films of our times, *Night of the Living Dead*. A former maker of industrial films, Romero claimed he was trying to make the most chilling film imaginable under a very limited budget, being a bit coy about the film's political ambitions. It is clear from where the "chills" flow. The film is one of the most scathing condemnations of postwar America imaginable at that moment of social/cultural history. The dead come back to life to become cannibals, the phenomena caused by vague antics of the space program, suggested here mostly as a military boondoggle rather than a quest for knowledge. A rocket may or may not have brought a virus back from the cosmos. Whatever the cause, a small group of survivors are led by a black man, Ben (the superb actor Duane Jones), a breakthrough in action cinema in part because the film never exploits his race—although his race is of consequence to the narrative, and Romero never assumes that we have "transcended" race. Throughout the course of the film, the white nuclear family is portrayed as monstrous—the child killing the mother—and Ben is forced to fight the hateful, stupid father for control of the little group of survivors. The redneck posse, led by a local sheriff, is quickly developed as at least as lethal and loathsome as the zombies ("Beat 'em or burn 'em—they go up real easy"). At the end, Ben is shot down by the posse—is he murdered because they thought he was a zombie, or because he is black? We are never sure, but the film's final images—stills behind the credits—show men placing bodies, including Ben's, on a bonfire, the grainy photos evoking both the Nazi genocide and Southern lynchings. When looking at this film today, I think of Daniel Goldhagen's 1996 book about the Holocaust, *Hitler's Willing Executioners*, wherein he informs us that ordinary German citizens freely took part in the mass extermination of Jews. The notion that the run-of-the-mill, middle-class individual would be more than willing to vent various grievances by shooting down fellow citizens is accepted by Romero as a commonplace notion.

Romero followed *Night* with *Dawn of the Dead* (1978) and *Day of the Dead* (1984), the first a comment on consumer capitalism and the imperialist rampage that was the US attack on Southeast Asia, the second a scathing critique of the Reagan period, with its renewed military mindset—the film's strongly feminist ethic is notable. Together, Romero's first trilogy constitutes one of the most scathing cinematic critiques of America from the 1960s to the 1980s. Its project is comprehensive enough to constitute the total dismissal of American ideology. Perhaps most important for the present writing, Romero's zombie films offer one of the horror film's greatest critiques of Otherness. Are the zombies of *Night* the monsters or the military, the awful family, or the redneck posse? The action of *Dawn* takes place mostly in a closed-down shopping mall, the zombies ambling about aimlessly, imitating the behavior of consumers—and their cannibalism makes the points that the real targets of capitalism are other people, who are consumed by work over which they have no control. The survivalists, the nominal heroes of the film, further extend Romero's critique of the other by way of their own jealousy, rapaciousness, and fight for their domain—a fight that becomes complicated indeed when they face off against a motorcycle gang, one of the cinema's emblems of a reversion to barbarism. *Day*, which takes place in a mammoth underground bunker, shows the remnants of humanity governed by an arrogant scientist and a lunatic army captain and his command. Made in 1984, *Day* evidences Romero's despair, his sense that whatever positive occurred in the 1960s was being erased by the Reagan mode of capitalism, sexism, and imperialism.

Romero undertook a second trilogy with the arrival of the Bush era. The films—*Land of the Dead* (2005), *Diary of the Dead* (2007), and *Survival of the Dead* (2009)—are, respectively, critiques of the increasing class divisions of American society, the worthlessness of the "new media" and its promised utopia, and the myths undergirding American violence. Romero's project may be considered the "second wave" of horror using the zombie as metaphor. Initially, the zombie is a tool of a terrible manipulator whose interests are involved in personal capital and slavery (as in the superb *White Zombie,* 1932), or closely associated with the exploitation of the female (the equally superb *I Walked with a Zombie,* 1943), or the control of power by aristocracy (*The Plague of the Zombies,* 1966). Many early zombie films are rooted in the folklore of Caribbean culture, as well as the connection of the zombie with the American and Spanish slave trade.

Although the popularity of the zombie film today is enormous, its value as social/political commentary is not only almost totally gone, it has been transformed by neoconservative culture into its opposite, with audiences invited to enjoy the decapitation or blasting-apart of shambling, decaying ghouls. The aesthetic (if this is the word) of the plethora of zombie films [at this writing, *Zombie Apocalypse* (2011), *Humans vs Zombies* (2011), *The Dead* (2010), *Undead Apocalypse* (2012), *Abraham Lincoln vs Zomb*ies (2012), *et al.* are on the racks of big-box stores] is derived very much from video games—hence their minimal exposition and character development, as well as little attempt at narrative. Instead of the zombie film asking questions basic to the horror genre like "who are the REAL monsters?," the contemporary zombie film revels in the notion of human beings as targets in a shooting gallery. One essential point of Romero's films is that the zombies are people, removed from the living by accident and the fact of disease and death. Their monstrousness (cannibalism) is clearly associated with the norm, with accepted human behavior under consumer capitalism. Most of this is now erased, most egregiously in the attenuated television series *The Walking Dead* (AMC 2010 —), a soap opera about the travails of human survivors after the zombie hordes have been unleashed. The principal concern here is the extent to which, over the course of seasons, the human group will fall apart, lose some of their number, or find their sensitivity to loss waning — elementary issues dealt with by the early Romero films. There is an assertion in this series and in the current deluge of zombie films that the Other deserves little or no empathy, except for the occasional twitch of concern that the human killers may become desensitized to violence.

In the age of the patently amoral and illegal invasions of Iraq and Afghanistan, the direction of the zombie film is not surprising. Except for a few (very few) documentaries on these topics, the assertion is that the Arab/Muslim world needs to be annihilated; the main concern is the affect of slaughter on "our boys." The devastation of ancient societies and the murder of thousands of people are represented in the media with indifference — the body count in the Middle East and Central Asia is rarely mentioned. In the new, militarized US society, it is hardly surprising that social metaphor be stripped from a genre that has historically been focused on questioning the Law of the Father, and the acceptable codes of conduct within white patriarchal bourgeois society.

A few distinct elements of the current zombie film are evident. Zombies and vampires have become interchangeable [putting aside vampires as focus of teen sex fantasy as in the execrable *Twilight* series (2008 – 2012)]. The 2004 remake of *Dawn of the Dead* (effectively shorn of politics), and *28 Days Later* (2002) introduce zombies/vampires as manic predatory beings who run incredibly fast rather than shamble, their mania jibing with, it seems, a sense of disintegration and dread in bourgeois society that sees itself coming apart, destroyed by the culture of predation that built it (the placid, conformist suburbs very suddenly under bloody siege at the start of the *Dawn of the Dead* remake). Zombies/vampires have for the most part lost the characteristics of their respective predecessors, their importance located solely in the issue of their nebulous origin in the unnamed plague that animated them, and the ability of the human survivors to fend them off (again, in an orgy of special-effects blood). But the sense of panic that informs some of these films (there are so many that are simply dismissible from any aesthetic, technical, or political perspective, and are straight-to-video write-offs) is notable, suggesting the legitimation crisis that has pervaded US society since the Vietnam/Watergate period, accelerating with the Reagan era, and reaching its nadir with the amorality of the Bush neoconservatives who wage war with impunity in an unabashed show of imperialist strength as they simultaneously shred the social contract.

The Love of Apocalypse

The idea of apocalypse has been central to American fiction, and has returned to the horror film with a certain insistence. The notion of apocalypse (revelation) is a religious discourse derived from perhaps the most fantastic book of the Bible.

The fixation on waiting for the end, which will bring divine revelation, stands in opposition to a historical materialist view of reality, an opposition that has existed in America since the Puritans, becoming entrenched in the antebellum era. As sectional tensions over the growth of slavery increased before the Civil War, so did the ideologies of Northern and Southern cultures, including within various churches (Northern Baptist vs Southern Baptist, etc.). The North tended to believe in the value of Good Works—and hard work, a staple of Protestantism—as well as civic improvements, such as new roads, bridges, and canals. The religiosity of the South emphasized personal salvation, and the Bible-based rightness of the immiseration of blacks as slaves. The notion of "God's will" prevailed in the thinking of both sections, but especially the South in their justification of slavery: human agency in the ending of slavery seemed out of the question, although the reliance on religious dogma was amply buttressed by racial and economic rationales for slavery. Of course both sections contained deeply-entrenched racist dogma (more codified in the South), and Lincoln's Second Inaugural, seen by many as his greatest prose, is nothing if not apocalyptic, with its admonitory assertions about the need for the Civil War's blood drawn by sword to compensate for blood drawn by the slaveholder's lash. In Reconstruction and post-Reconstruction America, as white supremacy was reasserted, the nation tended to rely on apocalyptic thinking as capitalism confronted regular crises—the Panic of 1873 was blamed on the excesses of Reconstruction, with avaricious blacks blamed for a national decline; Native Americans were seen as Red Devils overtaking land that should belong to the divine mission of whites, fomenting yet another wave of genocide to keep a sacred pact with Manifest Destiny (see Slotkin, 1985).

The apocalyptic is alive today in the fixation on the Rapture (only the faithful will be "saved"), the battle of Armageddon, and the arrival of God's kingdom. Human involvement in such issues as climate change or the rapaciousness of capitalism seems heretical or senseless, especially in those sectors of the US firmly embracing born-again evangelical Christianity—not ironically, the always-reactionary South, as well as the Southwest and the West, the territory wanted by the South for the extension of slavery. In these regions, the apocalypse is *desired* as an affirmation of divine will and a demonstration of the rightness of this form of reaction against the liberalism that has been the tempter of sectors of US society. The apocalyptic view rejects the worth of science, history, and all intellectual activity in favor of fairy-tale mysticism that affirms a form of social vindictiveness. But ahistorical visions of reality extend to all parts of the nation and much of the world in the era of global capitalism. The moral bankruptcy of finance capital, with its dependence on speculation and the migration of capital, brings a sense of despair and the collapse of human agency even within those sectors of the population outside of the Bible Belt expressing a progressive social view.

The adaptation of Cormac McCarthy's novel *The Road* (2009) represents one of the more serious-minded renderings of the apocalypse in postmodern cinema, its bleak, burnt-out *mise en scene* complementing the sense of a total reversion to barbarism. In it, the world is redeemed at the last moment when the dead father is replaced by a new one; the mother is written off quickly — it is unclear if she simply dismisses the endgame of the patriarchal world, or if she is (more likely given the lack of agency or worth allowed the female) merely betraying the family. It is a film that is another inversion of *Shane* (1952), important for its emphasis on the promise of the verdant land, the wholeness of the family, the goodness of community, and the self-sacrifice of the hero; the suggestion now being that such naiveté can today hardly be conceived of or articulated. *The Book of Eli* (2010) is another post-apocalypse film recalling in design and visual tropes the *Mad Max* films of the early 1980s, particularly in its unabashed messiah myth. While the *Mad Max* films tried for strained intellectual legitimacy by allusions to Joseph Campbell and his ilk (as well as earlier Hollywood), the hero of *The Book of Eli* is literally a walking Bible wanting to restore civilization through the Word. (As several commentators have noted, is it not this Word that caused the catastrophe in the first place?) Yet other films such as *2012* (2009) turn the disaster film into a thrill ride (with much emphasis on computer graphics), eschewing the depression/despair of post-Vietnam/Watergate disaster films, suggesting that the bourgeoisie will survive — even triumph — regardless of whatever cosmic or scientific catastrophe is awaiting us.

The horror film helps the notion of apocalypse retain some of the despair essential to the disaster cycle in the 1970s, when the credibility of the capitalist state fell into extreme doubt. *The Mist* (2007) refers most obviously to *The Birds* (1963), with its community under siege from a monstrous foe concealed by a dense fog. Like Hitchcock's film (I don't want to make a strict comparison here, since *The Birds* outstrips *The Mist* both in intelligence of concept and realized achievement), *The Mist*'s horror centers on social breakdown, beginning with the surliness of neighbors and culminating in the siege of the market/final redoubt of the town. It is there that the mean-spiritedness of all becomes the source of catastrophe, best represented in the lunatic female evangelist, the perfect embodiment of a culture that has opted for mysticism over reason, the essence of the apocalyptic worldview (Figure 4.2). The film's Rod Serling-like "twist" ending is its greatest equivocation. The father's murder of his son and their companions (one could say the father's slaughter of the family) comes a tad too soon, as the military suddenly emerges from the mist to drive back an alien force constructed as unstoppable. The father's despair is complete, but is the implication that he had so little faith in the state apparatus, a notion perfectly in keeping with our newly militarized age? The soldiers, with their tanks and weapons, seem quite ominous, and there is the issue that the state is responsible for the catastrophe in the first place, with the father's ostensible commitment to home and family tenuous. This reading may be a stretch — the ending of *The Mist* is less than consoling because its temperament is once again simply nihilistic, making it fully representative of the apocalyptic strain that refuses history and politics.

The Happening (2008) is of similar outlook, its affinities with *The Birds* also evident, as parts of the US see the population suddenly turn murderous and suicidal. Unlike *The Birds* or "revenge of nature" horror films of the 1970s, the cause of the catastrophe is rather intangible; an eerie breeze, which may or may not contain a toxin, causes people to go insane. It is tempting to talk about a "wind from the east"

Figure 4.2 The lunatic female evangelist (Marcia Gay Harden) from *The Mist* (2007), the perfect embodiment of a culture that has opted for mysticism over reason. Directed by Frank Darabont. Produced by Dimension Films, Darkwoods Productions, and The Weinstein Company.

causing disaster — such a wind has always been feared, an Eastern plague-bringer, precipitated by rats, Dracula, Muslims, or Mao. But this strange breeze is so evanescent it may not have meaning at all, and may function more as a dramatic device to signal further crises. An elderly woman (old women have always been suspect, since their sexual usefulness is over, they are "ugly," they prey upon or terrify the young, or, occasionally provide suspect comfort as sexless grandmothers) seems to lend a helping hand to the young survivors, but becomes hysterical (demonic) when she thinks her property is threatened. As in the better social apocalypse films, humans become monstrous over property, sometimes because of resentment over property they do not have — especially true of the white bourgeoisie toward minorities (see the opening of Romero's *Dawn of the Dead*, with the National Guard assault on the housing project).

Some millennial horror/apocalypse films deal with the topical, incorporating a form of social comment that judges the current generation "guilty" without explicitly naming the nature of the crime. *Cloverfield* (2008) responds to the attacks of September 11, 2001 ("9/11"). It is important, like *The Happening* and *The Mist*, for its refusal to provide consolations, but we find less an impulse to shock the bourgeoisie than express an anxiety that capitalism will not turn out the way the new yuppie culture expected. Many elements of the 9/11 attacks are replicated (clouds of dust rushing down streets), but there are no Muslim terrorists, just glimpses of a misshapen monster sporadically captured by the camera. Like a number of contemporary horror films [*The Blair Witch Project* (1999) is the most deplorable example for its very weak premises and articulation], *Cloverfield* makes use of "new media," with the group of yuppies giving us the action through their point of view via cell

Figure 4.3   Pervasive cinematic imagery since 9/11: New York City in flames after a monstrous sneak attack, as seen in *Cloverfield* (2008). Directed by Matt Reeves. Produced by Paramount Pictures and Bad Robot.

phones. The film's focus is not on the monster, but rather the wealthy young people, portrayed as self-indulgent, then easily panicked and largely helpless. A large amount of time is spent on the "set-up," the display of the foibles of the bourgeois community that the film appropriates from the 1970s disaster film. The party scene, wherein the young people say goodbye to one of their number, is a display of excess; the petty gossip, confused jealousies, and back-biting are typical of a spoiled bourgeois class with time on its hands, whose work cannot be considered productive in any reasonable sense, whose speech and relationships are alienated. Their total destruction by the catastrophe, especially if we indeed see the film as a meditation on 9/11, may constitute one of the most nihilist statements of the recent cinema. It comes close to asserting that the US class system deserved the crisis of 9/11, and perhaps deserves a great deal more, if one sees September 11 as the signal of the apocalypse. One wonders if the film was noted by the various offices of state power, given the new hyper-vigilance that has overtaken the nation! The particular nihilism of this film seems a negation of a generation's impulses and ambitions, not necessarily the goals of capitalism and imperialism (Figure 4.3).

The movement away from recuperation is also noteworthy in the remake of *The Crazies* (2010), which rigorously eschews most of the complex politics of George Romero's Vietnam-era original (1973). Still, the film's importance, like *The Mist*, is in its sense of the decay of middle-class life, the disintegration of the small town and its virtues, as the local sheriff is impotent in holding back the catastrophe. This remake is important for its sense of rural, small-town America under siege from the outside, the red-state nation beleaguered by the external and suspicious. The military/state apparatus is at the center of the apocalypse, as the film reintroduces once more the notion of the nation being destroyed by the enforcement system ostensibly designed to protect it. Again, the state is separated from the economic system it really *protects*; the film's despair has a populist appeal ("you can't trust anybody") that complements the disempowerment and paranoia overtaking American political discourse. *Vanishing on 7th Street* (2010) is slightly more radical, as it looks back (the disappearance of the Roanoke Colony) as well as at the present, deindustrialized US society (parts of the film were shot on the streets of Detroit — the filmmakers found they needed little police assistance with traffic since very little traffic existed in this near-abandoned city) in a post-apocalypse narrative where the population is overtaken by simple darkness, making people disappear in a canny inversion of The Rapture. Like *The Happening*, *Vanishing on 7th Street* is premised on a disaster that is articulated in the vaguest terms, presuming, it seems, that it takes precious little for bourgeois society to destroy itself entirely, or in this instance simply vanish — except for a pointless and misjudged note of recuperation at the end.

Torture Porn and the New Conservatism

The horror film's degeneration became most notable with the slasher cycle of the 1980s, which not incidentally coincided with the enormous reaction of the Reagan years. These films — whose monsters murder teens as they are on the verge of having intercourse — give their undermotivated bogeymen the job, it seems, of policing youth sexuality. [A few radical traces remain, if in undeveloped form: Tony Williams (1996: 112–126) notes that Michael, Freddy, and Jason are all sketched, if inadequately, as monsters who had been the subject of abuse.] The most notable damage caused by these films is their effectively throwing the politics of the genre, even at its weakest, into reverse, associating the monstrous Other unproblematically with the law of the father. Over the past 20 years, motivation of any type has faded as films tend increasingly to deluge the spectator with computer graphics and bloodshed entirely removed from narrative purpose.

The *Saw* franchise (2004–2010) brought a new moralism far exceeding the violence visited upon sexual transgressors in the slasher films (Sharrett, 2009). The monster of the *Saw* cycle is John Kramer, a serial killer also known as Jigsaw. Jigsaw is a cancer patient doomed to an early death by a callous medical establishment; he is driven to the brink when his pregnant wife suffers a miscarriage while helping a narcissistic drug user. A psychopath with the omniscient powers of Ming the Merciless or Dr. Mabuse — and the scenery-chewing of Hannibal Lecter — Jigsaw presides over a dark social liturgy. Clad in a hooded black robe with red trim (giving him the aspect of an Inquisitor), bald from chemotherapy, Jigsaw masterminds ornate punishments for transgressors, using impossibly complicated torture traps designed to teach the subject a moral lesson. If the tortured subject is able to solve Jigsaw's puzzle/trap, s/he will ostensibly know the "true meaning of life." Here we have the franchise's central conceit: an appreciation of life must be harshly taught in this day and age, an idea certainly not displeasing to the Puritans, and perfectly appropriate to the age of George W. Bush, wherein the US reasserted its idea that nations must be destroyed for their own good. However, the key thematic thievery of the *Saw* films is manifestly from *Se7en* (1995), the celebrated apocalypse-noir film of the 1990s. Like *Se7en*, the *Saw* films posit a "fallen world," with their urban settings swathed in black, their interiors lit with the sickly yellow-green of fluorescent lights that is a key signifier of the post-industrial world. Western culture in *Se7en* is portrayed as under siege—the older detective listens to Bach as he peruses Milton and Dante, texts that seem less about finding clues about the killer than providing meditative solace. Culture in *Saw* is peculiarly compromised, but in a way that gives the franchise a certain hip frisson. Jigsaw's lair is filled with odd detritus, including tangles of wire, rusted iron machinery, and broken dolls and mannequins—the lair recalls Dadaist assemblage, adding modernist sophistication to an absurdly retrograde project.

Jigsaw's capture and torture of drug addicts, bad parents, cheating husbands, and wife batterers has its share of defenders in the columns of horror fanzines; the new morality of born-again religious culture, with its insistence on chastity (bolstered by AIDS anxieties) jibes well with the "angry white male" narratives that have proliferated in the last decades of the twentieth century. Jigsaw's actual forbears are the pissed-off vigilantes of *Dirty Harry* (1971), *Death Wish* (1974), and *Walking Tall* (1973). It is notable that the vigilante cycle itself was rebooted in the 2000s, with *Death Sentence* (2007) (based on a novel by Brian Garfield, author of *Death Wish*), a new *Walking Tall* franchise (2004–2007), and *The Brave One* (2007), with the vigilante now a woman (played, astoundingly, by lesbian actor Jodi Foster) avenging her murdered spouse. Today some measure of "political correctness" permits the urban bourgeoisie to strike out with aplomb at perceived threats to its preeminence.

The *Hostel* films of Eli Roth are defined less by the "angry white male" temperament than by a focus on predation that looks more than a bit disingenuous. In the first *Hostel* (2005), a group of young male college students embark on a sex vacation in Europe that eventually takes them deep into deindustrialized, post-Soviet Eastern Europe, where they are set upon by a wealthy group of businessmen whose own notion of tourism is the murder of the young, facilitated by the locals. *Hostel II* (2007) has essentially the same story and structure, but female students replace boys, with the girls becoming perhaps more vicious in their revolt against the predators. *Hostel*, although only a three-film franchise thus far, is representative of torture porn for its emphasis on ever-escalating violence, the human body mangled in ever-more-baroque ways for the delectation of the spectator. Roth has argued a political agenda, stating that American predators, who take for granted their right to prey upon women, are themselves objects of predation. The thought is fine but not supported by the evidence of the films; the sex in these films looks largely consensual, and *Hostel* has much in common with the slasher films of the 1980s, as sex is consistently associated with violence: especially noxious is a scene in *Hostel II* where a young woman, the "nerd" of the group, is trussed up nude to be slashed to ribbons by a naked, statuesque woman in a "Countess Bathory" fantasy borrowed from the photography of Helmut Newton. The Other of these films is simply pursuit of sex by immature boys and girls. Beyond this, the films' monster is Eastern Europe and its inhabitants, all of whom are portrayed as sinister and calculating, unlike their

Western counterparts. By contrast, the college boys, said (by Roth) to be the villains of the piece, are naïve, and while boorish (and wholly lacking in interest), they are distanced from the monstrous topic of sex tourism and sex trafficking—while they have sexual appetites, their downfall is due to the appetite alone. Actual predation is associated solely with the Eastern European entrepreneurs from whom the boys (and girls) are distinct. The young sex tourists are seduced by the wiles of an alien land.

Torture porn has become a synonym, as such things tend to occur in nitwit popular journalism, with any form of bloody horror cinema deemed equally worthless. But a few films, such as Pascal Laugier's remarkable *Martyrs* (2008), are remarkable contributions to radical tendencies within latter-day horror. In *Martyrs*, a religious cult tortures young girls to the brink of death, until they gain a vision of the "hereafter" that will give solace to the decrepit, aging overseers of the group. The upper-class cult is clearly an image of organized religion itself, and their monstrousness merely the consequences of patriarchal religion on each generation, sapping the vitality of the young, proceeding systematically with a strategy of annihilation. *Martyr*'s radicalism has marginalized it, along with Laugier's subsequent *The Tall Man* (2012), another meditation on the destruction of the young, here by small-town America.

Conclusion

The horror film, like all forms of art, continues to embody the ideological circumstances of the moment that contains it. It has been some time since the genre has advanced the radical ambitions of its greatest epochs (the Weimar cinema, Hollywood in the 1930s, the horror renaissance of the 1960s), given the retrograde impulses of our society since the reaction of the 1980s. Yet these impulses are never totally dormant and continue to resist the worst tendencies of the rollercoaster cinema of the new, corporatized Hollywood. But neither do we see, nor can we much anticipate, the achievements of F. W. Murnau, Tod Browning, James Whale, George Romero, Tobe Hooper, Larry Cohen, or other horror innovators anytime in the near future. At this writing, reactionary politicians attempt to strip all rights from women, especially the basic right to control their own bodies, absolutely crucial within patriarchal society. At the same time, the patently illegal and immoral invasions of Iraq and Afghanistan are spoken of even by liberal journalists mostly in regard to their mistakes and blunders. The suppression of voters' rights, especially those of African-Americans and Latinos, takes the US back to the antebellum era. Barack Obama may have won a second term as the first African-American President of the United States, yet the US is spiraling downward ideologically (perhaps precisely because whites are once again so terrified of the "swarthy hordes"), with private and state power encouraging us to view the Other as simply the Other. Under these conditions, can we expect a vibrant, critical film culture?

References

Grant, B.K. and Sharrett, C. (eds) (2004[1984]) *Planks of Reason: Essays on the Horror Film*, Scarecrow Press, Metuchen, NJ.

Goldhagen, D.J. (1996) *Hitler's Willing Executioners: Ordinary Germans and the Holocaust*, Alfred A. Knopf, New York.

Sharrett, C. (2009) The problem of *Saw*: 'Torture Porn' and the conservatism of contemporary horror films. *Cineaste*, **XXXV** (1, Winter), 32–38.

Slotkin, R. (1985) *The Fatal Environment: The Myth of the Frontier in the Age of Industrialization*, Athenaeum, New York.

Williams, T. (1996) *Hearths of Darkness: The Family and the American Horror Film*, Associated University Presses, Madison, NJ.

Wood, R. (1979) An introduction to the American horror film, in *The American Nightmare* (eds R. Lippe *et al.*), Festival of Festivals, Toronto.

Wood, R. (1986) *Hollywood from Vietnam to Reagan and Beyond*, Columbia University Press, New York.

Wood, R. (2004) Forward: 'What Lies Beneath', in *Horror Film and Psychoanalysis: Freud's Worst Nightmare* (ed. S.J. Schneider), Cambridge University Press, Cambridge UK.

5

Avenging the Body
Disability in the Horror Film

Travis Sutton

"But for the accident of birth," the sideshow barker warns his tour at the opening of the movie *Freaks* (1932), "you might be even as they are." The barker's line relies upon an us-versus-them construction between the curious spectators and the freaks on display, yet the line also draws attention to the fluidity and mobility of the boundary between ability and disability; any individual on the tour (or in the viewing audience of the film for that matter) could have ended up on a carnival platform, laughed at or shuddered at by curious onlookers. In fact, horror movies often offer the possibility that their characters may end up on such a platform, or at least have a body that attracts attention in that way. With such possibilities of fate, identity categories that are measured against standards of human abilities and body types appear to be unreliable indeed, but such categories persist in spite of the growing, aging, and mutating nature of the human body.

As a genre, horror emphasizes the body. The body suffers. It dies. It changes. And it horrifies. On the set of *The Phantom of the Opera* (1925), Lon Chaney famously pulled his nose back with wire to capture the skeletal-like features of the villain behind the mask. His handiwork appears the moment Christine surreptitiously removes the phantom's mask while he plays the organ. The unexpected reveal of the phantom's face, along with his cry—"Feast your eyes—glut your soul on my accursed ugliness!"—reveals the capacity for the human body itself to generate fear and horror. Other notorious bodies include Frankenstein's monster, a creation of body parts that harness the life force; Dr. Jekyll who is powerless when forces inside his body turn violent; the werewolf's body that instantaneously transforms; and Dracula's body that never dies as long as he replenishes it with the blood of human victims. Accordingly, horror films persist in drawing upon and adapting these manifestations of the body: the bizarre, the fascinating, and the frightening. In this

A Companion to the Horror Film, First Edition. Edited by Harry M. Benshoff.
© 2014 John Wiley & Sons, Inc. Published 2017 by John Wiley & Sons, Inc.

way, the horror film not only addresses the fear of death but also of bodily difference, tapping into able-bodied assumptions about people who have disabilities. This essay identifies disability stereotypes that have been taken up by horror iconography, particularly the Obsessive Avenger and the Sweet Innocent, and how these images serve both the plot and tone of a horror narrative; additionally, these images reinforce cultural ideas about ability and disability, particularly in the way dominant heteronormative and able-bodied assumptions conflate disability and queerness. A Hollywood movie such as *Freaks* marginalizes disabled characters as a queer community and dramatizes the conflict between dominant and marginal spaces, potentially challenging cultural assumptions in the process. Perhaps, surprisingly, an independent horror film such as *Deafula* (1975) reimagines dis/ability standards only to rely upon the formulas and iconography of the genre that predictably (and paradoxically) reinforce heteronormative and able-bodied ideals.

Theorizing Disability; Queering Identity

The twentieth century saw not only the development of the movie industry but also shifts in the way human ability was perceived. In earlier periods of human history, disabilities were often assumed to manifest some interior character flaw or corrupt soul; nineteenth- and twentieth-century developments in medicine provided more insight into physical anomalies, focusing on causes and cures, and giving rise to the so-called medical model of disability. Advances in medicine also had a major effect during World War I: soldiers who would have died from certain injuries in previous conflicts were now being kept alive, albeit with physical disfigurements. As a consequence, people in the wider able-bodied culture had increasing opportunities to interact with people of different abilities, and assumptions (and fascinations) with disabilities began to change. Nevertheless, the medical model of disability treated physical anomalies as pathological, necessitating prevention and remediation. In cases where a cure would not be possible, the disabled individual was now to be perceived with pity, regarded as doomed to a life of suffering and reliant upon the good graces of the able-bodied world (Benshoff and Griffin, 2009: 360). In *Hideous Progeny: Disability, Eugenics, and Classic Horror Cinema*, Angela Smith demonstrates how eugenic discourse in American culture influenced the development of horror films in the early twentieth century, particularly the "effort to eject or eradicate the monstrous and disabled body" (2011: 87). In contrast, Smith also discovers how horror films of this time undermined eugenic thought in the way that audiences demonstrated "an attraction to physical variation and mutability, and a passion for discomfort and distress" (2011: 3).

The social climate changed significantly by the 1960s and 1970s: to be known as a freak in the American counterculture was then a badge of honor, a mark of individuality (Brottman, 2005: 21). Writers and thinkers began to apply the prominent questions of identity (already applied to race and gender) to further complicate the idea of disability, and thus contributed to the development of the social model of disability. This model challenges the way definitions of disability might be applied, especially as the traditional definitions had been used to exclude and oppress. In the words of writer and disability activist Irving Kenneth Zola, "We think of ourselves in the shadows of the external world. The very vocabulary we use to describe ourselves is borrowed from that society. We are *de*-formed, *dis*-eased, *dis*-abled, *dis*-ordered, *ab*-normal, and most telling of all, an *in*-valid" (quoted in Norden, 1994: 12). Marking an individual as disabled assumes that he or she falls below some standard of ability, as if there were a single standard of normal ability that all humans might agree upon. The social model of disability questions where this apparent standard of ability might be. In fact, one anecdote David Skal and Elias Savada share about the casting of the film *Freaks* emphasizes the potential for understanding disability as a social construction, malleable with individual perception and experience. While at Tod Browning's desk, Daisy Earles, who plays the little person Frieda in the film, casually browsed through photographs of freaks considered for casting. "She picked up one and clucked her tongue. 'Oh my,' the three-foot-high actress said … 'it must be dreadful to be like that.' Freakishness, clearly, was a matter of perspective" (Skal and Savada, 1995: 167). Many people who might be called disabled by an able-bodied culture reject the term forthrightly. Activists in the Deaf community shun the term *hearing impaired* or any term that marks their experience as deficient. These activists take pride in their community and language, and many argue that they would not choose to become hearing-abled even if medical science were to give them the option.

Members of the queer community are similarly interrogated with hypotheticals about "curing" their queerness. In *Crip Theory: Cultural Signs of Queerness and Disability*, Robert McRuer feels that scholarship on gender and sexuality can clarify the cultural hegemony at work with dis/ability. Queer theorists explore how people do not question heterosexuality because it is the assumed norm, consequently making it invisible. Heterosexuality is invisible, in the sense that early doctors and psychologists (who perceived homosexuality through the medical model) were more likely to wonder what caused homosexuality rather than what caused heterosexuality. McRuer believes this process of invisibility applies to able-bodiedness as well (2006: 1). There is an unspoken category of normality regarding the abilities of the human body, and rather than fully acknowledging that category of ability, people tend only to recognize and question those bodies outside of this unspoken standard of able-bodiedness. Queer theory aims to make visible such invisibilities by questioning both dominant and marginalized positions (McRuer, 2006: 6).

The invisibility of able-bodiedness, like the invisibility of heterosexuality, makes able-bodiedness compulsory, "a non-identity, as the natural order of things" (McRuer, 2006: 1). In fact, McRuer takes the compulsory nature of each system one step further: "the system of compulsory able-bodiedness is thoroughly interwoven with the system of compulsory heterosexuality that produces queerness: that, in fact, compulsory heterosexuality is contingent on compulsory able-bodiedness, and vice versa" (2006: 2). In other words, as dominant systems, the two compulsory systems rely upon one another. Exclusion from one likely means exclusion from the other. Consequently, the sexuality of disabled people is culturally marginalized as queer, even when the sexual activity between disabled persons might involve heteronormative (monogamous, reproductive) practices. In truth, dominant notions prefer to understand disabled bodies as non-sexual; if a disabled person is sexual with his or her body, then the sexuality is generally marginalized as perhaps curious or gratuitous but most certainly unusual/queer. Compulsory heterosexuality and compulsory able-bodiedness work in tandem as ideals that ultimately mark the Other. Historically and even today, the horror film is fundamentally "about" such considerations of normality and monstrosity, and works to reinscribe (or much more rarely critique) the allegedly heteronormative and able-bodied nature of human beings and human cultures.

Disabilities on the Movie Screen

In *The Cinema of Isolation*, Martin F. Norden describes movies that include images of disability as a cinema that isolates "disabled characters from their able-bodied peers as well as from each other" (1994: 1). This isolation can appear not only in the content of the story and the ideology behind it but also in the design of the mise-en-scène, as in how disabled characters are positioned in the frame. Isolation is a consequence of able-bodied perceptions, a perception that Norden summarizes in this way: "You're different because one or more of your physical attributes doesn't work properly, and that difference makes me uncomfortable but intrigues me at the same time" (1994: xii). This combination of discomfort and intrigue does a couple of things. First, the perception of discomfort motivates distance and isolation, and the isolation of the disabled character can make him or her appear as wholly Other. Second, with the separation of Otherness intact, able-bodied perceptions are free to objectify, usually with "objectifications of pity, fear, scorn, and so on — in short, objects of spectacle" (Norden, 1994: 1). Spectacle is what made possible the carnival freak show as a form of mass entertainment, and Gaylyn Studlar notes how the decline of sideshows by the mid-twentieth century owing to social pressures would prompt the movie industry to provide for this market of curious carnival goers (Studlar, 1996: 200).

Much of the way disability is represented on the movie screen is inherited from literature. Most notably, William Shakespeare's *Richard III* relies upon the title character's physical deformity to signal his inner depravity. "And while it might strike us as cruel and unjust to equate physical deformity with character or moral deformity," one literary guide explains, "Shakespeare is very much a product of his time in suggesting that one's proximity to or distance from God is manifested in external signs" (Foster, 2003: 194). While the medical and social models of disability have since challenged this cultural idea, the strategy to figuratively convey spiritual or moral weakness through physical difference in film and literature persists centuries after Shakespeare's time, especially in the horror film. When villainous characters with a disability are given little motivation for their evil behavior, then the horror film seems to fall back on these earlier notions of sin and disability. This appears to be the case with the original *The Hills Have Eyes* (1977), about a group of wilderness survivors who violently attack a family stranded with their camper van. Few reasons are given for the attackers' brutal behavior, aside from sadistic delight and their physical appearance. *Wrong Turn* (2003) similarly depicts a small group of people in the mountains of West Virginia who are severely deformed, apparently through generations of inbreeding. They howl and grunt as they entrap unsuspecting travelers, perhaps for sport or to satisfy their cannibalistic appetites; the motive is not clear, yet depravity is implied by their physical bodies.

Some horror films follow this pattern of linking disability with inner depravity by displacing the disability onto a character associated with the immoral endeavor of another character. This often appears in movies with disabled laboratory assistants and emphasizes the lab project itself as morally corrupt. The relationship of the assistant to his master is defined by the power of the able-bodied professional, so oftentimes a hunched back serves visually as a posture of subservience: the professional is the mind of the evil operation while the disabled figure is the doer of the deed, an extension of the professional's inner demons. In Tod Browning's *The Unknown* (1927), Cojo, a hunchbacked dwarf played by John George, assists the main character "Alonzo the Armless" (Lon Chaney), an able-bodied circus performer who passes as an armless knife thrower until he commits murder and decides to have his arms surgically removed. Alonzo's persistent deception as a performer and murderer relies upon Cojo's aid, so Cojo's disabled body, at least in part, embodies Alonzo's moral underhandedness. Once Alonzo is surgically altered and permanently disabled, however, his own body takes on the symbolic role, and Cojo disappears from the film. Gaylyn Studlar's work on masculine performance in classical Hollywood chronicles how Lon Chaney's star image relied upon the transformation of his body, not only attracting audiences accustomed to the carnival freak show but also signaling the cultural anxieties of ideal masculinity after the trauma of World War I (1996: 210).

Frankenstein might be the locus classicus of the hunchbacked assistant trope (even though the character type does not appear in Mary Shelley's novel). In *Frankenstein* (1931), Fritz (Dwight Frye) assists Dr. Frankenstein in gathering body parts and bringing the creature to life. However, Fritz is inept, and mistakenly steals an "abnormal" brain to be used for the monster. This raises the question of whether Frankenstein's experiment would have turned out differently had Fritz selected a normal brain. Since Fritz dies in the first film, he does not appear again in the Frankenstein franchise, although Dwight Frye plays a similar character in *Bride of Frankenstein* (1935).

Another kind of disabled assistant who appears in horror films is the "deaf-mute," a dated and misleading term used in these movies that assumes either a physical connection between the anatomy of the ear and the vocal chords or that deaf individuals are incapable of producing sounds (Schuchman, 1988: 30). (In reality, the condition of one individual being both mute and deaf is quite rare.) This process appears in *Mystery of the Wax Museum* (1933) and its remake *House of Wax* (1953). In the first film, a wax sculptor becomes trapped in a museum fire set by his former investor who is intent on acquiring funds from the insurance. As the fire disables the sculptor's use of his hands, he relies on assistants such as Hugo, identified as a "deaf-mute." As the assistants are not as skilled with wax as the sculptor was prior to the fire, they resort to using dead bodies as molds for the wax figures. The 1953 remake follows a similar plot, including the participation of a deaf assistant, now identified as Igor. As assistants, Hugo and Igor are denied voices, and their silent persona not only function as their "hunched back" to enhance their subservience but they also appear to have silent hearts, devoid of volition, passion, or any spark of human kindness.

The appearance of disabled individuals as assistants also points to perhaps the most pervasive use of characters with disabilities in horror films: supporting characters who contribute little to the narrative but a lot to the ominous tone a horror film frequently demands. At one point in *Mystery of the Wax Museum*, Hugo gestures to the heroine, Ms. Dempsey, only to moan as if he were a menacing animal. The effect serves its purpose, as it prompts Ms. Dempsey to run away. *The Old Dark House* (1932) does this as well with the performance of Boris Karloff as Morgan, the mute butler, who drifts through the house as a mysterious and ultimately threatening presence. Characters who aid in developing the mood of a horror film need not be dangerous characters. In *Poltergeist* (1982), a family tormented by ghostly hauntings calls upon a spirit medium for assistance, played by Zelda Rubinstein, a prominent activist for little people. In *The Others* (2001), a mother and her two children are haunted by the apparition of a blind old woman. Though her image is designed to be frightening at first, the figure also turns out to be a harmless spirit medium.

Horror films also make regular use of the various stereotypes of the disabled identified by Martin F. Norden in *The Cinema of Isolation*. Many of these stereotypes appear as far back as the silent film era, especially the stereotype of the Sweet Innocent, a regular feature of D. W. Griffith's films. The iconic Sweet Innocent of literature is Tiny Tim, the disabled boy who softens the bitter heart of Ebeneezer Scrooge in Charles Dickens's *A Christmas Carol*. When this stereotype appears in the horror film, it is often used to show the depths of a villain's cruelty. In *Eyes of a Stranger* (1981), for example, a serial killer terrorizes women in gruesome ways, catching the attention of an up-and-coming news reporter. As the reporter singles out a possible suspect, she realizes that she is not only putting herself at risk but also her young sister, who is deaf and blind. When the serial killer catches on to the reporter's trail and invades the apartment, he attempts to attack the Sweet Innocent, emphasizing his utter depravity. One of the many problems with this persistent stereotype is the way it denies disabled characters full moral agency. As innocents, they are also denied any kind of desire — sexual or otherwise – other than the hope to be supported and protected by able-bodied people. Another of Norden's common stereotypes, the Saintly Sage, is similar to the Sweet Innocent in the way that he or she is figured as pure and angelic. However, the Saintly Sage is usually older, and his or her disability, which is most often blindness, allegedly grants this character access to higher levels of wisdom, foresight, and morality. One of the most prominent Saintly Sages in the horror film is the blind hermit in *Bride of Frankenstein* (1935); because of his blindness, he cannot see the monstrosity of the creature, so he takes pity on him, inviting him inside and treating him as a friend. At this moment the viewer sees the monster's vulnerability as a lonely figure in a world he does not understand.

Opposite to the Sweet Innocent and the Saintly Sage stereotypes is the Obsessive Avenger. A good example of this stereotype is Captain Ahab in Herman Melville's *Moby-Dick*, "an egomaniacal sort, almost always an adult male, who does not rest until he has had his revenge on those he holds responsible for his disablement and/or violating his moral code in some other way" (Norden, 1994: 52). Revenge is a theme in all kinds of genres and is particularly useful in the horror film to justify monstrous behavior; however, when the revenge itself is tied to a disability, as it is with the Obsessive Avenger, then such stories draw upon able-bodied assumptions that people in the disabled community are usually bitter and angry about their disabilities. Media scholar Paul Longmore summarizes the prejudicial attitude that fuels this stereotype: "Disabled people resent the nondisabled and would, if they could, destroy them" (quoted in Norden, 1994: 28). This assumption — that people in the disabled community resent their disabilities and are jealous of able-bodied people — reveals more about the cultural hierarchy of dis/abilities and the insecurity of dominant positions rather than the wide spectrum of experiences and perspectives of those people who have a disability.

Nevertheless, the Obsessive Avenger is a character that permeates the horror genre from its inception till today. *Son of Frankenstein* (1939) and *The Ghost of Frankenstein* (1942) introduce the character of Ygor (Bela Lugosi), a man with a crooked back as a consequence of surviving his hanging for the conviction of grave robbing. Though not precisely the lab assistant often associated with the name, Ygor assumes the role of the mad scientist by taking control of Frankenstein's monster. The man with the crooked back is now the monster's master — an Obsessive Avenger figure forcing the monster to commit a series of revenge murders, which include the authorities who brought about his hanging and subsequent disfigurement. A rare female Obsessive Avenger appears in *The Hypnotic Eye* (1960), wherein the disfigured Justine (Allison Hayes) uses hypnosis to make other women mutilate their "normal" faces in spectacular ways. In the 2006 remake of the film *The Hills Have Eyes*, the radioactive fallout of the wilderness setting from decades of military testing, a point mentioned only in passing in the original film, allows for the depiction of sensational disabilities within the villainous clan, making them Obsessive Avengers. They attack the travelers who represent the modern, civilized world that brought about the damage done by military testing. "You made us what we've become!" one vengefully yells from his wheelchair.

Vincent Price's entire cinematic career is peppered with Obsessive Avenger roles, even down to playing a vengeful Richard III in *Tower of London* (1962) and *Theatre of Blood* (1973). He plays the wax sculptor in *House of Wax* who, with the aid of the "deaf-mute," seeks vengeance for the destruction of his original museum in the fire that disfigured his body. Price appears to play a similar role as the title character in *The Abominable Dr. Phibes* (1971), but Phibes does not entirely fit a single character type. In fact, the movie seems to break down the Obsessive Avenger trope. Phibes, who has been severely disfigured in a car accident, admits to being on a "quest for vengeance," but his revenge is against the medical professionals he believes are responsible for his wife's botched surgery and subsequent death. His disfigurement seems to figure insignificantly in his plotting as the movie repeatedly dramatizes his sorrow for his wife. Furthermore, it is predominantly the doctors and their assistants (rather than Phibes) who come across as arrogant, unsympathetic, and monstrous. Though his vengeance might be obsessive and carefully calculated, it is depicted for the most part as justifiable, particularly in the way his actions are modeled after God's systematic attack against the Egyptians in the Old Testament. Still, Phibes hides his disfigurement behind a mask for much of the film, only to reveal it for shock effect near the story's climax, which implies some level of shame with his disfigurement.

A few other horror movies introduce characters who have a disability, yet play against expected types. One of the victims in *The Texas Chain Saw Massacre* (1974) happens to be in a wheelchair, but he is far from a Sweet Innocent. At times affectionate and at other times crass, Franklin freely swings from being amiable to obnoxious, complaining for much of his time on screen. George Romero's *Monkey Shines* (1988) presents a more thoughtful and complicated take on issues of ability. It follows the story of a young athlete, Alan, who becomes a quadriplegic after an automobile accident. Alan works to adjust to his new way of life and remains a complex character with the inner conflicts and emotional range associated with being human. The movie includes a rare scene in movie history that acknowledges sexual desire (and activity) among people with disabilities as Alan and a young female scientist, Melanie, make love. The crux of the story, however, is not centered upon the romance or even the quadriplegia itself but Alan's relationship with a monkey assistant that turns dangerous. After Alan defeats the monstrous monkey in the end, the movie concludes with the trope of a miracle surgery that restores Alan's able-bodiedness, a scene that seems forced onto the narrative—and was apparently forced upon Romero by his studio bosses (Norden, 1994: 298).

Of course, the most (in)famous horror film to feature characters with disabilities is Tod Browning's *Freaks*, about a trapeze artist named Cleopatra who pretends to fall in love with Hans, a little person in the sideshow, because she hears he is set to inherit a fortune. After Cleopatra and Hans marry, the other freaks discover Cleopatra trying to poison Hans. The freaks retaliate against her one stormy night, physically muti-lating her body to the point of Cleopatra becoming an attraction in the sideshow herself. A central concern audiences and critics have with the movie *Freaks* is its depiction of deviant bodies, and whether the movie characterizes such bodies as monstrous or human. Even after the studio added a final scene with a repentant Hans finding comfort with another performer in the sideshow, *Freaks* continued to shock and horrify audiences at a level MGM did not anticipate. One female viewer threat-ened a lawsuit against MGM claiming the film had induced a miscarriage (Skal and Savada, 1995: 174). British censors banned the movie, and MGM pulled it from cir-culation after its dismal performance in New York (Skal and Savada, 1995: 180). The film was subsequently purchased by Dwain Esper, an exploitation filmmaker known for advertising his films as educational but with the intent to lure curious audiences with the promise of nudity or sex. "Can a full grown woman truly love a midget?" his advertisements asked about *Freaks*. "Do Siamese twins make love?" (Skal and

Savada, 1995: 222). While perhaps exploiting a fascination with sex and the unusual body, Esper drew attention to the capacity for queerness that critics find in the film today. For example, in her study of sideshows in American culture, Rachel Adams argues that *Freaks* is not about the abnormal but rather the questioning of normality altogether, particularly in matters of sex: an array of bodies demonstrating erotic possibilities (2001: 76).

In many ways, then, what the story of *Freaks* is about is the division between a dominant group and a marginal (disabled and queer) group. The groups delicately hang side by side in the carnival setting; members of the marginal group are invited in front of the gaze of the dominant group as performers and objects of spectacle, only to retreat again to the carnival back lot. Much of the conflict in *Freaks* occurs when the dominant group intrudes upon the marginal group and vice versa. The opening title card of the film can be seen as a metaphor of the boundary that separates the two groups. In a sense, the audience is positioned by the camera as looking from a dominant perspective, having purchased a ticket to the film, to peer into the queer space of the film. The word *Freaks* is written in bold letters; around each letter are caricatured drawings of many of the freaks who will appear on screen. This artistic rendition alludes to the ways the freaks appear when entering the dominant space: as caricature. Their image is constructed and performed. And while the title card fills the screen, a hand breaks through and tears it away. The boundary is breached, though the viewer cannot see how and by whom (Figure 5.1). Thus, this initial collision

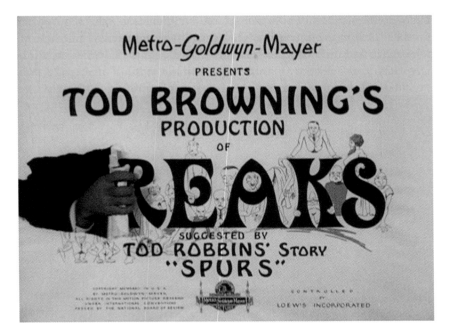

Figure 5.1 In *Freaks* (1932), the title sequence alludes to the ways the freaks appear when entering the dominant space (as caricature), as well as their startling potential to breach the boundary between "them" and "us." Directed by Tod Browning. Produced by Metro-Goldwyn-Mayer (MGM).

between dominant and marginal spaces stylistically attempts a moment of terror and unease, but as the movie continues, the viewer is immediately returned to the dominant space with the barker as their guide. Oddities might pervade the background of the shot, but the sideshow is a dominant space where "monstrosities" (as the barker calls them) are invited to stay on the condition that they take on the role of performer. The freaks appear to be looked at, never to return the gaze.

It is when a freak returns the gaze that trouble begins. Hans gazes upon Cleopatra as she performs her trapeze act. As any protagonist with a goal, Hans decides to venture (intrude) into the dominant group, claim his love for Cleopatra, and return with her to his marginal group. One notable scene in which Hans appears as an outsider in a dominant environment occurs in the main circus tent. Hans stands perched on the circus ring as if waiting at a territorial border, watching Cleopatra inside. While Hans is transfixed by Cleopatra, Hercules and the Rollo brothers play cards nearby, talking suggestively about Cleopatra, and this angers the jealous Hans to the delight of the card players. Cleopatra sustains the humor of the three able-bodied men by feigning muscle pain and sitting upon the structure of the circus ring, figuratively meeting Hans on the border between marginal and dominant worlds. Though played for laughs at Hans's expense, the little man and big woman engage in a queer encounter as she lowers her shirt off her shoulder for him to reach down her back and rub her muscles.

The circus tent itself is a useful, transient structure in the film that constantly moves between dominant and marginal spaces. The notorious wedding feast at the latter part of the film is the most pronounced marginal space as the group gathers to celebrate. "One of us, one of us," the freaks chant in unison. Hans successfully pulls Cleopatra into this marginal environment where she is horrified and does not intend to stay. It is doubtful she anticipated leaving the dominant position at all, given that her intentions for marrying Hans were underhanded. When Hercules, the able-bodied strong man in the show, laughs at Cleopatra from his dominant position, Cleopatra's performance of taking an interest in Hans begins to wane. "They're going to make you one of them," Hercules mocks, and the thought of her pretended desire for Hans potentially marking her as freakish or queer makes Cleopatra thunderously condemn the group of festive freaks. It is after her emotional outburst that Cleopatra and Hercules reclaim the tent as a dominant space. The other freaks are removed from the recaptured territory, and Hans is shamed as he returns to being the queer figure held up in mockery by Cleopatra. This reclamation of the feast by the dominant group with Hans as a prisoner becomes a call to war, and the freaks take up the fight.

The final scenes of the freaks' violent retaliation against Cleopatra and Hercules are designed to be horrifying, particularly the high angle shot into the sideshow display that reveals the aftermath of Cleopatra's mutilation. Viewers of the film still question whether the film is simply isolating the characters as monstrous Others or whether it affirms the humanity of the sideshow performers with the theme that maintaining oppressive divisions risks damage to all within the system. Most horror films that include images of disability are produced and/or distributed by an enter-tainment system that routinely acquiesces to dominant notions of able-bodiedness. That the movie *Freaks* is open enough to allow for various readings of the film in terms of its ideological position is rare indeed, particularly as it is a product of the Studio System. The following section examines *Deafula* (1975), a much more obscure film produced by members of (what might be called) a disabled community, espe-cially for its marginalized members, yet perhaps surprisingly, it ends up reaffirming the heteronormative binaries that *Freaks* potentially deconstructs.

"Blindness separates a person from things," Helen Keller once described, "but deafness separates him from people" (quoted in Gargiulo, 2012: 490). Keller's sum-mation has a flipside: deafness might separate a person from the dominant hearing world, but it also creates a world all its own, what many in the community iden-tify as the DEAF-WORLD. (Capitalized letters are the conventional way to refer to signed concepts in American Sign Language as the language has no written form.) "DEAF-WORLD" as a concept refers not only to the Deaf community but also to the physical spaces, such as residential schools or silent clubs, where members of the community gather (Lane, Hoffmeister, and Bahan, 1996: 125). Writers on Deaf culture explain that when Deaf people meet one another, they are quick to exchange personal histories, revealing their connection to the DEAF-WORLD. "For unlike other cultures, Deaf culture is not associated with a single place, a 'native land'; rather, it is a culture based on relationships" (Lane, Hoffmeister, and Bahan, 1996: 5).

As one of the first feature-length movies filmed entirely in American Sign Lan-guage, *Deafula* presents an imaginative rendering of the DEAF-WORLD: everyone in the diegesis uses sign language, doorbells connected to blinking lights, and tele-typewriters. As an independent film, the movie was a collaborative endeavor among members of the Deaf community for distribution predominantly within the Deaf community, although the videotape release of the movie includes an audio track with music and spoken English translations of the sign language on the screen. The clos-ing credits of the film specify the participants who identify as Deaf, including Peter Wolf (also known as Peter Wechsberg) who is credited as the writer, director, and star of *Deafula*. He studied at Gallaudet University and in 1967 was selected as part of a group of performers to inaugurate the National Theater of the Deaf (Baldwin, 1994: 31). Wolf also participated in a news show intended for Deaf audiences, for which he received two Emmy awards (McNally and Florescue, 1979: 296). Wolf's reinterpre-tation of the character Dracula through the lens of his own culture was not new. For example, *Blacula* (1972) exploits the sex, violence, and power of the vampire myth to dramatize tensions found in racial difference.

Deafula reimagines the vampire narrative for the DEAF-WORLD, and in so doing, it reaffirms compulsory heterosexuality through its depiction of monstrosity-as-queerness. This is striking, particularly in light of McRuer's argument about the discursive links between queerness and the cultural status of those people dominant culture marks as disabled. Furthermore, although *Deafula* dramatizes an entirely non-normative world (absent hearing/able-bodied characters), it succeeds not only in demonizing queerness but also disability itself. Because of its reliance upon Hollywood's narrative style, horror film iconography, and the imperatives of vampire mythology, *Deafula* ends up reaffirming and upholding the desirability of heteronormativity and able-bodiedness, despite having been made by Deaf filmmakers.

Deafula follows the story of Steve, a preacher's son who is studying to become a preacher himself; however, the movie opens with Steve murdering a man and a woman. As the victims' bodies exhibit telltale bite marks, two detectives investigating the crimes contemplate that a vampire is in their midst. When Steve is later attacked by a couple of robbers, the confrontation visually reveals that Steve can physically transform into Deafula, a vampire who in this moment uses hypnotic powers to coerce the attackers into driving off a cliff. The detectives meet with Steve at a restaurant, revealing that Steve is a good friend of one of the detectives. Afterward, Steve's father dies of a heart attack, prompting Steve to meet with Amy, an old friend of his mother, who reveals not only that Steve's mother had died giving birth to him, but also that she had an encounter with Dracula during her pregnancy. Amy then directs Steve to a museum where Dracula is sleeping. Dracula awakens, and he makes Steve's mother appear as well. She helps Steve kill Dracula, but she inadvertently turns to dust after the fact. After Steve becomes a preacher, the detectives confront him with the evidence that they know he is a vampire. Having been found out, Steve returns to the chapel, pleads for redemption from the Lord, and falls dead. Steve, whose vampirism is marked with queerness and disability, is destroyed by the power of traditional Christian morality, reaffirming heteronormative and able-bodied ideals.

The narrative of *Deafula* comes across as very Freudian, particularly as it combines popular conceptions of *Dracula* with elements from Robert Louis Stevenson's *The Strange Case of Dr. Jekyll and Mr. Hyde*. Steve can be linked with the good-natured Dr. Jekyll, the conscious individual (Ego) who functions according to the dictates of his preacher-father and religious law (Superego), but in moments of thirst and rage (Id) he transforms into Deafula to control and devour other humans, which is reminiscent of the violent behavior of Mr. Hyde. The divided nature of this central character is depicted visually as well: Steve has blonde hair and wears conventional clothing while Deafula has dark hair, a large nose, and a dark suit complete with a cape. As a cosmetic device, Deafula's enlarged nose is distractingly artificial on screen, but the way the nose draws attention to itself does serve to sexualize Deafula's persona, particularly as his nose is depicted as an organ that grows when Steve succumbs to his desire for other human bodies (Figure 5.2).

The sexual connotations of Deafula's attacks are instantly made clear. In the opening scene, the camera shows a close-up of Steve's hand gripping a doorframe with intensity, followed by Steve exiting the doorway and wiping his mouth, satisfied and exhausted. His first victim remains inside the room, motionless and slumped over on his knees. In the following scene, Steve sits in the park enjoying what could easily be interpreted as a post-orgasmic cigarette, considering that his second victim

Figure 5.2 Steve transforms into Deafula, complete with cape, dark goatee, and a large false nose. *Deafula* (1975). Directed by Peter Wolf (as Peter Wechsberg). Produced by Sign Scope/Holstrom.

is lying motionless on her back in front of him, her legs bound and strung up in the air. Both of these victims, male and female, appear in sexually submissive positions, suggesting the conflation of Steve's sexual appetites with his thirst for blood, repressed drives that conflict with the religious rule of his father. As Steve sits with cigarette in hand and he thinks back on his relationship with his father, it is clear that he feels some degree of remorse for his behavior. In flashback, Steve sits as a child watching his father's sermon in sign language. This flashback also reveals that Steve's father had been providing his own blood for Steve since childhood to sustain Steve's life and, presumably, to prevent the emergence of Deafula and his evil behavior. Like some forms of deafness, Steve's thirst for blood appears to be some sort of inherited condition.

Curiously, there are few successful heterosexual pairings in the imagined DEAF-WORLD of *Deafula*, or pairings of any kind for that matter. The detectives never speak of having wives or partners, though one mentions a granddaughter. Many of Deafula's victims are depicted as home alone when he appears. This absence of human relationships in the setting of the film enhances Deafula's need for human contact as well as emphasizing what few couplings do make it into the story, even as all of these heterosexual relationships are demolished by the end of the narrative. The robbers who witness Steve's transformation into Deafula are a romantic male–female duo, at least until Deafula forces them off a cliff. Deafula also encounters two young heterosexual lovers in the woods, only to murder them in his bloodlust. Steve's parents appear to be a model heterosexual pairing, but Steve's mother dies giving birth to him and only appears in flashback or as a ghostly image. Any and all heteronormative pairings that Steve touches become threatened, and this destruction of normative human relationships by a queer monster serves to intensify his villainy, as per usual generic conventions.

As a patriarch, preacher, and widower, Steve's father becomes the film's clear voice for heteronormative ideals. While on a drive in the mountains, Steve's father asks him if he is continuing with his studies to become a preacher, which Steve affirms. Then his father asks the inevitable question of a heteronormative parent with an aging, single son: "Why aren't you married?" Steve struggles to answer, confessing that he would like to marry. Unconvinced, the father persists with pressure: "I hope to have some grandchildren before I die!" The conversation is upsetting to Steve, and he stops the vehicle to vomit, a rather pointed response to his father's philosophy. While Steve is vomiting, his father collapses into a heart attack, which might be interpreted as the father's breaking heart over a son who resists marriage and children. In this moment of sickness and heartbreak, Steve's repressed urges again surface as he notices a young couple in the forest about to become intimate. Steve watches as they strip to enter a nearby lake, whereupon Steve transforms into Deafula and feeds on both of them, perhaps in lustful retaliation against his father's urgings to settle down and conform to the dominant order.

Compulsory heterosexuality thus plays out in the narrative by demonizing Deafula as a queer figure or embodiment of queer desire that must be repressed. The films' use of traditional horror iconography also links queerness to disability. For example, when Steve goes to visit his mother's friend Amy (who is a witch), he is waited upon by her disabled assistant who has no hands. Curiously, this assistant embodies both of the physical characteristics of subservience seen in previous horror films: the assistant has a hunched back, and his inability to sign (because he has no hands) renders him "mute" in the DEAF-WORLD (Figure 5.3). "The devil has his hands now," Amy explains about her assistant's physical condition, his hands having been taken as punishment for evil behavior. Amy's line, which is communicated through sign language, harkens back to previous era's assumptions about the links between sin and disability, a surprising theme in a film prepared by and distributed within a disabled community. The connection between physical difference and deviltry is also emphasized in the end of the film. For reasons that are not fully explained in the narrative, Amy gives Steve a ring and when he later touches it to a Christian cross in the church, the ring is destroyed and Amy, who is located elsewhere, dies in that moment as well. Amy's death restores her assistant's hands, and he no longer has his hunched back; thus, the assistant's disability is finally revealed to be a devilish curse that imprisoned him and necessitated divine correction and restoration.

Compulsory able-bodiedness in this dramatization of the DEAF-WORLD not only appears with the disabled assistant but also with the title character. Curiously, the condition of deafness is never commented upon in the narrative. Sign language is always appropriate and expected among the characters in the movie, and in the film there is a wide array of characterizations that show how the DEAF-WORLD

Figure 5.3 Amy and her disabled assistant in *Deafula* (1975), a play on the horror film cliché of the "deaf-mute"? Directed by Peter Wolf (as Peter Wechsberg). Produced by Sign Scope/Holstrom.

can be just as varied as the hearing world. A Deaf identity becomes the assumed norm in the world of the film. That said, the word "Deaf" appears only in connection with Steve's alter-ego, Deafula. He spells this out (literally, through fingerspelling) to Dracula, who is also Deaf, at the climax of the film. This father-son dynamic between Dracula and Deafula differs from traditional vampire mythology. Usually vampires create other vampires through the transfer of blood or some other kind of bodily fluid. In *Deafula*, Dracula seduces Steve's already pregnant mother. Because Dracula does not extract her blood or transform her into a vampire, Dracula's influence on Steve's mother seems explicitly sexual, and the only character permanently affected by this encounter is the unborn Steve. Steve, then, is divided between two fathers: one good (the preacher) and the other evil (Dracula). The iconic title of the film that marks Steve's deafness is thus the name tied to his evil father.

The hereditary nature of many forms of deafness has historically frightened the dominant hearing world. Prominent figures such as Alexander Graham Bell pushed for legislation to prevent deaf people from marrying and reproducing for fear of creating more instances of deafness. That the monstrous Dracula creates Deafula through sexual intercourse with a pregnant woman seems to mirror these fears of deafness and heredity. Therefore, even in a diegesis where deafness is the invisible norm, the only instance where deafness is commented upon is through a character's name in relation to being the offspring of a monstrous figure. Deafness, vampirism, and queerness are all figured as one interrelated and inherited curse. Paradoxically, this isolates deafness as Other and as something to be feared in a film that otherwise affirms d/Deaf identities and experience. As Steve/Deafula is marked as a monstrous Other by the compulsory heterosexual and able-bodied systems at work in the film (and the horror genre itself), his eventual demise is to be expected.

Conclusion

In the movie *Freaks*, queerness and disability appear to meld together within the marginal group, and the marginal figures appear to accept it to the point of celebrating it at the wedding feast. In contrast, *Deafula* relies upon the conventions of the Hollywood film, the horror genre, and the vampire myth; thus, this rare film that was mostly produced and distributed on the margins of able-bodied culture still recirculates the mutually dominant systems of compulsory able-bodiedness and compulsory heterosexuality. Heteronormative ideals are not separated from able-bodied assumptions in this movie, a story that includes the stereotype of a disabled assistant along with a central character whose inability to conform to the dominant order and control his repressed self leads to his destruction. As the barker in *Freaks* laments, "They did not ask to be brought into the world," a world that centralizes able-bodiedness as the standard, leaving those who are different to remain on the margins: disabled and queer. But this boundary between the dominant and the marginal is unstable, and the horror genre reveals that this instability can be used as a device to incite fear. Anxiety about disability typically reduces characters in the horror genre to objects of pity, spectacle, or rage, oftentimes returning to old cultural notions that link disabled bodies with sin and depravity. In spite of this, McRuer reminds his readers that "Everyone is virtually disabled, both in the sense that able-bodied norms are 'intrinsically impossible to embody' fully and in the sense that able-bodied status is always temporary, disability being the one identity category that all people will embody if they live long enough" (2006: 30).

References

Adams, R. (2001) *Sideshow U.S.A.: Freaks and the American Cultural Imagination*, U of Chicago P, Chicago.

Baldwin, S.C. (1994) *Pictures in the Air: The Story of the National Theater of the Deaf*, Gallaudet U P, Washington D.C. Web. 06 Dec, 2012.

Benshoff, H. and Griffin, S. (2009) *America on Film: Representing Race, Class, Gender, and Sexuality at the Movies*, 2nd edn, West Sussex, Wiley-Blackwell.

Brottman, M. (2005) *Offensive Films*, Vanderbilt U P, Nashville.

Foster, T.C. (2003) *How to Read Literature Like a Professor: A Lively and Entertaining Guide to Reading Between the Lines*, Quill, New York.

Gargiulo, R.M. (2012) *Special Education in Contemporary Society: An Introduction to Exceptionality*, Sage Publications, Thousand Oaks. Web. 06 Dec, 2012.

Lane, H., Hoffmeister, R., and Bahan, B. (1996) *A Journey into the DEAF-WORLD*, Dawn-SignPress, San Diego.

Longmore, P.K. (1985) Screening stereotypes: images of disabled people. *Social Policy*, **16** (1), 31–37.

Marinelli, R.P. and Dell Orto, A.E. (eds) (1984) *The Psychological and Social Impact of Physical Disability*, 2nd edn, Springer, New York, pp. 139–147.

McNally, R.T. and Florescue, R. (1979) *The Essential Dracula: A Completely Illustrated and Annotated Edition of Bram Stoker's Classic Novel*, Mayflower Books, New York. Web. 06 Dec, 2012.

McRuer, R. (2006) *Crip Theory: Cultural Signs of Queerness and Disability*, New York U P, New York.

Norden, M.F. (1994) *The Cinema of Isolation: A History of Physical Disability in the Movies*, Rutgers U P, New Brunswick.

Schuchman, J. (1988) *Hollywood Speaks: Deafness and the Film Entertainment Industry*, U of Illinois P, Urbana.

Skal, D.J. and Savada, E. (1995) *Dark Carnival: The Secret World of Tod Browning*, Anchor Books, New York.

Smith, A.M. (2011) *Hideous Progeny: Disability, Eugenics, and Classic Horror Cinema*, Columbia U P, New York.

Studlar, G. (1996) *This Mad Masquerade: Stardom and Masculinity in the Jazz Age*, Columbia U P, New York.

Zola, I.K. (1984) Communication barriers between 'the Able-Bodied' and 'the Handicapped', in *The Psychological and Social Impact of Physical Disability*, 2nd edn (eds R.P. Marinelli and A.E. Dell Orto), Springer, New York, pp. 139–147.

6

Horror Reception/Audiences

Matt Hills

It might come as no surprise that a genre premised on horrifying its consumers has given rise to explorations of audience responses. But horror has also often been mired in limiting perspectives on its relationship to audiences, caught up in "media effects" debates and fears surrounding violent imagery (Barker and Petley, 2001). And horror audiences have been poorly served by theories of the genre aiming to resolve its "paradox" (why do people enjoy seeing images that they should find repulsive?). Whether in Noel Carroll's *The Philosophy of Horror* (1990), or Julian Hanich's *Cinematic Emotion in Horror Films and Thrillers* (2010), horror becomes a puzzle to be solved on behalf of audiences; yet, without the empirical study of actual audiences (or, at least, without considering audience discourses; see Hills, 2005a).

We might suggest, then, that there has been another paradox surrounding horror scholarship. Many scholars are themselves fans of the genre they are writing about, but although their fandom frames the act of study, it does so implicitly rather than empirical audience emotion becoming an object of theorization. After all, academics who analyze horror are themselves audiences, but their audience identity is typically displaced by generalizing textual readings rather than offering an experience to be analyzed in its own right. The audience-related paradox of horror *studies* thus amounts to the following: why would so many people pick over horror's texts as a result of their lived (audience) experiences while effectively sidestepping the matter of lived (audience) experiences?

Horror's audiences are all too often spoken for. They are assumed to be enmeshed within specific socio-historical meanings; assumed cognitively to process films in "intended" ways; assumed to be part of settled fan interpretive communities. This chapter explores the work of scholars who have paid closer attention to horror's audiences, unhappy at the way they are ventriloquized in the theoretical frameworks of those who are themselves evidently passionate about horror.

The distinction which frames this chapter, "reception" as opposed to "audiences," can be fuzzy in some cases but it nevertheless grasps a difference between the institutional, mediated framing of textual meaning (publicity, promotion, press reviews, etc.), and audience-produced meanings (studied via qualitative data such as interviews and focus groups, or through naturally-occurring and user-generated content). The reception/audiences separation is somewhat unclear because audiences can (and increasingly do, thanks to so-called "web 2.0") produce their own mediated framings of textual meaning, for example, blogs and reviews. Audience-created paratexts hence circulate around horror films, and though they may not be as powerful as marketing paratexts (Gray, 2010: 162–163), it cannot be presumed that they are merely ephemeral "transitory media with little public visibility and low aesthetic and cultural status owing to their derivativeness and link to amateur enthusiasm" (Klinger, 2011: 196). Overall, though, "reception" work asks *How* does a text mean?" (Staiger, 2005: 2), typically examining Hollywood machineries of marketing, whereas audience studies focuses on *what* texts mean *for their viewers/fans*. This latter question is far easier to consider in relation to contemporary films: while reception studies can span longer histories by drawing on archival sources, empirical audiences usually need to be tracked through a more "presentist" lens. For instance, important analyses of horror's reception have focused on 1930s Universal horror pictures (Berenstein, 1996), on *King Kong* (1933) and its remakes (Erb, 1998), on the marketing of US horror in the 1950s and 1960s (Heffernan, 2004), and on the *Alien* franchise's shifting signifiers (Gough, 2010).

Where horror's audiences have been empirically approached, recent work has focused on "transmedia storytelling"—narrative extensions outside film texts—in the age of media convergence (Jenkins, 2006; Tryon, 2009). Even though scholars have sought to move beyond the text here, a tendency has remained for audience interpretations to be assumed on the basis of textual analysis. Angela Ndalianis's book *The Horror Sensorium* studies "viral horror" from *The Blair Witch Project* onwards without integrating actual audience responses into its framework (2012: 163–193). And Caetlin Benson-Allott's *Killer Tapes and Shattered Screens* studies how faux footage horror "imagines pirate spectators" and "build[s] ... paranoid spectatorial interpellations" (2013: 201), but again does so without addressing whether flesh-and-blood audiences are able to shake off, or negotiate with, these textual imaginings and interpellations. As Martin Barker has pointed out, "[a]udience research is *hard*, in many ways. Not doing it, however, and substituting untested 'figures' to be stand-ins ... is becoming inexcusable" (2013: 115). Problematically, both these text-focused analyses of "viral horror" and "imagined" file-sharers continue to duck the issue of what "film audiences 2.0" actually do with horror films (Monk, 2011).

Other writers have addressed this head-on, however. In *Reinventing Cinema: Movies in the Age of Media Convergence*, Chuck Tryon considers the practice of film blogging, challenging "digital cinema myths ... [that celebrate] a participatory culture in which power relationships seemed to have been leveled" (2009: 142), with fan campaigns supposedly gathering traction over Hollywood decisions. Rather than destabilizing Hollywood's corporate power, however, web 2.0 has facilitated experiments aimed at reaching horror's tech-savvy youth market, for example, web serials like *When Evil Calls* (2006) and *Beyond the Rave* (2008) — the latter forming part of Hammer's social media attempt (partnered with MySpace) to re-create itself for twenty-first century producers. Web 2.0 has also been used to support all-platform simultaneous releases, such as *A Field in England* (2013) from cult/horror director Ben Wheatley. Far from industry models and power relations being magically democratized, online horror instead proffers a domain where limited, industrially hemmed-in innovation can take place. At the same time, business as usual carries on. Corporate and fan interests are brought into alignment:

> [I]t is evident that marketing and fan activities can co-exist on official [web] sites.... [For example] the Hammer site offers a history of the studio and archival material on every Hammer film ... [T]hese features allow fans to build on their knowledge and competencies, and also to purchase merchandise. (Cherry, 2010: 78–79)

Paul Booth has also explored digital horror fandom, investigating *Saw* fan films. Just as Brigid Cherry sees no necessary tension between corporate agendas and fans' participatory culture, Booth likewise argues that the "contemporary mainstreaming of fandom ... has created a new type of fan — one that may identify the dominant ideologies of the media, but also supports them" (2012: 69). For Booth, fan trailers mimic the "intensity of ... *Saw* trailers" (2012: 75) rather than resisting *Saw*'s "torture porn" formula. He argues that by failing to "transgress the original" (2012: 79), *Saw* fan films exceed the norms of transformative fandom. But this assumes that fan activity must be transformative: what Booth's study demonstrates is less the transgression of transgression, and more the alignment of specific fan practices with "the commercial positioning of the *Saw* franchise" (2012: 79).

This emphasis on non-transgressive audiences draws on cultural studies to interrogate the cultural politics of horror. The author argues that the genre has played a key role in film studies' engagement with cultural studies. Adopting the latter's "interest in the pleasures of consumption and the experience of audiences" (Turner, 2012: 29), horror studies' "cultural turn" has been driven by the genre's subjection to controversial censorship, as well as by reactionary stereotypes of its (allegedly male) audience. Consequently, horror's consumers have been studied via a progressive cultural politics — one aimed at complicating censorship, thinking more carefully about gender, and exploring audiences' cultural identities via their memories of horror. Audiences are caught up in a series of power relationships (to State censors, to representations of "deviance," to different sections of generational fandom and anti-fandom) and a cultural studies-inflected approach enables these to be critically examined.

Restricting any overview purely to work on horror audiences would, however, miss contiguous debates in audience studies. Case studies from beyond the genre can offer new ways of thinking about horror's viewers. First, though, the debate surrounding "media effects" is examined. Peter Hutchings has pointed out that "the horror audience is heterogeneous, mutable, and decidedly elusive; just when you think you have it identified and neatly labeled, it has a habit of vanishing mysteriously into the dark" (2004: 95). Nowhere has this "labeling" of the audience, and denial of its heterogeneity, been more apparent than in paternalistic censorship practices.

Effected Audiences? Censorship in the UK Context

The audience for horror movies is typically assumed to be young men (Cherry, 2009: 40). Historically, this audience has been depicted as requiring protection from the graphic representations characterizing horror, with cultural concerns circulating that the genre might also be consumed by, especially, impressionable and vulnerable viewers, that is, children. Mark Kermode has argued that while an "X" certificate (introduced in the United Kingdom in 1951) supposedly prohibited those under-age from seeing unsuitable films, adult audiences have nonetheless been treated "as little more than advanced children" (2002: 11) by the British Board of Film Censors (or Classification, as they became from 1984 onwards). Censorship in the United Kingdom has continued to blunt horror's textual transgressions, just as the Production Code restricted what could be shown in the United States between 1930 and 1968 "when the last vestiges of the Code were abolished" (Prince, 2003: 1).

If the 1970s ushered in a somewhat more relaxed attitude to horror's representations, the genre has engaged in pushing at boundaries of taste and taboo ever since (Petley, 2011). The 1980s "video nasties," the "new brutalism" of the 1990s, and the "extreme cinema" of the noughties have all tested censors, acting as cultural attractors for debates surrounding acceptable imagery in screen entertainment. Different phases, cycles, or subgenres have also given rise to distinct audience studies: Annette Hill published *Shocking Entertainment: Viewer Responses to Violent Movies* in 1997, seeking to understand audience responses to a "new wave" of violent films released in the United Kingdom between 1990 and 1995 such as *Reservoir Dogs* (1992), *Natural Born Killers* (1994), and *Henry: Portrait of a Serial Killer* (1986) (Hill, 1997: 10). And Martin Barker *et al.* studied new "extreme" cinema 10 years later (2007). Hill's qualitative work (based on pilot interviews, questionnaires, and focus groups) illuminated how "portfolios of interpretation" were drawn on by audiences, as well as how viewers actively "self-censored" violent images (Hill, 1997: 106–107) based on personal thresholds, for example, a phobia of needles. Such findings suggest that audiences cannot be wholly reduced to membership in interpretive communities such as "fandom" because horror's challenging material can relate to individual anxieties and fears.

This is not simply an issue of horror in the nineties or noughties, however. Though the BBFC has adopted greater transparency, publishing its guidelines as well as

Figure 6.1 *The Human Centipede 2 (Full Sequence)* (2011) was initially denied a UK certificate by the BBFC. Here, the film's protagonist (played by Laurence R. Harvey) watches *The Human Centipede* on his computer. Directed by Tom Six. Produced by Six Entertainment Company.

making its reports available online, certain films continue to court controversy. For instance, *The Human Centipede 2 (Full Sequence)* (2011) was denied a certificate by the BBFC (Figure 6.1):

> There is little attempt to portray any of the victims in the film as anything other than objects to be brutalised and degraded for the amusement and sexual arousal of the main character and for the pleasure of the viewer. There is a strong and sustained focus throughout the work on the link between sexual arousal and sexual violence and a clear association between non-consensual pain and sexual pleasure. (BBFC, 2011)

The Bunny Game (2010) had been similarly banned by the BBFC the previous year, again owing to concerns that its depictions of violence were linked to sexual arousal. This has been a key concern for UK film censors, as witnessed by a research report commissioned on "Audiences and Receptions of Sexual Violence in Contemporary Cinema" (Barker *et al.*, 2007) which examined audiences for five films: *À Ma Soeur* (Catherine Breillat, 2001), *Baise-Moi* (Virginie Despentes and Coralie Trinh Thi, 2000), *The House on the Edge of the Park* (Ruggero Deodato, 1980), *Ichi the Killer* (Takashi Miike, 2001), and *Irreversible* (Gaspar Noë, 2002). This report sought to empirically establish "orientations" of meaning-making among audience members, studying "embracers" and "refusers" of the films along with ambivalent responses. Findings were based on a survey of 243 film-related web sites, 760 responses from a web survey plus 79 paper-based questionnaires, and 20 focus groups (Barker *et al.*, 2007: 1). The report flagged up "the issue of the BBFC's implicit models of the audience contained within its judgments about different films, whose evidential base may not be available for scrutiny" (Barker *et al.*, 2007: 9). And it stated that:

> There are considerable tensions surrounding the issue of finding screen representations of sexual violence "arousing" .... Yet there is strong evidence within our study (a) that many—both men and women—do find some such scenes arousing, but (b) that this can associate with *greater* condemnation of the violence because the arousal heightens awareness and involvement, and thus imaginative participation in the implications of the scene. (Barker *et al.*, 2007: 3)

This runs strongly counter to any implicit model of the audience that is imagined as being "effected" or corrupted by finding horror/"extreme" film images arousing. Yet, in choosing to downplay such empirical evidence in their policy-making, the BBFC grounded their decisions by referring to "the result of an extensive process of public consultation and research … reflect[ing] the balance of media effects research, the requirements of UK law and the attitudes of the UK public" (BBFC, 2010). However, it is hard to suggest that conclusions surrounding "media effects" can be "balanced," especially given that a range of scholars writing in the media/cultural studies' tradition have savaged this model as a hugely problematic approach. David Gauntlett, for example, lists "Ten things wrong with the 'effects' model" (2001: 52–59). Censorship rooted in the "effects model" restricts what horror material can be legally available to viewers, but it does so on the basis of *imagining* that certain audiences will be corrupted by the genre's narratives.

And yet this model remains, in effect, a folk theory: a matter of ideology rather than empirical study and theorizing. The BBFC can validate their stance by referring to "public attitudes" as "the public"—a shifting signifier if ever there was one—are unlikely to have kept up with debates in film studies, and may be rather more likely to consume regularly news reports reinforcing the hegemonic "common sense" status of the effects model. "Media effects" persist as a belief system, then, iterated within media coverage and by the persistence of pundits and politicians. But this "meta" possibility (that "media effects" might itself seem to resemble a media effect) is connected with the fact that "effects discourse" is highly moralizing, constructing those who appropriate it as mature, rational, and superior to the "unruly Other" (Gauntlett, 2001: 57) whether this Other is the lacking, impressionable child, the uneducated viewer, or the frequent, undiscriminating media consumer. The circulation of effects discourse enables a range of social actors to perform actively their self-identity as morally "good," protecting the vulnerable Other who does not know better.

What appears to be the predominant empirical outcome of under-age horror viewing is the creativity of horror fandom rather than depravity, with many writers and commentators discussing how they were inspired by childhood intensities of seeing horror films on TV (e.g., Kermode, 2001; Morris, 2006: 64–65; Gatiss in Rigby, 2011: 6–7). Fandom has been culturally-politically opposed to the censorship of horror films, partly because it denies fans the legal right to watch specific horror films, but also because such practices are premised on a notion of the horror genre as deviant — pathologizing fans as weird consumers (Hutchings, 2004: 84–86). However, censorship has also secured the "illicitness" and authenticity of hard-to-find titles for horror fans, for example, *The Evil Dead* (1981) prior to its uncut DVD release in 2001 (Egan, 2011: 30–31).

Despite this subcultural capital — latterly translated into sourcing censored or restricted materials online — fans have been denied any meaningful voice in political debates surrounding horror's UK censorship. It is thus unsurprising that fandom would applaud the work of researchers such as Martin Barker, who have challenged the cultural politics of the "video nasties" phenomenon and continue to question the BBFC's working practices (Barker *et al.*, 2007). Indeed, when Barker was a guest at FrightFest in 2010, his critical views on censorship were warmly welcomed by the fan audience, with one blogger describing him as "the secret hero of British horror fans" (Soufex, 2010). It should be noted that Barker does not write as an aca-fan of horror; his work is very much rooted in an "objective," social-scientific approach to audiences. Yet, at the same time, the cultural politics of Barker's scholarship evidently resonate with sections of horror fandom. The sense that horror's most faithful audiences have been the most disenfranchised by censorship debates is captured in Thomas Austin's (2002) work on *Natural Born Killers*. This title had its film classification delayed in the United Kingdom after fears over copycat violence, and one of Austin's questionnaire participants — blurring the line between institutionally constructed reception categories of "new violence fans" and "meat-heads" — concluded his response with a highly oppositional flourish: "Fuck the censors" (2002: 176 and 178).

Horror audiences have been silenced in censorship debates, with imagined audiences circulating in powerful discourses while flesh-and-blood fans are pathologized, marginalized, and subjected to a moralizing "common sense." This situation suggests the need to study actual audience interpretations of horror but it also suggests that we need to break down monolithic discourses, for example, assuming that "horror fandom" can be equated with one interpretive community when fans' "portfolios of interpretation" may contain moments, which surprise the self (and the analyst), connecting social and individual experiences in different ways. And there is a need to think more carefully about film "embracers," "refusers," and forms of ambivalence which horror/extreme cinema can generate, rather than focusing only on "cooperative spectators" who "respond in large part in congruence with the film's intended affective trajectory," as cognitive theory tends to do (Plantinga, 2009: 242). Cognitivists and film censors may seem like odd bedfellows, but both depend on imagined models of audience behavior. The next section considers another way in which horror audience practices can be complicated by a progressive cultural politics of analysis indebted to cultural studies: the gendering of fandom.

Gendered Audiences? The (Dis)pleasures of Horror

Horror may be a (sub)culturally masculinized genre, with its "gorehound" audience intent on tolerating extreme imagery (Bolin, 2000). But horror film can also be far more than a test of masculinity, as Brigid Cherry's work has demonstrated by analyzing horror's female fan following. Noting that "fandom per se is not necessarily gendered, but specific fan interests, activities and communities are often marked out as feminine or masculine" (2011: 140), she investigates how feminine interests define "good" horror. In "Refusing to Refuse to Look: Female Viewers of the Horror Film," Cherry asked female respondents to name their favorite horror movies. She found that "336 individual films were named by 107 of the participants," with *Hellraiser* (1987), *Alien* (1979), and *Interview With the Vampire* (1994) being the top three choices (2002: 171). This qualitative data enabled Cherry to argue for a gendered pattern in horror film tastes, with vampire films being the most popular in her study, and "subtlety of horror" being praised as a reason for liking certain films, for example, *The Haunting* (1963) (2002: 172). The appeal of gothic-horror vampires was linked to romanticization:

> A 41-year old respondent commented that "the vampire film is the closest the horror genre comes to the traditional romantic film. Vampires have most often been portrayed in literature and film as handsome, often foreign, exotic men who seem to have an uncanny knowledge of how to give pleasure ... " A 53-year-old participant suggested that "tragic hero figures" such as Heathcliff ... were similar to ... "magnetic vampire characters." (2002: 172)

Though this study was carried out before the rise of the *Twilight* franchise (2008–2012), given Cherry's "patterns of feminine readings in ... reference to the appeal of the hero" (2010: 82) then *Twilight's* success accords very well with her findings. Her work also stressed how "feminine interpretative strategies" (2002: 176) tended to focus on strong female characters such as Ellen Ripley in *Alien* while critiquing conventional, patriarchal horror narratives. Thomas Austin's audience study examining viewers of *Bram Stoker's Dracula* (1992) echoed Cherry's conclusions, with "a dislike of gratuitous gore, an enjoyment of involving and 'moving' characterization, and a sympathy for the dilemma of the vampire" being "pleasures [that] were less likely to be mentioned by men in the sample" (Austin, 2002: 136–137). Austin rejected any "simple and clear-cut gendered division" between male and female audiences (2002: 137), acknowledging that for a number of self-identified horror fans of both genders *Bram Stoker's Dracula* was positioned as a "'mainstream' mishandling of horror" (2002: 135) that failed to deliver horror's promised affect, displacing terror with romance. This discursive move recuperates a gendered division between the subcultural capital of "real" horror and devalued, culturally feminized "romance" horror.

Such cultural struggles over generic distinction have strongly marked the *Twilight* franchise. Fan discourses have recurrently sought to distinguish "'authentic' horror and '*real* horror fans' from the inauthentic interloper" (Jancovich, 2000: 29). Mark Jancovich's work has shown how this binary played out in the 1990s, with the *Scream* franchise allocated an analogous role to *Twilight*, acting as a marker of highly commercial, mainstream genre film that cannot be "authentic horror":

> subcultural capital is usually gendered as masculine, and the reference to "scantily clad, barely legal teen starlets" [in fan critique of the *Scream* franchise] once again associates the films with inauthenticity through the familiar trope of "mass culture as woman" … These films, it is implied, are not just inauthentic horror but they are made for, and consumed by, inauthentic fans: young girls. (Jancovich, 2000: 29)

It is striking how such a resolutely similar, and similarly reactionary, cultural politics emerged around the *Twilight* films. Lisa Bode (2010: 716) has shown how horror fans sneered at "sparkly" vampires as a marker of genre inauthenticity, replicating an audience discourse of masculinized, subcultural horror versus feminized, romantic *Twilight*. Although this subcultural reading may be shared by male and female horror fans—just as Austin observed in the case of *Bram Stoker's Dracula*—it nevertheless implies a strongly gendered construction of audience understandings.

Audience studies' work on the constructed "authenticity" of horror, and on how feminized "mainstream" film can be denigrated as improper horror, shows that we cannot merely identify one coherently imagined and "constellated community" of horror film spectators (Altman, 1999: 161). Instead, actual audiences often fragment into pro-subcultural and pro-mainstream camps, with genre fandom displaying a component of "anti-fandom" whereby texts construed as rivals to "proper" horror are symbolically attacked. *Twilight* and its (female teen) audiences have therefore been commonly derided by those invested in securing boundaries around the "scary" vampire and horror's promised affects (Sheffield and Merlo, 2010).

Horror's "constellated community"—the audience we imagine sharing our taste in film genre—is never without its own shifting in-groups and out-groups. As horror's genre conventions move in and out of commercial visibility, articulated with other genres such as the romance, they give rise to inter-fandom conflicts which, far from being imagined, have become increasingly realized and visible thanks to online fan forums and social media. However, gendered audience readings of horror do more than cleave it into masculinized-authentic and feminized-inauthentic discourses. Cherry noted that female fans qualified the sort of horror they enjoyed, not only favoring "subtlety," but also stressing "quality" in production values, art direction, set design, and acting as well as plot and character development (2002: 172). Of course, "quality horror" is not an institutionally recognized subgenre. And nor is thematically "smart horror," which was identified by audiences in a study of the *Ginger Snaps* films (2000, 2004) carried out by Martin Barker, Ernest Mathijs, and Xavier Mendik:

> "gender" and "identity" … break open the genre shackles. References to puberty, growing up, menstruation, and bonding were seen as signs to take the viewing of these films beyond the boundaries of the horror genre, into a not-really well defined category of "coming of age" metaphors. But, it also transpired that the liking of the film (and

roughly 75% of the audience liked it a lot) was less a matter of being a fan of the genre than of an appreciation of the themes.... [W]hen [producers] declared they wanted to make a "smart horror film" in order to get a ... "broader audience" they got exactly what they wanted, smartness included. (2006: 20–21)

In each case, gendered meanings are said to occur "beyond the boundaries of genre." Cherry's female fans specify the kind of horror films they appreciate, but in a way that exceeds genre classifications. The same is true for the *Ginger Snaps* audience studied by Barker, Mathijs, and Mendik, and for Austin's study of *Bram Stoker's Dracula* and its audience. Here, viewers overwrite established, public, and institutionally consolidated genre categories by using "'private' typologies" where "film genres are rewritten into idiosyncratic groupings" such as "cool intelligent films," "clever" movies, or indeed, "smart horror" (Austin, 2002: 134). Although Austin ultimately rejects using a public/private dichotomy to theorize these taxonomies, his analysis shows how horror films can be qualified below the level of (sub)genre, yet in line with specifically gendered understandings.

Just as horror's "constelled community" is partly fractured by masculine and feminine interests, this audience community is also fragmented by evaluative terms which can overwrite and (re-)gender the industry's genre categories. However, these performative labels are usually ones of clear approval: cool, smart, quality horror. Alternatively, audiences perform their gender through anti-fandom and disapproval: inauthentic, unscary, unreal horror. But, studying actual audiences can also allow us to think about ambivalent responses. This is one powerful reason for moving from reception to audience study (where possible). What are usually tidier activations of meaning in publicity and press reviews can become murkier in people's troubled engagements with horror films. These might involve defending against transgressive desires (Staiger, 2000: 186), or demonstrating "self-awareness of split reactions [and] the search for a missing meaning" in relation to David Cronenberg's *Crash* (1996) (Barker, Arthurs, and Harindranath, 2001: 132). Far from always being a well-defined experience of fandom or anti-fandom, audience studies of horror can illustrate how viewers work at comprehending their own discomfort. In such cases, there is empirically no paradox of horror, because unpleasant imagery does not smoothly give rise to viewer pleasure.

Presuming that horror films must predominantly be about one affect—the scare—misses the range of ways in which flesh-and-blood spectators relate to the genre. The next section considers another cultural-political aspect to audience studies' work: exploring how horror's history has been nostalgically recalled. The horror film is not merely read; it is *remembered*, with consequences for generational cultural politics rather than gendered constructions of "authentic" horror.

Nostalgic Audiences? Looking Back on Horror

Gathering audiences' accounts of horror film inevitably means tackling the issue of memory, as Janet Staiger has pointed out (2005: 186). And the genre's persistence over time also means that it appeals to different generations of viewers (Mathijs and Sexton, 2011: 202–203). Again, this raises the issue of how horror is recalled and how its pleasures are discursively framed.

Memory has been a key topic in cultural theorization of late (Garde-Hansen, 2011), with "collective memory" being understood as ideological, for example, reinforcing views that contemporary culture is wholly enlightened versus a prejudiced past. Contrasted to "collective memory," which can be circulated through a variety of mass and niche media, there is also "personal memory," or what Staiger terms "personal event memory" (2005: 188). This type of recollection focuses on moments that are especially significant for self-identity, linking "turning point" memories to spaces and times as well as "sensory images" and associated recollections. As Garde-Hansen has observed: "The focus upon fan collectivity … suggests that there is room for notions of collective and personal memory in audience research of fan behavior" (2011: 123).

Indeed, film scholars such as Kate Egan (2007) and Annette Kuhn (2002) have carried out important studies of personal and cultural memory, with Egan's work being particularly relevant to horror audiences. Constructions of genre "authenticity" are once more relevant here, as Egan demonstrates in her work on video nasties, interviewing horror fans who collect original video releases of these 1980s titles:

> When quizzed about why he continues to valorise VHS over DVD versions, when his VHS copies are often of bad quality and cut, John made the following comment: " … I like the fact you feel as if you've got a proper product — a bulky big tape, especially with the old ones." … [T]hese articulations of the authenticity of the original nasties relate not just to memories of their prior consumption in the pre-VRA age [i.e., before the 1984 Video Recordings Act], but also to their distinctive material appearance (Egan, 2007: 165 and 167).

Such practices may be relatively unusual — many horror audiences will not have collected "original" video nasties — but they nonetheless illuminate the "process of reviewing and remembering" that is common to genre consumption and fandom (Hutchings, 1993: 187). Even audiences who become subculturally tutored in film "originals" and "remakes" such as *Ringu* (1998) and *The Ring* (2002) may remain emotionally attached to the first version they saw (Hills, 2005b: 165) and memories of their own prior consumption.

David Church has argued that processes of remembering are enmeshed in the horror genre's consistent appeal to youth audiences:

> we may spend time gaining (sub-)cultural capital surrounding the genre, only to eventually find ourselves distanced in age and (sub-)cultural competence from the audience currently being catered to — hence the tendency to distrust current trends and seek refuge in nostalgia. (2010: 236)

Here, horror nostalgia emerges precisely when new generations of (youth) audiences have embraced more recent developments in horror, for example, "torture porn" or "found footage horror," leaving those who have grown up with a prior genre phase to conserve (sub)cultural knowledge of this film history — whether it concerns "video nasties" or, say, Hammer horror. There is thus an intense and recurrent "generational politics" to critical narratives of the horror genre (Jancovich, 2002: 9), as the cultural aging of fan audiences, and commodified conversion of "edgy" subcultural capital into "respected" cultural capital, has a marked impact on the cultural status of certain cycles or subgenres. Video nasties are released uncut on DVD and Blu-ray today. And Hammer horror enjoys DVD "Viewing Notes" in which fan archivists criticize "fanciful Film Studies theorizing" to indicate they are the "true" keepers of the crypt (Hearn and Rigby, 2003: 19). Peter Hutchings has bemoaned this recontextualization, saying specifically of Hammer's output:

> we must constantly be aware of British horror's disreputability, for this quality comprises an integral part of the genre's working … therein lies dispensation for its transgressions … Rendering these films worthy and respectable would be doing them a disservice. More, it would be like forcing them into the light and then watching helplessly as they crumble into dust. (1993: 187)

In the very moment that he decries horror's conversion into more genteel and archivist pleasures, Hutchings also performs a type of fan collective memory, aligning this loss of transgression with the closing moments of Hammer's 1958 [*Horror of*] *Dracula* where the titular vampire is reduced to dust (Figure 6.2). It is a moment, and an image, which circulates in the work of professional writers and scholars drawing on their generational fan passions, also occurring metaphorically at the end of Christopher Fowler's novel about Hammer (2012: 270) and as a structuring image

Figure 6.2 The Count crumbles into dust in Hammer's [*Horror of*] *Dracula* (1958), an iconic image suggesting a commentary on the genre's evolving meanings. Directed by Terence Fisher. Produced by Hammer Film Productions.

in Stephen Volk's novella *Whitstable* (2013: 24 and 111), released to commemorate actor Peter Cushing's centennial year. Such textual poaching—transforming a momentary image in Hammer's history into statements about sociohistorical contexts, the Studio's own decline, and the contrast between fantastical and real "monsters"—cuts across "collective" and "personal" memory.

By zeroing in collectively and personally on "moments" of horror (Rigby, 2011: 8), fans present a challenge to the traditions of film studies. As well as interacting with texts' whole narratives, horror fandom also circulates examples of what Victor Burgin calls the "sequence-image" (2004: 23). For Burgin, such textual excerpts are dimly remembered and brief, cropping up in voluntary recollections as well as involuntary associations, but they distinctively "present a configuration ... that is more 'object' than narrative. What distinguishes the elements of such a configuration from their evanescent neighbours is that they seem somehow more 'brilliant'" (2004: 21) or affectively laden. For fans, though, these bits of objectified memory that exceed their narrative framing are unlikely to be dimly grasped. Fanzines, magazines, blogs, forums, and interpretative machineries of fandom all aim to transform the "sequence-image" into knowledge with a degree of fan cultural capital.

Writers such as Fowler, Hutchings, and Volk draw on a filmic moment that has been collectively celebrated by Hammer fans, to be sure, but they also choose *this* moment to demarcate discursively Hammer's remembered authenticity. Metaphorical appropriation and creative retooling inserts a self-reflexive "distance between our contemporary selves and some romanticized past when ... the genre still seemed ... fresh and new," allowing "the rosiest of personal and cultural memories" to discursively secure a particular genre history (Church, 2010: 236). Such professionalized (scholar-)fan writings refuse to lump Hammer horror together into a formula, instead remarking specific textualities. Though Peter Hutchings argues that it has "become difficult to view the Hammer 1958 *Dracula* as a film in its own right" (2003: 97), with critical receptions blurring it into "Hammer horror generally," the collective and personal memories of a generation of "archivist" Hammer fans counteract this process. Fans constantly *re-specify* what they have loved about particular horror films. Nostalgia for how horror affected the past (often child) self is a strategy for countering discursive shifts in "contexts of mediation and consumption" where older horror films may not only be in danger of respectability, they might also be "seen as restrained or even laughable" (Jancovich, 2002: 10). Fan nostalgia recontextualizes aging horror films as "classics," understood fan-culturally and through "personal event memory" in terms of their "authenticity" (Church, 2010: 240).

These "personal event memories" can also take in the horror genre's actors and stars. Kate Egan has analyzed how some male fans celebrate Ingrid Pitt, especially her appearance in *The Vampire Lovers* (1970), in relation to memories of their sexual awakening. One fan notes that Pitt was his "first real fantasy" and another that she was among his "first crushes" (Egan, 2013: 216). This is not so different to how some female fans talk about actors embodying "handsome, exotic, and charismatic" vampire figures (Cherry, 2002: 174). Nor, for that matter, does it differ greatly from how the *Twilight* franchise might function for a section of its teenage audience. Different audiences, sometimes pitted against one another's generational and gendered cultural politics and memories of horror, may nonetheless share experiences of emergent sexuality in relation to the horror genre. That is not to say that youthful audience sexuality is somehow a transhistorical factor: discourses of sexual identity (hetero- and queer) remain historically variable (Benshoff, 1997). What it could have meant to have a crush on the vampiric Ingrid Pitt is liable to be somewhat distinct, therefore, from being part of the vampire-loving "Team Edward" (with all the productive, commodified discourse this implies).

Remembering and nostalgically defending moments of horror involves audiences in struggles surrounding who has the right to speak for, and articulate, horror's histories (critics/academics/fans/specific generations). Looking back on the horror films that viewers were fascinated by in their younger days, or embracing the horror "canon" across generations (Mathijs and Sexton, 2011: 203–204), suggests that horror audiences are somehow inherently past-oriented. But, while reception studies has been able to explore "how texts mean[t]" across the twentieth century in increasing detail, contemporary fandom has simultaneously embraced digital media and new possibilities for activity. The puzzle for scholarship, then, is how to best tackle the multivalent and multiple activities of horror audiences, whether viewers/fans are looking back on horror, challenging censorship, or engaging in gendered (anti-)fandom conflicts (Figure 6.3).

Work on horror film audiences has certainly benefitted from the emergence of web 2.0, and the greater visibility of diverse audience practices and paratexts which

Figure 6.3 The "Stab-a-thon" event depicted in *Scream 4* (2011) continued to play with horror audience understandings of audience activities. Directed by Wes Craven. Produced by Dimension Films, Corvus Corax Productions, Outerbanks Entertainment, The Weinstein Company, Midnight Entertainment, and Prime Focus.

would have been more subculturally secluded a generation ago. Today's scholars have access to a mass of searchable and naturally occurring audience data, ranging from blogs and 24/7 genre news sites to Facebook groups and Twitter feeds. It is not only media technologies that can offer assistance to students of horror film audiences but work in other, contiguous areas of audience studies may also offer fresh blood for the theorization of the genre. Indeed, horror has become a fertile area for the video game industry, suggesting that horror/audience studies needs to focus more intently on how genre conventions and audience experiences can intersect with gameplay (Perron, 2012; Ndalianis, 2012). There is yet another "paradox" here: not only that horror represents an enjoyable consumption of what should be repulsive, but furthermore that gaming represents the enjoyable performance of what itself should be displeasing, that is, moments of player "failure" that go to make up gameplaying processes (Juul, 2013). Bernard Perron argues that horror videogames intensify the "play of ratiocination" identified in Carroll's (1990) philosophy of horror as a key element of the genre's appeal (2012: 104). This desire to learn about the game environment gives rise to "*gameplay emotions*" (Perron, 2012: 96) that keep gamers invested in, say, *Silent Hill* or its sequels even while they run into instances of annoying failure. However, arguing for game/film distinctions can downplay the extent to which horror film — certainly in its "postmodern" variants — itself seeks a kind of spectator-player who participates in the film's "game" and whose participatory playfulness can be incorporated into a "community of knowledge and discussion" (Jess-Cooke, 2012: 62). For Carolyn Jess-Cooke, the *Scream* franchise aims to provoke audiences into playing with horror's competencies so that its branded, genre-gaming "discourses are re-circulated" (62) via paratexts and user-generated content.

Although Annette Hill's more recent audience studies' work has not focused directly on horror, she has usefully tackled *Paranormal Media* (2011), that is, the mainstream popularity of TV shows such as *Most Haunted* (2002). Just as Jess-Cooke stresses the "*connective* response" that postmodern, playful horror gives rise to (2012: 74) — where audiences generate textual continuations and viral marketing — Hill emphasizes how spirituality, magic, and the supernatural in popular culture offer "ambiguous cultural experiences" (2011: 35). Here, the very multiplicity of meaning facilitates a similar scenario to postmodern play: again, "the audience is the show" (Hill, 2011: 151), this time producing/debating beliefs. Detailed audience study such as Hill's can therefore supplement the theoretical directions which have been taken around postmodern horror, suggesting that how "audiences embody the culture they experience" (2011: 166) is important, with this not only being linked to community, but even more fundamentally to "feeling alive" (Hill, 2011: 181).

Encountering the fictionally threatening or the inexplicable illusion gives rise to audience affects which are not pre-subjective or impersonal flows (*contra* Deleuzian theories of horror, e.g., Powell, 2005) so much as "affective-textual encounters" (ATEs) (Skeggs and Wood, 2012: 127). These "ATEs" are open to empirical observation: Beverley Skeggs and Helen Wood explore them for audiences of reality television, but it is startling that so little audience study has sought to understand the "non-verbal response" (127) of actual horror audiences without setting up analysts' (cognitivist or Deleuzian) frameworks as a "stand-in" for flesh-and-blood audiences. Equally, much audience work has fallen back on discourses as evidence of how horror is interpreted (Hills, 2005a), thus potentially marginalizing the experienced affects of horror. Angela Ndalianis (2012) is surely right to call for a greater focus on *The Horror Sensorium*—both cognitive and affective—but this needs to be joined up with empirical audience investigation, for example, of the innovative kind carried out by Skeggs and Wood, rather than carried through into new master narratives of theory excluding horror's audiences. Contemporary audience participations sustained by postmodern horror film, videogames, and paranormal media (as well as the cinematic livecasting of plays such as Danny Boyle's *Frankenstein*: see Barker, 2012) all suggest that *the audience is increasingly the show in the age of media convergence and paratextual proliferation.* Horror audiences today are pop-culture cannibals: consuming "themselves" (their blogs and tweets), consuming horror. And by drawing on a cultural studies-inflected approach, empirical audience studies can address the cultural politics of the power relationships framing today's horror cinema, whether these involve the legality of specific (cut) horror films, the way in which web 2.0-faciliated audience groups represent one another in relation to gender and age, and the way in which horror's "authenticities" are claimed and counter-claimed by (anti-)fans.

References

Altman, R. (1999) *Film/Genre*, BFI Publishing, London.

Austin, T. (2002) *Hollywood, Hype and Audiences: Selling and Watching Popular Film in the 1990s*, Manchester University Press, Manchester.

Barker, M. (2012) *Live To Your Local Cinema: The Remarkable Rise of Livecasting*, Palgrave Pivot, London.

Barker, M. (2013) Watching rape, enjoying watching rape … : how does a study of audience cha(lle)nge film studies approaches?, in *The New Extremism in Cinema: From France to Europe* (eds T. Horeck and T. Kendall), Edinburgh University Press, Edinburgh, pp. 105–116.

Barker, M., Arthurs, J., and Harindranath, R. (2001) *The Crash Controversy: Censorship Campaigns and Film Reception*, Wallflower Press, London and New York.

Barker, M., Mathijs, E., and Mendik, X. (2006) Menstrual Monsters: The Reception of the Ginger Snaps Cult Horror Franchise, http://cadair.aber.ac.uk/dspace/bitstream/handle /2160/1988/Ginger+Snaps+Film+International+Article,+Barker.pdf?sequence=1 (accessed 25 July 2013).

Barker, M. and Petley, J. (eds) (2001) *Ill Effects: The Media/Violence Debate*, 2nd edn, Routledge, London and New York.

Barker, M. *et al.* (2007) Audiences and Receptions of Sexual Violence in Contemporary Cinema, http://www.bbfc.co.uk/sites/default/files/attachments/Audiences%20and%20 Receptions%20of%20Sexual%20Violence%20in%20Contemporary%20Cinema_0.pdf (accessed 25 July 2013).

BBFC (2010) *The Bunny Game*, http://www.bbfc.co.uk/releases/bunny-game-1970 (accessed 25 July 2013).

BBFC (2011) *The Human Centipede 2 (Full Sequence)*, http://www.bbfc.co.uk/releases/human-centipede-2-full-sequence (accessed 25 July 2013).

Benson-Allott, C. (2013) *Killer Tapes and Shattered Screens: Video Spectatorship from VHS to Filesharing*, University of California Press, Berkeley and London.

Benshoff, H.M. (1997) *Monsters in the Closet: Homosexuality and the Horror Film*, Manchester University Press, Manchester and New York.

Berenstein, R.J. (1996) *Attack of the Leading Ladies: Gender, Sexuality and Spectatorship in Classic Horror Cinema*, Columbia University Press, New York.

Bode, L. (2010) Transitional tastes: teen girls and genre in the critical reception of *Twilight*. *Continuum*, **24** (5), 707–719.

Bolin, G. (2000) Film swapping in the public sphere. *Javnost: The Public*, **7** (2), 57–74.

Booth, P. (2012) *Saw* fandom and the transgression of fan excess, in *Transgression 2.0: Media, Culture and the Politics of a Digital Age* (eds D.J. Gunkel and T. Gourneos), Continuum, New York and London, pp. 69–83.

Burgin, V. (2004) *The Remembered Film*, Reaktion, London.

Carroll, N. (1990) *The Philosophy of Horror*, Routledge, New York and London.

Cherry, B. (2002) Refusing to refuse to look, in *Horror, The Film Reader* (ed. M. Jancovich), Routledge, London and New York, pp. 169–178.

Cherry, B. (2009) *Routledge Film Guidebooks: Horror*, Routledge, London and New York.

Cherry, B. (2010) Stalking the web: celebration, chat and horror film marketing on the internet, in *Horror Zone* (ed. I. Conrich), I.B. Tauris, London and New York, pp. 67–85.

Cherry, B. (2011) Knit one, bite one: vampire fandom, fan production and feminine handicrafts, in *Fanpires: Audience Consumption of the Modern Vampire* (eds G. Schott and K. Moffat), New Academia Publishing, Washington, DC, pp. 137–155.

Church, D. (2010) Afterword: memory, genre, and self-narrativisation; or, why I should be a more content horror fan, in *American Horror Film: The Genre at the Turn of the Millennium* (ed. S. Hantke), University Press of Mississippi, Jackson, pp. 235–242.

Egan, K. (2007) *Trash or Treasure? Censorship and the Changing Meanings of the Video Nasties*, Manchester University Press, Manchester.

Egan, K. (2011) *Cultographies: The Evil Dead*, Wallflower Press/Columbia University Press, New York and London.

Egan, K. (2013) A *real* horror star: articulating the extreme authenticity of ingrid pitt, in *Cult Film Stardom: Offbeat Attractions and Processes of Cultification* (eds K. Egan and S. Thomas), Palgrave Macmillan, Basingstoke and New York, pp. 212–225.

Erb, C. (1998) *Tracking King Kong: A Hollywood Icon in World Culture*, Wayne State University Press, Detroit.

Fowler, C. (2012) *Hell Train*, Solaris, Oxford.

Garde-Hansen, J. (2011) *Media and Memory*, Edinburgh University Press, Edinburgh.

Gauntlett, D. (2001) The worrying influence of "media effects" studies, in *Ill Effects*, 2nd edn (eds M. Barker and J. Petley), Routledge, London and New York, pp. 47–62.

Gray, J. (2010) *Show Sold Separately*, New York University Press, New York and London.

Gough, K. (2010) Alien receptions: boundary contagion, generic pollution and Ripley as a shifting cultural signifier. unpublished PhD, awarded from University of Nottingham.

Hanich, J. (2010) *Cinematic Emotion in Horror Films and Thrillers: The Aesthetic Paradox of Pleasurable Fear*, Routledge, New York and London.

Hearn, M. and Rigby, J. (2003) The Quatermass Xperiment: Viewing Notes Hammer/DD Video, London.

Heffernan, K. (2004) *Ghouls, Gimmicks, and Gold: Horror Films and the American Movie Business, 1953 – 1968*, Duke University Press, Durham and London.

Hill, A. (1997) *Shocking Entertainment: Viewer Response to Violent Movies*, John Libbey/University of Luton Press, Luton.

Hill, A. (2011) *Paranormal Media: Audiences, Spirits and Magic in Popular Culture*, Routledge, London and New York.

Hills, M. (2005a) *The Pleasures of Horror*, Continuum, London and New York.

Hills, M. (2005b) Ringing the changes: cult distinctions and cultural differences in US fans' readings of Japanese horror cinema, in *Japanese Horror Cinema* (ed. J. McRoy), Edinburgh University Press, Edinburgh, pp. 161 – 174.

Hutchings, P. (1993) *Hammer and Beyond: The British Horror Film*, Manchester University Press, Manchester and New York.

Hutchings, P. (2003) *Dracula*, I.B. Tauris, London and New York.

Hutchings, P. (2004) *The Horror Film*, Pearson Education, Harlow.

Jancovich, M. (2000) "A real shocker": authenticity, genre and the struggle for distinction. *Continuum: Journal of Media & Cultural Studies*, **14** (1), 23 – 35.

Jancovich, M. (2002) General introduction, in *Horror, The Film Reader* (ed. M. Jancovich), Routledge, London and New York, pp. 1 – 19.

Jenkins, H. (2006) *Convergence Culture: Where Old and New Media Collide*, New York University Press, New York and London.

Jess-Cooke, C. (2012) *Film Sequels*, Edinburgh University Press, Edinburgh.

Juul, J. (2013) *The Art of Failure: An Essay on the Pain of Playing Video Games*, MIT Press, Cambridge and London.

Kermode, M. (2001) I was a teenage horror fan: or, "How I learned to stop worrying and love Linda Blair", in *Ill Effects: The Media/Violence Debate*, 2nd edn (eds M. Barker and J. Petley), Routledge, London and New York, pp. 126 – 134.

Kermode, M. (2002) The British censors and horror cinema, in *British Horror Cinema* (eds S. Chibnall and J. Petley), Routledge, London and New York, pp. 10 – 22.

Klinger, B. (2011) Re-enactment: fans performing movie scenes from the stage to YouTube, in *Ephemeral Media: Transitory Screen Culture from Television to YouTube* (ed. P. Grainge), BFI/Palgrave Macmillan, Basingstoke and New York, pp. 195 – 213.

Kuhn, A. (2002) *Dreaming of Fred and Ginger: Cinema and Cultural Memory*, New York University Press, New York and London.

Mathijs, E. and Sexton, J. (2011) *Cult Cinema: An Introduction*, Wiley-Blackwell, Malden and Oxford.

Monk, C. (2011) Heritage film audiences 2.0: period film audiences and online fan cultures. Participations, **8** (2), http://www.participations.org/Volume%208/Issue%202/3h%20Monk.pdf (accessed 21 February 2014).

Morris, M. (2006) *The Reptile* [1966], in *Cinema Macabre* (ed. M. Morris), PS Publishing, Hornsea, pp. 64 – 69.

Ndalianis, A. (2012) *The Horror Sensorium: Media and the Senses*, McFarland, Jefferson.

Perron, B. (2012) *Silent Hill: The Terror Engine*, University of Michigan Press, Michigan.

Petley, J. (2011) *Film and Video Censorship in Modern Britain*, Edinburgh University Press, Edinburgh.

Plantinga, C. (2009) Trauma, pleasure and emotion in the viewing of *Titanic*, in *Film Theory and Contemporary Hollywood Movies* (ed. W. Buckland), Routledge, New York and London, pp. 237–256.

Powell, A. (2005) *Deleuze and Horror Film*, Edinburgh University Press, Edinburgh.

Prince, S. (2003) *Classical Film Violence*, Rutgers University Press, New Jersey.

Rigby, J. (2011) *Studies in Terror: Landmarks of Horror Cinema*, Signum Books, Cambridge.

Sheffield, J. and Merlo, E. (2010) Biting back: *Twilight* anti-fandom and the rhetoric of superiority, in *Bitten by Twilight: Youth Culture, Media & the Vampire Franchise* (eds M.A. Click, J.S. Aubrey, and E. Behm-Morawitz), Peter Lang, New York, pp. 207–222.

Skeggs, B. and Wood, H. (2012) *Reacting to Reality Television: Performance, Audience and Value*, Routledge, New York and London.

Soufex (2010) Frightfest 2010, posted 1st September, http://soufex.tumblr.com/post/1046592030/frightfest-2010 (accessed 25 July 2013).

Staiger, J. (2000) *Perverse Spectators*, New York University Press, New York.

Staiger, J. (2005) *Media Reception Studies*, New York University Press, New York.

Tryon, C. (2009) *Reinventing Cinema: Movies in the Age of Media Convergence*, Rutgers University Press, New Brunswick.

Turner, G. (2012) *What's Become of Cultural Studies?* Sage, London.

Volk, S. (2013) *Whitstable*, Spectral Press, London.

7

A's, B's, Quickies, Orphans, and Nasties

Horror Films in the Context of Distribution and Exhibition

Kevin Heffernan

As the companion pieces in this volume demonstrate, horror cinema can be situated within an array of historical, industrial, technological, and cultural contexts. One often-overlooked aspect of the horror film is its distribution and exhibition. In fact, shifts in the relationship between the distribution and broadly-defined exhibition branches of the film and television industries — often in conjunction with trade policy, censorship, and other government interventions — are frequently the generative mechanisms that determine both long-range and smaller tactical innovations in film production, most notably in film financing, marketing, and the ebb and flow of genre cycles. The periodic reappearance of horror movies in successive guises is often as much a result of changes in distribution and exhibition as it is of social changes in the landscapes of fear. For example, the cycle of films during the period 1931–1934, which came to be called *horror pictures* were produced and received in the context of a vertically-integrated American and British film industry adapting to changes in international distribution after the coming of sound and the onset of the Great Depression. This situation drastically changed with the Second World War, the ensuing product drought, and declining audiences. These shifts led to fluidity between horror films and other styles, genres, and modes of filmmaking as independent exhibitors struggled to fill their screen time with an increasingly eclectic range of programming. The hugely controversial British release of *Peeping Tom* in 1960 illustrates many of these trends and demonstrates how historians' blind spots in the areas of distribution and exhibition can result in a series of ill-considered judgments of very important films in the history of cinema. Finally, the use of horror movies to fill shortages in the product pipeline provides a much-needed economic dimension to the histories of both the "video nasties" controversy in early 1980s Britain, as well as the rise of cult/paracinematic film culture 15 years later.

A Companion to the Horror Film, First Edition. Edited by Harry M. Benshoff.
© 2014 John Wiley & Sons, Inc. Published 2017 by John Wiley & Sons, Inc.

Vertical Integration, Import Quotas, and "The Horror Picture," 1931–1945

Before the term *horror picture* was even coined, much less associated for decades with derivative, low-budget movie making, the appearance of *Dracula*, *Frankenstein*, and *Dr. Jekyll and Mr. Hyde* (all 1931) initially left audiences and critics bereft of a generic category with which to understand them (Skal, 1993: 144). The production trend had its roots in changes in exhibition and distribution: Universal, which produced *Dracula* and *Frankenstein*, had briefly attempted to enter the ranks of the major studios through the purchase of a small circuit of theaters. When this proved unprofitable, the company fell back on its established market of non-affiliated circuits and smaller theaters in the neighborhoods and small towns. In order to ensure access to the deluxe downtown houses owned by the Big Five companies (Paramount, Warner Bros, RKO, Fox, and MGM), the company needed to produce "A" product, a strategy they began with the prestigious literary adaptation of *All Quiet on the Western Front* (1930) (Balio, 1993: 298). *Dracula* and *Frankenstein* (and their immediate imitator, Paramount's *Dr. Jekyll and Mr. Hyde*), were based less on their nineteenth century literary sources and more on hugely successful recent stage adaptations (Skal, 1993: 107). This modest but visible cultural pedigree was enhanced by period costumes and bold and stylized sets designed by Universal's art director Charles D. Hall and Paramount's Hans Dreier; however, the relatively brief running times of many of Universal's horror hits reveal that they never lost sight of their market of smaller exhibitors in need of supporting movies for high-turnover double features. What became known as *horror pictures* were characterized by a conspicuous display of technical virtuosity designed to make a splash in deluxe first-run situations, from Universal's expressionist production design to the innovative sound and visual effects of *Dr. Jekyll and Mr. Hyde* to Warner's use of two-strip Technicolor in *Dr. X* (1932) and *Mystery of the Wax Museum* (1933) to the revolutionary special effects in RKO's *King Kong (1933)*, which was premiered in not one but two deluxe theaters in New York, including Radio City Music Hall (Gomery, 1986: 146).

At the same time, Hollywood's international distribution system and the audiences to which it had been successfully catering were facing a language barrier in the years following the coming of sound. Anticipating stagnating or declining international revenue, and experimenting with multiple language versions of their showcase films while still refining the art of dubbing dialog into multiple languages, they set their sights on the UK market, always Hollywood's most lucrative customer abroad and one which presented no language barrier (Jarvie, 1992: 7). At the time of the horror picture cycle, Hollywood distributors' British branch offices ramped up their release schedules and inundated the UK market with sound movies with major stars and high production values (Jarvie, 1992: 80). The British government had already taken action against this attempt at market colonization with the 1927 Cinematograph Film Act, which established a minimum quota of British productions for exhibitors and distributors (Street, 1997: 17). Throughout the 1930s, the most profitable sectors of the British film industry came to be controlled by an oligopoly of vertically-integrated combines: British-Gaumont (Ryall, 1997: 27), Odeon (over which Rank gained controlling interest in 1941) (Porter, 1997: 122), and Associated British ABC chains. Each of these combines played the most popular British and American films, including the films from the early 1930s horror cycle (Ryall, 1997: 28). The British Board of Film Censors, led by Edward Shortt from 1929–1935, was deeply troubled by the horror films and banned, cut, or classified them under the "H" designation, a rating also awarded to British-Gaumont's *The Ghoul* (1933) (Richards, 1997: 170). This censorship of horror films was also, of course, a way to erect a barrier of entry to some of Hollywood's product. At the other end of the industry, smaller producers such as George "Quota" King produced low-budget genre pictures for working class provincial theaters to meet their Film Act quotas, including the Victorian Grand Guignol "strong meat" horror melodramas such as *The Demon Barber of Fleet Street* (1936) and *The Face at the Window* (1939) (Richards, 1998) starring Tod Slaughter.

Back in America, the severe market downturn at the box office during the Depression led small-town and neighborhood exhibitors to devise a number of promotional strategies to lure audiences back into the theaters, the most enduring being the wide adoption of double features. By 1935, the practice became a standardized aspect of exhibition, and distributors began to systematize their supply of product to the market, in which a subsequent-run engagement of a major studio hit booked for a percentage of the box office was paired with a shorter, supporting "B" film, usually booked for a flat fee (Balio, 1993: 28). All of the major and minor studios, as well as "Poverty Row" studios such as Monogram, Republic, and Producers Releasing Corporation, produced "B" pictures for these situations. It is this shift in exhibition and distribution, much more than the enforcement of the Production Code in 1934 that led to the decline in "A" horror films from the studios and their reappearance as modest program pictures. Universal, after a too-rapid attempt at expansion, was taken over by Standard Capital Corporation in 1936 (Balio, 1993: 17). They renewed the studio's earlier strategy of providing smaller pictures to exhibitors outside of the major studios' affiliated circuits, moving their production policy from period horror films to — most successfully — musicals starring Deanna Durbin, their version of mega-star Shirley Temple (Balio, 1993: 104). The company's two notable horror entries from mid-to-late decade, *Bride of Frankenstein* (1935) and *Son of Frankenstein* (1939), were modeled on previous production trends: the literary costume adaptation and Technicolor super production respectively, although *Son of Frankenstein* was eventually shot and released in black and white.

From the mid-1930s and throughout the boom years of World War II, during which wartime rationing made movies one of the only available consumer goods, and well into the postwar period, the horror film was the purview of "B" units of the major studios and Poverty Row companies (Schatz, 1999: 111). *The Wolf Man* (1941) began Universal's wartime series of "B" sequels to its 1930s hits, and

RKO, which had its own takeover in 1942 by the Atlas Corporation, also stopped producing high-budget prestige pictures such as *Citizen Kane* (1941) and *The Magnificent Ambersons* (1942) and focused instead on supporting features for smaller exhibitors. RKO's new production head Charles Koerner assigned producer Val Lewton to make a series of terse, stylish, and understated horror pictures such as *Cat People* (1942), *I Walked With a Zombie* (1943), and *The Body Snatcher* (1945). Although elsewhere in this volume Mark Jancovich argues that several critics fond of the pulpy elements in "B" horror offerings from Monogram and Producers Releasing Corporation (PRC) objected to the "pretentious" high-brow stylings of the Lewton films, the RKO horror cycle turned the many liabilities of "B" horror production—short running times, contemporary settings, leftover sets from other productions, and Production Code-mandated restraint—into assets of ambiguity, style, and understatement (Schatz, 1999: 185). Meanwhile in Britain, wartime rationing also fostered a boom in movie going, despite the dangers of German air raids (Eyles, 1997: 220), and throughout the war horror film elements were introduced into crime films, comedies, and fantasy films (Conrich, 1997: 228). Despite criticism of the horror genre by the British press throughout the war years, less than a month after the Axis surrender, Rank's Eagle-Lion released Ealing Studio's *Dead of Night* (1945), one of the great masterworks of British horror cinema.

Surviving the Fallow Post-War Years

The wartime prosperity of the American film industry came to an end in 1948 when the decade-long antitrust suit against the major studios was resolved in the US Supreme Court's decision *US v. Paramount Pictures, et al.*, which ruled that the studios' ownership of theater chains, its practice of block booking, and de facto local monopolies of profitable theater circuits constituted illegal restraint of trade. The studios were forced to sign a series of consent decrees ending the highly regularized system of distribution, which provided exhibitors with a predictable supply of features for their twice-weekly changes in double features. Over the next decade, the shift in population to the suburbs moved the audience away from the downtown movie theaters, and theater construction in the suburbs did not catch up to this development until the mid-1960s. The major studios' fewer, more expensive movies showcasing new technologies such as monopack color systems, widescreen, 3-D, and stereophonic sound played extensive first runs in the major houses and were passed along to subsequent run exhibitors, often with their audience appeal virtually exhausted. Theaters that had subsisted or even thrived during the studio era with a predictable supply of sub-run engagements of studio films frantically scrambled for product, and by the mid-1950s, many had shifted their programming policy to specialize in youth movies, exploitation films, features from abroad, and horror films (Heffernan, 2004: 5). In 1954, at the beginning of a catastrophic 15-year recession of the US film industry, James H. Nicholson and Samuel Z. Arkoff formed American Releasing Corporation, later American International Pictures, to create low-budget, pre-constituted double features for neighborhood theaters, drive-in chains, and even the deluxe down-town houses, all of which suffered from chronic or seasonal product shortages. They also courted exhibitors with iron-clad release dates, pre-tested titles, ad art, and trailer mockups, which preceded the production of the films themselves (Heffernan, 2004: 70).

Across the pond, Hollywood was attempting once again to compensate for its diminishing domestic box office by aggressively promoting its product in British cinemas through its own long-established distribution subsidiaries, and this had the catastrophic effect of funneling large amounts of hard currency out of Britain's devastated postwar economy (Jarvie, 1992: 215). The years 1947 and 1948 saw Britain impose a currency freeze and Hollywood retaliate with an export ban (Jarvie, 1992: 215). This, along with the major exhibition circuits ABC, Odeon, and Gaumont extending their first runs of the premiere product of both Hollywood and Britain, led to a product shortage in provincial and subsequent-run theaters at least as acute as the one faced by American exhibitors (Eyles, 1997: 221). It was in 1949, during the darkest days of this fallow period that British distributor Exclusive incorporated Hammer Film Productions to make program pictures for the starving British theatrical market. The following year saw the establishment of the British Film Finance Company (BFFC), a pool for domestic film production funded by a voluntary tax on each cinema ticket sold in Britain, the so-called "Eady Levy." When the levy became mandatory in 1956, Hollywood realized that it could establish nominally "British" production subsidiaries and have its investment augmented by as much as 50% with funds from the BFFC. British producers such as Hammer and Anglo-Amalgamated, and later Compton, Amicus, and Tigon could have the lion's share of their own investment in their production slate paid for with Eady funds (Heffernan, 2004: 47). By the late 1950s, Hammer's color remakes of Hollywood's golden age gothic horror movies were financed by a combination of Eady funds and Hollywood money from silent partner Associate Artists Productions (the future Seven Arts company), Columbia Pictures (who bought a huge interest in Hammer in 1958), and Universal.

Anglo-Amalgamated, similar to Exclusive, was independent of the vertically-integrated Rank and ABC groups and had been formed in 1949 to supply quota features to a wide range of exhibitors. After 1958, Anglo enjoyed a reciprocal distribution arrangement with AIP, with each handling the other's product line in their own home country. A number of Anglo's horror, comedy, and crime pictures were financed with a combination of Eady and AIP money, beginning with *Cat Girl* in 1957. Thus, we can see that two of the signature postwar exemplars of the English-language horror cinema—the black-and-white drive-in program pictures of AIP such as *I Was a Teenage Werewolf* (1957) and the colorful Gothic cinema of Hammer films, which began with *The Curse of Frankenstein* that same year—grew out of the changing relationship between the distribution and exhibition branches of the film industry and the two-decade-long product shortage which resulted from these changes.

In this period, both American and British subsequent-run exhibitors came to rely on an eclectic programming strategy to maintain their twice-weekly program changes, and smaller distributors began to acquire a number of films from continental Europe to release to these product-hungry theaters. Some American companies, such as Mayer-Burstyn, Janus Films, Times Films, and Films Around the World carefully built up an upscale, older, educated "lost audience" through their handling of postwar art films (Wilinsky, 2001: 70; Balio, 2010: 79). Many of these companies also handled exploitation films under their own moniker or that of a subsidiary (Heffernan, 2004: 114). The American leader in this release strategy was Joseph Levine's Embassy Pictures, which released horror films such as *Godzilla, King of the Monsters* (1956) and *Jack the Ripper* (1959), dozens of dubbed sword-and-sandal epics such as *David and Goliath* (1960) and *Hercules in the Valley of Woe* (1961), and art-house classics such as *Two Women* (1960), *Sky Above, Mud Below* (1962), *8½*, and *Contempt* (both 1963), all of which were promoted on their real, imagined, or added sensational content (Balio, 2010: 199).

In the United Kingdom, former ABC chain manager Tony Tenser and partner Michael Klinger began the Compton Cinema Club in 1961. Subscription-based private cinema clubs in Britain were not subject to BBFC restrictions, and they screened a range of both highbrow and lowbrow films from continental Europe. The Compton Cinema Club parlayed this success into the establishment of a circuit of provincial cinemas and a distribution subsidiary, Compton-Cameo. As Tenser told *Kine Weekly* in 1964, Compton-Cameo established a "policy of acquiring product to cater for the wider range of exhibitor requirements and public tastes," with a particular emphasis on X-certificate films that major circuits Rank and ABC were reluctant to book the early 1960s wave of Gothic horror films from Italy such as *Lo Spettro/The Spectre* and *Il Virgine del Norimberga/Horror Castle* (both 1963). As film historian Michael Ahmed (2011) notes, "Offering a range of different products on the same exhibition bill was part of a deliberate business strategy by Tenser and Klinger." When the company moved into film financing and production, this diversified approach characterized the company's output. Their first film was the nudist film *Naked—As Nature Intended* (1961), directed by pinup photographer Harrison Marks and starring his wife, the hugely popular glamour model Pamela Green. Subsequent Compton-Cameo films, all of which were released with the X-certificate, included girl-in-trouble "clinical melodramas" [*That Kind of Girl* (1963)], exploitation/"kitchen sink" amalgams [*Saturday Night Out* (1964)], and the fascinating reworking of Italian Gothic horror motifs *The Black Torment* (1964). Most apposite for our discussion of the fluid categories between horror, exploitation, and art cinema during this period, Compton-Cameo released Roman Polanski's *Repulsion* (1965), which had also been financed in conjunction with Columbia's Royal Films subsidiary. Shortly after, Tenser left Compton to form Tigon, a production/distribution firm, which produced or released some of the most accomplished British horror films of the period including *Witchfinder General* (1968), *Scream and Scream Again* (1970), *Blood on Satan's Claw* (1971), and *The Creeping Flesh* (1973) (Ahmed 2011).

Peeping Tom: "Without X Films, What Are Exhibitors Going to Show?"

The power of the major theater circuits, the severe distribution drought, the multiform programming strategies of exhibitors and distributors, the perplexing fluidity of genres, and pin-up model Pamela Green all come together in one of the most famous scandals in British horror cinema, the 1960 release of *Peeping Tom* by Anglo-Amalgamated. Histories of this greatest of *film maudits*—the story of a psychotic focus puller in a quota-quickie film studio who spends his spare time murdering young women to capture their dying expressions of fear on 16 mm film—have emphasized its career-ending effect on director Michael Powell who, 2 years prior to signing on with Anglo had broken with his longtime Archers collaborator Emeric Pressburger and was no longer supported by the powerful Rank Organization (Lowenstein, 2005: 82). Other histories of the film center on the intricate linguistic and psychoanalytic subtext of the film's screenplay by former wartime code breaker Leo Marks (Silverman, 1988; Bick, 1994). In this account, Powell and Marks used the resources of Anglo schlockmeisters Nat Cohen and Stuart Levy to produce a subversive, avant-garde film masquerading as a horror programmer that was decades ahead of its time and which was immediately pulled from release after public indifference and excoriating reviews (Christie, 1978: 53). The film then languished in obscurity until later critics such as Carlos Clarens and director Martin Scorsese, sensitive to its profound philosophical engagement with the deep structures of the horror genre and the institution of cinema itself, pressed for its radical re-evaluation (Clarens, 1968: 145; Gritten, 2010).

If we move the genuinely heroic figures of Powell, Marks, Clarens, and Scorsese to the side and examine *Peeping Tom* against the background of distribution and exhibition, a more complex picture emerges. At the time of *Peeping Tom*'s release, there were three tiers of exhibition in England. The West End of London was home to the country's showcase houses owned by Rank, ABC, *et al.*, and were the focus of publicity and high-profile premieres. The circuits, comprised of theaters owned by ABC, Rank's Odeon and Gaumont chains, and smaller chains such as Granada (who enjoyed an exclusive arrangement with Twentieth Century Fox), were key to suburban first run engagements. Finally, there were the 500-seat halls in the suburbs and industrial North, Midlands, and South, known as *nine-pennies* or *industrial* situations, which had suffered a 15% decline in attendance since the launching of ITV in 1955 and which were often starved for subsequent-run product, especially pictures which fulfilled their quota requirement.[1] In addition, the increasing number of X-certificate films, especially horror films, was a source of friction between these smaller exhibitors and local boards and watch committees. Sidewalk displays and publicity stunts, which had been common for genre pictures since the 1930s, now included hearses, ambulances, and coffins [for Exclusive's release of their Hammer *Dracula* (1958)],[2] and an improvised, gore-soaked operating theater in the lobby for a 1960 engagement of *Eyes Without a Face*.[3] Such tactics came under fire for excessive morbidity from both industry and trade publications[4] and, in a broader concern with the popularity of horror films, public bodies such as the British section of the International Union of Local Authorities[5] and Home Secretary R. A. Butler in a 1958 address to the House of Commons.[6] At the same time, lurid film posters for "films about horror, sex, and prostitutes"[7] were the subject of controversy and accused of "driving people away from the cinemas" by trade groups heavily representative of the Rank/ABC vertical combines such as the British Film Producers Association,[8] the Federation of British Film Makers, and the distributor-based Kinematograph Renters Society.[9]

Although many X-certificate films in a variety of genres enjoyed successful circuit bookings throughout this period, many producers submitted to cuts to obtain the A rating and thus an easier circuit release for their films,[10] particularly in theaters owned and controlled by the Rank Organization, but at a trade meeting of the Cinematograph Exhibitors Association, local exhibitor Jim Poole confessed, "I run both the good X films and the bad ones … If the producers will give us something to replace this type of product, we'll be glad to show it. Without X films what are exhibitors going to show?"[11] Throughout 1958–1960, several solutions to the quandary of X films and the desperate and varied programming strategies of the independent exhibitor were proposed, including a return to the "H" certificate for horror films[12] and the introduction of a new "AA" category for adult-themed films which did not merit the age restriction of the X certificate.[13]

At the same time that the horror film was fanning the flames of controversy, smaller British distributors (as did their American counterparts) began to book a range of imported Continental pictures into theaters suffering from the product shortage. Gala Film Distributors was exhibitor-backed and acquired its product with an eye to serving its own Gala chain and the Jacey Cinemas circuit, a group of broadly-defined art cinemas and subsequent-run houses in the London suburbs and the industrial North.[14] Beginning in the mid-1950s, Gala distributed art-house classics [*Shoot the Piano Player* (1960)], European thrillers [*Les Diaboliques* (1955)], exploitation movies such as the decade-old American nudist picture *Elysia* (1934), the Italian horror film *I Vampiri* (1956), the German JD drama *Teenage Wolf Pack* (1958), and a 1958 release of the 1956 Japanese *taiyozoku* "sun tribe" film *Crazed Fruit* (dubbed and trimmed to barely an hour under the new title, *Juvenile Passion*). The nudist film trend during 1958–1962 was able to take advantage of reclassification of nudist films by the BBFC as suitable for an A rating as long as nudity was featured "in a documentary way … [and not] in an erotic setting."[15] After this reclassification, a major hit in both ABC houses and non-circuit bookings in the provinces was *The Nudist Story* (1960), which was handled by Eros Films, another specialist in imports, quota program features, youth pictures, and X-certificate horror films such as *The Trollenberg Terror* and *Fiend Without a Face* (both 1958).[16] Even Anglo-Amalgamated, the largest and most successful independent distributor in Britain weighed in with a nudist double feature, *Nudist Paradise* and *Liane, Jungle Goddess* (1959), which was a huge hit in both West End and industrial bookings.[17]

Anglo produced and released *Peeping Tom* in the 1959–1960 season, a time in which the company was scoring big on the ABC circuit with *Horrors of the Black Museum* (1959), a gruesome Grand Guignol horror film, and *Carry On Nurse*, the second in the long-running "saucy" comedy series. The company was undergoing significant expansion in the year of their 10th anniversary, and company heads Nat Cohen and Stuart Levy trumpeted the rising production values of their features and announced their "First Fabulous Five" big budget releases of 1960, which cost a total of a million pounds[18] and included *Peeping Tom*, an "out-of-the-rut thriller" directed by Michael Powell. Anglo repeatedly invoked Powell's name in their announcements for the upcoming season, even as Cohen and Levy insisted that they would never make "prestige pictures" or become "arty, high-brow or long-haired … Our expanding production program will include comedies, thrillers, dramas, horror subjects and out-of-the-rut 'gimmick' pictures of all types."[19] The phrase "out of the rut" appeared several times during Anglo's sales drive and was designed to draw attention to the fact that the company's product was no longer quota-filler but rather a successful and distinctive entry in the annual British box office release schedule.

The marquee name of Michael Powell was ideally suited to convince the ABC circuit and its suburban first-run audiences of the film's box office potential, as Powell and Pressburger's features had scored consistently for over a decade in arch-rival Rank's Odeon and Gaumont chains. This impression was abetted by Powell himself, who described the upcoming production as a "Freudian thriller,"[20] and announced straight-faced to the press that "I think you will find that it has many points in common with *The Red Shoes*," not the least of which was the casting of Moira Shearer, the former teenage ballerina from the earlier Archers hit, in a minor role as a bit player at "Shepperfield Studios."[21] While *Peeping Tom* was before the cameras at Pinewood, Powell asserted that the stylized color by cinematographer Otto Heller and the meticulously rehearsed and well-crafted performance by leading actor Carl Boehm would mute the horrific elements of the story. "It is not a gruesome picture," Powell told trade journalist Bill Edwards. "How could I have got such a good cast (Moira Shearer, Anna Massey, Maxine Audley) if it was?" Edwards must have missed the memo from studio heads Cohen and Levy, because he referred to *Peeping Tom* as a "prestige picture," albeit one with a 5-week shooting schedule, an ostensible shooting ratio of 1.5 – 1, and extensive use of the Pinewood film studio itself as a "ready-made set."[22] Eventually, the budget of the film was slashed in half from the figure touted in trade ads to approximately one hundred thousand pounds (Figure 7.1).[23]

As were Anglo's other releases of 1960, *Peeping Tom* was clearly crafted with an eye toward the overseas market. Although its horror elements were more stylized

Figure 7.1 Moira Shearer in *Peeping Tom* (1960). Michael Powell, "I think you'll find that it has many points in common with *The Red Shoes.*" Directed by Michael Powell. Produced by Michael Powell (Theater).

than the overtly pulpy *Circus of Horrors* (1960), Powell's film was designed in part to replicate the success of *Horrors of the Black Museum* in locations as varied as Paris, Zurich, Bangkok,[24] as well as Greece, Italy, and, crucially, the United States,[25] the latter through its reciprocal distribution arrangement with AIP. [26] The casting of 21-year-old Austrian actor Carl Boehm as the deranged and ostensibly London-born Mark Lewis was a direct attempt to court audiences in continental Europe, where Boehm was "immensely popular,"[27] and London's *Evening News* described him to potential British filmgoers as "[a] Continental version … of Dirk Bogarde."[28] And speaking of "Continental versions" (British trade parlance for international release prints containing more nudity than their domestic versions), *Peeping Tom*'s earliest publicity trumpeted one of the movie's most singular attractions, "in her first screen role, lovely model Pamela Green, the famous 'Kamera' girl."[29] Green was the most famous nude pinup model in Britain at the time, and was married to glamour photographer George Harrison Marks; the two had started *Kamera* magazine in 1957. By the time of *Peeping Tom*, they were selling hundreds of thousands of calendars, magazines, and picture sets through both the mail and newsagent shops. Green was cast in the role of Millie, a nude model and one of Mark's victims. Although the nude shot of Millie was not seen in prints released in Britain, Green later recalled that Anglo had made sure that members of the trade and popular press were present at Pinewood on the day that she shot her pinup scenes (Figure 7.2).[30]

From this perspective, the wildly dissonant registers of *Peeping Tom*'s tonal and generic elements that generations of critics have perceptively ascribed to a self-conscious alienating effect designed to bare and reveal cinema's underlying

Figure 7.2   Glamour model Pamela Green recalled, "My pictures were used as there seemed to be hardly anything available from the publicity department." Green with Carl Boehm in *Peeping Tom* (1960). Directed by Michael Powell. Produced by Michael Powell (Theater).

sexual economy (Silverman, 1988; Bick, 1994) are as much a product of the movie's prospective distribution and exhibition demands as they are of Brechtian design. To be sure, *Peeping Tom* was crafted as a scalding satire on the British film industry by a director who was already at the time a casualty of the changing movie business, with the prestige star-driven cinema of the Rank empire nowhere in sight. Meanwhile, "legitimate" studio filmmaking was shading almost imperceptibly into the private "views" shot by Mark within the film, the sadistic psychological experiments inflicted upon him as a child, and the secret murder movies Mark screens in his private theater. This array of modes of exploiting film and photography, each heavily coded by social class and cultural capital, finds its parallel in the different stages of *Peeping Tom*'s theatrical playoff, which included a widely-promoted West End premiere, a national booking on the ABC circuit in May similar to other X-certificate horror pictures, hundreds of summer engagements in nine-penny theaters in the industrial North (where nudist pictures, exploitation films, and quota programmers flourished), and markets abroad including the Continent and the United States.

As might be expected, the use of the names Michael Powell and Moira Shearer featured prominently in the lead up to *Peeping Tom*'s West End premiere, and Anglo hyped its "intensely dramatic and intriguing thriller"[31] by placing an interview with Shearer and an excerpt from the film on the BBC television program *Picture Parade*.[32] In conjunction with theater owners, Anglo also provided a five-installment serialization of *Peeping Tom* for local newspapers,[33] a strategy characteristic of high-profile studio releases. When the film premiered at the Plaza Theater on April 7 for a 2-week engagement, on hand were studio heads Cohen and Levy, director Powell, and stars Carl Boehm, Moira Shearer, Anna Massey, and Pamela Green. Massey and Green recall the chilly reception they received from industry colleagues and members of the trade press at the premiere, and the critical response was swift and savage. Most famously, Leonard Moseley of *Daily Express* confessed that "neither the hopeless leper colonies of East Pakistan … nor the gutters of Calcutta — has left me with such a feeling of nausea and depression as I got this week sitting through a new British film called *Peeping Tom*." Nina Hibben of the *Daily Worker* opined that "from its slumbering, mildly salacious beginning, to its sadomasochistic and depraved climax, it is wholly evil," and Derek Hill of the *Tribune* suggested that "the only way to dispose of *Peeping Tom* would be to shovel it up and flush it swiftly down the nearest sewer. Even then the stench would remain" (all quoted in Macdonald, 1995: 54). Many of the negative reviews struggled to categorize the admittedly skillfully-made film which avoided the supernatural and gothic horror-film clichés easily "dismissed as risible,"[34] and which deftly engaged audiences emotionally in the inner lives of its characters.[35] Isabel Quigly in the *Times* was angered and bewildered by the film's juxtaposition of violent paraphilia with finely-crafted performances, moody longeurs, and psychological depth.[36] Trade sources, on the other hand, correctly predicted that its exploitable angles, vivid use of color, and excellent acting performances would help it "do very well as an X certificate booking,"[37] and a fortnight later, columnist Josh Billings noted that "a savagely hostile press didn't prevent *Peeping Tom* from scoring steadily during its two weeks stay at the Plaza."[38]

Much of the received wisdom of *Peeping Tom*'s "cursed film" status comes from its abbreviated run on the ABC circuit, which began on May 23. Derek Hill's jeremiad against the film ended with an entreaty to suburban audiences to avoid the film's circuit release once *Peeping Tom*'s West End engagement came to an end.[39] In fact, the film "opened to huge figures" in pre-release engagements in Bristol, Bath, Leicester, Doncaster, and other locations "in spite of, or because of, its extraordinary press reception,"[40] and was described by Billings on the eve of its circuit release as "the answer to every live showman's prayer."[41] But 2 years of controversy about lobby displays, posters, horror films, nudist films released with the A-certificate, exploitation pictures carrying the X-certificate, and nudie magazines such as *Kamera*, as well as the Anglo release's "titillating title" had laid a trap for the film which local constabularies and watch committees were only too eager to spring. The Reading watch committee banned the film from chain houses under its authority based solely on the synopsis in Anglo's press kit and "the reviews [they] read in responsible newspapers and journals which criticized the film."[42] The same thing occurred in other localities, and despite the film's "clicking"[43] in many engagements, the ABC chain (unlike subsequent-run and industrial theaters, who had to scramble for commercially viable product to book) removed *Peeping Tom* from its program after a week. This is the source of the legend that the film was quickly "yanked from distribution" and consigned to oblivion.

But on June 9, Anglo returned *Peeping Tom* to the West End for an engagement at the Gala Royal.[44] Gala was an exhibitor-backed distribution firm whose release schedule was comprised of a mix of art-cinema and exploitation, categories that blended seamlessly into each other vis-a-vis its affiliated Gala and Jacey houses and other sub-run theaters desperate for product. This West End release existed alongside other downtown summer bookings from Gala's distribution arm which included *Hiroshima Mon Amour* (1959), *Le Testament d'Orphée* (1959), and the 1958 French import *Sins of Youth* ("The Fire of Heaven is in Their Bodies, But The Parents See Only the Flames of Hell!").[45] For the Gala Royal run, manager Kenneth Rive festooned the theater's marble arch with signs quoting the most damning critical assessments of the film, including those by Moseley, Hibben, and Hill, and once again, long queues for *Peeping Tom* were seen in the West End. The *Daily Mail* noted that this sensationalist come-on at the Gala/Jacey Cinema circuit flagship coincided with the firm's purchase of an additional seven provincial theaters,[46] and the growing Jacey chain would parlay the *succès de scandale* of *Peeping Tom* into an effective launch of their expanded circuit during the last half of 1960.

This was not unanticipated: in the middle of the film's vituperative press reception during the Plaza engagement, Josh Billings asserted that "its time will come later."[47] The Gala Royal engagement marked the beginning of *Peeping Tom*'s successful release in smaller provincial houses that were suspicious of "prestige" films designed exclusively for West End audiences and who still needed Anglo features in commercial genres. During this phase of the film's playoff, Powell's name was seen less than that of "*Kamera* girl" Green, who noted in retrospect that "for most of the publicity purposes, my pictures were used as there seemed to be hardly anything available from the publicity department." Although removed at the last minute from British release prints, the brief glimpse of nudity before Millie's demise was designed to help bookings of the film on the Continent, with Powell's pre-release claim that he found both nudity and Continental versions of British films "boring," conveniently forgotten.[48] The film was increasingly booked as an adults-only engagement, and under these terms, Reading lifted its ban on the film for non-circuit bookings in July.[49] During the hot summer when attendance usually fell, *Kine Weekly* noted that *Peeping Tom* continued to bring in crowds at the Gala Royal and in "suburban and provincial halls."[50] By late summer, trade sources noted that the film was "playing to very large audiences all over the country." It was approved for adults-only exhibition in Ireland,[51] and Josh Billings could proclaim that "Critics threw the book at *Peeping Tom*, (but the Gala Royal and other Jacey and provincial cinemas) threw the book back."[52] However, AIP, Anglo's American partner, passed on the film, and its US release was handled by Gala-like art cinema/exploitation distributor Astor Pictures, who booked it into a range of supporting engagements in American drive-ins, inner-city theaters, and early adopters of the adults-only admissions policy (Heffernan, 2004: 130).

The case of *Peeping Tom* illustrates the centrality of distribution and exhibition to the production and reception of bold and experimental commercial cinema. Powell's film has been called an *independent* production, but it was independent only of former partner Pressburger and the powerful Rank interests that had sustained the pair for a decade. During 1959–1960, *Peeping Tom* was very much a product of its financer/distributor Anglo-Amalgamated and the exhibition environment in which they were operating. Powell would have been acutely aware of this, as the first of the five points in the Archers' 1942 manifesto read, "We owe allegiance to nobody except the financial interests which provide our money; and, to them, the sole responsibility of ensuring them a profit, not a loss" (Macdonald, 1994: 189); contrary to received wisdom, Powell appears to have met this responsibility with *Peeping Tom*. The commercially-driven conventions within which Powell and screenwriter Leo Marks were working in 1959 enabled, not debilitated, the bold striations of style and tone in *Peeping Tom*. The film grew out of rather than opposed important trends in the movie business of the time, most notably in distribution and exhibition. Further, the critical outrage which greeted the film was as much a result of its confounding categories between the prestige film, the circuit release, and the program feature for provincial halls as it was of the actual licentiousness and mayhem on display. In short, the same features which resulted in the film's lamented and lambasted commercial success in 1960 later led to its valorization as a masterpiece of modernist cinema.

Distribution and "Exhibition" on the Home Screen

As noted earlier, the introduction of the British commercial network ITV in 1955 was one of the major causes of decline in movie-going in the heavily working class industrial neighborhoods to which theater managers responded with X-certificate films and other exploitation fare. In the United States, the explosive rise in TV viewing was one of the major causes of Hollywood's postwar recession and the film industry's retooling to cater to the youth market. By the mid-1950s, TV stations needed programming for time slots not filled by the network feed, and older Hollywood films, especially westerns, crime pictures, and horror movies from Poverty Row studios were pressed into service during off-hours. In 1957, Columbia's TV subsidiary Screen Gems licensed the TV rights to dozens of Universal horror films from the 1930s and 1940s, and their "Shock Theater" and "Son of Shock" packages became hugely popular in specialized weekly late night showcases, which often featured a costumed host who camped up the films with commentary, magic tricks, or humorous non-sequiturs (Heffernan, 2004: 156). RKO, rapidly devolving after its sale to General Tire, placed dozens of its pre-1948 titles into TV syndication through its subsidiary C and C Television, and horror films such as *King Kong* (in its edited post-Code, re-release version) and the Val Lewton pictures turned up in heavy rotation on many local stations, leading to a steady re-evaluation of the latter by fans and critics.

For the next 30 years, horror movies became a staple of off-hours television programming. Two later developments in the 1960s, TV's conversion to color and the rise of UHF stations, renewed the scramble for product regardless of genre or country of origin, and the films which TV syndicators proffered to fill this vacuum were the now-familiar mélange of horror films, crime dramas, art-house releases, historical costume spectaculars, and spy movies in imitation of the hugely successful James Bond films (Heffernan, 2004: 165). Some of these were the same movies which had filled the bills at subsequent-run theaters for years, such as the Italian gothic horror pictures released in the United Kingdom by Cameo-Compton and in the United States by AIP. Others were "orphans," pictures imported from Italy, Spain, and Japan which had enjoyed no US theatrical release but whose programmability in genre showcase slots, audacious twists on genre conventions, and florid color palettes helped to create a new canon and a new type of film culture made up of what *Variety* called "really rabid movie buffs" (Heffernan, 2004: 175–176).

In the early to mid-1980s, the "exhibition" context of horror cinema came to include storefront videotape businesses hawking films of wildly disparate styles and genres for a large and diverse movie watching public. In many ways, the video rental shop replayed the histories of the post-war subsequent-run, art cinema, drive-in, and grindhouse theaters and the late-night TV horror movie showcases that they would ultimately render obsolete. Initially the major Hollywood studios fought home video, first in a lawsuit against Sony by MCA and Disney, then by an attempt to collect royalties on each blank videocassette sold, and, when the rental model threatened their total control of all commercial exploitation of their product, the invention of a video cassette that could only be rewound at the factory (Lardner, 1988: 240). Until mid-decade, video shops faced a severe shortage of product as both VCR sales and demand for a regular supply of new titles skyrocketed. As they had through several cycles of film distribution, horror films (along with their perpetual siblings the art movie and sex film), filled the vacuum. Movies which had been produced and financed outside of major studio channels and long played out in "underbelly runs" in drive-ins and grindhouses were quickly released on video, often with dodgy commercial custody credentials. Two of the most important regionally-produced independent horror films, Continental's *Night of the Living Dead* (1968) and Allied Artists' *Communion aka Alice, Sweet Alice* (1977) circulated through the rental market in battered "public domain" editions because their release prints had failed to include a copyright notice on their onscreen title cards.

Similar to the *Peeping Tom* scandal of 20 years before, the "video nasties" farrago of early 1980s Britain was also a direct outgrowth of changes in distribution and exhibition and the fluid categories of genre that followed in their wake. Before the video rental business in Britain was consolidated (with a regular system of timely distributed popular films from major studios), hire shops, convenience stores, and (one presumes) newsagent shops such as those owned by Mr. Peters in *Peeping Tom* were in constant need of product, and a range of very small manufacturers rushed to fill the gap with hastily acquired titles. Similar to the lurid lobby displays from the earlier period, large boxes with screaming copy, female cleavage, and gouts of gore promoted product in the absence of stars. A look at the 39 videos banned by the Director of Public Prosecutions reveals a catalog of small, short-lived video manufacturers who supplied films in an array of genres including horror, soft core sex, sports documentaries, and European and American independent

Figure 7.3   The rape-and-revenge film *I Spit On Your Grave* (1978) was one of the most pilloried of the "Video Nasties" in the United Kingdom. Directed by Meir Zarchi. Produced by Cinemagic Pictures.

movies and art films.[53] Three of the most pilloried of the nasties, *Blood Feast* (1963), *Snuff* (1976), and *I Spit on Your Grave* (1978) were released on video in the United Kingdom by Astra Video, the British distributor of the American company Wizard Video (Figure 7.3). Wizard, one of the companies to innovate the use of oversize boxes with grisly, low-down cover art, marketed a list of the by-then canonical drive-in/grindhouse product-shortage hodgepodge of horror films, comedies from the TV vaults, soft core sex movies, Southern-fried exploitation films, as well as John Waters's art-house cult hits *Pink Flamingos* (1972) and *Female Trouble* (1974). As had happened with the troubling hybrid status of *Peeping Tom* and its co-features in provincial nine-penny theaters, the fluidity and heterogeneity of the genres proffered by companies such as Astra/Wizard were eventually read into individual films themselves. Categories of horror, pornography, and documentary—in the case of the risible search for commercially-distributed "snuff films"—seemed to guardians of the public weal to give birth to frightening, hydra-headed spawn.

The clash of taste the public exemplified by the "video nasties" controversy became a defining feature of movie culture in the home video era. By the mid-1980s, Hollywood distributors embraced home video and regularized VHS release of theatrical features in its multi-platform playoff timetable. In addition, horror cinema became a staple of the direct-to-video market and its fraternal twin, the pro forma theatrical release designed for home viewing on video and cable. Video rental shops, which underwent a steady process of consolidation over the course of the decade, now stocked their shelves with mainstream titles and New Hollywood versions of former exploitation movie staples. Increasingly, postwar art-house, sexploitation, horror, porn, and martial arts films became the purview of specialized mail order companies such as Sinister Cinema, Luminous Film and Video Wurks, and Something Weird Video.

By the 1990s, a new generation of film buffs and cognoscenti was using these catalogs to define an alternative cinematic canon that Sconce (1995) has named "paracinema." Paracinema catalogs include "in addition to art film, horror, and science fiction films ... entries from such seemingly disparate genres as bad film, splatterpunk, mondo films, sword-and-sandal epics, Elvis flicks, government hygiene films, Japanese monster movies, beach party musicals, and just about every other historical manifestation of exploitation cinema from juvenile delinquency documentaries to ... pornography" (Sconce, 1995: 372). If we remove the non-theatrical films and the later splatterpunk movies from this list, we see an inclusive catalog of all of the pictures that were booked by malnourished subsequent-run theaters in the 1950s through the mid-1970s. Even the films on the list released by major studios and mini-majors such as AIP and Embassy—Elvis films, beach party films, and Japanese *kaiju-eiga*—usually premiered for a single week at downtown houses and were then released wide in ad hoc circuits of neighborhood theaters, grateful for the rare opportunity to be part of a saturation "first-run" release (Heffernan, 2004: 117). While Hawkins (1999: 22) sees this collection of highbrow and lowbrow offerings as celebrating "the two extreme tastes of the postwar, youthful filmgoing public," their proximity in the video catalog replays their coexistence in subsequent-run theaters and on local TV stations over the previous 25 years.

Sconce observes the rise of paracinematic film culture in, among other things, the disaffected institutional marginalization of the male humanities graduate student who, as a form of cultural resistance, came to "valorize all forms of cinematic 'trash' whether such films have been either explicitly rejected or simply ignored by legitimate film culture" (372) and the desire of other, less self-consciously theoretical movie fans to "explicitly situate themselves in opposition to Hollywood cinema" (381). But when we position these films in the history of American and British film distribution and exhibition, we find the origins of paracinema in another group of anxious, marginalized men, the hard-scrabble, working-class theater managers of the grad student's grandfather's generation, who were themselves rejected by Hollywood's production/distribution network and their cousins, the British vertical combines, and who booked these films into their theaters in what was for most, thankfully, a successful effort to narrowly avert the madness, uxoricide, and death by spine-shattering panic attack experienced by sub-run theater owner Ollie Higgins (Philip Coolidge) in William Castle's *The Tingler* (1959).

Conclusion

Postwar theatrical distribution patterns—such as those of art-film distributors who booked *Les Diaboliques* and *Eyes Without a Face* into extended runs in urban theaters to build up word of mouth as both prestige and horror entries before wider release—were used profitably for Warners' American playoff of *The Exorcist* (1973).

The release patterns of double features such as *I Was a Teenage Werewolf* and *Invasion of the Saucer Men* (1957) — booked into huge number of theaters while backed by massive saturation advertising — would be hailed as groundbreaking when applied to Universal's *Jaws* (1975). In Britain, the rise of the multiplex theater and the decline in double bills in the late 1980s would be one of the driving forces behind the rise of "Americanized British horror" films such as *Hellraiser* (1987) (Conrich, 1997: 232). Recently, new distribution pipelines, including cable channels devoted to sci-fi and horror programming, and the growth of online distribution portals such as Netflix, required product to fill their own voracious jaws, and here the horror movie served its time-honored function of providing program filler, often in complex hybridization with other genres and styles. Knowledge of paracinematic reading strategies is now entered into the mysterious algorithms which suggest movies we might want to watch or buy based on our previous choices at Amazon or Netflix. These new venues have consigned the video rental shop to the same historical dustbin as the marginal theatrical exhibition venues it had itself rendered obsolete. A thorough and nuanced history of horror films in the contemporary period will establish the many changes in film style, genre conventions and iconography, representations of gender and sexuality, portrayals of violence, and narrative strategies in the context of the still-evolving ways in which horror movies are distributed and reach the eyes and ears of their audience.

Notes

1. "Subsequent-Run Men Can't Find Good Quota Product" *Kinematograph Weekly* (Hereafter KW) October11, 1956, p. 8, "1958 Attendances Down" *KW* April 2, 1959, p. 6, and "Admissions Go Down Again" *KW* May 14, 1959, p. 103.
2. "His 'Horrormobile' Did the Trick for 'Dracula'" *KW* November 27, 1958, p. 22.
3. "A Ticket For Leslie Phillips" *KW* September 15, 1960, p. 20.
4. This Sort of Display is Bad Public Relations' *KW* 10 July, 1958, p. 27.
5. "Horror ... " *KW* September 18, 1958, p. 4.
6. "Home Secretary on Horror" *KW* December 11, 1958, p. 7.
7. "Bad Taste in Films: Producers to Meet" *KW* October 23, 1958, p. 1
8. "'Horror Film Posters Must Be Watched'" *KW* December 11, 1958, p. 6.
9. "KRS Will Act on Horror Posters" *KW* November 20, 1958, p. 6.
10. "How the Censor Aids the Producer" *KW* November 27, 1958, p. xii.
11. "Far Too Many X Films of the Wrong Type: John Davis" *KW* June 9, 1960, p. 14.
12. "H Certificate: CCC Will Not Support BFPA" *KW* May 14, 1959, p. 104.
13. "CCC Considers New Censorship Category AA" *KW* October 13, 1960, p. 1.
14. See "Business Has Never Been Better for Continental Pictures" *KW* September 19, 1958, p. 17, "Gala Has Something For Everyone" *KW* September 18, 1958, p. 19, and Gala trade ad, KW September 18, 1958, p. 16.
15. "Change in BBFC Policy" *KW* September 4, 1958, p. 1.
16. See "Eros Has Big Plans for the New Year" *KW* January 1, 1959, p. 12 and "Conference Men Told of Eros Product Line-up" *KW* March 12, 1959, p. 9.

17. "'Black Museum' Gets an ABC Release" *KW* March 26, 1959, p. 6.
18. "Anglo Spends a Million on Five Pictures" *KW* October 29, 1959, p. 6.
19. Stuart Levy and Nat Cohen, "Anglo Week" *KW* December 31, 1959, p. 3.
20. Bill Edwards, "Production" *KW* October 15, 1959, p. 21.
21. Bill Edwards, "Production" *KW* November 19, 1959, p. 22.
22. Bill Edwards, "Production" *KW* November 19, 1959, p. 22.
23. Pearson Phillips, "'Peeping Tom' Cuts Costs" *Daily Mail* June 8, 1960.
24. "'Black Museum' in the Money" *KW* December 24, 1959, p. 8.
25. Phillip Jacobs, "Anglo Product Goes Round the World—and Breaks Records" *KW* December 31.1959, p. 24.
26. "Anglo Signs Big Product Deal With U.S. Group" *KW* December 11, 1958, p. 1.
27. "Ambitious Five Year Plan: Continuity of Supply is Guaranteed" *KW* December 31, 1959, p. 37.
28. Jympson Harman, "Michael Decides to Take the Plunge" *Evening News* October 19, 1959.
29. "Ambitious Five Year Plan," p. 37.
30. Green, who passed away in 2010, presided over an incredibly detailed, profusely illustrated, and well-written web site and blog, "Never Knowingly Overdressed," in which she recounted her career with Marks and *Kamera* magazine. Her lengthy account of the casting and shooting of Peeping Tom is essential reading. As of early 2013, the site is still online at http://www.pamela-green.com/
31. "Anglo Sets Premiere For 'Peeping Tom'" *KW* March 31, 1960, p. 14.
32. "'Peeping Tom' For Picture Parade" *KW* April 7, 1960, p. 16.
33. "'Peeping Tom' Serial" *KW* May 26, 1960, p. 34.
34. Dilys Powell, "Focus-Pocus and Worse" *Sunday Times* April 10, 1960, p. 25.
35. Isabel Quigly, "Filthy Pictures" *The Spectator* April 15, 1960, p. 544.
36. "The Murderous Cameraman" *London Times* August 8, 1960.
37. "Reviews—Peeping Tom" KW April 7, 1960, p. 24, Josh Billings, "Your Films" *KW* April 14, 1960, p. 10.
38. Josh Billings, "Your Films" *KW* April 28, 1960, p. 10.
39. Derek Hill, "Films—Cheap Thrills" *Tribune* April 29, 1960.
40. "Renters' News—'Peeping Tom' Does Well" *KW* May 26, 1960, p. 18,
41. Josh Billings, "Your Films" *KW* May 19, 1960, p. 30.
42. "'But its Censors Never Saw X-Thriller" *Daily Mail* May 25, 1960.
43. Josh Billings, "Your Films—On Release" *KW* June 2, 1960, p. 131.
44. "'Peeping Tom' Back in West End" *KW* June 9, 1960, p. 15.
45. "Gala Product in Six West End Cinemas" *KW* June 9, 1960, p. 15.
46. Pearson Phillips, "Three Men and Peeping Tom" *Daily Mail* June 8, 1960.
47. Josh Billings, "Your Films" *KW* April 14, 1960, p. 10.
48. Bill Edwards, "Production" *KW* November 19, 1959, p. 22.
49. "Ban on 'Tom' is Lifted" *KW* July 14, 1960, p. 7.
50. Josh Billings, "Your Films" *KW* June 23, 1960, p. 11.
51. "Renters' News—Anglo's 'Peeping Tom' Approved in Eire" *KW* August 4, 1960, p. 22.
52. Josh Billings "Your Films—On Release" *KW* July 7, 1960, p. 14.
53. The Internet is full of shrines to the banned videos from this period and the sensationalist box covers which ensconced them. One of the most comprehensive is at http://www.melonfarmers.co.uk/nasties.htm (accessed January 2013).

References

Ahmed, M. (2011) Independent cinema exhibition in 1960s Britain: compton cinema. *Post Script*, **30** (3), http://www.freepatentsonline.com/article/Post-Script/281175261.html (accessed January 15 2013)

Balio, T. (1993) *Grand Design: Hollywood as a Modern Business Enterprise, 1930–1939*, Charles Scribner's Sons, New York.

Balio, T. (2010) *The Foreign Film Renaissance on American Screens, 1946–1973*, University of Wisconsin Press, Madison.

Bick, I. (1994) The sight of difference, in *Re-Viewing British Cinema, 1900–1992* (ed. W.W. Dixon), State University of New York Press, Albany, pp. 182–189.

Christie, I. (1978) The scandal of *Peeping Tom*, in *Powell, Pressburger, and Others* (ed. I. Christie), British Film Institute, London, pp. 53–59.

Clarens, C. (1968) *An Illustrated History of the Horror Film*, Perigee, New York.

Conrich, I. (1997) Traditions of the British horror film, in *The British Cinema Book* (ed. R. Murphy), British Film Institute, London, pp. 226–234.

Eyles, A. (1997) Exhibition and the cinemagoing experience, in *The British Cinema Book* (ed. R. Murphy), British Film Institute, London, pp. 217–225.

Gomery, D. (1986) *The Hollywood Studio System*, St. Martins Press, New York.

Gritten, D. (2010) Michael Powell's *Peeping Tom*: The Film That Killed a Career. *Telegraph* online August 27, 2010, http://www.telegraph.co.uk/culture/film/7967407/Michael-Powells-Peeping-Tom-the-film-that-killed-a-career.html (accessed January 15 2013).

Hawkins, J. (1999) Sleaze mania, euro-trash, and high art: the place of European art films in American low culture. *Film Quarterly*, **53** (2), 14–29.

Heffernan, K. (2004) *Ghouls, Gimmicks, and Gold: Horror Films and the American Movie Business, 1952–1968*, Duke University Press, Durham, North Carolina.

Jarvie, I. (1992) *Hollywood's Overseas Campaign: The North Atlantic Movie Trade, 1920–1950*, Cambridge University Press, Cambridge.

Lardner, J. (1988) *Fast Forward: Hollywood, the Japanese, and the VCR Wars*, New American Library, New York.

Lowenstein, A. (2005) *Shocking Representation: Historical Trauma, National Cinema, and the Modern Horror Film*, Columbia University Press, New York.

Macdonald, K. (1994) *Emeric Pressburger: The Life and Death of a Screenwriter*, Faber & Faber, London.

Macdonald, K. (1995) Poor Tom. *Index on Censorship*, **24** (6), 52–58.

Porter, V. (1997) Methodism and the marketplace: the rank organisation and British cinema, in *The British Cinema Book* (ed. R. Murphy), British Film Institute, London, pp. 122–131.

Richards, J. (1997) British film censorship, in *The British Cinema Book* (ed. R. Murphy), British Film Institute, London, pp. 167–176.

Richards, J. (1998) Tod Slaughter and the cinema of excess, in *The Unknown 1930s: An Alternative History of the British Cinema, 1929–39* (ed. J. Richards), I. B. Taurus Publishers, London, pp. 139–159.

Ryall, T. (1997) A British studio system: the associated British picture corporation and the Gaumont-British picture corporation in the 1930s, in *The British Cinema Book* (ed. R. Murphy), British Film Institute, London, pp. 27–36.

Schatz, T. (1999) *Boom and Bust: American Cinema in the 1940s*, University of California Press, Berkeley.

Sconce, J. (1995) "Trashing" the academy: taste, excess, and an emerging politics of cinematic style. *Screen*, **36** (4), 371–393.

Silverman, K. (1988) Masochism and male subjectivity. *Camera Obscura*, **2** (17), 31–68.

Skal, D. (1993) *The Monster Show: A Cultural History of Horror*, Penguin Books, New York.

Street, S. (1997) British films and the national interest, in *The British Cinema Book* (ed. R. Murphy), British Film Institute, London, pp. 17–26.

Wilinsky, B. (2001) *Sure Seaters: The Emergence of Art House Cinema*, University of Minnesota Press, Minneapolis.

8

Horror and the Censors

Julian Petley

Horror films tend to contain at least one element that acts as a magnet for censors and their allies, namely violence. Frequently there are sexual elements too, ranging from the suggested, as in *Nosferatu* (1922), to the overt eroticism of later Hammer to the European horrors of Jess Franco, Joe D'Amato, and others. These last represent the *ne plus ultra* of unacceptability for censors of one kind or another, and some are still cut, or even banned, in countries such as Britain with strict censorship regimes.

Although different countries' censors have had different *bêtes noires*—America has tended to be tougher on sex than violence, while in Sweden the reverse has been the case—there can be little doubt that horror, after pornography, has been cinema's second most censored genre. But note the tense. In many Western countries, horror movies, like pornographic ones, benefitted from a relaxation of censorship standards in the relatively liberal 1960s. Furthermore, from the 1980s onwards, new developments such as domestic video, satellite broadcasting and, in particular, the Internet have made censorship at the national level increasingly difficult (although not impossible) to operate and enforce. Most Western countries employ cinema and video classification systems for consumer guidance purposes and some northern European countries such as Norway, Sweden, Iceland, and Germany have been known to cut horror films, even in more recent times. But the European countries with the strictest regimes of film and video censorship—where horror films and videos are most heavily and frequently cut—are the UK and Ireland, the former having constructed an elaborate and statutorily-backed system of regulation, one which still frets over films which barely raise an eyebrow elsewhere in the West.

A Companion to the Horror Film, First Edition. Edited by Harry M. Benshoff.
© 2014 John Wiley & Sons, Inc. Published 2017 by John Wiley & Sons, Inc.

The Horror Wave Breaks

Horror films flourished in the United States in the early 1930s. Although the Motion Picture Producers and Distributors of America (MPPDA) had in 1930 introduced the Motion Picture Production Code (also known as the Hays Code after the organization's president Will H. Hays), it was not properly enforced until 1934. Nonetheless, horror films proved particularly problematic for the Studio Relations Committee (SRC). This had been created by Hays in 1927, with Colonel Jason S. Joy as its head, in order to vet scripts and completed films and to ensure that the MPDDA's standards were being observed; it was also their job to liaise with local censor boards. However, it was largely ineffective in enforcing the MPDDA's standards, and consequently found itself bombarded with complaints from local censorship boards, women's groups, and religious organizations. In December 1931, with *Dracula*, *Frankenstein* and *Dr. Jekyll and Mr. Hyde* either in distribution or about to be distributed, Joy wrote to Hays asking: "Is this the beginning of a cycle which ought to be retarded or killed?", while the following January he expressed his concern that horror films would be "straining for more and more horror till the wave topples over and breaks" (cited in Prince, 2003: 72).

As *Variety* noted in 1931, film producers soon discovered that the Code contained no provision

> which rules on the quality or extent of gruesomeness. Sex, crime, ridicule, politics, church, and school—all are taken care of in the censor book. [Yet] the Hays Office admits that under the Code it is powerless to take a stand on the subject. (Cited in Doherty, 1999: 297)

As Thomas Doherty puts it:

> As long as monsters refrained from illicit sexual activity, respected the clergy, and maintained silence on controversial political matters, they might walk with impunity where bad girls, gangsters, and radicals feared to tread. (1999: 297)

This may be one of the reasons why the SRC approved the scripts of the early Universal horrors in a fairly cursory manner. Thus *Dracula* escaped censorship in the United States, but was the subject of numerous complaints to the MPDDA. It was also banned in Singapore, Malaya, and British Columbia.

Regarding *Frankenstein*, the SRC expressed concern about the scene in which the monster hangs the dwarf, but otherwise stated that they believed it "satisfactory under the Code, and unless some of the official censor boards consider it gruesome, reasonably free from censorship action" (cited in Prince, 2003: 53). They were thus taken aback by the reaction to the film among some sections of the public and certain local censor boards. *Frankenstein* experienced its greatest difficulties with the Kansas board, which initially banned it entirely, claiming that it was cruel and would tend to debase morals. They then demanded so many cuts that the film would have been stripped of almost all its horrific elements (Prince, 2003: 59–60). The Kansas censors finally settled for fewer, although still considerable, cuts after the intervention of both Joy and Joseph Breen of the MPDDA. The *Kansas City Star* noted sardonically that:

> *Frankenstein*, the most popular picture of the year, is being kept from thousands of Kansans because it is not suitable for children and because three women do not like it. (Cited in Doherty, 1999: 297)

Frankenstein also encountered problems in several Massachusetts towns, and in Quebec, which initially banned the film. It was also banned in Belfast, South Australia, Czechoslovakia, and Sweden. When it was re-released in 1938, the Production Code Administration (PCA) which was formed in 1934 in order to enforce the Code more effectively, insisted on the removal of the child being drowned and of Frankenstein sticking the syringe into the monster's back, along with shortening the shots of Fritz tormenting the monster.

Dracula's huge popularity encouraged other studios to put horror films into production and also emboldened them against pressures to tone them down. Paramount entered the market with *Dr. Jekyll and Mr. Hyde*, which was presented to the MPDDA just after *Frankenstein* had enjoyed an extremely successful release. Still uncertain how to handle this new genre, Joy wrote to Paramount's chief, B.P. Schulberg, stating that:

> Because it is so well established a literary classic the public and the censors may overlook the horrors that result from the realism of the Hyde make-up, though we are frank to say we cannot estimate what the reaction will be to this, or to the other horror pictures. Certainly we hope that the excellence of the production will offset any apprehension that the theme is too harrowing. (Cited in Skal, 1994: 144)

As far as the United States was concerned, Joy was proved largely right, but the film was banned in Finland, the Netherlands, Rhodesia, and Czechoslovakia.

Less fortunate was *Freaks* (1932), a property which MGM had owned for some time that was given the green light in the wake of Universal's success, even going so far as to hire *Dracula*'s Tod Browning to direct it. The fact that such a film could be conceived of and made at all shows how relatively liberal was the industry's censorship apparatus at the time, and it is significant that the real damage done to the film resulted from self-censorship by MGM. During filming there was pressure from certain MGM executives to discontinue it, and after disastrous test screenings, nearly half an hour was cut from the film before the premiere. It was widely banned in the United States and also banned in Britain.

Freaks opened on the same day as Universal's latest horror offering, *Murders in the Rue Morgue* (1932), an extremely free adaptation of the Poe story. The SRC had approved the script, subject to a few rewrites, and thought it "reasonably safe from censorship difficulties" (cited in Prince, 2003: 66). However, after the film was completed, Joy wrote to Universal's Carl Laemmle Jr. about a scene in which a scantily-clad young woman is tied to a cross and injected with ape's blood. He pointed out that:

> Censor boards are very likely to think that this scene is over done in gruesomeness. We therefore suggest that you ought to consider making a new soundtrack for this scene, reducing the constant loud shrieking to lower moans and an occasional modified shriek. (Cited in Prince, 2003: 71)

This was duly done, but nonetheless the scene was cut entirely by censor boards in Pennsylvania, Chicago, and New York, and reduced to a mere suggestion by Virginia and Massachusetts. Ohio passed the film but, significantly, warned that:

> In the future, we are going to take more drastic action concerning such scenes of horror and realism to which we have found the public is reacting unfavorably. In this I am asking for the co-operation of the Producers not to include such sequences in pictures so it will not be necessary for us to cut into plots to remove them. (Cited in Prince, 2003: 71)

Abroad, the film was banned in Hungary, and first banned and then cut in Vancouver. When it was re-released in 1936, the PCA insisted on the scene's near elimination (Figure 8.1).

Figure 8.1 The gruesome laboratory torture scene from *Murders in the Rue Morgue* (1932) was censored in many locales. Directed by Robert Florey. Produced by Universal Pictures.

When Paramount first came up with the idea for an adaptation of H.G. Wells's novel *The Island of Dr. Moreau*, Joy warned Schulberg that a story which involved crossing animals with humans "should be abandoned, for I am sure you would never be allowed to suggest that sort of thing on screen" (cited in Doherty, 1999: 311–312). However, Paramount pressed on, and when the SRC received the script for *Island of Lost Souls* (1932) it merely warned that Moreau's line "Do you know how it seems to feel like God?" might cause problems. Again, the SRC was proved wrong both at home and abroad. It was banned by numerous local censor boards in the United States, and also in Singapore, New Zealand, Tasmania, Germany, India, Hungary, Italy, South Africa, the Netherlands, Latvia, and Britain. The fact that it could not be shown in a number of lucrative overseas territories almost certainly influenced the PCA's refusal to grant the film a reissue license in 1935. Joseph Breen, the head of the PCA, and also an ardent Catholic, was offended by its allegedly blasphemous qualities, as well as the horror of its scenes of medical experimentation. It was again refused a license in 1941, with Breen complaining of "the general flavour of excessive gruesomeness and horror" which made the picture "quite definitely repulsive" (cited in Prince, 2003: 67). However, after extensive cuts, the licence was granted.

Enter the Production Code Administration

In the early 1930s, then, Hollywood was faced with a dilemma. Horror films were extremely popular—*Variety* estimated that in the 10 years following the release of *Frankenstein*, horror films had made Universal alone over 10 million dollars. And as the MPDDA was an industry body, it was unwilling to kill the goose that was laying so many golden eggs and thus tended to take a relatively liberal attitude toward these films. On the other hand, horror films were extremely unpopular with many local censor boards, with certain sections of the population, and with various censorship bodies beyond the shores of the United States. And this concerned the MPDDA because outright bans on films limited their takings while controversies about sex and violence besmirched the medium's image and thus made cinema-going unattractive to sections of the population, which also impacted negatively on cinema's profitability. Matters reached a head in 1934 when the National Legion of Decency was formed, primarily to organize boycotts of films which its members, most of whom were Catholics, found offensive. For obvious economic reasons, the threat of boycotts seriously worried the film industry. The SRC was thus transformed into the PCA and given considerable powers. The gap in the Production Code through which horror films had slipped was filled by an amendment entitled "Brutality, Horror, and Gruesomeness," advising film-makers that:

> Scenes of excessive brutality and gruesomeness must be cut to an absolute minimum. Where such scenes, in the judgement of the Production Code Administration, are likely to prove seriously offensive, they will not be approved. (Reproduced in Doherty, 1999: 365)

From 1934 onwards, then, scenes of horror were considerably toned down. When Universal submitted a script based very loosely on Poe's story *The Black Cat*, they were informed that the film's climax, where a character is skinned alive, "will have to be handled with great care, lest it become too gruesome or revolting" (cited in Prince, 2003: 74). They were also warned that scenes involving the killing of cats and the display of women in glass coffins could be problematic. Much is thus suggested by shadows, and the sound in scenes of violence is relatively muted. Nonetheless, the flaying scene was either partially or wholly cut in Maryland, Ohio, and Chicago, and the film was banned outright in Malaya, Italy, Sweden, Austria, and Finland.

Similarly, when Universal submitted a film based on Poe's poem *The Raven*, Breen cautioned them about "the current accumulation of horror in motion pictures" and advised "great care" in dealing with scenes of "excessive horror and brutality" (Prince, 2003: 76). The story involves a surgeon obsessed with Poe who possesses a basement full of torture instruments, including a pendulum which is put to the same use as that in Poe's "The Pit and the Pendulum." The PCA forbade the showing of any detail of a scene of surgery, no blood was to be visible throughout, and in the climactic scene the pendulum was not to touch the victim's body. The film is thus relatively tame compared to its predecessors, but nonetheless censor boards in New York, Ohio, Pennsylvania, and Virginia cut some or all of the pendulum scene.

In July 1934, Universal submitted to the PCA the script of its *Frankenstein* sequel, which was released as *Bride of Frankenstein* (1935). Breen required the deletion of any references which compared Frankenstein's creation of the monster to God's creation of humankind, and noted that "all material which suggests that he [the monster] desires a sexual companion is objectionable" (cited in Gardner, 1987: 66). On receiving a revised script, Breen reiterated his objection to the parallel between Frankenstein and God, and also expressed concern about the number of killings, pointing out that:

> In a picture as basically gruesome as this one, we believe that such a great amount of slaughter is unwise and recommend very earnestly that you do something about toning this down. (Cited in Gardner, 1987: 67)

The film's director, James Whale, then met with the PCA and, as a result, Breen wrote to Universal, explaining that;

> It is our understanding that Mr. Whale intends to shoot various killings in this picture in a decidedly impressionistic manner, without devoting too much footage to them, and in such a way as to avoid the gruesome details. (Cited in Prince, 2003: 78)

However, when the PCA saw the finished film they felt that Whale had not kept his word, and rejected it for its "excessive brutality and gruesomeness." They also suggested cuts to make it more acceptable, although these would have robbed it of almost everything which made it a horror film (Gardner, 1987: 69–70). Finally a compromise was reached, with only a few cuts made, but the PCA warned Universal that the "the very nature of the production is such as to invite very critical examination" at both the local and international level, noting that "it is the kind of picture which is acceptable under the *letter* of our Production Code, but very dangerous from the standpoint of political censorship" (cited in Prince, 2003: 82). "Political censorship" was the term habitually used by the PCA when referring to film censorship practiced outside the United States. Sure enough, numerous cuts were demanded in Ohio, the film was banned in Hungary, Palestine, and Trinidad, and heavily cut in China, Singapore, Sweden, and Japan.

There were also problems with *Dracula's Daughter* (1936). Breen noted of the first draft of the script by R.C. Sherriff, that it "contains countless offensive stuff which makes the picture utterly impossible for approval under the Production Code," and in particular "a very objectionable mixture of sex and horror." Eventually a quite different script was submitted, and met with few objections, although the PCA warned Universal of "the necessity for care in avoiding any unduly gruesome shots" (cited in Naylor, 2011: 7). The script of *The Walking Dead* (1936) also underwent significant rewrites at the behest of the PCA, as did *The Devil Doll* (1936). The latter, based on the novel *Burn Witch Burn* by A. Merritt, was originally conceived as a horror film, but was subjected to such changes at the behest of the PCA that the press book proclaimed:

> IT IS NOT A HORROR PICTURE … in any sense of the word. It is a thriller, a melodrama, a punch, sock, dynamic story that is real entertainment … but most of all it has novelty. (Cited in Naylor, 2011: 8)

Similarly, when Columbia began to develop *The Man They Could not Hang* (1939) they were informed that it was unacceptable because of "the excessive number of gruesome and brutal killings," following which they agreed to develop it "as a murder mystery rather than a horror story" and to leave the killings largely off-screen (cited in Naylor, 2011: 9).

Horror and the British Board of Film Censors

Before I turn to the fate of these films in Britain, it is first necessary to outline the attitude of the British Board of Film Censors (BBFC) in the 1920s and 1930s to horror films. From its beginnings in 1912 until the start of World War II, the BBFC cut or even banned films for a vast number of reasons, and these were also reflected in censorship practices across the British Empire. Reasons for cuts or bans included "the exhibition of profuse bleeding," "gruesome murders, suicides, strangulation scenes, and massacres," and "excessive cruelty and torture to adults" (cited in Trevelyan, 1973: 32–34), all of which impacted on horror films. In 1922 *Nosferatu* was banned (although this may have been because of problems with Bram Stoker's estate). Three years later, alarmed by adverse press comment based on American screenings, the

Cinematograph Exhibitors Association (CEA) took a public stand against Rupert Julian's *The Phantom of the Opera* (1925) even before the BBFC could view it. In Britain local councils possessed (and indeed still do possess) the power to override the classifications handed out by the BBFC, and presumably the CEA feared a re-run of the kind of local censorship which had caused the industry to create the BBFC in the first place. Universal withdrew the film from Britain until 1930, when it was passed uncut. Cuts were made to *The Cat and the Canary* (1927), as well as to *The Terror* and *Sweeney Todd* (both 1928), and *The Cabinet of Dr. Caligari* (1920), belatedly submitted to a wary BBFC in 1928.

When mainstream Hollywood turned to horror in 1931, it rang alarm bells with the BBFC, local councils, and bodies such as the National Society for the Prevention of Cruelty to Children (NSPCC) and the Order of the Child. At this time, only two censorship certificates existed: "U" for films especially suitable for children, and "A" for films generally suitable for public exhibition. Under the regulations governing cinema licensing, children under 16 could be admitted to "A" films only if accompanied by an adult. However, as Sarah J. Smith has illustrated, the regulation was easily circumvented and only patchily enforced, although certain local authorities in Liverpool, Newcastle, Leicester, Sheffield, and Birmingham did ban children from attending "A" films at all (2005: 61–70). Consequently, in 1931 the Home Secretary, Sir Herbert Samuel, established the Film Censorship Consultative Committee (FCCC) to address the issue. This consisted of Samuel himself, the President and Secretary of the BBFC, and representatives from county and local councils.

The classification of *Frankenstein* with an "A" brought this whole matter to a head. Even though the print submitted to the BBFC was already missing four minutes, and even though the BBFC cut it by a further three, it became the object of considerable controversy. Children were banned from seeing it in various towns and cities, and the CEA recommended "in very strong terms that all exhibitors showing this film should make an announcement [that] *Frankenstein* is not .... suitable for children" (quoted in Smith, 2005: 70). The same procedure was followed for *Dr. Jekyll and Mr. Hyde* and *Murders in the Rue Morgue*. As a result of the *Frankenstein* furor, the Order of the Child asked the BBFC to introduce a new category specifically for films which "cannot under any circumstances be shown to children" (quoted in Smith, 2005: 71), and this was the origin of the "H" (for "horrific") category which came into being in May 1933. This was not, at first, a separate certificate; however, films that fell within this category had to carry a warning that they were liable to frighten or horrify children, although they could still be admitted with an adult unless the local council decided otherwise. Other local authorities refused to allow cinemas to show "H" films at all. The first film passed in the "H" category was *Vampyr* (1931).

The BBFC was unhappy about this state of affairs. It could and did discourage at script stage the production of home-grown horrors (e.g., a proposed remake in 1936 of *The Cabinet of Dr. Caligari* was blocked), and it saw the "H" category as in many respects making it easier to distribute and exhibit Hollywood horrors. But the measure had significant support from both central and local governments, and the

BBFC, being an arm of the commercial film industry, could not completely stem the flow of movies which were undoubtedly popular and thus profitable. As its 1935 *Annual Report* complained:

> Although a separate category has been established for these films, I am sorry to learn that they are on the increase, as I cannot believe that such films are wholesome, pandering as they do to the love of the morbid and horrible ... Some licensing authorities are already much disturbed about them, and I hope the producers and writers will accept this word of warning, and discourage this type of subject as far as possible. (Cited in Phelps, 1975: 36)

This was not the end of the horror controversy, however. In July 1935 the London County Council (LCC) proposed to the FCCC and the Home Office that children should be banned from attending films in the "H" category, and in December Middlesex excluded children from all films which the council itself deemed horrific, with Surrey and Essex following suit in 1937. From October 1936 onwards, the LCC tried to persuade the BBFC to introduce an actual "H" certificate for films to which children could not be admitted; the topic was debated in Parliament in 1937, and in February of that year the head of the Odeon cinema chain, Oscar Deutsch, announced that, because of the child problem, his cinemas would no longer show "H" category films. Faced with all these pressures, the BBFC agreed to introduce a stand-alone "H" certificate with an age limit of 16, and the first film to be given such a certificate was *The Thirteenth Chair* (1937).

In all, 18 "A" films were placed in the "H" category, and 37 were awarded a stand-alone "H" certificate (Robertson, 1985: 183). Most of these were in the horror genre, although there were oddities such as *J'Accuse* (1937), *A Child is Born* (1939), and the *United Nations War Crimes Film* (1945). This did not mean, however, that horror films were exempt from cuts, although no horror film was actually rejected by the BBFC in the 1930s after the introduction of the stand-alone "H." But during World War II several councils banned horror films altogether, and in 1942 the BBFC banned two — *The Corpse Vanishes* (1942) and *The Mad Monster* (1942) — before deciding not to allocate any more "H" certificates. It banned 23 films over the next three years. After the war the "H" was restored, but certain councils, such as Huddersfield and Oldham, banned all horror films for several more years, and the BBFC itself banned *Bedlam* (1946). The "H" lasted until 1951, when it was incorporated into the new adults-only "X" certificate which, as we shall see, by no means marked a free-for-all as far as horror films were concerned.

"Horror Films Taboo in Britain"

Let us now return to the fate of *Dracula* and its successors at the hands of the BBFC. *Dracula* came before the Board in 1931 but the fact that it was seven minutes shorter than the American version suggests that the distributors cut it before submission. The film was passed with no further cuts, but *Frankenstein*, as already noted, was less fortunate. Other American horror films which suffered cuts at this time were *Dr. Jekyll and Mr. Hyde*, which lost almost a quarter of its length, *Murders in the Rue Morgue*, *Doctor X* (1932) (even though the print had already been shortened by six minutes), *White Zombie* (1932), *The Most Dangerous Game/The Hounds of Zaroff* (1932), *Mystery of the Wax Museum* (1933), *King Kong* (1933), *The Vampire Bat* (1933), *Life Returns* (1935), and *The Walking Dead* (1936). As noted earlier, both *Island of Lost Souls* and *Freaks* were banned outright; the ban on the latter was upheld in 1952, and the films were not passed until 1958 and 1963 respectively, each with an "X." And when the first draft of *Dracula's Daughter* (1936) was submitted to the BBFC in 1935, its senior script examiner and Vice-President, Colonel J. C. Hanna, commented:

> *Dracula* was ghoulish-weird-eerie and every other adjective in the language which expresses Horror, but *Dracula's Daughter* would require the resources of half a dozen more languages to adequately express its beastliness. I consider this absolutely unfit for exhibition as a film. (Cited in Robertson, 1989: 66)

The Raven also ignited a great deal of protest in the British press, one critic calling it "quite the most unpleasant picture I have ever seen, exploiting cruelty for cruelty's sake" (cited in Skal, 1994: 195). On 23 August 1935, the Associated Press ran an article headlined "Horror Films Taboo in Britain — *The Raven* Last," which reported BBFC Secretary Joseph Brooke-Wilkinson as stating that this would be the last such film passed by the BBFC, and quoted BBFC President Edward Shortt as warning the industry that such films were "unfortunate and undesirable" and needed to be curbed (cited in Skal, 1994: 195). And when the following month Breen wrote to Warners about *The Walking Dead*, he pointed out that:

> Horror stories of all kinds are a precarious undertaking in these days, especially with respect to their likely reception at the hands of political censor boards. I think you know that the British Board in London has indicated a disposition not to approve out-and-out horror stories . . . . (Cited in Naylor, 2011: 7)

In fact, as Alex Naylor (2011) makes clear in a significant corrective to the commonly accepted view, no actual "ban" existed, although on 6 May 1936 *Variety* reported that Universal would not be making any more horror films after *Dracula's Daughter* for at least a year:

> Reason attributed by U[niversal] for abandonment of horror cycle is that European countries, especially England, are prejudiced against this type product. Despite heavy local consumption of its chillers, U[niversal] is taking heed to warning from abroad ... Studio's London rep has cautioned production exec to scrutinize carefully all so-called chiller productions to avoid any possible conflict with British censorship. (Cited in Naylor, 2011: 5)

Indeed, just before this article was published, when Universal had sent the PCA the synopsis of the proposed horror film *The Human Robot*, Breen had responded by pointing out that "[British] opposition to this kind of screen entertainment suggests that the making of a horror picture is a somewhat hazardous undertaking" (cited in Naylor, 2011: 8). The project was shelved, although eventually filmed as *Man Made Monster* (1941). However, it is also worth noting that Universal effectively changed hands at the start of 1936 and the new management appeared to be more receptive than Laemmle to the PCA's warnings about horror films, announcing in the *Los Angeles Daily News*, 17 June 1936, that "Universal this year will go in for less tense drama and so-called 'horror' pictures, and make more pictures to amuse and enthuse audiences" (cited in Naylor, 2011: 4).

But Universal continued to make horror films. When they expressed the desire to make a second *Frankenstein* sequel, *Son of Frankenstein* (1939), Breen cabled BBFC Secretary Joseph Brooke-Wilkinson and asked: "Would you be disposed to approve horrific picture like *Frankenstein*?" only to receive the rapid reply:

> Film created considerable public outcry and partly instrumental in bringing into existence Horrific category. Film would today unquestionably come within this category. We use every endeavour to prevent such productions. (Cited in Naylor, 2011: 9).

A different source also cites Brooke-Wilkinson as responding that:

> We have had so much trouble in [the] past with films … in the "horrific" category that the trade have come to the conclusion that they are more trouble than they are worth … Representations have been made to us by the trade asking us to curtail this type of film as much as possible. (Cited in Skal, 1994: 205)

Although threats and actions by the BBFC did not put even a temporary stop to the production of horror films in the United States, these were routinely invoked by the PCA in its efforts to persuade Hollywood film-makers to avoid explicit horror. What this suggests is that the activities of both the PCA and the BBFC, taken together, contributed to a significant toning down of such films, at least those from the major studios. Those produced by Universal in the first half of the following decade such as *Frankenstein Meets the Wolf Man* (1943), *House of Frankenstein* (1944), and *House of Dracula* (1945) are indubitably tamer than their precursors.

Pathological Reactions to Post-War Horror

With the introduction of the "X" certificate in 1951, the censorship of horror films in Britain became rather more lenient. However, like the PCA in the case of Hollywood movies, the BBFC was able to exert control over the pre-production stage of home-grown films. Witness BBFC Secretary John Trevelyan's remark that:

> Horror films were rarely a problem since most of them came to us from Hammer Films, the most successful production company in the field, from whom we always had full co-operation … I remember a talk that I had with Sir James (Jimmy) Carreras many

years ago in which we agreed that his company's horror films would avoid mixing sex with horror and would avoid scenes which people could regard as disgusting and revolting. (1973: 165–166)

However, this is quite simply untrue. It was not until writers such as Wayne Kinsey (2002, 2007) and David Pirie (2008) began to delve into the BBFC and Hammer archives that the truth emerged, namely that BBFC examiners absolutely loathed Hammer films, along with other contemporaneous British horrors, and did their utmost to censor them. And if the BBFC did modify its views, it was only because of remarkable persistence on Hammer's part. Trevelyan himself seems not to have experienced the almost pathological reactions these films invoked in his staff, but he did appear to have regarded this body of work as beneath contempt, remarking in his memoirs that "nobody took these films seriously; this included the people who made them as well as the audiences" (1973: 166).

It was only when Pirie came to prepare the new edition of his seminal *A Heritage of Horror* that he discovered the reality behind what he rightly calls Trevelyan's "absurd assertion." Of his epiphany Pirie writes:

The files of the BBFC reveal that far from being, as I naively expected, detached urbane and objective, the British censor's office during his tenure was, it now emerges, utterly disgusted and enraged by the British horror films, constantly waging a frantic and hysterical campaign against them, with most of the examiners secretly trying to stop them being made at all. (2008: 37)

His description of some of the material in the files as "quite disturbing, massively prejudiced and oddly violent in its expression" (37) is entirely accurate. Take for example, the examiner who wrote in large capitals on their report on *Horrors of the Black Museum* (1959): "THROW IT OUT AND LET THERE BE NO MERCY" (cited in Pirie, 2008: 120–121).

In the following pages, I will attempt to give a critical account of the factors that lay behind the examiners' neuralgic responses. The situation was rendered even more toxic by the hatred—not too strong a word—that most critics displayed toward these films, a hatred which clearly impacted upon the manner in which BBFC treated horror movies. At times, it seems as if the BBFC examiners saw themselves as civilization's last line of defense against an inrushing tide of cinematic barbarism. For example, of *Circus of Horrors* (1960) Audrey Field proclaimed:

This disgustingly strident script fills me with nausea. Everything which we have objected to in excessively violent and horrible "horror films" is here outdone … It seems to be the product of a diseased mind … There ought to be a point at which the Board, regardless of the consequences, will not allow its certificates to impart a semblance of respectability to that which is not respectable. (Cited in Pirie, 2008: 127)

It should be pointed out, however, that although many of the films discussed below appear to have been released with only fairly minor cuts, it could be argued

Figure 8.2   A new degree of explicit color violence in post-war British horror films, seen here in *Circus of Horrors* (1960). Directed by Sidney Hayers. Produced by Lynx Films Ltd.

that the bulk of any censorship which took place did so before a frame was shot. On the other hand, scripts submitted to the BBFC very probably contained scenes which the film-makers knew would never pass muster with the Board, their purpose being either to distract the examiners' attention away from those which were less lurid but to which they might otherwise have objected, or to serve as bargaining cards in censorship negotiations, or indeed both. But there again, it is clear from Kinsey (2002, 2007) that, in many cases, the prints of the films which were finally passed by the BBFC were themselves the result of a good deal of post-production but pre-classification negotiation between the Board and the film-makers, so cuts noted in the BFI's *Monthly Film Bulletin* may not always tell the full censorship story (Figure 8.2).

The censors' main objection to the new wave of British horror unleashed by Hammer was quite simply that it was too horrific. Faced with the second script of Hammer's first Gothic horror, *The Curse of Frankenstein* (1957), examiner Field exclaimed that it was "really evil. A lip-smacking relish for mutilated corpses, repulsive dismembered hands and eyeballs removed from the head, alternates with gratuitous examples of sadism and lust" (cited in Pirie, 2008: 38). Her colleague Frank Crofts complained that the "author has done his best to pile horror on horror in a way that in my opinion makes it unlikely that we should be able to pass such a film as this." A third examiner fulminated that "the writer of this script seems to think that the X category is a depository for sewage" (both cited in Pirie, 2008: 38). Field thus wrote to Hammer and requested a revised script "in which the overall unpleasantness should be much mitigated" (cited in Kinsey, 2002: 61 – 62). Similarly, in the case of the script of *Dracula* (1958), examiner John Nicholls wrote to Hammer, taking exception to its "nauseating and repulsive details" and drawing the company's attention to "the importance of discretion and restraint in the treatment throughout" (cited in Kinsey, 2002: 115–116). A similar prescription was made by another examiner, Newton Branch, who argued that horror "should never be disgusting. The true elements of the real horror film are terror, suspense, action, the unknown, the macabre" (cited in Kinsey, 2002: 115), a classic example of confusing the tale of terror and the tale of horror, a subject discussed at some length in Petley (2002). Other examiners committed an even more elementary category mistake and judged the films as if they were works of historical fiction, inevitably finding them more than wanting on these grounds. Thus Crofts lambasted the script of *The Curse of Frankenstein* as "ludicrously written, with a complete disrespect for history" (cited in Kinsey, 2002: 60).

A third major objection to many of these films was their mingling of sex and horror (Figure 8.3). This was particularly the case with the vampire cycle, since sex and vampirism are inextricably intertwined. Thus the examiners wanted the removal of any sexual suggestion from *Dracula* and, in particular, were concerned at "the whole episode of Dracula and Mina together whenever either of them shows sexual pleasure. There must, for instance, be no kissing or fondling" (cited in Kinsey, 2002: 111). The intermingling of sex and horror became of increasing concern to the Board in the 1960s as film-makers attempted to take advantage of the changing tenor of the times in sexual matters. Thus when presented with the script of *Dracula Has Risen from the Grave* (1968), Trevelyan informed Hammer that the Board would be concerned about "any close association between blood-sucking and sex" (cited in Kinsey, 2007: 73), while of *Taste the Blood of Dracula* (1970) he observed that "I have always advised keeping vampirism and sex apart" (cited in Kinsey, 2007: 192). Imagine, then, the consternation caused by a film like *The Vampire Lovers* (1970) in which the sexual

Figure 8.3 *Circus of Horrors* (1960) was one of many post-war British horror films to push at the allowable boundaries of sex and horror, a combination that outraged many of the era's censors. Directed by Sidney Hayers. Produced by Lynx Films Ltd.

element was more overt than in any previous British horror film. After reading the script, Trevelyan told Hammer:

> I can only hope that it is a gross exaggeration of what will be put on the screen, since it contains a lot of material that we would be unhappy about even with an "X" at 18 .... Our policy is that we have always been strongly against a close association between horror and sex, especially when horror includes sadism and brutality. (Cited in Kinsey, 2007: 169)

Trevelyan also provided a long list of suggested cuts and modifications but by the time the finished film was submitted, the Board had revised its classification categories and raised the minimum age of admission to an "X" film from 16 to 18, which meant that more "adult" content was permitted in this category, although this by no means ushered in an era of "anything goes." And examiner Branch still saw fit to complain that:

> We are very concerned with the combination of nudity (transparent nightdresses, pubic hair showing etc.) with horror. There are some very sick things here ... We do feel that this film without considerable cuts will set a bad precedent. It has a very morbid atmosphere in parts. (Cited in Kinsey, 2007: 207–208)

A fourth worry about these films from the point of view of the BBFC concerned exhibitors' recurring unease that anything too explicit might encourage local authorities to exercise their powers of censorship, particularly if prodded into action by hostile accounts of horror films in the press. Of *The Revenge of Frankenstein* Field observed: "The policy to be adopted in regard to it is important at a time when sections of the trade are anxious about 'horror' films'" (cited in Kinsey, 2002: 115). Writing to Hammer about the film, examiner Nicholls stated: "All we are concerned about is any danger of any horror film being too 'sexy': we often find that the juxtaposition of sex and horror gives rise to unfavourable criticism" (cited in Kinsey, 2002: 119). A propos *Horrors of the Black Museum*, Trevelyan wrote to Herman Cohen, the film's producer, warning him that:

> You will appreciate that there has been a great deal of criticism about horror pictures generally and in particular about scenes such as the murders in this film. This is the reason why we have to be very careful when dealing with a picture like this. (Cited in Pirie, 2008: 122)

Similarly, of *Jack the Ripper* (1959), Trevelyan noted that "this kind of film is one which causes us great concern ... we run the risk of considerable criticism" (cited in Pirie, 2008: 125).

At the root of the critics' and censors' fear and loathing of the horror film there undoubtedly lay worries about the possible "effects" of these films on their viewers, and especially their younger viewers. So, for example, when faced with the script of *Horrors of the Black Museum*, Field warned:

I do not think the makers should be encouraged to hope for a certificate from us. The X certificate, if given, would merely serve as an umbrella for out-of-the-way sadistic ideas to try the patience of decent people rather too far ... We should not I think lose sight of the fact that a sharp increase in crimes of violence has accompanied a relaxation in our standards. (Cited in Pirie, 2008: 120)

It is also possible to trace the impact of a prior moral panic about "media effects" on examiners' attitudes to these films: namely the one sparked off in the early 1950s by imported American comic books. Thus examiner Branch was concerned that the script of *The Reptile* (1965) "goes far too much into the realm of the horror-comic" (cited in Kinsey, 2002: 332), while of the script of *The Plague of the Zombies* (1966) he demanded that "the horror-comic elements must go" (cited in Kinsey, 2002: 324).

A film which suffered particularly badly at the hands of the BBFC was *The Curse of the Werewolf* (1961), and the Board's treatment of it usefully illustrates most of the organization's concerns about horror films in general. One of Hammer's and Terence Fisher's very finest films, it was indubitably a victim of the savage critical backlash caused by *Peeping Tom* (1960), which turned into an onslaught on horror films in general. As usual, the trouble started at the script stage, Field calling *Curse of the Werewolf* "intolerable" and delivering the judgment that "this is not the legitimate thrill of horror, but caters for very debased and perverted sexual tastes." Branch referred to it as "obscene muck". Even the normally moderate Trevelyan found in it "scenes of bestial nastiness which we would want you to change" (all cited in Kinsey, 2002: 197–198). Changes were duly made, but when the examiners and the BBFC President saw the final product, they argued that it should be banned outright. Even at this late stage, very considerable (and costly) cuts were demanded, and the version of the film released in the UK was two minutes shorter than the one released in the United States. Trevelyan's explanation to Hammer of the Board's mauling of the finished film is extremely revealing. He first of all noted that:

Unlike your previous horror films, there is a good deal in this film which provides a combination of horror and sex. We have always taken the line that this is a dangerous cocktail and we feel this strongly. This is the kind of thing that runs into so much public criticism.

He then elaborates at some length on this last point:

Since we last had a horror picture from your company there has grown up quite a considerable criticism of the Board for passing such pictures. Admittedly this criticism sometimes comes from people who do not go to the cinema and who do not see such films, but I can assure you that it would be most unwise at the present time to provide these people with ammunition which they can use not only to criticise us but to harm the industry ... If you think that we are treating your picture more roughly than we would have treated a similar picture two years ago, you may have some justification, but you must realise that we stand between the industry and such pressures and that it is part of our job to assess the potential danger of pressures at any given time. (Cited in Kinsey, 2002: 214–215).

But if, during this time, British horror films suffered at the hands of the BBFC, films from further afield were treated even more harshly. Throughout the 1960s and 1970s the BBFC assiduously guarded British cinemagoers from the murky depths of the American and Italian cinema industries, with their sex-leavened horrors and their increasingly bizarre cast of cannibals, Nazis, and assorted maniacs. Films which were cut by the BBFC included *Les yeux sans visage* (1959), *Psycho* (1960), *La maschera del demonio/The Mask of Satan* (1960), and *Hexen bis aufs Blut gequält/Mark of the Devil* (1969). Mario Bava's *Reazione a catena/A Bay of Blood* (1971), Wes Craven's *Last House on the Left* (1972), and Tobe Hooper's *The Texas Chain Saw Massacre* (1974) were all banned outright, but such bans were relatively rare—distributors knew perfectly well that there was no point in wasting money to submit them to the BBFC only to have them banned, or else cut to such an extent that their very *raison d'être* was excised.

Conclusion

No wonder, then, that when in 1979 the advent of temporarily unregulated home video showed the British public what it had been missing thanks to the tender mercies of the BBFC, strict video censorship was urgently called for; this was subsequently imposed by the Video Recordings Act 1984. This is a lengthy story in itself (for a detailed account see Petley, 2011), but for the purposes of this chapter it is sufficient to note that the bulk of what came to be known as "video nasties" were horror movies that were trashed by the critics and other guardians of public morality, and that this greatly helped to legitimize their evisceration or complete banishment once video censorship began. This was carried out by the BBFC, this time armed with statutory powers which gave its classifications legal force. Just how little its attitudes toward horror films had changed is neatly illustrated by the Board's *Annual Report 1994–95* which notes that "The return of horror as a video genre rested mostly in 1994 on the revival of old shockers from the '70s, and cuts here were more or less what they were for the cinema in that distant decade" (1995: 18). The next year's *Annual Report* similarly revealed that close-ups of a gouged neck and of flesh eating

> were removed from an old British vampire movie revived on video, while two other revivals featured sexual mutilation, in one case by a murderous nun and in the other by female zombies. This last, a French horror film from the early '80s, contained the most appalling images cut by the Board's examiners in 1985. (1996: 17)

As always the Board had, and to some extent still has, particular problems with films which mingle horror with sex: witness the banning in 1994 of Jess Franco's even then rather aged *Sadomania—Hölle der Lust/Sadomania* (1981), which was denounced in the *1994–95 Report* for its "peaks of evil and atrocity" (21). That this was passed in 2005 with 17 seconds of cuts shows that the BBFC's attitudes have certainly become more liberal in the new millennium, but films of a horrific nature which also contain sexual elements are still liable to be heavily cut [e.g., *I Spit on Your Grave* (2010) and *Srpski film/A Serbian Film* (2010)], or even banned outright as in the case of *Gurote-suku/Grotesque* (2009) and *The Bunny Game* (2010). Only time will tell whether these actions will look as odd in 20 years time as the examiners' fits of hysterics over Hammer horrors and their contemporaries.

References

British Board of Film Classification (1995) *Annual Report 1994–95*, British Board of Film Classification, London.

British Board of Film Classification (1996) *Annual Report 1995–96*, British Board of Film Classification, London.

Doherty, T. (1999) *Pre-Code Hollywood: Sex, Immorality, and Insurrection in American Cinema 1930–1934*, Columbia University Press, New York, NY.

Gardner, G.G. (1987) *The Censorship Papers: Movie Censorship Letters from the Hays Office 1934 to 1968*, Dodd, Mead & Company, New York, NY.

Kinsey, W. (2002) *Hammer Films: The Bray Studios Years*, Reynolds & Hearn, Richmond.

Kinsey, W. (2007) *Hammer Films: The Elstree Studio Years*, Tomahawk Press, Sheffield.

Naylor, A. (2011) A horror picture at this time is a very hazardous undertaking: did British or American censorship end the 1930s horror cycle? *The Irish Journal of Gothic and Horror Studies*, 9, February, http://irishgothichorrorjournal.homestead.com/1930shorroban.html (accessed 2 January 2013).

Petley, J. (2002) A crude sort of entertainment for a crude sort of audience: the British critics and horror cinema, in *British Horror Cinema* (eds S. Chibnall and J. Petley), Routledge, London, pp. 23–41.

Petley, J. (2011) *Film and Video Censorship in Modern Britain*, Edinburgh University Press, Edinburgh.

Phelps, G. (1975) *Film Censorship*, Victor Gollancz, London.

Pirie, D. (2008) *A New Heritage of Horror*, I.B. Tauris, London.

Prince, S. (2003) *Classical Film Violence: Designing and Regulating Brutality in Hollywood Cinema, 1930–1968*, Rutgers University Press, New Brunswick, NJ.

Robertson, J.C. (1985) *The British Board of Film Censors: Film Censorship in Britain, 1896–1950*, Croom Helm, London.

Robertson, J.C. (1989) *The Hidden Cinema: British Film Censorship in Action, 1913–1975*, Routledge, London.

Skal, D.J. (1994) *The Monster Show*, Plexus Publishing, London.

Smith, S.J. (2005) *Children, Cinema and Censorship: From Dracula to Dead End Kids*, I.B. Tauris, London.

Trevelyan, J. (1973) *What the Censor Saw*, Michael Joseph, London.

Part II

The Form of Horror

9

Carl Dreyer's Corpse
Horror Film Atmosphere and Narrative

Robert Spadoni

Horror films are "atmospheric" compared to most other genre films. It would be hard to reach a different conclusion following even the most cursory survey of writing on the genre, from the earliest newspaper reviews to scholarly works published this year. Even if one takes into account the widespread opinion that the films became less atmospheric when *Psycho* (1960) influentially introduced a greater degree of explicitness to the genre, still, the genre as a whole has always been distinctive as much for the quantity as for the quality of the atmosphere it pumps into its films.

But what is horror film atmosphere? Any attempt to answer this question must ask what parts of a film contribute to its atmosphere. Most of this essay is devoted to exploring this question, paying particular attention to the role narrative plays in atmosphere's creation, a role that has, to date, been undervalued and misunderstood.[1] One should also ask what sorts of things an atmosphere can evoke. Here is a good starting question for us, because even the quickest sketch of an answer points to one of several problems facing anyone hoping to flesh out a productive definition of horror film atmosphere. My approach to these problems, and a definition, will consist mostly of examining statements that have been made about the atmosphere in various horror films. These statements show, broadly speaking, two things: first, that writers through the decades have minimized and overlooked atmosphere as an analytical concept and as a formal component of horror films; and second, that these writers know more about atmosphere than they realize. Making some of their implicit knowledge explicit is an aim of this essay. I conclude by briefly considering work by German philosopher Gernot Böhme, whose thinking on atmosphere in relation to media other than cinema can help us better understand and appreciate what everyone agrees is an especially atmospheric genre of film.

Before beginning, let me acknowledge that by looking at statements across a wide span of decades, and by not discriminating between popular and academic writing,

A Companion to the Horror Film, First Edition. Edited by Harry M. Benshoff.

I may seem to be taking an ahistorical and undiscerning approach to a vast body of discourse. Certainly this body deserves more attention than I give it here, for I believe a fascinating history of film atmosphere *as an idea* remains to be written. But I suggest that this idea exhibits, through the decades, a stubbornly untheorized quality. It has almost always been atmosphere with a small *a*, a concept far more often invoked than even lightly probed. What the word means has been mostly taken for granted, and what it has to teach us about how horror films cohere and how they affect viewers remains poorly understood.

Problems of Definition

What sorts of things can a horror film atmosphere evoke? An atmosphere can be redolent of an idea, frequently (although not always) one soaking in emotion. For example, in the Bates house in *Psycho*, "the Victorian decor, crammed with invention, intensifies the atmosphere of sexual repression" (Wood, 1989: 147); while in the opening hotel-room sequence, "the heat, the bleached feel of the visuals, the half-nakedness, evoke an atmosphere of unsatiated sensuality" (Durgnat, 2000: 42). An atmosphere might also conjure up the spirit of a literary author—Wodehouse in *Ghost Story* (1981), Poe in *The Black Cat* (1934)—or a film subgenre or cycle, as in "the atmosphere of the vampire genre" in *Daughters of Darkness* (1971) (Zimmerman, 1996: 384). And of course an atmosphere can evoke a time and place, nineteenth century London in a *Jekyll and Hyde* adaptation, the 1980s (and its horror films) in *House of the Devil* (2009).

Films that call to mind an author or historical period suggest that an atmosphere can seem to point outside itself, to connect a film to the world around it. But the word "atmosphere," with its roots in meteorology, also suggests a kind of *internal* weather system, one a film whips up and sustains within its own textual borders. *The Fall of the House of Usher* (1928) "resides within its sealed world, as if—yes, as if buried alive" (Ebert, 2005: 142); *White Zombie* (1932) exudes "an atmosphere of fusty timelessness" (Rigby, 2007: 109); Universal classic horror movies created "a tight, false world of studio-built landscape, where … every actor was caught in the closing ring of horrors, untouched by the possibility of a normal world beyond" (Gifford, 1973: 192, my ellipsis). An atmosphere can forge a link to the outside world or cut a film off from it.

These are only some of the things a film atmosphere can do and evoke; enough, I hope, to suggest that it might be difficult to come up with a description that encompasses such a broad range of possibilities. Another problem of definition is that the concept is itself often characterized as "ineffable," as in this screenwriting guide from 1944:

> Sometimes, we find a place with a certain something which we call atmosphere. But this certain something is of almost miraculous appearance, too volatile to be defined . . . . It seems that this attribute of a place escapes all crystallization into a rule. (Vale, 1944: 56, my ellipsis)

If atmosphere is indeterminate and ineffable, how can we hope to define it with any concreteness? A related problem is that the term has historically been applied less for purposes of analysis than for ones of evaluation. Atmosphere is elusive, but a good critic knows it when she sees it. And a good filmmaker knows how to create it. The vagueness of what everyone means by the word makes it easy for critics to assert their superior taste while advancing opinions that are purely subjective.

More conceptual murkiness arises from the tendency to use the word interchangeably with "mood." Still more confusing is when writers string these words together, implying that they mean different things without explaining what this difference might be: "Horror movies of mood and atmosphere are interesting for how they treat moral struggles with evil" (Freeland, 2004: 191); "Art-dread is associated with horror movies based on mood and atmosphere" (Cherry, 2009: 164). Are the words synonyms or do they partially overlap or do they mean different things? I suggest that these words function, in many kinds of film writing, as a kind of padding, appearing together when a sentence has a more pleasing cadence ticking off two attributes rather than just one. While, as I suggest below, some statements that have been made about mood can help us understand atmosphere, I prefer to focus on "atmosphere" because the "weather system" sense of the word invites us to consider the *spatiality* of a film—the space filled by all the big and small atmospheric shifts and disturbances—and so it encourages us to construe the concept in terms of a film's concrete formal particulars.

This is what Julian Hanich does in his study of emotion in horror films and thrillers. He identifies a film's atmospheric elements as "setting, daytime, weather and season" (2010: 171). By linking atmosphere to just a few elements, Hanich advances a definition that not only grounds the term in the film text but also steers clear of the vague and impressionistic language that has characterized nearly all its applications. But Hanich goes too far by linking atmosphere to too few elements. He extends a longstanding tradition of shoehorning atmosphere into too small a box within the total filmic system. In much film writing, typically in an off-hand and unreflective manner, atmosphere is insulated from those parts of a film with which it is assumed not to overlap. This thinking works to constrain our sense of the concept, when it should be moving in the opposite direction.

Take atmosphere and meaning. Writers seldom look to atmosphere for elements that centrally convey a film's themes, and when such elements do, this can be judged distinctive enough to warrant a mention: David Bordwell finds *Vampyr* (1932) developing "death motifs … not solely for atmosphere but also to build up a reserve, as it were, of connotative energy to be discharged at a later phase in the narrative" (1981: 95, my ellipsis). But this double functioning is not unusual at all. Returning to Wood on *Psycho*, is "sexual repression" an atmosphere of the film or a meaning? Clearly it is both. Similarly, Vivian Sobchack (2001: 122) refers to the "convincing atmosphere of paranoia" in *Invasion of the Body Snatchers* (1956). But anyone focusing on paranoia in this film is likely to find the concept characterizing more than just what most would call its atmosphere. Where is the line separating meaning from atmosphere? Here is the better question: What is wrong with trying to draw any such line at all?

More bewildering than statements that distinguish atmosphere from mood, and atmosphere from meaning, are ones that implicitly partition atmosphere from style, as when a writer notes that "films of Gothic horror are expressionist in their style and atmosphere" (Ross, 1972: 2). This might just be another example of sentence padding, but such casual statements, taken in sum, constitute the picture of atmosphere that film studies has drawn for itself; and it is hard to imagine what parts of a film are creating its atmosphere if not, in large measure, its style. But writers know this, and the picture is more complicated (contradictory, really), because many of these same writers indicate their intuitive grasp of the dense web of connections that binds atmosphere to every part of a film — not just nondiegetic ("mood") music, off-screen diegetic sound, and mise-en-scene, but elements of style routinely cordoned off from atmosphere, including framing and editing. And if atmosphere cannot be separated from *any* other aspect of a film, and if these other aspects are not merely "colored" by atmosphere but directly take part in its creation, then we need to rethink atmosphere's relationship to the filmic whole. For reasons of space, I will devote the rest of this essay to the relationship between horror film atmosphere and narrative.

Narrative

What is the relationship between atmosphere and narrative? One pattern in the literature suggests that they represent two poles around which one might structure an artwork. For example, Jean Epstein's *The Fall of the House of Usher* (1928) "was based on a Poe story that is more atmosphere than plot" (Ebert, 2005: 171). And with *Vampyr*, Dreyer "focuses on mood and atmosphere rather than exploring the emotions of his characters" (Senn, 1996: 77). A film with deficiencies in one area can compensate by beefing up its reserves in the other: *Ringu 2* (1999) "lacked the clearly defined narrative of *Ringu* but what it lacked in clarity it made up for in atmosphere" (Hutchings, 2008: 264). Such statements find artworks foregrounding atmosphere over narrative considerations, with favorable results.

This same foregrounding can also meet with criticism. In *Isle of the Dead* (1945), a Val Lewton film directed by Mark Robson, a scene involving a ghostly female figure lacks something found in Lewton films directed by Jacques Tourneur:

> There is a slow track forward into the black rectangle formed by the open door of her tomb as her faint white figure emerges, but the dimension of uncertainty omnipresent in Tourneur is absent here: we are dealing with stylistic effects to create atmosphere and nothing more, however effective they are. (Humphries, 2002: 53)

We should note, in addition to a camera movement creating atmosphere, this writer's opinion that a movement that does *only* this is wasting the viewer's time. Similarly, David Denby writes that the makers of *Hereafter* (2010) "clearly wanted to work soberly and realistically and to avoid routine scare techniques and the banalities of 'atmosphere'" (*New Yorker*, 1 Nov. 2010: 26). It is unclear why Denby encloses the word in quotes. Perhaps it is to signal his disdain for atmosphere for atmosphere's sake, which would put him in the company of writers who view such a prioritization as a weak and even irritating aesthetic choice.

More disregard for the concept is suggested by the sense of atmosphere as a kind of aesthetic leftover. Considering a film heavily edited for US distribution, one writer notes that "with the deletion of all of Mario Bava's sado-masochistic scenes from *La frusta e il corpo*, its American remnant *What!* is reduced to an hour of atmospheric, but meaningless, corridor-wandering" (Erickson, 2000: 272). Delete a film's plot action and what remains behind is poetic air that no longer serves a worthwhile purpose. The extreme result of defining atmosphere in terms of what it is not — not meaning, not style, not narrative — is to push it to the margins and view it as little more than textual dressing, or garnish. It makes the meal nicer but, far from the main course, it is not even a side dish.

Such statements point to the widespread tendency to see atmosphere as secondary to almost everything else in a film, including, and perhaps especially, its narrative. Atmosphere is subordinate. It is background. This is why some critics get annoyed when filmmakers devote too much energy to atmosphere when they should be attending to the textual "foreground," where one finds the characters and story. Reflecting this bias, an *American Cinematographer* article describes the instructions followed by the costumers working on a big-budget film:

> The atmosphere on the whole in "The Hunchback of Notre Dame" is little short of a miracle in variety and breath-taking splendor. And yet, no matter how much they like the styles and general effect of the costuming, they have the same orders as every other person on the unit: "The costuming must be subdued. We are spending money on it primarily to make it so correct that it will be inconspicuous." (Arthur Q. Hagerman, "Costuming a Super-production," Feb. 1923: 20)

Good atmosphere is atmosphere that does not call too much attention to itself or get in the way. It must be, above all, *appropriate* to the narrative's unfolding.

It is this entrenched view of the hierarchical relationship between atmosphere and everything else in a film that needs to be challenged. More specifically, atmosphere should not be thought of as separable from narrative. Nor is it sufficient to say that they exist in a tightly integrated relationship, and that the line dividing the two can be fuzzy. Many examples of this sort of qualification can be found in Hanich, who notes, for example, that "separating atmospheric *components* from the *whole* contains the risk of distorting matters" (2010: 171, his italics). But then he proceeds to separate them anyway. To do so is to misconstrue the essence of the dynamic that defines their relationship.

Consider characters, those major movers of the narrative, the figures whose actions propel the plot and whose goals we care about. In the conventional view, characters move against the atmospheric backdrop, which colors and supports their activities. But characters support the atmosphere as well. In *Night Monster* (1942), "old hands at the game like Bela Lugosi and Lionel Atwill are simply present for atmosphere purposes" (*New York Herald Tribune*, 30 Nov. 1942). In *House of Frankenstein* (1944), "through successive locales, the monsters carry with them their own violent environment" (Denne, 1972: 127). In *The Golem* (1915), the "creature of inadequacy is surrounded by an atmosphere of sadness: a melancholy sense of doomed efforts to reach the unattainable." This figure moves across a "soul-suffused landscape" (*Die Schaubühne*, xi, 1915: 225–227; quoted in Prawer, 1980: 29). But where is the "soul" coming from? Is it seeping into this yearning creature or pouring out of him?

More recognitions of this two-way dynamic abound. In *Psycho*, Lila wades into a space thick with dread when she enters the Bates house: "As we can't make up our mind whether the danger's coming from in front (Mom) or behind (Norman) we're no longer thinking very coherently, but yield to the atmosphere" (Durgnat, 2000: 46). Lila is caught in a riptide of horror that appears to stream out of two characters. Atmosphere here functions not as a background but as the medium that transmits and sustains this character's and the viewers' emotions. Lastly, when Rick Worland writes that *Cat People* (1942) "diverged from Universal predecessors by substituting suggestive horror effects and psychological atmosphere for the attacks of physical monsters" (2007: 176), he suggests that there is no point in trying to distinguish between character psychology and at least certain kinds of horror film atmosphere.

Raymond Durgnat (2000: 43–44) further blurs the line between atmosphere and narrative when he writes that, in *Psycho*, Norman's

> friendliness is all the more reassuring in contrast with the sinister atmosphere (the stuffed birds, the Victorian house with the petulant, tyrannical old mother), though he seems tainted by it. The over-obvious horror cliches shift our suspicions from Norman to the atmosphere; they camouflage the inevitable stiltedness of his relationship with Mrs. Bates.

Atmosphere thus provides camouflage that helps preserve a later surprise. Something that does the same is the camera that, when Norman is carrying Mother upstairs, climbs to an extreme high-angle, from which her status as a corpse remains concealed. This crane suppresses narrative information, and no one would disagree that the movement belongs in a discussion of *narration*, itself at the center of any discussion of narrative. But atmosphere, Durgnat finds, is working a deception, too. Is this not *also* narration at work? Where is the line, however indistinct one might claim that it can be, separating atmosphere from narration? It is impossible to locate.

I have been suggesting some ways we can problematize the accepted understanding of the relationship between horror film atmosphere and narrative. Keeping in this vein, let us turn to a narrative process that is arguably as characteristic of the genre as its celebrated atmosphere: suspense.

Suspense and Dread

That atmosphere and suspense are thoroughly entwined could not be a less controversial claim. *Jane Eyre* (1914) benefits from "an atmosphere of suspense, due in a measure to the spooky situations" ("Jane Eyre," *Moving Picture World*, 14 Feb. 1914: 810); *The Cat Creeps* (1930) creates a "'creepy' atmosphere of suspense and terror" ("Mystery Held Over Another Spooky Week," *Washington Post*, 16 Nov. 1930: A2); *Night Watch* (1973) "creates a nice atmosphere of suspense over who's going to wind up dead in the wing-chair" (Alexander Walker, rev. of *Night Watch*, *Evening Standard*, 6 Sept. 1973: 30). The stock phrase "atmosphere of suspense" crops up in every kind of film writing. But what does it—and the less ubiquitous but still common "atmosphere of dread"—mean?

The standard understanding is that a film's atmosphere is appropriate to and supports the narrative operations called *suspense* and *dread*. Hanich subscribes to this view, writing that certain atmospheric elements "are not a necessary condition for dread, but fear can thrive against their backdrop since the experiences they enable are concomitant to those of dread. Hence atmospheres of constriction and isolation do not create but *facilitate* and *enhance* dread and are therefore almost always part of it" (Hanich, 2010: 171, his italics).

A different interpretation of these phrases would see suspense and dread permeating a film's atmosphere and understand them to contribute to, and support, the atmospheric whole. My working definition of dread is that it fosters (unlike the broader category of suspense), less a state of hopeful expectancy (when will James Bond defuse the bomb?) than one of awful near certainty that the imminent outcome for a character will be bad. In the case of a horror film, this outcome is often death at the hands of a monster or other stalker waiting somewhere nearby in the darkness. In its most conventional configurations, the threat is unseen, or partially seen, and manifests itself in things like indeterminate off-screen noises and shadowy movements in the out-of-focus background. This is dread, which again is a form of suspense—for as Noel Carroll notes, "one still has suspense even if evil triumphs" (1996: 102). With this understanding of dread, let us now consider atmosphere's relationship to it. I begin my approach to the question by briefly cataloging some of the attributes that have been assigned, separately, to these two dimensions of the cinematic text.

Atmosphere is diffuse. Hanich writes that "atmospheres are gushed out spatially, but cannot be pinpointed locally," and calls them "diffuse emotive colorations of the lived-body without concrete object" (2010: 170 and 171). For Greg M. Smith, moods are "low-level emotional states that tend to be more diffuse and longer lasting than emotions" (2003: 38). *Dread is likewise diffuse.* One writer finds that dread is "different from fear because it is looser and less focused on an object" (Freeland, 2000: 238). Calling it by a different name, another notes that "terror is always of the indeterminate and incomprehensible, of the unseen but sensed or suspected, or of the imperfectly seen" (Rockett, 1988: 46). Also working with a different name, and making a pertinent comparison, S.S. Prawer writes that "to be *unheimlich*, a work need not provide shocks of horror: the uncanny may be diffused over the whole as an atmosphere like fogs that blanket London in the more macabre pages of Dickens" (1980: 111; he relates the uncanny to dread on p. 124).

Atmosphere can be sustained or it can leak out of a film. In *White Zombie*, "the macabre atmosphere is evenly maintained (*Variety*, 2 Aug. 1932: 15); whereas in *The Hearse* (1980), "atmosphere builds strongly for the first hour, but then just dissipates" (Muir, 2007: 103). *Suspense and dread also can be preserved or allowed to fizzle*. The zombies in *The Fog* (1980) "fail to inspire sustained dread" (Newman, 2011: 230); while in *Monster* (2003), "there is little of the repetitious, pseudo-sexual buildup and release of suspense so much a staple of mainstream thrillers"(Simpson, 2010: 137).

Atmosphere is background, not only because it frequently refers to settings, but because it routinely is judged to be of secondary importance and so stakes out the figurative background as well: "*Ah, Wilderness* is a first-class atmosphere piece ... Practically all of it that is good is background, in the way of local color" (Otis Ferguson, "To Act One's Age," *New Republic*, 25 Dec. 1935: 198, my ellipsis). Also, recall Hanich, referring to "atmospheric elements," writing that "fear can thrive against their backdrop." *Dread is background, too*, in the indiscriminate off-screen noises that can constitute a sonic backdrop for the shadowy contents of the frame, in smudges of movements glimpsed in mirrors, in the slow advance of figures from the blurry depths (Figure 9.1). In *Halloween* (1978):

> Having established the threatening aspect of the background and periphery of his compositions, Carpenter uses that disparity between his characters' restricted viewpoints and his audience's inevitably more encompassing field of view to sustain the general atmosphere of tension and expectation.(Telotte, 1987: 123)

Figure 9.1 The Woman appears in the deep background in *The Woman in Black* (2012). Directed by James Watkins. Produced by Cross Creek Pictures, Hammer Film Productions, Alliance Films, UK Film Council, Talisman Productions, Exclusive Media Group, Film i Väst, Filmgate Films, and Filmgate.

Dread is background for Hanich as well; in *Psycho*, expectations of imminent violence constitute a "background assumption that dominates the character of dread and feeds it" (Hanich, 2010: 158).

Atmosphere makes certain events and outcomes seem more likely; it facilitates, is conducive; it primes. One type of film atmosphere "initiates uneasiness in the audience even before the manifestation of the phenomenon so that when that occurs, terror comes upon the audiences all the more readily" (Rockett, 1988: 93). *Hellraiser* (1987) "creates such an atmosphere of dread that the astonishing visual set pieces simply detonate in a chain reaction of cumulative intensity" (Pym, 2004: 512). As noted, for Hanich atmospheres "*facilitate* and *enhance* dread," while for Ed. S. Tan, "mood is a disposition that encourages certain emotions and inhibits others" (2011: 204; and see Smith, 2003: 38–40, 42). *Dread primes, too*, since it is all about what is going to happen, about anticipation. Matt Hills, considering "objectless affect such as anxiety"—and so what we are calling dread—writes that "this affective process would predispose audiences to seek an object to attach their objectless affect to, priming them to experience the emotion of art-horror when a suitable object (whether a 'horrifying' monster of a 'horrific' force) is represented" (2005: 28).

Atmospheres can be thick, enveloping, saturating. In *Alien* (1979), "an eerie atmosphere seems to engulf everything" (Creed, 1993: 16); "a brooding sense of death permeates *The Black Cat*" (Jensen, 1974: 76); *The Old Dark House* (1932) "is thick with horror atmosphere (Paszylk, 2009: 23). *So can dread.* As Hills notes, "objectless anxiety … potentially saturates a *mise-en-scéne*" (Hills, 2005: 27, my ellipsis). Most eloquent on this dimension of dread is Hanich, who describes viewers' "thickening inner-time experience" during scenes of anticipatory fear (2010: 160, his italics). He finds that dread scenes cause viewers to experience duration "as *denser* than average scenes," and writes that "time in dread swells up and distends" (2010: 187, his italics; 191).

I present this catalog not to show that atmosphere can be complementary and appropriate to dread, nor to underline how many attributes the two share, but to challenge the idea that these dimensions of the cinematic text can be—even through the most delicate and provisional means imaginable—disentangled. More to the point, I claim that the atmospheres that permeate dread scenes do not *accompany* these scenes at all, but rather constitute their *culmination*. To understand what an "atmosphere of dread" is, one must first understand which is the cart and which is the horse.

Before arguing for atmosphere as a culmination, let me give an illustration of the fruitlessness of trying to separate atmosphere from suspense. As I find with film atmosphere generally, older writings tend to shed more light on this fundamental inseparability than more recent ones. Here is Béla Balász in *Theory of the Film*:

> It often happens that the camera shows not the person or scene itself but only its image in a mirror, or a shadow of it on the wall. This may be a means of preparation, destined to increase the effect of what is coming; this applies especially to the case of shadows cast before, which by making us imagine the figure belonging to them, create in advance an appropriate atmosphere. Such indirect indications of something to

come always contain some threatening, promising or curiosity-arousing mystery. No horror can be so horrible, no beauty so enchanting, if really seen, than the horror or enchantment suggested by its shadow . . . . In a direct shot we see only the scene itself; for instance a man about to shoot himself, a revolver in his hand, the hand raised to fire the shot. Even if something else is actually visible on the screen, the glaring nature of the scene blots it out. But if we see only a shadow of the scene on a wall, then we see the wall, the room of which it is a part and the physiognomy of the things which witness the deed. If we see something in a mirror, we see the mirror and its character together with the reflected image. Man and the scene he plays do not stand before us so nakedly, so without atmosphere. The real animation of the background increases the real animation of the scene itself. (1953: 109–110, my ellipsis)

Richly, Balász lays out this sequence in a way that scrambles attempts to see atmosphere and dread working tightly in unison to lay groundwork for an event to come. An image in a mirror, a shadow on a wall, act as "means of preparation" that are "destined to increase the effect of what is coming." So these elements are priming viewers. But how to label them? Balász claims they "create in advance an appropriate atmosphere" and refers to them as "the real animation of the background," so he would seem to agree with those who find atmosphere mainly *facilitating* what is going on in the scene. But what is going on and how do we apprehend it?

A man raises a gun to his head. This we register, even though neither the man nor the gun is visible. Instead we see a shadow or a reflection, bits of surface that are embedded in the mise-en-scene and telegraphing essential plot actions. A wall, a mirror, elements in the setting, are generating this hypothetical scene's primary narrational output. The sequence is spreading story information across the frame, so *something* is diffuse—but what? There is no meaningful distinction to be made between what is atmosphere and what is narration. It is not enough to say that the two are closely related and intertwined. They are *fused*. Notions of "foreground" and "background" do not help us conceptualize this relationship. We need a better model. Guidance on what shape this model might take can be found, again, in older writings—for if dread scenes are driven, and made, by the unseen and the partially seen, then Boris Karloff knew, as did Balász, which is the cart and which is the horse: "The mightiest weapon of the writer of the terror tale is the *power of suggestion*—the skill to take the reader by means of that power into an atmosphere where even the incredible seems credible" (1943: 12). Atmosphere is not a handmaiden but a destination.

Dreyer's Corpse

For a definition of film suspense, we go back to the most famous one, Hitchcock's, from his interview with François Truffaut:

We are now having a very innocent little chat. Let's suppose that there is a bomb underneath this table between us. Nothing happens, and then all of a sudden, "Boom!"

There is an explosion. The public is *surprised*, but prior to this surprise, it has seen an absolutely ordinary scene, of no special consequence. Now, let us take a *suspense* situation. The bomb is underneath the table and the public *knows* it, probably because they have seen the anarchist place it there. The public is *aware* that the bomb is going to explode at one o'clock and there is a clock in the decor. The public can see that it is a quarter to one. In these conditions the same innocuous conversation becomes fascinating because the public is participating in the scene. The audience is longing to warn the characters on the screen: "You shouldn't be talking about such trivial matters. There is a bomb beneath you and it is about to explode!"

In the first case we have given the public fifteen seconds of *surprise* at the moment of the explosion. In the second we have provided them with fifteen minutes of *suspense*. The conclusion is that whenever possible the public must be informed. Except when the surprise is a twist, that is, when the unexpected ending is, in itself, the highlight of the story. (quoted in Truffaut with Scott, 1985: 73, italics original)

Hitchcock explains how unrestricted narration (viewers knowing more than the characters) can pull viewers into a scene, intensifying their involvement and producing the immersive emotional experience that lovers of suspense relish. Such a narrational strategy can arch across a whole film, as in Hitchcock's *Rope* (1948), in which two accomplices murder a man, put him in a trunk, then host a dinner party that might or might not result in their eventual exposure and capture. This principle shapes films in moment-by-moment ways as well, for we see it at work in *The Woman in Black* (2012; see Figure 9.1) when camera placement combines with staging to inform viewers, but not a character, of an approaching threat.

At macro and micro levels, viewer knowledge can "saturate" a mise-en-scene and every other part of a film as well. In Hitchcock's scenario, we have a clock, a table, two chairs, two figures, and some dialogue. All these elements, spread across the sequence (and so diffuse), are colored by what viewers know — that is, by the classic suspense setup. This knowledge blankets everything, like the fog in Prawer's analogy concerning the uncanny. Operating in the background, never forgotten, this knowledge transforms every image and sound. Hitchcock has suffused the scene with an "atmosphere of suspense."

Compare his scenario to one sketched by another filmmaker. Carl Dreyer explains the effect he was after when he made *Vampyr*:

Imagine that we are sitting in an ordinary room. Suddenly we are told that there is a corpse behind the door. In an instant the room we are sitting in is completely altered: everything in it has taken on another look; the light, the atmosphere have changed, though they are physically the same. This is because *we* have changed, and the objects *are* as we conceive them. That is the effect I want to get in my film. (quoted in Neergaard, 1950: 27, his italics)

It takes only a couple of alterations to bring Dreyer's description into line with Hitchcock's. Imagine this is a scene *in a film* and that *viewers* are told there is a corpse behind a door. Now we can say that at the moment viewers learn of the corpse, the narration becomes less restricted. This time, the elements weighing on our (but not the characters') minds are not a bomb and a clock but a corpse and a door. Helpfully, Dreyer is explicit in ways Hitchcock is not. Everything has changed, though nothing has. Let us say it is the same room as in Hitchcock's scenario. The same table and chairs, the same figures, even the same clock (which, in Dreyer's scene, means nothing to us). Picture the same mundane dialogue and ordinary high-key lighting. Now viewers are not bracing for an explosion, and straining to hear ticking, but processing the discomfiting knowledge of something close by and disgusting. As Dreyer notes—and we can say the same thing about Hitchcock's scene—this narrational shift effects a change in the *atmosphere*, one that engulfs, overpowers, and redefines everything, from what the men are saying to what the wallpaper looks like to how the scene is lit.

I am not claiming that narrative is the sole or even the most important source of film atmosphere, only that it is a neglected and poorly understood one. Certainly stylistic choices generate atmosphere as well. A camera creeping over a moonlit swamp, accompanied by sounds of snapping branches and indistinct gurgling, will be atmospheric, even if this is the first shot in the film and viewers have no narrative context in which to set it. But confining a scene's atmosphere to setting, time of day, season, and weather—and even if one adds other aspects of film style—can only account for atmosphere in an incomplete and inaccurate fashion, for the sum of these elements will be less than the atmospheric whole.

Underestimating how many parts of a film flow into its atmosphere will lead to problematic claims. Cinematographer John Alton, after considering the mood-altering effects of weather, writes that "next to the elements is the setting, which influences mood also. A cemetery, for example, cannot even in the brightest sunlight look a happy place" (1995: 120). But filmmakers shooting a cemetery scene are less constrained than Alton believes. In the anthology film *Paris, je t'aime* (2006), in the "14e Arrondissement" segment, an American tourist visits a cemetery on a sunny day. In her guidebook, she reads about the famous people buried there while she stops at their graves. The scene is accompanied by carefree and upbeat nondiegetic music that is about as menacing as what you might hear in an elevator or a dentist's office. This vignette, about a lonely middle-aged woman whom love has passed by, is colored by a mild melancholy, but it is far from maudlin, and it has a happy ending. And if the music and bright sunlight were not enough to encourage viewers to construe the cemetery scene as other than gloomy, following it, after contemplating her own mortality, the character says in a voice over: "But I am not a sad person. Au contraire." Director Alexander Payne takes chances and reaps rewards undreamed of by Alton.

Likewise, in *The Poetics of Space*, Gaston Bachelard writes that compared to anything one might encounter in an attic, "creatures moving about in the cellar are slower, less scampering, more mysterious," adding that "in the attic, fears are easily 'rationalized.'" Whereas in the cellar, "'rationalization' is less rapid and less clear" (1994: 19). But, as with a cemetery, absolute affective attributes cannot be assigned

Figure 9.2 A shot that shows Melanie's point of view. *The Birds* (1963). Directed by Alfred Hitchcock. Produced by Universal Pictures and Alfred J. Hitchcock Productions.

to an attic setting. Hitchcock's *The Birds* (1963) shows that narrative and stylistic choices can swamp an attic in as much menace and mystery as any other location. Late in the film, off-screen fluttering noises serve roughly the same function as the strange creaks that, in another horror film, might draw a heroine toward a cellar. Mitch is asleep; Melanie takes her flashlight and investigates. Representing her point of view, the camera tracks forward and tilts up, her flashlight illuminating a stairway ascent that is as scary as any other horror film's twisting descent into a basement (Figure 9.2). And there is nothing "rational" about the threat scene awaiting her at the top of these stairs.

The tendency to see affective potentials immanent to a setting persists in more recent writing as well. After quoting Bachelard on forests, Hanich asks: "Why … is the immensity of the forest (as in *The Blair Witch Project*) frightening while the immensity of the prairie (as in *Dances with Wolves*) is not?" (2010: 176, my ellipsis). Here is the kernel of his answer:

> While the prairie gives you the feeling of standing *on top* and the sky creates an impression of being *under* their horizontal expansions, you are always *inside* the forest, enwrapped by its horizontal *and* vertical immensity. (176, his italics)

Hanich adds that in a forest, darkness, twigs, and other obstructions limit our vision, and this "enables a *depth* experience that we do not have in the prairie where vision can reach expansively out to the horizon" (177, his italics). But just as a scene of elation and delight can unfold in a tangled forest, so can fear set in under open skies—a corn field for example, and the flat land surrounding it, in broad daylight.

I am describing the setting of the famous crop-dusting sequence in *North by Northwest* (1959), in which Hitchcock ignores conventions and plays with our expectations, including ones held by writers who would explain how a setting is supposed to make us feel. A more prudent and supple approach would concede that, without knowing how a film's narrative is making use of the setting, we have no idea. And once Hitchcock saturates a setting, any one he chooses, in an "atmosphere of suspense," then suspense not only is what we feel; it also is the principal galvanizing core, and source, of the sequence's atmosphere. Ignore the role narrative plays in creating atmosphere and one is bound to make claims that inventive filmmakers will easily prove wrong. Atmosphere will always escape and exceed such limiting views.

Conclusion

For every case of a writer reflexively sectioning off atmosphere from the other parts of a film, one finds another writer acknowledging, however implicitly, that such a thing is impossible. Sometimes it is the same writer doing both these things at once, which shows that in our thinking, as in films, atmosphere is always percolating up, pushing forward, touching everything. It cannot be confined to a background, even if we insist that it is a background of the most supportive, enabling, and indispensable kind. Atmosphere sifts *downward*, too. In the hierarchy we construct for understanding what films do, what they are about, narrative tends to sit at the top. But narrative does not sit "on top" of film atmosphere; it feeds the atmosphere, which is bigger and more important than the story the film is telling.

The summative, global nature of atmosphere has been recognized by some writers. Smith, for example, argues that "the primary emotive effect of film is to create mood" (2003: 42).[2] One can find likeminded views by looking outside film studies. In *Supernatural Horror in Literature*, H. P. Lovecraft calls atmosphere "the all-important thing, for the final criterion of authenticity is not the dovetailing of plot but the creation of a given sensation" (2000: 23). And Mark Wigley writes that "atmosphere might even be the central objective of the architect" (1998: 18). These writers provide guidance on how film studies can begin to develop a more comprehensive and enlightened understanding of atmosphere in horror and other sorts of films. Much more of the same can be found in writing by Gernot Böhme.

A number of points in my argument echo claims Böhme has made about atmosphere in relation to stage productions and other media. This brief passage shows how we contemplate some of the same problems of definition and how, in general, he takes a view highly sympathetic to mine:

> The phenomenon of atmosphere is itself something extremely vague, indeterminate, intangible. The reason is primarily that atmospheres are totalities: atmospheres imbue everything, they tinge the whole of the world or a view, they bathe everything in a certain light, unify a diversity of impressions in a single emotive state. And yet one cannot actually speak of "the whole," still less of the whole of the world; speech is analytical and must confine itself to particulars. (Böhme, 2012: 2)

Böhme (1993, 1998a, 1998b) writes lucidly about the word's meteorological roots; atmosphere's diffuseness as a textual entity and, necessarily and productively, as an analytical concept; how atmosphere radiates from persons and things; and more. For Böhme, the atmosphere of an artwork amounts to no less than the sum total of the work's constituent elements plus its affective power. Not only coalescing the work into a unified entity, atmosphere also circumscribes the work and its perceiver. It constitutes the intersubjective experience that defines the work in the context of its reception. According to this view, within a horror film, dread and narrative are mere pieces of the atmospheric whole. Böhme articulates an opposite approach to ones that would too rigidly compartmentalize a film's formal workings, undervalue the interconnectedness of — and fluid interplay between — its elements, and place atmosphere in a bottom (or rear) compartment in the total system.

In conclusion, I have argued that horror film narratives create atmosphere in direct and largely unappreciated ways, but this is not to say that *lapses* in narrative — films with a minimum of plot, ones, like *Vampyr*, with attenuated or incomprehensible narratives — do not generate atmosphere in distinctive ways as well. Atmosphere may have as special a relationship to the *absence* of narrative as it does to narrative.[3] I believe further study would find such a view to be complementary to the one expressed here.

Notes

1. Signs that this has begun to change include Kristi McKim's *Cinema as Weather: Stylistic Screens and Atmospheric Change* (2013), in which she construes cinematic weather as an "atmospheric" dimension of a film that bears a strong relationship to narrative.
2. Smith is not without critics, some who uphold distinctions I challenge in this essay. For example, considering Smith, Carl Plantinga writes: "It isn't the mood that causes the suspense … If the scene is successful, it is the narrative situation that elicits suspense" (2009: 142, my ellipses).
3. I explore this possibility in Spadoni (2014).

References

Alton, J. (1995) *Painting With Light*, U of California P, Berkeley.

Bachelard, G. (1994) *The Poetics Of Space*. Trans. Maria Jolas, Beacon P, Boston. Orig. publ. 1958.

Balász, B. (1953) *Theory of the Film*. Trans. Edith Bone, Roy Publishers, New York.

Böhme, G. (1993) Atmosphere as the fundamental concept of a new aesthetics. *Thesis Eleven*, **36**, 113–126.

Böhme, G. (1998a) Atmosphere as an aesthetic concept. *Daidalos*, **68**, 112–115.

Böhme, G. (1998b) The atmosphere of a city. *Issues in Contemporary Culture and Aesthetics*, **7**, 5–13.

Böhme, G. (2012) March 16–17 The art of the stage set as a paradigm for an aesthetics of atmospheres, keynote address, *Understanding Atmospheres: Culture, materiality and the texture of the in-between* conference, Aarhus, DK: University of Aarhus.

Bordwell, D. (1981) *The Films of Carl-Theodor Dreyer*, U of California P, Berkeley.

Carroll, N. (1996) *Theorizing the Moving Image*, Cambridge UP, Cambridge.

Cherry, B. (2009) *Horror*, Routledge, New York.

Creed, B. (1993) *The Monstrous-Feminine: Film, Feminism, Psychoanalysis*, Routledge, London.

Denne, J.D. (1972) Society and the monster, in *Focus on the Horror Film* (eds R. Huss and T.J. Ross), Prentice-Hall, Englewood Cliffs, pp. 125–131. Orig. publ. 1967.

Durgnat, R. (2000) The subconscious: from pleasure castle to libido motel, in *Horror Film Reader* (eds A. Silver and J. Ursini), Limelight, New York, pp. 39–49. Orig. publ. 1962.

Ebert, R. (2005) *The Great Movies II*, Broadway Books, New York.

Erickson, G. (2000) Women on the verge of a gothic breakdown: sex, drugs and corpses in *The Horrible Dr. Hichcock*, in *Horror Film Reader* (eds A. Silver and J. Ursini), Limelight, New York, pp. 269–279. Orig. publ. 1997.

Freeland, C. (2000) *The Naked and the Undead: Evil and the Appeal of Horror*, Westview P, Boulder, CO.

Freeland, C. (2004) Horror and art-dread, in *The Horror Film* (ed. S. Prince), New Brunswick, Rutgers UP.

Gifford, D. (1973) *A Pictorial History of Horror Movies*, Hamlyn, New York.

Hanich, J. (2010) *Cinematic Emotion in Horror Films and Thrillers: The Aesthetic Paradox of Pleasurable Fear*, Routledge, New York.

Hills, M. (2005) *The Pleasures of Horror*, Continuum, London.

Humphries, R. (2002) *The American Horror Film: An Introduction*, Edinburgh UP, Edinburgh.

Hutchings, P. (2008) *Historical Dictionary of Horror Cinema*, Scarecrow, Lanham.

Jensen, P.M. (1974) *Boris Karloff and His Films*, A. S. Barnes, South Brunswick, NJ.

Karloff, B. (1943) Introduction, in *Tales of Terror*, World Publishing Co, Cleveland.

Lovecraft, H.P. (2000) *Supernatural Horror in Literature*. (ed. S.T. Joshi), Hippocampus, New York. Orig. publ. 1927.

McKim, K. (2013) *Cinema as Weather: Stylistic Screens and Atmospheric Change*, Routledge, New York.

Muir, J.K. (2007) *Horror Films of the 1980s*, MacFarland, Jefferson.

Neergaard, E. (1950) *Carl Dreyer: A Film Director's Work*, BFI, London.

Newman, K. (2011) *Nightmare Movies: Horror on Screen Since the 1960s*, Bloomsbury, London.

Paszylk, B. (2009) *The Pleasure and Pain of Cult Horror Films: An Historical Survey*, McFarland, Jefferson.

Plantinga, C. (2009) *Moving Viewers: American Film and the Spectator's Experience*, U of California P, Berkeley.

Prawer, S.S. (1980) *Caligari's Children: The Film as Tale of Terror*, Da Capo P, New York.

Pym, J. (ed.) (2004) *Time Out Film Guide*, 12th edn, Penguin, London.

Rigby, J. (2007) *American Gothic: Sixty Years of Horror Cinema*, Reynolds and Hearn, London.

Rockett, W.H. (1988) *Devouring Whirlwind: Terror and Transcendence in the Cinema of Cruelty*, Greenwood P, New York.

Ross, T.J. (1972) Introduction, in *Focus on the Horror Film* (eds R. Huss and T.J. Ross), Prentice-Hall, Englewood Cliffs, NJ, pp. 1–10.

Senn, B. (1996) *Golden Horrors: An Illustrated Critical Filmography of Terror Cinema, 1931–1939*, McFarland, Jefferson.

Simpson, P.L. (2010) Whither the serial killer movie?, in *American Horror Film: The Genre at the Turn of the Millennium* (ed. S. Hantke), Jackson, UP of Mississippi, pp. 119–141.

Smith, G.M. (2003) *Film Structure and the Motion System*, Cambridge UP, Cambridge.

Sobchack, V. (2001) *Screening Space: The American Science Fiction Film*, Rutgers UP, Brunswick. Orig. publ. 1987.

Spadoni, R. (2014) Horror film as anti-narrative (and vice-versa), in *Merchants of Menace: The Business of Horror Cinema* (ed. Richard Nowell), Bloomsbury, New York, pp. 109–128.

Tan, E. (2011) *Emotion and the Structure of Narrative Film: Film as an Emotion Machine*. Trans. Barbara Fasting, Routledge, New York.

Telotte, J.P. (1987) Through a pumpkin's eye: the reflexive nature of horror, in *American Horrors: Essays on the Modern American Horror Film* (ed. G.A. Waller), U of Illinois P, Urbana, pp. 114–128. Orig. pub. 1982.

Truffaut, F. and Scott, H.G. (1985) *Hitchcock*. Rev. edn., Simon and Schuster, New York.

Vale, E. (1944) *The Technique of Screenplay Writing*, Crown, New York.

Wigley, M. (1998) The architecture of atmosphere. *Daidalos*, **68**, 18–27.

Wood, R. (1989) *Hitchcock's Films Revisited*, Rev. edn., Columbia UP, New York.

Worland, R. (2007) *The Horror Film: An Introduction*, Blackwell, Malden, MA.

Zimmerman, B. (1996) *Daughters of Darkness*: the lesbian vampire on film, in *The Dread of Difference: Gender and the Horror Film* (ed. B.K. Grant), U of Texas P, Austin, pp. 379–387. Orig. publ. 1981.

10

Horror Sound Design

William Whittington

Every good horror story has its secrets. In fact, the uncanny has been described as "something that ought to have remained secret and hidden but has come to light" (Cherry, 2009: 126). The film sound track is no different. In creating the innovative sound effects for horror cinema, contemporary sound designers strategically embrace a measure of deception, especially when naming audio effects. During the process of postproduction, traditional mixing cue sheets (which list dialogue, music, and sound effects) have been replaced by computer software like *Pro Tools*, and as a result, mix "sessions" now detail every aspect of a sound from its location on the editorial timeline down to its waveform. These "sessions" include the names of the various effects, which generally evoke a sense of poetic onomatopoeia in the way that they describe sound — *whoosh, rip, stab, moan*, and *drip*. These descriptions chart not only the thematic breadth of a story, but also the overall architecture of a film's sound design. However, in the process of labeling effects, sound designers never reveal the primary sources or "roots" of the recordings. Instead, they remain conspicuously silent about the methods by which these sounds are captured and constructed.

The rationale is simple. Root effects are often drawn from mundane sources ranging from animal noises like dog growls or pig squeals to the manipulation of foodstuffs during the Foley process.[1] For instance, the sound associated with the crack of a bone beneath the skin can be achieved by wrapping a celery stalk in chamois and breaking it in half (Hoen, 2012: 1). This is not to suggest that these "ready made" sounds are by any means without complexity or stylistic design. They are embedded with ideological concerns, historical allusions, and even visceral intents, which will be explored throughout this chapter. Nonetheless, these root effects serve as the foundation for creating entirely new and "refined" sound effects, which are meant to shock or jolt filmgoers. When a description such as "moan

A Companion to the Horror Film, First Edition. Edited by Harry M. Benshoff.
© 2014 John Wiley & Sons, Inc. Published 2017 by John Wiley & Sons, Inc.

of ghost" appears on the computer screen during the final mix of film, it might actually be the sound of a revolving door at a bank pushed in the wrong direction, but then slowed down during the editing and re-recording process in order to produce a "guttural groan" (Rydstrom, 2004). This was, in fact, the sound source and method by which sound designer Gary Rydstrom [*Terminator 2: Judgment Day* (1991) and *Jurassic Park* (1993)] created the ethereal effects for the 1999 remake of *The Haunting*.

This conspiracy of silence around the origins of horror sound effects suggests ideological and even political aims. In general, the relabeling strategy serves two specific purposes during the postproduction process. First, it establishes a descriptive illusion, akin to a trick of misdirection, that sound personnel use to both focus and support the overall goal of audiovisual unity within a horror film. These descriptions function like costumes in that they convey the narrative meaning and visceral intent of an effect. In the example from *The Haunting*, the label supports the narrative goal of establishing a spectral presence in a secluded mansion, which is being used by a research team to study the paranormal. Thematically, the sound and its description serve to anthropomorphize the setting by evoking the notion of a *house in pain*. For filmgoers, it is important to note that the displacement of a root sound from its visual referent like the revolving door contributes to this overall project of misdirection by creating intellectual uncertainty or cognitive dissonance. Filmgoers may recognize fragments of the sound design, but not the entire structure, frame, or context. In the horror genre, hesitation of belief is at the heart of the uncanny effect.

The second reason for the mislabeling of sound effects deals with trust or rather the lack of it. It should come as no surprise that trust is also a major thematic concern of horror films, which constantly pose the question: "Whom do I trust?" John Carpenter's *The Thing* (1982) plays this out on a grand scale as a crew of scientists in the Antarctic is attacked by an invasive alien species with the ability to assimilate and mimic all life forms that it encounters. In order to restore trust among the team members, a gruesome blood test is devised to determine who is still human. Mistrust is rendered sonically when the alien blood held in a petri dish *screams* at the touch of a cauterized wire. During the often high pressure and contentious sound mix process for a film, similar questions and concerns around trust and authenticity arise. A uniquely genre-specific label for a sound effect eliminates any second-guessing (or screaming) by producers and directors about the appropriateness or suitability of a sound design created by the audio team. When placed in the context of a horror film, the description "moan of ghost" establishes credibility more readily than the label "sound of revolving door." In the end, sound designers understand that to reveal the truth about a sound source is to unmask its mystery and allure and consequently compromise its intention of establishing a link to the uncanny. On this point, they *must* remain silent. Part of the effectiveness of a horror sound effect resides in its naming as well as its evocation of dark emotion. In general, the depth and shocking nature of any hidden horror depends on the conspiracy of silence that surrounds its origin.

The aim of this chapter is to break the conspiracy of silence in regard to sound design and horror. In the past, the music score generally held together classic horror films like *Bride of Frankenstein* (1935) and *Cat People* (1942), but today, sound effects take up a larger portion of the sound track in this function. As a result, reading strategies and generic expectations in horror have shifted to fall in line with the tropes of contemporary Hollywood cinema, which foreground self-reflexivity, visceral intents, and audiovisual spectacle. These are the new pleasures of sound and horror in addition to the traditional narrative mayhem. While thematic and genre analysis will frame much of this study, I am equally interested in understanding how contemporary horror cinema has expanded the aesthetic range of sound design as an artistic movement. As a genre, horror is an aggregator of anxiety, informed by our fears of mortality and modernity, but horror also considers long suppressed primal terrors of fears of the natural and supernatural. The horror sound track maps the terrain between these extremes by offering a range of sound effects from the "raw" to the "refined," in order to challenge perception and question rationality. The intent of both horror and sound design in this context is to render an unfamiliar landscape filled with anxiety, fear, and dread. Uncertainty is key to unlocking the unconscious and accessing primal terrors. As a result, the aesthetic style of the horror sound track is never fixed because the "rules" of both sound and horror are constantly shifting.

Rather than provide a unifying lexicon of sonic grammar, the organization of the horror film sound track accesses a cabinet of sonic curiosities within which can be found an assemblage of found audio objects; familiar echoes from sound effects libraries; and unexpected mash-ups of organic and inorganic sounds. These disparate elements come together on the film sound track to establish their own organizing principles that are unpredictable and intentionally shocking. Additionally, traditional recording and re-recording techniques for sound, which were cultivated during the classical Hollywood period, are thwarted in order to directly challenge the expectations of filmgoers. Contemporary horror film sound habitually embraces abstract design strategies to promote both visceral and symbolic readings by filmgoers. For this reason, a voice from the afterlife may roam throughout the surround channels, or a low frequency effect (LFE) — like a cannon *boom* — might accompany the slam of a door with a dramatic finality that signals immanent death.[2]

While the visual design of horror has often been linked to German Expressionism, the movement of Surrealism provides an equally useful set of understandings and vocabulary for evaluating the horror film sound track. Surrealist art, photography, and filmmaking engage in techniques such as the collision of scale, amplified perception, disjunction, and cognitive dissonance, all of which have equivalents in the audio realm, particularly within the context of horror films. Similarly, Surrealism and sound design in horror also seek to create disjunction and discord in order to better understand "truths" that have been openly hidden by normative perception and social convention. Both approaches challenge the conception of perceived "reality," acknowledging that it is highly subjective, constructed, and suspect. It is fitting then that a movement that consciously sought to deny aesthetic method in order to understand the unconscious should be reapplied to help understand a genre that challenges traditional aesthetic methods, creating a cinema of nightmares and the subconscious. This study ends as it begins with a consideration of silence and its symbolic resonance with death.

Sound Design and Contemporary Horror

In my previous work on *Sound Design and Science Fiction* (Whittington, 2007), I argue that the term *sound design* arose in part to describe an aesthetic approach centered on the creation of specific audio effects. These designs were often achieved through highly innovative recording, editing, and mixing processes and were made possible due to the introduction of portable audio technologies, shifts in labor practices, and a renewed interest by New Hollywood filmmakers in sound as an art form. Subsequently, sound design has become a means by which we understand and critique the film sound track, as well as a way to consider the deployment of sound within the theatrical environment through the use of 5.1 multichannel audio formats like Dolby Digital and DTS.[3] While the creators of science fiction cinema were eager to embrace *sound designer* as a "Tiffany title," filmmakers working in horror have been less inclined to take up the designation or to use the term *sound design* to describe their work (Ondaatje, 2011: 53). In part, their reticence relates to the status of horror itself as a less valued genre, but equally important, their restraint emerges from a professional understanding that considers sound work in horror as a matter of craft rather than an artistic endeavor.

In the post-*Psycho* era, horror cinema moved away from the traditional gothic and atmospheric narratives of the past toward more violent, exploitative, and (sometimes) socially aware narratives that were hypercritical of the American economic and cultural landscape. The influence of Vietnam and the political scandals of the Watergate era infected the films of this period with a heightened level of paranoia and mistrust. Most relevant to sound, *The Conversation* (1974) embodied these concerns by presenting a conspiracy narrative that centered on professional eavesdropper Harry Caul (played by Gene Hackman) and his link to a corporate killing. Moments of horror *are* folded into this thriller as Caul records yet misinterprets the various conversations that lead up to the murder, but unmistakably, the film follows the aesthetic and theoretical underpinnings of the French New Wave imported into Hollywood at that time. As a result, the film firmly established director Francis Ford Coppola as a New Hollywood auteur, and Walter Murch as a "sound designer," whose work with "sound montage" demanded attention as an essential aspect of film art.

In contrast, horror filmmakers of this same period including George Romero [*Night of the Living Dead* (1968)], Wes Craven [*The Last House on the Left* (1972)], Tobe Hooper [*Texas Chain Saw Massacre* (1974)], and John Carpenter [*Halloween* (1978) and *The Fog* (1980)] were primarily seeking access into the Hollywood system by working in a marginalized yet highly profitable genre. Significant box office receipts would undoubtedly insure future work as a director. [Many young filmmakers continue to pursue this strategy in the era of "found footage" horror films like *The Blair Witch Project* (1999) and *Paranormal Activity* (2007)]. John Carpenter seemed most interested in the sound track, but his focus was primarily on music. He famously created the unsettling and spare theme for *Halloween*, which featured a rhythmic piano motif in 5/4 time signature with electronically produced undertones. But his contributions were in part driven by the fact that the production did not have enough money in its budget to hire a composer to do the job. Big budget horror auteurs such as Roman Polanski [*Rosemary's Baby* (1968)] and William Friedkin [*The Exorcist* (1973)] did emerge, but they quickly distanced themselves from horror when opportunities to work in other genres arose. Steven Spielberg also began his career working in horror at first on network television [*Rod Serling's Night Gallery* (1969–1973) and *Duel* (1971)] and then, in cinema [*Jaws* (1975) and *Jurassic Park*]. He also helped to raise the status and budgets of horror cinema within the industry, producing *Poltergeist* (1982), *Twilight Zone: The Movie* (1983), and *Gremlins* (1984). This shift in status was achieved in part through hybridization, a process by which narrative and audiovisual elements migrated between adjacent genres, giving rise to hyphenated categories such as the horror-thriller, the horror-action film, and horror-black comedy, and more recently, the rom-zom-com or the romantic zombie comedy like *Shaun of the Dead* (2004).

These filmmakers and their films bracketed the extremes of the horror cycle during this period, and sound track design was tied to this scale in terms of economic resources and aesthetic innovation. These works were a study in contrasts. Some were hailed by academics as narratively subversive, while others were reviled in the popular press. Film critic Roger Ebert consistently questioned the necessity of what he termed the *dead teenager movie*, which he noted "begins with a lot of living teenagers and … ends with all of them dead, except for one who is necessary to come back in the sequel" (Ebert Clip, 2012). Yet all of these films were easily marketable due to their shock value as well as highly profitable, often spinning off a series of sequels. Historically, they challenged censorship boundaries (most received [R-ratings for violence, nudity, and profanity), embraced new make-up and visual effects processes, and shifted expectations in regard to spectacles of gore and violence, aided in part by the sound track.

This is not to suggest these films lacked style; but rather, in regard to the sound track, budgetary constraints necessitated innovative acoustic shortcuts and aesthetic scavenging that established a kind of "house style" that had no specific studio home but instead developed within the horror genre itself. Low-budget horror films of this period embraced the strategies of cinema verité and the tropes of documentary style as a means of presenting a more objective, "raw," and confrontational point-of-view. Audio was recorded in close perspective, closing the distance between microphone and subject, and consequently, creating a sense of sonic claustrophobia. The quality of the recordings affirmed the materiality of the recording medium, as sound editors left in place volume distortions and equipment handling noise, which in most films would render the audio unusable. Ambiances such as wind and thunder were drawn from stock material found in sound libraries, and edited liberally throughout entire

Figure 10.1　The sound design functions as an overture, presenting a layering of *raw* and *refined* sound effects. *Texas Chain Saw Massacre* (1974). Directed by Tobe Hooper. Produced by Vortex.

sequences. "Castle thunder," an effect from the Universal horror films of the 1930s, was used so much in the horror of radio, television, and film that it has become a recognizable acoustic cliché. The "Wilhelm scream" has achieved similar status and can be heard in hundreds of films; its use is now considered an "inside geek joke" among sound designers (Lee, 2007: 1).[4]

Low-budget horror films blurred the line between "professional" and "amateur" filmmaking, but in doing so evoked a sense of immediacy and authority common to on-the-spot broadcast recording found on both radio and television. *Night of the Living Dead* adopted the look and sound of civil rights footage from network news broadcasts, while *The Texas Chain Saw Massacre* embraced the audiovisual codes of "hand-held" documentary, incorporating close perspective recordings of breathing and screaming, which caused a distorted screeching when transferred to the optical medium. Sound became an essential means by which these films engaged with codes of cinematic "realism," and subsequently, established credibility among filmgoers as "true." Voiceovers and title cards telling filmgoers the events depicted were "based on real events" also supported the illusion. In general, these sound tracks embraced a sense of urgency and perceived "liveness," but with a wider critical range than broadcast media. *The Texas Chain Saw Massacre*, for example, begins with the sounds of digging and heavy breathing, which a radio bulletin details as an incident of rural "grave robbing" (Figure 10.1). The sound montage and voiceover adeptly collapse time. A police investigation is implied through the sound of a high-pitched screech of a flashbulb filament, which accompanies the gruesome images of body parts that appear from the darkness. In addition, the underscoring presents a rising jangle of clanging and scrapping metal, foreshadowing the cutting surfaces and hooks that will be found in the slaughterhouse. Initially, these sounds function to represent the mere "capture" of events (i.e., police evidence gathering), but the not-so-subtle iso-lation of filament effect resonates in a highly symbolic way. On the visual track, the camera zooms out to reveal a mountain of body parts draped over a graveyard head-stone, creating a gruesome monument. The sound of the camera flash presents a twisted commentary on tourism and the American family's obsession with photog-raphy, specifically the need to visit historical monuments to document them through staged family portraitures. In this instance, the mundane becomes the macabre, and foreshadows the unsettling family portrait the film's narrative will eventually offer. To borrow an understanding from Surrealism, this stylistic approach isolates the "com-monplace" (in this case a sound rather than an image) in order to:

> confer a dignity and poetic value on the things of the everyday life, to turn them into what Freud called *thing-representations*, indices of the unconscious. In isolating objects, magnifying them, and recombining them in new ways, things were revealed … in all their fulsome, hieratic mystery. (Hammond, 2000: 7)

But does this innovative sound work rise to the level of "sound design" or encour-age sound personnel to take on the designation of "sound designer"? To those work-ing in horror at the time, the answer was no. In terms of economics, few productions spent much money or time on the postproduction sound process, typically contract-ing it out to the lowest bidder or allowing distributors to cover the cost of "sweeten-ing" the sound track with additional Foley or sound effects. For those engaged in the sound work, low-budget films offered little more than a steady paycheck, regard-less of the genre. In this sense, the sound track was more about crafting a work that satisfied the producer and director and coming in under budget, than in shaping an overall aesthetic design. Re-recording mixer Bill Varney, who worked with Tobe Hooper on *Poltergeist*, sums it up in this way: "That term came about in the San Fran-cisco Bay area . . . .Up there, you're a sound designer. In the Hollywood or New York world of filmmaking, you're a sound editor or creator" (Chell, 1987: 107). For sound personnel working in the horror genre, perhaps the greater fear embedded in the term *sound designer* was the appearance of professional hubris. Even on big-budget horror films like *The Exorcist*, the sound methods were somewhat primitive and mat-ter of fact. As Foley artist Ross Taylor explains, "I did the scene in *The Exorcist* when Linda Blair throws up in bed on the exorcist. I drank a warm 7-Up, waited a few minutes, and then I had this terrible belch that they recorded, and that's what they used. You have to create as you go" (quoted in LoBrutto, 1994: 63).

In terms of labor practices, the credit of "sound designer" was not a designation recognized by either the Hollywood unions or the Academy of Motion Pictures Arts and Sciences. So for union postproduction houses, the designation was not allowed, and if a film were nominated for "Best Sound," the Oscar would be given to those per-sonnel on the sound team in the categories of "Sound Mixing" or "Sound Editing." For non-union houses in the Los Angeles area, the term might have raised questions about labor hierarchies and division of duties, which would have led to fines or sanc-tions. However, the popular press and filmgoers did take up the term *sound design* and began to apply it across all genres from science fiction to action films, and so it is now firmly positioned within the lexicon of cinematic culture and criticism. Looking back on the history of the horror sound track, it is important to acknowledge that while many of these audio "techniques" may have been the unintended consequences of inadequate resources coupled with time constraints during the postproduction process, they do constitute an overall aesthetic within the horror genre that continues to be influential even today. The sound tracks for *The Blair Witch Project* or *Cloverfield* (2008) would not have been as effective or widely accepted without these earlier experiments in horror sound style. Overall, the planning and patterns of these post-studio-era sound tracks are part of the historical poetic of horror cinema, and they contribute significantly to an expanded understanding of sound design as an artistic movement and the horror genre in general.

Horror Sound Design: From the Raw to the Refined

Unlike sound in the science fiction genre, sound design in contemporary horror cinema is by no means unified or standardized, rather these sound track strategies align themselves with the cycles of the genre. These trends are dependent upon film economics, fan enthusiasm, and the ability of these films to reframe the anxieties of the moment. Historically, horror film cycles emerge from a successful work like *Halloween* or *A Nightmare on Elm Street* (1984), and then echo for years to come through various sequels and knock-offs, until declining box office revenues end the pattern. But these films, like their killers, never die. Instead, they are referenced, remade, and rebooted with regularity. New horror films embrace older aesthetic approaches as a means of creating retrograde ("retro") designs, paying homage to past horror films and embracing a sense of nostalgia for bygone forms and fears. The 2009 film *House of the Devil*, for instance, created a hybrid slasher film and ghost story in the style of 1980s horror, embracing not only the techniques of that era but also the technology for the production. Similarly, Japanese horror filmmakers like Takashi Shimizu borrowed heavily from 1970s and 1980s horror to create the J-horror trend, which has been globally influential (McRoy, 2005: 177). In this context, horror sound aesthetics are unmoored from industrial imperatives, traditional standards of "good sound practices," and even nations of origin in regard to genre and sound track design.

Thematically, horror sound design moves along a wide aesthetic spectrum ranging from the primal to the ethereal. As previously noted, sound effects design of early 1970s horror adopted the codes and stylistic tendencies of documentary and cinema verité, and as a result, the sound tracks can be defined as somewhat "raw." This style went into remission as big-budget films like *Poltergeist* and *An American Werewolf in London* (1981) supplanted these approaches with highly refined sound tracks, and led to a series of big budget horror remakes from John Carpenter's *The Thing* to David Cronenberg's *The Fly* (1986). It was not until new consumer recording technologies arose that the cycle of "raw" sound effects re-emerged and embraced the retrograde and regressive sound style of the 1970s. The newer cycles included video verité [*Henry: Portrait of a Serial Killer* (1986)], which provides a twisted and horrific take on the "home movie," and more recently, computer and HD verité (*Paranormal Activity*), which considers the anxieties around surveillance, voyeurism, and privacy.

One of the key qualities of the "raw" sound for these films is its self-reflexivity, specifically in regard to an awareness of its own construction. These sound tracks acknowledge the materiality of the various capture mediums from videotape to computer hard drives. In doing so, the sound designs include artifacts from recording devices like onboard camera microphones, which have limited pickup patterns and reduced dynamic range. Due to the point-of-view (POV) shooting style, the sound tracks include residue of cable-handling noises, camera bumps, and battery failures. The most notable examples of these can be heard on the sound track for *The Blair Witch Project*, evoking an intimacy and directness that was part of its improvisational production style.

"Raw" sound also emerges as a category of audio effects, which are typically collected and archived in sound libraries. During the Foley process, these sounds are often cultivated from organic sources such as fruits, vegetables, chicken carcasses, entrails of larger game and even eggs. According to John Post, who did Foley on John Carpenter's *The Thing*, the alien autopsy scenes required "goopy sounds" which were achieved by using animal "guts" dropped into a bowl with raw eggs to achieve the "liquid quality" of the decaying alien remains (Stone, 2009). Similarly, cantaloupes are sometimes used to create the sound of guts being pulled from bodies, while the viscous juice is repurposed to create the sound of blood spattering on surfaces like walls and floors. In her essay "Film Bodies: Gender, Genre, and Excess," Linda Williams notes that horror is a "body genre" dependent on "gross displays" around bodily functions, which establish spectacles of "excess" (2009: 602–603). "Raw" sound effects support this understanding as they acoustically get beneath the skin of both characters on the screen and filmgoers, and render an understanding about the fragility of the human body. From the head turning sequence in *The Exorcist* to the chest buster scene in *Alien* (1979), the images are only half the story. Sound effects explore the body in ways that visuals cannot.

It is important to note that the deployment of a "raw" sound effect interacts with filmgoers both cognitively and *physically* in order to create the visceral responses necessary for horror cinema. When any individual is presented with any moment of terror in real life or on film, the event (in the form of audiovisual stimuli in this case) takes two pathways through the brain, which neuroscientist Joseph E. LeDoux terms the "high road" and the "low road" (Foley and Johnson, 2003). One path seeks a conscious understanding of the event through intellectual evaluation and insight. The second path connects the moment of terror to the physical (via the amygdala—a storehouse of primal fears and emotional memories), which triggers increased adrenaline flow, rapid breathing, and an elevated blood pressure and heart rate; subsequently, "the entire body is suddenly in a state of high alert, ready for fight or flight" (Foley and Johnson, 2003). These are the physical cues and sensations for the *feelings* of fear. Horror sound designers are effectively crossing the wires when they use "raw" effects or body effects like heartbeats, breathing, and bone breaks to represent a character in peril. These sound designs preemptively trigger the physical pathways in filmgoers' brains and cause a perceptual matching telling the body acoustically to feel fear. What the sound effects do not offer is enough information to make an intellectual evaluation of the situation. Similarly, this is why the image track seeks to hide the killer, monster, or creature in a horror film for as long as possible. The intellectual disconnection amplifies anxiety and heightens the physical responses even further. This model sonically represents the fear of the unknown, a key theme of the horror genre, and necessitates that filmgoers draw from the wellspring of the subconscious to dredge up primal as well as personal fears and anxieties. To make matters worse, horror sound designers do not play fair in the organization of these sonic moments. Just when a stylistic strategy establishes a pattern that allows filmgoers to anticipate the terror, horror sound designers and directors change the rules. Like an unreliable narrator, the sound track design cannot be trusted in a horror film.

At the other end of the spectrum of the horror sound track are the highly refined effects and affiliated design processes like multichannel mixing and deployment, which filmgoers have come to expect from contemporary Hollywood cinema. While the horror genre still clings somewhat to its outsider status as exploitation or cult cinema, the design of contemporary horror sound tracks can be as refined as those found in any recent blockbusters, due to advances in digital recording and editing technologies and multichannel formats. Even the "shaky cam" horror films present something of a paradox in this regard as they combine both the "raw" and the "re-fined" aspects of sound. While it should be easy and cost effective to capture and cut "bad sound" effects into a horror film, this is not always the case in the multichan-nel era. The sound is no longer limited to one channel of hissy optical sound. *The Blair Witch Project* had a reported shooting budget of $35,000 dollars, but the post-production and finishing costs for the film incurred by its distributor Artisan cost a reported $341,000, and included the addition of new effects, a multichannel mix, color timing, and the 35 mm blowup (Leland, 1999: 48). The filmmakers turned the sound "sweetening" duties over to Dana Meeks at the Wilshire Stages in Los Angeles. According to one of the directors of the film, Daniel Myrick,

> The mixing people cleaned up a lot of very raw audio and really took the film to a new level … We told them to go ahead and add things, but it had to be in keeping with the sensibility of the film. They really understood what we were going for, and so they were able to add background ambient noise like crickets, cracking sticks, wind, and other things that really helped the film. (CreativePlanetNetwork.com, 2012: 1)

In this case, the multichannel mix provides an aspect of immersive terror to the film. The off-screen sound effects of breaking branches and rustling leaves in the surround channels establish an unseen menace that lurks just out of reach, eventually eroding the sanity of the three young filmmakers. Despite the expanse of the open woods, the multichannel sound serves to encircle the characters in a sonic noose. Filmgoers feel the squeeze as well through perceptual matching.

Multichannel sound design has been transformative within the horror genre not simply in establishing off-screen threats, but also in establishing metaphysical challenges. Traditionally, multichannel formats serve to localize sound effects, to achieve audio separation so sounds do not "mask" or sit on top of each other, and to establish a sense of spatial and cinematic immersion like the one described above. Horror films can subvert these drives toward seamless continuity by pushing the use of multichannel sound toward disunity and fragmentation in order to disorient filmgoers. Freddy Krueger from the *Nightmare on Elm Street* series consistently uses the surround channels to taunt his victims from the nightmare dreamscape off-screen. Sound theorist Michel Chion identifies this practice as "the acousmêtre," or an off-screen voice that has not as yet attached itself to an onscreen representation, and consequently is engaging in a game of "primal hide-and-seek" (1999: 17). Horror cinema is replete with such games and sonic lures, but the genre's thematic interests in the afterlife complicate these sound strategies (Figures 10.2 and 10.3).

Figure 10.2   The sound of the voice reaches out from the afterlife through the surround channels. *Poltergeist* (1982). Directed by Tobe Hooper. Produced by Metro-Goldwyn-Mayer (MGM) and SLM Production Group.

Figure 10.3   The sound design superimposes the ethereal plane over the "real world." *Poltergeist* (1982). Directed by Tobe Hooper. Produced by Metro-Goldwyn-Mayer (MGM) and SLM Production Group.

In the film *Poltergeist*, for example, the surround channels serve as a means to represent the ethereal space beyond the borders of not only the film frame, but also lived experience. In the film, Carole Anne Freeling (played by Heather O'Rourke), the daughter of a real estate developer and his wife, is pulled into another dimension by paranormal forces. Paradoxically, the surround channels (as well as the left center and right center channels) serve as the "place" where she is "trapped." The cage is not visual but sonic. The child's voice, which is best heard from the television set, is separated from her body, and becomes a sonic spectacle of discontinuity with heavy reverberations and echoes to imply distance. In this instance, the traditional strength of the surround channels indicates not location but rather dislocation. Within the horror genre, disembodied voices and ghosts linger in the surround channels to establish a link to the afterlife, a place that visual design in cinema has been reluctant to explore.

Horror Sound Design and Surrealist Impulses

In order to understand the range of sound refinement and design within horror, it is important to consider some of the methods by which specific sounds are conceptualized, constructed, and organized. While the connection between cinematic horror and German Expressionism has been well documented in regard to subjectivity and mise-en-scene (specifically how madness is represented through lighting and set design), the influences of Surrealism have not yet been fully explored, particularly in regard to the film sound track. In the early 1920s, Surrealism emerged in Paris, France as a cultural movement in response to the trauma of World War I. It sought to challenge rationalism and the socio-economic conditioning that contributed to the state of the world consumed by global conflict. The movement coalesced around founder André Breton, who wrote the initial *Surrealist Manifesto* in 1924, which challenged the restrictions and understandings of traditional artistic method. Nonconformity was prized, and various poets, writers, and artists embraced the challenges set forth in the manifesto to liberate themselves from social conditioning and cultural expectations in regard to art. The most famous surrealist film was *Un chien andalou* (1929) which sprang from the collaboration of Salvador Dalí and Louis Buñuel and evolved from a comingling of recollected dreams. The project of surrealism was "the overthrow of rational thought and of the barriers between art and life" and to achieve this aim, artists engaged in a variety of disruptive practices that rejected a singular or dogmatic method (Rees, 1999: 41). The movement was particularly invested in exploring dreamscapes as theorized by Sigmund Freud in works such as *The Interpretation of Dreams*. The hallucinatory qualities of surrealism have subsequently influenced fashion photography, advertising, punk rock music, and Hollywood cinema. Alfred Hitchcock staged several dream sequences modeled on surrealism, in particular for the film *Spellbound* (1945). Surrealism has more recently influenced a variety of contemporary filmmakers including Terry Gilliam [*Brazil* (1985) and *The Fisher King*

(1991)], David Cronenberg [*Videodrome* (1983), *Naked Lunch* (1991), and *eXistenZ* (1999)], and David Lynch [*Blue Velvet* (1986), *Twin Peaks* (1990–1991), and *Mulholland Dr.* (2001)].

While Surrealism challenged the notion of method, the strategies by which the movement eventually engaged the various mediums of poetry, photography, and cinema were transformative as well as disruptive. In the efforts to challenge traditional art forms and audience expectations, these works leave splinters in the conscious mind that are disturbing and often irreconcilable. The aim of horror cinema is then uniquely aligned with these Surrealist intents, and for this reason, Surrealist approaches to style, which have been well documented in critical writing, migrate deftly to the task of characterizing the various complexities of horror film sound design. Specifically, these techniques and interests have been characterized as challenges to hierarchy, collision of scale, amplified perception, disjunction, and cognitive dissonance. Rather than focus on the drive to interrogate visual processes as the Surrealists have done, the sound track in horror presses filmgoers to question subjectivity as it relates to the perception of hearing. From the noise and mayhem, the listener must cup their ears and sort the truth from the horror.

Challenges to Hierarchy through the Collision of Scale

Traditionally, the sound track mix adheres to the hierarchy of dialogue, music, and effects, and tends to foreground the voice in order to promote narrative intelligibility. In short, dialogue functions to "tell the story." During the classical period, this hierarchy assured that sound effects were functional and unobtrusive, establishing a sense of unbroken continuity. However, in contemporary horror cinema, the opposite is true. As previously noted, sound effects have become a form of spectacle through multichannel deployment and isolation of focus, thus demanding notice by filmgoers. Another form of sound spectacle relates to changes in volume, which are engineered during the mix process. This most basic form of collision of scale emerges in the clash between loud and soft sounds. The initial aim of unexpected level changes is to create a "startle response," a jolt that triggers a basic reflex of shock or surprise, but sound designers often coordinate this primal intent with an attack on expectation and reason (Baird, 2000: 12). For example, in *Paranormal Activity 3* (2011), the character of Dennis (played by Chris Smith) rigs a video camera to the base of an oscillating floor fan so that it can survey the domestic landscape of the family home from the kitchen to the front door. Sonically sweetened with the light hum of the fan's motor, the camera movement is hypnotic and lulling, but the intent is to capture evidence of the unsettling supernatural events that have beset the family. At one point, a knock lures Dennis's girlfriend Julie (played by Lauren Bittner) from the kitchen where she is on the phone with her mother to the front door, but she calls out and finds no one there. When she and the camera sweep back toward the kitchen, everything is missing within the space from the phone to the furniture. The scene is in part a homage to a similar incident in *Poltergeist*. But suddenly, all of the contents of the kitchen crash to the floor from the frame above, and Julie screams. The sound design presents a high-volume cacophony of crashing pots, plates, chairs, and glass, providing filmgoers with a visceral jolt. The sound designers even dip the sound of the fan just before the impact in order to create a psychoacoustic effect of increased volume by tricking the ear's protective "aural reflex," which actively "turns down the volume" during loud sonic bursts, into a state of micro-relaxation (Holman, 1997: 31). Beyond the startle effect, the audiovisual moment thematically challenges the understanding that the suburban kitchen is the domestic command center of the nuclear family. The supernatural forces (in part controlled by Julie's mother) and the sound design literally upend this traditionally organized and safe domestic space. Even gravity is called into question. In true Surrealist fashion, mundane elements of the everyday become malevolent through inversion of hierarchy and collision of scale.

Amplified Perception

Traditionally, sensory perceptions establish a normative subjectivity, specifically a means by which we formulate an understanding of lived experience. Both Surrealism and horror question this "normative" status through an exploration of amplified perception. By challenging perceptual balance, new points of view emerge. Horror films are particularly interested in exploring both primal and supernatural subjectivity. Supernatural thrillers posit the ability of amplified perception in the notion of extra sensory perception or ESP. In *The Sixth Sense* (1999), the young protagonist Cole Sear (played by Haley Joel Osment) expresses his secret of perceptual imbalance in the now famous line of dialogue "I see dead people." In thematic terms, sight and insight are connected, and even his name speaks to his supernatural ability. Beyond dialogue and the voice, sound effects design tends to characterize the act of hearing with the primal, blurring the distinctions between man and beast. In the Mike Nichols film *Wolf* (1994), Jack Nicholson plays Will Randal, a book editor, who has been bitten by a wolf. Over the course of the film, he undergoes a transformation that heightens his acoustic and olfactory senses. As he stands at the top of the interior stairway of his office building, his ears visibly twitch, and he begins to truly "hear" the world around him. The sound track montage includes footfalls, doors closing, building ambiance, and fragments of conversations including the telling line of dialogue: "You can't trust anybody." In this sonic landscape, secrets and trust are intertwined to create a heightened sense of paranoia. The character's point of audition not only underscores his condition of lycanthropy, but also provides a critique of the post-human condition—a reversion in the form of primal privilege necessitated by the demands of corporate capitalism.

Disjunction

When considering sound theory, early Surrealist filmmakers embraced "the call for a non-naturalistic sound cinema" characterized by the 1928 manifesto ("A Statement") by Soviet theorists S. M. Eisenstein, V.I. Pudovkin, and G.V. Alexandrov (Rees, 1999: 51). The "Statement" called for "contrapuntal use of sound" in order to "perfect" the conceptual aspects of montage (Eisenstein *et al.*, 1985: 84). The artifice of "naturalism" was to be avoided. True to the subversive nature of the genre, however, horror sound adopts and transforms this approach to challenge expectation and cultural convention. In regard to film music, contemporary horror films dislocate popular music standards, displacing them from their cultural context. *A Clockwork Orange* (1971) recalibrated the associations related to the song "Singin' in the Rain" by twisting it into a spectacle of violence as Malcolm McDowell, playing a street thug, sings the song during a rape scene. Similarly, the pop hit song "Hip to Be Square" by Huey Lewis and the News serves as the "needle drop" sound track for the ax murder scene in *American Psycho* (2000). The intent of these disjunctions is the defacement of the sacred cultural reception of popular music.

Disjunction is also specifically tied to sound design and montage. Sound designers actively cultivate and construct a cabinet of sonic curiosities—scrapes, knocks, screeches, creaking doors, groans, body hits, and falls—for horror sound libraries, and during the editorial process, they lay out these effects as if on an autopsy table, mixing and matching them against the visuals. The aim is to create the sonic grotesque. In *The Texas Chain Saw Massacre*, the sound editors incorporated pig squeals into Leatherface's dialogue, underscoring his reversion from human to inhuman killer and cannibal. Like surrealistic imagery, the sound design combines incongruous elements, which are generally recognizable, but when they are decontextualized, re-mixed, or layered, they provoke revulsion by association. This is horror colliding with the contrapuntal use of sound.

Cognitive Dissonance

The horror sound track extends the project of cognitive challenges in the form of sonic dissonance, which mimics madness. The sound track picks up a kind of automatism of the unsettled mind, which manifests as incomplete and unresolved sonic ideas, chords, and movements. Composer Bernard Herrmann established this aesthetic design in his music scores for films like *Vertigo* (1958) and *Psycho* (1960). In *Friday the 13th* (1980), composer Harry Manfredini pays homage to Herrmann but incorporates new techniques of sound montage and re-mixing. Manfredini reworked the killer's final lines of dialogue "Kill her mommy" into the familiar sonic rift of "Ki Ki Ki Ma Ma Ma." Through the techniques of close perspective microphone positioning and syncopated delivery, Manfredini recorded his own voice saying the lines, then processed the abbreviated version with heavy reverberation and echo and used the results liberally throughout the film. The sonic abstraction provided not only a recurrent leitmotif that represented the killer Mrs. Pamela Voorhees (played by Betsy Palmer), but also, it provided an underlying critique of the origins of her psychosis—the loss of her disfigured son, whose persona she incorporated into her own. The leitmotif comes to represent an irrational mode of thought, critiquing the boundaries between sanity and insanity, mother and son. In the end, this sonic dissonance and the narrative are an adept inversion of Freud's notions about "castration" and motherhood, and in true Surrealist fashion, both mother and later son wear masks that mirror the abyss of the other. The mother's mask is one of grief, rage, and revenge that manifests in her dual personality, while Jason's (physical) mask reflects all of these emotional characteristics as well as a sense of moral judgment. In a metaphysical sense, he is a variation of "The Grim Reaper," who dispenses judgment on the unsuspecting teens that populate the films with a machete rather than a scythe.

Conclusion: The Long Silence

The horror sound track offers its own version of the existential abyss in the form of silence. But paradoxically, silence in film has never been silent. It is filled with both noise and meaning—most readily it symbolizes death. In the early years of cinema sound, a gloved hand slipping over a mouth in order to stifle a scream often represented imminent death. The sound of this loss was not meant to reach the filmgoer's ears, but the hiss of the optical track was always the unintended underscoring of such moments. In contemporary cinema, sound design has inverted these moments of "silence" and ended them all together, which is ironic given that digital formats can now offer nearly complete silence. However, cinematic "silence" is often represented by ambient footfall recorded at a distance or "white noise" culled from the sounds of traffic, wind, or air conditioning. But within the horror genre, this "silence" is still cause for alarm. When the wind stops or the footfalls cease, death is near. So now more than ever, characters must listen if they are to survive. Horror filmgoers must also do the same because through the act of listening, they hear the secrets that were meant to remain hidden; the whispers of madness in the mundane; and the calls of those trapped in the afterlife. These are the true soundings of the horror film sound track.

Notes

1. Foley is the process by which sound effects are created on a sound stage in synchronization with the picture. The technique is named after Jack Foley, a sound effects editor at Universal.
2. LFE are deep, low-pitched sounds like thunder and animal growls. In digital theater venues, specific speakers have been designed to reproduce sounds within the 3–120 Hz

range and are generally located behind the screen. Localization is not a consideration when directing sound to this channel; rather, sound designers are concerned with the visceral impact the sound offers to filmgoers.

3. Dolby Digital is 5.1 channel audio format, which features six discrete channels of sound—an array that includes left, center, right, left surround, right surround and LFE channels. The format is commonly used in theatrical and home theater venues. Similarly, DTS (Digital Theater System) is a discrete format developed by Universal and Amblin Entertainment, which encodes the sound track on a CD-ROM, which runs in synchronization with the film through time code.

4. Sound Scholar Benjamin Wright chronicles the history of the Wilhelm Scream in his online essay found at http://www.offscreen.com/Sound_Issue/wright_forum1.pdf. Wright notes that this "sonic signature" originated from the production of *Distant Drums* in 1951 and was named after a character in that film by Sound Designer Ben Burtt.

References

Baird, R. (2000) The startle effect: implication for spectator cognition and media theory. *Film Quarterly*, **53** (3), 12–24.

Chell, D. (1987) *Moviemakers at Work*, Microsoft Press, Redmond.

Cherry, B. (2009) *Horror*, Routledge, New York.

Chion, M. (1999) *The Voice in Cinema*, Columbia University Press, New York.

CreativePlanetNetwork.com (2012) Behind The Blair Witch Project, http://www.creativeplanetnetwork.com/dcp/news/behind-blair-witch-project/44043 (accessed 1 November 2012).

Hammond, P. (2000) Available light, in *The Shadow & It's Shadow—Surrealist Writings on the Cinema* (ed. P. Hammond), City Lights Books, San Francisco, pp. 1–45.

Ebert, R. (2012) http://www.youtube.com/watch?v=rUjawc8PQpw (accessed 1 November 2012).

Eisenstein's, S.M., Pudovkin, V.I., and Alexandrov, G.V. (1985) A statement, in *Film Sound Theory and Practice* (eds E. Weis and J. Belton), Columbia University Press, New York, pp. 83–85.

Foley, D. and Johnson, S. (2003) Emotions and the brain: fear, in *Discovery—The Magazine of Science, Technology and the Future* http://discovermagazine.com/2003/mar/cover#.UMUAJKXR3wx (accessed 1 November 2012).

Hoen, T. (2012) *The Credits*. Did You Hear That? Nightmare on Elm Street Foley Artist Gary Hecker Reveals How Horror Movies' Scariest Sound Effects Are Made, http://www.thecredits.org/2012/10/did-you-hear-that-nightmare-on-elm-street-foley-artist-gary-hecker-reveals-how-horror-movies-scariest-sound-effects-are-made/ (accessed 18 March 2014).

Holman, T. (1997) *Sound for Film and Television*, Focal Press, Boston.

Lee, J. (2007) Cue the Scream: Meet Hollywood's Go-To Shriek. *Wired Magazine*, 15.10, http://www.wired.com/entertainment/hollywood/magazine/15-10/st_scream (accessed 1 November 2012).

Leland, J. (1999) The Blair Witch Cult. *Newsweek*, pp. 44–51.

LoBrutto, V. (1994) *Sound-on-Film*, Praeger, Westport, Connecticut.

McRoy, J. (ed.) (2005) *Japanese Horror Cinema*, University of Hawai'i Press, Honolulu.

Ondaatje, M. (2011) *The Conversations — Walter Murch and the Art of Editing Film*, Alfred A. Knopf, New York.

Rees, A.L. (1999) *A History of Experimental Film and Video*, BFI, London.

Rydstrom, G. (2004) *Sound Design*, Lecture at University of Southern California, Los Angeles.

Stone, D.E. (2009) *Event Curator. The Sound Behind the Image III: Real Horror Show*, Academy's Science and Technology Council, Los Angeles.

Whittington, W. (2007) *Sound Design and Science Fiction*, University of Texas Press, Austin.

Williams, L. (2009) Film bodies: gender, genre, and excess, in *Film Theory and Criticism* (eds L. Braudy and M. Cohen), Oxford University Press, New York, pp. 602–616.

11

Mellifluous Terror

The Discourse of Music and Horror Films

Joe Tompkins

The scene is distinctly familiar: a dark moonlit night, a deserted city street, a solitary man leaving his girlfriend's apartment, a killer on the loose. Following a cautious glance around the corner, the man edges his way out from the door and down the stairs. There is no dialog, no background noise — just the quavering sounds of some high-pitched string music and an incessant piano loop that adds a layer of agitation and suspense. The man peers right, then left. Suddenly a discordant blast ruptures forth onto the soundtrack and the man stops dead in his tracks. Out of the depths of the fog-shrouded alleyway emerges a hulking shape, lurching forward in silhouette, holding what appears to be a mangled object in one hand — perhaps a severed head — and a large, pointed instrument in the other, possibly a dagger. The music intensifies: an atonal din of brass and strings, high and low, seems to reflect aurally the man's shock and alarm, while at the same time registering our own emotional turmoil … that is, until the laugh track ensues.

"Lopper!" exclaims Jerry before scuttling back into the apartment; meanwhile a funky bass-guitar cue overtakes the musical tension, as Kramer's friend, "Slippery Pete," ambles past with a car battery and an electrical extension chord — he is looking for "holes" (a power source). This gag from an episode of *Seinfeld* (called *The Frogger*) offers a knowing acknowledgment of horror film-music conventions even as it satirizes those conventions for an altogether different generic purpose: television comedy. Despite the fact that the scene is set for laughs not scares, the pragmatic effect is still uncanny: we know, for instance, that Jerry is in no real danger of becoming the lopper's next victim (lest the series come to an abrupt and gruesome conclusion), yet the musical codes oblige us to consider otherwise. That is, if we are to apprehend Jerry's own folly (his laughable misrecognition of the situation at hand) and, hence, "get" the joke, we must be astute "readers" of horror movie music: we must

A Companion to the Horror Film, First Edition. Edited by Harry M. Benshoff.
© 2014 John Wiley & Sons, Inc. Published 2017 by John Wiley & Sons, Inc.

be competent enough to recognize (consciously or unconsciously) the grouping of atonal clusters and jarring musical dissonances as distinctly that: "horror music," and not simply some unnerving combination of oddly misplaced cues that sound rather inappropriate to the context of a prime-time network sitcom.

Put simply, the reference to horror film music is, in this context, less a matter of pure dramatic underscoring than overt cultural signage: that is to say, it appears indicative, on one hand, of a peculiar set of stylistic codes and conventions that guide our response to generic moments of fright, tension, and danger, while on the other, it seems to require little in the way of outside visual or narrative support to achieve those effects. Rather, horror's distinctive cinematic-musical codes are so clearly familiar that even when removed from their filmic context, these codes manage to evoke the same terrifying ideas and images usually associated with the genre. As K. J. Donnelly (2005: 89) writes: "music for horror films is often as distinctive and easily identifiable as the films themselves ... [it] is often very distinct from music used in other film genres." And hence horror film music epitomizes what Donnelly calls the "mental frameworks" of the genre (2005: 14), those *extra*-musical relations and textual structures that work to articulate different meanings and listener expectations through the power of cultural association. Taken together, these expectations reference certain ideals of what horror film music *should* sound like: ideals that work to set it apart as an identifiable type and also position it within the broader field of musical discourse. For this reason, horror film music cannot be reduced to certain kinds of formal features, for it is also a cultural discourse that encompasses certain kinds of listening habits.

Accordingly, this chapter will attempt to explain horror's musical conventions in light of their aesthetic and discursive components. Its aim is to describe not only the way horror films make use of different types of music for generically specific ends, but also how such music works to solicit generically specific listening practices by drawing upon prior audience knowledge and certain cultural associations. Along the way, different sections will make reference to a number of "exemplary" texts in the genre; however, these references will not take the form of a canonical history of "great" horror film scores and their composers. Rather, they will focus on the broader stylistic norms that govern horror scoring practice, the critical debates that underwrite these approaches, and the generic assumptions that motivate the use of various types of music in horror films. As I hope to make clear, the discursive dynamics of music and horror entails not only aesthetic strategies for shaping mood, atmosphere, and identification; it also involves routine audiovisual articulations that affect the codes, competencies, and affective terrains that organize our investments in and evaluations of specific musical styles and genres.

Aesthetics and Exemplars

One of the best ways of grasping the musical identity of the horror film is to consider it aesthetically, that is, in relation to the genre's distinctive textual strategies. Whereas

numerous scholars have argued, for instance, that horror's primary aesthetic function is to horrify—and this finds clear manifestation in the genre's penchant for
"startle effects" (Baird, 2000; Donnelly, 2005)—others have been less keen to identify
any essential qualities in the genre, arguing instead that the category is too stylistically and historically varied to permit such reductions. Peter Hutchings (2009), for
example, has sought to explain the distinctive character of the music in relation to
the "peculiarly protean" nature of the genre, suggesting that the latter has experienced numerous transformations over the years, and these "reinventions" coincide
with producers' attempts to maintain audience interest:

> Arguably as a by-product of this, the genre has throughout its history housed a variety
> of musical styles: including not just orchestral and choral scores but also electronic, jazz
> and rock-based music as well as some avant-garde experimentation. In certain respects
> this music has served the same sort of functions that music serves in other genres . . . .
> However, horror's moods, characters and effects often exhibit a generic specificity that
> seems to require not just particular types of music but also particular deployments of
> that music within films. It follows that trying to identify what is distinctive about music
> in horror films requires a sense not just of how horror music changes in relation to the
> genre's history but also the extent to which horror music deviates from the more general
> norms and conventions of film music. (2009, 221)

Accordingly, one of the central questions encompassing debates over horror movie
music concerns not just the different types of music used, but the way these different types get used to produce distinctive generic effects. In other words, how are the
technical codes of film music manipulated so as to bring about the appropriate kinds
of aesthetic response (terror, fright, dread, anxiety, and so forth)? One answer lies
with the listening strategies afforded by conventional *usage*, which is to say, the aesthetic possibilities to which music is put in horror films, and, as a part of this, the
generic expectations that are discursively maintained through such conventions. As
Hutchings suggests, horror music is not defined by some single, overarching stylistic
feature, but by recurrent patterns of deviation that permit "licensed transgressions"
(2004: 130) in film scoring practice.

One such transgression involves the classical scoring principle of inaudibility,
the idea that film music should be scarcely noticed (if noticed at all) in popular
cinema—that it should subordinate itself to dialog, visuals, and other primary
vehicles of cinematic storytelling (cf. Gorbman, 1987). To be sure, some of the
most iconic musical moments in the horror film have been distinguished in terms
that blatantly contradict this practice. Consider the shrieking violins in Alfred
Hitchcock's *Psycho* (1960): not only is this cue often cited as the most famous (if not
infamous) in cinematic history (Siegel, 2000; Sullivan, 2006; *Chicago Tribune*, 2012),
it is also credited with having "overturned the convention that music must remain
subliminally in the background" to be effective (Sullivan, 2006: 244). In other words,

Figure 11.1 "The Knife." *Psycho* (1960). Directed by Alfred Hitchcock. Produced by Shamley Productions.

when music is heard in *Psycho* it is not deployed like the more traditional scores of the classical era; rather the "slashing dissonances" draw attention to themselves in a way most other scoring techniques do not. As Jack Sullivan writes, "'The Knife' in *Psycho*'s shower scene has been ripping through our culture ever since [film composer] Bernard Herrmann secretly created it. This is the cinema's primal scream … it is a force of aggression as frightening as the flashing knife" (Sullivan, 2006: 243–244) (Figure 11.1).

To that end, other horror scores have been canonized according to the same aesthetic criteria underwriting *Psycho*'s patently "aggressive" music cues. Stephen Thrower (2011), for instance, defines the "art of horror movie music" in reference to soundtracks for *The Texas Chain Saw Massacre* (1974) and *Suspiria* (1977), two films that ostensibly "set out to disprove the argument that the best film music is that which you don't hear." And indeed the latter mobilizes a veritable grab bag of horror music tropes and conventions: everything from speed guitars to shrieking violins, spastic drums to synthesizer cues and sounds of the human voice (e.g., whispers, screams and wails). By contrast, more prominent horror films like *The Shining* (1980) and *The Exorcist* (1973) rely on preexisting art music to achieve their effects. Nonetheless, they have been analyzed (and distinguished) in terms that are directly opposed to incidental "background" music. As K. J. Donnelly (2005: 43) writes, "art music in *The Shining* seems to dominate the image … at times it seems this 'foreground' music is too dominant to occupy a role in the background." Accordingly, the use of avant-garde music in *The Shining* is described not only as a central convention of the genre but also as "an alien object to mainstream film … the antithesis of popular and mainstream film music" (Donnelly, 2005: 44).

In this way, scholars and critics maintain horror movie music as a legitimate aesthetic category, through reference to "anti-mainstream" exemplars. More specifically, horror's musical conventions are said to constitute a special category on two fronts: first, in terms of an aesthetic ideal of noticeability or "foreground music," a presence on par with the images that ultimately works as a "force of aggression" on listeners; and second, in terms of stylistic deviation from classical Hollywood norms, insofar as the latter traditionally emphasize romantic-symphonic idioms and accessible musical structures (i.e., tonal harmony and melodic themes). By contrast, the "music of terror" (as Sullivan labels it) ostensibly takes on its unsettling qualities via those aesthetic features that "deviate in some way from what would be [considered] appropriate elsewhere in cinema either because of the weirdness of the sounds or the incongruity of their use" (Hutchings, 2004: 146). In effect, these features bear the imprint of musical vocabularies deemed outside the purview of "normal" film scoring practice—features that, in turn, afford horror moviemakers and composers the opportunity to create strong emotional reactions such as fear, shock, and revulsion.

Affect and Emotion

But how, one might ask, do these affects play out in practice? How is it that horror music gets configured to manipulate our emotional perceptions of characters and events? And to what extent are these affects and manipulations bound up with stylistic trends in the genre? As already noted, horror music is largely designed to have an "assaultive character." But this can be achieved through a variety of means, including sheer volume (as in "noisy" outbursts that erupt on the soundtrack each time a monster appears or violence ensues), musical timbre (in characteristic instrumental sounds like "screeching" violins or "haunting" electronic synthesizers), or specific musical techniques, such as repetitious drones (tension built in and through sustained notes), clashing dissonances (unusual combinations of notes), and stingers (sudden musical blasts that coincide with moments of shock and revelation). Moreover, many of these techniques are readily familiar to most horror moviegoers, and accordingly they draw upon norms and expectations that ultimately reward aesthetic competency in the "language" of horror music. As Kay Dickinson (2007: 175) writes, the tacit "rules" of horror scoring often embody strategies deemed culturally appropriate for representing screen violence. As such, the "lion's share of horror soundtracks deploy instruments that sound as close as possible to humans in pain: instruments like violins and even the voice that linguistically tag alongside the victim and most pointedly provoke our empathy." To that end, horror's musical affects carry a decisive moral connotation as well, one that works to implicate certain sounds and structures with the overall "negative" implications of horrific action and events. As Dickinson continues:

Music itself can also function as a perpetrator of brutality, so much so that assertive sonic spasms are commonly known in the scoring trade as "stabs." Dissonance rears its head frequently, although it does so mainly to tell us that things aren't quite right, to provoke an unease, certainly, but one in keeping with our sense of both moral and musical right and wrong.

Thus, most horror films make use of the same affective strategies in order to convey a generally "suitable" tone that corresponds with our (culturally constructed) "sense of moral and musical right and wrong" — with what we imagine we *should* hear when confronted with violent imagery and horrific situations. Within this context, horror music is often considered as a signifier of emotion, a culturally specific approach to musical "mood" conventions.

However, whereas these conventions often derive from people's shared experience of horror movie soundtracks, they also become entangled in our broader cultural understanding of musical meanings and values; in other words, they help to constitute certain musical sounds and structures as more "horrific"-sounding than others, and thus they make up a series of listener expectations that become embedded in concrete practice. And yet (as we shall see below) the link between concrete practice and emotional impact remains an unresolved point of contention among film music scholars. For instance, horror music is often said to have direct physical effects — sending "shivers" down the spine, making audiences jump or raising neck hairs; however, the extent to which this process is attributable to basic sensory experience remains open to debate. While one theory suggests that horror music is somehow uniquely and purposefully of the body, for example, another proposes that it can be studied in terms of distinct musical traditions, which in turn represent particular affective-emotional states. In either case, the category of horror music is distinguished as a special type of movie music on the basis of its affective character — its ability to cue spectator responses through "startle effects" and/or emotional signification.

Horror Music as "Startle" Effect

For his part, Hutchings (2009: 222) observes the distinctive manifestation of startle effects in the genre's penchant for stinger chords, a scoring device "which for all intents and purposes entails the idea of music as noise." As he writes:

> Imagine a potential victim in a horror film foolishly straying into some shadowy location. The tension builds as the victim moves further away from safety and the audience increasingly anticipates that the killer will leap out from the shadows. And when the attack does occur, the shock or startle thereby provided will be accompanied by a discordant crash of music. It might be argued that in many cases startle effects of this kind are actually generated more by the sudden musical outburst than they are by the visuals themselves.

As a substantive part of the horror movie world, then, the stinger chord acts in a manner that is constitutive of that world rather than a mere stylistic appendage; it operates in conjunction with other components of the narrative (image, sound, and dialog), while also contributing strongly to the representation of horrific events. Thus, when we hear a discordant crash of music (as, say, when the killer emerges from the shadows), the cue is not merely reinforcing the dramatic aspects of a scene but forming them. It presumes the capacity to shape emotional perception and trigger sensory reactions, acting as a potent stimulus for the kinds of musical affects we typically associate with the genre.

For this reason, scholars like Donnelly have been inclined to assign the stinger chord a central place within the overall horror score, pointing out how "deep stinging blasts" are crucial to horror's "material effects." As Donnelly writes, there is something of a "physical aspect" to horror movie music, which arrives most clearly during moments of "deep stinging blasts." Here, stinger chords not only manage to underscore the horrific aspects of a scene but also "partially manifest the horror itself," causing audiences to respond directly to the "sonic aspect of the attack" (2005: 92–93). One example of this sort of "attack" might be the famous "head-in-a-hole" scene in *Jaws* (1975), where Matt Hooper (played by Richard Dreyfus) is investigating Ben Gardner's sunken boat. As he pulls a shark tooth from the boat's hull, Gardner's severed head suddenly appears in the hole, just as a sharp musical *sforzando* (a sudden blast of brass and string music, augmented by the sound of human screams) is engaged on the soundtrack. No doubt, the music works to convey Hooper's instantaneous shock and surprise; however it also works to prompt a similar affective reaction in the audience: eliciting a "jump scare," as it were, via our involuntary reflex to the suddenness of the cue itself (Figure 11.2).

In turn, this sort of reaction raises questions about the nature of horror music in general, and specifically whether generic conventions like the stinger chord are simply a matter of "conditioned reflex" or, alternatively, a consequence of "learned

Figure 11.2 "Head in a Hole." *Jaws* (1975). Directed by Steven Spielberg. Produced by Zanuck/Brown Productions and Universal Pictures.

triggers", which work by coding particular musical moods and affects. For his part, Donnelly argues that musical stingers need not be interpreted through learned associations and musical codes; rather, when considered "as absolutely fundamental blasts of sound ... stingers underline that there is a primary level that precedes learned responses, precedes complex mental cognition and responses" (2005: 95). In other words, so long as music proceeds loudly and abruptly, it triggers appropriate startle reflexes, and thus "the most primitive (and primal) musical moments in cinema are stingers, which engage with the audience on the most basic levels" (2005: 95). Grounding this assessment is a self-styled "behaviorist" model of cinematic experience, which suggests that musical horror acts in a more-or-less biologically determined way: much like the buzzer in Pavlov's famous dog experiments (Donnelly, 2005: 6), stinger chords are conceived as a means of directly stimulating audience reactions. The more basic the stimuli (the theory goes), the more powerful the effect. Thus, researchers working in this area tend to regard horror film music as a visceral experience: as some combination of physiology and aesthetics which is "measurable via heart rate, EEG (electro-encephalogram) readings of brain waves and respiration" (Donnelly, 2005: 95).

This "science of scary music" (Haggin, 2012) resonates with the practical assumptions of many horror film composers. For instance, Christopher Young, composer for films such as *A Nightmare on Elm Street 2* (1985), *Trick or Treat* (1986), *Hellraiser* (1987), *Species* (1995), *Urban Legend* (1998), *The Grudge* (2004), and *Drag Me to Hell* (2009), comments that horror movie music has to be "aggressive" and, above all, it "needs to generate a kneejerk reaction" that will "make the audience jump out of their seats" (quoted in Ellison, 2012). Similarly, Tyler Bates describes his music for *Dawn of the Dead* (2004) as something that "engages your senses on a very primal level" (quoted in Loring 2012); meanwhile John Frizzell, whose scoring credits include *I Still Know What You Did Last Summer* (1998), *Ghost Ship* (2002), and *The Following* (2013–2014), labors under the assumption that audience reactions to horror music are essentially hardwired, and that our sensory experience of the genre is relatively less "complex" when compared to other types of film. He explains:

> Fear is a very two-dimensional, rudimentary feeling—I don't even want to call it an emotion. It's a very primal, simple thing. You're afraid or you're not afraid. This creates the challenge of writing a good, scary score. If you're dealing with drama, you might have the complexity of someone who is elated but slightly anxious and maybe envious, but hopeful. Writing a cue that has those things in it is a lot easier than simply scoring fear. Fear is not a terribly complex feeling ... it's something very primal, deep down in our brain stem that evolved very early and doesn't have the complexities of higher emotional functions. And that's what makes a scary score hard. (quoted in Donnelly, 2005: 105–106)

Setting aside the possibility that a "good, scary score" might also encompass a wide variety of musical styles and genres, or that horror movies might be capable of generating a range of emotional responses beside fear (dread, anxiety, exhilaration, amusement), the question still remains as to whether musical horror is inherently frightening or if it derives its power from differences from other types of film (e.g., drama). To be sure, whereas composers like Frizzell and scholars like Donnelly assume that music works on listeners by dint of basic physiological processes, others prefer to view horror's musical affects as equally bound up with stylistic codes and conventions — narrative and stylistic patterns which have become ingrained over time as a function of our collective experience. Hutchings, for example, makes the point that horror movie stinger chords may well have something in common with "primal" emotions like fear, but these techniques do not exist within a cultural vacuum. Rather they are engaged in very specific dramatic and narrative contexts (i.e., horror films), and these contexts are in turn "dependent on audience expectations and competencies" (2009: 221). As a result, "audiences familiar with horror's musical conventions will know that the maximum threat occurs once any atmospheric music ceases and we are left with a menacing silence that could at any moment be breached by an ear-splitting stinger" (2009: 221). Thus, depending on our awareness of generic codes and conventions, stinger chords potentially activate a mishmash of aesthetic reactions that, not infrequently, derive their power from a knowing appreciation of "a good, scary score."

Consequently, it might be more useful to suggest that audiences make sense of musical horror on a number of different levels (emotional, cognitive, and physiological), and that these levels include an amalgamation of sensory triggers and culture-based responses (cf. Smith, 1999). Of course, this does not obviate the notion that horror movie music constitutes a truly distinctive aesthetic category — the cornerstone of some genuinely "unnerving" cinematic experience — but it does complicate the notion that musical horror works *primarily* in one of two directions: either through direct sensory stimulation (the arousal of "rudimentary feelings") or through a codified set of institutionalized practices. Returning to our example from *Jaws* then, we might realize that scenes like "head-in-a-hole," which clearly establish music's physiological dimensions, also draw upon an extended filmic tradition of composers using musical noise to fit conventionalized narrative patterns. To be sure, this is a tradition with deep roots in the genre, one that extends back at least as far as the 1940s, with Val Lewton's famous "bus sequence" in *Cat People* (1942), and continuing up through other renowned musical moments in horror from the canonical shower scene in *Psycho* to the routine musical "stabs" that accompany slasher killers Jason Voorhees or Michael Myers. Without a doubt, such music takes on a peculiar function as a sensory trigger in these contexts. However, it also operates not so much as an *essential* or defining feature of the genre (as in Donnelly's account) but as a stylistic trope that gets used intermittently, as befits certain generic traditions. Indeed, as Hutchings (2009: 222) points out, it is not until the 1950s that the startle effect "becomes a significant feature of horror cinema … [as it] was increasingly reliant on shock effects." In this context, stinger chords emerge as a central hallmark of the genre to the degree they become associated with certain *types* of horror films and horror film scoring practice.

Discourse and Tradition

Perhaps the best way of accounting for these practices, then, is by offering an abbreviated snapshot of horror's musical traditions, with an eye toward the various conventions routinely used to achieve horrific effects and associations. Whereas most histories, for example, tend to highlight the 1950s as the period when horror music begins to separate itself out as a distinctive category of film music, it is arguable that some of the earliest genre films — those associated with Universal's gothic cycle, for example — contain a fair amount of stylistic novelty and eclecticism. Franz Waxman's score to *Bride of Frankenstein* (1935), for instance, is often recognized as a landmark of horror film scoring, and includes both late romantic styles and leitmotif structures (in the Monster and Bride themes), as well as indices of early atonal music (Dr. Pretorius's theme). Furthermore, it also contains orchestral bursts (akin to the stinger chord) which underwrite moments of dramatic spectacle: Waxman recalls using a "big dissonant chord" at the end of the film in order to underscore the monster's destruction of the laboratory (quoted in Rosar, 1983: 411). Music here also proves to be a source of ironic commentary, as in the church bells that accompany the Bride's creation scene.

By and large, however, these practices remain the exception, not the rule, as most early horror films contain little (if any) musical accompaniment outside the opening titles. *Dracula* (1931) and *Frankenstein* (1931), for example, consist mostly of track music (as opposed to original scoring), which is made up of a repertoire of classical selections carried over from the concert hall (e.g., Wagner, Tchaikovsky, and Schubert). Likewise, scores for *The Mummy* (1932), *The Black Cat* (1934), and *The Invisible Ray* (1936) maintain relatively conservative scoring practices insofar as they draw on related conventions of romantic-symphonic music. As Randall Larson (1985: 30) sums up this early cycle: "these early Universal horror films share a similarity in musical approach, both stylistically (most favored a romantic, leitmotif style) and with regard to the repetition of the same library tracks and classical material (such as Tchaikovsky's *Swan Lake*)." As a result, there is arguably "little about the music itself, or the use of music within these films, which separates it out from music elsewhere in Hollywood" (Hutchings, 2004: 142); as such, many of these scores were subsequently recycled for films associated with other genres.

Nonetheless, as an early model of horror scoring, these films contain a fair amount of stylistic materials now associated with "scary" music (dissonance, chromatic chords, extensive use of the pipe organ), and so provide an early glimpse into what was (and indeed still is) considered musically horrific. Likewise, Roy Webb's original scores for RKO (and Val Lewton) during the 1940s supply a fairly standard model of "eerie" mood music, one geared more toward atmosphere and suspense rather than impulsive moments of shock. Films like *Cat People* (1942), *The Seventh Victim* (1943), and *I Walked with a Zombie* (1943) adhere to classic norms of "unheard melodies" (Gorbman, 1987) — restrained narrative cueing and subtle melodic themes—which are inflected by harmonic dissonance to punctuate sustained suspense sequences. This practice parallels the ways in which critics have discussed Lewton's films more generally, as "artful" applications of atmospheric *mise-en-scene* and sound effects (Jancovich, 2012; Hutchings, 2004: 134–140). As one reviewer noted of the score for *Cat People*: "Roy Webb's music conveys an undercurrent of menace without becoming obtrusive, adding immeasurably to the gathering atmosphere of dread" (quoted in Larson, 1985: 45). In these terms, Webb's scores are set apart from subsequent trends in the genre, which tend to feature startle effects more blatantly.

By contrast, Hammer horror films of the 1950s and 1960s are notable for incorporating startle effects as the central aspect of their overall scores—this owing largely to the work of studio composer James Bernard, who scored films such as *The Curse of Frankenstein* (1957), [*Horror of*] *Dracula* (1958), and *The Plague of the Zombies* (1966). Bernard's work tended to rely on techniques that exploit what Donnelly (2005: 99) calls music's potential for "instant effect," utilizing a variety of "scare tactics" (e.g., brass stingers, crash chords, string harmonics, and percussion taps) noted for their loud, piercing qualities. Bernard was also famous for using his scores to play with the title of a given film as well, and so one hears the idiosyncratic three-note horn motif blasting "DRA-cu-laaa!" in Hammer's many *Dracula* films. The technique prefigures a wide-ranging strategy of studio composers utilizing loud brass and percussion instruments as aural punctuation to previously unseen levels of Technicolor gore. As Hammer musical director Philip Martell described this approach in 1976:

> there is a pattern. As long as it's horror you have to make frightening sounds, and they do come in a pattern . . . . The general practice is to make a great deal of noise on your titles and give everybody the impression that this is a terrifying and very important film. But it is true that on horrors as a rule you need a lot of brass … you've got to make a lot of noise to terrify the audience. (quoted in Buscombe, 1976: 101)

To be sure, such assumptions may hardly come as a surprise to horror film audiences; however, they also suggest a broader discourse for *conceptualizing* the experience of horror music—that is, the type of music used to activate particular sorts of generic listening strategies. Here, the idea of "horrors as a rule" entails a set of enculturated associations regarding not only the kind of musical devices best suited to the genre (a lot of brass, a great deal of noise), but also a series of shared cultural expectations. Undoubtedly these expectations derive significance from musical traditions outside the cinema (Donnelly, 2005: 96–97), but it is also arguable that the suppositions people bring to such music achieve their most stable articulation in proximity to the horror film, wherein putatively "frightening" sounds take on clear visual/thematic associations and the value of aesthetic norms. As evidenced above, these norms operate as part of a codified set of practices that production personnel (like Martell) and horror composers bring to bear on horror film-music aesthetics. However, whereas such assumptions routinely manifest in a more practical understanding of the genre, they also work to construct an implicit discursive framework for *thinking about* the music. In other words, they indicate the extent to which the generic coding of musical moods and affects (e.g., horror, fear, and anxiety) belies its own set of normative expectations about stylistic practice.

Horror and the Musical Avant-Garde

One such practice entails the repeated association of dissonant or "atonal" music with horror films of the post-war era. Within this context, horror composers grow increasingly reliant on "awkward and jarring musical sounds and combinations of notes" — a reliance that has since developed into "one of the most characteristic and most straightforward aspects of horror film music" (Hutchings, 2004: 146): namely a penchant for "weird" styles and structures associated with musical avant-gardism. As genre composer Les Baxter states: "With a horror score … the notes can be extremely strange. That gives you a lot of leeway. You can be as far-out or as weird as you want to musically" (quoted in Larson, 1985: 1). And certainly some of the most "far-out" scores have been for horror films: everything from the strange "electronic tonalities" heard in 1950s monster movies to the "slashing dissonances" that permeate horror film music post-*Psycho*, from the blending of popular idioms and synthesized scores in works by Ennio Morricone and John Carpenter to the increasing reliance on atonal clusters and ambient, industrial-type noise in contemporary horror films.

In all, these trends have allowed for considerable experimentation in scoring practice, affording composers the somewhat rare pop-culture entry point for avant-garde techniques that (at one time, anyway) seemed outside the stylistic purview of mainstream film music. At the same time, the use of musical avant-gardism in horror cinema serves particular representational functions as well: not the least of which being a depiction of the world "out of kilter" (Donnelly, 2005: 51). As music theorists David Neumeyer and James Buhler (2001) point out, this practice takes on a particularly unsettling character in the context of tonality, the schema that forms the basis of most popular and mainstream film music and charts a "closed system" of major and minor modes and hierarchical pitch relations. By contrast, music in the horror film presents genre composers with fewer restrictions on musical organization, due in no small part to horror's characteristic emphasis on monstrosity, otherness, abnormality, and dystopia. As Neumeyer and Buhler put it, music in horror "often embodies a kind of dystopian projection, a means of figuring the unintended consequences of the system, which take musical shape as tonality gone awry to the point of incomprehension" (2001: 23).

It follows, then, that the main manifestation of this sort of musical (and metaphorical) breakdown is atonality, or music that, in the broadest sense, lacks a tonal center—music that invariably portrays "the dissolution of … [normal, tonal] order through its own logic" (David Neumeyer and James Buhler (2001)). In all those 1950s SF/horror monster movies, for instance, wherein prehistoric beasts are uncovered amidst far away lands, the narrative movement away from ordinary reality is usually met with shrill atonal effects: a flat or sharp in the wrong place, or harsh discordant themes whenever horrific elements arise. Thus, in *Creature from the Black Lagoon* (1954) a variety of minor melodic passages are used to convey the tranquility of the lost lagoon, only to be ritualistically torn asunder by dissonant brass cues and clattering cymbals whenever the Creature attacks. While not atonal in the strictest sense, the score nonetheless effectively hinges on the conspicuous disruption of tonality, with jarring sounds and structures used to "signify not only the emergence of the Creature into the unknown but also the cataclysmic collapse of harmonious existence up until that point" (Brophy, 1998: para 5).

Similarly, many contemporaneous SF/monster movie scores also utilized electronic sound manipulation (formerly an avant-garde enterprise) to achieve their effects. *The Thing From Another World* (1951) and *It Came From Outer Space* (1953), for example, indicate the presence of alien beings through the spacey, otherworldly sounds of the theremin, an electronic instrument whose tremulous pitch and volume are controlled by a performer's hand movements through radio waves. Equally, monster movies like *Them!* (1954) and *Tarantula* (1955) blend electronically produced sound effects with orchestral music to suggest the beastly horrors of the atomic age; in doing so these (and other) "creature features" of the 1950s call upon avant-garde timbres (via electronic instrumentation) to underscore the "dystopian projections" of modern scientific America.

In turn, these scores begin to take on the character of full-fledged musical discourse, furnishing wider cultural associations between unconventional timbres and distinctly modern (some would say, paranoid) threats posed by "other" worlds. In short, they adopt fairly irregular practices for relatively generic purposes, and thus tend to maintain clear ideological distinctions: on one hand they help to underline generic representations of monstrosity and abnormality, while on the other they also work to reiterate the peculiar status of the music itself as something altogether "different," something that disrupts "harmonious" existence and thus bears a direct kinship to the horror movie monster. As film/music scholar Philip Brophy (1998: para 2–3) writes, atonality in the film score signifies "the Other: the monstrous, the grotesque, the aberrant." The "birth of the monstrous" in 1950s horror films reflects a situation in which "pastel smears of classical music [are reserved] for the correctly socialized human; dark sludges of avant-garde music [are reserved] for the deviant being." Indeed, the resulting antagonism seems to echo the fracas caused by the horror movie monster: unleashed to arouse fear and anxiety, the threat of "deviant" music (and its monstrous visualization) is mostly—if arbitrarily—contained once the end credits roll.

Thus, many post-1950s Gothic and supernatural horror movies utilize dissonance, atonality, and unusual configurations of instruments to signify all sorts of anomalous, paranormal activity. *Black Sunday* (1960) and *The Haunting* (1963), for example, make use of atonal clusters, which operate in sharp contrast to tonal music and thus provide antagonistic symbols for supernatural evil and good (respectively). Likewise, *The Amityville Horror* (1979) and *Poltergeist* (1982) employ various thematic materials ranging from soft-sounding lullabies to atonal outbursts. In *Poltergeist*, which earned composer Jerry Goldsmith an Oscar nomination, the score follows a clear trajectory from lyrical themes (representing Carol Anne and the Freeling family) to more frightful, quasi-religious music (for depictions of "the light" and the souls caught between worlds). Eventually the score culminates in a series of jagged atonal orchestral strikes (in low registers) and synthetic sound effects (involving the rub rod, slide whistle, musical saw, resin drum, and other percussive sounds) all of which are used to connote various aspects of "the other side" and "the beast." In this way, Goldsmith's score stages a thematic confrontation between "light" and "dark," which conveys the gradual collapse of musical and metaphorical cohesion (Figure 11.3).

By the same token, contemporary (or near contemporary) music in the horror film draws upon a substantial vein of musical modernism to evoke analogous textual responses. Discordant music (broadly construed) can result in equally discordant

Figure 11.3 "Night of the Beast." *Poltergeist* (1982). Directed by Tobe Hooper. Produced by Metro-Goldwyn-Mayer (MGM) and SLM Production Group.

generic effects, as in the famous shower scene in *Psycho*, which exploits a handful of modernist strategies (dissonant harmonies, erratic rhythms, high-pitch timbres) for invoking terror; many post-*Psycho* films including Brian De Palma's *Carrie* (1976), Sam Raimi's *The Evil Dead* (1981), and Sean Cunningham's *Friday the 13th* (1980) have relied on the same "string stab" strategy. By contrast, Benjamin Frankel's twelve-tone serial composition for *The Curse of the Werewolf* (1961) develops a more methodical approach to symphonic modernism, whereas Wayne Bell's atonal score for *The Texas Chain Saw Massacre* (1974) operates more in the style of *musique concrète*: an avant-garde practice that electronically distorts everyday, nonmusical sounds (e.g., chainsaws, chicken clucks, seed-shakers, and heart beats) to create the impression of an unconscionable musical din. Alternatively, films in the tradition of *Night of the Living Dead* (1968), *Sisters* (1973), and *It's Alive* (1974) incorporate synthesized musical timbres in a manner reminiscent of 1950s monster movies. However, given the clear shift of emphasis in these later, so-called modern horror films—where the roots of monstrosity stem not from "external" realms but familial, private, and "internal" disorders (madness, psychosis, sadistic desires)—the use of synthetic sounds both correlates to and augments altogether different thematic purposes.

Contrast this with the more familiar work by director-composer John Carpenter, whose relatively unembellished, melodic synthesizer scores for *Halloween* (1978) and *The Fog* (1980) derive more from minimalist art music than twentieth-century modernism (Donnelly, 2005: 102). As a number of critics point out, Carpenter's music is generally devoid of symphonic touches; however, the repetitious character of the music builds on a fairly limited selection of standard musical devices (e.g., droning chords and weird tonalities, including thorny percussive musical stingers) that ultimately work to create a sense of tension and release. Perhaps for this reason, droning synthesizers and electronic effects became a viable model of horror film scoring post-*Halloween*, inspiring a host of imitators seeking to build upon Carpenter's tense build-up and climax structure and keyboard aesthetic [some examples include *Phantasm* (1979), *The Boogey Man* (1980), *Maniac* (1980), *Graduation Day* (1981), and *Slumber Party Massacre* (1982)] (cf. Larson, 1985: 280–285; Donnelly, 2005: 102). Conversely, a host of horror soundtracks during the 1980s mingled electronics and orchestral music, layering traditional instrumentation alongside generally "horrendous" synthesizer sounds. For example, Howard Shore's music for *Scanners* (1981) and *Videodrome* (1983) grows increasingly electronic as the narratives become more involved in bizarre, psychic occurrences. Alternatively, Ennio Morricone's music for Carpenter's *The Thing* (1982) upholds a more traditional association between synthesized sound and extra-terrestrial Otherness.

There are also those films that compile avant-garde music from preexisting sources (e.g., *The Exorcist*, *The Shining*), as well as those which blend pop idioms and modernist effects. The latter include Morricone's unique intermingling of modern jazz, orchestral music, and psychedelic rock in giallo-thrillers like *The Bird with the Crystal Plumage* (1970) and *A Lizard in a Woman's Skin* (1971); Donald Rubinstein's self-styled "Baroque-jazz" scoring for George Romero's *Martin* (1976); David Hess's blend of folk rock and country bluegrass in Wes Craven's *Last House on the Left* (1972); and the various progressive rock-style scores written and performed by Goblin for Dario Argento's films *Profondo Rosso* [also known as *Deep Red* (1975)], *Suspiria*, and *Tenebre* (1982). Indeed the latter approach foreshadows a trend that has become a defining feature of the genre in its engagement with popular music in subsequent years: namely, a well-worn association with hard rock and heavy metal, which operates as a "lifestyle referent" for horror's presumed target audience (Hutchings, 2009: 227; Tompkins, 2009). The combination of pop idioms and modernist effects shares a similar musico-representational strategy with that of the modernist scores discussed above: these scores also rely on a selective "othering" of popular styles and genres (modern jazz, folk rock, heavy metal) which have not featured much (if at all) in other types of films. As a result, they enlist such music as a generic indicator of difference, while reinforcing the notion that it remains at odds with more "normal" musical practice.

Conclusion: Horror Films as Music Pedagogy

What is perhaps most important about this mélange of musical horror and avant-garde and popular styles, then, is not only how it structures our affective and cognitive experience, but also how it impacts upon the reception of such music. These mixtures raise questions about the cultural value of such music, and why it is that certain styles can be said to "work" better than others, or how it is that certain musical strategies just seem to "fit" with horrific situations of violence and monstrosity. No doubt these questions belie common-sense attitudes about the aesthetic construction of horror films (and the various procedures mobilized by film composers); however, they also impact the consumption of horror movies (and the various listening strategies and expectations solicited from horror audiences). As composer Howard Shore once noted of his score for *The Brood* (1979): "when I thought 'horror movie,' I thought 'avant-garde' … I just used any kind of technique I could think of! There's some Bartók in it, some Stravinksy. Parts of it are twelve-tone. It's a pretty strange score" (quoted in Brown, 1994: 337). In the same way, scholars like Donnelly admit to gaining knowledge of Bartók's *Music for Strings, Percussion and Celesta* via *The Shining*. He writes: "Consequently, when I listen to sections of the piece, I think of the film. Moreover, when I listen to sections of the piece that are not in the film, I still associate them with the film" (2005: 37). Each of these examples, then, illustrates the degree to which horror's penchant for musically avant-garde styles inevitably influences the reception of such music, just as the heavy-handed use of atonality and dissonance reciprocally influence the reception of horror movies.

This is not to suggest that musically avant-garde styles are somehow "co-opted" or degraded as a result of their incorporation within horror cinema—although this claim has been made many times over. Rather it is to suggest that such styles are recodified within the musical language of horror film as a popular field of discourse. Thus, while interactions between horror and the musical avant-garde inevitably alter the reception of such music, this does not mean (as some would have it) the "cultural downfall" of high art, as if "pressing [avant-garde musical styles] into clichés for all manner of manifestations of the 'Other'" somehow cheapens the authentic cultural value of otherwise "difficult" music (Barham, 2009: 139; cf. Donnelly, 2005: 43). Instead, one might suggest that horror's extra-musical associations entail a modification, or "fine-tuning" of avant-garde practices, which inevitably informs the way audiences and practitioners alike conceptualize the genre's music.

As a result, music in horror can serve broadly pedagogical functions, functions that have less to do with expressing Otherness or horrific emotions than with evoking certain types of listener competency. As Kay Dickinson (2007) points out, music in horror, particularly in the tradition of *Psycho*, has become so deeply ingrained in our cultural experience that it comes to inform not only the way we conceive of such music but also how we understand the interaction between the "right" kinds of music and the "right" kinds of aesthetic effects. In the same vein, Stan Link (2004) has suggested that "late romantic and early modernist styles" represent the most sustained model for depictions of psychopathology in horror film; they are, in effect, "what we imagine we should hear when music is brought into explicit connection with deeply unhinged personalities and actions" (2004: 1). As a result, these styles have become, over time, the proverbial way of "suturing" horror audiences to the perceived emotions of a scene. Not only do they give the impression of expressing the inner feelings of characters (the victim's fear, the killer's rage), but they also guide the affective involvement of spectators, directing us toward the "appropriate" generic emotions.

Of course, modernism is not the only model for scoring horror films, and indeed, as Link's essay makes clear, even the most superficial, seemingly "anempathetic" sorts of music (tonal or otherwise) can become utterly terrifying when articulated to generic representations of psychopathology, torture, and violence. It follows that in addition to its characteristically visual, dramatic, and storytelling functions, the horror film is also a potent musical medium, for it musters the capacity to serve as both a system of representation *and* a form of musical pedagogy: a medium with the power to construct and naturalize a particular framework for engaging in music culture. Accordingly, different musical forms may be called upon to mark fear, otherness, and/or monstrosity, but these articulations engender their own musical aesthetics—a way of conceptualizing the cultural value of "horror music," which inevitably bleeds out from the screen to enter into dialog with other traditions. In this sense, the stability of horror's musical conventions implicates not only certain types of music but also certain types of listening habits and responses. To the extent these responses impact people's knowledge and expectations of the genre, the horror film might itself be considered a distinctive way of embodying musical experience, with the overall effect of sanctioning certain types of listener associations.

References

Baird, R. (2000) The startle effect: implications for spectator cognition and media theory. *Film Quarterly*, **53** (3), 12–24.

Barham, J. (2009) Incorporating monsters: music as context, characterization and construction in Kubrick's *The Shining*, in *Terror Tracks: Music, Sound and Horror Cinema* (ed. P. Hayward), Equinox, London, pp. 137–170.

Brophy, P. (1998) Picturing Atonality: the Birth of The Monstrous, http://www.philipbrophy.com/projects/scrthst/AcademyPeril.html (accessed 8 February 2013).

Brown, R. (1994) *Overtones and Undertones: Reading Film Music*, University of California Press, Berkley.

Buscombe, E. (1976) *Making Legend of the Werewolf*, BFI Publishing, London.

Chicago Tribune (2012) 10 scariest Movie Soundtracks Ever, http://www.chicagotribune.com/entertainment/movies/chi-20121024-movie-scary-soundtracks-pictures,0,4566974.photogallery (accessed 10 March 2013).

Dickinson, K. (2007) Troubling synthesis: the horrific sights and incompatible sounds of video nasties, in *Sleaze Artists: Cinema at the Margins of Taste, Style, and Politics* (ed. J. Sconce), Duke University Press, Durham, NC, pp. 167–188.

Donnelly, K.J. (2005) *The Spectre of Sound: Music in Film and Television*, BFI Publishing, London.

Ellison, V. (2012) Composer Christopher Young: 'Horror Film Is the Idiot Bastard Son of Hollywood' (Q & A), *The Hollywood Reporter.com*, http://www.hollywoodreporter.com/heat-vision/composer-christopher-young-horror-film-379342 (accessed 23 March 2013).

Gorbman, C. (1987) *Unheard Melodies: Narrative Film Music*, Indiana University Press, Bloomington.

Haggin, P. (2012) Why Is Scary Music Scary? Here's the Science, *TIME.com*, http://newsfeed.time.com/2012/06/19/why-is-scary-music-scary-heres-the-science/ (accessed 29 January 2013).

Hutchings, P. (2004) *The Horror Film*, Pearson, London.

Hutchings, P. (2009) Horror: music of the night: horror's soundtracks, in *Sound and Music in Film and Visual Media: An Overview* (ed. G. Harper), Continuum, New York, pp. 219–229.

Jancovich, M. (2012) Relocating Lewton: cultural distinctions, critical reception, and the Val Lewton horror films. *Journal of Film and Video*, **64** (3), 21–37.

Larson, R. (1985) *Musique Fantasique: A Survey of Film Music in the Fantastic Cinema*, Scarecrow Press, London.

Link, S. (2004) Sympathy with the devil: music of the psycho post-*Psycho*. *Screen*, **45** (1), 1–20.

Loring, A. (2012) Talking Scary Scores, Getting Away with Murder, and All Hallows Eve with Horror Composer, Tyler Bates, *Filmschoolrejects.com*, http://www.filmschoolrejects.com/features/interview-tyler-bates-alori.php (accessed 23 March 2013).

Neumeyer, D. and Buhler, J. (2001) Analytical and interpretive approaches to film music (I): analysing the music, in *Film Music: Critical Approaches* (ed. K.J. Donnelly), Continuum, New York, pp. 16–38.

Rosar, W. (1983) Music for the monsters: universal pictures' horror film scores of the thirties. *The Quarterly Journal of the Library of Congress*, **40** (4), 390–421.

Siegel, R. (2000) Bernard Herrmann's Score to *Psycho*, NPR.org, http://www.npr.org /2000/10/30/1113215/bernard-herrmanns-score-to-psycho (accessed 3 March 2013).

Smith, J. (1999) Movie music as moving music: emotion, cognition, and the film score, in *Passionate Views: Film, Cognition, and Emotion* (eds C. Plantinga and G. Smith), John Hopkins University Press, Baltimore, MD, pp. 146–67.

Sullivan, J. (2006) *Hitchcock's Music*, Yale University Press, New Haven, CT.

Thrower, S. (2011) From Goblin to Morricone: the Art of Horror Movie Music, http://www .guardian.co.uk/film/2011/aug/18/horror-film-movie-music (accessed 8 January 2013).

Tompkins, J. (2009) What's the deal with the soundtrack album: metal music and the customized aesthetics of contemporary horror. *Cinema Journal*, **49** (1), 65–81.

Part III

A History of the (Western) Horror Film

12

Horror Before "The Horror Film"

Harry M. Benshoff

This chapter explores some of the antecedents of what eventually became known as the classical Hollywood horror film. Conventional wisdom and most histories of the genre mark its start with the release of *Dracula* in 1931. That film's success and the subsequent reiteration of its formula over the next several years within the Hollywood studio system—especially at Universal Studios—established generic criteria that have affected horror filmmaking across the decades and around the globe. And while those developments are reflected in various other chapters within this volume, this particular chapter surveys the roots of the classical Hollywood horror film from within preceding texts of Western horror, from various nations as well as various genres. Productively, historian David J. Skal (2001) has argued that the American horror film primarily arises from two divergent sources: gothic literary traditions in eighteenth and nineteenth century Europe, and the rise of the carnival or freak show during those same epochs. Arguably those two trends are still at work in the genre today, from those films that recall or rewrite classic Gothic traditions [*Gothika* (2003), *Splice* (2009), *The Woman in Black* (2012)] to those concerned primarily with shocking their viewers with ghastly deaths or grotesque situations [*Final Destination* (2000), *Hostel* (2005), *The Human Centipede* (2009)]. Of course, gothic narratives and freakish attractions are deeply intertwined within the genre: *The Human Centipede* may be notorious for its off-putting subject matter, but where would its mad scientist be if not for Dr. Frankenstein and his mad scheme to usurp and pervert the power of creation?

Elaborating on his model, Skal further suggests that the American horror film is fueled by four primary icons: "Dracula, the human vampire; the composite, walking-dead creation of Frankenstein; the werewolfish duality of Dr. Jekyll and Mr. Hyde; and perhaps most disturbing, the freak from a nightmare sideshow"

(Skal, 2001:19). And while those icons are certainly among the best known, one might also wish to add ghosts, ghouls, zombies, phantoms, creatures, serial killers, witches, and even giant sharks to the list. The history of Western horror (as is the history of the Western horror film) is nothing if not prolific and diverse. In addition to the Gothic classics and the carnival's sideshow, horror has been figured for centuries across media as diverse as oil painting (Fuseli's *The Nightmare*, Munch's *The Scream*), sketches and wood cuts (by Goya and Hogarth among others), folk tales, poetry, theater, pulp fiction, religious texts, and even travelogs (Twitchell, Frayling, and Kendrick). Horror has been inspired by nightmares and "real life" atrocities, and fueled by creative imaginations and the influence of mind-altering drugs. Blood, sex, and death bookend and comprise the human experience as well as Western horror. Focusing primarily on literary and cinematic precursors, this chapter explores some of the various ways Western horror was figured before the development of "The Horror Film."

Literary Precursors to the Classical Hollywood Horror Film

In the introduction to his book *Dreadful Pleasures*, James B. Twitchell (1985: 3–7) reports that monsters and other fantastic creatures appear in the cave drawings of the earliest human civilizations, arguing, as many critics do, that horror is somehow a primeval and essential aspect of the human experience. The iconography (if not the narrative structure or effect) of the classical Hollywood horror film is more often traced back to ancient Greek mythology and theater (Clarens, du Coudray, and Frayling). Greek gods such as Zeus, Hera, and Poseidon were fantastic enough in their own right, interacting with the natural world and a panoply of animistic spirits. Greek myths also contain creatures we today might describe as more forthrightly monstrous, such as giants, sea serpents, and a host of human–animal hybrids including the Minotaur (man-bull), the Centaurs (human-horses), and the Harpies (women-birds). Chantal Bourgault du Coudray (2006: 12) notes that human-wolf transformations appear in the Greek classics *Metamorphoses* and *Satyricon*. However, these monsters' narrative function was usually a bit different from those found in more contemporary horror genres: ancient Greek monsters were less likely to horrify *per se* and were more likely to be used for other narrative purposes. For example, in *Metamorphoses*, Zeus punishes the King of Arcadia for serving a meal of human flesh by transforming him into a wolf. In a great many other Greek myths, monstrous beasts serve as unique obstacles for stalwart Greek heroes to overcome. Thus the Cyclops Polyphemus may have captured and threatened Odysseus and his men, but his narrative function was primarily to allow Odysseus to demonstrate his heroism. Killing the Gorgon Medusa was just another heroic task for Perseus. Similarly, Scylla and Charybdis are thought to be mythic manifestations of natural phenomena (rocky shores and a whirlpool, respectively) who tested

Greek sailors from Odysseus to Jason and the Argonauts. Greek mythology also gives us the story of Prometheus, "the titan who," according to certain versions, stole heavenly fire from the gods to infuse life into his own creation (Clarens, 1967: 12). Centuries later, Mary Shelley would subtitle her famous gothic novel *Frankenstein* "The Modern Prometheus," even as the dream of man creating artificial life (animating a "homunculus") was an obsession of alchemists throughout the Middle Ages.

Ancient Greek culture gave rise to a few other creatures that seem similar to those found in later Western folklore and Gothic literature, such as the Lamia, the incubus, and the succubus. All were somewhat sexualized figures who stole into sleeping bedchambers to feed upon unsuspecting victims, sometimes having intercourse with their victims while draining them of their vital essences. The Lamia is a demon associated with children, while an incubus is a male spirit who preys upon women, and the succubus is his female counterpart who preys upon men. Arguably, early Greek and Roman myths developed into folkloric traditions and superstitions all over Europe throughout the Middle Ages. Concepts such as the Lamia persisted within Greek culture, while the Wurdalak came to describe a kind of Russian vampire. Eastern European myths of werewolves and vampires became the grist for Western Europe's fascination for allegedly true tales of terror from far-off places, and thus monsters made their appearance in a new literary genre, the travelog (Frayling, 1991: 16–36).

The rise of Christianity provided a new roster of monstrous forces out to wreak havoc upon unsuspecting Europeans: chiefly the Devil himself, various assorted minions and minor demons, and the figure of the witch. Werewolves and vampires now became associated with corrupted priests and "theological confusion" (Frayling: 25–26). Importantly, Christianity's Manichean system of absolute good versus absolute evil dovetails neatly into the usual narrative pattern of much classical and contemporary Western horror. Thus, while Greek myths featured monstrous or magical figures which may or may not have worked to do evil, within the Christian cosmology monsters like demons and witches became the irrevocable Other to Holy Christian dogma. (National cultures steeped in religious traditions not founded on a binary opposition between good and evil—such as Shinto or Buddhism—are more like ancient Greek culture in that their fantastic figures are just as likely to be playful or even helpful than solely monstrous and destructive.) Surely, Christian belief systems gave rise to horrific real world terrors: the torture and murder of those suspected to be in league with the devil, men and especially women branded as witches. Slowly, however, as the Middle Ages and the Renaissance gave way to the Age of Enlightenment (circa 1700), science, logic, and philosophy worked to bring Europe out of the Dark Ages. Thinkers, writers, and scientists such as Locke, Spinoza, Voltaire, and Newton battled superstition, folklore, religious abuse, and intolerance. The new European was expected to set aside his (and by implication her) ignorance in favor of intellect, logic, and rational thought.

Cultural movements inevitably seem to give rise to counter-movements, and thus the rise of Romanticism and especially Gothicism in literature and the arts during the late eighteenth and nineteenth centuries has been theorized as a response or backlash to the Age of Enlightenment. As Noel Carroll has succinctly put it, "the Enlightenment supplied the horror novel with the norm of nature needed to produce the right kind of monster" (Carroll, 1990: 57). Broadly put, Romantic artists turned away from logic and toward emotion and sensation. Gothic writers steeped themselves in the architecture of previous centuries, reveling in the antique, uncanny, and supernatural elements that Gothic architecture seemed to suggest. While ghost stories became prevalent on the continent, among the first developments in this shift in England was the work of the so-called Graveyard Poets. The Graveyard Poets (including William Cowper, William Parnell, Oliver Goldsmith, and Thomas Gray) wrote works that explored themes of death, decay, and mortality. Thomas Gray's "Elegy Written in a Country Churchyard" (1751) is among the most well known of these pieces, famous for its moody evocation of a moldering graveyard and its philosophical musings about death and remembrance. Literary historians often position the Graveyard Poets as important precursors to the Gothic novel, and the Gothic movement in general. In fact, Graveyard Poet Thomas Gray was a close friend of Horace Walpole, the man credited with "inventing" the Gothic as a literary (as opposed to architectural) form.

Walpole's *The Castle of Otranto* (1764) establishes many of the Gothic novel's central iconographic and thematic conceits. First is its alleged (faux) authorship, a trope that works to mediate or question the tale's veracity (as well as place it within a Gothic and foreign past): Walpole claims that his book is a translation "from the Original Italian of Onuphirio Muralto." Second is the book's central Gothic castle, a space that mirrors the protagonist's twisted and shadowy psyche (herein the titular castle and its owner, Manfred). Strange supernatural goings-on, such as a gigantic helmet that mysteriously crushes Manfred's son, commingle with all sorts of family melodrama including murder, deceit, and unwanted sexual advances made toward virginal heroines. As later critics of the form have suggested, the Gothic is often all about diseased or haunted domestic spaces, a sort of supernatural queering of heteronormative expectations and rituals (Haggerty, 2006). In that light it is important to note that Walpole was himself something of a bachelor dandy (as a homosexual or queer man of the era might have been called) who exhibited camp taste and behavior in his personal life as well as in his writings (Bleiler, 1966: vii–x; Sedgwick, 1985: 91–92; Kendrick, 1991: 38–42). Most famously, he refashioned his family's ancestral home Strawberry Hill into an imitation Gothic castle and referred to himself the "The Abbot of Strawberry." [Recently this architectural experiment was renovated and reopened to the public (Morris, 2011).]

Following *The Castle of Otranto*, other novels in the Gothic tradition soon appeared. Among the more famous are *Vathek* (1786), a sort of Orientalist nightmare written by William Beckford. Ann Radcliffe's *The Mysteries of Udolpho* was published in 1794, and her novel *The Italian* followed in 1797, establishing a narrative template for what many critics would later call the Female Gothic, wherein a young ingénue must deal with the dark mysteries and even darker desires of a domineering patriarch. In the United States, Charles Brockden Brown brought a New World sensibility to the Gothic novel in books such as *Wieland* (1798) and *Edgar Huntley* (1799). One of the more pulpy and popular of the era's Gothic novels was Matthew G. Lewis's *The Monk* (1796). In addition to incest, rape, murder, crumbling monasteries, and shadowy passageways, the book features a murderous monk named Ambrosio and a transsexual demon named Matilda. By the early 1800s, the gothic was ripe for multiple knockoffs and parodies such as T. J. Horsley Curties's *The Monk of Udoplho* (1807) and Jane Austen's *Northanger Abbey*, written in 1799 but not published until 1817. It was during this period that the werewolf made his first official *fictional* appearance, in Charles Maturin's 1824 Gothic novel *The Albigenses* (du Coudray, 2006: 14).

However, it was during a summer retreat at the Villa Diodati on Lake Geneva in 1816 that two works were conceived that would have an even greater impact on the horror film genre. The Villa Diodati was the residence of romantic poet and ladies man Lord Byron, and that year his guests included fellow romantic poet Percy Bysshe Shelley, Shelley's future wife Mary Godwin, Mary's stepsister Claire Clairmont (who was also Byron's lover), and Byron's physician John Polidori. As the well-known historical anecdote is told, the group amused themselves on rainy nights by reading German ghost stories popular at the time, and then decided to try writing their own. Perhaps ironically, the two important works that emerged from this challenge were not written by the renowned poets, but by Polidori and the 16-year-old Mary Godwin, soon be known as Mary Wollstonecraft Shelley. Her *Frankenstein* was published in 1818 and became a popular success, especially as multiple stage versions brought it to life in the ensuing decades (and centuries). A tale of a doctor usurping the powers of God and fashioning—and then abandoning—his own man-made man, *Frankenstein* has been hailed as an important feminist tract, a critique of the Enlightenment, and as one of the most important milestones in the development of both the science fiction and horror genres. John Polidori's short work "The Vampyre" (published in 1819) also created an iconic horror character: the vampire as seductive nobleman, as opposed to the more common folkloric image of the vampire as ravening beast. Polidori's vampire, Lord Ruthven, was allegedly based on Lord Byron, and especially Byron's penchant for profligate seductions that left some of his conquests ruined and/or dissipated. This aspect of "The Vampyre" was immediately repeated in other works of literature and on the stage, and consumed by eager audiences willing to believe that Lord Byron truly was a monster (Frayling: 37–38). Almost 70 years later, Bram Stoker's *Dracula* (1897) would also portray its vampire as an aristocrat who feeds off the blood of young innocents, but Polidori's "Vampyre" is more accurately credited with creating the trope.

Meanwhile, in America, another strain of Gothic literature was developed by writers like Edgar Allan Poe (1809–1949) and Nathaniel Hawthorne (1804–1964). Following in the footsteps of Charles Brockden Browne and Washington Irving ("The Legend of Sleepy Hollow"), Poe and Hawthorne wrote Gothic tales with more subtle historical or psychological emphases, such as Poe's "The Tell-Tale Heart" and "The Fall of the House of Usher," or Hawthorne's *The House of the Seven Gables* (1851). Later in the century, the misanthropic journalist Ambrose Bierce wrote many short stories with bizarre or fantastic premises ("The Damned Thing," "An Occurrence at Owl Creek Bridge"), and Robert W. Chambers authored a collection of weird tales entitled *The King in Yellow* (1895). Other American writers of greater renown occasionally wrote ghost stories, including Edith Wharton ("Afterward") and Henry James [*The Turn of the Screw* (1898)]. The cult figure H. P. Lovecraft (1890–1937) published his weird tales of "cosmic horror" in pulp magazines during the 1920s and 1930s. Lovecraft sometimes employed (but more regularly eschewed) the subtle psychological terrors of writers like Hawthorne or James, focusing instead on fantastic otherworldly creatures that inhabit his *Cthulhu Mythos*, a term that refers to his (and his emulators') interrelated short stories. While visualizing any of Lovecraft's gigantic tentacled monsters would have been difficult for early cinema, films based on his work continue to be made both commercially and by his dedicated fans. In 2005 for example, The H. P. Lovecraft Historical Society released *The Call of Cthulhu*, a faithful adaptation of one of Lovecraft's most famous works. The film is a loving "What if?" movie, a black and white silent film homage to Lovecraft's story, had it been filmed in the era in which it was written.

Back in mid-nineteenth century England, the realist novel flourished and Gothic horrors were more likely to be found in cheap serial pulp fictions (sometimes called *penny dreadfuls*) and on theater stages than in literary salons. Significantly, penny dreadfuls usually featured illustrations of the horrors contained within, mirroring the visceral shocks of the era's freak shows as well as predating horror cinema's visual appeal. Two of the more famous of these penny dreadfuls are *Wagner the Wehr-wolf* (1846–1847) and *Varney the Vampyre; or, The Feast of Blood* (1845–1847). A close examination of them reveals many similarities between them and what would become the classical Hollywood horror film. For example, *Wagner the Wehr-wolf* contains one of the first man-to-wolf transformation scenes in modern literature, a narrative point that could and would be effectively exploited by later werewolf films (du Coudray: 51). Similarly, the first chapter of *Varney the Vampyre* contains a prototypical version of a vampiric attack that predates *Dracula* by 50 years. As *Varney the Vampyre* is less well known than *Dracula*, it is worth quoting some of its opening scene as it contains actions and iconography that would heavily inform most subsequent vampire narratives, both literary and cinematic. The chapter begins as "[t]he solemn tones of an old cathedral clock have announced midnight." A violent storm rages outside of "an antique chamber in an ancient house," wherein a "creature formed in all fashions of loveliness lies in a half sleep." A large latticed bay window "filled with curiously painted glass and rich stained pieces" dominates the stage-like setting, as does the portrait "of a young man, with a pale face, a stately brow, and a strange expression about the eyes." The "lightning streams across that bay window, for an instant bringing out every color in it with terrible distinctness," while also revealing a "tall gaunt figure in hideous relief." The vampire breaks the glass and "from without introduces a long gaunt hand, which seems utterly destitute of flesh." As it approaches the bed, the paralyzed-with-fear ingénue can see that its face is "perfectly white—perfectly bloodless. The eyes look like polished tin; the lips are drawn back. And the principal feature next to those dreadful eyes is the teeth—the fearful looking teeth—projecting like those of some wild animal, hideously, glaringly white, and fang-like." As the vampire "approaches the bed with a strange, gliding movement," his victim's "bosom heaves, and her limbs tremble, yet she cannot withdraw her eyes from that marble-looking face." The chapter ends as the monster "drags her head to the bed's edge. He forces it back by the long hair still entwined in his grasp. With a plunge he seizes her neck in his fang-like teeth—a gush of blood, and a hideous sucking noise follows. *The girl has swooned, and the vampyre is at his hideous repast!*"

Varney the Vampyre's purple prose and thinly-disguised sexuality could be said to be a hallmark of the Gothic and sensation novels that flourished in England during the Victorian era. [Sensation novels, epitomized by Wilkie Collins's *The Woman in White* (1859), were written to provide chills but were less likely than their Gothic counterparts to involve supernatural events and/or far flung locales.] Elaine Showalter's *Sexual Anarchy: Gender and Culture at the Fin de Siècle* (1990) explores this tumultuous era, cataloguing the literary, artistic, and even medical texts that directly or indirectly expressed the era's hysterical concerns over (newly coined) concepts such as feminism and homosexuality. The era also saw the publication of dozens of soon-to-be famous Gothic novels, most of which deal with sex and horror in more or less overt ways, and most of which have been adapted into horror films throughout the twentieth century. Among the most well known of these works is *Carmilla* (1872), by J. Sheridan Le Fanu. It features the titular female vampire, and has arguably served as the template for an entire subgenre of horror, the lesbian vampire story. Robert Louis Stevenson's *The Strange Case of Dr. Jekyll and Mr. Hyde* (1886) introduced another iconic character into the canon: the "normal" Dr. Jekyll whose inner demon Mr. Hyde is unleashed via a transformative potion. Although better known as a work of science fiction, H. G. Wells's *The Island of Dr. Moreau* (1895) contains a fin-de-siècle mad scientist investigating the connections between humans and beasts; the book would later be turned into numerous horror films, including the classical Hollywood horror film *Island of Lost Souls* (1932). Similarly, Oscar Wilde's homosexual allegory *The Picture of Dorian Gray* (1891) has been filmed multiple times over the last century. Wilde's book is also linked to another "monstrous" artistic and literary tradition of the era, the so-called Decadent Movement, whose poets and painters—inspired by Edgar Allan Poe among others—were prone to rhapsodize in necrophilic ways over the bodies of beautiful dead women. Arguably the best known Gothic novel of the Victorian era is Bram Stoker's *Dracula* (1897). Featuring a powerful foreign aristocrat who unleashes the repressed sexualities of both men and women, monstrous shape shifting between humanoid form and beast, the walking undead, decaying castles and crypts, and patriarchal science as both powerful and perverse, *Dracula* is a culmination of Gothic tropes and themes, and one of the major progenitors of twentieth century horror. As Showalter notes, "by 1980 over 133 full-length film versions had been recorded" (1990: 182). Broadening out the category a bit, in 2012 the Internet Movie Database listed over 650 horror films found under the key word "vampire."

Horror was also quite popular on the stage throughout the Victorian era and into the 1920s. As noted above, theatrical adaptations of *Frankenstein* and "The Vampyre" appeared soon after their appearance in print and were popular throughout the century. Historians have also noted that stage versions of *Frankenstein* and *Dracula* were extremely popular in the 1920s, and that the classical Hollywood films based on them owe as much to these theatrical versions as they did to their original source novels (Skal, 1990: 2001). Probably the most famous theater devoted to horror was the Grand Guignol, founded in the Montmartre district of Paris by Oscar Metenier in 1897. Run by Max Moray for the next several decades, the Grand Guignol became famous for its gruesome melodramas and gory stage effects. "The sadistic and bloody plays produced at the Grand Guignol from 1897 until its closing in 1962 established important precedents for popular horror entertainment that took the cinema many years to match" (Worland, 2007: 36). In other words, the Grand Guignol contributed to the "freak show" appeal of the contemporary horror genre by giving its audiences graphic depictions of bodily mutilation, a trend that only continues to increase in global horror filmmaking as censorship and regulation of the medium continues to decline. (See also Chapters 17, 18, 20, 23, and 25.) However, when the Grand Guignol brought its theatrical excesses to New York City in 1923, it was excoriated in the press (Skal, 2001: 60). As the next section explores in greater detail, American audiences of the 1920s were loathe to experience anything too gruesome either on stage or on screen, and producers tended to shy away from introducing actual supernatural themes.

Cinematic Precursors to the Classical Hollywood Horror Film

Some film buffs cite *Frankenstein* (1910), a short adaptation of Mary Shelley's tale made by Thomas Edison's production company, as the first "horror" film. Perhaps D. W. Griffith's *The Avenging Conscience* (1914) — a filmic adaptation of Edgar Allan Poe's "The Tell-Tale Heart" — deserves the honor. But to call either film a horror film would be a historical misnomer: as recent film historians have argued, the term *horror film* was not really used by the film industry or its audiences in any consistent way until the 1930s, and even then it was used in conjunction with other terms such as chiller, thriller, and/or mystery (Studlar, 1996: 205). Thus, most of the films discussed in this section would have been thought of upon their releases as something other than horror, be it literary adaptation, mystery, or even comedy. To invoke one model of generic formation and evolution, before the 1930s the horror film might be said to have been in its "experimental" phase (Schatz, 1981: 36–41). That means that certain elements and conventions that would become strongly identified with the genre in its classical phase—such as old dark houses, menacing mad men or supernatural monsters, low key and chiaroscuro lighting—were being "isolated and established" by filmmakers, even as no one recognized that a genre called the *horror film* yet existed (Schatz, 1981: 37). In truth, generic evolution and/or change is always a complicated process, and as many (if not most) of the essays in this volume demonstrate, the horror film—whatever it is or has been called—has always been an exceedingly plastic form, readily adapting itself to technological innovation, as well as historical, national, and industrial contexts.

Carlos Clarens (1967), in his seminal tome *An Illustrated History of the Horror Film*, suggests that the horror film begins with George Mélies, the magician turned filmmaker responsible for hundreds of short "trick" films during cinema's first decade. While monsters, moon men, and devils do populate his films, Mélies is today more remembered as a progenitor of the fantasy and science fiction genres, thanks to films such as *A Trip to the Moon* (1902) and *The Impossible Voyage* (1904). Other early filmmakers adapted more truly Gothic tales from the Victorian era. *The Picture of Dorian Gray* was filmed at least seven times during the era (Mank, 1994: 298), as was *Dr. Jekyll and Mr. Hyde*; Selig released a version of the latter tale as early as 1908. Phil Hardy (1993 [1986]) describes the Vitagraph short *Conscience*, also known as *The Chamber of Horrors* (1912: 17), as "a cautionary moral tale [that] makes use of a setting that was to become a horror movie favourite." He also notes Maurice Tourneur's Edgar Allan Poe adaptation *The System of Dr. Tarr and Professor Feather* (1912), Bison's *The Werewolf* (1913), "seemingly the first werewolf [film], attaching the theme to American Indian mythology" (18), and *Life Without Soul* (1916), "the first feature-length version of … *Frankenstein*" (20).

The first movement of something that closely resembled the horror film *as a coherent genre* arose in Germany as an outcropping of German Expressionist painting, sculpture, design, and theater—especially the theater of Max Reinhardt. *The Haunted Screen* (2008 [1969]), Lotte Eisner's groundbreaking study of German Expressionist cinema, notes the movement's Gothic themes (the fantastic, the doppelganger) as well as its remarkable formal elements: high contrast and chiaroscuro lighting, skewed and irrational visual design (especially in corridors and staircases), "geometric grouping" of crowds and landscapes, exaggerated gesture and costume, and the moving camera. Broadly, German Expressionist cinema includes crime serials and costume dramas as well as *Schauerfilme*, a term translated as "films of fantasy and terror" (Cook, 1990: 121). Among the most famous of the *Schauerfilme* are *The Student of Prague* (1913, 1926), three film versions of *The Golem* (1915, 1917, and 1920), *The Cabinet of Dr. Caligari* (1920), *Der Januskopf* (1920), *Nosferatu*

(1922), *The Hands of Orlac* (1924), *Waxworks* (1924), and the groundbreaking science fiction epic *Metropolis* (1925).

The best known of these films, *The Cabinet of Dr. Caligari* created an international sensation because of its unique Expressionist style, as well as its twisting narrative about a street mountebank named Caligari (Werner Krauss) who uses a zombie-like sleepwalker named Cesare (Conrad Veidt) to commit a series of murders. The tale has obvious antecedents in *Frankenstein* (the mad doctor, the creature he creates and tries to control), as well as the genre of vampire literature (Cesare sleeps in a coffin-like box and enters the bedchamber of one female victim through a broken window as did *Varney the Vampyre*). The film uses its Expressionist style in ways akin to Gothic style: its distorted lines and angular shadows serve as a visual corollary for the distorted psyches of the film's villains. Intriguingly, while the original idea behind the film was to present the story as an allegory for how Germany had been manipulated by its leaders into the First World War, a framing story was added by its producers that reduced the whole cautionary tale to a mad man's nightmare (Cook, 1990: 118). Nonetheless, the film's blending of Gothic and Expressionist motifs would come to define the look and feel of the classical Hollywood horror film 10 years later. It even served as a template of sorts for the classical Hollywood horror film *Murders in the Rue Morgue* (1932), albeit with a giant ape replacing Cesare as the mad doctor's accomplice. Other critics have noted how Dr. Caligari's unique bespectacled and top-hatted look was used to characterize menacing figures in later American films like *The Bells* (1926) and *The Cat and the Canary* (1927) (Clarens, 1967: 57, 63) (Figure 12.1).

Produced several years before *Caligari*, *The Student of Prague*—based on Edgar Allan Poe's "William Wilson" and E. T. A Hoffmann's "The Sand Merchant"— is less Expressionist in style but nonetheless an important precursor to later horror films (and *Schauerfilme*) that explore the theme of the doppelgänger, or double. *The Golem* films are based on a Medieval legend about a Rabbi who creates and animates a man of clay in Prague's Jewish ghetto; however, this "monster" is a protector of his people, not a force of evil. Critics have noticed similarities between Paul Wegener's performance as the Golem and Boris Karloff's performance of the Frankenstein monster in 1931. Writing on the (still extant) 1920 version of *The Golem*, Clarens (1967: 20) also notes the scene of "the little girl who will be his [the Golem's] innocent nemesis" or foil, a scene that will be replayed in many later film versions of *Frankenstein*, including *The Ghost of Frankenstein* (1942). *The Hands of Orlac*, based on a novel by Maurice Renard, was directed by *Caligari*'s director Robert Wiene. Its tale of stitched together body parts with a "mind" of their own would be remade in classical Hollywood as *Mad Love* (1935), a film that also draws upon the legend and lore of the Grand Guignol theater.

While *Der Januskopf* was yet another version of *Dr. Jekyll and Mr. Hyde*, *Nosferatu* was the first (unauthorized) screen adaptation of *Dracula*. Mrs. Florence Stoker, the wife and executor of author Bram Stoker's estate, successfully sued the filmmakers: all copies of the film were ordered to be destroyed, but fortunately some survived (Skal, 1990). The film does depart from the novel in certain ways, most

Figure 12.1 Dr. Caligari's unique look was used to characterize menacing figures in later American films like *The Cat and the Canary* (1927). Directed by Paul Leni. Produced by Universal Pictures.

clearly in its characterization of the vampiric Count. While Stoker's Count Dracula grows younger and better looking throughout the book, *Nosferatu's* Count is a hideous feral creature with crooked teeth and spider-like claws. Employing a less flamboyant style of Expressionism, *Nosferatu* still makes excellent use of shadow and light. *Metropolis*, which is usually classified as science fiction, also contains significant elements that would influence the classical Hollywood horror film. For example, besides its Expressionist visual design, *Metropolis* contains a creation scene that certainly seems to have inspired the one in James Whale's *Frankenstein* (1931) as well as its many subsequent imitators. It also contains a sequence in which the villain chases the heroine through dark twisting catacombs that would not be out of place in either a Gothic novel or a more recent slasher film.

Der Januskopf and *Nosferatu* were both directed by F. W. Murnau, and *Metropolis* was directed by Fritz Lang, who would also direct *M* (1931), one of the first films about a serial child killer. Both men were luminaries within German Expressionist cinema, and like many of their colleagues, both men emigrated to America to escape the rise of Nazism. In doing so, German Expressionist filmmakers entered directly into the Hollywood studio system where they would influence the classical Hollywood horror film, and in the following decade *film noir* (Davis, 2004). Murnau made just a few films in America before he died in a car accident, just as the first Hollywood horror cycle was beginning. Lang went on to a decades-long Hollywood career directing *films noir*, gothic melodramas, and terrifying mysteries like *The Woman in the Window* (1944) and *Secret Behind the Door* (1947), films that many critics of the era did classify as horror films (Chapter 14). However, other German and European ex-patriots including Paul Leni, Karl Freund, Michael Curtiz, Lothar Mendes, Ludwig Berger, Conrad Veidt, Robert Florey, Robert Siodmak, and James Whale carried the German Expressionist style into the first wave of American horror films. As even a cursory study of the issue reveals, the impact of German Expressionist style on the classical Hollywood horror film was profound, and is still being invoked by auteur directors from Guy Maddin to Tim Burton.

In America's so-called Golden Age of Silent Cinema (the 1920s), there were also films that might be considered "experimental" horror films, although they usually stopped short of presenting outright supernatural creatures such as vampires or homunculi. The Lon Chaney classics *The Hunchback of Notre Dame* (1923) and *The Phantom of the Opera* (1925) have been retroactively added to the canon of classical Hollywood horror films (and marketed by Universal Studios as such), but during the 1920s they were more likely to be classified as historical melodramas or literary adaptations (of Victor Hugo and Gaston Leroux, respectively). Similarly, although later events, such as the publication and circulation of the fan magazine *Famous Monsters of Filmland* beginning in 1958, have positioned Lon Chaney as the "first horror movie star," in the 1920s he was known as a talented character actor who specialized in weird parts, especially those requiring extensive make up or bodily alteration. The press dubbed him "The Man of a Thousand Faces" and a popular joke of the day went thusly: "Don't step on it—it might be Lon Chaney." As such, Chaney's Hunchback is only monstrous because of his misshapen body, created with a great deal of physical suffering on the actor's part. Arguably the film's most horrifying scene is when Quasimodo is flogged in the public square, making him a highly sympathetic human monster, a trait that would characterize classical Hollywood monsters such as Frankenstein's creature, *King Kong* (1933), and *The Wolf Man* (1941). That said, the Phantom of the Opera is a more traditional Gothic villain, with sexual and/or romantic designs on the young ingénue, and the film was designed by Parisian-born Ben Carré with many Expressionist touches, such as shadow shots of the Phantom and the decaying Gothic spaces inhabited by the Phantom underneath the opera house. While it may not have been called a *horror film* upon its release, *The Phantom of the Opera*, along with its many remakes and adaptations, has nonetheless become a key text of the horror film genre.

Although Lon Chaney appeared in many weird tales and criminal melodramas throughout the 1910s and 1920s, later critics have championed the films he made with Tod Browning at MGM as some of his most interesting. These films include *The Unholy Three* (1925, remade as a sound film in 1930), *The Road to Mandalay* (1926), *The Unknown* (1927), *London After Midnight* (1927), and *West of Zanzibar* (1928). Tod Browning, who began his career in traveling circuses and sideshows, would go on to direct *Dracula* and *Freaks* (1932) during the classical era, and many of his thematic obsessions are on display in the films he made with Chaney. As one pair of critics put it, "The commercial glue that held Browning and Chaney together … was their mutual interest in themes of boiling sexual frustration and concomitant, visceral revenge" enacted by Chaney's blind, crippled, or otherwise physically deformed villains (Skal and Sevada, 1995: 93). The films were perceived by many critics of the era as perverse and morbid, and have more recently been the subject of explication by critics like Gaylyn Studlar, who argues that "the masculine self exposed in Chaney's films was in the freak show mold of the Other constructed in contradictory terms: stigmatized yet aggrandized, grotesque and yet still romantically capable of suffering for love" (1996: 210). Studlar finds many of Chaney's films to be perverse Oedipal narratives reflective of the era's "antimodern fascination with suffering." Certainly they represent the dark side of American masculinity as represented by someone like Douglas Fairbanks, but they also seem to speak to the shattered and deformed men returning from the horrors of World War I (Skal, 2001: 66–70). While the Chaney–Browning films included gothic themes of troubled familial or romantic relationships, they also visualized for the public the grotesque and abnormal. The freak show itself as a cultural phenomenon was dying out during the 1920s (as medical models of disability and eugenics came into prominence), but Studlar suggests that Chaney's films arose to fill the void, fulfilling many of the same cultural needs.

Among the more audacious of these films is *The Unknown*, in which Chaney plays Alonzo the Armless, a circus performer who throws knives with his feet at his young assistant Nanon (Joan Crawford), with whom he is also in love. But Alonzo is only faking his disability in order to escape suspicion for a previous murder he committed: he actually has arms, although one of his hands is deformed by having two thumbs. When Nanon tells Alonzo she cannot bear to be touched by any man, Alonzo blackmails a doctor into surgically removing his arms. After the operation Alonzo discovers Nanon has gotten over her fears of being touched, and is now seeing the circus strongman Malabar (Norman Kerry). Alonzo devises a plan to have Malabar's arms ripped from their sockets by a team of horses; however, the plan fails and Alonzo is trampled to death in the process. The critical reaction to *The Unknown* was similar to that Browning and the entire horror film industry would face several years later when the horror film came under attack by moral watchdog groups like the Legion of Decency and the Production Code Administration. For example, the film critic for *Harrison's Reports* opined that the film could only be enjoyed by "a moral pervert of the present day, or professional torturers of the times of the Spanish Inquisition.... it is difficult to fancy average men and women of a modern audience in this enlightened age being entertained by such a thoroughly fiendish mingling of bloodlust, cruelty and horrors ... " (quoted in Skal and Sevada: 115).

The critical backlash to outright horrors such as those depicted in *The Unknown* forced many filmmakers of the 1920s to hedge their bets, diluting horror with either comedy or an "it was all just a dream or an elaborate ruse" plot twist. The Chaney-Browning collaboration *London After Midnight* illustrates the latter trend toward mitigating horror. Ostensibly America's "first" vampire film, *London After Midnight* features Chaney as "The Man in the Beaver Hat," a squat vampire with a bat-like cape, pop-eyes, lank hair, and mouthful of razor-sharp teeth. However, the vampire and his bat-girl assistant are revealed to be actors taking part in an elaborate scheme devised by a Scotland Yard detective (Chaney again, in a dual role) designed to catch a murderer. *London After Midnight* was the most commercially successful of the Chaney-Browning collaborations (Skal and Sevada: 118). Critics may have decried the more gruesome work Chaney and Browning did together, but the public was certainly interested, and looked forward to the duo's planned production of *Dracula*. However, Chaney died of cancer before the collaboration could take place, and the role went to Bela Lugosi. *London After Midnight* was remade by MGM in 1935 as *Mark of the Vampire*, with Browning again directing. But *London After Midnight* remained a cult item, famous throughout ensuing decades as a much sought after lost film. In 2002 it was "reconstructed" from existing production materials and still photographs and is available for study in that form on DVD.

Other important cinematic antecedents to the classical Hollywood horror film were the stage plays and film versions of what have been called *old dark house mysteries* or *clutching hand thrillers*. Old dark house mysteries have all the iconographic elements of Gothic horror — deserted cobwebbed mansions, creaking doors, secret passageways, dark clouds skirting across the moon — but are more likely to include comedic characters instead of angst-ridden gothic heroes. And instead of some supernatural or otherworldly force, the "monster" in these films is usually revealed to be a perfectly human being merely *costumed* as some sort of frightful creature (as in *London After Midnight*). According to Walter Kendrick (1991: 209), "spooky-house comedies reached their peak in the middle and late 1920s; by 1925 their conventions were already so familiar to theatergoers that (playwright Ralph) Spence could spoof them in *The Gorilla*," a Broadway hit that would be filmed in 1927, 1930, and 1939. Perhaps the best known film of this type is *The Cat and the Canary*, based on a 1922 stage play written by John Willard. Directed by German émigré Paul Leni [who also directed the *Schauerfilme Waxworks* (1924) and the Victor Hugo-based proto-horror movie *The Man Who Laughs* (1927) for Universal], *The Cat and the Canary* uses depth of field cinematography, traveling camera shots, multiple dissolves, and superimpositions to create a highly visual Expressionist atmosphere. At one point a distorting mirror is used to suggest the subjective state of a crazy old aunt, a technique that James Whale would use a few years later in his film version of the clutching hand thriller, the aptly titled *The Old Dark House* (1932). True to this subgenre's narrative pattern, *The Cat and the Canary* reveals that the strange cat-like creature who has been haunting the gothic mansion is really just a disgruntled heir, attempting to frighten the heroine into a state of insanity so he can claim the family fortune (Figure 12.2).

MGM's 1925 release *The Monster* is another good example of the era's old dark house mystery or clutching hand thriller, and it also happens to star Lon Chaney. Based on a stage hit by Crane Wilbur, the film was directed by Roland West, who also directed the similar films *The Bat* (1926) and *The Bat Whispers* (1930). After its opening scene, in which a car is forced off the road by a mysterious figure in a

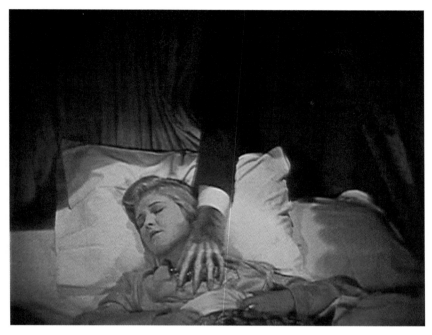

Figure 12.2 *The Cat and the Canary* (1927) was one of the era's most famous "old dark house" mysteries; this shot demonstrates why they also became known as *clutching hand thrillers*. Directed by Paul Leni. Produced by Universal Pictures.

cloak, the film seems to become a vehicle for Johnny Arthur, a Harold Lloyd type comedian herein playing Johnny Goodlittle, an effeminate nebbish who aspires to be a detective. Investigating the scene of the crash at night, he sees both the man in the cloak — Rigo — who is setting up for another car crash, and Daffy Dan, an eccentric goon who asks for a match to light his imaginary cigarette. Johnny falls into a hole that transports him via a chute into the interior of the local sanitarium, and he is shortly joined there by his paramour Betty and his rival for her hand, Amos. At about the half-hour mark of this 86-min film, Lon Chaney as Dr. Ziska arrives via an expressionist shadow shot of his hugely menacing hand. Dr. Ziska attempts to drug his guests so he can perform a "remarkable operation" on Betty, but various hijinks ensue with Dr. Ziska, Rigo, Daffy Dan, and Caliban — a dark-skinned bare-chested hulk of a man — menacing the romantic triangle. By the end of the film, the "monster" and his three henchmen are revealed to be mental patients who have taken over the sanitarium. Johnny, disguised as Rigo, saves the girl and tricks Caliban into electrocuting Dr. Ziska in his own electric chair. Johnny frees the real doctors from their prison cell and receives due accolades from the local police and a hired detective.

The Monster is not very well known today, and it has escaped much critical attention, partly because of its formulaic nature and partly because it does not give Chaney that much to do. Nor is Chaney's makeup all that striking. As Studlar has noted, Chaney's best and most memorable roles are those in which he is both tortured and torturing, a true Gothic antihero who has the capacity to love as well as destroy. In comparison to his Hunchback or his Phantom (or even Alonzo the Armless), Chaney's Dr. Ziska is a one-note character whose designs on the heroine are at best rather murky. He certainly has no overt heterosexual interest in her. In fact, the operation he wants to perform on Betty is rather queer — somehow placing a male soul into her female body — but Ziska is foiled before the experiment can begin. Nonetheless, the film makes good use of its soon-to-be iconic "electric laboratory" set filled with Expressionist shadows, as well as its soon-to-be iconic mad scientist chortling over the supine figure of the ingénue, here strapped onto a medical gurney and wearing a flimsy nightgown (Figure 12.3). As such, the film draws from both *Frankenstein* and Victorian science's penchant to investigate and pathologize the female body (Showalter, 1990: 127–143). As Ziska puts it, "It is only from a woman that I can learn the secret of life!" Just as surely as do vampires and werewolves and most other Gothic villains, the mad scientist attempts to rape and despoil — in whatever displaced form — his victim's (usually female) body.

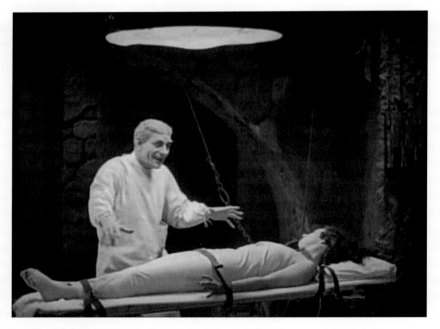

Figure 12.3   MGM's comedic thriller *The Monster* (1925) contains countless narrative and iconographic elements that would later characterize the horror genre; in this scene mad Dr. Ziska (Lon Chaney) prepares some nefarious experiment on a scantily clad female victim. Directed by Roland West. Produced by Metro-Goldwyn Pictures Corporation.

Hollywood's transition to sound in the late 1920s would eventually contribute to the eerie atmosphere of the classical Hollywood horror film, but the industry's first sound "horror" films were talking versions of the already creaky old dark house stage thriller. Clarens (1967: 60) reports that Warner Bros.' *The Terror* (1928, directed by Roy Del Ruth), MGM's *The Thirteenth Chair* (1929, directed by Tod Browning), and Universal's *The Cat Creeps* (1930, directed by Rupert Julian) all received lukewarm reviews, and did little to inspire what would become the classical Hollywood horror film. But one other theatrical novelty would: a stage version of *Dracula* starring Bela Lugosi that opened on Broadway in October of 1927. While reviews were mixed, audiences were thrilled, accepting both the supernatural aspect of the title character as well as Lugosi's oddly inflected speech patterns. Several years later, when Lugosi intoned the immortal words "I am Dracula — I bid you welcome" in the Universal Studios film adaption of the play, he helped usher in a new era of cinematic horror: the start of the classical Hollywood horror film. And the rest, as they say, is history.

References

Bleiler, E.F. (ed.) (1966) *Three Gothic Novels: The Castle of Otranto, Vathek, and the Vampyre*, Dover Publications, Inc., New York.

Carroll, N. (1990) *The Philosophy of Horror; or, Paradoxes of the Heart*, Routledge, New York.

Clarens, C. (1967) *An Illustrated History of the Horror Film*, G. P. Putnam's Sons, New York.

Cook, D.A. (1990) *A History of Narrative Film*, 2nd edn, W. W. Norton & Company, New York.

du Coudray, C.B. (2006) *The Curse of the Werewolf: Fantasy, Horror, and the Beast Within*, I. B. Tauris, New York.

Davis, B. (2004) Horror meets noir: the evolution of cinematic style, 1931–1958, in *Horror Film: Creating and Marketing Fear* (ed. S. Hantke), University Press of Mississippi, Jackson, pp. 191–212.

Eisner, L. (2008[1969]) *The Haunted Screen*, University of California Press, Los Angeles.

Frayling, C. (1991[1978]) *Vampyres: Lord Byron to Count Dracula*, Faber & Faber, Boston.

Haggerty, G.E. (2006) *Queer Gothic*, University of Illinois Press, Chicago.

Hardy, P. (ed.) (1993[1986]) *The Overlook Film Encyclopedia: Horror*, The Overlook Press, New York.

Kendrick, W. (1991) *The Thrill of Fear*, Grove Press, New York.

Mank, G.W. (1994) *Hollywood Cauldron*, McFarland and Co., Inc., Jefferson, NC.

Morris, R. C. (2011) The Gothic Pioneer Horace Walpole Finally Gets His Due. *The New York Times*, www.nytimes.com/2011/03/23/arts/23iht-rartberry23.html (accessed 26 March 2012).

Schatz, T. (1981) *Hollywood Genres*, McGraw-Hill, Inc., New York.

Sedgwick, E.K. (1985) *Between Men: English Literature and Male Homosocial Desire*, Columbia University Press, New York.

Showalter, E. (1990) *Sexual Anarchy: Gender and Culture at the Fin de Siècle*, Penguin Books, New York.

Skal, D.J. (1990) *Hollywood Gothic: The Tangled Web of Dracula from Novel to Stage to Screen*, W. W. Norton & Co., New York.

Skal, D.J. (2001) *The Monster Show: A Cultural History of Horror*, Revised Edition, Faber and Faber, Inc., New York.

Skal, D.J. and Sevada, E. (1995) *Dark Carnival: The Secret World of Tod Browning*, Anchor Books, New York.

Studlar, G. (1996) *This Mad Masquerade: Stardom and Masculinity in the Jazz Age*, Columbia University Press, New York.

Twitchell, J.B. (1985) *Dreadful Pleasures: An Anatomy of Modern Horror*, Oxford University Press, New York.

Worland, R. (2007) *The Horror Film: An Introduction*, Blackwell Publishing, Malden, MA.

13

Classical Hollywood Horror

John Edgar Browning

Of monsters following the Wall Street Crash of 1929, acclaimed horror film historian David J. Skal (2001: 111) writes poetically:

> Risen from slab and box, jolted alive by jazz-age energies, they were strong enough to make their own way, in a bleak and transformed America.
>
> It was a moment the dark gods had waited for. In a new world of social upheaval and economic eclipse, their night could be endless.

Enter the year 1931. There was little question that the public mood had veered markedly astray when, during a 12-month stretch considered by those who lived it to be the most critical period of the Great Depression, consecutively four of Hollywood's horror icons-to-be were either unleashed to the public or nearing postproduction. In short, "America's worst year of the century," Skal (2001: 115) reasons, "would be its best year ever for monsters." What Americans were then witnessing was, unequivocally, the birth of a cinematic genre: the horror film. As Skal (2004: 165) puts it, "Horror movies of the genuinely fantastic, supernatural variety had not been invented yet, at least not in America, where conventions dictated that supernatural occurrences always be 'explained away'." Indeed, no decade of horror's cinematic history has been so thoroughly treated by—nay, *strip-mined* by—scholar and fan alike as this period; doing so here seems doomed to redundancy. Thus, following Robert Spadoni's (2007: 45) example in *Uncanny Bodies: The Coming of Sound Film and the Origins of the Horror Genre*, this chapter explores what has been termed Hollywood's "classical era" of horror during the 1930s but does so in a fashion concerned less with critiquing the production value

A Companion to the Horror Film, First Edition. Edited by Harry M. Benshoff.
© 2014 John Wiley & Sons, Inc. Published 2017 by John Wiley & Sons, Inc.

of the films that emerged during the period than considering their reception and cultural significance, in order that we may uncover, as it were, "some of the[ir] lost original power, and strangeness."

The same decade during which sound was to come into prominence in the cinema found Americans peering anxiously down the (figurative) lens at a gaggle of supernatural monsters. These new *noms de macabre*—Dracula, Frankenstein, the Mummy, King Kong—were indeed far from the counterfeit men and women of earlier silent pictures who merely masqueraded in monstrous garb. What here followed, in 1931, was truly, as Manchel (Frank, 1970: 60) called it, "A Time of Kings." Patterns would emerge, standards would be set, foundations would be laid, and impressions unforgettable would be left upon millions. Horror's first age—the American age—had arrived in grim earnest.

Why *Dracula*, Why Now?

More precisely, "Why horror?" was in 1931 the question being asked in the press. As Skal (2004: 103–138) exhaustively lays out in his book *Hollywood Gothic: The Tangled Web of Dracula from Novel to Stage to Screen*, *Dracula*'s first officially licensed stage play (1924), with the Hamilton Deane troupe, had for 3 years enjoyed a successful provincial tour in England, where it "packed [theatres] … to a degree never previously exceeded" ("'Dracula' at the Grand Theatre," *The Derby Daily Telegraph*, May 14, 1925: 3). American publisher and stage producer Horace Liveright, while being piloted around the British capital by John L. Balderston ("Return of a Native," *New York Evening Post*, November 16, 1929), discovered the vampire play during its London run and soon thereafter commenced negotiations with Bram Stoker's widow, Florence, to bring it back with him to the States [see also Skal (1993)]. Deane's *pronouncedly* English play would eventually be "Americanized" (Forecasts and Postscripts) by no less than Balderston himself, and the previously English lead was quickly refitted with Hungarian-born actor Bela Lugosi (Béla Ferenc Dezső Blaskó). Lugosi was visibly "foreign" (i.e., non-American), and *Béla* was such "a mysterious sort of name [that it] seem[ed] to fit the part," told reporter Wood Soanes to Lugosi during an interview ("Jane Fooshee Will Open Special Fulton Season Following Lugosi Week," *Oakland Tribune*, July 6, 1930: 8-S). When asked by the *New York Evening Post* what his greatest difficulty had been "in mastering the English language sufficiently to enable American audiences to understand him," Lugosi responded, smiling first, "Mastering? You flatter me . . . . I am still struggling with it. However, my highest jury is the audience—and if they are satisfied I suppose I should not complain" ("Including the Hungarian," December 17, 1927: 12). And satisfied they were, if titillatingly so. Historians and scholars alike have for decades remarked on Lugosi's enunciation and voice inflections as playing a key part in his archetypication of the Dracula *rôle*, and his rather peculiar style being the unintentional result of his learning the lines phonetically. However, there was, at least according to Lugosi, much more skill and style involved:

> I first "get" a part in my own Hungarian, thinking it out as though I were going to act it in my native tongue ... you see? I study it and seek to perfect it, just as though I were going to act it to Budapest, for Hungarian audiences. Then, when I begin to feel quite at home in it, I begin to concentrate on speak *[sic]* the part as it should be spoken for the American audiences. ("Including the Hungarian")

Regardless of whether it was Lugosi's craft or simply the public's fascination with his delicious alterity, the play became a raving financial success.

By the time the American stage tour descended upon California, it had already set attendance records in New York, reportedly even turning away patrons "at every performance" at the Fulton ("Shudder Play Sets Record at Fulton Theater," *Oakland Tribune*, August 17, 1929: 4-B). Even baseball legend Babe Ruth was reportedly spotted attending a New York performance ("Left at the Post," *New York Evening Post*, December 9, 1927: 14). Curiously, horror was making money, and fear was fast becoming the tonic of the day, but few, if anyone, were asking *why* yet. The *Oakland Tribune* commented, "The play 'Dracula' deals seriously with the subject (of vampires) and depends for its success upon its ability to instill belief that there are such things in the minds of its modern-day audiences — at least during the time they are in the theater" ("Shudder Play Sets Record at Fulton Theater"). What a spectacle it must have been indeed, for these contemporary audiences, to see Lugosi *as* Dracula appearing and behaving so realistically, so methodically on the stage. Yet, in the end, it was *just* a stage, was it not? The players were *only* people whom the audience could see and touch, and at curtain call and a final bow from the theater company, stage-goers could escape with relative ease. This was not to be the case, however, when Dracula appeared upon the screen.

Dracula's leap (swoop?) onto the big screen as a "talking picture," an innovation at the time, together with an entire industry of special effects and exotic, elaborate set changes that were impossible in stage productions, served to confront audiences with what could only be likened then to some sort of new, believable "unreality," much like CGI would be to audiences 60 years later. Immediately following the film's production, Lugosi (1990: 7 – 8) wrote of its influence: "'Dracula' is a story which has always had a powerful effect on the emotions of an audience, and I think that the picture will be no less effective than the stage play. In fact, the motion picture should even prove more remarkable in this direction, since many things which could only be talked about on the stage are shown on the screen in all their uncanny detail." Lugosi no longer played Dracula: he simply *was* Dracula, a condition that would haunt him for the rest of his life. It was as if the medium of film had existentially distanced, or removed entirely, the audience from the story reeling before them in a way the stage never could, so much so that disbelief was more readily suspendable. What is more, a trend was begun in *Dracula* that would become a hallmark of subsequent vampire pictures.

Profiling Dracula, Interrogating Culture

In *The Horror Film: An Introduction*, Worland (2007: 56) aptly notes that Tod Browning, the film's director, "renegotiated the thematic expectations of Hollywood horror. After this there would be no jokes, no last-minute revelation of a criminal scheme. Dracula drank blood." And, indeed, to film audiences Lugosi's Dracula did just that. He was, after all, according to Skal (2001: 126), "a 'castrated' seducer who cannot penetrate in the conventional way": instead, "all sex energy is displaced to his mouth." Of the film version, Skal (2001: 126) adds:

> sex in general was toned down. The play, for instance, contained directions for a long, passionate lip-lock between Dracula and his victim, leading up to the bite; in the film, Lugosi does no more than stiffly kiss Helen Chandler's [Mina's] hand.

Indeed, something peculiar did happen during translation from stage to screen, but it went far deeper than Dracula's bite. That is to say, the "unreality" that so convinced *Dracula*'s audiences at the time had taken on simultaneously shades of truth that communicated the rather conservative socio-politics of the day. Critics familiar with the novel expected great things of what the Universal film could unleash from Stoker's novel. Wood Soanes (1930: 8-S) wrote in the *Oakland Tribune*:

> I refer to that episode describing Dracula's voyage by sea to England. He starts on a vessel containing a full complement of sailors. Each night the vampire, in order to retain his earthly form, must drink the blood of one human. Each morning there is a dead sailor. Finally the vessels *[sic]* comes within view of the coast of England. Only one sailor remains and Dracula takes his hideous toll.

> As the vessel comes onto the rock-bound coast Dracula is at the wheel of the charnal *[sic]* vessel but the countryside has been aroused. The Britons are awaiting him, prepared to drive the stake through his heart that will stop him from further walkings on the earth. Dracula runs the ship on the rocks, wrecks it and turns himself into a wolf. As they shoot at him, he changes to a bat, flies away and escapes. It should make a most stirring picture.

Unfortunately, as Skal (2001: 126) is apt to point out, Universal's executive Carl Laemmle, Jr., was "apparently uncomfortable" with some of the script's "homoerotic displacements." Laemmle wrote, for example, about Scene B-14 (*The wreck of the Varna [later "Vesta"] has just arrived at harbor and the captain is found dead at the wheel*) in his personal copy of the Bromfield-Murphy script (September 8, 1930): "What happened to the crew? Explain in dialog? How? Dracula should go only for women and not men" (quoted in Riley, 1990: 56). In the final cut, the fate of the ship's crew is attributed (through voiceover) to a storm out at sea. In short, *Dracula*, though it may have "liberated the dormant [irrational and macabre] impulse in America, reestablishing an essential connection between film and the unconscious" (Skal, 2001: 127–128), also awakened a sleeping giant in Stoker's novel, an up to now widely unexplored, but nevertheless integral branch of Dracula's teratology in film: the political subtext of Dracula's victimology.

Dracula's cinematic retellings, with and since the Universal picture, reveal the progression of Western political ideologies about normative sexuality, race, and class, so much so in fact, to borrow Laurence A. Rickels's (1999: 7) phrasing in *The Vampire Lectures*, that "we will find that we must first be sure we know what is being sucked and what or who exactly is doing the sucking." Scholars like Joseph Valente (2002) have treated the xenophobic implications of inferior, "non-Germanic" blood exchange in Bram Stoker's *Dracula* (1897), but blood politics in the novel extend decidedly beyond racial hegemony, cross-pollinating with Dracula's filmic progeny. More precisely, the classed and sexed demographics of Dracula's victims in the novel, and in subsequent films, have gone relatively unexamined. Beginning with Universal's treatment of Stoker's novel, the markers of race, class, and sex prompt studios to segregate particular victims into either visualized or censored representations, even going so far as to disqualify some victims from the privilege of being "turned" (or "vamped") or, in some cases, even from serving as mere nourishment for Dracula. Dracula's procreatively- and consumptively-defined victimology reveals that the physical attack itself (and subsequent "turning") is a much more regulatory, even discriminatory process than previously accepted, one that continues to gesture toward, with considerable regularity, outdated Victorian sexual politics concerning procreation and "good-breeding." With future treatments of Stoker's novel on screen, Victorian bourgeois discourses about class and miscegenation which initially informed Dracula's victim pattern will eventually diminish. For example, by the end of Christopher Lee's run as Dracula in England during the early- to mid-1970s, we see the evolution of these politics in full force. Lee's Dracula bites, on-screen, white *as well as* "non-white" females of noticeably lower means in Hammer's *Dracula A.D. 1972* (1972), though he does not turn them and discards their bodies; he does bite and turn a male victim but does so off-screen (i.e., out of view). Thus, even 40 years after the Universal film, Dracula's pathology continues to denote an ideologically conservative, and particularly heteronormative victim pattern, in keeping with Victorian prescription of restrained sexual activity.

Little had changed by the time of Columbia's *Bram Stoker's Dracula* (1992), a film in which there are few, if any, indications of male-on-male biting (with the exception of Dracula's journey to England aboard the *Demeter*, where, ingeniously, he viciously attacks the all-male crew in wolf form, effectively desexualizing the entire experience). It is not until TriStar's *Dracula 2000* (2000) that Dracula bites, and turns, a male victim onscreen, one who also happens to be "non-white," albeit the exchange is quick, violent, and forced, not unlike many early cinematic visualizations of gay male kissing. In sexually, racially, and socially encoding Dracula's victim pattern, film has afforded Dracula a seriality that is as much criminological as it is mythic. Reassessing

Figure 13.1   In *Dracula* (1931), a homoerotic encounter between the Count and Renfield is suggested but never explicitly shown; in this scene he waves away his vampire brides so he himself may drink from Renfield. Directed by Tod Browning and Karl Freund (uncredited). Produced by Universal Pictures.

the censorial and representational development of Dracula's bite, his victims, and their respective typologies in relation to sexed, raced, and socially classed demographics allows us to uncover, beginning with the Universal picture, the complex ways in which blood politics are manifested across Dracula's cinematic evolution. Interrogating Dracula's victimology in this way offers an insightful and relatively uncharted perspective into the ongoing negotiation between ideologically progressive and conservative forces at work in such cinematic narratives (Figure 13.1).

Dracula and Gothic Economics

Charles P. Jones called *Dracula* in *The Times-Picayune* "the best substitute for black coffee" ("Post-view," September 3, 1933: 8), and for audiences of the 1930s, unaccustomed as they were to the moving terror on the screen, it was precisely that. *Dracula* paved the way, thematically as well as economically, for what would become horror cinema's most influential decade. The Universal film "scored so heavily at the box office," wrote Mollie Merrick on location in Hollywood, California in 1931, "that it prompted the producer to essay something, a little more so." She continued: Were "horrors becoming the favorite entertainment of the American public? .... could motion pictures create a 'Grand Guignol' for these United States that would be as well patronized as France's palace of things horrible, gruesome, and weird?" Either there was, Merrick continued, "a minimum of normally sensitive people in the world today or the public [had] become so bored that novelty [meant] more to them than anything else in the entertainment lines." The "turn" Merrick observed was not restricted to the English-speaking viewing public either. Universal concurrently produced *à la mode* an equally lucrative Spanish-language version entitled *Drácula* (1931) starring Carlos Villar (Carlos Villarias) as the infamous Count. It is interesting to note, too, that despite the secondary status many early American studio foreign-language "talkies" received, Villarias's portrayal was and still is regarded by no small number of Spanish- and English-speaking viewers as comparable to Lugosi's; even the Spanish version's cinematography and direction are generally deemed superior, underscoring the pervasiveness of this new "weird" aesthetic that was at the time coming into fashion across multiple, culturally divergent communities (Figure 13.2).

Americans today should have little difficulty understanding why a vampire would do so well at the box-office during economic hard times. Observe, for example, the recent economic recession and the vampire/undead "boom" that accompanied it, a

Figure 13.2   Lobby entrance of the Kentucky Theatre at 214 East Main, decorated to promote *Dracula* (1931). Reprinted by courtesy of the Lafayette Studios Collection, University of Kentucky Archives.

boom that in many ways is still surging in 2013. So, when times are tough financially, the United States routinely turns to the vampire, and monsters generally, for
help. Ironically, before the Universal film appeared, *Dracula*'s stage play was already
helping to fight the Depression in America before it even started, grossing profits
that would keep theaters afloat ("'Dracula' Makes Money," *The New York Evening
Post*, May 25, 1929: M7). *The Seattle Daily Times* reported, "With heavy advance seat
sales the Pantages Theatre will reopen tonight as one of the leading legitimate play-
houses of the Pacific Coast, playing for its first attraction the sensational thrill-drama,
'Dracula'," with the play's "Los Angeles cast intact" ("Advance Sales for 'Dracula' Are
Reported Heavy," June 24, 1929: 5). Among the superstitions that began to surround
the play's "eerie occurrences" during its New York run, "there is one," wrote *The
Seattle Daily Times*, "that any person who plays a part in 'Dracula' will become successful." Movies were the next logical step, offering, according to Skal (2001: 115),
"an instinctive, therapeutic escape," and the Depression was their galvanizing force.
Skal (2001: 115) records Gilbert Seldes as saying, "The rich could still go to the South
Seas Islands; the intellectuals went to Mexico; the poor went to the movies." Merrick
(1931) called the success of Lugosi's portrayal "one of those strange freaks of popular
approval"; however, things were about to get even weirder.

Frankenstein's Monster and Spooks on Parade

Enter *Frankenstein* (1931) starring Boris Karloff. Backed by the financial success of
Dracula, Laemmle, Jr., authorized the production of Mary Shelley's famous Gothic
masterpiece. As the novel had long been in the public domain, Universal had merely
to purchase the rights to the stage adaption by Balderston and Peggy Webling (at a
mere half of what was paid to Stoker's widow for *Dracula*) to bar outside competition
and begin production of its second horror picture (Skal, 2001: 128). What followed
shocked, as *Dracula* did months before, the sensibilities of film-goers and critics
alike. The ever-vigilant Mollie Merrick (1931) of *The Times-Picayune* observed:

> Ladies have fainted—and gentlemen also—and little children, brought to the picture
> [*Frankenstein*] by unsuspecting parents have cried out in terror. But did papa and
> mamma take them home? They did not. They stayed to see the finish and made little
> Johnny hide his eyes on the paternal shoulder. In short, "Frankenstein" seems to be
> what the public wants this year, with lack of work, hunger, panhandling, and other
> disastrous elements.

Yet, "where 'Dracula' merely drew aside the veils of the mysterious and
blood-curdling things as yet hinted at in other motion picture productions,"
Merrick notes, "'Frankenstein' went the whole gamut": "Nothing put on in the
Grand Guignol had anything on this film. In color—and what a fine touch that nice
ruby blood would have added to the scheme—it would have bowled them over."
　　Skal (2001: 132) in retrospect describes the Frankenstein monster as a "'Grotesque
mannequin'...an amalgam of conventional bodies torn apart and reassembled

according to new, logical-angular, electromechanical principles. The square head ... powerfully evokes the plight of an old consciousness forced to occupy a new paradigm, a round brain bolted uneasily into a machine-tooled skull." The effect was disturbing. "Why did you make such a picture?" Merrick asked of Laemmle, Jr. following a press viewing. His "answer was straightforward, truthful and interesting: 'Because we made so much money on "Dracula'." Merrick continued, noting that the rise of a new horror genre "is not an arraignment of Carl Laemmle, Jr." "If there is an arraignment of any kind," she offers, "it is the taste of the American public that is on trial," a public that "would seem to have gone over wholeheartedly for a type of entertainment which formerly was attributed to the vitiation of Old World audiences. The Grand Guignol has entered the American movie theater and there seems to be a definite place for it. Yes—even a demand for it. How come?" Motion pictures, Merrick concluded,

> must provide thrills and they have run the gamut thus far. Realism has entered into movie making and most of the thrills which gangland, war, and life in general can furnish, have been exhausted. There is left, ladies and gentlemen, horror. And it looks as if we will have plenty of it.

One wonders if Merrick could possibly have known just how right she would be. The 1930s were only just getting started.

Universal unleashed over the next 5 years a stream of supernatural monsters who today are, as they were then, the kings of their kind. Yet beyond Universal, there were two exceptions in Skal's view. Just before the New Year, Paramount released *Dr. Jekyll and Mr. Hyde* (1931) staring Fredric March as Dr. Henry Jekyll/Mr. Hyde. And while also not a Universal film, Metro-Goldwyn-Mayer released in February of 1932 Tod Browning's pre-Production Code sideshow narrative entitled *Freaks*, which featured cast members with real deformities who did not have to rely on special makeup and costumes. The film's taboo nature would force it into "hibernation" for several decades, yet the film, as Skal (2001: 159) rightly contends, "would eventually have as large an imaginative impact as any of its fellow creations" of the previous 12 months. What Skal (2001: 159) terms the "four archetypes" of the American horror film had all "sprung into mass consciousness in response to the trauma of the Great Depression":

> They contained perceptible, if unintended, metaphors of economic and class warfare. Dracula, a sanguinary capitalist, relocates from Transylvania after draining the local peasants. The bourgeois Dr. Jekyll exploits and destroys a woman of the lower classes. The freaks live in a literally unbalanced social competition — "big people" against "little people." And the Frankenstein monster is a poignant symbol for an army of abject and abandoned laborers, down to his work clothes and asphalt-spreader's boots.

To return to Universal, the studio gave audiences, the same year as *Freaks*, Karl Freund's unforgettable *The Mummy* (1932) starring Boris Karloff, then released James Whale's *The Invisible Man* (1933) starring Claude Rains the following year.

Figure 13.3   James Whale directed one of the best and most iconic horror films of the classical era, Universal's *Bride of Frankenstein* (1935), even as the cycle was beginning to wane. Directed by James Whale. Produced by Universal Pictures.

Universal's first horror cycle wound down in 1935 with James Whale's *The Bride of Frankenstein*, and in 1936 with *Dracula's Daughter* (1936), arguably the last installment in Universal's classical horror pictures (Figure 13.3).

Notably, Universal looked not only to European Gothic literature for its steady supply of reliable and (with the exception of *Dracula*) public domain "cash crops," but found equally lucrative adapting the dark works of American Gothicist Edgar Allan Poe, with the haunting darkly envisaged productions of *Murders in the Rue Morgue* (1932) starring Lugosi, and *The Black Cat* (1934) and *The Raven* (1935), both starring Lugosi and Karloff. The latter two titles, however, felt the increasingly long arm of the MPPDA (Motion Pictures Producers and Distributors of America), and across the Atlantic horror fared even worse under the new restrictions in Britain. By the release of *Dracula's Daughter* the following year, the title character of the de-feminized (i.e., butch) Countess Marya Zaleska fell, too, under the heavy hand of the MPPDA "like many other post-Code 1930s female characters," Benshoff (1997: 81) is keen to note, such that her propensity for attractive, female "victim-lovers" is all but vaguely nuanced. Strictly prohibited under the newly enforced production code were portrayals, or mere suggestions, of homosexuality on the screen, resulting in the strange, ambivalent exchange between Lily (Nan Gray) and the Countess in the Countess's art studio, a scene that underwent several rewrites before receiving approval from the censors. Nevertheless, these were but mere warning tremors of what was to come in the 1940s. *Dracula's Daughter* looked ahead to "an increasing domesticization" of monsters during the war years, "the idea of monstrous communities, less interest in the so-called normal couple, and a more vigorous interest in psychiatry or medical science as a tool for treating and/or eventually 'curing' the monster" (Benshoff, 1997: 77). Frequent change of hands in Universal's management, combined with the new "morality" fueling the censors and the public's increased awareness of sex crimes through the media, conspired to usher in the horror dearth of the late-1930s.

Universal had become a factory of horror, unwittingly developing, with its motley gaggle of monsters and other horror programmers, a self-sustaining franchise, one whose economical benefits helped to ease the financial burden of many of the studio's toughest years. For Skal (2001: 114), "the most lasting and influential invention of 1931" — (or indeed of the decade, I would add) — was modern horror cinema, because it "served as a kind of populist surrealism, rearranging the human body and its processes, blurring the boundaries between Homo sapiens and other species, responding uneasily [not only] to new and almost incomprehensible developments in science" but the challenges these developments posed to previously stable structures, like society, religion, and psychology.

The power of horror films, their essential place in the human experience, is underscored, even today, by their unwavering lucrativeness. In 1938, this became painfully obvious to conservative groups and institutions bent on the censure of horror pictures on moral and psychological grounds when a Los Angeles film exhibitor paired *Dracula* and *Frankenstein* together in the hopes of making a quick buck. Instead, the double billing "broke all records" and afterwards spawned similar dual revivals in other cities like Philadelphia and Manhattan. Universal executives began scratching their chins again, and so was the way paved for the 1940s, a decade that would produce, for Universal in particular as well as other studios, monster match-ups, horror films as wartime propaganda, and hybrid genres like horror-comedy. But for other studios, amid a decade that produced a world war even bloodier and more horrible than the previous one, it was to "psychological horror" and a newer, darker *mise-en-scène* that the human psyche had turned.

References

Benshoff, H.M. (1997) *Monsters in the Closet: Homosexuality and the Horror Film*, Manchester University Press, Manchester.

Jones, C.P. (1933) Post-view. *The Times-Picayune* (Sep 3), p. 8.

Lugosi, B. (1990) Special introduction, in *Dracula: The Original 1931 Shooting Script (Universal Filmscripts Series)*, vol. 13 (ed. P.J. Riley), Hollywood, Atlantic City, pp. 7–8.

Manchel, F. (1970) *Terrors of the Screen*, Prentice-Hall, Inc., Englewood Cliffs, NJ.

Merrick, M. (1931) Hollywood — in Person. *The Times-Picayune* (Dec 27), p. 2.

Rickels, L.A. (1999) *The Vampire Lectures*, University of Minnesota Press, Minneapolis, MN.

Riley, P.J. (1990) *Dracula: The Original 1931 Shooting Script (Universal Filmscripts Series)*, vol. 13, Atlantic City, Hollywood.

Skal, D.J. (1993) *Dracula: The Ultimate, Illustrated Edition of the World Famous Vampire Play*, St. Martin's Press, New York.

Skal, D.J. (2004) [1990] *Hollywood Gothic: The Tangled Web of Dracula from Novel to Stage to Screen, Revised Edition* edn, Faber and Faber, Inc., New York.

Skal, D.J. (2001[1993]) *The Monster Show: A Cultural History of Horror*, Faber and Faber, Inc., New York.

Soanes, W. (1930) Jane Fooshee Will Open Special Fulton Season Following Lugosi Week. *Oakland Tribune* (July 6), p. 8-S.

Spadoni, R. (2007) *Uncanny Bodies: The Coming of Sound Film and the Origins of the Horror Genre*, University of California Press, Berkeley and Los Angeles, CA.

Valente, J. (2002) *Dracula's Crypt: Bram Stoker, Irishness, and the Question of Blood*, University of Illinois Press, Champaign, IL.

Worland, R. (2007) *The Horror Film: An Introduction*, Blackwell Publishing, Malden, MA.

14

Horror in the 1940s

Mark Jancovich

The 1940s are rarely seen as a distinct period within the history of the English-language horror film, but merely as the decadent tail-end of the 1930s production. For example, many films are accused of having a "rehashed plot" (Gifford, 1973: 131) while others are condemned for using the kind of tricks that "helped stuntman Edwin Parker look like Chaney look like Tyler look like Karloff" in *The Mummy's Tomb* (1942) (Gifford, 1973: 139). The implication here is not simply that these films were imitations of earlier films but that the process of imitation obeyed a law of diminishing returns. For Tudor, the war period "simply extends the patterns already established in the 1930s," and in ways that were often taken to "desperate limits" (Tudor, 1989: 34). Similarly, John Brosnan claims that 1940s horror films "were but pale shadows of the original versions produced a decade earlier" (1976: 73) and that each "sequel was worse than the one before" (Butler, 1971: 46). However, the nadir of this process of degeneration is usually seen as being *Abbott and Costello Meet Frankenstein* (1948), which is supposed to be a "mockery of the once-serious monsters" and to confirm "the decline in the serious side of the genre" (Frank in P. Hardy, 1985: 74). Similarly, Butler describes the 1940s as "the sad path to the Abbott and Costello travesty" (1971: 56), while Twitchell sees the film as the culmination of "the process of vulgarization" that distinguishes the period (1985: 55).

Against this narrative of deterioration, the only exceptions or significant contributions are presumed to be the films produced by Val Lewton at RKO. For Brosnan, these films "have a unique place in the history of the horror film" (1976: 73), while David Punter claims that the 1940s was a "period of comparative infertility" that was "relieved only by the undoubted but minor-key successes of the Lewton/Tourneur production team" (1980: 347). Not only have these films inspired a series of studies

A Companion to the Horror Film, First Edition. Edited by Harry M. Benshoff.
© 2014 John Wiley & Sons, Inc. Published 2017 by John Wiley & Sons, Inc.

(see for example Nemerov, 2005; Newman, 1999; Siegel, 1972; Telotte, 1985; and Wood, 1972) but most of these studies distinguish the Lewton films both from their period and from the horror film more generally. According to Clarens, "the movies of Val Lewton stand out as chamber music against the seedy bombast of the claw-and-fang epics of the day" (1967: 111). They are claimed to be "ambitiously literary" works (Clarens, 1967: 112) that are notable for their "poetry" (Butler 1971: 78), and compared to "the beauty of Cocteau's *La Belle et La Bête* (1946), or Autant-Lara's *Sylvie et le Fantome* (1946)" (Everson, 1974: 186).

In this way, they are disassociated from other "monster movies" through their supposed "atmospheric and imaginative" qualities (Butler, 1971: 76) and described as "eerie and understated" (Frank, 1977: 46). They are claimed to be restrained films that privilege the "suggested" over the "explicit" (Butler, 1971: 76), and Lewton is attributed with the belief "that it was not the thing seen but the thing unseen that truly terrified" (Gifford, 1973: 161). In other words, the Lewton films are supposed to elicit the imagination of their viewers more than other horror films, something that is partly accomplished through their "distinctive use of light and shade" (Tudor, 1989: 34), which not only obscures the monster but is also related to the thematics of these films. For many critics, the Lewton films are crucially concerned with the "shadow" as the sign of repression and the unconscious, and they call the apparently normal world into question. The shadow is an alter-ego or dark self that haunts the world of light, and a film such as *I Walked With a Zombie* (1943) is claimed to be "built around an elaborate set of apparently clear-cut structural oppositions: Canada—West Indies, white—black, light—darkness, life—death, science—black magic, Christian—Voodoo, conscious—unconscious, and so on—and it proceeds to systematically blur all of them" (Wood, 1986: 86).

Despite the current consensus surrounding the Lewton's films, they were not so positively received during the 1940s and the *New York Times* was particularly hostile towards them (Jancovich, 2011). If most critics today suggest that 1940s critics could not see beyond the lurid titles used to market these films, publications such as the *New York Times* actually demonstrated a high degree of affection for lowbrow horror (Jancovich, 2010) and did not object to the Lewton films for being lowbrow horror films but quite the reverse: they accused them of being "pretentious." For these publications, the Lewton films were middlebrow efforts that threatened the distinction between the lowbrow horror films associated with Universal and Columbia, and a prestige horror cycle that was exemplified by films such as *Rebecca* (1940), *Jane Eyre* (1944), and *The Spiral Staircase* (1946) (Jancovich, 2010; Jancovich, 2013).

The point here is not to present the 1940s critics as "right" but rather, as Barbara Klinger (1994) and others have noted, to recognize that criticism is a form of "social discourse" and that current accounts of the period rely on assumptions that need to be identified, examined, and even challenged. For example, as Peter Hutchings puts it, the "negative perception of sequel-heavy 1940s Universal horror is often intertwined with a prejudice against the sequel itself as a particular cinematic format, with the sequelization process seeming to mark the moment where innovation ends and exploitation begins" (2004: 20).

"Creepy Pix Cleaning Up": Production Trends in 1940s Horror

If the 1940s horror films start to look very different when one begins to work with definitions of horror current at the time rather than definitions that are imposed retrospectively, these films also look very different when one acknowledges that they constituted a separate and distinct cycle of production. Indeed, despite presenting the 1940s as simply the tail-end of the 1930s, most accounts of the genre's history acknowledge that the 1930s horror cycle had largely come to an end by 1936 and that production only restarted in 1939, after a small cinema in Los Angeles, the Regina, had phenomenal success in late 1938 with the triple bill of *Frankenstein* (1931), *Dracula* (1931), and *Son of Kong* (1933). In response, Universal quickly made *Frankenstein* and *Dracula* available as a nationwide double bill and organized a personal appearance tour by Bela Lugosi to promote it. As Bela Lugosi observed shortly after, "One day, I drove past [the Regina] and see my name [on the theater marquee], and big lines people all around. I wonder what is giving away to the people — may be bacon or vegetables. But it is the comeback of horror, and I come back." (Quoted in Lennig, *The Immortal Count: The Life and Times of Bela Lugosi*. Lexington: University of Kentucky Press, 2003: 260)

Universal then took the step of putting a new horror film into production, *Son of Frankenstein* (1939), and by 1939 almost every major motion picture studio had a horror project in production: Universal released *Son of Frankenstein* and *Tower of London*; Fox countered with *The Hound of the Baskervilles*, *The Gorilla*, and *The Adventures of Sherlock Holmes*; Warner's contribution was *The Return of Dr. X*; Paramount had a major hit with the comedy-horror film, *The Cat and the Canary*; RKO cast Charles Laughton as *The Hunchback of Notre Dame*; Columbia began a series of four Boris Karloff vehicles with *The Man They Could Not Hang*; and United Artists distributed Samuel Goldwyn's *Wuthering Heights*.

After this explosion of productivity, 1940 was a period of reflection for most of the studios, although the year also witnessed the monumental critical and commercial success of United Artist's film version of *Rebecca*, a film that was clearly understood as a horror film at the time and became the most requested release by women in the early 1940s ("ARI Report 163, Princeton 25th July 1942", in *Gallup Looks at the Movies: Audience Research Reports 1940–1950*, Delaware: Scholarly Resources, 1979). *Rebecca* also established two key trends in horror during the 1940s. First, not only was it a horror film but also a woman's film, and it clearly demonstrated the potential market for horror films targeted at women. Second, it was a prestige

Figure 14.1   A dark mansion, a sinister housekeeper, and a haunting specter made *Rebecca* (1940) one of the era's most successful horror films. Directed by Alfred Hitchcock. Produced by Selznick International Pictures.

production that demonstrated that horror need not be relegated to the less profitable, low budget end of the market (Figure 14.1).

Elsewhere, other studios continued to experiment with the horror film. Paramount sought to recapture the success of *The Cat and the Canary* with *The Ghostbreakers* (1940), while also releasing the spectacular *Dr. Cyclops* (1940), with its use of vivid color and special effects. Columbia released two more Karloff vehicles and cast Peter Lorre in *Island of Doomed Men* (1940). Indeed, during the 1940s, Lorre was understood as one of the major horror stars of this period, appearing in a wide range of pictures for Columbia. For Warner Bros., he also starred in the now classic horror film *The Beast with Five Fingers* (1946). However, it was Universal that responded most vigorously and exploited its brand as a horror producer, a strategy that did not necessarily depend on the grinding out of horror sequels. Instead, it initially focused on new properties and even when it did turn to series production, its key series were not Frankenstein or Dracula but its creations of the 1940s.

In 1940, then, Universal's only sequel was to James Whale's 1933 film, *The Invisible Man*, and most of its productions were new efforts such as *Black Friday* and *The House of the Seven Gables*. Its biggest horror success, however, was with *The Mummy's Hand*, which was not a sequel to *The Mummy* (1932) but featured a whole new cast of characters and most particularly a new monster that was markedly different in both its motivation and its powers from Karloff's creation nearly a decade earlier. The studio was quick to capitalize on this success and the new mummy became central to one of Universal's key series during the 1940s. The other key series was developed the following year with *The Wolf Man* (1941), which was a break from *Werewolf of London* (1935) that featured new characters and a new monster with its own mythology. In contrast, neither Frankenstein nor Dracula really became fully fledged series during the 1940s. *The Ghost of Frankenstein* was not released until 1942, 3 years after *Son of Frankenstein*, and only once Universal had had success with the Mummy and the Wolf Man.

Even then there were no more productions that solely focused on Frankenstein's monster, and when the monster appeared in his next film, *Frankenstein Meets the Wolf Man*, the narrative of the film was centered on Lon Chaney Jr.'s Wolf Man. Frankenstein's monster became very much a secondary figure, a situation exacerbated by the studio's decision to cut the monster's role still further due to anxieties about Bela Lugosi's accent. The same is true of Dracula. The only follow-ups to the 1931 *Dracula* were *Dracula's Daughter* in 1936 (at the end of the 1930s cycle) and *Son of Dracula* in 1943, just before Universal turned to films such as *House of Frankenstein* (1944), *House of Dracula* (1945), and *Abbott and Costello Meet Frankenstein*, where the studio brought their monsters together while still privileging the Wolf Man over their other monsters.

Instead of depending on the monsters of the 1930s, then, Universal concentrated on developing other series during the 1940s and, in 1942, it started a series of Sherlock Holmes films, which, as I have shown elsewhere, were clearly understood as horror films at the time (Jancovich, 2005). For example, the *New York Times* praised *The Pearl of Death* (1944) for its "horror-chills," although other films in the series were attacked for being too clichéd in their horror materials (P.P.K., "Holmes At it Again," *New York Times*, August 26, 1944: 15). In 1943, the studio also launched the *Captive Wild Woman* films; and, in 1944, it initiated the *Inner Sanctum* series. It also continued to produce horror films that were not part of any series, including *Man Made Monster* (1941), *Horror Island* (1941), *The Black Cat* (1941), *The Mad Doctor of Market Street* (1942), *The Strange Case of Doctor Rx* (1942), *Night Monster* (1942), *Phantom of the Opera* (1943) *The Mad Ghoul* (1943), *The Climax* (1944), *Phantom Lady* (1944), and *Cobra Woman* (1944).

If 1940 and 1941 can therefore be seen as a moment of experimentation and reflection, 1942 was one of the key pivotal moments in the period due to the commercial success of Val Lewton's *Cat People*. As we have seen, the film is usually regarded today as a unique and original intervention in the genre but it was seen very differently at the time. Indeed, as Kim Newman (1999) has claimed, *Cat People* was an overt attempt to hybridize the werewolf themes of Universal's *The Wolf Man* with the female-centered narrative of Selznick's *Rebecca*. After all, when RKO approached

Lewton to set up the horror unit at RKO, he was working for Selznick as a script editor on films such as *Gone With the Wind* (1939) and *Rebecca,* and was developing Selznick's adaptation of *Jane Eyre,* a film that was referred to by critics as a "romantic horror tale" (Bosley Crowther, "'Jane Eyre,' a Sombre Version of the Bronte Novel with Joan Fontaine and Orson Welles, Opens at the Music Hall," *New York Times,* February 4, 1944: 12). Indeed, as Biesen (2005), Hanson (2008), and Worland (1997) have all demonstrated, manpower shortages, and government propaganda designed to encourage women to taken on war work, all contributed to the trend for female-centered narratives. In the case of *Return of the Vampire* (1944), for example, a female scientist takes the place of the customary (male) Van Helsing figure as the vampire's nemesis (Figure 14.2).

Although *Cat People* may not have been a unique and unprecedented film, it had profound and direct impact on the development of the horror film during the 1940s. Despite its modest budget, *Cat People* became a phenomenal commercial success: its estimated budget was $134,000 but reports of its gross takings are between $2,000,000 and $4,000,000 (Siegel, 1972: 39). Throughout 1943, Lewton also put out a range of other horrors that were modestly budgeted, culturally ambitious, and heavily targeted at female audiences: *I Walked with a Zombie, The Seventh Victim, The Leopard Man* and *The Ghost Ship,* although the last of these was a brief departure from his other female-friendly fare.

By 1943, then, *Variety* was openly commenting on a new period in the horror film, and the title of one article, "Creepy Pix Cleaning Up," captured the key issues through the use of a pun. "Creepy Pix" were not just "cleaning up" at the box office, but were cleaning up their act in the process (Jim Cunningham, "Creepy Pix Cleaning Up: Studios Cash in on Cycle", *Variety.* March 31, 1943: 7). In his work on cinema exhibition, Douglas Gomery (1996: 51) notes that one of the key ways in which the major studios maintained their power was through their control of a small number of first run picture houses: "From their theatres the Big Five took in three quarters to seven-eighths of all dollars. Only after they granted their own theatres first runs and soaked up as much of the box-office grosses as possible did they permit smaller, independently owned theatres to scramble for the remaining bookings, sometimes months, or even years, after a film's premiere." As the *Variety* article made clear, it was not simply that these "creepy pix" were "cleaning up in most spots around the country" but that they were "even getting first run and downtown bookings in an unprecedented manner" (Cunningham: 7). In other words, while some of the 1930s horror films were clearly major productions, the horror film had come to be associated with the lower end of the market, a process that was changing in 1942 and 1943. Not only were they securing a strong footing within the most profitable markets but also "their usually low budgets" meant that horror films were "reaping comparatively greater profit than other picture types." The horror film was going up market and was making considerable profits as a result.

Figure 14.2   Universal's *Captive Wild Woman* (1943) cashed in on the female-centered horror of both *Rebecca* (1940) and *Cat People* (1942), albeit in far less subtle ways. Directed by Edward Dmytryk. Produced by Universal Pictures.

Consequently, it was not only claimed that these films were "stacking up more importantly daily on most Hollywood lots" so that more and more projects were being given the "go-ahead," but also that horror films were changing their image. This involved both greater cultural ambitions and a tendency to be more ambiguous about their generic associations. Although it was clear that the studios had long had problems getting horror films past the Production Code Administration (PCA), the *Variety* article displaces this problem onto Britain: "To meet toning down requirements of the British, studios here are not only who-dun-iting horrors to permit their classification as mystery yarn, but also interpolating with comedy, slapstick and nightclub sequences" (Cunningham: 46). Indeed, although the article is about "creepy pix," the issue of generic classification is immediately apparent in the first line, which refers to these "creepy pix" as a category that includes "Horror pictures, horror in whodunits and just plain whodunits" but then proceeds to describe all of these as "chillers" and then as "horrors" (Cunningham: 7), even if some of these horrors are "who-dun-iting" themselves. In other words, the "whodunit" is at one moment a separate category, at another merely a subgenre of horror, and then at yet another, merely a disguise for horror.

Horror, Mysteries and Thrillers

As we have already seen, the Sherlock Holmes films were one of Universal's key horror series and their marketing described them as "whodunits," "mysteries," *and* "horror" (Jancovich, 2005). Not only are generic categories hardly impermeable but also, despite claims to the contrary, marketing campaigns rarely explicitly identify films in generic terms. As Rick Altman (1999: 128) has put it:

> Since naming a genre is tantamount to taking a political stand, and always runs the risk of alienating potential spectators who systematically avoid the genre, Hollywood studios prefer instead to imply genre affiliation rather than actually to name any specific genre (except films specifically designed to take advantage of a "hot" genre). The goal is of course to attract those who recognize and appreciate the signs of a particular genre, while avoiding repulsion of those who dislike the genre.

Consequently, films rarely play to one set of genre tastes and their marketing campaigns often stress a range of different pleasures, such as the "comedy, slapstick, and nightclub sequences" mentioned by Cunningham above.

However, even the terms "whodunit," "detective story," and "mystery" have a complex relationship, and "mystery" was not simply equivalent to the previous two. While the term *whodunit* suggests that the solving of a puzzle is central to the narrative, the term *mystery* was not primarily associated with puzzle- solving as is common today. Rather it was concerned with the strange, uncanny, and *mysterious*. For example, in his account of the story types used to organize production and marketing strategies in the period, Handel (1950) demonstrates that mystery and horror were seen as virtually synonymous terms, although mystery implied suggestion and restraint and was therefore a much less problematic term for the PCA than horror. In other words, as Cunningham makes clear, the studios had much less trouble with the censors if they could classify a project as a "mystery yarn" rather than a "horror film."

In the 1940s, then, understandings of horror were different from those common today and one of the main reasons that the period is currently seen as a relatively unproductive one is that many of the films identified as horror at the time have been reclassified since then. The point here is not to reclaim specific films for the category of horror but to refute claims about the essential characteristics of a genre, and to concentrate instead on historically specific definitions of genre — to reconstruct how genres are understood in specific periods rather than to retrospectively impose later definitions back onto earlier periods, or vice versa. As such, this project is similar to that which Steve Neale undertook in relation to melodrama, in which he surveyed *Variety*'s use of the term between 1920 and 1950 and found that it was very different from the use made by film critics in the 1970s and 1980s, by which time it was strongly associated with woman's genres: "The mark of [the films identified as melodrama between 1920 and 1950] was not pathos, romance, and domesticity, but action, adventure, and thrills; not 'feminine' genres and woman's films but war films, adventure films, horror films, and thrillers, genres traditionally thought of as, if anything, 'male'" (1993: 69).

Nor was the association between mystery and horror new. It had a long history that goes back at least as far as the late eighteenth century when many Gothic novels were explicitly identified *both* as tales of horror and as mysteries, such as *The Mysteries of Udolpho*. This association was still in circulation in the early 1970s when monster hunters Scooby Doo and the gang began traveling the countryside in their van, the *Mystery* Machine. Thus, while descriptions of the Sherlock Holmes films did refer to Holmes as a detective, the films were explicitly identified as horror films, and often associated with the terms "fear," "terror," and "horror" in their market campaigns and even in their titles. Furthermore, they were also claimed to feature the "weird" and "eerie" and concern events that were inexplicable and uncanny, sometimes appearing to be the result of ancient curses. The films were also described as "chillers" or films that provided both "thrills and chills."

Like "mystery," the term *thriller* also had a very different meaning during the 1940s to that which is common today. Rather than being limited to realist dramas of crime or espionage, the thriller was directly associated with the "chiller," and the terms *thrills* and *chills* were often used together as a combination term rather than as two

separate terms. Like the chiller, the thriller was a film targeted at the "thrill seek-
er" and the films identified as such were supposed to be "terrifying," "hair-raising,"
and/or "spinetingling"; they were also supposed to make one's "flesh creep" or induce
"goosepimples." Many films that would still clearly be defined as horror today were
therefore described as thrillers by reviewers during the 1940s, films such as *The Phantom of the Opera* and its follow-up *The Climax* (1944), *The Return of the Vampire*,
and *House of Dracula*. In 1944, Karloff even put his name to a collection of horror
stories in which he distinguished thrillers from horror in ways that might surprise
many readers today. For Karloff, horror was identified with stories that we would
commonly identity with the thriller today:

> Horror carries with it connotations of revulsion which has nothing to do with clean
> terror. If we are not careful we will end up by giving simple terror a bad name. The
> well-told tale of a really juicy murder, with grisly undercurrents of lust and hatred, the
> carnage and what-have-you, topped off with intimate and gory details of how the corpse
> was dismembered and disposed of, and what a time the murderer had cleaning up the
> mess, makes exciting and even shocking reading, with a direct appeal to our morbidity
> and sadism. But we are not really frightened. After all, however cunningly it has been
> dressed up, it is still rather old hat. (Boris Karloff, *Tales of Terror*, Cleveland: World,
> 1943: 10)

Alternatively the thriller is identified with stories that sound much more like the
classic Universal horror films, stories in which "the essential element" is "fear … of
the unknown and the unknowable" (Karloff: 11).

Similarly, many films that we would now describe as thrillers were either explicitly
identified as horror films or discussed in terms that strongly associated them with
horror. For example, *The Maltese Falcon* (1941) was described as a story of "monstrous but logical intrigue" and as "one of the most compelling nervous laughter
provokers yet" (Bosley Crowther, "'The Maltese Falcon,' a Fast Mystery-Thriller With
Quality and Charm, at the Strand," *New York Times*, October 4, 1941: 18), at a time
when references to nervous laughter was one of the ways in which reviewers indicated the success of a horror film (Berenstein, 1996). *This Gun for Hire* (1942) was
also claimed to be "truly hair-raising" (Bosley Crowther, "'This Gun for Hire,' Seen
at The Paramount, Introduces a New 'Tough Guy,'" *New York Times*, May 14, 1942:
23), while Hitchcock's *Foreign Correspondent* (1940) featured "much flesh-creepy
business" (Bosley Crowther, "The Screen: At the Rivoli," *New York Times*, August
28, 1940: 15). Similarly, Hitchcock's *Saboteur* (1942) was simply claimed to "terrify" (Bosley Crowther, "'Saboteur,' Alfred Hitchcock Melodrama, Starring Priscilla
Lane, Robert Cummings and Otto Kruger, at Music Hall," *New York Times*, May 8,
1942: 27). *Shadow of a Doubt* (1943) was described as "a bumper crop of blue-ribbon
shivers and chills" from a director who "can raise more goose pimples to the square
inch of flesh than any other director of thrillers in Hollywood" (Bosley Crowther,

"'Shadow of a Doubt,' a Thriller With Teresa Wright, Joseph Cotton, at Rivoli," *New York Times*, January 13, 1943: 18).

Similarly, the espionage thriller *Journey into Fear* (1943) was described as "a tale of terror" and "a tense invitation to heart failure from fright" (T.S., "At the Palace," *New York Times*, March 19, 1943: 15), while the four major films of 1944 that are seen as establishing film noir—*Phantom Lady*, *Double Indemnity*, *Laura*, and *The Woman in the Window*—were explicitly identified as horror or strongly associated with it. *Phantom Lady* had a "hair-raising climax" and was one of its director's "superior chillers" (Archer Winsten, "'Phantom Lady' Opens at Loews and Let—A Chiller Diller," *New York Post*, February 18, 1944: 466), while *Double Indemnity* was "a spine-chilling film" [Eileen Creelman, "'Double Indemnity,' Billy Wilder's Exciting Version of James M. Cain Novel," *New York Sun*, September 7 (Republished in *New York Motion Picture Critics' Reviews, 1944*: 254)] that was "no picture for the kiddies, nor for adults with faint hearts or weak stomachs" (Crowther, "'Double Indemnity,' a Tough Melodrama, With Stanwyck and McMurray as Killers, Opens at the Paramount," *New York Times*, September 7, 1944: 21). If *Laura* was seen as a rather restrained and elegant film, critics still claimed that it "packs as much wallop, and more, than the deliberate pulse quickening shocker" [Irene Thirer, "'Laura', Superb, Sophisticated Screen Thriller at Roxy," *New York Post*, October 12 (Republished in *New York Motion Picture Critics' Reviews, 1944*: 213)] and "builds up an eerie atmosphere" [Eileen Creelman, "Laura," *New York Sun*, October 12 (Republished in *New York Motion Picture Critics' Reviews, 1944*: 214)]. Finally, *The Woman in the Window* "will give you the screaming meemies" [John McManus, "A Murder Rap at the Window," *New York PM*, January 26 (Republished in *New York Motion Picture Critics' Reviews, 1945*: 484)] and was deliberately engineered to "scare the audience and keep it in a constant state of horror" (Manny Farber, "Crime Does Pay," *New Republic* 1945: 296).

By 1944, then, RKO's *Cat People* had given new impetus to the 1940s horror cycle and the *New York Times* claimed, "Every studio has at least one such picture in production and others coming to a witches boil" (Fred Stanley, "Hollywood Shivers," *New York Times*, 28 May 1944: 13). This chapter refers to Paramount's ghost story, *The Uninvited* (1944), but it also identified other films with this trend, many of which have become disassociated from horror. In addition to films such as *Phantom Lady*, *Laura*, and *The Woman in the Window*, it also referred to films now identified as examples of the Gothic (or paranoid) woman's film such as *Gaslight* (1944) and *Dark Waters* (1944). It also identifies *Hangover Square* (1945) as part of this horror cycle along with "'The House of Dr. Edwardes,' which Alfred Hitchcock will direct for David O Selznick," a film that was later renamed *Spellbound* (1945). Interestingly both of these films have been associated with *both* films noir and the Gothic (or paranoid) woman's film.

Consequently, while it is now common to identify horror, film noir, and the Gothic (or paranoid) woman's film as three distinct and separate types, neither film noir nor the Gothic (or paranoid) woman's film were categories that existed within the United States during the early to mid-1940s. These categories were developed in later periods and then retrospectively imposed on the period, in ways that may have their uses in certain contexts but can also hinder our understanding of the past in other ways. For example, one of the reasons that contemporary critics do not define the Gothic (or paranoid) woman's film as horror is due to the assumption that horror is a masculine genre. For example, Diane Waldman explicitly opposes horror and the Gothic on the grounds that, despite their shared "hesitation between two possible interpretations of events by the protagonist and often, in these filmic presentations, by the spectator," the Gothic (or paranoid) woman's film differs from horror in that "this hesitation is experienced by a character (and presumably a spectator) who is female" (1984: 31). Alternatively, Mary Ann Doane sees horror as being inherently opposed to the concerns of the woman's film, and repeats Linda Williams' equation of horror with the male spectator, so that it is assumed that horror "prompts the little girl (or grown woman) to cover her eyes" and refuse to look (Doane, 1987: 136; Williams, 1984).

Psychology, Realism, and Generic Transformation

An acknowledgement that these three genre categories were not distinguished from one another within the 1940s, but were all identified as horror, can help us observe features that had previously been obscure. For example, despite the claim that film noir (like horror) is a male-centered drama, many key examples of noir were female centered. For example, the main character and chief investigator in *Phantom Lady* is a young secretary who turns "amateur detective to unravel a strange murder" (*Variety*, January 26, 1944: 12) and, as one reviewer observed, the "whole story is the girl's quest" [Cook, "Franchot Tone a Villain in Macabre *Phantom Lady*," *New York World-Telegram*, February 18 (Republished in *New York Motion Picture Critics' Reviews 1944*: 467)]. Conversely, while the Gothic (or paranoid) woman's film is supposedly organized around the protagonist's difficulty seeing and making sense of their world, this feature is also supposed to be a central feature of film noir. Nonetheless, many critics read this problem of vision in the Gothic (or paranoid) woman's film as being a peculiarly feminine dilemma (Waldman, 1984: 31). Doane even claims that these films deny women the investigating gaze or punish them for it: "The violence associated with the attribution of a desire to see to the woman reaches its culmination in the gothic paranoid films, where the cinematic apparatus itself seems to be mobilized against the female spectator, disabling her gaze" (1987: 37). In other words, the female protagonist of these films is presented "as impotent in terms of the actual ability to uncover the secret or attain the knowledge that she desires" (Doane, 1987: 135). The films perform an "invalidation of female perception and interpretation, equating female subjectivity with some kind of false consciousness, as the male character 'corrects' the heroine's impressions" (Waldman, 1984: 33).

However, this argument is ultimately tautological. It ignores the equally insistent problem of vision within film noir or simply asserts that film noir and the Gothic (or paranoid) woman's film are different due to their gendered dynamics: if film noir features problems of seeing, it is associated with masculinity and signifies a crisis in male power; while if the Gothic (or paranoid) woman's film features a problem of seeing, it is associated with femininity and signifies an insistence on woman's inferiority. However, there is an alternative way of understanding these films, many of which feature women who actively investigate and make sense of their world; and despite the claims of Waldman and Doane, these investigating females were rarely invalidated. Indeed, when they were invalidated, as in the case of *Suspicion* (1941), reviewers declared their invalidation to be both illogical and an insult to audiences. Consequently, as John Fletcher has pointed out, these films did not prohibit or punish their female investigators but quite the reverse: like Paula in *Gaslight* (1944), these women are not presented as victims due to some psychological inadequacy but rather due to an "internalized prohibition against recognizing what she knows," a prohibition that she must overcome if she is to save herself (1995: 364). In this way, these investigating women share much in common with the heroines of the Gothic novel, who must refuse the separation of spheres that keeps them ignorant of the world of men. As Kate Ferguson Ellis puts it, these novels allowed "the heroine to purge the infected home and to establish a new one, by having her re-enact the disobedience of Eve and bring out of that a new Eden 'far happier'" (1989: xii). To put it another way, the Gothic (or paranoid) woman's films did not suggest that women were incapable of investigating their world but rather that such an investigation was essential to their survival within it.

The problem of vision within these films was therefore part of a broader generic feature and the *New York Times* stressed that many films in this "new horror cycle" were "fresh psychological efforts" along the lines established by Selznick and Hitchcock with *Rebecca* and exploited by Lewton in *Cat People* (Stanley, 1944: X3). On the one hand, these films were supposed to be suggestive horror films that had indirect marketing and lacked explicit or fantastic material but on the other, they were supposed to be psychological dramas with distraught protagonists and/or psychologically deranged villains. As Kracauer pointed out in 1946, in an article on what he termed the "terror films" or "horror-thrillers" of the period, these films often featured villains who were not only motivated by some psychological compulsion but also performed psychological violence upon their victims: they "no longer shoot, strangle or poison the females that they want to do away with, but systematically try to drive them insane" so that these horror films featured "the theme of psychological destruction" (Siegfried Kracauer, "Hollywood's Terror Films: Do They Reflect an American State of Mind," *Commentary*, 2, 1946: 133).

Nor was this theme restricted to women or simply the result of psychologically disturbed villains. In many cases, it is the male lead that finds himself on the verge of mental breakdown, or explicitly undergoing such a breakdown. Indeed, one of the most celebrated examples of the type was *The Lost Weekend* (1945), in which Ray Milland plays an alcoholic going through a crisis, a film that was explicitly identified as horror at the time. Furthermore, these films do not present either their villains or their victims as psychologically inferior or Other, as Waldman, Doane, and others suggest in relation to the female victim of the Gothic (or paranoid) woman's film — or as Wood, Tudor, and others claim of the psychological horror film prior to *Psycho* (1960). On the contrary, Kracauer and others were highly critical of the absence of such clear distinctions within these films and claimed that "many a current melodrama suggests that normal and abnormal states of mind merge into each other imperceptibly and are hard to keep separate" (Kracauer, 1946: 133). In other words, while Kracauer found this refusal to distinguish clearly between "normal and the abnormal states of mind" to be unhealthy, later critics would not only champion horror films that refused such clear distinctions but also suggest that this trope was a feature of the post-*Psycho* horror film, distinguishing this later period from earlier horror films.

If the psychological aspects of these films were, at least in part, due to their "far more ambitious level" (Stanley, 1944: X3), their ambition was also demonstrated by the upscaling of horror that *Variety* had begun to discern in 1943 but attained new levels in 1944, 1945, and 1946. As the *New York Times* noted, many of these films were "being dressed up in full Class 'A' paraphernalia, including million-dollar budgets and big name casts" (Stanley, 1944: X3). By 1945, MGM had invested so heavily in its production of *The Picture of Dorian Gray* (1945) that *Variety* observed that it was "reported to have cost over $2 million" and doubted whether "the negative cost will be returned" (*Variety*, March 7, 1945: 20). However, this film does not simply demonstrate the scale of investment in horror but also the levels of cultural ambition. This was a prestige literary adaptation, and many horror films of the period sought prestige and respectability, even if critics often accused these films of using cultural materials to disguise or distract attention from their lowbrow elements. Elsewhere, horror films were also taking on serious social issues, as in the case of *The Lost Weekend*, which critics celebrated as a major and important intervention.

Consequently, although Janet Staiger (1992) identifies Rossellini's *Rome, Open City* (1945) as marking a turning point when film critics started to champion realism as a value, the critical reception of *The Lost Weekend* demonstrates that this shift in critical values was well underway before the critical reception of Rossellini's classic, and that such shifts were predominantly bound up with the horror film. Indeed, the process even predates *The Lost Weekend* and can clearly be seen in relation to *Double Indemnity* (1944), which had long been seen as an unfilmable novel due to the restrictions of the PCA. Wilder's 1944 adaption, then, was not only identified as a horror film, but was also "described by some producers as an emancipation for Hollywood writing" (Fred Stanley, "Hollywood Crime and Romance,"

New York Times, November 19, 1944: X1). Furthermore, both *The Woman in the Window* and *The Strange Affair of Uncle Harry* (1945) were seen as horror films at the time and pushed at censorship restrictions through their use of twist endings. Both films evaded censorship by eventually revealing that the stories that they told were simply dreams, a strategy that antagonized some critics who were "more outraged than surprised" by these twists [Archer Winsten, "'Strange Affair of Uncle Harry' Opens at Loew's Criterion," *New York Post*, August 24 (Republished in *New York Motion Picture Critics' Reviews 1945*: 240)]. Others were more sympathetic and saw these twists as overtly ridiculing the Hollywood Production Code: "The ending and the circumstances of censorship and prissiness which obviously dictated it, should have the effect of plaguing the Hays Office out of its high moral collar and into something more comfortable for all of us" [John McManus, "Good to the Last Drop," *New York PM*, August 24 (Republished in *New York Motion Picture Critics' Reviews 1945*: 241)].

Even Kracauer's discussion of the "terror films" clearly places them within the context of these larger shifts and overtly compares them to *Rome, Open City*. Ultimately, Kracauer privileges Rossellini's neo-realism over the terror films on the basis that the latter simply incite terror, while Rossellini's "shocks" were claimed to be a confrontation with social reality that sought to diagnose its problems. As Kracauer claimed, fear can only "be exorcised … by an incessant effort to penetrate it and spell out its causes" (1946: 136). In other words, the "shock" of Rossellini's realism was directly associated with the terror of the 1940s "shockers," even if figures such as Kracauer saw the terrors of Rossellini's film as infinitely superior to those of the Hollywood horror cycle.

However, others saw things differently. There was a clear distinction drawn in the period between "verisimilitude" and "realism" (Robert Hatch, "The New Realism", *New Republic*, March 8, 1948: 27), a distinction that became central to many critics' dissatisfaction with the documentary style thrillers that emerged after *The House on 92nd Street* (1945). For these critics, realism was not simply about resemblance but about the attempt to confront social problems; and it was on this basis that the films were deemed justified in handling materials that troubled the PCA. In other words, the attack on censorship did not suggest that "anything-goes" but that films should escape censorship on the condition that their handling of taboo materials was necessary for social commentary and not simply as a form of sensationalism. Of course, it was acknowledged that the handling of taboo materials would (and should) prove shocking, and this capacity to shock directly identified many realist films with horror while many horror films were presented as being realist.

However, this process would also result in a transformation in horror during the late 1940s. In the early 1940s, there was such a strong association between the horror film and the psychological film that, in its review of *Phantom Lady*, the *New York Times* could claim that its director, Robert Siodmak, was "a former director of German horror films," a term that it used interchangeably with the phrase "German psychological films" (Bosley Crowther "'Phantom Lady,' a Melodrama of Weird

Effects, With Ella Raines and Franchot Tone, Has Premiere at Loew's State," *New York Times*, February 18, 1944: 15). In the early 1940s, psychological films were associated with fantasy and their psychological materials were often dismissed as simply unconvincing explanations for the preposterous behavior of their characters. Of course, this sense did not necessarily oppose the psychological film to realism at the time, given that both were associated with artistic shock tactics that many critics found fantastical and pretentious. However, by the mid-1940s, as psychology gained prestige through its use with veterans of the war, psychology and realism became associated in new ways. No longer was psychology associated with fantasy but came to signify realism, a process that was consolidated by their shared interest in handling repressed or taboo materials in order to diagnose problems. Although horror initially figured heavily in this process, as can be seen in the case of *The Lost Weekend*, the decade also began to see a shift, in which horror became associated with fantasy on the one hand, and the thriller with realist drama on the other, a process that increasingly identified horror with the Gothic and with science fiction, while realist dramas (even those that featured terrifying psychopaths) started to be distinguished from horror.

By 1946, however, the horror cycle was coming to an end. Although many critics today claim that the supposed lack of interest in horror during the 1940s was due to war itself, either because people did not want to be confronted with horror when the world was full of the real horrors of wartime, or that the horrors of the war meant that the old monsters were no long frightening anymore, the highpoint of horror production during the 1940s seems to coincide with the war years. Of course, this does not imply a causal relationship between the end of the war and the decline of the cycle, which may simply have been due to the inevitable tendency to overproduction in cycles. By 1945, the popularity of horror led studios to invest heavily in the genre and so created a situation in which too many films were competing with one another. Certainly, after 1946, films continued to contribute to the cycle, but the period of intense productivity was over by 1947. When Frankenstein, Dracula, and the Wolf Man finally encountered Abbott and Costello in 1948, this encounter was not the end of a process, but rather the start of a new one, in which Universal sought to regenerate the monsters and combine them with the comic duo, a double act that had been crucial to the studio's finances during the 1940s, but whose popularity was also in need of regeneration. However, it was not the Gothic monsters that were to prove central to the next cycle of horror production but rather the monsters associated with another form of fantasy — science fiction.

References

Altman, R. (1999) *Film/Genre*, BFI, London.

Berenstein, R. (1996) *Attack of the Leading Ladies: Gender, Sexuality and Spectatorship in Classic Horror Cinema*, Columbia University Press, New York.

Biesen, S.C. (2005) *Blackout: World War II and the Origins of Film Noir*, Johns Hopkins University Press, Baltimore.

Brosnan, J. (1976) *The Horror People*, Macdonald and Jane, London.

Butler, I. (1971) *Horror in the Cinema*, Paperback Library, New York.

Clarens, C. (1967) *An Illustrated History of the Horror Film*, G. P. Putnam, New York.

Doane, M.A. (1987) *The Desire to Desire: The Woman's Film of the 1940s*, Indiana University Press, Bloomington.

Ellis, K.F. (1989) *The Contested Castle: Gothic Novels and the Subversion of Domestic Ideology*, University of Illinois Press, Urbana.

Everson, W.K. (1974) *Classics of the Horror Film: From the Days of Silent Film to the Exorcist*, Citadel, Secaucus.

Fletcher, J. (1995) Primal scenes and the female Gothic: *Rebecca* and *Gaslight. Screen*, **36**, 4.

Frank, A. (1977) *Horror Films*, Hamlyn, London.

Gifford, D. (1973) *A Pictorial History of Horror Movies*, Hamlyn, London.

Gomery, D. (1996) The economics of the horror film, in *Horror Films: Current Research on Audience Preferences and Reactions* (eds J.B. Weaver III and R. Tamborini), Routledge, New York, pp. 49–62.

Handel, L. (1950) *Hollywood Looks at its Audience: A Report on Film Audience Research*, University of Illinois Press, Urbana, IL.

Hanson, H. (2008) *Hollywood Heroines: Women in Film Noir and the Female Gothic Film*, I.B. Tauris, London.

Hardy, P. (ed.) (1985) *The Aurum Film Encyclopedia: Horror*, Aurum, London.

Hutchings, P. (2004) *The Horror Film*, Longman, London.

Jancovich, M. (2013) Bluebeard's wives': horror, quality and the paranoid woman's film in the 1940s. *Irish Journal of Gothic and Horror Studies*, **12**, http://irishgothichorrorjournal .homestead.com/IJGHS_Issue_12.pdf.

Jancovich, M. (2005) The meaning of mystery: genre, marketing and the Universal Sherlock Holmes Series of the 1940s. *Film International*, **17**, 34–45.

Jancovich, M. (2011) Relocating Lewton: cultural distinctions and generic negotiations in the critical reception of the Val Lewton horror films. *Journal of Film and Video*.

Klinger, B. (1994) *Melodrama and Meaning: History, Culture, and the Films of Douglas Sirk*, Indiana University Press, Bloomington, IN.

Kracauer, S. (1946) Hollywood's terror films: do they reflect an American state of mind. *Commentary* **2**, 132–136, and republished in *New German Critique*, pp. 105–111.

Neale, S. (1993) Melo talk: on the meaning and use of the term 'melodrama' in the American trade press. *Velvet Light Trap*, **22**, 66–89.

Nemerov, A. (2005) *Icons of Grief: Val Lewton and the Home Front*, University of California Press, Berkeley.

Newman, K. (1999) *Cat People*, BFI, London.

Polan, D. (1986) *Power and Paranoia: History, Narrative and the American Cinema, 1940–1950*, Columbia University Press, New York.

Punter, D. (1980) *The Literature of Terror: A History of Gothic Fictions from 1765 to the Present Day*, Longman, London.

Siegel, J. (1972) *Val Lewton: The Reality of Terror*, Secker and Warburg, London.

Staiger, J. (1992) *Interpreting Films: Studies in the Historical Reception of American Cinema*, Princeton University Press, Princeton, NJ.

Stanley, F. (1944) Hollywood Shivers. *New York Times.* (May 28), p. X3.

Telotte, J.P. (1985) *Dreams of Darkness: Fantasy and the Films of Val Lewton*, University of Illinois Press, Urbana.

Tudor, A. (1989) *Monsters and Mad Scientists: A Cultural History of the Horror Movie*, Blackwells, Oxford.

Twitchell, J. (1985) *Dreadful Pleasures: An Anatomy of Modern Horror*, Oxford University Press, New York.

Waldman, D. (1984) 'At last I can tell it to someone!' female point of view and subjectivity in the Gothic romance film of the 1940s. *Cinema Journal*, **23** (2), 29–40.

Williams, L. (1984) When the woman looks, in *Re-Vision: Essays in Feminist Film Criticism* (eds M.A. Doane, P. Mellencamp, and L. Williams), University Publications of America, Frederick, pp. 83–99.

Wood, R. (1972) The shadow worlds of Jacques Tourneur. *Film Comment*, **8**, 64–70.

Wood, R. (1986) *Hollywood from Vietnam to Reagan*, University of Columbia Press, New York.

Worland, R. (1997) OWI meets the monsters: hollywood horror films and war propaganda, 1942–1945. *Cinema Journal*, **37** (1), 47–65.

15

Science Fiction and Horror in the 1950s

Steffen Hantke

Often a cinematic cycle comes most sharply into focus, both in regard to its characteristic morphology and its political/ideological agenda, when rediscovered. 1950s horror films—frequently a blend of horror and science fiction—were first rediscovered in the Reagan era, but it has been post-9/11 America, first under Bush and then under Obama, that has seen a renaissance of the form. Thus, a classic like Don Siegel's *Invasion of the Body Snatchers* (1956) has proven its lasting relevance by way of three remakes (1978/1993/2007), and the three versions of *The Thing from Another World* (1951/1982/2011) have provided dire apocalyptic takes on the Cold War, the Reagan era, and post-9/11 America. Blockbuster remakes of signature 1950s sci-fi horror films like *The Day the Earth Stood Still* (1951/2008) and *War of the Worlds* (1953/2005) continue this trend, as do numerous reworkings of period-specific tropes, such as the giant creature film [*Cloverfield* (2008), *The Mist* (2007)], and the alien invasion film [all of the above-mentioned titles plus television series like *Threshold* (2005), *Surface* (2005), and *Invasion* (2005)]. All of these remakes and reimaginings continue to speak to audiences' fears of ubiquitous enemies both at home and from abroad.

Earlier remakes aside, the "primary political significance" of this most recent rediscovery of 1950s sci-fi horror is in "announcing [its] historical origins and thus asserting an analogy between the 1950s and the Bush years" (Hantke, "Bush's America," 2010a: 149). This gesture may be conceived of as inherently critical of post-9/11 America, undermining the right-wing view of the 1950s as a prelapsarian utopia of affluence and social harmony and highlighting instead Cold War paranoia, suffocating political and social conformity, and apocalyptic anxieties surrounding new military technologies (Hantke, "Return of the Giant Creature," 2010b: 235–257). Contrary to nostalgic retrospection of 1950s sci-fi horror—which often comes with

A Companion to the Horror Film, First Edition. Edited by Harry M. Benshoff.
© 2014 John Wiley & Sons, Inc. Published 2017 by John Wiley & Sons, Inc.

fond memories of film titles that begin with "It Came from …," the spooky wail of a theremin on the soundtrack, and/or a man in a rubber suit with a zipper up its back—the 1950s were a nervous, skittish, neurotic decade, its stability perpetually teetering on the verge of phantasmagoric social panics about Communist fifth columns, the travails of the suburban housewife, juvenile delinquents, the corruption of innocent children through horror comics, and the arrival of flying saucers (Hollings, *Welcome to Mars*, 2006). Horror films of the 1930s and 1940s seemed incapable of keeping up with this emergent zeitgeist. Sold off by the studios in package deals to the newly booming medium of television, their late-night presentation either drained them of their topical life blood or, at best, enshrined them as objects of harmless nostalgia.

Although it contributed to the demise and "camping up" of the horror film's previous cycle (via parodic "Shock Theater" hosts such as Vampira and Zacherley), television also helped elevate 1950s horror films to what was to become their iconic status. While late 1940s and early 1950s television had followed the format of science fiction adventure serials [e.g., *Captain Video* (1949–1955) and *Space Patrol* (1950–1955)], television from the late 1950s and early 1960s began repeating and reinforcing the sci-fi horror iconography prevalent in 1950s cinema. Following an anthology format with each weekly episode standing as an independent story, shows like *Tales of Tomorrow* (1951–1953), *The Twilight Zone* (1959–1964), *One Step Beyond* (1959–1961), and *The Outer Limits* (1963–1965) recycled and entrenched, but also reinterpreted and broadened the scope of cinematic horror during a time when the number of pulp magazines and horror comics was diminishing [due to their investigation by the Senate Subcommittee on Juvenile Delinquency (1953–1954)].

Although this thematic continuity and exchange between film and television could still be seen as market competition, the Paramount Decision in 1948, limiting the major studios' oligopoly by cutting back on their control of distribution and exhibition, opened film production to a wider variety of players. Smaller production companies like American International Pictures, formed in 1954 by James H. Nicholson and Samuel Z. Arkoff, as well as some of its occasionally affiliated independent producer–directors like Roger Corman, Herman Cohen, and Bert I. Gordon, managed to establish themselves with low-budget projects in this more accommodating marketplace. While the major studios continued to make successful and significant horror films during the era—among them Warner Bros.' *House of Wax* (1953) and Universal International's *The Creature from the Black Lagoon* series (1954, 1955, 1956)—low-budget independent films helped to define the era by solidifying the youth market, making the drive-in a (if not *the*) major outlet for the era's horror films. And although the Production Code was still in place, the more variable distribution and exhibition opportunities during the 1950s would pave the way for more daring and graphic horror of subsequent decades.

While these economic conditions helped to ensure the prolific production of horror films, the uncertainties and anxieties concomitant with the transition from World War II to the Cold War provided fertile ground for the genre's thematic preoccupations. Vivian Sobchack reads the thematic inventory of (broadly speaking) fantastic films during the period as "a symbolic response to an America transformed by heightened public recognition of the vast power and sociopolitical consequences of rapid advances in science and technology; a new consciousness of the relativity of spatial and temporal distance and the planet as a connected global community; and by a lived sense of political enmity and geophysical vulnerability" (2005: 262–263). From Henry Luce's declaration that the twentieth century was going to be the "American Century," to the Truman Doctrine and America's first steps toward its new global ambitions in Greece, Hungary, and on the Korean peninsula, the 1950s marks a period in which popular culture helped to recruit Americans into a new imperial paradigm.

The films of the period contribute to this recruitment process: through fear and desire, positive and negative viewer identification, aggression and pacification, and, specifically, the dynamic of sadism and masochism that animates the horror film. These films arrive, inevitably it seems, at the moment when American authority, military power, and social and political values and thought are to be triumphant. Compelling as this recruitment may be on the level of narrative cohesion and closure, its celebration of American superiority—"victory culture," as Tom Engelhardt has called it (2007: 9)—begins to crumble at the level of the isolated moment, revealing an underlying and thus more profound emotional and ideological complexity, what Engelhardt diagnoses as "triumphalist despair" (2007: 9). It is at this level of the era's horror films—the frisson, the sharp shock, the gasp, or the shudder—that paranoia, fear, and abjection reign unchallenged. It is at this level that those left out of the postwar economic boom—the radiation victim, the traumatized WWII veteran, the homosexual, the juvenile delinquent, the wayward child, and the medicated suburban housewife—among others—remain visible against the allegedly seamless background of American victory culture.

Horror and Science Fiction: Abjection and Technoscience

Any survey of what might loosely be termed cinematic fantasy during the 1950s is likely to turn up a number of films that will be listed either as science fiction or as horror. A film like Jack Arnold's *Tarantula* (1955) positions itself exactly on this boundary between genres. Its basic premise—that a scientist develops a technology which escapes his control and, having wreaked havoc across the countryside, ultimately kills him before it is contained and destroyed—has been at the heart of the gothic tradition since Mary Shelley's *Frankenstein, or The Modern Prometheus* (1818), a text that combines horror's emphasis on physical abjection with science fiction's use of scientific rhetoric as a means of legitimizing the presence of the fantastic. Mad scientists, like the one in *Tarantula*, had appeared in horror films before the 1950s, most famously in Universal's *Frankenstein* films (1931, 1935, 1939) as well as in *Doctor X* (1932) and *The Invisible Ray* (1936). Though the science practiced by these scientists often took its cue from technological advances of their time, the films lack a coherent framework to render them relevant as a phenomenon with broader social consequences. Only during the 1950s, which harnessed postwar affluence to technological progress in a synergy of civilian and military life famously described by President Eisenhower as the "military industrial complex," did such a framework come into existence. While scientists in 1930s horror films primarily replayed the mythical dimensions of the "modern Prometheus," those in 1950s horror films reflect back on the concrete realities of a technoscience intensified and accelerated by wartime research and transformed by the postwar security state into an omnipresent institutional force that permeates military and civilian life alike. Unlike their more mythical predecessors, the agents of this force operate in a world of grant proposals, commercial applicability, and institutional accountability.

With its mad scientist, its references to radioactivity and acromegaly, *Tarantula* is still doing what Shelley did, mobilizing the rhetoric of science in order to literalize its central metaphor and legitimize its uncanny state (within a diegesis that insists on conventional cinematic realism). Repeatedly, the film manages to construct scenes of intense emotion around the menacing appearance of its eponymous central monster. The film's giant spider also inspires a persistent and unsettling paranoia even when it is not on screen; after its escape from the laboratory, its presence haunts the Southwest desert and turns it into an eerie place, an agoraphobic nightmare setting notable for its departure from horror's usual preference for small claustrophobic enclosures. Like the vertical threat inherent in the Cold War mantra "Keep watching the skies," the wide open horizontals of panoramic landscapes are infused with anxieties close to horror. However, the tarantula's sheer size — by the end of the film it appears as large as a city block — as well as its somewhat arbitrary, almost accidental destruction of its creator's house — lacks horror's predilection for the abject. As a response to being crushed beneath its bulk or killed by falling pieces of debris, terror would perhaps be a more appropriate response — an emotion that moves these scenes in *Tarantula* and other giant creature films closer to the disaster film than the horror film.

Films released during the 1950s would parse this play on size so differently that the distinction between science fiction and horror vanishes amidst a variety of finely differentiated local phenomena. While the re-release of *King Kong* in 1952 came, as a result of the Production Code, without the original shots that featured Kong crushing villagers beneath his feet or sticking them in his mouth in graphic medium close-ups, films inspired by its success did sometimes feature small-scale destruction to the human body alongside the more massively staged mayhem. *The Beast from 20,000 Fathoms* (1953), which was to become, in turn, the inspiration for Ishiro Honda's *Gojiro* (1954), features a scene in which the dinosaur rampaging through New York singles out a foolishly heroic police officer, snatches him in his jaws, and chews him up in gruesome explicitness (courtesy of soon-to-be famous stop-motion animator Ray Harryhausen). The horrific moment remains submerged, however, within the more richly textured sequence that emphasizes the destruction of the city itself and the mass panic that ensues — a vision associated more urgently with urban fears of nuclear war. That vision seems to have been exacerbated more than alleviated by Cold

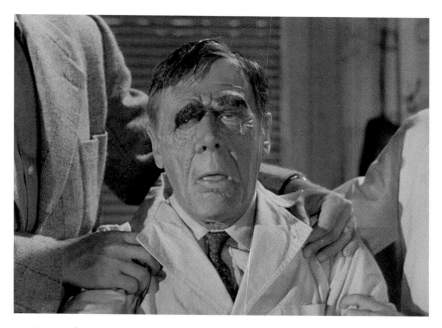

Figure 15.1 Abject spectacle in the sci-fi horror hybrid *Tarantula* (1955): Professor Deemer's experiments lead to monstrosity and horror. Directed by Jack Arnold. Produced by Universal International Pictures (UI).

War security regimens that included air-raid drills, public safety bulletins, backyard bomb shelters, and early-warning systems which haunted the affluent and supposedly secure civilian sphere with the specter of sudden military disaster.

Horror in *Tarantula* emerges most impressively from the viewers' encounter not with the massive spider's body, but with that of the grotesquely disfigured body of its scientist creator, Prof. Deemer (Leo G. Carroll). When we see the effects of his contamination for the first time, we are confronted with his face and body as abject spectacle (Figure 15.1). Though his physical transformation marks a significant psychological shift that, in effect, humanizes him (Jancovich, 1996: 190), the close-up of Deemer's disfigured body is geared toward an immediate audience response. The moment takes place within Deemer's laboratory, an intimate space more conducive to medium shots and close-ups than the vast open landscapes wherein the spider's attacks take place. Unlike the anonymous destruction caused by the tarantula's outsized body, the size of the interaction in this scene is measured by the dimensions of the human body: its accessibility, permeability, and vulnerability are experienced as horror, physical disgust, and revulsion. To the degree that giant creature films of the 1950s stage scenes of mass panic, evacuation, and destruction, they fall more into the purview of science fiction. Gigantic size translates into awe, into visions of the technological sublime, whereas the human dimension is more readily accessible to the affective and thematic reach of horror. Other films of the giant creature subcycle—like Gordon Douglas' *Them* (1954) or Edward Ludwig's *The Black Scorpion* (1957)—hardly ever bring events down to the scale of the individual human body with any graphic efficiency, and thus might be said to gravitate more toward science fiction than horror.

More Abject Bodies: Fluids Coming Alive

While *Tarantula*'s eponymous creature wreaked a type of havoc on Professor Deemer's house akin to the percussive wave of nuclear test explosions, the melting features of Deemer himself, contaminated with the radioactive substances used in his experiments, brought nuclear fears down to a more intimate bodily level. Nuclear technology, since its horrifically triumphant display of effectiveness in Hiroshima and Nagasaki, occupied a strangely ambiguous position within public consciousness during the postwar period, reflected by its use in horror films. On the one hand, the "stylized image [of the mushroom cloud] pervaded popular culture during the late 1940s and the 1950s" (Titus, 2004: 107), a symbol of nuclear technology in all its promise and menace. Discussion in popular media abounded. And yet control of the technology, especially in regard to its spread to the Soviet Union in the context of Cold War rivalries, also demanded tight control of information and visibility (Wills, 2010: 7–24). Again, this applied to the ubiquitous imagery of the mushroom cloud. Though "promoted by various administrations to generate support for an arms race designed to win the Cold War" (Titus, 2004: 105), the image itself "focused the public's collective eye on the aesthetics of the mushroom cloud and glossed over the dangers that resulted from radioactive fallout" (Titus, 2004: 107), promoting a panoramic, sublime view of the technology over its impingement upon, and intrusion into, the individual's intimate bodily space.

However, just as the development of the technology within the confines of the Manhattan Project had generated a security apparatus that controlled public discourse (as well as much of the geographic space around Los Alamos and other primarily Southwestern sites), so did this apparatus remain in place during the 1950s. While it managed public opinion by suppressing some types of information, it also provided Foucauldian "incitement to discourse" in regard to others. In other words, this tension between discursive overexposure on the one hand and secrecy on the other opened up a space of speculative imagination into which the era's horror films happily inserted themselves. To this extent, the era's sci-fi horror films reify fears about nuclear technology, providing the discursive means of using such technology (and both its real and imagined consequences) as a metaphor for whatever ailed 1950s America.

Though 1950s horror films still feature monsters that fit the mould of previous decades' creatures, both civilian and military nuclear technology provided a backdrop against which new concepts of monstrosity began to emerge. Prosthetic technology had not advanced significantly since Jack Pierce designed many of the classic Universal monsters. Consequently, the transformed test pilot in *First Man into Space*

(1959), an American film that takes its cue from the British *Quatermass* franchise developed by Nigel Kneale for the BBC (1953, with sequels in 1955 and 1957), is still an actor covered in a crude body suit, suggesting vaguely reptilian surface textures superimposed upon a stubbornly anthropomorphic human frame. Though some of the iconic films of the period succeeded in producing abject imagery of startling intensity by way of "men in rubber suits" (perhaps most notably *The Creature from the Black Lagoon*), effects of this type remained limited to the body's surface and restrained by its shape. Events transgressing this boundary—intrusion, penetration, explosion, expulsion—which were to make horror films in subsequent decades far more visually striking, were difficult to stage, with one exception: the appearance of slime.

There is a hint of novelty in the fact that the surface of the transformed body in *First Man into Space* is glistening with moisture. Wetness—not that of blood or exposure to water—but one that remains mimetically undefined and thus altogether more evocative and repulsive—testifies to a deeper investment in abjection on the part of 1950s horror films than that of their immediate predecessors. As in canonical horror films of the 1970s and thereafter, the slimy, drippy, glistening wetness of the monstrous surface suggests the inside of bodies, the excretion of unspeakable bodily fluids that breach the boundary between inside and outside and, even worse, communicate the threat of contamination.

Slime even detaches itself from monstrous bodies in films like *It Came from Outer Space* (1953), wherein the alien creatures leave wet trails like snails, or takes on a life of its own as in *The Blob* (1958), in which the monster's body consists entirely of abject liquid. Perhaps unsurprisingly, Japanese horror films from the same period go even further in the pursuit and display of such bodily abjection. In Ishiro Honda's *The H-Man* (1958), characters liquefy completely, while Honda's *Matango* (1963) has characters transformed into mushrooms, a reference perhaps less to the mushroom cloud as to a life form that flourishes in dark and damp places and is associated with primeval and prodigious yet oddly amorphous and fluid growth. It is hardly far-fetched to see the high degree of abjection in both films as responses to the experience of Hiroshima and Nagasaki. Neither is it difficult to see the gender politics at work in these images of manly American men—from the first man into space to your average middle-aged scientist—altered beyond human recognition. Phallic masculinity becomes itself softened or even liquefied just when its maintenance was proving essential for postwar American "containment culture" posited against Communism as much as women dangerously empowered by World War II (Nadel, 1995: 117–155; Theweleit, 1987: 229–249).

In the Bedroom with the Stranger(s): Uncanny Sexual Politics

As long as monstrosity was produced by means of special effects, the operative metaphor was abjection. Whenever abjection would mask its presence, or would be altogether absent, however, the monstrous metaphor would shift from abjection to a state of altered cognition. Together with giant creatures and mutated bodies, the monstrous other in our midst masquerading as "normal"—as is perhaps most famously dramatized in Don Siegel's *Invasion of the Body Snatchers*—provides yet another signature theme of 1950s horror. Conventionally, critical discourse has cast these alien impostors as a metaphor for Communist subversion, a reification of the "loss of free will, loss of identity, and disintegration of the family and community" (O'Donnell, 2003: 177). Implied in this reading is an ambiguity about the social origins of these dehumanizing forces, the question "of whether pods were anticommunist conformists or invading Communists" (O'Donnell, 2003: 184). By recognizing that social conformity might emanate from hysterical McCarthyism, mindless consumerism, or the corporate structures of the postwar economy (just as it might from alleged Communist subversion), the metaphor of the mindless alien impostor provides a differentiated view of the politics of many 1950s horror films. As such they are suspended between films that were "apocalyptic and hysterical about *them*" and films that showed the same sense of discomfort "about *us*" (Engelhardt, 2007: 102, emphasis added).

That the metaphor proves flexible even beyond the boundaries of this polarity can be traced in the multiple readings the film *I Married a Monster from Outer Space* (1958) has generated. [This film has also been remade in recent years, roughly reimagined as *The Astronaut's Wife* (1999).] *I Married a Monster from Outer Space* posits a central character, a newlywed husband named Bill Farrell (Tom Tryon) who, on the night before his wedding, is replaced with an alien impostor. David Seed reads this as a "compensatory fantasy" in response to "revelations in the mid-1950s of American POWS collaborating with their Korean captors" (1999: 133). Harry Benshoff traces the film's unease with the film's alien husband and his opaque sexuality to the cultural afterlife of Alfred Kinsey's two reports on male (1948) and female (1953) sexuality (1997: 123–132). Since public discourse at the time habitually linked the deviance of homosexuality with that of Communism (Benshoff, 1997: 130), the insufficiently resolved tension between the husband's sexual aggressiveness and sexual reluctance complicates the Cold War requirement of stable heteronormative arrangements. Just what is Bill Farrell "up to" whenever he abandons his young, attractive wife in favor of a group of men meeting in bars, diners, and, worse, in the woods adjacent to the town?

Bill's aberrant behavior suggests yet another historical context. Given the list of odd behaviors he displays—his emotional coldness alternating with moments of intense though unconsummated sexual interest, his penchant for violent outbursts, his secrecy and inconsistency—one might also diagnose Bill as suffering from post-traumatic stress disorder. Possible physical disfigurement in the war is displaced from Bill's immaculate body to those of the aliens in their true form; like Deemer's face in *Tarantula*, these aliens' melted faces evoke graphic memories of severe burns, the most common physical disfigurement, together with amputated limbs, of returning WWII veterans. Given this displacement, as well as the lack of an explicit reference to Bill having served in the military or having seen combat in the course of WWII or the Korean War, reading Bill's pathology as that of a veteran seems like a stretch. However, given the character's age, and the release date of the film, it would not be far-fetched to see it as linked to what thousands of American GIs went through upon their return to (what Henry Miller so aptly named) "the air-conditioned nightmare" of suburban America. The absence of an explicitly named causal link between Bill's erratic behavior and war trauma, however, is not automatically grounds to rule out this scenario. Rather it can be read as a symptom of postwar America's collective amnesia. The few films of the period which explicitly addressed war trauma, like the enormously successful *The Best Years of Our Lives* (1946), also testified to a collective desire to leave the war and all its concomitant trauma behind. Meanwhile, the era's countless psychological Westerns and films noir — with their dead-eyed, cynical, antisocial, and misogynist protagonists whose prior trauma is rarely named — are perhaps more adept at capturing the dynamic of the era's tortured gender relations, whatever their multiple and overdetermined causes (Figure 15.2).

In *I Married a Monster from Outer Space*, the subtext of repressed war trauma also links up thematically with the anxieties surrounding Bill's ambiguous sexuality, situated uneasily between a surplus of sexual energy (the hypermasculinity of the alien rapist), and its lack (the emasculated sexuality of the traumatized war veteran who cannot or will not perform his marital duties). To the degree that Bill seems to prefer homosocial bonds with other men in his circle — every one of them a member of the alien conspiracy — the film expresses a retroactive anxiety about conscripted American men having lived exclusively in male company during the war years. Within the affective and thematic registers of the horror film, *I Married a Monster from Outer Space* flirts with the possibility of reading their camaraderie as a sign of suspicious sexual otherness. Much of the wartime propaganda displaying, and excusing, the

Figure 15.2   Newlywed Bill (Tom Tryon) in *I Married a Monster from Outer Space* (1958). Just what kind of monster is he? Directed by Gene Fowler, Jr. Produced by Paramount Pictures.

sexual aggressiveness of the American soldier at home and abroad, is retroactively cast as a discourse of sexual anxiety over a beleaguered heterosexual masculinity.

Yet, as much as Bill is sexually suspect, so is Marge, his wife (Gloria Talbott). To the degree that sexual politics during the postwar period are "congruent to and commensurate with the American foreign and domestic policy of containing communism" (Nadel, 1995: 117), and that, at the heart of this sexual politics is a "cult of domesticity" focused on the suburban home as a space emblematic of both social coherence and economic efficiency (Marling, 1994: 242–284), Marge is both the victim and instigator of her husband's sexual otherness. As the presumptive benefactor of the married suburban household, Marge has incurred a debt of agency greater than that of her husband. Initially, she suspects herself and not her husband to be the one who must take the initiative to correct the fledgling marriage; or, as Nadel puts it, the "responsibility for this containment [for the sexual energies that might otherwise run rampant and attach itself to the wrong object] in the postwar era fell on women whose role was to resist and channel the 'natural' sexual energies of men," a burden of responsibility that requires a strange "duplicity: the woman had to attract and stimulate male sexual drives but not gratify them" (1995: 117). Marge's ability to perform this duplicitous function on her wedding night—or rather her failure to perform it—provides the foundation for the film's sense of sexual paranoia which includes women as much as men. At its resolution, the film steers Marge back into a marriage which, despite the elimination of the impostor and his replacement with the real Bill Farrell, promises to be as haunted as the one she has experienced before.

To the degree that 1950s horror films include women among those replaced by alien impostors—*Invasion of the Body Snatchers* features among its signature moments the voiceover line, "I never knew fear until I kissed Becky"—more general anxieties of voracious, castrating female sexuality and concomitant male sexual regression are also present in 1950s horror (Creed, 1993: 17). At the core of the mutated anthill in *Them* is, after all, a queen, and for every sexually menaced woman like Marge Farrell there is a sexually menacing one like the eponymous killers of men in *The She-Creature* (1956), *The Wasp Woman* (1959), and *The Leech Woman* (1960). Heterosexual masculinity is also threatened (albeit in a more camp fashion) in films like *Cat Women of the Moon* (1953) and *Queen of Outer Space* (1958). Again, these readings are supported by historically specific discourses, such as "Momism," a derisive term coined by Philip Wylie in his attacks on the cult of domesticity, which he saw as weakening traditional American masculinity (Hendershot, 2001: 117).

Nonetheless, as hostile takeovers progress in the majority of the era's alien invasion films, their targets are less frequently single women (or single men) than entire populations, spreading from the individual through the family to society at large. For example, the alien invasion in *Invaders from Mars* (1953) begins with a father, then spreads to a mother, and, as it threatens to absorb the son and complete its conversion of the 1950s nuclear family, is poised to spill over into the public sphere. The frequency with which men are the first targets of these invasions, and with which men's harsh, aggressive, and erratic behavior often betrays their status as alien impostors, suggests that the destructive effects of masculine war trauma spreads from the central agent of patriarchal power through families, communities, and ultimately the nation.

Abject Geography: Global Threats in the American Century

If films like *I Married a Monster from Outer Space* and *Invaders from Mars* gothicized the newly emergent suburbs, another strand within the same cycle took on space from an altogether more lofty vantage point, following Sobchack's insight that 1950s horror was informed by "a new consciousness of the relativity of spatial and temporal distance and the planet as a connected global community" (262). The same nervous panopticism, which appears on the level of the individual body and of the domestic sphere in the paranoid invasion films, reappears in what one might call its agora-phobic manifestation in the subcycle of giant creature films (Seed, 1999: 68–81). Southwestern desert landscapes of the United States provide the setting for a consid-erable number of 1950s horror films, be they giant creature films (*Them*, *Tarantula*) or alien invasion films [*It Came from Outer Space*, *The Monolith Monsters* (1957)]. As a key site of the Manhattan Project, the Southwest remained an important testing ground for nuclear weaponry during the postwar years. Cordoned off no-go areas under the control of the US military, like those giving rise to the Area 51 mythol-ogy in Nevada, increased a sense of geographic otherness, even as the expansion of the Interstate Highway system provided growing incentives for tourism in the region (Rugh, 2008: 5–17). Instead of seamlessly continuing in the tradition of the West-ern, which had enjoyed a virtual cinematic monopoly on the representation of the Southwestern United States, the 1950s horror film rewrote the landscape according to a new agenda, infusing it with a pervasive sense of "physical threat, ubiquitous yet vague" (Goin, 2004: 82). Eerie long shots of the supposedly empty landscape accompanied by voiceover musings about the limits of human knowledge became a staple of these films, as did the cinematically ubiquitous Joshua Trees which, against the botanical reality of their limited spread throughout the Mojave Desert, intrude menacingly into virtually every film of this type.

Containing this uncolonized geographic other — or attempting to, at least — were technologies such as the telephone, the automobile, and the airplane, all of which are prominently on display in many of these films. In *The Monolith Monsters*, the land-scape itself has come alive under the influence of an invasive alien life form, and the film's characters continuously test, analyze, measure, and map the desert in order to locate and contain the source and spread of the infection (Figure 15.3). *It Came from Outer Space* features several helicopter shots that travel alongside telephone wires crisscrossing the desert. Ownership of these technologies often blurs the boundaries between corporate and military control, with technoscience as an adjunct to both; nonetheless, their success in mapping and subjugating the natural landscape remains precarious at best. In fact, whoever or whatever is traveling along those telephone wires unobserved in *It Came from Outer Space* is turning the tables on those tracking them by using the wires to listen in on their pursuers in return. Just as the landscape

Figure 15.3   In the 1950s, even the landscape is threatening: the premise of *The Monolith Monsters* (1958) is that an alien species has transformed the desert into giant killer crystals. Directed by John Sherwood. Produced by Universal International Pictures (UI).

feels haunted, the technology used to civilize it does, too. As the historical connotations of the landscape changed, 1950s horror films turned the Southwest back into a geographic other, challenging the ideological narrative of the Frontier, the myth of progress as geographic expansion elaborated upon by the Western film genre.

Alongside the defamiliarization of domestic geography, 1950s horror films are equally invested in exotic locations, not as the dehistoricized allegorical backdrops typical of 1930s and 1940s horror films, but as imaginary spaces available to the United States in its expanding sphere of influence. American adventurers, no matter if they are scientists, submarine captains, or entrepreneurs, operate with self-evident entitlement within a global theater that includes the Amazon (*Creature from the Black Lagoon*), Mexico (*The Black Scorpion*), Asia [*Cult of the Cobra* (1955)], and the polar regions. This latter part of the world especially provides the setting for a significant number of the era's monster movies, from *The Thing from Another World* and *The Beast from 20,000 Fathoms* to *The Deadly Mantis* (1957) and *The Atomic Submarine* (1959). The Arctic Circle was also the setting of the DEW (Distant Early Warning) line, a series of radar stations designed to guard against potential Soviet missile attacks; again, it is not hard to see the logic of metaphor at work in these films, wherein actual fears are displaced onto fantastic cinematic ones. And not only do these regions harbor threats that will eventually intrude upon the US mainland, but their representation replays, on a global geographic register, the logic of abjection prevalent among bodies, suburban homes, and domestic geography. As E. Leane has put it, "The South Pole, and by extension the Antarctic region, is a place where borders are breached, a hypothetical hole in the surface of the Earth that collapses the division between interior and exterior" (2005: 231).

The Pod's Inhuman Stare: Challenging Usual Modes of Spectatorship

According to most histories, horror films of the 1950s predate a self-reflexive quality in the genre that critic Philip Brophy has named "horrality," a trait that has come to define the genre from the advent of 1960s horror to the present day. "The contemporary horror film," Brophy writes, "knows that you've seen it before; it knows that you know what is about to happen; and it knows that you know it knows you know" (2000: 279). Combined with the self-aware and explicit textuality of contemporary horror is an emphasis on intense affect in the present moment, achieved through graphic transgressive imagery, often centered upon the body, which triggers "a nervous giggle of amoral delight as you prepare yourself in a totally self-deluding way for the next shock" (Brophy, 2000: 279). Given this aesthetic of structure and affect and its arrival and ascent to dominance at a particular moment in the history of the genre, one might suspect that it is exactly the pronounced *lack* of horrality that is responsible for the affinity that later audiences have seen between 1950s horror films and camp; after all, no other period and no other genre have provided *Mystery Science Theater 3000* (1988 – 1999) with more fodder for ridicule. 1950s horror films are perhaps the most dated of all horror films, due to their earnest overreaching toward melodrama; they are seemingly free from any redeeming sense of self-irony in both their thematic ambitions and technical execution.

However, although this critical assessment may be accurate in the broader sense, individual moments in 1950s horror film suggest otherwise. For instance, the blank stare of the dehumanized human being—the zombie, the pod person, the victim of hypnotism, and the sleepwalker—is not the invention of the 1950s, yet it is that era's horror films that show an interest in that motif as a way of introducing a level of self-reflexivity to the discourse. Famously, the prehistory of the zombie film begins with films like *White Zombie* (1932) and *I Walked with a Zombie* (1943), which both feature characters whose state of dehumanization is marked by an unwavering stare into blank space. The pervasive interest that horror films had in this motif during the 1930s and 1940s was based on a broader fascination with mind control, on display most strikingly in films like *Svengali* (1931) or *Dracula* (1931), in which the vampire is defined less by his bloodsucking and more by his hypnotic control over others.

The 1950s expanded this notion of outside manipulation into a broader one of dehumanization. Films of the 1950s created "a paranoid style (and spectatorship) in which alien 'difference' was marked not [always] by special effects but by the wooden demeanor and small failures of the human-looking aliens to respond appropriately in ordinary human situations" (Sobchack, 2005: 265). The pod people in *Invasion of the Body Snatchers* or the alien husband in *I Married a Monster from Outer Space* have moments in which their affectless, blank stare reveals them as alien impostors posing as humans. However, the emphasis has slightly shifted: Dracula's victims are capable of concealing their otherness only to the degree that their controller is capable of upholding the fiction of normality. The blank stare of the 1950s alien impostor is often reserved for the camera, and thus for inspection by the audience, alone. For example, in *Invaders from Mars*, after the father has been altered by the aliens, there is a small scene with his nuclear family. Director William Cameron Menzies blocks the scene so that the father has his face turned toward the camera, with his wife and son flanking him in profile, unable to look him straight in the eye. Their access to visual information is less clear and direct than that of the audience. Though the actor never looks directly at the camera—a violation of classic Hollywood style that would tear down the fourth wall rather more aggressively—his gaze is directed to either side of the camera, to a space outside the frame that does not warrant such close scrutiny. Even worse, the film denies the audience the pleasure of being sutured into this diegetic gaze by cutting, as convention would demand, to a subjective shot revealing what Father is so fixedly looking at. This is a small but noticeable transgression against the classic Hollywood style, which the scene never makes good on. The only consolation offered to the spectator is not stylistic but diegetic, when, in the final instance, the audience is rescued from what Sobchack calls paranoid spectatorship by a shot of a little scar on Father's neck—indisputable proof that he is not the man he used to be.

Similarly, horror films of the 1950s frequently feature scenes in which the camera lingers on the face of the alien impostor after any other human character has exited the frame, or continues to linger on that face for a few seconds after stylistic conventions would have demanded a cut, fade, or dissolve. As a convention that marks the appearance of the uncanny in an otherwise inconspicuous moment, the significance of these moments rests to a large degree in their very conventionality; in other words, once audiences learned to read these moments properly, it did not matter any longer what exactly they expressed specifically. They became shorthand, an arbitrary code for otherness. By subtly manipulating formal conventions such as these, the films draw attention to the existence of such conventions, and thus to conventionality itself.

Invaders from Mars also provides a striking counterpoint to Peter Biskind's dismissive description of the visual idiosyncrasies of 1950s horror films. Stylistically, Biskind argues, "these films were much more restrained [than their gothic 1930s and 1940s predecessors] mostly shot in flat, matter-of-fact black and white and employ[ing] a series of colorless, almost interchangeable actors," the actors' "affectless performances" contributing to the films' overall sense of "visual blandness" (1983: 102–103). There is ample evidence that contradicts Biskind's remark about "visual blandness"—one might think, for example, of the "unusually high … color saturation" of the original release prints of *Invaders from Mars* which contributed to the film's "eccentric view of small-town America" and gave it its "aura of unreality"

(Di Fate, 2004: 64). Similarly, the choice of "interchangeable actors" appears relevant as part of the films' investment in a larger paranoid logic. Authenticity thus emerges as an overarching theme. By substituting what Sobchack calls a "paranoid style" for the classical Hollywood style, and substituting a paranoid spectatorship for classical Hollywood spectatorship, horror films of the 1950s self-reflexively replay the theme of substituting, replacing, masquerading, impersonating, imitating, and internally subverting on a formal and stylistic level what their use of the alien pods enact on a diegetic level. This metadiscursive operation is not exactly "horrality" as Brophy defines it, but it is also something that, in its full complexity, challenges the idea that 1950s horror films are earnest, overreaching, and free of redeeming self-irony.

Movie Monsters at the Monster Movies

While the pod's inhuman stare might sneak self-reflexivity into the 1950s horror film, a monster getting loose in a crowded movie theater announces that self-reflexivity more openly and explicitly. William Castle's *The Tingler* (1959) is not the only film of this kind: the eponymous monster in *The Blob* also invades a movie theater, one filled with teenagers laughing, making out, and enjoying the film. In fact, their communal experience is reminiscent of the scene in *Rebel Without a Cause* (1955) wherein James Dean and his fellow classmates are lectured in the planetarium on their own insignificance in the universe. Both scenes illustrate the era's emergent teenage subculture and its ritualized attachment to spaces removed from parental oversight. Given their social and economic prominence during the postwar years, teenagers became increasingly important to Hollywood revenue, and teenage characters began to crop up in a variety of cinematic genres: from James Dean and Marlon Brando in the signature melodramas of their (early) careers, to films like *Gidget* (1959), manufactured around teen idol Sandra Dee. Similarly, Howard Hawks's *Rio Bravo* (1959) added teen heartthrob Ricky Nelson to an otherwise middle-aged cast to attract the youth demographic. But teenagers reigned supreme in the era's horror films, from central characters confronting monsters in films like *Invasion of the Saucer Men* (1957) and *Ghost of Dragstrip Hollow* (1959), to the titular monsters themselves in films like *I Was a Teenage Werewolf* and *I Was a Teenage Frankenstein* (both 1957).

To the degree that *The Blob* self-consciously reflected its own demographics, it also performed a function that is visible in *The Tingler*. Though the audience in *The Tingler* is not primarily one of teenagers—there is only one couple that looks like it came from *The Blob*—the film very explicitly comments on the alignment of the fictional and "real" film viewers. Both films come with deliberations about the similarities or differences between the violence and/or horrors watched by the diegetic audience and those watched by the actual audience. In *The Blob*, the implied significance is hardly subtle: new horrors have entered the postwar world and have rendered classic gothic horror films like *Daughter of Horror* obsolete, a source of light entertainment at the late show as much as on late-night TV. Castle's choice of the silent non-horror film *Tol-able David* (1921) for *The Tingler* is more difficult to decode. Kevin Heffernan provides a valuable clue when he cites the performance of actress Judith Evelyn as the deaf-mute Martha Higgins as "the centerpiece of the film." Her "neurotic pantomime (screenwriter White gives her a full range of obsessive and phobic tics) sets her off from all the other characters in the film. She is, in the words of critic Tim Lucas, 'truly a silent character in a sound movie'" (Heffernan, 2004: 100). This gesture links deaf-mute Martha with the showing of the silent film *Tol-able David* during *The Tingler*'s key scene, in which the creature runs amok in the movie theater. As in *The Blob*, the use of *Tol-able David* suggests the dawning of a new era of visceral and shocking horror films—ones ready to make use of sound, and color, and all the various technologies the era could provide. (*The Tingler*'s use of several color inserts—of garishly red blood—in its otherwise black and white cinematography works to make the same point.)

For Castle, this scene also marked the opportunity to stage one of the stunts for which he became famous, this one a gimmick named "Percepto," which involved selected theater chairs being fitted with "vibrating motors under the seats" designed to administer calculated jolts to viewers during the moment when the titular creature is supposed to be running amok in both the diegetic theater *as well as* the theater screening *The Tingler*.

Castle is often criticized as a crass entrepreneur in pursuit of sensational stunts to draw attention to essentially mediocre films. The accuracy of this critique notwithstanding, Castle's approach is representative of the entire film industry floundering after the Paramount Decision and the advent of television. From Cinemascope to the roadshow format, to 3D (e.g., *House of Wax*, *It Came from Outer Space*, *The Creature from the Black Lagoon*), larger budgets were the only thing that put the major studios ahead of Castle's low-budget gimmicks like "Percepto" and "Emergo" [a model skeleton that flew over the theater audience during the climax of *House on Haunted Hill* (1959)].

Hence, Castle deserves credit for serving the flipside of horrality, the one that complements self-reflexivity: the moment of visceral shock, unencumbered by the necessity to legitimize itself—a short, sharp pang of pleasurable discomfort. Practical or not (not to mention legally advisable), the idea of wiring theater seats for vibration and goading audiences into individual or collective hysterics, makes films like *The Tingler* precursors of things to come. All showmanship aside, Castle deserves credit for opening the horror film to the exploration of its own space of consumption, the movie theater, as a nexus of social interaction and individual psychological experience. *The Tingler* addresses, thematically and affectively, the experience of watching a horror film—that precarious balance between menace and safety, emotion and simulation, suffering and pleasure, sadism and masochism.

Still, if the dominant cycle of 1950s horror films unpacked and explored this complex dynamic through the characters, spaces, and technologies of the emergent American Century and the Cold War, this did not mean that the genre had expunged all traces of its deep gothic heritage. Eventually, the Cold War, after the peak of the Cuban Missile Crisis, would lose some of its urgency and settle into a tolerable long-term arrangement; the triumphalism of the American Century would be bogged down by costly wars in Southeast Asia and social unrest on college campuses like those of Kent State and Berkeley. In search of new relevance, it was to be horror's gothic heritage, demoted for a decade, that was about to make a comeback. With help from various independent American producers and a British production company whose name was to become synonymous with horror, the classic monsters of the 1930s were about to return in all their gory glory.

References

Benshoff, H. (1997) *Monsters in the Closet: Homosexuality and the Horror Film*, Manchester University Press, Manchester.

Biskind, P. (1983) *Seeing is Believing: How Hollywood Taught Us to Stop Worrying and Love the Fifties*, Pantheon, New York.

Brophy, P. (2000) Horrality—the textuality of contemporary horror films, in *The Horror Reader* (ed. K. Gelder), Routledge, London/New York, pp. 276–285.

Creed, B. (1993) *The Monstrous-Feminine: Film Feminism. Psychoanalysis*, Routledge, New York.

Di Fate, V. (2004) 'This means something!': *Invaders from Mars*, in *The Science Fiction Film Reader* (ed. G. Rickman), Limelight, New York, pp. 60–68.

Engelhardt, T. (2007) *The End of Victory Culture: Cold War America and the Disillusioning of a Generation*. New York: HarperCollins, 1995, Revised edn, University of Massachusetts Press, Amherst.

Goin, P. (2004) The nuclear past in the landscape present, in *Atomic Culture: How We Learned to Stop Worrying and Love the Bomb* (eds S.C. Zeman and M.A. Amundson), University Press of Colorado, Boulder, pp. 81–101.

Hantke, S. (2010a) Bush's America and the return of cold war science fiction: alien invasion in *Invasion*, *Threshold*, and *Surface*. *The Journal of Popular Film & Television*, **38** (3), 143–151.

Hantke, S. (2010b) The return of the giant creature: *Cloverfield* and the Political Opposition to the War on Terror. *Extrapolation*, **51** (2), 235–257.

Heffernan, K. (2004) *Ghouls, Gimmicks, and Gold: Horror Films and the American Movie Business, 1953–1968*, Duke University Press, Durham/London.

Hendershot, C. (2001) *I Was a Cold War Monster: Horror Films, Eroticism, and the Cold War Imagination*, Bowling Green State University Press, Bowling Green, OH.

Hollings, K. (2006) *Welcome to Mars: Ken Hollings Presents a Live Twelve-Part Series of Unscripted Reflections on the Fantasy of Science in the Early Years of the American Century*, http://www.simonsound.co.uk/podcasts/marspodcast.xml (accessed 24 February 2007).

Jancovich, M. (1996) *Rational Fears: American Horror in the 1950s*, Manchester University Press, Manchester/New York.

Leane, E. (2005) Locating the thing: the Antarctic as alien space in John W. Campbell's "Who Goes There?". *Science Fiction Studies*, **32** (2), 225–239.

Marling, K.A. (1994) *As Seen on TV: The Visual Culture of Everyday Life in the 1950s*, Harvard University Press, Harvard.

Nadel, A. (1995) *Containment Culture: American Narratives, Postmodernism, and the Atomic Age*, Duke University Press, Durham/London.

O'Donnell, V. (2003) Science fiction films and cold war anxiety, in *The Fifties: Transforming the Screen 1950–1959*, History of the American Cinema General Ed. Charles Harpole (ed. P. Lev), University of California Press, Berkeley, pp. 169–197.

Rugh, S.S. (2008) *Are We There Yet?: The Golden Age of American Family Vacations*, University Press of Kansas, Lawrence.

Seed, D. (1999) *American Science Fiction and the Cold War: Literature and Film*, Edinburgh University Press, Edinburgh.

Sobchack, V. (2005) American science fiction film: an overview, in *A Companion to Science Fiction* (ed. D. Seed), Oxford University Press, Blackwell, pp. 261–275.

Theweleit, K. (1987) *Male Fantasies; Volume 1: Women, Floods, Bodies, Histories* (1977), University of Minnesota Press, Minneapolis.

Titus, C.A. (2004) The mushroom cloud as kitsch, in *Atomic Culture: How We Learned to Stop Worrying and Love the Bomb* (eds S.C. Zeman and M.A. Amundson), University Press of Colorado, Boulder, pp. 101–123.

Wills, G. (2010) *Bomb Power: The Modern Presidency and the National Security State*, Penguin, New York.

16

The Gothic Revival (1957 – 1974)

Rick Worland

In the decade after World War II, the American film industry underwent a series of structural changes in response to converging pressures from within and without. Perhaps not coincidentally the horror genre largely disappeared. Following a record box office take in 1946, the domestic audience began to shrink year by year. The 1948 Paramount anti-trust case forced the major studios out of exhibition, though as it turned out, it did so just as the business of running theaters was becoming riskier and more difficult. During this decade, television grew slowly at first, then rapidly expanded after 1952 when the Federal Communications Commission lifted a 4-year "freeze" on issuance of new station licenses. Hollywood at first resisted the new medium and then began to establish close connections with the broadcasting networks to produce most prime time shows. One of the most important and lasting changes was the steady demographic shift in which teenagers and young adults increasingly made up greater portions of frequent moviegoers. Though the big studios saw their business continue to decline, the exhibition sector was enlivened by the new drive-in theaters that mushroomed in cities and towns across the country, drawing increasing audiences and becoming a major venue through which the horror genre would see a revival.

Although the genre's return took several forms, it had one highly distinctive branch, the mid-budget gothic horror story built on traditional marks of a period setting, (mostly) supernatural monsters, and the shadowy backdrops of castles, crypts, and dungeons, conventions derived from the earliest literary expressions of the form in eighteenth century English novels including *The Castle of Otranto* (1764), *The Mysteries of Udolpho* (1794), and *The Monk* (1796). The movies were noted for their increasing gore and sexual explicitness, usually in potent combination, but also for their rich atmosphere evoked through careful attention to

A Companion to the Horror Film, First Edition. Edited by Harry M. Benshoff.
© 2014 John Wiley & Sons, Inc. Published 2017 by John Wiley & Sons, Inc.

sets, costumes, lighting, and camerawork. The most famous and influential were the products of Britain's Hammer Films, notably those starring Peter Cushing and/or Christopher Lee that began the trend. The American Edgar Allan Poe series with Vincent Price answered, as did many fine efforts from Italian, German, Spanish, and other British producers. The Euro-American gothic revival stretched from Hammer's *The Curse of Frankenstein* (1957) into the 1970s by which point its violence was rivaled by major Hollywood releases, while its sexual content grew closer to soft-core porn, particularly in continental examples. Throughout this period though, the settings, plots, and imagery of gothic horror came to seem as familiar and conventionalized as that of the Western. Because the cycle was so abundant, presented here is an overview of some essential or representative films that reflect the stylistic and industrial trends of this particular era of gothic cinema.

Though Hollywood horror production largely stopped after the war, by the mid-1950s the industry was recognizing that for the first time a major segment of its audience consistently liked science fiction, though producers struggled to find winning formulae. As Thomas Doherty (1988: 142–178) noted, the trades called such unpredictably successful offerings "weirdies," a broad term that might encompass a well-produced monster movie like Universal-International's *The Creature From the Black Lagoon* (1954) that featured sharp underwater photography and the new 3D process but more often meant low-budget efforts like Republic's *The Beginning of the End* (1957) with its less impressive swarm of giant grasshoppers. Other weirdies were emerging from small companies like American International Pictures (AIP) and Allied Artists that targeted drive-ins and neighborhood theaters hungry for product as the big studios reduced their outputs in the face of falling attendance. AIP's *It Conquered the World* (1956), directed by Roger Corman who would soon make a much stronger mark, was about as weird as they came, shot in 2 weeks with a tiny budget and featuring a squat, toothy space monster someone once described as resembling an angry carrot. With its atomic mutants and invasion anxiety, science fiction at least seemed strongly contemporary whatever the merits of particular movies, which aided its appeal to the youth audience, an impression that may have temporarily obscured the venerable attractions of the gothic.

Forthright gothic horror reappeared in the late 1950s in the form of low- to medium-budget exploitation movies, a type usually dependent on lurid titles, topical or risqué subject matter, and heavy promotion. Like the weirdies, they too were aimed at a narrower and younger audience segment in drive-ins and subsequent run houses. Yet, following the Hammer precedent, successful gothic horror films would also need to raise budgets and production values sufficiently to evoke the look of a studio costume drama, and further separate themselves from threadbare sci-fi. In the American market horror's revival began in 1957 with two hit movies and an important Hollywood venture with television. AIP's

I Was A Teenage Werewolf (1957) and the British import *The Curse of Frankenstein* (distributed by Warner Bros.) each wrung up $2 million grosses that summer from modest outlays. In the fall, Columbia's television subsidary, Screen Gems, having acquired some of Universal's back catalog, began to syndicate a package of vintage horror movies to stations across the country. The immediate success of the package promoted under the name *Shock!* introduced *Frankenstein* (1931), *The Mummy* (1932), *The Wolf Man* (1941), and so on, to a new generation and helped fuel a monster fan phenomenon among children and teenagers. The movies typically aired late on Friday or Saturday nights, often introduced by a local host costumed as some macabre figure who also did corny skits and jokes during commercial breaks (Heffernan, 2004: 157–179). The growing popularity of these old films on TV reinforced the surge of new movies from AIP, Hammer, Columbia, and other producers. It may have been the year of the Soviet Union's Sputnik satellite triumph, but as if to signify a moment of genre transition, AIP offered *I Was A Teenage Werewolf* in some venues as a double feature with *Invasion of The Saucer Men* (1957).

A model for vital elements of the new phase had actually appeared a bit earlier in the United Artists release *The Black Sleep* (1956), a low-budget feature made by Bel-Air Productions with a cast of studio-era veterans and intended for drive-ins as part of UA's integrated approach to distributing prestige dramas, exploitation features, and foreign art films to target all parts of the post-war exhibition landscape (Balio, 1987: 117–124). *The Black Sleep* has a Grand Guignol-worthy plot with Basil Rathbone as a nineteenth century London surgeon attempting to cure the catatonia into which his beloved wife has fallen, by conducting gruesome experiments on the brains of unwilling patients, mostly maiming or rendering them demented or mindless if they survive. The film's supporting cast includes Lon Chaney, Jr., John Carradine, and in his final performance, Bela Lugosi, troupers who had logged endless hours in horror programmers. Also present, as if to indicate the abject path to which the genre might yet descend was burly ex-wrestler Tor Johnson, like Lugosi now part of the entourage of the legendary Edward D. Wood, Jr. with appearances in *Bride of the Monster* (1955) and the notorious *Plan Nine From Outer Space* (1959). Instead, *The Black Sleep* displays the look and feel of a solid studio B picture with passably creepy sets and makeup, good performances, and a mix of atmosphere and graphic effects. Seasoned studio director Reginald LeBorg provided a basic but discernable level of craft that would only improve in the coming years.

As such, *The Black Sleep* straddles two eras of the genre but was more inclined to trends of the future: it relies on mature stars either previously associated with horror roles or subsequently specializing in such; features a period setting, usually the mid-nineteenth century to underscore the gothic's fundamental theme of a traumatic and unresolved past typically symbolized by the decaying manor or castle. Crucially, *The Black Sleep* flaunts a more cynical attitude toward graphic and bloody content, effects rooted in the cold, amoral irony of the *Grand Guignol* (See Gordon, 1988). In one scene, Rathbone and his assistant open a victim's skull and stimulate regions of his brain with scalpel and electrical probe, the kind of vivid gore that would become Hammer's trademark. When the shocked assistant realizes they are dissecting a living brain, Rathbone darkly responds, "In the interests of science … anything, *anything* is justified," sounding like a depraved Nazi doctor, a charge critics soon leveled at Hammer for the acts of Peter Cushing's conscienceless Baron Frankenstein. Yet in the climax, the tormented victims rise up against the mad doctor, driving him to his death, a common genre pattern from decades earlier that brought a traditional catharsis (Figure 16.1).

Regardless, the movie is foremost an exploitation product dependent on shocks, violence, and the flaunting of taboos, in this case those surrounding narcotics. The "black sleep" of the title results from a supposed East Indian potion that induces a death-like coma, which Rathbone uses as an anesthetic. Yet combined with the horrific doings in the film's hilltop castle setting, part medieval torture chamber and hellish insane asylum, the intravenous drug lends the tale an undercurrent of hallucinogenic nightmare, content expressly forbidden by the old Hollywood Production Code along with the explicit surgical scenes depicted here. ("The terror-drug that wakes the dead!" the ads now shouted.) Yet with the censor's

Figure 16.1   Studio horror veterans Basil Rathbone, Bela Lugosi, and Lon Chaney, Jr. straddle two eras of the genre in UA's exploitation feature *The Black Sleep* (1956). Directed by Reginald Le Borg. Produced by Bel-Air Productions.

grip steadily loosening after the mid-1950s, such boundary-pushing effects in relation especially to sexuality and violence would become central to postwar gothic filmmaking.

Hammer, Cushing, and Lee

In 1949, a small but established film production and distribution business founded in the early 1930s was reorganized as Hammer Film Productions and set about making a range of genre films including comedies and crime stories (See Meikle, 1996 among others). The studio took a decisive turn, however, after a major hit with *The Quatermass Xperiment* (1955), a well-made science fiction tale adapted from a popular British television series. The movie's odd title referred to Professor Quatermass (Brian Donlevy), a scientist in charge of a manned space flight that returns with its crew controlled by malevolent aliens. His work became an "Xperiment" in Britain to capitalize on the 1951 change in the censorship system that replaced the old "H" certificate (for Horrific) with a new designation, the "X" to indicate that no one under 16 could be admitted without an adult. Though the Quatermass movie was both low-key and suspenseful, Hammer was flaunting its restrictive rating in the familiar manner of the exploitation producer. The tactic was revealing because while foreign films were meeting success in American art houses, Hammer sought wider access to drive-ins and neighborhood theaters with its mid-budget genre movies. Indeed, its *Xperiment* was successful in US release via United Artists even with a clumsy new title, *The Creeping Unknown*. Regardless, Hammer would find its greatest and lasting success with its particular brand of gothic horror.

Soon after *Quatermass*, American producers Milton Subotsky and Max J. Rosenberg (later the founders of UK-based Amicus Productions, a Hammer competitor) pitched *The Curse of Frankenstein*, the film that crystallized major elements of the gothic revival, starting with overall production values. While *The Black Sleep* was shot in black and white like most 1950s exploitation features, Hammer used color and wide-screen as signs of its up-market aspirations as well as to accentuate the film's gory effects. Detailed sets and period costumes also added flavor. This raised their movies (and subsequently those of AIP from 1960 onward as the American company reacted to this new competition) to more respectable ranks even on still modest budgets. Upon announcement of the project in the trades however, Universal notified Hammer to expect legal difficulties if any of its copyrighted elements were violated, especially the iconic makeup design worn by Boris Karloff in 1931. This threat forced the British producers to be especially original in features of plot and conception and in the process they helped reinvent the character for a new age and audience.

Starting from Subotsky's original script, screenwriter Jimmy Sangster, one of the principal architects of the Hammer style, devised a new model of the doctor. Mary Shelley's young scientist turns frantic and indecisive after bringing his creation to life before finally engaging in a mutually vengeful duel that results in both their deaths. In James Whale's telling, Colin Clive's Dr. Frankenstein veered between obsession and remorseful collapse, making Karloff's Monster the most fascinating figure. However, Peter Cushing's icy but compelling Baron Frankenstein essentially became the monster of Hammer's version. He would never suffer remorse and remained patiently, methodically fixed on his work to the exclusion of any moral or legal concern, facilitating his acts with all the charm, calculation, and presumption of his aristocratic station. Moreover, with a different look in each movie, the Baron's patchwork creature became less a character than grisly variations of a corpse-like killer. The first time out, Christopher Lee played the monster and although his mute role was quite limited and memorable largely for its grotesque makeup, he would become Hammer's second reigning star as the Master Vampire in [*Horror of*] *Dracula* (1958). The studio had gone back to the same two gothic characters (originally conceived by English authors after all) with which Universal had inaugurated the American horror genre in the 1930s and found new blood.

Yet where filmmakers at Universal had featured off-kilter sets and deep shadows inspired by German expressionism, Hammer director Terence Fisher flaunted what Mary Shelley's doctor had called "my workshop of filthy creation", reveling in gore around securing corpses, murdering innocents, and sewing up bloody pieces of flesh and bone to construct the monster. In *The Curse of Frankenstein* he visits a morgue to buy a pair of eyeballs that float in a liquid-filled jar, attaches severed hands, and cuts a rotted head from an otherwise usable body. Cushing's doctor casually wiping a bloody hand on his lab coat or leather apron was a common gesture in the series, and a mystery parcel wrapped in burlap became a thing of dread. This grisly business intertwined with positing the Baron as the monster became literal in *The Revenge of Frankenstein* (1958), which climaxes with the doctor's brain transplanted into a conveniently identical body. Moreover, in place of the hunchbacked servant, a character originating in the first stage adaptation in 1823 but to which Universal could make some claims given Dwight Frye's vivid performance as Fritz, Hammer supplied handsome medical assistants. Though often portrayed as earnest young men who might feature in a heterosexual couple, the genre's traditional figuration of the "normal," this too got complicated. In *Frankenstein Created Woman* (1967), for example, he puts the assistant's brain into a woman's body.

Earlier versions of *Frankenstein* stress the interplay between the doctor's experiments and his sexual drives to indicate just how radically his work had intervened in traditional conceptions of both nature and society. In the novel, the angry Monster promises his creator, "I shall be with you on your wedding night" and then kills Frankenstein's bride; in the 1931 version, Elizabeth (Mae Clarke) reveals that "the very day we announced our engagement, [Frankenstein] told me of his experiments" suggesting how the scientist channels his sexual urges into the creation of life by most unconventional means. Hammer's Baron cynically manipulates both sides of the equation, indulging in an affair with his maid Justine, while continuing his work and planning to marry Elizabeth besides. Yet when Justine becomes pregnant, he traps her with the monster for an implied rape-murder and then listens intently at the door, heaving a sigh of relief that is itself nearly orgasmic. Worse, a fade out on Justine's screams dissolves to a pleasant breakfast next morning. "Pass the marmalade, would you, Elizabeth?" the doctor asks with droll politeness, followed by discussion of their wedding plans.

Hammer's first *Frankenstein* was made under legal warning but after its international success, the producers again looked to Universal's record and saw *Dracula* as the proven follow up. Moreover, as Universal had paired Karloff and Lugosi in several horror vehicles after their initial triumphs, Hammer realized that Cushing and Lee might serve in a similar, highly marketable capacity. For the 1958 film simply titled *Dracula* in UK release, Cushing played a traditionally cool and resolute Dr. Van Helsing while Lee with his height and regal bearing became a commanding vampire. Jimmy Sangster and Terence Fisher had recognized the charnel house atmosphere as the most popular undercurrent of *Frankenstein* and similarly emphasized the illicit sexuality at the core of Bram Stoker's tale. Where Lugosi had played the Count as courtly and quietly threatening, Lee made Dracula an athletic figure of great strength whose appetite for blood was a thin disguise for sexual hunger. Cushing's Baron may have been a cunning aristocrat but Lee became an aggressively violent thing when angered or aroused. When the Count intercedes to stop a vampire bride from attacking Jonathan Harker, a shock cut to a wide-angle close up depicts a snarling Dracula baring his fangs in a blood-smeared mouth, blood-red eyes aglow with rage (Figure 16.2). He then leaps across a table to hurl down the bride, toss the man aside,

Figure 16.2 Christopher Lee's rabid Count Dracula proclaims the gory new Hammer style in *Horror of Dracula* (1958). Directed by Terence Fisher. Produced by Hammer Film Productions.

then hoist her into his arms and disappear down a hidden passageway, leaving Harker gasping on the floor. The Lugosi image was countered in physical combat.

Additionally, settings memorably frame the performances here and in the best of Hammer's output. The art and craft of such mid-budget production lay in making the movies look more expensive than they really were. Apparently spacious and well-dressed sets in conjunction with careful production design and color cinematography were always Hammer's strong suit. In *Horror of Dracula*, not only do we see a detailed castle exterior with drawbridge and moat (plus background matte paintings blended in) but a large entrance hall, corridors, a library, and a subterranean crypt. Castle décor is subtly detailed to evoke the Count's bloodlust with red drapes, tapestries, furniture cushions, and even a chess set in Harker's room with pieces cast in an unusual white versus red scheme. Moreover, when it came to photographing exteriors, it is perpetually late autumn in Hammer horror films with bare trees and gray skies that evoke the chill of death, a cruel and foreboding naturalism in counterpoint to the stylized gothic interiors.

Lee's Dracula has dialog only in his initial meeting with Jonathan Harker after which both his violence and enslaving sexual power are expressed in astute visuals that combine performance, mise-en-scene, and careful editing. His initial appearance in England depicts the once-victimized Lucy Holmwood (Carol Marsh) in diaphanous gown opening the French windows of her bedroom, removing her protective crucifix, then lying down and sighing expectantly. His attack on Mina (Melissa Stribling), however, is a combination of an aggressive invasion of her room and a seduction. Dracula backs her onto the bed then begins to kiss and caress her face before dropping his head to her neck, before a shock cut to a screeching owl. Van Helsing and Mina's husband find her splayed across the bed, blood staining her gown and shoulders, the posture and setting suggesting awful violation. Sometime later though, she returns home from a rendezvous with the Count, throat notably covered, exuding a previously unseen confidence, and even a satisfied smirk. Sex is apparently the "true" horror of Dracula, though as often before, repressed Victorian women seem to be enjoying it to the greater horror of the men losing control of them. As such, when Harker staked the bride in Dracula's castle, she reverted to her evidently true age as a gray-haired crone. Upon Van Helsing's destruction of Lucy however, she loses her scarred and "wanton" appearance and returns to a more softly feminine look, much to the relief of her brother, Arthur (Michael Gough).

Following a distribution deal with Universal in 1958, Hammer began near exclusive devotion to the horror genre with only occasional trips into science fiction or dinosaur fantasies heavy on cave girls in fur bikinis. (Throughout this period, Hammer struck deals across Hollywood for the best terms, partnering at different times with Warner Bros., Universal, Columbia, United Artists, Twentieth Century-Fox, and even AIP in the early 1970s.) The Universal deal facilitated remakes of *The Mummy* (1959) with Cushing and Lee and the more original *Curse of the Werewolf* (1961) with neither. Returns to Frankenstein and Dracula were commercially requisite for the next 15 years. Universal allowed the creature (Kiwi Kingston) to resemble Karloff's square-headed monster for *The Evil of Frankenstein* (1964), for example, a movie that demonstrated both the strengths and weaknesses of Hammer's market position.

For this outing, the studio standard for vivid photography was a given for director Freddie Francis. In a highly interesting career, Francis alternated acclaimed work as a cinematographer [*Room At The Top* (1959), *The Elephant Man* (1980), *Glory* (1989), and so on.] with steady success as a genre director for Hammer and Amicus. Here his creation scene uses bright splashes of red, yellow, and blue liquids as well as green-hued glass insulators and a blue electrical arc crackling above the operating table, colors that pop from subdued backgrounds. Hammer could now not only quote the famous makeup (whose skull-like shaping and coloration photographed better at a distance) but also depict the monster coming to life in a laboratory filled with the buzzing electrical machinery that had to be largely avoided the first time. Hammer also varied older plot points including the monster's body discovered frozen in a glacial cave as seen in *Frankenstein Meets the Wolf Man* (1943). To complain (as some fans and critics have) that this was at once pale imitation of Universal and dilution of Hammer's original touches is to miss the point of the studio's shrewd negotiation of the postwar production and exhibition environment in which the popularity of Universal's "golden age" horror tradition was ascendant and fueling the very gothic mode in which Hammer thrived.

The more serious problem with *The Evil of Frankenstein* was a weak third act. In order to awaken the creature's dormant brain, the Baron must enlist the aid of carnival hypnotist who of course schemes to control the monster himself. Despite a promising tack to the carnival demimonde as a setting for the fantastic that dates from *The Cabinet of Dr. Caligari* (1920), there is something wrong with the brilliant Baron needing the questionable talents of a sideshow performer to assist in his work. At best, we could say it continued the occasional rough justice of the Grand Guignol repertoire as the venal and greedy hypnotist inevitably falls victim to the monster. Yet when the rampaging creature tears up the lab and sparks a fatal fire, the mute Beggar Girl and servant Hans fleeing as the tower laboratory explodes, it seems more a repeat of the most basic gothic finale than any reimagining of it. In any case, both doctor and monster seemingly perish in the blaze, a fitting end for this bumpy foray into stylistic collaboration between Hammer and the old Universal tradition.

Though the *Dracula* series too fell into repetition, Lee remained menacing, physically intimidating, and sexually forceful but could seldom get scenes that allowed anything more. Baron Frankenstein remained the richer part. Of course, Frankenstein is a complex if deeply flawed human being and Dracula is an ethereal, undead creature, yet it is easy to see why Lee soon chafed under the role, mainly serving as a threat in the shadows before striking out in rage. Still, as with any popular series, the interest lies in the variations. In *Dracula, Prince of Darkness* (1966), an often wild-eyed and snarling Lee has no lines whatsoever, a conception that keeps him at once ghostly and animalistic as the script works variations on both Stoker's novel and Hammer's first outing. Here the Van Helsing figure is gruff Father Sandor (Andrew Keir), an earthy, rifle-toting priest on horseback making Dracula's opponent a more traditional action hero if unconventional cleric. The vampire's socially unhinging sexual power is directed at two British couples on holiday in the Carpathian Mountains. (Hammer's cultural geography was as vague as Universal's: a similar mixture of Germany and Eastern Europe where everyone speaks with British accents.)

The familiar gothic conventions predominate however, as an unnerved coachman refuses to take the group further as sundown nears and abandons them just below Castle Dracula. Weirdly, a driverless coach arrives and whisks them straight to it where they find a dinner table set for them. A sinister servant, Klove (Phillip Latham), explains his master is dead but left instructions for the castle always to be ready to receive visitors. Helen (Barbara Shelley), the older, more repressed woman is deeply frightened but the others insist they have no choice but to stay. Confident Charles proposes a toast to their late benefactor. "May he rest in peace" he smiles, as a gust of wind flickers the candles, a touch almost amusing in its directness as a sign of foreboding. Still, the combination of gore and high style that Hammer perfected appears in the sequence of Dracula's resurrection. In the amber light of sundown, Klove murders Alan and then hoists his body over Dracula's crypt, and cuts his throat as if butchering a lamb. The blood streams onto the vampire's ashes and revives him. In a polite nod to Lugosi though, Dracula's spider-like hand crawls over the rim of the sarcophagus as he materializes.

Moreover, Hammer's knack for combining sex and violence appears in victimized Helen's return as a vampire, wherein like Stoker's Lucy Westenra before her, she becomes a sexually aggressive predator, her matronly garb replaced by a flowing, low-cut gown. Vampirism's often uninhibited bisexual lust manifests itself when she confronts innocent Diana, smiling, "We've been waiting for you, Diana" and "Come, sister," advancing with arms extended. "Where's Charles?" Diana asks nervously of her husband. "You don't need Charles" Helen purrs, an invitation to the orgy as a hissing Dracula suddenly appears as well. When Charles intervenes and grabs a sword to defend his wife, Dracula seizes it and snaps it in front of him, clear demonstration of who wields the greater sexual power. In an even more frank and sexualized episode taken from the novel, Dracula later traps Diana in her bedroom, opens a gash on his chest with his fingernail and pulls her to him to drink his blood, a gory communion rite but also a thinly disguised enactment of oral sex.

Skillful writing and direction, quality production values, graphic violence, and increasingly overt eroticism all helped Hammer achieve a strong international market presence throughout the 1960s. They also built success on another mainstay of commercial cinema, the star system. Had Peter Cushing and Christopher Lee worked in big studio movies at this time, they would likely have become familiar and respected character actors (as indeed they did later). In Hammer horror films, they were stars. As prefigured by *The Black Sleep*, the gothic revival also revived the careers of actors like Basil Rathbone and John Carradine who had once played plum supporting roles in studio A pictures and leads in second features. Bela Lugosi died in 1956 but had he lived longer, he surely would have appeared in some of the same exploitation horror films where Karloff, Chaney, Jr., and Peter Lorre labored in the 1960s, or even worked alongside the new crop of specialists including AIP's Vincent Price.

Once Upon a Drive-In Dreary

For the first few years after its formation in 1954, AIP specialized in preconstituted double features that would appeal to the growing drive-in audience — genre quickies about hot rods, juvenile delinquents, the Korean War, and monsters from outer space. They were made fast and cheap in black and white, with the company's real talent for titles, trailers, and promotion compensating for a highly variable product. Still, by 1959 the market for exploitation features had gotten crowded with independent competitors. With the appearance of Hammer's polished color horror movies backed by the distribution might of Warner Bros. and then Universal, AIP was increasingly pressed. Roger Corman had by then directed or produced about two-dozen movies and was itching to tackle productions with longer schedules and bigger budgets. With AIP resolved to take the risk, Corman proposed adaptations of Edgar Allan Poe titles to be shot in color and CinemaScope. Starting with *House of Usher* (1960) and *The Pit and the Pendulum* (1961), Corman ultimately directed eight such movies, seven starring former Fox contract player Vincent Price who had recently been emphasizing horror roles with William Castle's *House on Haunted Hill* (1959) and *The Tingler* (1959). While still cheap by major studio standards, the Poe series marked a big step up for AIP: instead of making two movies in black and white for $100,000 apiece, a single Poe feature would be shot in color for about $270,000 (Corman and Jerome, 1990: 77–79 and Arkoff and Trubo, 1992: 86). Corman's practiced ingenuity in getting most of a meager budget up on the screen would prove a major asset in the success of these movies and AIP's new strategy.

Though never planned as a series, the steady success of the Poe movies kept them in production for 5 years. Their appeal lay in stylish elaboration of gothic conventions built around Vincent Price's alternately brooding and histrionic performances and Corman's drive to create new variations. Fantasy novelist turned screenwriter Richard Matheson made *Pit and the Pendulum* a livelier take on his script for *House of Usher*, the latter a comparatively faithful adaption of Poe's short story. The only real connection to Poe's tale in the second movie was a helpless man strapped to the torture device of the title. Matheson's challenge was to take that central image and create an original story that led up to it, using the common method of exploitation filmmaking practiced by AIP and others in which a bankable title and promotional ideas often came first and a fully structured story later. Accordingly, the terrified victim bound beneath the swinging scimitar blade graced most every poster and advertisement for the movie.

AIP's promotional acumen was needed because the company was still at a disadvantage against their British rivals. Comparable production budgets went further in Britain and Hollywood majors picked up their US distribution costs. Moreover, Hammer poured virtually all its resources into horror-fantasy after 1959, whereas AIP's horror releases were always part of a broader program that included beach party movies, biker gang tales, and genre-crossing comedies like Price's campy James Bond villain parody *Dr. Goldfoot and the Bikini Machine* (1965). Still, Corman had a lot of talent in his corner. Besides the unique verve of Vincent Price supplemented by old pros like Boris Karloff and Peter Lorre, accomplished fiction writers Matheson and Charles Beaumont (both of whom were contributing scripts to *The Twilight Zone* at this time too), able production designer Daniel Haller, and veteran cameraman Floyd Crosby helped AIP match Hammer's standard. Moreover, Corman's cycle was flexible enough to cover experiments like the anthology format in *Tales of Terror* (1962), which included two horror segments bookending a fine comic interlude with Price and Lorre ("The Black Cat"), replicating the *Grand Guignol*'s program of alternating terror plays with farces to keep the audience emotionally off balance. Its success prompted making *The Raven* (1963) wholly as a comedy with Karloff and Price vying for the spotlight and Lorre in mugging support. *The Masque of the Red Death* (1964) featured exceptional color photography (by Nicholas Roeg) and reflected both the influence of Hammer and the emergent Italian gothic cinema with which AIP was already partnering on US distribution.

After several Poe outings, Corman had sought a different feel in the source material and turned to pulp horror writer H.P. Lovecraft and his 1941 novella *The Case of Charles Dexter Ward*. Though loose adaptations were the cycle's stock in trade, AIP insisted on maintaining the established brand, and the film went out under the title of Poe's poem *The Haunted Palace* (1963), barely motivated by Price reciting its final stanza in voice-over after the movie's Early American prolog. Regardless, the film is a virtual primer on conventions of gothic storytelling. In the prolog, Joseph Curwen (Price) is burned as a warlock outside his medieval manor by a torch-waving mob that seizes him just after he conducts some unseen ritual before a dark altar with a young village woman. The titular structure is a European castle that Curwen has brought to New England in pieces, literally importing the key gothic symbol to loom over the town. Curwen has already stolen the mob leader's wife who now lives with him in the castle, the pair's radical sexuality caught in a highly charged shot exchange of the woman presenting the virgin girl to his lecherously appraising gaze. The gothic's fundamental theme of sins and traumas of the past returning to haunt the present is met when the mob binds him to a tree for burning as he swears revenge on them and their descendants. A century later, Curwen's own descendant Charles Dexter Ward (Price again) arrives in town with his wife Ann (Debra Paget) and the curse continues.

Unlike many gothic tales though, the horror of Curwen's palace is not just repressed and contained within its walls, a convention often marked by a suspicious servant refusing entry to outsiders, rather it has spread like a sickness throughout the town. The community still suffers from the curse, its nightmare quality emphasized by a parade of blind, nearly faceless figures shuffling through the foggy streets as well as the contemporary villagers played by the same actors from the prolog including Leo Gordon, Elisha Cook, and Frank Maxwell. Corman shrewdly varied this entry too by casting outside the charmed circle of horror veterans, using performers generally known for playing tough guys in westerns and crime movies. This group ought to have made formidable opponents for the often epicene characters Price usually played were they not confronted here by the stronger and crueler figure he could embody as well. Once the Wards enter the castle though, Lon Chaney, Jr. makes a scary entrance as Simon, the menacing servant, who like Klove in *Dracula, Prince of Darkness* seems perpetually in wait to assist the resurrection of his master. In another common gothic trope, Ward regards an ominous, glaring portrait of Curwen and starts to be possessed by his ancestor's evil spirit.

In terms familiar to readers of Lovecraft—the mystical book called the *Necronomicon*, the ancient and monstrous Elder Gods—Dr. Willet (Frank Maxwell) explains that Curwen was trying to "open the gates" to the netherworld and mate the Gods with local women. Some kind of illicit mating is going on in the castle to be sure, as in most gothic tales. As a result of the curse, Weeden (Leo Gordon) has a mutant son, a growling "thing" locked in an upstairs room, which he feeds with raw meat. Still, the film skillfully balances its several narrative motifs. As two personalities struggle for control of Ward's body, the servants exhume a coffin and carry it through a secret door by the fireplace (the house's hidden anatomy again marking its repressed secrets). Curwen speaks an incantation over his long dead mistress and when the corpse rises, a quick cut depicts Ann bolting up in bed. Besides this familiar gothic doubling, when Ward/Curwen begins his revenge, he releases Weeden's offspring to attack him, and they fall into the fireplace together burning, followed by Price tearing Weeden's name from a death list. After he stalks Elisha Cook and immolates him with kerosene, he tears another name from his list, acts that anticipate Price's methodical avenger in AIP's *The Abominable Dr. Phibes* (1971) and variations with which Price finished his horror career (Worland, 2003).

In the climax, another mob storms the palace as the warlock is offering Ann to what we glimpse through a grate beneath the altar as some green-faced horror. When the villagers burn Curwen's portrait though, it seems to free Ward, who releases Ann. Corman again stages a big fire as the traditional gothic finale, yet with an important difference. Rescued from the flames, Ward shelters against the tree where his ancestor perished at the beginning. Yet with his back to the group, we can see by Price's darkly satisfied smirk that Joseph Curwen has finally triumphed, an ironic refusal of catharsis pointing to the genre's coming shift after 1968 that generally refuses to completely repress the monster. Corman left gothic horror after *The Tomb of Ligeia* (1964) but his talented unit had led AIP into a more competitive position by mid decade. Although the company returned to Poe films starring Price a few years later, only Michael Reeves's *The Conqueror Worm/Witchfinder General* (1968) was a critical success. In any case, the creation of the MPAA ratings system that year coupled with the growing social and political tremors of the late 1960s soon yielded a much more graphic and disturbing strain of horror in contemporary settings, signaled by George Romero's *Night of the Living Dead* (1968).

Horror *all'italiana*

Like other film companies reacting to a changed global market after World War II, AIP became truly international in the early 1960s. They both imported European movies for domestic distribution (dubbing, recutting, and sometimes shooting new footage to shape them for the American market) and took productions abroad in conjunction with European partners to take advantage of policies that European nations had enacted to help their recovering economies compete with the Hollywood colossus. For example, *Masque of the Red Death*, *The Haunted Palace*, and *Tomb of Ligeia* were shot in Britain to tap into the "Eady Levy" tax fund intended to finance national production (Arkoff and Trubo, 1992: 125–126). Moreover, just as Hammer's gothic films began to thrive, the Italian film industry was beginning an extended period of prosperity. Auteurs like Federico Fellini and Michelangelo Antonioni had brought prestige to Italian cinema but the booming business around Rome's Cinecitta studios arose from production of low-cost genre movies with wide commercial appeal, perhaps most famously the innovative "Spaghetti Westerns" made by Sergio Leone *et al*. Italian filmmakers also showed great flair for horror—all the more remarkable since Italy had no tradition of gothic literature or cinema.

Horror films had been largely prohibited in Fascist Italy even though many American movies were distributed on the peninsula until 1939. As such, Italian filmmakers and audiences had little exposure to the mythic characters and images at the foundation of the genre's commercial popularity. Tim Lucas (2007: 171–172) argues that the eventual appearance of *Dracula* and *Frankenstein* in Italy in the early 1950s plus the release of Warner Bros.' *House of Wax* in 1953 provided examples and impetus. Though it had little commercial impact, *I Vampiri* (1956), directed by Riccardo Freda, was Italy's first genuine gothic horror film. Its cameraman,

Mario Bava finished directing the movie when Freda quit after a dispute with the producers. Both men would go on to make some of the most memorable Italian horror films of the 1960s, often exceeding their Anglo-American competitors in both formal and thematic complexity.

Like Freddie Francis, Bava would always bring his considerable technical skills as a cinematographer to projects he directed, from devising clever in-camera optical effects to displaying great facility with lighting and composition in either black and white or color. As such, Italian horror rose to international attention with Bava's *La maschera del demonio* (1960), distributed by AIP in 1961 as *Black Sunday*, which as Lucas argues, continued "one of the key premises in Italian horror" established in *I Vampiri*: "men and women doomed to replay the loves and hates of their ancestors" (174). *Black Sunday*'s famous prolog depicts the execution of an accused witch who is bound to a stake before a spike-filled metal mask is set on her face and pounded into place by a mallet-wielding executioner, blood spurting through the openings. Two centuries later, she returns as a vengeful ghost taking possession of a contemporary descendant. British actress Barbara Steele played the awful witch and her victim, becoming the only international star of Italian horror, her dark beauty and luminous, wide-set eyes used to great advantage by assorted directors. Almost immediately a cult sensation, Steele personified a gothic figure not unlike Vincent Price in that in any given role she might be monster, victim, or both. Indeed, she has a small but pivotal part opposite Price in *Pit and the Pendulum* where both alternate as villains and victims.

Riccardo Freda's *The Horrible Dr. Hichcock* [*L'Orribile segreto del Dr. Hichcock*] (1962) is a prime example of Italian cinema's take on gothic horror. On the surface it is well within genre norms of the time with striking color photography and requisite gothic conventions from a creepy manse riven with hidden passages to an ominous servant to the lingering burden of an oppressive past. It was mainstream in no other way however as the "horrible secret" of the Italian title is that the upstanding doctor is an obsessed necrophiliac. Immediately after the credits, Freda gets to the point with remarkable directness. In a nighttime cemetery that recalls the opening of Whale's *Frankenstein*, a gravedigger is bashed from behind by a shadowy figure. The camera pans over to a coffin waiting beside the grave as the assailant opens the lid. Inside is the corpse of a young woman. The mysterious figure proceeds to run his hands provocatively across the body and is clearly climbing atop her as the scene fades. (One longs here for the comfort of Cushing's *sangfroid* or Price's hysterics but neither is forthcoming.)

In 1885 London, Dr. Bernard Hichcock (Robert Flemyng) is a gifted surgeon who has developed a new anesthetic that holds great promise for risky operations. At night, however, the doctor and his young wife Margherita (Maria Teresa Vianello) engage in a perverse sexual game in which after he administers the drug and she falls into a coma, he can indulge his fixation. Though the wife is a willing participant, stretched out on a special couch awaiting his arrival and greeting him

Figure 16.3 Barbara Steele trapped in a coffin by her perverse husband in the visually elegant *The Horrible Dr. Hichcock* (1962). Directed by Riccardo Freda (as Robert Hampton). Produced by Panda Film.

with a breathy smile of anticipation that would make Dracula envious, there is an implicit problem: the body is still just too warm . . . . One night the doctor goes too far. The uncertainty of his motives is part of the film's artful ambiguity. Hichcock perhaps only half-consciously administers a lethal dosage and seems genuinely shocked and anguished at Margherita's (apparent) death. Crushed, he leaves his home and devoted servant Marta (Harriet White), only to return 10 years later with a second young wife, Cynthia (Barbara Steele). His subsequent actions toward Cynthia, while more malevolent, are finally revealed to be in service of restoring the damaged Margherita, who survives prematurely aged and seemingly mad. In any case, experimentation on Cynthia holds out the added bonus of producing another "alluring" corpse (Figure 16.3).

Flemyng plays Hichcock as a hopeless addict: his drives recognizable if not remotely sympathetic. His antecedents include major gothic figures from Dracula and Dr. Jekyll down to Norman Bates, one of several implicit references to the work of Alfred Hitchcock in the movie. (The film's title deliberately misspelled the character's name to avoid potential legal problems with Alfred Hitchcock's trademarked name and image: see Erickson, 2000.) Uncertainty about the doctor's motives recur when (apparently atoning for the death of his wife) he refuses to use the anesthetic to operate on a patient who subsequently dies; but then tight point of view shots reveal him closely watching the body being moved to the morgue. At home that night with Cynthia he nervously smokes, preoccupied with returning to the hospital to molest the corpse. One can only speculate on how this movie got made in Italy or most anywhere in 1962. Whereas today such a film would be heavily marketed as an outré art house offering like *The Human Centipede* (2009) and discussed in the *New York Times*, *The Horrible Dr. Hichcock* played on drive-in double bills with Jess Franco's *The Awful Dr. Orloff* [*Gritos en la noche*] (1962), while taking the exploitation movie's typically lurid content to unsurpassed levels.

Still, what likely explains the movie's commercial acceptance is the generally low regard in which the horror genre has long been held (it simply escaped notice), an effect bolstered by Freda's mastery of the gothic film vocabulary. Expert visual conception includes the rendering of Cynthia awakening in a coffin, with shots from inside as she frantically tries to escape, and a lingering shot from outside of her contorted face, hands slapping against its small window with no sound emitting. More conventionally, finely constructed suspense sequences describe the gothic heroine's increasingly anxious discovery of the household's secrets: waking up on a stormy night to see a ghostly woman outside by the family mausoleum; or searching the passage hidden behind a full-length mirror (a traditional symbol for doubling and alter egos) that leads to the crypt. Freda even provides traditional relief at the end when Kurt, the young intern who is drawn to Cynthia, rescues her from the doctor, the mad Margherita, and the flames of another climactic fire that destroys the house. Still, for all its superb gothic stagecraft, the episodes of Dr. Hichcock fondling the dead linger unwanted in the mind. Though likely without conscious connection, Freda had taken the basic premise of *The Black Sleep* (the "terror-drug," the doctor's obsession with restoring his stricken wife, the awful results of his efforts) into realms the genre's main currents would take nearly another decade to approach.

Twilight of the Gothic, 1968–1974

Without question, the end of prior restraint of content with the institution of the MPAA ratings system in late 1968 affected the horror film as it did most every other kind. On the one hand, nudity, greater violence, and more complex themes now became permissible, which in theory broadened the horizons for filmmakers even as it curtailed stories built on the accumulation of foreboding atmosphere and limited (if effective) episodes of shock. It also implied that horror elements could become a thin veneer for soft-core sex. For example, Hammer's response was a cycle of female vampire films including *The Vampire Lovers* (1970) and *Countess Dracula* (1971) that opened onto subversive sexual possibilities but also presented many opportunities for gratuitous female nudity. Similarly, Jess Franco's *Daughter of Dracula* (1972) contained explicit lesbian sex scenes and an episode in which the dutiful daughter offers a young woman to the Count, placing the nude victim atop him in a coffin and discreetly closing the lid. Franco provides all the familiar gothic trappings but this hardly seems the main attraction. However, Hammer's undervalued *Dr. Jekyll and Sister Hyde* (1972), starring Ralph Bates and Martine Beswick, balanced these competing pressures with an inventive take on the story that also spoke to a moment of profound social changes around sexuality and gender roles.

Still, the masters of the earlier era also adapted more successfully to "the new freedom of the screen" including Fisher and Cushing's gory *Frankenstein Must Be Destroyed* (1969) and Price's turn as a pitiless witch-hunter in the bleak *Conqueror Worm/Witchfinder General*. While Lee and Cushing made an ill-advised trip to modern London in *Dracula A.D. 1972* (1972), Price found a satisfying end to his horror career in the slyly self-reflexive *Dr. Phibes* films (1971, 1972) and *Madhouse* (1974), the latter an AIP-Amicus coproduction. *Madhouse* varied a similar tale of theatrically staged revenge killings with Price as an aging horror star who may have snapped and turned to committing murders costumed as his screen character, Dr. Death. A smart, poignant scene finds Price's Paul Toombes watching highlights of what are supposedly his Dr. Death roles, really clips from the Corman/Poe movies, and reminiscing with fellow actor Herbert Flay, played by none other than Peter Cushing. The era of the "horror star" was officially at an end.

Significant industry realignments and social shifts had produced the gothic revival in the late 1950s and such changes would contribute to its end. By the mid-1970s, Hammer, AIP, and their like were being squeezed by a convergence of forces like those that struck the Hollywood majors after World War II. The big studios were now featuring more graphic content than ever before, even as brilliantly conceived yet explicit independent films like *Night of the Living Dead* and *The Texas Chain Saw Massacre* (1974) made the old gothic style seem quaint. Indeed, Peter Bogdanovich's *Targets* (1968) had presciently contrasted Boris Karloff's horror roles with the image of a psychotic serial gunman shooting patrons of a Los Angeles drive-in from a perch behind the screen. In a commercially shrewd but telling instance, AIP, which had always been cautious about extremes of sex and violence, distributed Wes Craven's hideously violent *Last House On the Left* (1972) but kept its name off posters and advertising (Szulkin, 2000). The move suggested the company might adapt to changed circumstances but the leap was too great. In any case, by decade's end, both Hammer and AIP were defunct, done in by a combination of the Hollywood blockbuster, cable television, and the beginning of home video, developments that also contributed to the rapid waning of drive-in exhibition and neighborhood theaters. Even so, the postwar gothic cinema Hammer inspired remains a highlight of the genre's history.

References

Arkoff, S. and Trubo, R. (1992) *Flying Through Hollywood by the Seat of My Pants*, Birch Lane Press, New York.

Balio, T. (1987) *United Artists: The Company That Changed the Film Industry*, University of Wisconsin Press, Madison.

Corman, R. and Jerome, J. (1990) *How I Made a Hundred Movies in Hollywood and Never Lost a Dime*, Random House, New York.

Doherty, T. (1988) *Teenagers and Teenpics: The Juvenilization of American Movies in the 1950s*, Unwin Hyman, Boston.

Erickson, G. (2000) Women on the verge of a Gothic breakdown: sex, drugs, and corpses in *The Horrible Dr. Hichcock*, in *Horror Film Reader* (eds A. Silver and J. Ursini), Limelight, New York, pp. 269 – 279.

Gordon, M. (1988) *The Grand Guignol: Theatre of Fear and Terror*, Amok Press, New York.

Heffernan, K. (2004) *Ghouls, Gimmicks, and Gold: Horror Films and the American Movie Business 1952 – 1968*, Duke University Press, Durham.

Lucas, T. (2007) *Mario Bava: All the Colors of the Dark*, Video Watchdog, Cincinnati.

Meikle, D. (1996) *A History of Horrors: The Rise and Fall of the House of Hammer*, Scarecrow Press, Lanham, MD.

Szulkin, D.A. (2000) *West Craven's 'Last House on the Left': The Making of a Cult Classic. rev. expanded ed*, FAB Press, Guildford, UK.

Worland, R. (2003) Faces behind the mask: Vincent Price, *Dr. Phibes*, and the horror genre in transition. *Post Script: Essays in Film and the Humanities*, **22** (2 winter/spring), 20 – 33.

17

International Horror in the 1970s

Peter Hutchings

Is 1970s horror cinema really "the last truly celebrated period in the history of the genre," as Ian Olney suggested in his recent book on European horror (2013: 97)? Possibly not everyone would agree, but nevertheless there is a pervasive sense in much horror history and criticism that the 1970s represents at the very least, in Rick Worland's words, "an exceptionally rich period for the form" (2003: 20). Indeed, the fact that both Olney and Worland offer these as passing remarks suggests that the importance of the 1970s is so widely accepted that it does not require much by way of justification or elaboration. One does not have to look far for evidence to support such a view. Genre landmarks from the 1970s include *Daughters of Darkness* [*Les lèvres rouges*] (1971), *Don't Look Now* (1973), *The Exorcist* (1973), *The Wicker Man* (1973), *The Texas Chain Saw Massacre* (1974), *The Omen* (1976), *Suspiria* (1977), *Dawn of the Dead* (1978), and *Alien* (1979), to name but a few. The decade also saw the rise to prominence of horror and cult auteurs such as Dario Argento, Larry Cohen, David Cronenberg, Tobe Hooper, Jose Larraz, Jean Rollin, and George Romero, again among many others, as well as a fully internationalized roster of horror production in Australia, Brazil, Canada, France, Great Britain, India, Italy, Japan, Spain, the United States, West Germany, and other locations across the world.

More than this, the 1970s has often been presented either as a period in which the horror genre underwent fundamental change or, more commonly, as the period in which changes initiated in earlier decades manifested themselves most visibly and obviously. It is therefore during the 1970s that what we now think of as the modern horror film comes to full fruition, with this involving a greater orientation across a range of films to the contemporary, the psychological, the explicit, and the shocking than had ever been seen before in the horror genre.

A Companion to the Horror Film, First Edition. Edited by Harry M. Benshoff.
© 2014 John Wiley & Sons, Inc. Published 2017 by John Wiley & Sons, Inc.

One of the more influential elucidations of the horror film's journey toward the 1970s has been provided by Andrew Tudor, who in his book *Monsters and Mad Scientists: A Cultural History of the Horror Movie* differentiates between what he terms "secure horror" and "paranoid horror". For Tudor, secure horror, which is broadly speaking pre-1960s horror, "presumes a world which is ultimately subject to successful human intervention" (1989: 103). This is a world in which

> human beings possess significant volition, while authorities and institutions generally remain credible protectors of social order. There is rarely any sense that the monster will survive and prosper long enough to overwhelm the movie's principal protagonists, let alone the whole of humanity, and our anticipatory involvement in both dramatic event and character always presumes secure narrative resolution. (1989: 103)

By contrast, paranoid horror, which is post-1960 horror, is an altogether more disturbing and apocalyptic affair.

> Expertise is no longer effective; indeed experts and representatives of institutional order are often impotent in the face of impending apocalypse. Threats emerge without warning from the disordered psyche or from disease, possessing us and destroying our very humanity. Lacking control of our inner selves, we have no means of resisting, and there is a certain inevitability to humanity's final defeat. (1989: 103)

Paranoid horror thus promotes a diminution in or a collapse of social authority, with monstrosity increasingly presented as immanent or internal (as opposed to the generally external threat posed by monsters evident in secure horror films of the 1930s and 1940s).

Other terms have been used to describe these two types of horror. Isabel Cristina Pinedo (1997), for instance, prefers "classical" and "postmodern," while Mark Jancovich (1992) has offered "Fordist" and "post-Fordist." Shifts of emphasis are also evident in the characterization of the emergence of the new horror, with both Tudor and Pinedo focusing primarily on the 1960s as the key decade—with in particular *Psycho* (1960) and *Night of the Living Dead* (1968) figured as portents of things to come—while Jancovich looks back further into the 1950s for signs of change. Ameliorating at least in part the general thrust of these accounts of horror history is an acknowledgment that these different types of horror can coexist, and that this is especially the case during the 1950s and 1960s, which is presented in this regard as a transitional period for the genre. Nevertheless, there is an underlying sense that by the time that horror cinema reaches the 1970s, it has become more anxiety-ridden and less inclined to assuage those anxieties.

The tone of these various accounts is studiously neutral inasmuch as one type of horror is not favored over the other. However, the paranoid/postmodern version often sounds more challenging and dynamic and possibly more interesting than its secure/classical predecessor. Indeed, the accounts of horror's development provided by Tudor and Pinedo in particular mimic, intentionally or otherwise, a strategy evident in a number of American horror films from the late 1960s and 1970s: that of associating a complacent and illusory sense of security with older forms of horror, with the new modern horror by comparison offered as more relevant and meaningful. One thinks here of the opening sequence of *Night of the Living Dead* where someone offers a Boris Karloff impersonation before falling victim to the modern zombie, as well as an aged Karloff himself coming face to face with another modern horror monster, this time a psychotic sniper, in *Targets* (1968) (Figure 17.1). Similarly, both the title of *It's Alive* (1974) and a discussion of old Frankenstein films within the narrative work to distance that 1970s film from what is presented as an outmoded form of horror, with something comparable evident in the more nostalgic *Young Frankenstein* (1974).

Bearing this in mind, one might question the extent to which "secure" and "classical" horror films are actually as closed, safe, and reassuring as Tudor and Pinedo (or for that matter horror filmmakers of the 1960s and 1970s) make them out to be, and indeed by implication whether post-1960s "paranoid" or "postmodern" horror films are as disturbing and on the edge as is sometimes claimed. Certainly other critics, notably Harry Benshoff (1997) and Rhona Berenstein (1996), have found in 1930s horror cinema provocative and critical elements that are not neatly contained by the narratives in which they feature, and some of those early horrors proved as controversial at the time of their original release as anything that came along later in the genre.

Figure 17.1 Boris Karloff in *Targets* (1968), a film that explicitly compares "old horror" (Karloff) to "new horror" (a psychotic sniper on a shooting spree). Directed by Peter Bogdanovich. Produced by Saticoy Productions.

The applicability of what is, for all the qualifications and caveats that come with it, a "big picture" account of horror history to what is by the 1970s a wide international range of production also merits some consideration. Although both Tudor and Pinedo incorporate non-English speaking horror films into their models, the emphasis is very much on American and British horror production. In particular, Tudor's basing his sample of horror films on those released in Britain inevitably excludes a significant number of non-English films that did not receive a British cinematic release. To what extent then does a movement from security to paranoia, however it is defined, primarily relate to English-language horror cinema? Are, say, Spanish or Italian or Japanese horror films of the 1970s as paranoid or as postmodern as their American counterparts, or are they operating in different, nationally specific ways?

Looking at 1970s horror production as something that not only cuts across national borders but also contains a variety of formats has the potential to introduce significant elements of diversity into the genre in ways that at the very least complicate some of the grand narratives of horror history. Focusing on just one year's worth of production can be revealing in this regard. For instance, the list of 1973 horror films included in *The Aurum Film Encyclopedia: Horror* (which is by no means an exhaustive or complete list) numbers 65 films in total: 22 from the United States, 15 from Great Britain, 11 from Spain, and 9 from Italy alongside offerings from Canada, France, the Philippines, and West Germany (Hardy, 1985). It is difficult to find any obvious, or indeed obscure, overall shape to this material, which ranges from art-horror productions such as the German film *The Tenderness of Wolves* [*Die Zärtlichkeit der Wölfe*] (1973), which some might not consider a horror film at all, to examples of US blaxploitation horror including *Blackenstein* (1973), *Ganja and Hess* (1973), and *Scream, Blacula, Scream* (1973); the British horror anthologies *From Beyond the Grave* (1973), *Tales that Witness Madness* (1973), and *Vault of Horror* (1973); and Hammer's final gothic horror productions of the decade, *Frankenstein and the Monster from Hell* (1973), *The Legend of the 7 Golden Vampires* (1974) and *The Satanic Rites of Dracula* (1973). There are films from cult favorite directors Jess Franco and Jean Rollin as well as the British cult classic *The Wicker Man*, three films from Spanish horror star Paul Naschy (real name Jacinto Molina), the deliriously excessive *Blood for Dracula* (1973) and *Flesh for Frankenstein* (1973), and idiosyncratic and hard to classify one-offs such as Oliver Stone's *Seizure* (1973) and Laurence Harvey's *Welcome to Arrow Beach* (1973). Not least, there is also, of course, *The Exorcist*, the most controversial and most commercially successful horror film of the decade. And more besides, with vampires, werewolves, mummies, zombies, and Frankenstein's monsters all present in various forms and in various locations.

This does seem a thoroughly disorganized sprawl of horror production, with different kinds of horror jostling for our attention in both national and international markets. On this basis, it could be argued that the more detailed and localized our critical engagements with the horror genre are—the more we focus on specific periods of production or types of film—the less amenable the genre as a whole is to being shaped thematically, structurally, or historically. Overarching accounts of the genre, such as those offered by Tudor and Pinedo, necessarily operate from a distance, using a series of films to illustrate what are presented as underlying principles of particular categories of horror film but generally not addressing differences between films that do not accord with those categories. These differences could relate to nationally specific characteristics, or to stylistic features, or to the particularities of certain horror formats or cycles of production.

The dispersal of 1970s horror across different locales and markets poses all sorts of difficulties so far as the basic business of genre definition and evaluation is concerned. An inclusive approach that engages with the full range of production during this period will likely have to operate as much in terms of generic disconnection and the parallel development of different kinds of horror film as it does in terms of any underlying generic functions or principles; in this sense it could become as chaotic as horror production itself. If one does engage with 1970s horror as a totality at that level of detail, then there is probably no neat, cohesive story to be told about it. For all its iconic status as a key period in horror history, 1970s horror thus starts to look more than a little opaque, mysterious, and hard to grasp. At the same time, the decade is central to some of the most influential accounts of horror history, particularly as they relate to the development of modern horror.

The remainder of this chapter explores some of the ways in which 1970s horror has been analyzed, discussed, and valued from the 1970s onwards. What is perhaps most striking about these various accounts is their partiality. Generally eschewing large-scale synoptic views of the genre, they explore instead specific elements of significance and meaning within the 1970s, with this involving the prioritization of some horror films and the marginalization or exclusion of many others. From this perspective, the value of 1970s horror, and indeed the richness assigned to it by Rick Worland, lies not just in the sheer variety of production that it encompasses but also in its ability to sustain often radically different interpretations of its nature and its worth.

From American Nightmare to Euro-Cult

The 1979 book *The American Nightmare*, edited by Robin Wood and Richard Lippe, and Cathal Tohill and Pete Tomb's 1994 book *Immoral Tales: Sex and Horror Cinema in Europe 1956–1984* could hardly be more different from each other. Separated by decades and continents, they offer entirely different versions of 1970s horror. They are presented here both as influential texts in their own right and as emblematic of broader approaches to 1970s horror cinema. Neither book restricts itself to the

1970s but that decade figures large in each as a key period in the growth of their own particular type or brand of horror.

For the contributors to *The American Nightmare*, an edited collection including work by Andrew Britton, Richard Lippe, Tony Williams and, most notably, Robin Wood, American horror films of the late 1960s and 1970s, or at least some of them, connect with and express a historically specific crisis in American society to do with the erosion of dominant social norms and authority. The causes of this crisis are not set out in detail in *The American Nightmare*, but later accounts of 1970s American horror, both by contributors to the book and other writers, have listed, variously, concerns over the Vietnam War and the protests against it, the Watergate scandal, the civil rights movement, feminism, and environmentalism as factors underpinning a widespread discomfort with and questioning of dominant social structures and belief systems. The terms of horror's engagement with this are ideological, with horror's monsters in particular representing, usually in coded form, that which has been socially repressed. In the troubled times that are the 1970s, this "return of the repressed" can lend itself in certain circumstances to a radical interrogation of the repression at the heart of the American way of life, and thus certain American horror films of the period acquire a politically progressive tenor, at least from the leftist perspective that characterizes all the *American Nightmare* entries.

A passage from Robin Wood's chapter "An Introduction to the American Horror Film" crystallizes this approach:

> If we see the evolution of the horror film in terms of an inexorable "return of the repressed," we will not be surprised by this final emergence of the genre's real significance—together with a sense that it is currently the most important of all American genres and perhaps the most progressive, even in its overt nihilism—in a period of extensive cultural crisis and disintegration, which alone offers the possibility of radical change and rebuilding. (Wood and Lippe, 1979: 17)

This way of understanding and valuing horror brings to the fore a series of mainly low-budget American horror films that are seen as fulfilling to some degree horror's radical potential, primarily through provocatively confusing distinctions between what is perceived as normal and what is perceived as monstrous. These include the films of Larry Cohen—including *It's Alive*, *God Told Me To* (1976) and *It Lives Again* (1978)—and Brian De Palma's *Sisters* (1973), which for Wood is "one of the great American films of the 1970s" precisely because of its critique of social normality (60). Tobe Hooper's *The Texas Chain Saw Massacre* also looms large, although not garnering unanimous praise: for Wood, "Hooper's cinematic intelligence ... becomes more apparent on every viewing, as one gets over the initial traumatizing impact and learns to respect the pervasive felicities of camera placement and movement" (19), while, by contrast, for Andrew Britton, writing in the same volume, *The Texas Chain Saw Massacre* is "eminently mediocre and objectionable" (41).

Horror is generally presented in *The American Nightmare* as a culturally marginal form, and indeed it is this marginality that permits a freer expression of potentially socially critical or radical views likely to be censored out of bigger budgeted productions. This does not mean that all low-budget films are received favorably, however. For example, Wood identifies David Cronenberg's Canadian shockers *Shivers* (1975) and *Rabid* (1977) as exemplars of what he terms the reactionary wing of horror, primarily for what he sees as their negative portrayal of sexuality in general and female sexuality in particular. In this, if not in budget, Cronenberg's work is aligned with *The Exorcist*, which—as it has been so often since—is presented in *The American Nightmare* as the epitome of reactionary or conservative horror.

It is easy to criticize such an approach; Tudor has described it as relying on "an inordinately reductive form of analysis" that produces "esoteric readings" (1989: 3). Nevertheless, the presentation of 1970s American horror cinema both in politico-ideological terms and as the product of a troubled society has certainly left its mark on subsequent horror criticism. It is now commonplace for horror films to be labeled as politically progressive or reactionary (and not just 1970s American horrors). For instance, Michael Ryan and Douglas Kellner's claim in their *Camera Politica: The Politics and Ideology of Contemporary Hollywood Film* that horror cinema potentially "provides a vehicle for social critique too radical for mainstream Hollywood production" feels very *American Nightmare*-like in tone and meaning (1988: 169). The idea that the various crises and disasters experienced by 1970s America end up in the horror films of the period has also found its way into recent accounts of the genre from the perspective of trauma studies, with both Adam Lowenstein (2005) and Linnie Blake (2008) offering case studies of 1970s American horror films as exemplary products of social trauma. And the 2000 documentary about horror cinema entitled (appropriately enough) *The American Nightmare* emphasized yet further the connection between fictional horror and troubled times by intercutting newsreel footage of Vietnam and scenes of social disorder in the United States with scenes from horror films from the period.

By contrast, the opening sentence of *Immoral Tales* establishes a different mood entirely.

> During the 1960s and 1970s, the European horror film went totally crazy. It began to go kinky—creating a new type of cinema that blended eroticism and horror. This heady fusion was highly successful, causing a tidal wave of celluloid weirdness that was destined to look even more shocking and irrational when it hit countries like England and the U.S.A. (1994: 5)

Compared to what is presented as the boring conventionality of US and British horror (and by implication the boring conventionality of the *American Nightmare* approach), the European *fantastique* is seen as offering opportunities for film-makers to "go sexy, get perverse and turn bizarre" (6). There is no interest in the ideological credentials of Eurohorror, or European exploitation cinema more generally. Instead the emphasis is on the experiences of delirious excess offered by European horror films, with a particular focus on the 1970s as the decade that benefits most from the loosening of the "shackles of censorship." Horror is shown to be thoroughly embedded in a broader exploitation field that flourished in Europe during the 1970s and within which boundaries were blurred, not just between horror and sex films but also between low culture and high cultural forms. Accordingly, the directors showcased in *Immoral Tales* are an eclectic bunch, ranging from figures from the avant-garde (Alain Robbe-Grillet) to exploitation specialists such as Jess Franco, Jose Larraz and Jean Rollin, and to Walerian Borowczyk, whose career encompassed both art house and pornographic elements. In all cases, however, the careers of these filmmakers were at their height during the 1970s.

In key respects, the films of Jess Franco sum up this kind of cinema in their exploitative sensationalism, their dispersal across national borders, and their blurring of distinctions between low and high culture. Franco began making horror films in his native Spain in the early 1960s, most notably the surgical themed and for the time rather conventional *The Awful Dr. Orlof* [*Gritos en la noche*] (1962), but by the 1970s he had become an astonishingly prolific director of lurid and mannered horror films, often international coproductions, across Europe. At his best—for example in the German-Spanish coproduction *Vampyros Lesbos* (1971)—his films combine explicit sex and violence with obscure, dream-like, and hallucinatory imagery. At his worst, his films are, for some at least, pornographic, tedious, and unwatchable. Although not as prolific as Franco, the work of Jean Rollin and Jose Larraz can be characterized in similar ways. Rollin began an influential series of French "sex vampire" films with *The Rape of the Vampire* [*Le Viol du Vampire*] in 1968, followed by *The Nude Vampire* [*La Vampire Nue*] (1970), *Requiem for a Vampire* [*Vierges et vampires*] (1971), and *The Shiver of the Vampires* [*Le Frisson des Vampires*] (1971) and other horror and sex-themed projects. *Vampyres* (1974), which is Larraz's best-known 1970s Eurohorror, was actually shot in Britain and, much like Rollin's work, placed scenes of intense eroticism and violence within very loose and often obscure narrative structures. Indeed, the narrative ambiguities and ellipses on offer in all these films serve to separate them out from much US horror of the period to the extent that a recent account of Eurohorror noted that it "has quite a bit in common with European art cinema" (Olney, 2013: 42).

This is 1970s horror viewed from the perspective of cult cinema, or, to use terms developed since then, *paracinema* or *trash cinema*. (For relevant discussions, see Sconce, 1995 and Hawkins, 2000.) Of course, cult cinema is not limited to 1970s Eurohorror, but the sheer volume of exploitation-related European productions during the 1970s, coupled with its penchant for nontraditional narrative structures

and a willingness to go further in explicit imagery than much American product, means that Eurohorror of this period is still afforded a significant place in
cult discourses.

The cult-based approach emerged after the *American Nightmare* approach and on
occasion its exponents have sought to distance themselves from the work of Wood
and his associates. For example, Ian Olney, in his book on Eurohorror, clearly references Wood's ideas when he critiques an engagement with horror films in terms
of whether they are "ideologically pure," and in so doing devalues some of those
American horror films identified by Wood as key achievements.

> This has been the case, for example, with some low-budget, independent American
> horror movies of the 1960s and 1970s, such as George Romero's *Night of the Living
> Dead* (1968), Tobe Hooper's *The Texas Chain Saw Massacre* (1974), and Wes Craven's
> *The Hills Have Eyes* (1977), which are typically lauded in academic writing on the genre
> for their radical gender, race, or class politics despite their formal and narrative defi-
> ciencies. (2013: 34)

The rejection of a politico-ideological approach in favor of an experiential engagement with 1970s horror that is attuned to notions of transgression rather than
political progressiveness becomes more obviously generational in Stephen Thrower's
Nightmare USA, which explores US exploitation cinema of the 1970s and 1980s and
which focuses on films that Wood *et al.* never discussed and probably never even
knew existed.

> The social response thesis (as expanded upon in 2000 by Adam Simon's documentary
> *The American Nightmare*) smacks of a middle-aged grasp for respectability by those
> uncomfortable with the atavistic, sadistic, masochistic, and sensationalist qualities of
> the genre. (2008: 17)

It is just as easy to criticize this kind of approach as it is the one presented in *The
American Nightmare* book. Here one might question a cultural politics that seems
based primarily on a fetishization of marginality and transgression accompanied
by simplistic definitions of mainstream cinema and mainstream culture. A rejection of ideological engagement with horror can also lead to an acceptance of, or, in
some cases, a revelling in scenarios and imagery that can be construed as misogynist,
racist, or in other ways demeaning of groups in society. Robin Wood himself, in a
rare comment on the kind of Eurohorror valued so positively by the cultists, found
the Italian horror films of Mario Bava and Dario Argento (the latter a significant cult
director who came to the fore during the 1970s) "obsessively preoccupied with violence against women, dramatized in particularly grotesque images" (2004: xvii). This
can be usefully juxtaposed with a moment in Danny Shipka's *Perverse Titillation: The
Exploitation Cinema of Italy, Spain and France, 1960–1980*, a book firmly grounded
in an Eurocult approach, where the author recalls a female student's response to his
description of the "Nazisploitation" film *SS Hell Camp* (1974) which includes the
genital torture and rape of women: "The student's response was something along the

lines of 'Well it's still disgusting,' to which I smiled from ear to ear and said, 'Yep, I love it'" (2011: 8).

While it is not difficult to find accounts of 1970s horror that draw upon elements from both the *American Nightmare* and the cult approaches, these approaches are at the same time not readily compatible. Indeed, tensions between them generally can be seen as marking a fault line in contemporary horror studies, and this is particularly evident in the contrasting versions of 1970s horror that each approach has conjured, with different films and film directors focused on and with the experience of horror characterized and valued in fundamentally different ways. The extent to which the shocks delivered by 1970s horror in terms of a new explicitness in subject matter and an assaultive aesthetic — coupled with an increased international proliferation of the genre — has fed and encouraged this split is not clear. However, ideas or notions of the 1970s continue to retain a place at the heart of what most horror historians and critics still think of as modern horror cinema.

National Distinctions in 1970s Horror

National distinctions between horror films figure in both *The American Nightmare* and *Immoral Tales*. *The American Nightmare* contains a chapter on the 1922 German vampire film *Nosferatu*, and Wood's "An Introduction to the American Horror Film" includes passing references to British horror films *Death Line* (1973) and *Frightmare* (1974) as works that share some of the properties he associates with 1970s US horror. *Immoral Tales* flits freely across the European continent in its presentation of Eurohorror as an international smorgasbord of transgressive delight, with national differences inflecting but not interfering with the kinds of cinematic experience that provide the book's focus. However, telling the story of 1970s horror cinema in terms of nationally specific schools of horror does have the potential to produce a more nuanced and inclusive account of the period but also a more fragmented one. Although, as noted above, 1970s horror production was widely internationalized, there were national centers within this, at least so far as volumes of production were concerned — namely the United States, Great Britain, Italy, and Spain. In each case, there are nationally specific contexts and cultural traditions to which particular sets of films can be related. At the same time, however, there was also a variety of production within each national cinema to an extent that renders questionable some of the broader generalizations about the nature of any national horror movement.

Take 1970s US horror, which is clearly distinct from what had gone before in US horror — not least in its eschewal of the European influences evident in the 1930s and 1940s and its refocusing on contemporary American settings and subjects — but which is difficult to sum up in a way that successfully captures all of its aspects in a cohesive manner. Wood and others have offered a powerful contextualization of the decade's horror, but it is striking how few films are focused on in detail in *The American Nightmare* or in related accounts of US horror such as Ryan and Kellner's.

It does not require much effort to find clusters of horror films that challenge or simply exist beyond the progressive/reactionary evaluative schema while also contributing to the richness and vitality of the genre at this time. For example, Matt Becker (2006) and others have identified a cycle of counterculture-influenced films or "hippie horrors" running from the late 1960s to the early 1970s, which could be seen historically as the missing link between *Night of the Living Dead* and *The Exorcist*. These include iconic films such as *Night of the Living Dead* and *The Texas Chain Saw Massacre* but also lesser known but still notable productions such as *Let's Scare Jessica to Death* (1971) and *Messiah of Evil* (1973), which together offer a different kind of cultural politics from that found elsewhere in the 1970s. Also noteworthy as yet another indicative instance of variety in 1970s US horror production is a blaxploitation cycle of horror production running from the early through to mid-1970s, including *Blacula* (1972), *Blackenstein*, *Ganja and Hess*, *Abby* (1974), *Dr. Black, Mr Hyde* (1976) and *J. D.'s Revenge* (1976). Harry Benshoff has argued that "many blaxploitation horror films reappropriated the mainstream cinema's monstrous figures for black goals, turning vampires, Frankenstein monsters, and transformation monsters into agents of black pride and black power" (2000: 37), and on this basis one can question the extent to which these films fitted neatly or at all into the more general interpretative categories and classifications that have been devised to explain 1970s US horror.

In his history of 1970s American cinema, David Cook notes that during the decade "horror moved from the margins of the exploitation field into the mainstream to become a vital and disturbingly influential genre" (2000: 220), and thinking about the "mainstreaming" of US horror (to use Cook's term) in the 1970s draws attention to another group of films that bring elements of distinctiveness to the field, and that is mid-budget adaptations of bestselling horror novels, of which notable examples are *The Mephisto Waltz* (1971), *The Other* (1972), *The Reincarnation of Peter Proud* (1975), *Burnt Offerings* (1976), *Audrey Rose* (1977), and *Magic* (1978). Tasteful, restrained, presold, and, especially in the case of *Audrey Rose*, directed at female audiences, such productions do not sit well with any account of American horror, or indeed horror in general, that values marginality or transgression, and they are generally ignored by critics and historians. Yet they do comprise a significant feature of US horror in the period, one that reflects the commercial influence of the genre not just in cinema but in the popular literature market.

Finally, but by no means least, is the slasher film, or, to use *Variety*'s phrase, "teenie-kill pic," which is generally seen as first appearing in US cinema in 1978 with the release of John Carpenter's *Halloween* but which does not mature as a subgenre until the early 1980s. The advent of this particular horror format has already been written into the ideological approach to 1970s horror as marking the moment when the progressive potential of American horror is finally closed down as both US cinema and US society adopt more conservative attitudes. (For example, see Wood, 1983.) With the exception of Carpenter's artful film, these stories of teenagers being stalked and killed by masked male killers were not critically well received at the time. However, they have since been recuperated, partly at least, via Carol Clover's influential formulation of the concept of the Final Girl, which denotes the female hero who in many slashers takes on and defeats the killer, and which at the very least complicates the charges of misogyny frequently leveled at this type of film (Clover, 1992). From another perspective, Richard Nowell, in his history of the slasher cycle, has traced what he terms the "female friendly teen film" back to Brian De Palm's telekinetic thriller *Carrie* in 1976, while others, including Clover, have considered *The Texas Chain Saw Massacre* as an early or proto-slasher project (Nowell, 2011: 9). It seems from this that the slasher was not entirely the end-of-decade excrescence which some have made it out to be but instead was firmly rooted in the 1970s.

Hippie horror, blaxploitation horror, adaptations of bestselling horror novels, and slashers: add to this all the other groupings and cycles that one can find in 1970s US horror, and which are too numerous to list here, along with those idiosyncratic films that do not fit easily into any category, and one has a complex national horror school. It is arguably more productive to view this as an ecology housing diverse sets of elements in ever shifting motion and interaction than it is as a generic entity possessing overall shape, cohesion, and purpose. Certainly one can detect some unexpected revelations looking across this material — for example, the importance of women in the audiences for both the novel adaptations and the slasher films in a genre often associated more with male audiences — but these relate to specific generic configurations rather than applying across the board.

Comparable principles of diversity apply to British, Italian, and Spanish horror during the 1970s, albeit in a scaled-down version, especially for British and Spanish horror which markedly fade away in the second half of the decade. They all exploit a relaxation in censorship with a greater emphasis on sex and violence than seen before in the genre. There is an evident focus on psychological horror (although supernatural horror retains its hold), and elements of social critique are also present. However, this manifests in different ways and in different contexts. For example, the case of 1970s British horror is somewhat paradoxical inasmuch as it experiences a decline in its international popularity coupled with a renewed creative vitality. This is evident at Hammer where a new generation of filmmakers introduced socially critical elements into the gothic horror format in films such as *Hands of the Ripper* (1971) and *Demons of the Mind* (1972). Grimmer, contemporary set-horrors such as *Death Line*, *Frightmare*, and *Satan's Slave* (1976) appeared closer to the US approach in their iconoclasm (and indeed, as already noted, Wood name-checks the first two in his "An Introduction to the American Horror Film") while at the same time proving thoroughly parochial in their engagement with the British class system. Other distinctive British horrors included the rural horror films *Blood on Satan's Claw* (1971) and *The Wicker Man* as well as the Vincent Price vehicles *The Abominable Dr. Phibes* (1971) and *Theatre of Blood* (1973), both of which are structured around a series of artful death scenes in a manner that parallels the Italian *giallo* films (more on which below) and anticipates the US slasher film.

Similarly, 1970s Spanish horror cinema offers a range of different kinds of films that do not necessarily add up to a cohesive whole. For example, Andy Willis has identified a series of films that contain coded critiques of "the established male social order of Franco's Spain" (2003: 77), among them *The Blood-Spattered Bride* [*La novia ensangrentada*] (1972) and *The Bell from Hell* [*La campana del infierno*] (1973). Spanish horror also produced one of the few fully fledged 1970s horror cycles with four "Blind Dead" films, beginning with *Tombs of the Blind Dead* [*La noche del terror ciego*] (1972), in which undead Knights of the Templar terrorize modern Spain. And there is also Spain's horror star, Jacinto Molina, better known as Paul Naschy, who began making horror films in the late 1960s and who throughout the 1970s develops his own horror cycle via his signature character, the werewolf Waldemar Daninsky, as well as playing Dracula, the Mummy, and a host of other horror roles, many of which can be seen to endorse precisely those machismo values that other Spanish horrors critiqued.

During the 1960s, Italy, like Britain, had specialized in period gothic tales, but in the 1970s the emphasis shifted mainly to contemporary-set psychological thrillers. While established Italian horror directors such as Mario Bava and Antonio Margheriti continued to work into the 1970s, the major director of this period was Dario Argento, whose visceral imagery in a series of films commencing with *The Bird with the Crystal Plumage* [*L'uccello dalle piume di cristallo*] (1970) has since procured him a substantial cult following. His signature success was the hyper-stylized supernatural drama *Suspiria* but his psychological crime-horrors or *giallo* films, of which *Deep Red* [*Profondo Rosso*] (1975) is probably the most significant, comprise his most enduring work. Weird, overly elaborate plots combined with bravura set pieces render these a distinctive format that, especially in the very capable hands of Argento, is unlike anything else one finds elsewhere in 1970s horror.

Opening the door to national distinctions in 1970s horror cinema produces an almost overwhelming sense of differentiation and variety, especially given that what has been set out above is merely a sketch of what is going on in different parts of the world. The fact that many of these films circulated internationally, and in some instances were influenced by horror films from other countries, complicates matters yet further, as indeed does the fact that other nations too, among them Australia, France, India, and Japan, were producing horror films during the 1970s, albeit in smaller numbers. Of particular interest in this context, both intrinsically and in terms of what it might have to say about the relationship between national horror cinemas, is Canadian horror. In the past, not least by the Canadian-based Robin Wood, this was generally subsumed into American horror cinema. More recently, critics such as Caelum Vatnsdal (2004) have found a distinctive Canadian aesthetic in, for example, the 1970s work of David Cronenberg, notably *Shivers* and *Rabid*. Richard Nowell (2011) has also pointed out the important contributions made by Canadian cinema to the development of the slasher film, not just through the Canadian proto-slasher *Black Christmas* (1974) but also via post-*Halloween* productions such as *Prom Night* (1980) at the end of the decade. This sense of national horror cinemas possessing their own distinctiveness but also existing in relation to other nations is arguably a widespread feature of 1970s horror. National borders have proved important in defining different kinds of horror but they are usually permeable, and mapping the movements of particular horror films and horror formats through different contexts arguably provides the best way of capturing the simultaneously national and international qualities of 1970s horror.

Thematic Distinctions in 1970s Horror

If thinking about 1970s horror in terms of national difference divides up the genre and magnifies its diversity, approaching it through shared themes has the potential to start putting things back together again, if only partially or provisionally. Clearly, specific themes do come to the fore during the 1970s. In "An Introduction to the American Horror Film," Wood listed the following thematic motifs: the monster as human psychotic, the revenge of nature, Satanism and diabolic possession, the Terrible Child, and Cannibalism (Wood and Lippe, 1979: 16–17). Clearly these themes have an international reach as well, and could readily be supplemented by other themes peculiar to the period—for example, the remarkable international proliferation of vampire films during the 1970s.

Thematic groupings have been used to underpin interpretations of the genre, and tell synoptic stories about its development, in ways that exist beyond the national or at the very least are not limited by it. However, one needs to guard against an overly general approach. For example, the US horror films *Frogs* (1972) and *Day of the Animals* (1977) and the Italian production *The Living Dead at Manchester Morgue* [*Non si deve profanare il sonno dei morti*] (1974) all exhibit concerns with the environment but are distinct from each other in terms of tone, intent, and effect. An environmental theme might underpin them all and connect them in that regard, but their respective treatments of this theme take them in radically different directions.

Bearing this in mind, it is worth turning to one of Wood's themes and considering how it might be used both to connect but also distinguish between horror films. Possession is a key 1970s thematic motif. It accords with Tudor's notion of paranoid horror in its sense of a threat that is immanent, close to home, coming from within the body. But it has a commercial nature as well, for the most successful of all 1970s horror films, *The Exorcist*, is a possession film. Possession as a theme predates the release of *The Exorcist*; for instance one can find it in the 1971 production *The Mephisto Waltz* and *The Possession of Joel Delaney* (1972). But let us focus on possession films that would not have existed without

Figure 17.2 Possession—Italian style in *The Antichrist* (1974). Directed by Alberto de Martino. Produced by Capitolina Produzioni Cinematografiche.

The Exorcist, films that manifestly attempt to exploit its phenomenal success. There were numerous such films but the ones to be discussed here are the Italian production *The Antichrist* [*L'anticristo*] (1974), the Spanish production *Demon Witch Child* [*La endemoniada*] (1975), and the official sequel *Exorcist II—The Heretic* (1977) (Figure 17.2).

Of these, *The Antichrist* and *Demon Witch Child* are the most obviously exploitative. Bearing this in mind, it is perhaps surprising how little they actually take from *The Exorcist*, the film in relation to which they are generally seen as opportunistic "rip-offs." As was the case in *The Exorcist*, they both feature a female who is possessed and who is ultimately exorcised by a priest. The possessed character's voice grows deeper in timbre and she spews forth obscenities, much like Regan, the possessed child in *The Exorcist*. Both also show the character levitating Regan-style and causing furniture to move around a bedroom, while *The Antichrist* also features projectile vomiting and a scene in which a man's head is turned round 180 degrees, in so doing referencing two of *The Exorcist*'s more notorious elements. Yet even these familiar elements are presented in these films differently from their presentation in the original. For example, the levitation sequences occur earlier than they do in *The Exorcist* and serve merely to clinch the idea that the female involved is possessed, as opposed to the much more climactic use of levitation in *The Exorcist*. The exorcism scene in *Demon Witch Child* is short and perfunctory while, as if to underline its Italian-ness, *The Antichrist*'s final exorcism scene takes place not in a Georgetown bedroom but instead in the Colosseum.

This difference between "rip-off" and original is most evident in *The Antichrist* where the possessed female is not, as in *The Exorcist*, a child but instead an adult.

The film also brings in reincarnation as a central plot device, when it is revealed that the woman in question had become involved with Satanists in an earlier incarnation, and that her current possession represents unfinished business for the Devil. Much of this is conveyed via an elaborate dream sequence which arguably owes more to *Rosemary's Baby* (1968) than it does to *The Exorcist* or any other 1970s horror film. In contrast, *Demon Witch Child* retains the idea of the possessed child, although here it is not diabolic possession, as it is in *The Exorcist*, but rather possession by the spirit of a witch out for revenge against the people who tormented her.

A subtler, but still important, difference lies in the presentation of the families of the possessed in all three films. Critics have made much of the fact that Regan's father does not appear at all in *The Exorcist*, and moreover that the idea of the absent father underpins and drives forward the film's increasingly desperate attempts to find a viable male authority to contain the threat posed by Regan. However, it is the mother who is missing from *The Antichrist* and *Demon Witch Child*, and instead we are given weak fathers unable to protect their daughters (especially in *Demon Witch Child* where the exorcism kills the child). The presentation of troubled patriarchy thus becomes in these films literal and therefore limited, and they consequently lack the resonance of *The Exorcist* in its depiction of a world in which all traditional gender roles are being thrown into question.

Exorcist 2: The Heretic was a much more prestigious and expensive project, although it is generally seen now as something of a disaster, commercially, critically, and creatively. What is of interest here is that while the film clearly follows on from *The Exorcist*, and features members of the original cast, it is also provocatively different from its predecessor. Indeed, one could argue that for all of its many flaws, its attempt to critique and challenge the worldview offered by *The Exorcist* was what disappointed critics and audiences the most. It is difficult to think of any other 1970s horror film that is so deeply (and for the period unfashionably) committed to the idea of goodness prevailing over evil. While *The Exorcist*, and indeed *The Antichrist* and *Demon Witch Child*, offer us gloomy worlds that have fallen and are probably beyond redemption, *Exorcist 2 — The Heretic* offers hope. In this, it was clearly out of step with much of 1970s horror. Nevertheless, its climactic episode in which images of Regan calming a swarm of locusts in the Georgetown setting of the original film are intercut with scenes of an African boy (like her an avatar of goodness), similarly calming locusts in an African desert, remains one of the more powerful moments in 1970s horror cinema.

Possession brings together these and other films. But it will not do to lump them together. They are clearly and obviously different from each other, with those differences to do in some ways with national distinctions and in other ways with the creative sensibilities of the people who made them. The same applies to all the other groups of horror films discussed here. This chapter began with "big picture" accounts of the 1970s before plunging into what seemed a more chaotic picture of the 1970s defined through multiple differences between a wide range of horror films. The latter part of the chapter has explored some of the ways in which

1970s horror films can be meaningfully grouped, while still retaining the idea that there is more than one way of doing this. Any particular strategy for shaping or interpreting these films will be necessarily and unavoidably partial, and will omit or marginalize films that arguably do not merit such treatment. The importance of 1970s horror cinema in this regard lies not just in the quality and influence of the many and diverse films that came out of it, but also in the way that it has provoked, encouraged, and inspired debate about the nature and value of modern horror. That debate continues.

References

Becker, M. (2006) A point of little hope: hippie horror films and the politics of ambivalence. *The Velvet Light Trap*, **57**, 42–59.

Benshoff, H. (1997) *Monsters in the Closet: Homosexuality and the Horror Film*, Manchester University Press, Manchester.

Benshoff, H. (2000) Blaxploitation horror films: generic reappropriation or reinscription? *Cinema Journal*, **39** (2), 31–50.

Berenstein, R. (1996) *Attack of the Leading Ladies: Gender, Sexuality, and Spectatorship in Classic Horror Cinema*, Columbia University Press, New York.

Blake, L. (2008) *The Wounds of Nations: Horror Cinema, Historical Trauma and National Identity*, Manchester University Press, Manchester.

Clover, C.J. (1992) *Men, Women and Chainsaws: Gender in the Modern Horror Film*, British Film Institute, London.

Cook, D.A. (2000) *Lost Illusions: American Cinema in the Shadow of Watergate and Vietnam 1970–1979*, University of California Press, Berkeley and Los Angeles.

Hardy, P. (ed.) (1985) *The Aurum Film Encyclopedia: Horror*, Aurum Press, London.

Hawkins, J. (2000) *Cutting Edge: Art-Horror and the Horrific Avant-Garde*, University of Minnesota Press, Minneapolis.

Jancovich, M. (1992) *Horror*, Batsford, London.

Lowenstein, A. (2005) *Shocking Representation: Historical Trauma, National Cinema, and the Modern Horror Film*, Columbia University Press, New York.

Nowell, R. (2011) *Blood Money: A History of the First Teen Slasher Film Cycle*, Continuum, London and New York.

Olney, I. (2013) *Eurohorror: Classic European Horror Cinema in Contemporary American Culture*, Indiana University Press, Bloomington.

Pinedo, I.C. (1997) *Recreational Terror*, State University of New York Press, New York.

Ryan, M. and Kellner, D. (1988) *Camera Politica: The Politics and Ideology of Contemporary Hollywood Film*, Indiana University Press, Bloomington and Indianapolis.

Sconce, J. (1995) "Trashing" the academy: taste, excess, and an emerging politics of cinematic style. *Screen*, **36** (4), 371–393.

Shipka, D. (2011) *Perverse Titillation: The Exploitation Cinema of Italy, Spain and France, 1960–1980*, McFarland, Jefferson, North Carolina and London.

Thrower, S. (2008) *Nightmare USA: The Untold Story of the Exploitation Independents*, FAB Press, Guildford.

Tohill, C. and Tombs, P. (1994) *Immoral Tales: Sex and Horror Cinema in Europe 1956–1984*, Primitive Press, London.

Tudor, A. (1989) *Monsters and Mad Scientists: A Cultural History of the Horror Movie*, Blackwell, Oxford.

Vatnsdal, C. (2004) *They Came from Within: A History of Canadian Horror Cinema*, Arbeiter Ring, Winnipeg.

Willis, A. (2003) Spanish horror and the flight from "art" cinema, 1967–73, in *Defining Cult Movies: the Cultural Politics of Oppositional Taste* (eds M. Jancovich, A. Lazaro Reboll, J. Stringer, and A. Willis), Manchester University Press, Manchester, pp. 71–83.

Wood, R. (1983) Beauty bests the beast. *American Film*, **8** (10), 63–65.

Wood, R. (2004) What lies beneath?, in *Horror Film and Psychoanalysis: Freud's Worst Nightmare* (ed. S.J. Schneider), Cambridge University Press, Cambridge, pp. xiii–xviii.

Wood, R. and Lippe, R. (eds) (1979) *The American Nightmare*, Festival of Festivals, Toronto.

Worland, R. (2003) From behind the mask: Vincent Price, *Dr Phibes*, and the horror genre in transition. *Post Script*, **22** (2), 20–33.

18

Slasher Films and Gore in the 1980s

James Kendrick

Horror films of the 1980s have been popularly understood as being dominated by two interrelated trends, one generic and one aesthetic. In terms of the genre as a whole, horror's dominant film-type during this period was undoubtedly the slasher film, which emerged in significant numbers in the late 1970s and early 1980s. Although slasher films never topped the box office charts, they became a regular mainstay of the cineplex-centered American youth culture, and by mid-decade had found even more success in the rapidly emerging markets of home video and cable television. More importantly, they lodged themselves into the cultural unconscious, where they continue to exert their influence over the horror genre while being regularly reinvented via parodies, remakes, and new sequels. In terms of aesthetics, the most notorious hallmark of 1980s horror was the use of graphic violence and explicit gore, which was made possible by new developments in prosthetic make-up and mechanical special effects. In fact, gore arguably became the central organizing principle of horror films in the 1980s. Lacking name actors, large production budgets, or complex plotlines, horror filmmakers instead relied on the tried-and-true shock value of graphically maiming the human body on screen, which made the slasher film even more disreputable among discerning critics (and more enticing to youthful audiences looking for a rebellious cinematic thrill). As such, the genre became more visually transgressive than ever before, significantly shifting away from both the literary-based Gothic tales of previous eras as well as the gritty, socially provocative horror films of the politically embattled 1970s.

Horror film production in the United States was not consistent throughout the 1980s, but rather went through an initial phase of overproduction that led to a 5-year period in which producers scaled back considerably, before launching back into the genre in the latter half of the decade. While a *Washington Post* article described 1980

A Companion to the Horror Film, First Edition. Edited by Harry M. Benshoff.
© 2014 John Wiley & Sons, Inc. Published 2017 by John Wiley & Sons, Inc.

as having "the biggest glut of nightmare movies in film history" (Williams, 1980), that year's production of 70 horror films was quickly surpassed the following year by 93 more. After that, horror film production declined steadily for 5 years before ramping back up in 1986 with 89 horror films, which was then eclipsed in 1987 with 105 (Prince, *A New Pot of Gold*, 2000: 298). Meanwhile, an entirely new market of cheaply made shot-on-video horror films emerged around mid-decade, which gave extended, albeit greatly degraded, life to the slasher film, whose narrative and characterological simplicity was inherently appealing to low-budget do-it-yourself horror entrepreneurs.

Generally speaking, the member studios of the Motion Picture Association of America (MPAA) — Paramount, Universal, 20th Century-Fox, Warner Bros., MGM/UA, Columbia/Tri-Star, Orion, and Disney — steered clear of either producing or distributing horror films, despite it being one of the decade's most consistently popular and profitable genres (Prince, *A New Pot of Gold*). While more than 700 horror films were theatrically distributed during the 1980s, the major studios were involved in fewer than 80 of them and tended to lean toward productions that had some air of respectability, usually via the involvement of an important filmmaker like Stanley Kubrick [*The Shining* (1980)] or Steven Spielberg [*Poltergeist* (1982)], or a known literary figure such as Stephen King, whose works supplied material for more than 15 films between 1980 and 1989 alone (Kendrick 2009, 139). The majority of horror films were therefore handled by smaller, independent production and distribution companies such as New Line Cinema [the *Nightmare on Elm Street* series (1984–), *Critters* (1985), *976-EVIL* (1988)]; Empire Pictures [*Ghoulies* (1985), *Re-Animator* (1985), *Rawhead Rex* (1986)]; New World Pictures [*Humanoids From the Deep* (1982), *C.H.U.D.* (1984), *The Stuff* (1985)]; and Analysis Film Releasing [*Maniac* (1980), *Basket Case* (1982)]. There was also a strong influx of European horror titles that made their way to theaters and home video via the smaller distribution companies, including films by Lucio Fulci, Dario Argento, Lamberto Bava, Bigas Luna, and Clive Barker [*Hellraiser* (1987), *Hellbound: Hellraiser II* (1988)].

Subgenres and Production Cycles

While it is commonplace to associate horror in the 1980s primarily with the slasher film, there were a number of other cycles and trends that met with varying degrees of box-office success. Traditional horror movie monsters were reborn via color and widescreen cinematography and, more importantly, significant advancements in make-up and mechanical special effects. Ghosts could be found in a number of films, including *The Fog* (1980), *Ghost Story* (1981), *The Entity* (1982), and *Lady in White* (1988), as well as two of the decade's biggest commercial hits, *The Shining* and *Poltergeist*; the latter film also produced two sequels (1986 and 1988). Werewolves and other shape-shifters were given new life in films like *Wolfen* (1981), *The Howling* (1981), *An American Werewolf in London* (1981), and *Cat People* (1982). *An American Werewolf in London* was particularly instrumental in defining the

Figure 18.1   *An American Werewolf in London* (1981). Directed by John Landis. Produced by PolyGram Filmed Entertainment and Lyncanthrope Films.

new parameters of what was possible to show on-screen with its detailed, entirely convincing man-to-wolf metamorphosis designed and executed by Rick Baker, who won the inaugural Academy Award for make-up effects the following year (Figure 18.1). Vampires were perhaps not as prevalent, although they appeared in a number of productions including *The Hunger* (1983), *Fright Night* (1985), *Fright Night II* (1988), *Vamp* (1986), and *Near Dark* (1987): many of these films sought to redefine the blood-sucking undead in a modern, self-aware guise. Zombies were consistently popular throughout the decade, lumbering through *Creepshow* (1982), *The Evil Dead* (1982), *Day of the Dead* (1985), *Re-Animator* (1985), *Return of the Living Dead* (1985), *Night of the Creeps* (1986), *Evil Dead II* (1987), and *The Serpent and the Rainbow* (1988).

Ridley Scott's genre hybrid *Alien* (1979), which effectively incorporated elements of the slasher film and the haunted house story with traditional elements of science fiction, helped spawn a series of sci-fi/horror hybrids, including *Scanners* (1981), *The Thing* (1982), *The Deadly Spawn* (1983), *Lifeforce* (1985), *Aliens* (1986), *The Fly* (1986), and *The Hidden* (1987). In addition to genre hybridity, horror filmmakers also reached into the cinematic past and remade classics from the golden era of horror and science fiction for modern audiences. Paul Schrader's 1982 remake of Val Lewton and Jacques Tourneur's expressionistic *Cat People* (1942) as a pop-music-infused erotic thriller was something of an anomaly, as most of the remakes seemed motivated primarily by the opportunity to take full advantage of advancements in special effects technologies. Thus, John Carpenter's *The Thing*, a remake of Howard Hawks and Christian Nyby's *The Thing From Another World* (1951), replaced the original's man-in-a-suit monster with Rob

Bottin's shape-shifting prosthetic and mechanical effects that provided some of the decade's most surreal horror imagery. In a more philosophical vein, in 1986 David Cronenberg turned the campy Vincent Price vehicle *The Fly* (1958) into a deeply unnerving exploration of human frailty and disease; rather than simply seeing a man whose teleportation accident leaves him stranded with a giant fly head and arm, audiences witnessed the gradual decay of Jeff Goldblum's body as he turned into a repulsive fly-human hybrid, literalizing his character's assertion about "society's sick, grave fear of the flesh."

The prevalence of genre hybrids and remakes suggested a postmodern turn in the genre, which found its apotheosis in the self-aware humor of a new breed of horror film that reveled in a previously untapped sense of perverse playfulness, making guts and gore funny and campy rather than sick and disturbing. Philip Brophy (2000) coined the term *horrality* to describe this new turn in horror and identified humor as one of its defining characteristics: "mostly perverse and/or tasteless, so much so that often the humour might be horrific while the horror might be humourous" (284). This trend was evident in the first year of the decade with *Motel Hell* (1980), although it reached an immediate pinnacle with the clever, low-budget horror "splatstick" of Sam Raimi's *The Evil Dead* and its sequel *Evil Dead II*, which took graphic horror violence to new and comically ludicrous heights. Other films of this type include *Creepshow*, *Gremlins* (1984), *Fright Night*, *Return of the Living Dead*, *Return of the Living Dead Part II* (1988), *Re-Animator*, *House* (1986), and *Beetlejuice* (1988), all of which, to varying degrees, found humor in the horrific.

The Centrality of Gore

Despite the wide range of horror subgenres and production cycles, all of them were bound together by a newly intensified emphasis on make-up special effects and explicit gore. The subtle horrors of Jacques Tourneur and Robert Wise were out, and "body horror" was in. To describe this shift in visceral impact, John McCarty (1984) coined the term *splatter movies* to describe films that "aim not to scare their audiences, necessarily, nor drive them to the edges of their seats in suspense, but to mortify them with scenes of explicit gore" (1). Such gruesome horror is arguably rooted in the Théâtre du Grand Guignol, which flourished in France from the late 1890s to the 1950s, and set new limits on what could be shown in terms of the mutilation and destruction of the human body. As P. E. Schneider (1957) noted, at the Grand Guignol "torrents of blood have flowed, eyes have been gouged, faces singed by fire or disfigured by vitriol, bodies dissolved in acid baths, arms and heads chopped off, and women raped and strangled" (13). Such gruesome gore made the transition to the screen in the early 1960s via a former college literature professor-turned-director of nudie films named Herschell Gordon Lewis, who began making so-called gore films largely because he felt that on-screen nudity was becoming too common: graphic on-screen violence became a new visual taboo to exploit on the drive-in circuit. Lewis's *Blood Feast* (1963), *Two Thousand Maniacs!* (1964), and *Color Me Blood Red* (1965), among others, were built around flimsy plots that functioned as little more than an excuse to generate situations in which people could be gouged, dismembered, crushed, beheaded, gutted, or otherwise killed in some imaginatively grisly manner. Although the effects were often crude and unconvincing, they signaled the beginning of a crucial shift in which explicit, gory violence was becoming more and more central to the genre.

In the 1980s gore made its way from the margins to the mainstream via horror films—especially slasher films—whose directors routinely sought to top what others had done; thus, while an innocent bystander's head was exploded with a shotgun in *Dawn of the Dead* (1978), the entirety of John Cassavetes's body exploded at the end of *The Fury* (1978). The MPAA ratings administration sought to crack down on the increasingly explicit violence (Kendrick, 2009), and while many films were trimmed in order to receive a market-friendly R rating, numerous horror films including *Dawn of the Dead, Re-Animator, Day of the Dead*, and *Evil Dead II* were released unrated in order to keep their gore fully intact. To these grisly ends horror filmmakers turned to a new breed of make-up special effects artists who honed and refined their skills in realistically depicting the maiming of the human body. Inspired by the "golden age" work of legendary effects men like Lon Chaney Sr. and Jack Pierce, and the more recent innovations of Dick Smith [*The Exorcist* (1973)] and Carlo Rambaldi [*Flesh for Frankenstein* (1973)], these new effects artists became *auteurs* in their own right, as horror aficionados became familiarized with their various techniques and specialties that, in their view, often transcended the rest of the film.

Rick Baker, who to date has won more Oscars for make-up special effects than any other effects artist, was renowned for his ability to create shape-shifting mutations and transformations in films like *An American Werewolf in London* and *Videodrome* (1983). His apprentice Rob Bottin designed the werewolf effects in *The Howling* and the sublimely unnerving alien transformations in *The Thing*. Stan Winston began his career in the horror genre on films like *Mansion of the Doomed* (1976), *The Hand* (1981), and *Dead & Buried* (1982), but he became best known for his work in the science fiction genre, creating horrific creature designs and gruesome bodily damage in films like *The Terminator* (1984), *Aliens*, and *Predator* (1987). The most famous and renowned of the make-up effects artists of this era was undoubtedly Tom Savini, whose ingenuity in crafting clever means of bodily damage was partially inspired by his work as a combat photographer in Vietnam. While his most famous early effects were in collaboration with George A. Romero, particularly the gruesome bullet wounds, dismemberments, and disembowelings in *Dawn of the Dead*, he became most famous for his work on films involving

Figure 18.2   The grisly gore effects of *Friday the 13th: The Final Chapter* (1984). Directed by Joseph Zito. Produced by Paramount Pictures and Georgetown Productions Inc.

knife-wielding maniacs, including *Friday the 13th* (1980), *Maniac* (1980), *Eyes of a Stranger* (1981), and *Friday the 13th: The Final Chapter* (1984) (Figure 18.2).

Baker, Bottin, Winston, and Savini, along with numerous other effects artists (including Chris Walas and Tom Burman), became particularly well-known via their coverage in the fan magazine *Fangoria*, which was introduced in August 1979. Unlike previous horror fan magazines like *Famous Monsters of Filmland*, *Fangoria* unabashedly celebrated the goriest, sickest, and most visually depraved elements of the genre, reproducing some of the most gruesome still images they could find, often accompanied by cheeky, ironic, or sarcastic captions. Most of the editorial content was focused on the "splatter film," particularly lengthy profiles of and interviews with make-up effects artists about the specifics of their trade. Savini, for example, was profiled three times in the first seven issues alone. Thus, the magazine was able to celebrate gore through graphic color imagery, but disavow its impact and any social significance by focusing on the techniques used to create the illusions, rather than their meaning (Kendrick, 2009).

Etymology and Structure of the Slasher Film

Despite the heterogeneity of the genre in the 1980s, the decade is best remembered for its prevalent slasher films, which Richard Nowell (2011) rightly notes was "arguably the most high-profile production trend of its time" (137). Regular use of the now commonplace term *slasher film*, however, was somewhat long in coming, as it was not until the mid-point of the decade that it was consistently used as a descriptor. Instead, critics, filmgoers, and various commentators employed a wide range of adjectival modifiers, including "stalker," "dead teenager," "women in danger," "psycho," "slash-and-chop," "stalk and slash," "teenie-kill," and "slice-'em-up" movies. In fact, the cinematic use of the term *slasher* dates back at least as far as the 1930s. When the 1935 French film *The Mysteries of Paris* was released in the United States in 1937, the character known as *Le Chourineur*, a butcher who has been imprisoned for 15 years for murder, is referred to in the credits as *The Slasher*. *Without Warning!* (1952), a low-budget police procedural about a paranoiac who kills blondes with garden shears, was known variously as *The Ripper* and *The Slasher* (The Fiends, 1952). The term *slasher* to refer to a psychotic killer was not, of course, limited to films, but was also used in relation to real-life serial killers. Vaughn Greenwood, who killed nine vagrants in Los Angeles between December 1974 and February 1975, was nicknamed by police the "Skid Row Slasher" (The Skid Row Slasher, 1975); he was later turned into a fictional character in the low-budget exploitation film *The Hollywood Strangler Meets the Skid Row Slasher* (1979).

The interplay of cinematic and real-life bloodshed was heightened around this same time as rumors of so-called snuff films, which purportedly contained real murders staged specifically for the camera, were rampant enough that Senator John C. Byrnes introduced a bill in 1979 making it illegal to sell, distribute, or view such films. The fact that a newspaper article about the impending legislation refers to these films as "snuff or 'slasher' film[s]" (Bertorelli, 1979: 6) suggests that the term *slasher film* already had not just a negative connotation, but one that suggests they are literally dangerous. By the early 1980s, the term *slasher* was being routinely used to describe killers in various horror movies and thrillers; for example, Vincent Canby of *The New York Times* described the transvestite killer in Brian De Palma's *Dressed to Kill* (1980) as a "slasher," while Robert Hatch in *The Nation* described Michael Biehn's character in *The Fan* (1981) as a "berserk slasher." Thus, by the time Vera Dika wrote her dissertation on this particular film-type in 1985, she could unproblematically note that her objects of study are known as *slasher films*.

Chicago film critics Gene Siskel and Roger Ebert's episode of *Sneak Previews* dedicated to slasher films in September 1980 is instructive regarding both the already entrenched familiarity and confusion with this type of film early in the decade. Siskel and Ebert both refer to the films repeatedly as "woman in danger films," thus highlighting what they saw as the subgenre's repulsive gender politics that encouraged viewers to root for male killers as they stalked and murdered objectified, helpless female victims. Both critics recognized certain formulaic elements in these films, including subjective camerawork, drawn-out sequences in which potential victims are stalked by an unseen killer, and the use of graphic violence. Yet they also failed to make any mention of the fact that the lone survivor is often female, ignored some qualifying issues in the use of subjective camerawork (particularly in *Friday the 13th*, where it functions at least partially to hide the killer's identity), and mischaracterized the films as frequently involving rape, which is actually extremely rare in the slasher film. This error, repeated several times during the episode, likely stems from their inclusion of the notorious rape-revenge film *I Spit on Your Grave* (1978), which along with their mention of *The Howling*, further suggests that a thorough understanding of the slasher film's parameters was not yet fully in place.

At its most basic, slasher films tell "the story of a blade-wielding killer preying on a group of young people" (Nowell, 2010: 16). By 1981, these films had coalesced into a generally recognized cycle within the horror genre, although it did not yet have a consistent label by which it was known and it was several years before critics and scholars attempted to systematize and analyze it. Due to the slasher film's fundamentally repetitive nature, many critics have found the structuralist perspective, which examines how a genre's constituent parts function together and generate meaning, to be one of the most useful modes of analysis. Robin Wood (1983) offered one of the earliest serious examinations of slasher films, arguing that they address certain "needs" in a capitalist consumer-oriented culture by using the slasher as a superego figure to punish sexual freedom and liberated female sexuality. John McCarty (1984) and William McCarty Schoell (1985) also wrote about slasher films, albeit within the framework of books dedicated to a wider analysis of graphically violent films (dubbed "splatter movies" and "shockers," respectively). Vera Dika (1985, 1987) and Carol Clover (1987, 1992) were the first scholars to pose detailed definitions and structural/ideological analyses of the slasher film, and others have followed, including Adam Rockoff (2002), Kent Byron Armstrong (2003), and Richard Nowell (2010, 2011). While there is some degree of variance in the definitions posed by these scholars, there is also a considerable amount of overlap, more than enough to generate a relatively stable, coherent description of the slasher film's major aesthetic and narrative characteristics, themes, and production strategies—what Clover (1992) calls its "inventory of generic components" (25). Although there has been some variation in terms of how the structural components of the subgenre have been understood, one could argue that, following Clover's analysis, they all contain, with minimal variation, a psychotic killer, a terrible place, a variety of weapons of death, a group of young victims, and a "Final Girl" who survives either to be rescued or dispatch the killer herself.

The psychotic killer is the most important of the slasher's structural components, a fact embodied in the subgenre's very name, as well as the widespread recognition of the most successful series' blade-wielding villains: Jason Voorhees (*Friday the 13th*), Michael Myers (*Halloween*), and Freddy Krueger (*A Nightmare on Elm Street*). The killer is typically human (or human-like), male, and vaguely supernatural to the extent that he appears to have mastery over space and vision that far outstrips that of his victims, allowing him to appear and disappear at will as well as constantly rebuke even the most vigorous attempts to kill him. Although Clover argues

Figure 18.3   Michael Myers of John Carpenter's *Halloween* (1978). Produced by Compass International Pictures and Falcon International Productions.

that slasher films are traditionally "unmediated by otherworldly fantasy" (1992: 22), many a slasher film bears some hint of the supernatural. Michael Myers is the proto-typical slasher in this regard; his psychiatrist, Dr. Loomis (Donald Pleasence), can only explain Myers as "pure evil," and the idea that he is simultaneously human and inhuman is implicitly suggested in his dehumanizing nickname, "The Shape" (Figure 18.3). *A Nightmare on Elm Street* (1984) introduced the first fully supernat-ural slasher in Freddy Krueger, a child killer murdered by angry parents and resur-rected as a murderous ghost that haunts (or, one might say, possesses) the dreams of the parents' teenage children. Freddy paved the way for other supernatural slashers, including Jason Voorhees, who was reanimated as a murderous zombie in *Friday the 13th Part VI: Jason Lives* (1986), and Chucky, a doll possessed by the soul of a serial killer in *Child's Play* (1988) and its numerous sequels.

The gender of the slasher has been complicated throughout the cycle's history, beginning with *Friday the 13th*, whose actual killer is a middle-aged mother seeking vengeance for the accidental drowning of her son. Similarly, in *Psycho II* (1982), it turns out that Norman is no longer the killer, but rather a kindly old woman named Mrs. Spool (who also reveals herself to be Norman's *actual* mother). *Sleepaway Camp* (1983) plays complete havoc with gender roles by revealing the killer to be a bullied, withdrawn teenage girl—whom the formula would seem to dictate would be the Final Girl—and then revealing that said teenage girl is actually a boy who has been forced by his aunt to live as such.

Although Dika (1987) originally argued that the killer is not typically psychol-ogized, distinguishing the slasher formula from structurally similar films such as *Maniac* and *Fade to Black* (1980), Clover and others have pointed out that the killer is often "propelled by psychosexual fury, more particularly a male in gender distress" (27), which tends to stem from some kind of childhood trauma. More generally, Rockoff describes the slasher film killer as "an ordinary person who has suffered some terrible—and sometimes not so terrible—trauma" (5–6). Examples include *The Burning* (1981) whose slasher is the much despised caretaker of a summer camp burned into an unrecognizable monstrosity by a prank gone wrong, and *The Prowler* (1981), whose slasher may or may not be a young soldier from World War II who was dumped by his girlfriend. The idea of a "past trauma," rather than specific "psychosexual rage," aligns more closely with Dika's conception of the "stalker," which she positions as an archaic relic of a previous era that returns to disrupt the present stability of a young community. Either way, the killer is key to the subgenre's two-part temporal structure, which is composed of a past event (presented either at beginning of the film or in flashback) that explains the killer's trauma and subsequent madness, and a present event in which the killer returns to take revenge on the guilty parties or their symbolic substitutes (Dika; Rockoff).

The setting of the slasher film is usually non-urban and is invariably removed from a larger community, which helps to isolate the film's young victims from intervention by adults, if not the rest of society in general (Dika; Nowell). Rockoff notes that while slasher films take place in a wide variety of settings, these settings are almost always directly connected with the adolescent American experience in some way, since teenagers generally comprise the film's victims. Thus, summer camps (*Friday the 13th, The Burning, Sleepaway Camp*), high schools (*Prom Night, Graduation Day, Return to Horror High*), colleges (*Black Christmas, Night School, The Prowler, Hell Night, Splatter University*), and small town suburbia (*Halloween, A Nightmare on Elm Street, Slumber Party Massacre*) are the most common locations in slasher films, connected primarily by their apparent banality and isolation. Yet despite the ordinariness of these locations, they also feature what Clover (1992) refers to as "a Terrible Place, most often a house or tunnel, in which victims sooner or later find themselves" (30). This element is not in any way unique to the slasher film, but is rather "a venerable element of horror" (Clover: 30) that can be traced back to Dr. Frankenstein's laboratory and Dracula's castle. The Terrible Places of slasher films are as varied as the settings themselves—the decaying Myers house in *Halloween*, the makeshift backwoods shrine to Jason's dead mother in *Friday the 13th Part 2* (1981), or even the dreams of sleeping teenagers in *A Nightmare on Elm Street*.

While the killers in slasher films are rarely if ever defined exclusively by a specific weapon (Freddy Krueger's unique knife-fingered glove being a major exception), they predominantly kill with bladed instruments such as knives, machetes, axes, spears, pitchforks, meat cleavers, and ice picks. Penetration of victims' bodies with sharp metallic instruments is one of the most consistent and expected elements of slasher films and a constituent part of their horrific appeal; not only do stabbings, garrotings, and gougings allow for the ample deployment of gory make-up effects, but they also emphasize the close proximity of killer and victim. Unlike being shot from a distance, as is typical in most action-adventure films and thrillers, being stabbed is a deeply personal, physically close violent action that leaves a lingering sense of discomfort in the viewer. Clover compares the close, tactile violence of slasher films to the violence in revenge-of-nature, werewolf, and vampire films: "Knives and needles, like teeth, beaks, fangs, and claws, are personal extensions of the body that bring attacker and attacked into primitive, animalistic embrace" (32).

Nevertheless, there has always been a wide range of weapons used in slasher films, and not all deaths arrive at the end of a bladed instrument. Sometimes victims are dispatched with found objects or even by the killer's bare hands. In *Halloween*, for example, Michael Myers stabs two of his victims but strangles another with a phone cord. In *Black Christmas* (1974), which is perhaps the true prototype for the slasher film, a character played by Margot Kidder is killed with a crystal unicorn that sits on her bedside table. As the slasher film developed throughout the decade and its formulaic elements became fully entrenched, enterprising filmmakers realized that creativity in killing was of paramount importance to attracting audiences. While knives and machetes and axes would always have their place, slashers quickly began to employ all manner of weapons, which at times brought the films well into the range of absurdity. The *Nightmare on Elm Street* series was perhaps the most inventive in terms of gruesome deaths, if only because Freddy was not limited to the physical laws of reality and could kill using any number of fantastical means. However, even those slashers who were still subject to the laws of physics found ways to turn almost anything into an instrument of death: a football with a sword attached in *Graduation Day*, garden shears in *The Burning*, a shish-kabob skewer in *Happy Birthday to Me*, a curling iron in *Sleepaway Camp*, and even a sleeping bag in *Friday the 13th Part VII: The New Blood*.

Because the threat of violent death is a constant in the slasher film, each entry must supply a convenient group of would-be victims. As Dika (1987) has pointed out, these victims are almost invariably young (either high school- or college-age), attractive, healthy, and normal. While the victims are often organized in social hierarchies with more and less popular members, they are still well within the broad parameters of "normality" according to typical American adolescence. Their youth, health, and energy are usually coded in sexual terms, and the victims are sexually active, which results in a frequent correlation between sexual activity and endangerment. While Wood (1983) argued that sexuality is unambiguously punished by the slasher (the victims are often killed in the moments following a sexual encounter), others have argued for a more nuanced understanding of post-coital death. Unlike the killer, who has visual power and sees but is not seen, his victims die precisely because they are unable to see the danger around them. Their deaths are sometimes preceded by lengthy "stalking" sequences, often from the slasher's first-person perspective. The victims have individual personalities, but they rarely develop as unique characters, partially because their screen time is limited by their victim status, but also because their actions have little or no narrative significance; that is, their activities are "transitional," simply filling time before their inevitable demise. And, while critics of the slasher film routinely accuse the films of misogyny and an obsession with violence against women, the victims in these films tend to be fairly evenly distributed in terms of gender, with just as many male as female victims (Nowell, 2010: 251–252). While scholars concede that violence against female victims is usually "more sensational or featured more predominantly" (Dika: 90) and "filmed at closer range, in more graphic detail, and at greater length" (Clover: 35), accusations of misogyny against the films cannot be sustained solely by the sex of the victims, but must also rely on the assumption that the slasher is not only male, but that his controlling gaze is inherently "masculine."

Accusations of misogyny against the slasher film are also undermined by the repeated presence of what Clover (1992) calls "the Final Girl": "the one who encounters the mutilated bodies of her friends and perceives the full extent of the preceding horror and of her own peril; who is chased, cornered, and wounded; whom we see scream, stagger, fall, rise, and scream again. She is abject terror personified" (35). More importantly, though, the Final Girl is a survivor, the one person among the young group of victims who not only avoids death, but actively appropriates the power of the gaze (she is able to *see*, while her friends cannot) and turns the killer's violence against him. The Final Girl is much like her friends, in that she is young and healthy, but unlike them, her youthful vitality is not immediately coded as sexual. Rather, the Final Girl is either explicitly virginal (e.g., Laurie Strode in *Halloween*) or simply has more sexual restraint than her friends (e.g., Nancy in *A Nightmare on Elm Street*). As a result she is not easily reduced to a sexual object. The Final Girl's victory over the slasher is central to Clover's understanding of the complex gender dynamics of the slasher film, arguing that the Final Girl is ambiguous in her sexual identity. Although she is physically female, she often has more masculine interests, and during the course of the film she is both explicitly feminized in undergoing the agonizing trials of victimhood, and then masculinized by destroying the killer and saving herself, often impaling him with his own (phallic) weapon. In gendered terms, then, the Final Girl literally turns the table on the slasher, symbolically castrating him while she is phallicized via her appropriation of his violence, which Clover argues is key to male viewers' ability to identify with and cheer for a heroine while all their male on-screen surrogates (boyfriends, police officers, etc.) have been killed.

More recently, Nowell (2011) has argued against Clover's reading of the masculinized Final Girl. Contrary to Clover's assertion that such characters are geared toward male viewers, Nowell asserts that filmmakers saw such characters, especially after the success of *Alien*, which featured Sigourney Weaver as a "Final Woman," as "an invaluable instrument with which to attract females, on the basis that a projection of female empowerment promised to resonate with female ticket buyers" (131). While Clover provides plenty of evidence that many Final Girls cross gender lines with their masculine interests and names, Nowell counters that just as many are overtly feminine, such as Jamie Lee Curtis's beautiful prom queen in *Prom Night* or Linda Blair in her provocatively low-cut dress in *Hell Night*. In essence, Nowell argues that the Final Girls of slasher films are really younger versions of the "new woman" heroines that were prominently featured in late-1970s television shows such as *Wonder Woman* (1975–1979) and *Charlie's Angels* (1976–1981). Either way, the Final Girl clearly plays a crucial role in slasher movie narratives, and challenges any simple preconceptions of the subgenre's deployment of non/traditional gender roles.

A Brief Genealogy: The Evolution of the Slasher Film

Alfred Hitchcock's *Psycho* is most often posited as the slasher film's originating text—its "appointed ancestor," as Clover (1992: 23) puts it—due to the fact that it is arguably the first film to assemble virtually all of the slasher's structural components into a single film: the psychotic, gender-confused killer; an attractive female victim who is "punished" for her sexual transgressions; stabbing deaths; a Terrible Place; and explicit, bloody violence, which at the time was considered so extreme that many critics panned the film because they were so disturbed by its graphic nature. However, while Adam Rockoff has gone so far as to call *Psycho* "the first true slasher film" (26), Richard Nowell (2010) has challenged this widely accepted lineage on the grounds that *Psycho* "exhibited only tangential similarities to teen slashers and … did not influence teen slasher film production or content in any meaningful way" (58). While Nowell is correct that there are distinct differences between *Psycho* and later slasher films (particularly *Psycho*'s lack of young characters), the fact remains that in a broad sense *Psycho* "signaled the start of a major shift in the American horror film … the popular definition of a horror film would be routinely understood to encompass predatory sexual psychopaths stalking everyday domestic settings as much as supernatural doings in the gothic manors" (Worland, 2007: 87).

England and France also each produced a canonical horror film that fundamentally altered the genre both visually and ideologically. The year before *Psycho* was released, Michael Powell's *Peeping Tom* (1960), a powerful psychological thriller about a soft-spoken serial killer who uses his camera tripod as a weapon to kill young women and immortalize their terror on film, was released in England. Powell elegantly and frighteningly captured the metaphorical essence of the horror genre, and his career was virtually ended by the vitriol heaped on the film by British critics. A year later, Georges Franju scandalized France with his second feature film, *Eyes Without a Face* (1960). The story of a plastic surgeon who murders young women in a failing effort to restore the disfigured face of his beloved daughter, *Eyes Without a Face* is a visually elegant, but deeply disturbing portrait of a scientist playing God for intensely personal reasons. Taken together, *Psycho*, *Peeping Tom*, and *Eyes Without a Face* were crucial in the very modern project of relocating horror from the fantastical to the mundane, generating chills with the uneasy notion that the guy next door might be flaying the skin from someone's face or being sexually aroused by self-made snuff films.

Psycho spawned a rash of similarly named imitations including William Castle's *Homicidal* (1961) and a series of thrillers from Hammer including *Maniac* (1963) and *Paranoiac* (1963). There were also a number of other film cycles in the 1960s and early 1970s that helped pave the way for the slasher's eventual emergence as its own subgenre. In addition to the drive-in splatter films of Herschell Gordon Lewis, a number of Italian filmmakers began to pioneer a new genre of horror-thrillers known as *giallo*. *Giallo* have a number of conventions that are similar to the slasher film, including masked psychopathic killers and elaborately choreographed and protracted murder sequences, although their use of baroque set design, flashing and colored lights, and overbearing and often inappropriate music is distinctly different from the stalk-and-slash formula of slasher films (see Chapter 22). Although not as well known as many other *giallo* films, Sergio Martino's *Torso* (1973) is a particularly acute progenitor of the slasher film. It features a knife-wielding psychosexual maniac, a cast of nubile college students-cum-murder victims, and a seemingly reactionary connection between sex and violent death. Most importantly (unlike most *giallo* films) *Torso* features a Final Girl who must quietly hide her presence in a large house while the killer, who kills women to avenge a childhood trauma, saws up the bodies of recently dispatched victims. However, unlike the Finals Girls of later slasher films, *Torso*'s Final Girl is denied the opportunity to have her final say against the killer as she is rescued at the last minute by her boyfriend.

Tobe Hooper's *The Texas Chain Saw Massacre* (1974) was another formative moment in the development of the slasher film. It tells the story of a group of young people who wander into a rural area owned by a family of cannibals who kill them off one by one. Even more than *Psycho*, *The Texas Chain Saw Massacre* includes a number of formal characteristics that would come to be associated with slasher films, particularly a community of young people threatened by a relic from the past as well as a Final Girl, albeit one who merely escapes with her life, leaving the cannibalistic clan largely alive and intact. Arguably, Bob Clark's Canadian horror film *Black Christmas* (1974) was the first to include all of the fundamental elements of the slasher film in a manner that is immediately recognizable. Clark envisioned a murder-mystery in which the viewer never sees the killer, which he accomplished by relying almost entirely on the then relatively new and decidedly unsettling point-of-view camera. The story takes place during the Christmas holidays on an unnamed college campus where a group of sorority sisters fall victim to an unseen stalker lurking in the attic of the sorority house. *Black Christmas* parts ways from later slasher films primarily in terms of its relative restraint, as it relies heavily on mystery and atmosphere to sell the horror, rather than graphic violence and nudity.

Many histories of the slasher film mark its beginning with John Carpenter's *Halloween*. Word-of-mouth and surprisingly good critical notices led it to become one of the most economically successful independent movie at the time. The film's opening sequence, in which Michael Myers kills his sister, is depicted (like the opening of *Black Christmas*) with an extended, gliding point-of-view shot that is intended primarily to obscure the killer's identity—until the crucial moment when the film cuts to a shot of Michael's parents removing his mask, revealing to the audience that the killer is a child. Apart from the point-of-view shots, Carpenter also proves himself a master of utilizing the horizontal space of the widescreen. In one of the film's most striking moments, Laurie backs up into a dark corner, and as her eyes adjust to the darkness, the ghostly face of Michael's white mask slowly appears in a doorframe behind her. The widescreen is crucial in this regard, as Carpenter plays with the audience's sense of security that the center of the frame is the place to look, instead forcing them to scan the entirety of the frame, always checking the corners.

By the summer of 1980, it was clear that the slasher film had developed into a significant trend. Richard Nowell (2011: 118) has noted that this trend actually emerged from four similar production trends that emerged out of the late 1970s: the now-familiar teen slasher film; a variation of the slasher film, likely inspired by *The Town That Dreaded Sundown* (1976) in which the victims are not teenagers, but rather unrelated adults [*Schizoid* (1980), *He Knows You're Alone* (1980)]; lurid thrillers about urban-dwelling psychotics modeled on *Taxi Driver* (1976) [*Don't Answer the Phone* (1980), *Maniac*]; and slick, adult-driven mystery thrillers about knife-wielding killers [*The Eyes of Laura Mars* (1978), *Dressed to Kill* (1980), *Cruising* (1980)].

One of the most famous of the early slasher films, *Friday the 13th* tells the story of camp counselors at the fictional Camp Crystal Lake being killed one by one by an unseen assailant. Director Sean S. Cunningham had always been a filmmaker willing to work with any formula that might be lucrative, and was previously notorious for producing the Wes Craven-directed *The Last House on the Left* (1972), one of the most shocking movies of the early 1970s drive-in circuit that is also frequently mentioned as a precursor to the slasher film. Cunningham knew the intrinsic value of controversy, and *Friday the 13th*, which he funded independently before getting a distribution deal with Paramount, produced it in droves. Gene Siskel made it his personal mission to destroy the movie, not only by lacerating it in his review and encouraging readers to write Paramount chief Charles Bluhdorn and star Betsy Palmer, whose addresses he conveniently supplied, but by joining with *Chicago Sun-Times* critic Roger Ebert on an all-out media campaign against the slasher film.

Although often compared to *Halloween*, *Friday the 13th* actually has more differences than similarities. The basic formula is the same (especially the role of the Final Girl), but screenwriter Victor Miller mixes Carpenter's stalk-and-slash rhythms with an older tradition of rural isolation, thus turning the film into less of a suburban nightmare than a folkloric warning about not going into the woods alone. *Halloween* derives its underlying sense of dread from what we know about the killer, namely that he is an unstoppable force who embodies dispassionate evil in such a way that the only explanation for his rampage is supernatural. *Friday the 13th*, on the other hand, revels in mystery, with a stalker whose identity is not revealed until the final reel, (providing the film's one true stroke of genius by reversing the *Psycho* dynamic) making the killer a mother who has internalized her dead son, rather than the other way around. This mystery element also reveals the film to be influenced by Italian *giallo* films, particularly *Twitch of the Death Nerve* (1971), some of whose 13 murders are copied almost verbatim.

Both *Halloween* and *Friday the 13th* spawned a series of sequels. In *Halloween II* (1981), Michael Myers continued stalking Laurie Strode, who is revealed to be his sister. *Halloween III: Season of the Witch* (1983) was a rare sequel that had—with the exception of a few musical notes—nothing whatsoever to do with its predecessors. In it, Michael Myers, who supposedly died a fiery death at the end of *Halloween II*, is replaced by a *Twilight Zone*-ish plot about a nefarious corporation's plans to kill kids on Halloween using lethal masks activated by a commercial video signal. Myers returned at the end of the decade when the series was revived in 1988 with *Halloween 4: The Return of Michael Myers*, which was followed by *Halloween 5* (1989), *Halloween: The Curse of Michael Myers* (1995), *Halloween H20: 20 Years Later* (1998)—which was notable for the return of Jamie Lee Curtis as Laurie Strode—and *Halloween: Resurrection* (2002).

For *Friday the 13th Part 2*, director Steve Miner and screenwriter Ron Kurz had to come up with a new killer, which they did by resurrecting Jason himself, now spurred to vengeance after the killing of his mother (a plot development that necessarily rights the original's inversion of *Psycho*'s mother–son dynamic). Thus, Jason became the face of the *Friday the 13th* series, which in the decade of the 1980s alone consisted of seven sequels, each of which offered some kind of twist, however slight, on the slasher formula. *Friday the 13th Part III* (1982) was shot and presented in 3D, and also introduced Jason's iconic hockey mask. The misleadingly titled *Friday the 13th: The Final Chapter* (1984) returned the series to a gorier, more expressly horrific tone via the return of Tom Savini. *Friday the 13th Part V: A New Beginning* (1985) attempted to return to the series' roots by disguising the identity of the killer and setting up a murder-mystery, but it failed due to particularly poor writing, directing, and acting. However, with *Friday the 13th Part VI: Jason Lives* (1986), writer/director Tom McLoughlin beat the *Scream* movies to the punch by a decade with his use of self-reflexive humor to parody the very film-type he was making without undermining its effectiveness. Still gory and occasionally scary, *Jason Lives* is above all funny, a largely enjoyable near-spoof of slasher films in general and the *Friday the 13th* series in particular. *Friday the 13th Part VII: The New Blood* (1988) matches Jason against another supernatural entity, in this case a sensitive and troubled teen girl who happens to be telekinetic. And, while *Friday the 13th Part VIII: Jason Takes Manhattan* (1989) would seem to suggest parody in the vein of *Part VI*, writer/director Rob Hedden played most of the film straight, despite the inclusion of several surrealistic visions and flashbacks.

The other dominant slasher film series during the 1980s was launched in 1984 by writer/director Wes Craven's *A Nightmare on Elm Street*. Drawing on ancient myths about the realm of dreams, the film is an inventive and literate mixing of fantasy and terror that does not fit in easily with the era's other slasher films (despite the popular press's attempts to lump them all together). *A Nightmare on Elm Street* introduced the villainous character of Freddy Krueger (Robert Englund), a truly frightening presence who immediately caught on in people's imaginations. The film also features one of the most determined and resourceful Final Girls in Nancy (Heather Langenkamp). While not as explicit as other slasher films of its era, *A Nightmare on Elm Street* has the distinction of being more creative in its death scenarios because it plays with the notions of fantasy versus reality and dreaming versus waking. Freddy is scarier because he does not have to play by the laws of physics, and unlike the numerous sequels that followed, this film keeps him mostly confined to the shadows. Unfortunately, with each subsequent sequel—*A Nightmare on Elm Street 2: Freddy's Revenge* (1985), *A Nightmare on Elm Street 3: The Dream Warriors* (1987), *A Nightmare on Elm Street 4: The Dream Master* (1988), *A Nightmare on Elm Street 5: The Dream Child* (1989), and *Freddy's Dead: The Final Nightmare* (1991)—Freddy became more wise-cracking than terrifying, returning again and again to torment sleeping teenage victims in increasingly elaborate dream scenarios while dropping bad one-liners.

While the *Halloween*, *Friday the 13th*, and *A Nightmare on Elm Street* franchises proved to be the most popular at the box office, there were numerous other entries in the subgenre that both solidified and tweaked the formula. In the years between the release of *Halloween* in 1978 and *Friday the 13th Part 2* in 1981, Dika (1987) identified nine additional films that "incorporate the greatest number of conventions from the formula": *Prom Night* (1979), *Terror Train* (1979), *My Bloody Valentine* (1980), *Night School* (1980), *The Burning* (1981), *Graduation Day* (1981), *Happy Birthday to Me* (1981), and *Hell Night* (1981). Other films from that era worth mentioning are *Silent Scream* (1979), *Final Exam* (1981), *The Prowler* (1981), *The Dorm That Dripped Blood* (1982), *Just Before Dawn* (1982), *Madman* (1982), and *Slumber Party Massacre* (1982). The latter film is particularly notable for being intended as a parody of the film-type and for having been directed and written by women—Amy Holden Jones and feminist author Rita Mae Brown, respectively. Even early in the decade, the slasher film was so fully entrenched in the popular mindset, especially among its teenage fans, that both Brian De Palma's *Blow Out* and Tobe Hooper's *The Funhouse* (both 1981) could open with nearly identical parodic point-of-view stalk-and-slash sequences. *Student Bodies* (1981), written and directed by Mickey Rose, a former writing partner of Woody Allen's, spoofed the subgenre entirely.

The speed with which the first cycle of slasher films took over the horror genre was matched by its relatively slow decline over the next 10 years; having peaked in mid-decade, by the early 1990s it was virtually dead, at least within the realm of mainstream theatrical distribution. The repetitiveness of the formula began to show, and fewer and fewer films were being made outside of increasingly absurd sequels—particularly the much maligned *Halloween: The Curse of Michael Myers* and *Freddy's Dead: The Final Nightmare*. The *Friday the 13th* series also continued to devolve, and as it shifted studios from Paramount to New Line Cinema, it produced another misleadingly titled "final" installment, *Jason Goes to Hell: The Final Friday* (1993). The film introduces the rather ludicrous idea that Jason's heart is its own parasitic creature that can be regurgitated from one person's mouth to another and ends with a promise of a meeting in hell between Jason and Freddy Krueger (eventually realized in 2003's *Freddy vs Jason*). However, the slasher film's demise was only temporary, a half-decade lull that set the stage for its re-emergence via Wes Craven's *Scream* (1996), which successfully reimagined the subgenre in postmodern self-aware fashion. *Scream* led to new cycles of both original slasher film series (including the *I Know What You Did Last Summer*, *Urban Legend*, and *Final Destination* franchises) and eventually remakes of virtually every notable slasher film from the 1980s. Like the relentless celluloid killers on which they center, the slasher film continues to defy all efforts to kill it.

References

Armstrong, K.B. (2003) *Slasher Films: An International Filmography, 1960 Through 2001*, McFarland, Jefferson, NC.

Brophy, P. (2000) Horrality: the texture of contemporary horror films, in *The Horror Reader* (ed. K. Gelder), Routledge, London, pp. 276–284.

Clover, C.J. (1987) Her body, himself: gender in the slasher film. *Representations*, **20**, 187–228.

Clover, C.J. (1992) *Men, Women, and Chainsaws: Gender in the Modern Horror film*, Princeton UP, Princeton, NJ.

Dika, V. (1985). Games of terror: a definition, classification, and analysis of a subclass of the contemporary horror film, the Stalker film, 1978–1981. Dissertation. New York University, Abstract. (n.d.): n. pag.

Dika, V. (1987) The Stalker film, 1978–81, in *American Horrors: Essays on the Modern American Horror Film* (ed. G.A. Waller), U of Illinois P, Chicago, pp. 86–101.

Bertorelli, P. (1979) Bill Would Ban 'Snuff' Movies. *Cumberland News* (Jan 31), p. 6.

Canby, V. (1980) Film: 'Dressed To Kill,' De Palma Mystery: Comedy and Terror. *New York Times* (July 25), p. C10.

The Fiends (1952) *Time* (May 19).

Hatch, R. (1981) Films: The Fan, The Four Seasons, A Second Chance. *The Nation* (June 13), pp. 739–741.

Kendrick, J. (2009) *Hollywood Bloodshed: Violence in 1980s American Cinema*, Southern Illinois UP, Carbondale.

McCarty, J. (1984) *Splatter Movies: Breaking the Last Taboo of the Screen*, St. Martin's Press, New York.

Nowell, R. (2010) *Blood Money: A History of the First Teen Slasher Film Cycle*, Continuum, New York.

Nowell, R. (2011) 'There's more than one way to lose your heart': the American film industry, early teen slasher films, and female youth. *Cinema Journal*, **51** (1), 115–140.

Prince, S. (2000) *A New Pot of Gold: Hollywood Under the Electronic Rainbow, 1980–1989*, U of California P, Berkeley.

Rockoff, A. (2002) *Going to Pieces: The Rise and Fall of the Slasher Film, 1978–1986*, McFarland, Jefferson, NC.

Schneider, P. E. (1957) Fading Horrors of the Grand Guignol. *The New York Times Magazine* (March 17), pp. 13, 56, 58, 60.

Schoell, W. (1985) *Stay Out of the Shower: 25 Years of Shocker Films, Beginning With Psycho*, Dembner Books, New York.

The Skid Row Slasher (1975). *Time* (Feb 10).

Williams, C. (1980) The Terror-Movie Boom: Why It's Making a Killing at the Box-Office. *The Washington Post* (Nov 2), p. M1.

Wood, R. (1983) Beauty bests the beast. *American Film*, **8**, 63–65.

Worland, R. (2007) *The Horror Film: An Introduction*, Blackwell, London.

19

Millennial Fears

Abject Horror in a Transnational Context

Adam Charles Hart

As the last dregs of the slasher cycle dissipated in the early 1990s (the major franchises of the period—*Friday the 13th, Halloween, Nightmare on Elm Street*—having stretched their premises past the point of absurdity), American horror seemed stagnant, struggling to find voice and direction. The decade would see several of the most commercially successful films in the history of the genre, along with occasional critical respectability, although horror films as a whole—American horror especially—seemed to be in a "slump" (Hantke, 2010). The decade began with the Oscar-winning success of *Silence of the Lambs* (1991), which was followed by a brief burst of largely unsuccessful prestige genre productions, including Francis Ford Coppola's *Bram Stoker's Dracula* (1992), Kenneth Branagh's *Frankenstein* (1994), and Mike Nichols's *Wolf* (1994). Hollywood studios briefly showed a renewed interest in horror at the end of the 1990s after the success of *Scream* (1996), with horror briefly becoming an arena for stars and cutting-edge CGI special effects with films like *Sleepy Hollow* (1999), *The Haunting* (1999), and *House on Haunted Hill* (1999).

However, 1999 also saw the release of two very different American horror films that became massive cultural phenomena: *The Sixth Sense* and *The Blair Witch Project*. The former film was made by the rising studio Miramax, a company already known for crowd-pleasing (and Academy Award-winning) art house fare that often crossed over into mainstream success. Featuring a major star in Bruce Willis, M. Night Shyamalan's *The Sixth Sense* told a carefully plotted, classically styled story with a surprise ending that became a major factor in the film's word-of-mouth success. *The Blair Witch Project* was independently funded on a micro-budget, featuring unknowns in the cast and boasting a style and format that were effectively new. The faux-documentary format had been used to great effect in comedy [*This Is Spinal Tap* (1984) and *Waiting for Guffman* (1996) had substantial cult followings],

A Companion to the Horror Film, First Edition. Edited by Harry M. Benshoff.
© 2014 John Wiley & Sons, Inc. Published 2017 by John Wiley & Sons, Inc.

but was, in 1999, a novelty in mainstream horror. *The Sixth Sense* distinguished itself among a number of studio horror releases as a critical and audience favorite, and established Shyamalan as a major new talent who continued to make "event" movies for much of the subsequent decade. It seemed to indicate an audience for intelligent, well-made horror that expanded beyond the usual teen demographic. *The Blair Witch Project*, meanwhile, seemed to herald a new viability for horror produced far from Hollywood. Neither success, however, registered much of an impact on the genre as a whole. Hollywood quickly fell back into cycles of remakes and CGI-heavy spectacles, while *The Blair Witch Project* was treated as a novelty and failed to spark much interest among distributors and audiences for low-budget independent productions.

It was, rather, the international success of *Ringu/The Ring* (1998) and the arrival of "J-horror" that reinvigorated the genre and showed the way forward, in part by marking horror in the new millennium as fundamentally international. Of course, America had never been the sole maker of major horror films, but in the twenty-first century the genre has become so thoroughly dispersed internationally that by 2013 it might be said to effectively have no center. Each new horror production, from anywhere in the world, enters into dialog with films from around the world. It is not a one- or even two-way conversation with Hollywood or other production centers in Japan or South Korea but a diverse international network of films and filmmakers that constitute the contemporary genre. The spooky otherworldliness of *Ringu/The Ring* proved to be incredibly influential but was quickly supplanted by the "extreme" bodily horror of Takashi Miike in Japan and filmmakers like Park Chan-wook in South Korea, Alexandre Aja in France, Greg Maclean in Australia, and Rob Zombie in the United States, among others. The emphatic focus on wounded bodies in these films would crystallize into series of films that explicitly thematize torture. The so-called torture porn films of the *Saw* and *Hostel* series would be predictably condemned by critics for their perceived amoral brutality, but their commercial and cultural impact was significant (Edelstein, 2006). The *Saw* franchise would become the most successful horror series of the decade, a new entry arriving like clockwork each fall for 7 years. In spite of that series' great success, however, the rest of the torture porn, or "spectacle horror" (Lowenstein, 2011) cycle ran out of steam by 2007.

In 2007 and 2008, a spate of "found footage" films picking up on *Blair Witch*'s structuring gimmick were released. In these films, the willfully excessive spectacles of gore and bodily suffering of the torture porn cycle were minimized in favor of the mounting tension and relatively uneventful narratives of the *Paranormal Activity* films or the partial, urgent glimpses of monsters in *Cloverfield* (2008) and *[REC]* (2007) (Figure 19.1). Found footage films foreground and thematize the anxious characterization of offscreen space that has dominated modern horror (especially since the early slasher films). The view provided by the camera in these films is insistently inadequate, never able to reliably capture all those spaces in which the monster may be hiding. Even the attacks may be only partially captured, seen in glimpses as the camera jostles wildly. This is true even of the *Paranormal Activity* films, which

Figure 19.1 Señora Izquierdo (Martha Carbonell), the first of the infected, prepares to attack in *[REC]* (2007). Directed by Jaume Balagueró and Paco Plaza. Produced by Castelao Producciones, Filmax, Televisión Española (TVE), Canal+ España, Instituto de la Cinematografía y de las Artes Audiovisuales (ICAA), Instituto de Crédito Oficial (ICO), ICF Institut Català de Finances, and Generalitat de Catalunya - Institut Català de les Indústries Culturals (ICIC).

are more concerned with surveillance than with the hand-held reportage-style filming that characterizes most of the other films in the cycle. That series, at least in its first two installments, presents near totalizing surveillance of suburban interiors, but does so at the expense of real-time observation within the film: if the characters who have set up video cameras ever do watch the footage they have recorded, they can only do so after the fact.

To reiterate, horror production has always been internationally dispersed. It was perhaps only as a nascent genre in the early 1930s that Hollywood could be seen as the dominant, near-exclusive producer of popular horror. The 1970s saw an eruption of hugely influential non-studio horror films from North America, but also a golden age of Italian horror and fascinating (and under-studied) horror cinemas in Spain and France. The films of Mario Bava and Dario Argento would be touchstones for the slasher cycle, while George Romero's first two *Dead* films were direct inspirations for Italian films by Lucio Fulci and Lamberto Bava, which in turn influenced American gore films of the 1980s.

Nonetheless, the 2000s saw a qualitative leap in the internationalization of the genre. Unlike previous influential cycles of films from England or Italy, these were films that were not in English, did not feature Hollywood (or well-known British) actors, and were rarely financed by American producers or distributors. With the arrival of VCDs and DVDs, *Ringu/The Ring* and other J-horror films were able to reach a broad global audience even in the absence of wide theatrical releases. The success of these films would help to create an audience—and a brand—for international horror in America, Britain, and elsewhere, and that would pave the way not just for other Japanese films, but also for films from Thailand, South Korea, even France. A demand for non-English language horror films emerged and modestly budgeted productions became more commercially viable on video (and on the festival and art house circuits). If J-horror established a creative center for the genre outside of the United States and proved that there was an audience for non-English language horror in the English-speaking world, the idea/brand of the "Asia Extreme" film helped to cement horror as an expanding transnational genre in the 2000s.[1] That is to say that the exchanges between films and audiences that define the genre freely cross national boundaries. The viewing habits of horror fans in the digital age ensure that the genre maintains a fully international character without neglecting the specificities of national cinemas. The online availability of DVDs and, later, torrents, would ensure that, to some extent, fan exposure to certain works would no longer be dependent on official distribution channels. In America, specialty video stores such as Seattle's Scarecrow Video rent and sell European and East Asian DVDs and VCDs, often in advance of official US theatrical releases. Torrenting and other online file sources have made this, of course, even easier, and cheaper. This, along with the eclectic library of films on streaming web sites such as Netflix and Hulu, has made more horror films available for home viewing than ever before, and has made genre fans less reliant on the curatorial choices of theatrical and video distributors.

The 2000s have thus seen a remarkable proliferation of independent horror films, only a small fraction of which ever make it to theaters, in the United States or elsewhere. Hollywood horror in the era has been largely defined by sequels and remakes, often relegated to specialty production houses like Platinum Dunes and Ghost House. Hollywood has plundered the American horror canon, especially of the 1970s and 1980s, as well as a number of East Asian films, in search of material. For critics and fans, the results have been mixed, to say the least, and the most vital films within the genre have been found in independent productions from around the world. With the rest of this essay I will look at horror's uneasy, shifting relationship with mainstream Hollywood, in particular the action blockbuster franchises (and their B-level doppelgangers like the *Resident Evil* films), before presenting a formal and structural account of films in the found footage cycle.

Monsters in the Mainstream

The box-office dominance of one-time underground gore-horror maestros Sam Raimi (the *Spider-Man* trilogy, 2002–2007) and Peter Jackson (the *Lord of the Rings* trilogy, 2001–2003) in the early 2000s heralded new directions in Hollywood. In particular, these and other big-budgeted action extravaganzas would become the home for the decade's most notable creature effects. With significant exceptions such as Guillermo Del Toro's *El Labirintho Del Fauno/Pan's Labyrinth* (2006), the most impressive monsters and fantastic creatures in contemporary cinema are more likely to be found in the big-budget blockbuster action movies than they are in what would be considered to be horror. Science fiction and fantasy continue to be homes for creatures, but there has, perhaps, never been a time when the genres, as a whole, were so far from the realm of horror. The contemporary action blockbuster is largely a vehicle for showcasing special effects, and creatures are often an essential element of the spectacle, while fantastical monsters have become relatively rare in a horror genre dominated by independent and low-budget productions. One cannot help but feel that horror is no longer a cinema distinguished by its monsters but rather by its victims, that the privileged horrific spectacle is no longer based in monstrous physicality but in abject, wounded bodies.

As the decade progressed, Hollywood continued to import horror elements into other genres, or would file away the horrific edges of the source material in order to make films like *The Mummy* (1999) or *I Am Legend* (2007) more appealing to broader international audiences. So, while horror—at least in the United States—may or may not be in a "slump," Hollywood blockbusters have, in the twenty-first century, become a cinema filled with monsters and horror tropes. The teen romance of the *Twilight* films (2008–2012) features vampires and werewolves, while the initial offering of *The Hunger Games* (2012), another young adult-marketed franchise, covers the same grim territory associated with quintessential cult horror favorite *Battle Royale* (2000). Action films are showcases for fantastic characters who often cross over into monstrosity, whether horror-esque psychopaths, *a la* the Joker in *The Dark Knight Returns* (2008), or fantastic creatures as with the wild beasts in *Avatar* (2009), the zombies and sea monsters of the *Pirates of the Caribbean* films (2003–2011), the orcs, trolls, and dragons of Peter Jackson's Tolkein films, or the Decepticons of the *Transformers* films (2007–2011), with many of Hollywood's largest budgets being employed toward their digital realization.

In Hollywood, 1999—the year of unexpected blockbusters *The Sixth Sense* and *The Blair Witch Project*—also saw the release of several larger budgeted studio projects, including the remakes *The Mummy*, *The Haunting*, and *House on Haunted Hill*. Digital effects figure prominently in all three. With the exception of Shyamalan's output, Hollywood studios tended in the new millennium to follow this familiar formula of approaching genre themes through investment in CGI, remakes, and stars. *The Mummy*, a very loose reimagining of Karl Freund's 1932 film in the vein of Spielberg's *Indiana Jones* films, would be followed by several sequels. As the series progressed, its horror movie origins became even less prominent. Similarly, the *Blade* franchise (1998–2004) mixed comic book superhero tropes with the conventions of vampire movies and stories. (Indeed, the half-human, half-vampire Blade fit nicely with the brooding, conflicted superheroes of the new millennium.) *Resident Evil* (2002) and *Underworld* (2003) both launched similarly action-oriented franchises with almost latent horror origins, and both franchises are closely related to the superhero genre. The latter's narrative, about a prophesied werewolf/vampire hybrid character pursued by warring clans, is reminiscent of *The Matrix* (1999), itself probably the major stylistic influence on the superhero films of the new decade. The visual style of the *Resident Evil* series often evokes the video game franchise that spawned it, and the narrative structure often seems to mimic a game's succession of distinct levels with individual challenges. However, the overall tone changes considerably in its cinematic translation. While the games are populated with monsters lurking in the shadows that result in a persistent feeling of dread and paranoid attentiveness for the gamer, the movies present a relatively conventional action heroine in physical combat. *Mummy* director Stephen Sommers would contribute again to the trend with the 2004 film *Van Helsing*, which turned Bram Stoker's elderly doctor into an action hero (a literally divine superhero: he is revealed to be an amnesiac Archangel Gabriel) fighting not just vampires but werewolves, a giant Dr. Jekyll, and Frankenstein's monster in an action-oriented tribute to the original Universal horror films. All of these films use themes, characters, and imagery from the horror genre to tell action-adventure stories, indicating a fascination with monsters that divorces them from horrific contexts.

Vampires and zombies have been unexpectedly dominant pop cultural forces in the new millennium, their reach extending far beyond the horror genre. In the *Twilight* series, the mythology behind vampires is rewritten so that vampirism is more about self-control, superpowers, and eternal beauty than the darker, more abject associations with death, disease, and parasitism seen in previous vampire films and literature. Similarly, *Twilight*'s werewolves do not terrorize the community with bloody, uncontrollable rampages, but transform into giant wolves at will. In both cases, the monsters represent an abstract danger that the sympathetic, heroic vampires and werewolves are able to resist due to willful self-control. Their villainous counterparts evidence the dangers associated with indulging in one's baser drives. *Twilight*, in other words, imports supernatural monsters into stories that disregard the traditions associated with the monsters in the horror genre. They scrub the unsavory elements of monstrosity in service of a narrative that marries conventions of the superhero genre to a mostly chaste teen romance plot—the problems of *Twilight*'s vampires are more closely related to those of the teenage heroes of *X-Men* (2000) or *Spider-Man* (2002) than they are to other more conventional vampires.

At the opposite end of the romantic spectrum [*Warm Bodies* (2013) and the erotic zombie films of Bruce LaBruce aside], there has been a remarkable resurgence of fascination with zombies, one that is largely associated with videogames such as *Resident Evil* but includes films such as *28 Days Later* (2003), the *[REC]* series, several new Romero films (starting with 2005's *Land of the Dead*), the parodic (but sincere and often effectively frightening) homage *Shaun of the Dead* (2004), and the only runaway blockbuster among them, the coming-of-age comedy *Zombieland* (2009). George A. Romero's 1968 film *Night of the Living Dead* and its brightly colored sequel, *Dawn of the Dead* (1978), had set the agenda for much of the zombie films that were to follow, not only in their intense interest in the display of opened, wounded bodies, but in their fluid, constantly-changing boundaries between monster and victim (Figure 19.2).

Sympathy for the monster has been an essential component of the genre's appeal from its inception, with the monster often being the most intriguing, fully developed character in a given film. But zombies are less sympathetic than they are pathetic.

Figure 19.2 Zombies used as literal target practice in *Land of the Dead* (2005). Directed by George A. Romero. Produced by Universal Pictures, Atmosphere Entertainment MM, ExceptionWild Bunch, and Romero-Grunwald Productions.

In the Romero tradition, zombies are little more than walking corpses, semifunctional reminders of death and decay looking literally to swallow any remaining living humans. In the process, of course, they spread the abjection they embody, making zombies of their victims as well. This is a long-held tradition in horror: vampires make victims into vampires, as do werewolves. The nature of the transformation is different, however. Zombies are corpses, sometimes barely ambulatory, and the transformation into a zombie is a very direct depiction of physical deterioration and death. Turning into a zombie entails a removal of the subjectivity that would seem to characterize a being as human (Shaviro 1993) — although as his filmography progresses George Romero grows increasingly concerned with finding the humanity in what appear to be soulless beings. In Romero's films, becoming a zombie is a slow, painful process that spectacularizes an exaggerated realization of more familiar mortal illness. Zombies chase the living, threatening to make their victims just like themselves. A zombie is a corpse that forces acknowledgement upon the survivors; it cannot be buried and ignored. It dies, rising again *as that which is discarded*: the physical, material substance of the body without the intellect that holds it together as a human subject. Zombies produce spectacles of wounded bodies, blurring the line between monster and victim, and making the victim's wounds the very marker of monstrosity. The genre's general emphasis on wounds and abjection in the 2000s links the figure of the zombie to the screaming, anguished victims of *Saw* or *Martyrs* (2008).

Much of this changes during the twenty-first-century zombie renaissance in films like *28 Days Later*, the *Resident Evil* series, and Zack Snyder's *Dawn of the Dead* remake, all of which feature quicker, even athletic zombies. Rather than being constantly encroaching reminders of mortality, such zombies present more urgent threats. George Romero credits video games with this shift in the nature of the zombie: in video games, zombies are handy target fodder, creatures that can be killed without moral compunction on the part of characters or gamers/audiences (Keogh, 2010). The curious mass-cultural popularity of zombies in the 2000s — of which the immense success of the AMC television show *The Walking Dead* (2010-present) is the most visible instance—suggests that the figure of the zombie has been recuperated fully into the culture, no more necessarily confrontational for the spectator than the Transylvanian aristocracy.

Time magazine declared in 2009 that zombies had become "the new vampires," claiming that the vampire craze sparked by *Twilight* was being displaced by a cultural fascination with zombies. Such hyperbole should be somewhat tempered, as *Twilight* films continued to be released to enormous box office until the series (supposedly) ended in 2012, and no single zombie film has come close to competing with that series. There has been, however, a remarkable *quantity* of zombie films produced in the first years of the new millennium. In the past 10 years, hundreds of feature-length zombie films have been made. The proliferation includes zombie musicals and operas, participatory events such as zombie pub crawls and zombie 5K runs (in which participants are expected to arrive in full zombie make-up), mass re-enactments of John Landis's video for Michael Jackson's "Thriller" (and persistent rumors of a Broadway adaptation), and so on. The mass popularity of zombies seems to have transmuted the abject, often revolting creatures into domesticated pop cultural images. It does seem significant that the most visible creatures in and around horror in the twenty-first century have been those which blur the lines between monster and victim, and which are defined by their wounded, abject bodies.

The Walking Dead, based on the comic book written by Robert Kirkman, returns to Romero's model of the slow-moving horde. In the television series, survival is articulated as a delay of inevitable death and transformation. The overwhelming numbers of "walkers" (as the characters refer to them) ensure that any security is only temporary. Characters contemplate and debate suicide as an appropriate means of taking control of their fate in the face of the endless masses. The central protagonist, Rick, and his wife fight over the extent to which they should shield their young son from the violent tasks they must undertake. The proximity to death (and the grim tasks that fighting it off requires) has drastically changed the demeanor of the protagonists. The series, in other words, takes seriously Romero's subtext of zombies being not only dangerous, but forcing confrontation with the fact of mortality.

Found Footage and Offscreen Space

The Blair Witch Project, though not the originator of what would soon become known as the *found footage horror* film, surely set the template for what would become a major element of early twenty-first-century horror. Ruggero Deodato had used a similar conceit in the film within a film in his notorious *Cannibal Holocaust* (1980), but the extremity of that film's imagery ensured that it would remain a cult item. Even among horror fans, however, documentary and horror were most closely associated pre-*Blair Witch* with the "Mondo" films and videos and the *Faces of Death* video series, both of which mixed documentary and staged footage in presenting footage intended to shock audiences. *The Blair Witch Project* was a phenomenon, a no-budget faux-documentary whose savvy exploitation of its innovative central gimmick turned it into a massive hit. The film claims to be the recovered footage of young filmmakers who were lost in the woods of Burkittsville, MD, while shooting for a documentary on a local legend. All images in the film come from cameras located within the diegesis, every shot supposedly filmed by one of the characters. In spite of its surprise success, it would take several years for another film to capitalize on *The Blair Witch Project*'s structural innovation. Not even the film's sequel [*Book of Shadows: Blair Witch 2* (2000)] maintained the structural conceit of the first film, instead opting for a conventional storytelling style. There were a handful of found footage horror movies in the subsequent few years, none of which made much of an impact at the box office or with critics, but in 2007 found footage horror suddenly announced itself as a major genre trend. That year saw the release of *Paranormal Activity* and [*REC*], followed shortly thereafter in early 2008 by *Cloverfield* and George A. Romero's *Diary of the Dead*, among others. The next few years would see the release of a number of successful found footage films from the United States and Japan, but also from the United Kingdom, Spain, Australia, and Norway, including *Lake Mungo* (2008), *Atrocious* (2010), *The Last Exorcism* (2010), *Trollhunter* (2010), *Apollo 18* (2011), *Chronicle* (2012), *The Bay* (2012), *The Devil Inside* (2012), *Chernobyl Diaries* (2012), the omnibus *V/H/S* (2012), and *Area 51* (2013), as well as several sequels to *Paranormal Activity*, and a sequel ([*REC*] 2 [2009]) as well as an American remake [*Quarantine* (2008)] to [*REC*].

These found footage films seemed to have supplanted torture porn as the dominant mode of horror in America, although by 2013 the trend was abating. Complaints about the shaky images began with *Blair Witch*, and once the format's novelty wore off, such reservations contributed to a quick decline. The nearly bloodless *Paranormal Activity* became a surprise hit by offering a seemingly drastic alternative to the insistently spectacular and visceral *Saw* and *Hostel* films, usurping *Saw* in the popular imagination, and at the box office, as an annual Halloween release. Moments of gore or splatter in the *Paranormal Activity* series are exceedingly rare. These are films that are built around suspense and anticipation, with few moments that offer release or realization of that build-up. Where the *Saw* films consistently offer shockingly violent images, *Paranormal Activity* is relatively devoid of them. The feeling that *Paranormal Activity* offered an alternative to the gross-out brutality and visceral horror of torture porn undoubtedly contributed to its appeal.

However, I would note that both trends share an emphatic focus on the display of the victims, rather than the monsters. The screaming, terrorized characters of the *Paranormal Activity* films might not display the kind of bodily abjection that is associated with *Saw*, *Martyrs*, and *Hostel*, but they nonetheless display what might be thought of as an emotional abjection. The screaming victim is, to be sure, nothing new to the genre, but it is a relatively recent development to make the victim the privileged horrific spectacle while keeping the monster almost totally offscreen. Slasher films in the 1980s would rely heavily on offscreen space, often keeping their monsters or killers out of the frame until a climactic confrontation with the protagonist. The found footage movies follow a similar method, except that the display of the monster is even further marginalized. In the *Paranormal Activity* series, with a

Figure 19.3 Katie (Katie Featherston) addresses the cameraman in *Paranormal Activity* (2007). Directed by Oren Peli. Produced by Solana Films and Blumhouse Productions.

few momentary exceptions for glimpsed reflections or bodily possession, the demon remains un-visualized throughout. The horrific spectacle in the *Paranormal Activity* films is entirely dominated by frightened victims (Figure 19.3).

The style of horror films that dominated the North American genre in the 1980s — particularly associated with *Friday the 13th* and the slasher subgenre — relied increasingly on offscreen space. The frame became an almost diegetic category as Mrs. Voorhees and Jason, and countless imitators throughout the genre since, seemed to exist just outside of the camera's view, ready to jump out at any moment. A film such as *Friday the 13th Part 2* (1981) or the more recent *The Strangers* (2007) builds its mise-en-scene around the viewer's perception of the scene rather than around considerations of diegetic coherence or predictability. The sudden appearance of the villain (or his/her/its arm or weapon) into the frame, or the feint of a cat jumping into the image or a similarly nonthreatening but sudden shock, became commonplace in the slasher cycle and entered into the general sensational vocabulary of horror. It should also be noted that, while the found footage horror film and the slasher film are both often characterized by a type of POV camerawork, the slasher genre primarily — almost exclusively — associates the subjective camera with the monster, while it is the protagonist or victim who wields the look (and the diegetic camera) in nearly all found footage horror films.

David Bordwell emphasizes the importance of predictability in the construction of space in the classical narrative style. For Bordwell (1985: 161), the classical film is heavily invested in redundancy, particularly regarding what he calls "necessary story data," among which diegetic space is one of the primary elements. Disagreeing with film critics associated with "apparatus theory" in the 1970s, Bordwell asserts that the role of most shots is not to reveal new information but to confirm what the viewer already knows or assumes about diegetic space. This predictability is one of the defining characteristics of classical film space. Becoming conventional with the arrival of the slasher film, in offscreen space, the modern horror film does not communicate an exact terrain but rather the unspecified, un-placed presence of a potential threat. The scenographic space outside the frame is best understood less as one inhabited by material objects than it is a space of threats, a paranoid space constantly sending signals of anxiety to the audience and, seemingly, the characters as well. It is rare in the horror film to have an attack without some sort of apprehension on the part of the victim. These films systematically blur diegetic and scenic space: the space of the frame becomes an important scenographic category when a character is tiptoeing through a dark basement and a knife-wielding stalker lurks in the shadows. The viewer's understanding of the narrative must include a conscious acknowledgement of the limits of the frame as a semi-diegetic device. What the viewer cannot see does seem to determine, in some cases, what the characters can see. What is important is the sudden eruption of the monster into the frame, regardless of the nature of the implied diegetic space from which he or she emerges: just because a character *should* be able to see a monster approaching does not mean that will be the case if the monster is offscreen. These attacks are presented so as to address the viewer's perspective first and foremost, with the character's reaction seeming to follow, cue, or support that of the viewer. Such a structure requires that characters as well as audiences adopt a paranoid style of viewing in reaction to the constant but uncertain signals of danger coming from unseen or offscreen space.

Found footage films normalize this activation of offscreen space and further the mode of paranoid viewing that results by placing this incomplete, inadequate camera perspective within the diegesis. If modern horror films in general are expected to withhold important information about the location and physicality of the monster or killer, the found footage film exaggerates this tendency with constant reminders that the camera's perspective is neither privileged nor optimal in terms of classical notions of display: the monster is potentially located just outside the range of the camera at any given time. These films frequently thematize this inadequacy — the characters are trying to detect any and all threats simultaneously with the audience.

The first two *Paranormal Activity* films are built largely around stationary, machinic surveillance, but *[REC]* and *Cloverfield* are structured around handheld cameras and movement through unfamiliar, dangerous spaces. The latter two films share with the popular style of "first-person shooter" video games this uncertain, fraught exploration of space. In those games, the diegetic world is seen from the literal point-of-view of the gamer-controlled protagonist. The gamer controls not just the movement through space and the employment of weapons but also the frame — and the "camera" must be in a constant state of vigilance to detect and defend against incoming attacks. Indeed, some of the most popular first-person shooter games (i.e., games in the *Doom*, *Resident Evil*, and *Left 4 Dead* series) are of the "survival horror" genre, in which the threatening creatures that populate the diegetic world are monsters. In found footage films, this anxious exploration of potentially dangerous offscreen space is central to their effectiveness. As a character looks through a lens, he or she is equally reliant on the camera's display to detect potential danger.

The recent anthology horror film *V/H/S* includes multiple sequences in which characters are wearing hidden recording devices in glasses or in hats, which, again, aligns the viewer's perspective more or less directly with that of a character, but which has the added benefit of explaining the diegetic cameraperson's continued insistence on recording while his or her life is in danger. *[REC]*'s primary protagonists are reporters who claim a journalistic responsibility to film everything (and the need to rely on the camera's "night vision" setting to see in darkness accounts for its continued usage in the film's final scenes after the building's power is cut off). *Cloverfield*'s non-journalist cameraman espouses a similar ethic, although his goals are mostly left unarticulated (a problem the film glosses over by making the cameraman the film's comic relief, a clueless friend of the main protagonist who is trying to use the camera to gain the attention of a romantic crush). Romero's *Diary of the Dead* is considerably more thoughtful about its format. His film critically analyzes, and even pathologizes, its cameraman's obsessive need to record as dangerous and perverse. The film ends with another character securely locked away in a safe room, editing together the footage her friend shot and uploading it onto the internet (which is still operational), while watching the undead hordes in and outside of the house on surveillance monitors. The film taps into a longer tradition of introspective critiques of camera-based voyeurism, most acutely and influentially expressed by Michael Powell's *Peeping Tom* (1960) and Alfred Hitchcock's *Rear Window* (1954), in order to explore the isolation and disengagement that Romero associates with seeing the world through the lens of the camera. Where *[REC]* and *Cloverfield* see the camera as a vehicle for truthful documentation within the narrative, *Diary of the Dead*'s diegetic camera is implicated in an attempt to avoid and morally distance its operator from the horrors he is witnessing. (See Steven Shaviro's 2008 review of the film for a discussion of the media critique in *Diary*, along with the film's characterization of the camera as a weapon.)

The *Paranormal Activity* films are primarily built around surveillance rather than handheld reportage. In each, a family records the interior of its large suburban house as a way of detecting the supernatural threat. Unlike other found footage films, *Paranormal Activity*'s cameras are (mostly) not connected to a specific human operator; rather, their cameras run on their own, mounted in the corners of rooms or left on a tripod. That means that the footage can only be seen at a later time (if it is ever watched within the diegesis — a significant amount of the footage is never watched by one of the characters). In these films, surveillance is a means of detecting an intrusive presence, but never of actually defending against or defeating that presence. It is not the penetrative camera of *Peeping Tom* or even a particularly probing or revealing documentary camera; the camera is in itself a signifier of impotence and helplessness.

The passive camera watches as invisible demons terrorize wealthy suburbanites, only to indicate to them later the danger *they had been in*. It is revealed in the first film that the demon will pursue the family wherever they go, and that trying to escape will only make it worse. Each victimized family attempts to combat or escape the demon (which is, again, invisible to the camera, though not necessarily to all the characters), and each is unsuccessful.

It is remarkably consistent among found footage horror films that they do not end happily. From the doomed expedition within *Cannibal Holocaust* to the crew in *The Blair Witch Project* to the post-2007 films discussed above, the only surviving protagonist is *Diary of the Dead*'s Debra, who survives by locking herself away, alone, in a safe room that is surrounded on all sides by zombies. She survives, but with no visible means of escape. It is perhaps notable that she is not the primary cameraperson until the very end of the film. The format seems to indicate an essential vulnerability that is often built into the narrative structure. The conceit of a number of these films is that the footage has been found and compiled by the authorities, so the subjects' doom is already assumed at the beginning of the film. Whether or not it is explicitly signaled by an opening title card, there seems to be a close association between the found footage format and the demise of the diegetic cameraperson. Unlike the mastering, sadistic gazes of the monsters and villains of previous generations of horror films, the found footage film's diegetic camera is always in a position of either utter vulnerability (the handheld camera) or passive, unresponsive surveillance. The owners of the look in found footage horror are doomed, and their susceptibility to attack is directly linked to the act of looking. Attacks, and retreats, register themselves through the shakiness of the image, its visible instability. Here, looking makes a character vulnerable, and the audience shares that exact perspective. This upends the traditionally privileged position occupied by the owner of the gaze in horror (and in narrative film more generally), offering what seemed, at least initially, to be a more insidious experience of dread. In found footage horror, a tragic ending seems inevitable.

Conclusion

As the twenty-first century approached, American horror was achieving some of its biggest mainstream successes, along with newfound cultural capital associated with the validation of critics and of the Academy Awards, while simultaneously seeming adrift and generally in a sorry state. The successes were isolated and unpredictable, and studios' attempts to put their resources into high profile horror films yielded minimal success. Indeed, such impulses would soon be directed more frequently toward bringing elements of horror into action, science fiction, and even romance films rather than attempting to make what most would consider to be horror films. The rejuvenation of the genre provided by Japanese films, *Ringu/The Ring* especially, is difficult to understate. "J-horror" gave the genre a new direction that included a conscious level of stylistic artistry that would bode well for horror's slow creep into the art house and into prestigious festivals in the 2000s with filmmakers like Guillermo del Toro, Lars Von Trier, and Michael Haneke. Perhaps more importantly, it also helped to open up the genre to a conception that was not primarily centered on American productions. *Ringu/The Ring*'s success paved the way for the enthusiastic reception of films from South Korea and other East Asian countries, but also from France and Spain. The genre's center would become globally dispersed in the twenty-first century, and, more than that, the films often seem to be in conversation with each other. An account of torture porn, for example, requires citing precedence and inspiration in films from South Korea, Japan, France, and Italy. When the found footage cycle began, it started in Spain at the same time it did in the United States. And, of course, *Saw* was written and directed by Australians James Wan and Leigh Whannell, while *Paranormal Activity* originated with Israeli filmmaker Oren Peli. Both series are set in the United States, but the international character of American-produced horror is now more apparent than it has been since, perhaps, the 1930s, when American and European sensibilities combined to create Universal's iconic monster movies. A number of prominent foreign horror filmmakers have migrated to the United States to produce or direct higher-budgeted films within the genre, including Del Toro, Alejandro Amenabar, Alexandre Aja, Park Chan-wook, and Bong Joon-ho.

The United Kingdom has also seen a flowering of independent horror films in the 2000s, with several—most notably *28 Days Later, Shaun of the Dead, The Descent* (2005), and *Attack the Block* (2011)—achieving substantial international success. British horror has yet to produce a single coherent style, mode, or subgenre, at least in the eyes of the rest of the world, an aspect so important in branding a national genre cinema. What makes contemporary British horror so interesting, however, is its close relationship to the rest of British independent filmmaking. Speaking in very broad terms, what connects the above-mentioned films and many other British horror films is a focus on character rather than plot or spectacle (though these films often provide that as well). Intensity in these films comes as often from conflicts among the various human characters as it does from the impending danger of monsters, and those conflicts are what drive and structure the narratives. The stylistic and thematic proximity of British horror to social dramas and to independent comedy (as well as television—Edgar Wright, Simon Pegg, and Joe Cornish all had fruitful careers on television before their first feature films) mark it as a vital national genre, but one that has yet to be embraced as such in the way that recent French horror's focus on wounded bodies has resulted in international fans' embrace of the "New French Extremity."

The heterogeneity of British horror may be its greatest strength, even if it has yet to result in a lucrative national branding. However, this also serves as a reminder of the genre's overall lack of a monopolizing style. If the mid-2000s seemed to be dominated by the spectacular display of pain and torture, it also saw the rise of art-house horrors, supernatural teen romance, the rise of the zombie film, and found footage films. Although the past 15 years have seen a number of trends cycle in and out of popularity, these trends tend to obscure the broad range of films that are being made, and occasionally finding success. The precise direction of horror's future trends seems once again to be uncertain as the found footage cycle loses steam, but the increased attention to international productions and remarkable quantity of independent productions in the United States and around the world give fans reasons to be optimistic. The sheer number of horror films being produced has made the job of fan web sites and horror-oriented publications seem almost curatorial (and, indeed, publications such as *Fangoria* and *Bloody Disgusting* have begun to produce and distribute films as well).

After the success of *The Blair Witch Project* and *The Sixth Sense*, it would have been difficult to predict that the most influential works for the genre as a whole would rather have been modestly budgeted films from Japan. And although there was perhaps an inevitable backlash against the visceral shocks of torture porn, the widespread revival of *Blair Witch's* found footage style is difficult to extrapolate from *Saw* or *Hostel*. As such, horror remains a volatile, unpredictable genre marred by long stretches of repetition and a seeming lack of novelty. That lack of activity, however, might be seen instead as an indication of variety and dispersal—the lack of a dominant trend or larger generic narrative is not necessarily an indication of a lack in terms of quantity or quality of productions. It remains to be seen whether the increased diversity of styles, themes, and approaches engendered by the genre's current international character and the proliferation of independent American productions will translate into an equivalent diversity of themes and styles.

Note

1. Joan Hawkins and Chi-Yui Shin have written about the ideological and aesthetic limitations of Tartan's Asia Extreme DVD label. In general, the company's film choices do not necessarily reflect the best or even most popular films of their home countries—some of these releases were outright flops at home. In general, as Joan Hawkins has argued, international distribution favors gimmicky premises and exploitation plots, while removing the films from the specific national context in which they originated. This process overlooks certain kinds of filmmakers and gives simplified, distorted pictures of diverse national cinemas. See Hawkins (2009) and Shin (2008). As both authors point out, international distributors tend to favor films with graphic violence, films with a strong (or broad) narrative hook or gimmick, and films that are reminiscent of previous successes. Thus, after *Ringu/The Ring*, other films about haunted technology received international distribution, including Takashi Miike's *One Missed Call* (2003), Kiyoshi Kurosawa's avant garde *Pulse* (2003), Byeong-Ki Ahn's *Phone* (2002), and Banjong Pisanthanakun and Parkpoom Wongpoom's *Shutter* (2004).

References

Bordwell, D. (1985) *Narration in the Fiction Film*, University of Wisconsin Press, Madison.

Edelstein, D. (2006) Now Playing at Your Local Multiplex: Torture Porn. *NY Magazine*, http://nymag.com/movies/features/15622/ (accessed 1 December 2012).

Hantke, S. (2010) Introduction: they don't make 'Em like they used to: on the rhetoric of crisis and the current state of American horror cinema, in *American Horror Film: The Genre at the Turn of the Millennium* (ed. S. Hantke), University Press of Mississippi, Jackson, pp. 7–32.

Hawkins, J. (2009) Culture wars, *Oldboy* and some new trends in art horror, in *Horror Zone: The Cultural Experience of Contemporary Horror Cinema* (ed. I. Conrich), I.B. Tauris & Co. Ltd., New York, pp. 112–138.

Keogh, P. (2010) Interview with George Romero (2010), in *George A. Romero: Interviews* (ed. T. Williams), University Press, Jackson, pp. 169–177.

Lowenstein, A. (2011) Spectacle horror and *hostel*: why 'torture porn' does not exist. *Critical Quarterly*, **53** (1), 42–60.

Shaviro, S. (1993) *The Cinematic Body*, University Minnesota Press, Minneapolis.

Shaviro, S. (2008) Diary of the Dead. *The Pinocchio Theory*, http://www.shaviro.com /Blog/?p=631 (accessed 24 June 2013).

Shin, C.-Y. (2008) Art of branding: Tartan 'Asia extreme' films. *Jump Cut: A Review of Contemporary Media*, **50**, 85–100 http://www.ejumpcut.org/archive/jc50.2008/TartanDist /index.html (accessed 1 December 2012).

20

Torture Porn

21st Century Horror

Isabel C. Pinedo

Torture has been thematically present as a trope in the horror film since its inception in the 1930s Hollywood cycle. But the thematic treatment of torture has largely been characterized by its oblique or off-screen presentation. Torture alone does not make a horror film a work of torture porn. Torture porn refers to a specific cycle of ultra-violent films that dominated the box office between 2004 and 2008, films that focus on the capture and torture of sympathetic characters who are subjected to extended and graphic torment, shot in spectacular close-ups that dwell on the details of injury. Torture porn is part of the post-9/11 shift in the horror film expressing a resounding surge in fear of terrorism and, specifically with torture porn, of our own ambivalence about torture and invasive government surveillance (Briefel and Miller, 2011; Wetmore, 2012). The controversial cycle emerges during a heightened period of national self-questioning and debate over the Bush administration's policy of "enhanced interrogation."

Historically, the thematic treatment of torture has been mired in controversy. The gothic fiction of Edgar Allan Poe inspired films such as *Murders in the Rue Morgue* (1932), in which a woman is abducted, bound, stripped down to a slip, and forcibly injected with an experimental serum that causes excruciating pain. In most of the scene her image is sustained within the frame as she writhes in pain. Her screams are unrelenting until she dies onscreen, tortured to death. Her screams amplify the violence of the scene beyond what could be presented visually, but at the insistence of censors, the audio track was remixed, toning down its violence. By the time *The Black Cat* (1934) was produced, the Production Code Administration was taking a harder line. In the climactic scene, the antagonist ties his nemesis to an embalming rack in the dungeon and tells him he is going to skin him alive. However, the flaying is approached obliquely, depicted only in shadowed silhouette; the victim's

A Companion to the Horror Film, First Edition. Edited by Harry M. Benshoff.
© 2014 John Wiley & Sons, Inc. Published 2017 by John Wiley & Sons, Inc.

anguish is shown only through his contorting hands. By this time, the political situation had changed and the Production Code Administration was working to suppress the use of sound to convey physical pain. According to Stephen Prince, "This suppression would have lasting consequences for American film, helping to make screen violence into the largely pain-free phenomenon that it remains even today" (2003: 75).

In the 1960s and 1970s, torture was thematically key in Inquisition-based films, including the notorious *Mark of the Devil* (1970, Michael Armstrong, WGER), whose original title *Hexen bis aufs Blut gequält* literally translates to the more exact "witches tortured to death." (Although a work of exploitation, the film incorporates a range of historical practices of the Inquisition, whose instruments of torture are preserved at the Criminology Museum in Rothenburg, Germany, including medieval technologies of punishment used to force captives into stress positions for prolonged periods of time for the purpose of extracting confessions.) The film follows an eighteenth-century witch finder and his apprentice at work in Austria. The witch finder, driven by lust and greed in his pursuit of Satan's disciples, tends to target attractive young women who are disrobed, tortured, and killed. Multiple sequences depict his victims subjected to medieval torture-techniques including whipping, branding, burning, the rack, water torture, ripping out tongues and fingernails, eyeball impalement, and rape, all in fairly realistic detail by the standards of the time. The price of admission included a vomit bag, to promote the film's visceral appeal, which would prove to be a major marketing component of torture porn films to come.

Torture Porn as Film Cycle: What's in a Name?

Torture porn as a filmic category or cycle of the horror film exceeds the thematic treatment of torture. Although some critics reject the label [Lowenstein (2011) argues that torture porn is just another iteration of the splatter film], torture porn is defined by its extensive and graphic depiction of torture. It dwells on the details of incisions in spectacular close-up. It utilizes special effects technology to deliver verisimilitude and a sense of immediacy. The term was coined in and circulated via film critic David Edelstein's 2006 *New York Magazine* article, "Now Playing at Your Local Multiplex: Torture Porn." In it, Edelstein used the term to refer to a variety of recent films with good production values and wide distribution that centered on the torture of relatable characters. The viewer is placed in both the victim's and the torturer's point of view, making the viewer complicit in brutal violence. Most of the titles Edelstein mentions are horror films—*Saw* (2004), *Hostel* (2005), *Wolf Creek* (2005), *The Devil's Rejects* (2005)—though others are not, notably *The Passion of the Christ* (2004). (*The Passion of the Christ*, as a passion play, is designed for a different purpose: emotional Catholic mortification of the flesh in sympathy with the character of Christ.) These films did well at the box office not despite, but because of their intense subject matter. Edelstein goes on to tie these films to the national debate about torture, a debate catapulted by 9/11 and fueled by the wide availability of evidence that by 2004 ordinary American soldiers were torturing prisoners in Iraq, and the fact that many Americans found these practices acceptable.

The mainstream success of *Saw* and *Hostel* also made it hard to ignore a trend of increasingly graphic and extended horror sequences in profitable horror films released starting in 2003: *House of 1000 Corpses* (April 11), *Wrong Turn* (May 30), *28 Days Later* (June 27), *Freddy vs. Jason* (August 15), *Cabin Fever* (September 12), and the *Texas Chainsaw Massacre* remake (October 29). Early 2004 also saw the release of the *Dawn of the Dead* remake (March 19). Edelstein was not alone in connecting the popularity of these films to "9/11," a term which connotes not only the attacks of that day, and an abiding fear of terrorism, but its aftermath in public policy decisions domestically and overseas, particularly the "war on terror." The United States was primed for fear and an escalated threat to the body.

Despite Edelstein's expression of ambivalence toward these films, the appellation of "porn" together with the masochistic and sadistic aspects of the film-viewing experience imply that viewers get some form of sexual gratification from these images. His assessment aligns with a larger pattern of critics historically linking horror and pornography in order to condemn the horror film. In 1968, for example, an article in *Variety* referred to *Night of the Living Dead* as "pornography of violence" (October 16: 6). In 1976, the charge was leveled at *The Texas Chain Saw Massacre* (1974) in a *Harper's Magazine* review by Stephen Koch entitled "Fashions in Pornography" (November: 108–111). In 1984, cultural historian Morris Dickstein referred to "the portrayal of explicit sex and of graphic violence developed in tandem" in slasher films as "a hardcore pornography of violence" (1984: 51). The coupling of pornography and violence is a semiotic move to condemn films deemed to violate representational taboos, films that go too far, something for which the horror film frequently strives. But unlike these earlier attempts to link horror and pornography, in the first decade of the twenty-first century the term *torture porn* caught fire among critics, social commentators, and filmgoers alike.

The use of the porn moniker conveys not only the sensual excess of the display of naked flesh, but also the horror film's physical manipulation of reflex reactions, for instance startle or disgust, and its use of sexual imagery to arouse the audience. Both horror and pornography are "body genres," designed to elicit intense physical reactions in viewers, fear and sexual arousal, respectively, though horror traffics in both (Williams, 1991). Horror has a long history of including sex scenes, and of eroticizing the depiction of violence. Beyond market consideration of appealing to an adolescent target audience, there is an affective logic to this pairing. Neurologically, if you stimulate viewers sexually, it not only draws their attention but also primes them to react more strongly to other feelings, such as suspense and fear. Strong emotions make for more memorable experiences, and that can add up to bigger box-office revenues (Plantinga, 2009: 6, 61).

Edelstein's inclusion of *Irreversible* (2002), a work of New French Extremity—a term coined by art critic James Quandt in 2004 to describe a body of violent French films—is instructive in how the term *torture porn* muddies the waters. Although the films of New French Extremity overlap with torture porn in their use of graphically gory scenes, tightly framed and shown in extended take, the French films tend to combine explicit sex and graphic torture in a single scene. Although the violence in torture porn is sexually charged, it is usually not presented in the same frame as sex (Weissenstein, 2011: 54). Furthermore, the sexual encounters in New French Extremity films are joyless, devoid of any emotion except aggression and rage. The depiction of sex in torture porn varies from duplicitous [*Hostel*, *Captivity* (2007)], or menacing [*Hostel: Part II* (2007)], to absent (*Saw*). The French films also differ in tone. Unlike the profitable torture porn films, the French films are designed to be deliberately hard to watch and deliberately hard to like, drawing on stylistic elements of the avant-garde, such as "drawn out sequences of passive meditation [or] inscrutable character interactions" (Palmer, 2006: 29).

Three Exemplary Films

The lucrative torture porn cycle was launched in 2004 with the success of *Saw*. It was released by "mini-major" production and distribution house Lions Gate, which established itself as a firm willing to take on films considered too controversial by the major studios. Made for an estimated 1.2 million dollars, the worldwide box office raked in 103 million. Production costs were kept low by utilizing narratively effective minimal sets, hiring a first-time creative duo, as well as unknown or has-been actors. The film is effects-driven, featuring high levels of graphic violence. It was screened at the Sundance Film Festival in January 2004 where it was so successful that Lions Gate decided on a theatrical rather than the previously planned straight-to-video release (McKendry, 2008: 49). Advertising concentrated on low-cost targeted posters, billboards, and horror websites such as BloodyDisgusting.com. The film was released around Halloween and became one of the most successful movies of 2004. Its enormous cost-profit ratio launched a wave of torture films in subsequent years.

The premise of *Saw* is deceptively simple: two men play a game in which survival is at stake. Adam and Larry awaken in a squalid industrial bathroom, chained to pipes, with a dead body of a man lying in a pool of blood in the room, a gun and tape recorder clutched in his hand. With no notion of how they got there or who is responsible, they try to puzzle out the situation. Cooperating with each other, they play tapes they find, in which Jigsaw's modulated voice reveals that he has had them under surveillance. He instructs Larry that the aim of his "game" is to kill Adam before 6 o'clock or his wife and daughter will be killed and he too will be left to die. When the captives conspire to fake Adam's death, Adam is subjected to a strong electric shock. The only way out seems to be to use the hacksaws they find to cut themselves free, but since the saws are unfit to cut chains, the only resort is to cut through their ankles.

To complicate the story, the film uses flashbacks to provide backstory and reveal how the men were surveilled and captured by the "Jigsaw Killer." The flashbacks also depict vignettes of earlier captives subjected to Rube Goldberg-like contraptions, who are permitted only brief, sudden countdowns before their gruesome deaths. The novelty and angst of their short-lived situations center around the imminent kill. The temporal progression discloses the nature of the trap; the (self-)mutilating task the captive must perform while the timer ticks down, and the trap's execution, all in gripping visual detail. The narrative purpose of these vignettes is twofold. First, they serve as a condensed distillation of the temporal flow of the torture process — anticipation (to generate dread), the actualization of wounding (to induce startle or disgust), and destruction of the self. Secondly, they hone the viewer's sense of suspense and dread for the possible fate of Adam and Larry. Together with the scenes in the bathroom, the film builds interest in what happens to the men, and sympathy for the anguish they undergo.

The film employs a videogame aesthetic, conveyed explicitly in Jigsaw's signature line, "I want to play a game." As such, the story starts in media res; people are thrown into an unknown situation where they have to explore their environment for clues. They receive basic instructions but most of the rules are unstated and have to be figured out in the course of "play." Players have to master tasks or, in the parlance of the film, tests, to reach the next level, mindful that there is a time element at work. Success depends on figuring out the underlying algorithm of the game, but the game is also built on deception. People and situations are not what they appear to be, and for the most part characters, and viewers, discern this too late (Johnson, 2005). In the end, desperate to save his family, Larry saws off his foot and crawls off presumably to bleed to death, Jigsaw eludes the police, and Adam is left in the bathroom to die because time is up, or as Jigsaw puts it, "Game over!" The film ends with Adam's screams playing over the credits.

Jigsaw's messages take on a tone of retribution. He accuses his captives of wrongs they have committed. In Inquisitional style, they are put to trials of the flesh. The characters are disciplined (trapped, admonished, shocked), inflict grievous harm on themselves or each other, and are mentally tortured. Jigsaw's moral conceit is that he does not kill anyone; he always provides captives with a way to save themselves. He rejects the blame for their almost inevitable deaths, despite the fact that he engineers both their captivity and the torture apparatuses, because he uses surrogates to torture people in a way that echoes the policy of outsourcing torture, known as *extraordinary rendition* or *torture by proxy* (Association of the Bar of the City of NY and Center for Human Rights and Global Justice, 2004: 104). There is thus a jarring disjuncture between Jigsaw's stated intention to teach people the value of life and his callous disregard for the lives of his captives. The gaming framework of the film also extends to the entire *Saw* franchise, whose sequels, released every year through 2010, traffic in surprises, throwing curveballs not only at the characters but also at their viewers. Although they reprise the basic setup, they also advance the backstory of Jigsaw and his accomplices, providing the viewer with both the game of the immediate film and the larger game of the cumulative narrative that the films comprise together. Sequels reference and advance the events of preceding films, at times providing flashbacks to events from earlier films, in ways that change our understanding of the latter.

Saw's model of low budget, frugally marketed, and graphically violent filmmaking, featuring unsuspecting characters surveilled, abducted, and confined in a torture chamber are repeated in *Hostel*, made for 3.8 million and directed by Eli Roth. It premiered at the Toronto International Film Festival in 2005 and was released commercially in January 2006, earning a worldwide box office take of 80 million dollars. *Hostel* is about three young male backpackers, two Americans (Josh and Paxton) and one Icelander (Oli), in Amsterdam enjoying the sex industry. They meet a Russian man, Alexei, who appeals to their arrogance and entices them with stories about a hostel in Slovakia where beautiful women throw themselves at Americans. Once there, they meet two beautiful women (Natalya and Svetlana) with whom they share a semi-naked steam bath, a night at the disco, and sex. The next morning, Oli and another tourist are missing. That night at the disco, Josh and Paxton are drugged. Paxton accidentally stumbles into a storage room where he passes out. The next morning Josh wakes up, stripped, with a hood over his head, chained to a metal chair in a grimy dungeon where a leather-aproned man begins to drill holes in his body. Screaming, crying, and begging for mercy, Josh offers to pay him to stop. To this the man, now revealed to be a Dutch businessman the three met earlier, replies that on the contrary, he is paying to be able to torture Josh. In a 5-min-long scene, the businessman viciously mutilates him.

His trepidations mounting for his missing friend, Paxton tracks down Natalya and Svetlana, now no longer looking glamorous (indeed looking pale and drawn), and forces them to take him to a factory on the outskirts of town. There, in one of many chambers along a dimly lit corridor, he witnesses Josh's corpse being cut up by the businessman. Natalya laughs at an enraged Paxton, and boasts that they are paid good money to deliver tourists. He is captured by facility guards who take him past an array of cells where different people are being tortured. This scene parallels an earlier one in the film in which Paxton, Josh, and Oli walk down a neon-lit Amsterdam brothel corridor past rooms where different sexual acts are being performed, suggesting that the tables have turned; the tourists are now the peddled flesh. Bound and gagged in a cell, a client amputates some of Paxton's fingers with a chainsaw, but due to a series of events, Paxton is able to break free, kill his torturer and a guard, and disguised as a client, make a run for it. In the course of his escape, Paxton learns that the police are complicit with Elite Hunting, a highly profitable international firm that sells tourists to torturers. Americans fetch the highest price. To gain his freedom, Paxton kills seven people, all complicit in some way with the hunting club. Exacting retribution, he runs down Alexei, Natalya, and Svetlana with a car, and after torturing him, slits the throat of the man who killed Josh. Like *Saw*, *Hostel* also asks, how far would you go to survive? But *Hostel's* protagonist is more in line with the slasher film's "Final Girl" than with the doomed characters of *Saw*. Paxton is pursued by relentless killers, cannot turn to the authorities, has to improvise with what he finds in his environment, and must kill to survive.

Although not as seminal as *Saw* and *Hostel*, the Australian film *Wolf Creek* is also regularly described as torture porn. Shot on high-definition video for 1.1 million dollars, the film grossed 28 million dollars worldwide. *Wolf Creek* avails itself of both Australian national symbols and internationally recognizable tropes of previous horror films. "Like many other Australian films, *Wolf Creek* plays with the powerful iconography of the bush as both a national defining symbol and an unknowable and fearful place" (Murray, 2008: 3). In its story of Kristy, Liz, and Ben, three hitchhikers stranded in the bush, the film taps into Australian criminal history, invoking the actual disappearances of hitchhikers. Thus, the film situates itself in an Australian context that resonates with local audiences, and also falls into the category of what Linnie Blake (2011: 190) calls "hillbilly horror," which international audiences would be familiar with since John Boorman's *Deliverance* (1972) and Tobe Hooper's *The Texas Chain Saw Massacre*.

What distinguishes *Wolf Creek* from other torture porn films is its (relatively) detailed character development, sustained by compelling performances; its effective use of the sublime landscape of Australia, where it was shot on location; and its sustained use of dread. The first 52 of its 104-min running time elapse before the backpackers' captivity begins. In this way, the film exploits the viewer's anticipation of torture, which is not ancillary but part of the process of torture itself (Scarry, 1987). As the film unfolds, revealing the likeable characters, the threat of harm that awaits them looms larger. The wide-angle shots of the vast and beautiful Australian wilderness provide a sense of scale that dwarfs the characters, making them seem vulnerable, as when the film departs from its handheld camera work to an aerial shot of the enormous Wolf Creek crater and the vast emptiness surrounding it. The natural beauty of the Outback, and its isolation, induces dread. When the travelers stop in a dilapidated outpost to fuel up, the hostile behavior of the bush men suggests the danger that awaits them. But the film makes the viewer wait, and wonder how and when the characters will be captured.

The backpackers' ordeal begins when they return from the hike to the crater to discover their car will not start. In the night, a driver named Mick discovers them. He offers to tow them to camp so he can repair the car. After an interminable drive, they arrive at the abandoned mine where Mick is based. Cautious, they refuse his offers of food or alcohol, but the parched travelers accept water. Late the next day, Liz awakens from a drugged sleep, bound and gagged in a shed. After freeing herself, and about to run from the mining camp, she hears Kristy cry out. Liz follows the sound to the garage, where she peers through a window. She sees an abject Kristy tied to a post, crying, screaming, and cursing. Her pants are off and she is bloodied. Mick shoots at her, and threatens to cut off her breasts and rape her. There is a dismembered human torso hanging nearby. He points to it and boasts that she lasted "good few months." Liz creates a diversion to get to Kristy, and eventually wounds Mick. They flee in his truck but he comes after them. Before he can overtake them they stage an accident, hide, then double back to the mine to take another car. Liz leaves a distraught Kristy outside, with instructions to run if she does not return promptly.

In the garage, Liz finds a large array of cars and tourists' possessions, including video cameras, one of which records a similar encounter with Mick at Wolf Creek by a stranded family. When she looks through Ben's footage, she spots Mick's truck in the background, demonstrating that he had them under surveillance long before they met him. Horrified, she struggles to start up a car when she is stabbed through the seat with Mick's hunting knife. When he pulls out the knife she crawls away. He toys with her, hacks off three of her fingers and stabs her in the spine, paralyzing her. He jests that she is now "a head on a stick" and begins to interrogate her about Kristy's whereabouts.

By early morning, a bloody, barefoot Kristy has found the highway. A car stops to help, but before he can rescue her, Mick kills the driver with a sniper rifle. Kristy takes off in the car and Mick pursues. When she runs him off the road, he blows out her tire, causing the car to flip over. A dazed Kristy crawls out of the car. Mick shoots her, dumps her body in the trunk and sets the car on fire. The film then cuts to Ben, bound and nailed to a crucifix in a cave. Vicious, possibly starving dogs are caged in front of him, with the tattered remains of a similarly nailed torso to his right. As with *Saw*, the dead body in the chambers where Kristy and Ben are held is there to torment the victim with the specter of tortures to come, underlining that anticipation of torture is an active component of the process long after captivity is achieved. Like Liz before him, Ben endeavors to escape. He pulls his forearms through the nails, tearing his flesh, to extricate himself. When he steps out into the early light, the shot situates him in Mick's campsite. Barefoot, he flees into the brush, under the parching sun. Dehydrated and desperate, he eventually finds a road but passes out. As night falls, a pair of tourists find him and take him to safety. An epilog reveals that Ben fell under suspicion for the disappearance of Liz and Kristy, whose bodies—like Mick's campsite—were never found.

Unlike other torture porn films, in *Wolf Creek* there are no disposable characters, no easy kills of a few anonymous victims as there are in *Saw*'s sudden countdowns or glimpsed along *Hostel*'s corridors. The narrative may be thin, but all three characters are fleshed out and sympathetic. The ordeals they endure may be conveyed in detail, their escape attempts largely futile, but they are all the more intense for happening to fleshed out characters. Kristy is the only one who dies onscreen, and given what Mick had in store for her, her death by bullet is a mercy. Liz's fate is chillingly unknown. Ben survives, but delivers no retribution at the end, and the suspicion he comes under further diminishes any sense of narrative relief or justice. Torture porn films' ability to effectively put the viewer in the victim's position is particularly acute in *Wolf Creek*.

Stylistic Strategies and Affect

In films of the torture porn cycle, the torture of characters, and (in mitigated form) of viewers, is constructed not only through narrative accounts of captivity and duress, but also through a range of stylistic choices. As such, the intensity of these films is worth exploring on a nonnarrative aesthetic level. Torture porn is characterized by excess on both axes of film violence that Stephen Prince describes: the subject matter depicted (torture in myriad forms), and *how* it is depicted, that is to say its stylistic amplitude, including aspects of graphicness and duration. Among these stylistic choices are a host of traditional horror conventions: minimalist or deserted settings, tight framing, a focus on faces and hands, fragmentation of the body through close-ups or obstructed shots, extended scenes of threatening and wounding, and the use of sound to amplify emotion.

Minimalist sets — the trap chamber in *Saw*, the cell in *Hostel*, the shed in *Wolf Creek* — serve to intensify the torture processes on display. They "limit visual complications, making sure [the] eye focuses on the torture and does not find solace in complicated background images. The cold, hard, monotone backgrounds offer a visual juxtaposition to the soft, red, easily broken human body that will take over the screen" (McKendry, 2008: 7). (In this way it might be thought of as the visual correlate of hard-core pornography's non-distracting musical score.) These spaces are squalid, dimly lit, deserted places where victims are secreted away at the mercy of their captors. Similarly, deserted settings — the uninhabited wilderness environment of *Wolf Creek*, the abandoned warehouse of *Saw* and the factory of *Hostel* — make the threat of torture more plausible. If the victims do escape confinement, they have nowhere to run, no one to turn to for help.

Tight framing is used to mimic the narrative confinement of victims, and to display the array of weapons at the disposal of the torturer — grimy, bloodied tools with bits of viscera caught in them, or the intricate torture apparatuses of *Saw*. Close-ups of the faces of the victims convey their terror, as they succumb to stunning pain, tears, and nausea in the face of injury or imminent threat (Figure 20.1). Torment is conveyed in close-ups of their contorted faces, hands, and feet, body parts that discernibly register pain and shock. Thus the victim's body is fragmented through shots and edits before and during the attack, though sometimes the view of the body is partially obscured. Close-up work of incisions, cutoff body parts, viscera, bodily spasms, and blood spurts visibly fragment the body, and prominently display realistic special effects technologies. Since the process of torture includes not only its execution and variations, but also its anticipation, considerable screen time is dedicated to verbal and nonverbal threats, as well as the use of assorted instruments to wound. This chronology is extended by using multiple camera angles — which also allow for a detailed rendering of the process — and incorporating them through editing. The lingering shots of the suffering body that characterize torture porn, particularly when they involve a sympathetic character, make for an intense viewing experience. What the viewer feels is not identical to what a character feels, but if the viewer is sympathetic to the character the viewer experiences attenuated congruent emotions (Plantinga, 2009: 101).

Ambient sounds — the clang of metal, the ticking of a timer, the hyperventilation of a victim — serve to induce suspense and dread in the build up to injury. The violence itself is accompanied by harrowing sound effects — bones breaking, the

Figure 20.1 Tight framing of the terrified figure of Liz in *Wolf Creek* (2005) mimics her narrative confinement. Directed by Greg Mclean. Produced by The Australian Film Finance Corporation, The South Australian Film Corporation, 403 Productions, True Crime Channel, Best FX, and Emu Creek Pictures.

oscillating whine of a power tool cutting through flesh — as well as the abject human voice as it pleads for mercy, sobs in anguish, or squeals in pain. Music typically accompanies the attack, rising in pace and volume to mirror the pitch of violence. A sound mix of screams, tearing flesh, and music accompanies the increasingly quick montage. The musical pacing usually accelerates to achieve what has been called *auditory entrainment* (Plantinga, 2009: 146). This is the process by which the human pulse synchronizes with music, or beats at equal time intervals to an external rhythm. The goal of musical pacing, in concert with the visual elements and narrative events, is to quicken the viewer's pulse and sense of agitation, generating emotional intensity in the viewer. Torture porn uses the musical conventions of the horror film to intensify its graphic and extended display of body horror. According to horror film convention, atonal, dissonant sounds are used to create an unsettling effect. The final sections of horror films are characterized by irregular rhythmic music based on film cuts (Hayward and Minassian, 2009: 246). "Irregular or unpredictable rhythms attract our attention by confounding our expectations and, depending on the violence of the deviation, can unsettle us physiologically through increased stimulation of the nervous system" (Kalinak, 2003: 18, quoted in Hayward and Minassian, 2009: 246).

The sound design of *Wolf Creek* provides a good case in point for the effective use of stylistic choices. In typical genre manner, the scoring is absent or subtle in the beginning, where its absence adds to the sense of being in the middle of nowhere. Then the sound becomes loud in the middle, and prevalent in the conclusion.

Sound volume mirrors the development of narrative intensity. In addition to volume, the strangeness of music can be used to unsettle the viewer. In keeping with the film's sustained use of sublime elements of the Australian landscape, the film employs the music of Australian sound artist Alan Lamb, who sets up installations of large-scale wind harps in rustic settings. Long humming wires resonated by wind produce low-pitched drones, subtle metallic twangs, and buzzing walls of sound. The composer for the film also used highly processed sounds from conventional musical instruments. Using the guts of a piano without the keys, it was struck with hands, mallets, and coins to accompany the torture scenes. These metallic sounds interact with the metal of the shed and the cold-blooded mindset of the captor (Hayward and Minassian, 2009: 245–247), producing unsettling effects.

Critical Reception of Torture Porn

Critical reception of the torture porn cycle, given both its timely, controversial subject matter and its high voltage emotional impact, was heated, spurred interest, advanced box office, and in time furthered the decline of the cycle. Poster and billboard marketing featuring dismembered limbs and head traps were used to sell *Saw*, as part of a business plan designed to churn out profit by keeping to a frugal budget, using targeted ads with memorable shock value. The denunciation of these images, displayed in public spaces such as the subway, drew attention to the film and served as free publicity. But by 2007, the box office for torture porn films started to decline and ads generated more controversy than usual. For example, *Hostel: Part II* used a poster featuring a chunk of gristled meat; but one in which a naked woman, shot from the neck to the knees, is holding her decapitated head in her hands was "banned," or so blogs reported. It had merely been rejected by some small town newspapers in favor of another poster for the film, but the marketing machine exploited the appeal of the forbidden (McKendry, 2008: 37, 57–58). Similarly, *Captivity's* use of a billboard and taxicab poster drew heavy fire. It was divided into four parts, each labeled and displaying a young woman in close up who is subject to "abduction," "confinement," "torture," and "termination." The poster met with public outrage, but the free publicity failed to spur box office. New entries in the cycle sought to salvage their films by redirecting their advertising focus from torture. *I Know Who Killed Me* (2007) focused on miscast star Lindsay Lohan's sex appeal, and *Untraceable* (2008) drew attention to the detective, played by Diane Lane, pursuing the torturer. Given the torture-centered nature of the films, the strategy was misleading and failed (McKendry, 2008: 60–61). Only the *Saw* franchise continued to be profitable, but even here the trend was one of diminishing returns.

The rise, popularity, and critical appraisal of torture porn films were influenced by the larger socio-historical context of their release. Edelstein and other critics

Figure 20.2   Josh is stripped, hooded, and bound, a shot that draws a visual parallel with an Abu Ghraib photo. *Hostel* (2005). Directed by Eli Roth. Produced by Hostel LLC, International Production Company, Next Entertainment, and Raw Nerve.

identified a link between the extensive media coverage of ordinary American soldiers torturing prisoners at Abu Ghraib in 2004, including the ready availability of still and video images online, and the escalation of uninhibited images of torture, degradation, and mutilation in fiction film. In fact, the phrase torture porn more aptly applies to the Abu Ghraib photos, with their S&M coding—dog collar and leash, bondage, masks—and the sexualized violence they depict, such as forcing prisoners to simulate sodomy. They were further sexualized by their status as souvenirs, swapped and intermingled with photos of soldiers having sex (Sontag, 2004). Moreover, Edelstein suggested that the popularity of torture porn reflected the fact that many Americans found these practices acceptable, but that is not the only way to read their popularity (Figure 20.2).

Eli Roth, the politically conscious director of *Hostel*, locates his film in a politically different interpretive framework. He sees it as narratively acting out American antipathy abroad, and aesthetically as resonating with online terrorist videos depicting the decapitation of Western abductees such as journalist Daniel Pearl. He defends the film, which was singled out in Edelstein's article, as socially relevant and cathartic. As evidence, he cites a letter he received from a soldier in Iraq. The soldier and his buddy had been out on patrol and had seen a dead body with its face blown off. That night, back on base, they watched *Hostel* along with 400 other soldiers. According to Roth:

> … [E]verybody was screaming. When you see that kind of violence—somebody with his face blown off—you can't emotionally respond to it. You're not allowed to be scared….They have to tactically respond to a situation and be brave, and all of that fear gets stored up day after day after day and there's no release for it. But when they put on *Hostel*, it says for the next 90 minutes not only are you allowed to be scared, but you are encouraged to be scared. It is socially acceptable. (quoted in Collura, 2007: 3)

Roth sees this as the civilian experience writ large, connecting torture porn to the horror film's historic role of obliquely engaging with and representing traumatic violence and historical trauma. However, not all filmmakers of the cycle attach sociological significance to their movies. James Wan, for instance, denies that *Saw* is a piece of social commentary, but he leaves an opening, noting that as a filmmaker " … you cannot help but be influenced by what's happening around you … " (quoted in Collura, 2007: 2–3).

These low-budget films managed to reach a mainstream audience in part because torture was a national pressing concern. In contrast, although films that dealt directly with 9/11 such as *Fahrenheit 9/11* (2004), *United 93* (2006), and *World Trade Center* (2006) were profitable, many of the films that directly tackled the Iraq or Afghan War, and specifically torture (including the policies of "extraordinary rendition" or torture by foreign proxy) such as *Redacted* (2006), *In the Valley of Elah* (2007), *Rendition* (2007), *Lions for Lambs* (2007), and *Stop-Loss* (2008) all lost money despite star power and social relevance. In contrast, two "war on terror" related films were profitable. Torture was obliquely dealt with in the absurdist comedy *Harold and Kumar Escape from Guantanamo Bay* (2008), and avoided in *The Hurt Locker* (2009), a film about a bomb disposal army unit in Iraq during the war. *Harold and Kumar* used its comic license to render the oblique suggestion of torture more palatable, and *Hurt Locker* was an exceptional entry, which won Best Picture and five other Oscars.

Edelstein's suggestion that torture porn consumption was leading to public apathy toward military torture conflates film and real life in simplistic ways. Desensitization to images of torture in fiction film cannot be equated with lessened sensitivity to torture practices in real life. It *is* disturbing that despite the shocking impact of the Abu Ghraib photos, "nearly half of Americans consistently said that the torture of terrorists to gain key information was at least sometimes justified" (Pew Research Center, 2008). Support for torture against suspected terrorists has consistently been correlated with political affiliation, with two-thirds of Republicans saying it is justified (65%) often or sometimes, while two-thirds of Democrats justify the practice (66%) rarely or never (Pew Research Center, 2009). But the effort to pin the blame on torture porn is and was mislaid. The films are not the problem, but real problems drove the films. In fact, I would suggest that Edelstein's apprehension that the mainstream success of torture porn films was due to eroding cultural taboos against torture practices in the military misses the mark. Body horror did escalate in the post-9/11 horror film, and the release of the Abu Ghraib prison photos did spur the escalation of uninhibited images of torture, degradation, and mutilation in film, but the relation is more complex than that. The wide dispersal of the prison photos was propelled by the high-profile joint release of the story on *60 Minutes* and *The New Yorker* in April 2004, followed by their availability online. But the availability of explicit images of real-world body horror online predates 2004.

Even before this it was possible to view violent videos online, including staged media events such as the beheading of American journalist Daniel Pearl in 2002, as well as American businessman Nick Berg in 2004. Since then the world has witnessed numerous other scenes of high-profile political violence such as the beating and killing of insurgents in Iran in 2009, as well as videos of accidents, suicides, and crimes, uploaded without a moralizing framework. Sue Tait argues that increased access to portable video technology, the ease of video upload, and the speed of viral dispersion have expanded public exposure to explicit images of body horror which has in turn redrawn the ethical boundaries for the viewing of graphic imagery (2008: 91, 93). I argue that this rise in the level of explicit body horror available online has changed the context of expectations for viewers, has raised the ante for the horror film industry, and has driven the rise in the level of explicit body horror in fiction film. Horror films have to compete with this to sustain their shock value, and digital technology has improved the quality of realistic special effects while lowering the cost. The result has been a higher level of explicit body horror in film. This is not a new phenomenon for the horror film. Audiences become accustomed to prevailing thresholds of violence and death, and films have to push the boundaries to evoke the same response (Prince, 2003: 84).

The labeling of horror films that traffic in this high watermark of graphic violence, and center their screen time around acts of torture as "torture porn" has confounded the critical discussion of these films. The stigmatizing effect of the term locates it in the discourse of media effects research, which draws a discursive link between sexual arousal, sexually violent imagery, and criminal sexual acts, and so concludes that sexual arousal is itself a form of harm or deviance when connected to violent films (Cronin, 2009: 10). Although Edelstein is far from advocating censorship, his critique played out in this larger discursive field. Cultural commentary has also designated the online content referred to earlier as "pornographic" or "pornographies of violence." The term *pornography* functions to stigmatize the films and, to extend Tait's argument, to displace concerns about one set of eroding cultural taboos (against actual torture practices) onto another (fictional torture depictions) without articulating what is truly at stake (2008: 92–93).

It is also possible that Edelstein is partially right. Perhaps for viewers who support torture practices as warranted, the retribution plot lines of these films reinforce their justification of torture, most notably in *Hostel*. As Jason Middleton (2010) argues, although *Hostel* critiques American arrogance and torture policies by placing young, white, middle-class American men in the position of torture victim, it ends up affirming the neo-conservative agenda of the Bush administration by depicting the American's brutal retaliation against "evil doers," in the jargon of President Bush, as justified. But for those who oppose torture practices, the films reinforce their repugnance for torture. Key here is the idea that torture porn films "bring us face to face with what is routinely denied in the process of … government sanctioned 'torture,'" namely that torture's primary purpose is not to interrogate but to use sustained and excruciating pain and isolation to break a captive's sense of self in order to bolster the torturer's own jeopardized sense of power (Murray, 2008: 2; Scarry, 1987).[1]

Conclusion

Horror has historically been a symptomatic and supple genre, tapping into social anxieties. The horror film helps us deal with deep and disturbing emotions, especially in contexts of threats such as wartime or terrorism, when the popularity of the horror film increases (Skal, 1993: 386). Torture porn is part of the post-9/11 shift in the horror film described by critics, expressing a resounding surge in fear of terrorism and, specifically with torture porn, of our own ambivalence about torture and invasive government surveillance (Briefel and Miller, 2011; Wetmore, 2012). This is in keeping with the horror film's larger role of articulating historical trauma in cinematic allegory (Lowenstein, 2005: 10). As it did in the 1970s during the tumult and national self-questioning of the Vietnam War era, so it has in the wake of the 9/11-induced national discussion about torture. Specifically, the torture porn cycle corresponds to the period between the exposure of torture practices in Abu Ghraib and the end of the Bush administration that crafted the policy of "enhanced interrogation" and declared the "war on terror" (Middleton: 2–3).

As Kristiaan Versluys characterizes it, 9/11 (and I would add here the torture sanctioned in its name) is an event that can be expressed only through "allegory and indirection" (2009: 14). Indeed, the torture porn cycle gave voice to the fascination with, unease toward, and fear of torture. It did so deploying the visual discourse of the splatter film, the tropes of the gothic, and the economics of the exploitation film. It generated great profit for several years until interest declined around 2008, but its sustained effect has been to raise the threshold for graphic violence and gore in the horror film, to effectively shift audience expectation. As it has done in the past, the genre competes with explicit images of body horror available elsewhere. It escalates to compete with photographic evidence of real violence in order to maintain its shock value. And in the process, it helps us process violent and traumatic collective experience.

Acknowledgment

This work draws from a larger project for which Panda Selsey and Jessica Wilson have supplied much appreciated research assistance. Support for this project was provided by a 2013 President's Fund for Faculty Advancement Award at Hunter College of the City University of New York, and a 2009–10 PSC–CUNY Award, jointly funded by The Professional Staff Congress and The City University of New York.

Note

1. During Q&A following a screening of *The Poughkeepsie Tapes* (2007) at the Tribeca Film Festival, director John Erick Dowdle denied that the use of stress positions and water

boarding by the film's serial killer was inspired by accounts of torture at Abu Ghraib. Rather, these scenes were fashioned after the activities of actual serial killers. Having clearly seen the earmarks of political torture, I was frankly disappointed with his answer, until I realized the implications. The film was not copying what was done at Abu Ghraib; Abu Ghraib was copying what some sadistic killers do.

References

Association of the Bar of the City of NY and Center for Human Rights and Global Justice (2004) *Torture by proxy: international and domestic law applicable to "extraordinary renditions"*, ABCNY and NYU School of Law, NY.

Blake, L. (2011) "I am the Devil and I'm here to do the Devil's Work": Rob Zombie, George W. Bush, and the limits of American freedom, in *Horror After 9/11: World of Fear, Cinema of Terror* (eds A. Briefel and S.J. Miller), University of Texas Press, Austin, pp. 186–199.

Briefel, A. and Miller, S. (eds) (2011) *Horror after 9/11: World of Fear, Cinema of Terror*, University of Texas Press, Austin.

Collura, S. (2007). Torture Porn: When Good Times Go Bad, http://movies.ign.com/articles/804/804194p1.html (accessed 18 May 2009).

Cronin, T. (2009) Media effects and the subjectification of film regulation. *Velvet Light Trap*, **63**, 3–21.

Dickstein, M. (2004[1984]) The aesthetics of fright, in *Planks of Reason* (eds B.K. Grant and C. Sharrett), Scarecrow Press, Metuchen, NJ, pp. 50–62.

Edelstein, D. (2006) Now playing at your local multiplex: torture porn. *New York Magazine*, **39** (4), 63–64.

Hayward, P. and Minassian, H. (2009) Terror in the Outback: *Wolf Creek* and Australian horror cinema, in *Terror Tracks: Music, Sound, and Horror Cinema* (ed. P. Hayward), Equinox Publishing, London, pp. 238–248.

Kalinak, K. (2003) The language of music: a brief analysis of *Vertigo*, in *Movie Music: The Film Reader* (ed. K. Dickinson), Routledge, London, pp. 15–23.

Johnson, S. (2005) *Everything Bad is Good for You: How Today's Popular Culture is Actually Making Us Smarter*, Penguin Group, NY.

Lowenstein, A. (2005) *Shocking Representation: Historical Trauma, National Cinema, and the Modern Horror Film*, Columbia University Press, NY.

Lowenstein, A. (2011) Spectacle horror and *Hostel*: why 'torture porn' does not exist. *Critical Quarterly*, **53** (1), 42–60.

McKendry, R.W. (2008). America and torture porn: the history, marketing, and meaning of American torture porn films. MA thesis. City University of New York.

Middleton, J. (2010) The subject of torture: regarding the pain of Americans in *Hostel*. *Cinema Journal*, **49** (4), 1–24.

Murray, G. (2008) *Hostel II*: representations of the body in pain and the cinema experience in torture porn. *Jump Cut*, **50** http://www.ejumpcut.org/archive/jc50.2008/TortureHostel2/index.html (accessed 12 June, 2011).

Palmer, T. (2006) Style and sensation in the contemporary French cinema of the body. *Journal of Film and Video*, **53** (3), 22–32.

Pew Research Center (2008). Bush and Public Opinion, http://www.people-press.org/2008/12/18/bush-and-public-opinion/ (accessed 1 June, 2011).

Pew Research Center (2009). Obama Faces Familiar Divisions over Anti-Terror Policies, http://pewresearch.org/pubs/1125/terrorism-guantanamo-torture-polling (accessed 1 June, 2011).

Plantinga, C. (2009) *Moving Viewers: American Film and the Spectator's Experience*, University of California Press, Berkeley.

Prince, S. (2003) *Classical Film Violence: Designing and Regulating Brutality in Hollywood Cinema: 1930–1968*, Rutgers University Press, New Brunswick, NJ.

Quandt, J. (2004) Flesh and blood: sex and violence in recent French cinema. *Artforum*, **42** (6), 126–132.

Scarry, E. (1987) *The Body in Pain: The Making and Unmaking of the World*, Oxford University Press, New York.

Skal, D. (1993) *The Monster Show: A Cultural History of Horror*, Faber and Faber, New York.

Sontag, S. (2004). Regarding the Torture of Others. *New York Times Magazine*, pp. 23, 24–30.

Tait, S. (2008) Pornographies of violence? Internet spectatorship on body horror. *Critical Studies in Media Communication*, **25** (1), 91–111.

Versluys, K. (2009) *Out of the Blue: September 11 and the Novel*, Columbia University Press, New York.

Weissenstein, C. (2011). Negotiating the non-narrative, aesthetic and erotic in new extreme gore. MA thesis. Georgetown University.

Wetmore, K. (2012) *Post-9/11 Horror in American Cinema*, Continuum Publishing, New York.

Williams, L. (1991) Film bodies: gender, genre, and excess. *Film Quarterly*, **44** (4), 2–12.

Part IV

Selected International Horror Cinemas

21

Spanish Horror Cinema

Ian Olney

Compared to when it appeared elsewhere in Europe, horror cinema arrived rather belatedly in Spain; it was not until the 1960s that the country produced its first horror movies. However, once the genre took root in Spanish soil, it blossomed with amazing speed and fecundity, yielding a riotous profusion of new films, directors, stars, narrative forms, and stylistic approaches. Today, Spanish horror cinema ranks among the most vibrant and influential national expressions of the genre not just in Europe, but in the world. In this chapter, I provide a brief history of the Spanish horror film, as well as a consideration of several of its key facets: its characteristic patterns, themes, and motifs; its often subversive treatment of sex and gender; and its longstanding relationship with Spanish art cinema. My aim is to show that although it has often been overlooked or underappreciated in scholarly work on the horror film, Spanish horror cinema represents a rich national tradition and a vital contribution to global horror.

A Brief History of Spanish Horror Cinema

The history of Spanish horror cinema can be roughly divided into three periods. A classic era running from the early 1960s to the early 1980s saw the birth of the Spanish horror film, the emergence of the country's first horror directors and stars, and the development of a distinctive national horror cinema. A transitional era lasting from the early 1980s to the early 2000s was comparatively fallow, marked by a sharp decline in production and a shift to more self-aware and reflexive modes of horror that could be described as postmodern. Finally, a contemporary era stretching from the early 2000s to the present has witnessed a genre renaissance fueled by the

A Companion to the Horror Film, First Edition. Edited by Harry M. Benshoff.
© 2014 John Wiley & Sons, Inc. Published 2017 by John Wiley & Sons, Inc.

resurgent popularity of horror cinema among Spanish viewers, the debut of a new generation of Spanish horror directors, and the unprecedented success of Spanish horror movies on the international stage.

The beginnings of Spanish horror cinema can be traced back to the 1960s. Excepting, perhaps, the Méliès-like fantasy shorts made by motion picture pioneer and innovator Segundo de Chomón in the early 1900s, or the moody mysteries directed by Edgar Neville in the 1940s, there were no horror movies made in Spain before then. The reasons for this were both cultural and political. Initially, the tastes of Spanish filmgoers and filmmakers simply ran in other directions. Spain had no real tradition of the gothic or the *fantastique* and the general preference was for films that drew on familiar, indigenous genres—particularly the *zarzuela* (light operetta) and the *sainete* (comic playlet) (Stone, 2002: 17). Following the Spanish Civil War (1936–1939), however, the absence of horror movies in Spain had as much to do with politics as it did with culture. The country's new fascist regime, run by dictator Francisco Franco with the support of the Catholic Church, tightly regulated cinema in the immediate postwar era, permitting only films that conformed to its political and religious precepts. Horror movies, of course, conformed to neither and almost certainly would not have been approved by government censors even had there been an interest in their production. When the genre finally established a foothold in Spain in the 1960s, it was largely thanks to a pair of serendipitous developments. First, Franco embraced a new national policy of *aperturismo* or "openness" in an effort to repair the country's reputation as a repressive dictatorship and boost its ailing economy. As a consequence, censorship was relaxed and directors were allowed more freedom to serve the "special interests" of popular audiences, as opposed to the "national interests" of the fascist regime. At the same time, England's Hammer Films triggered a major international horror boom with a series of gothic chillers that reintroduced classic monsters such as Dracula and Frankenstein in eye-popping color with newly explicit levels of sex and violence. These wildly successful movies resuscitated the genre, and sent filmmakers across Europe scurrying back to the crypt. Liberated from the political restrictions of the immediate postwar era and recognizing horror's commercial potential, Spanish directors and producers followed suit, cautiously at first and then with great enthusiasm. In just a few years, Spain was host to a thriving horror industry. And although Franco tightened censorship again at the end of the 1960s, the country's horror output actually increased in the early 1970s. Filmmakers found various ways around government restrictions; it was common, for example, to prepare two cuts of each movie—a tamer version for domestic audiences and a more graphic version for export (Tohill and Tombs, 1994: 65). Filmgoers, having developed a taste for horror, now actively sought it out—often going so far as to cross the border into France to see movies banned in their homeland (Tohill and Tombs, 1994: 64). The classic era of Spanish horror cinema had begun.

The first true Spanish horror movie was *Gritos en la noche* (*The Awful Dr. Orlof,* 1962). In it, the brilliant surgeon Dr. Orlof (Howard Vernon) becomes obsessed with restoring the beauty of his daughter Melissa (Diana Lorys) after she is horribly disfigured in a fire. With the aid of his blind assistant Morpho (Ricardo Valle), he kidnaps young women and brings them back to his isolated chateau, where he attempts to transplant their faces onto Melissa's. Orlof's reign of terror is finally brought to an end by police inspector Edgar Tanner (Conrado San Martín), whose resourceful fiancée Wanda (also Lorys) goes undercover to help him solve the case. To a certain extent, the film relies on established genre formulas. The title character was borrowed from British crime writer Edgar Wallace's 1924 novel *The Dark Eyes of London*, while the narrative premise was lifted straight from Georges Franju's influential medical shocker *Les yeux sans visage* (*Eyes without a Face*, 1960). Meanwhile, the look of the movie — particularly its gothic sets, chiaroscuro lighting, and oblique camera angles — was modeled after that of classical Hollywood horror. However, *The Awful Dr. Orlof* distinguishes itself from earlier genre fare in several key ways. In addition to surpassing even the Hammer films that preceded it in terms of overt violence and gore, it upped the ante with regards to sex, offering glimpses of female nudity and creating an unsettling atmosphere of erotic horror. It presents us with a rare sympathetic monster in Morpho, who is the victim of Orlof's inhumane experiments and sadistic abuse. It also gives us in Wanda a heroine whose "active, inquiring, investigative gaze" (Hawkins, 2000: 103) transgresses the gender norms of classical horror. These elements set the film apart in a very crowded field, and it found appreciative audiences in Spain and abroad (Figure 21.1).

Figure 21.1 Orlof (Howard Vernon) and Morpho (Ricardo Valle) in *The Awful Dr. Orlof*, Spain's first true horror movie (Sigma III Corp.). Directed by Jesús Franco. Produced by Hispamer Films, Leo Lax Production, and Ydex Euerociné.

The Awful Dr. Orlof also launched the career of its director, Jesús "Jess" Franco, who remained a key figure in the history of Spanish horror cinema until his death in 2013. There were few developments in the genre at the time with which this astonishingly prolific filmmaker was not in some way associated. Following the success of *The Awful Dr. Orlof*, Franco turned out a number of sequels—beginning with the stylish *El secreto del Dr. Orloff* (*Dr. Orloff's Monster*, 1964), which restored the original spelling of the title character's name—as well as other mad scientist movies such as *Miss Muerte* (*The Diabolical Dr. Z*, 1966), a haunting, surreal tale of revenge scripted by Luis Buñuel's frequent collaborator, Jean-Claude Carrière. He directed gothic horror films, from the relatively restrained *Nachts, wenn Dracula erwacht* (*Count Dracula*, 1970) with Hammer star Christopher Lee to the truly delirious *La maldición de Frankenstein* (*The Rites of Frankenstein*, 1972), which pits Dennis Price's Doctor Frankenstein and his silver-laminated monster against Howard Vernon's hypnotist Cagliostro and his blind, oracular bird-woman. Franco helped establish the popular lesbian vampire subgenre with *Vampiros lesbos* (*Vampyros Lesbos*, 1971). He also made possession films, zombie pictures, and slasher movies. His most important contribution to the genre, though, may be his pioneering of what I have described elsewhere (2012) as S&M horror cinema—a type of horror that incorporates sadomasochistic imagery and themes, blending sex and violence in a unique and disconcerting manner. Franco's S&M horror movies run the gamut from kinky gothic melodramas such as *La mano de un hombre muerto* (*The Sadistic Baron Von Klaus*, 1962) to more modern, experimental films such as the densely layered *Necronomicon - Geträumte Sünden* (*Succubus*, 1968). He took the women-in-prison picture into the realm of S&M horror with *Der heiße Tod* (*99 Women*, 1969), essentially inventing a new category of erotic terror, and applied the same formula to the inquisition film in *Il trono di fuoco* (*The Bloody Judge*, 1970) and the nunsploitation film in *Die Liebesbriefe einer portugiesischen Nonne* (*Love Letters of a Portuguese Nun*, 1977). He even adapted (albeit loosely) the work of the Marquis de Sade and Leopold von Sacher-Masoch for movies such as *Marquis de Sade: Justine* (*Marquis de Sade's Justine*, 1969) and *Paroxismus* (*Venus in Furs*, 1969). Made quickly and on shoestring budgets for less-than-scrupulous producers across Europe, Franco's films are wildly uneven. As Tohill and Tombs (Tohill and Tombs, 1994: 101) put it: "Some scenes are shot with quirky precision and painstaking attention to detail, while others are cobbled together cheaply." They are undeniably personal, however, and most contain at least flashes of spontaneity and brilliance that offset their more mundane or risible moments.

Another key director who emerged during the classic era was Narciso Ibáñez Serrador. Serrador got his start in television, creating the hugely popular horror series *Historias para no dormir* (*Stories to Keep You Awake*, 1966–1982). This program helped cultivate a taste for horror in Spain and guarantee the genre's future there. Its success also enabled Serrador to make two of the most important films in the history of Spanish horror cinema: *La residencia* (*The House That Screamed*, 1969) and *¿Quién puede matar a un niño?* (*Who Can Kill a Child?*,

1976). *The House That Screamed* is set at a boarding school for girls run by the repressive headmistress Madame Fourneau (Lilli Palmer), with assistance from a cohort of sadistic upperclassmen. The film opens with the arrival of a new student, Teresa (Cristina Galbó), who discovers that several girls have disappeared under mysterious circumstances in recent months. It is finally revealed that Madame Fourneau's adolescent son Luis (John Moulder Brown), driven mad by his domineering and possessive mother, murdered the missing girls in an attempt to assemble the "perfect woman" from their body parts. Unconventionally plotted, elegantly shot, and sharply edited, *The House That Screamed* inspired a number of subsequent horror films, from Dario Argento's celebrated occult thriller *Suspiria* (1977) to Juan Piquer Simón's gruesome slasher *Mil gritos tiene la noche* (*Pieces*, 1982).

Equally significant was Serrador's second horror movie, *Who Can Kill a Child?*, which also details the devastating effects of violence and repression on the young. It concerns a vacationing couple, Tom (Lewis Fiander) and Evelyn (Prunella Ransome), who travel to the remote island of Almanzora, only to find that the adult inhabitants have been systematically slaughtered by their offspring. When Tom and Evelyn are themselves targeted by the children, they face the dilemma suggested by the film's title: can they bring themselves to do what is necessary to survive? Not surprisingly, as its graphic violence is perpetrated by (and eventually directed against) children, *Who Can Kill a Child?* was very controversial at the time of its release and even banned in several countries. While undeniably chilling, however, the film's violence is neither gratuitous nor exploitative. It is in the service of a deeply serious meditation on the failure of the old in their moral responsibility to the young—a failure made clear by the movie's prolog, which catalogues twentieth-century atrocities (the Holocaust and the Vietnam War among them) that, although engineered by adults, had a devastating impact on children. The film implies that the massacre of the old at the hands of the young should be viewed as an act not of senseless murder but of self-preservation. Together with *The House That Screamed*, *Who Can Kill a Child?* expanded the genre celebrity Serrador had earned on television, making him perhaps that era's "most culturally prominent image of horror in Spain" (Lázaro-Reboll, 2004: 157).

In addition to major directors such as Franco and Serrador, the classic era of Spanish horror also produced an iconic star: Paul Naschy. Born Jacinto Molina in Madrid in 1934, Naschy developed a passion for the genre as a youth and decided early on that he wanted to be an actor; nevertheless, he studied architecture and jobbed variously as a record label designer, a comic book artist, a pulp fiction writer, and a professional weightlifter before drifting into film work as an extra in Spain-based Hollywood productions such as *El Cid* (1961) (Tjersland, 2003: 69). His career in horror began in the late 1960s, when he was hired to script *La marca del Hombre-lobo* (*Frankenstein's Bloody Terror*, 1968). Modeling the film after his favorite boyhood horror movie, Universal's *Frankenstein Meets the Wolf Man* (1943), Molina crafted the tragic tale of a Polish aristocrat, Count Waldemar Daninsky, who is bitten by a werewolf and can only be released from the curse of lycanthropy by his death at the hands of a woman who loves him. The role of Daninsky was intended for Lon Chaney, Jr., the star of *Frankenstein Meets the Wolf Man*, but when Chaney proved too ill to take the part, the producers reluctantly offered it to the eager Molina, on the condition that he adopt a screen name that sounded "less Spanish" than his own to aid international sales (Tjersland, 2003: 70). Rechristened "Paul Naschy," Molina played the character with gusto, using his brooding good looks and powerful physique to imbue Daninsky with a brutish sensuality. Thanks largely to the strength of his performance and the movie's lavish production values—conceived as Spain's first horror super-production, it was shot on 70 mm color film stock and in 3D—*Frankenstein's Bloody Terror* was an enormous success. It established Naschy as the leading star of Spanish horror and forever linked him with the character of Waldemar Daninsky. He went on to play the role in a dozen other films, some of which he directed himself and the most recent of which was released just a few years before his death in 2009. Rather than expanding on the original like most sequels, these movies retell the same story again and again with only a few minor variations—as in León Klimovsky's *La noche de Walpurgis* (*Werewolf Shadow*, 1971) or Carlos Aured's *El retorno de Walpurgis* (*Curse of the Devil*, 1973). Each time, Daninsky/Naschy struggles bravely but futilely against his lycanthropy and must be put out of his misery by a woman who loves him. As Antonio Lázaro-Reboll (Lázaro-Reboll, 2005: 133) puts it: "Hero and victim, that is the sempiternally doomed nature of Paul Naschy's character." As closely as Naschy became identified with this role, however, it was by no means the only one he essayed. Indeed, he became known as the Spanish Lon Chaney for the sheer variety of his parts; over the years, he played almost every movie monster imaginable, including Dracula, Mr. Hyde, the Mummy, the Hunchback—even Satan. It is his versatility and prolificacy as an actor, as well as his unwavering commitment to his signature role, that merits Naschy's special star status in Spanish horror cinema.

Franco, Serrador, and Naschy are generally regarded as the titans of classic Spanish horror cinema, but there are many other figures who made important contributions to the genre during this period, both in front of and behind the camera. For example, Amando de Ossorio's *La noche del terror ciego* (*Tombs of the Blind Dead*, 1972), introduced perhaps the most original and indelible monsters in the history of Spanish horror: skeletal Knights of the Templar who, cowled and sightless, rise from their graves at night to hunt the blood of the living. The Blind Dead, as they became known, were so popular with audiences that de Ossorio built three sequels around them, creating a vital genre series that helped define the era. Working in England, José Ramón Larraz turned out a number of memorable horror movies, such as *Symptoms* (1974), an atmospheric psychological thriller, and *Vampyres* (1974), a violent and erotic lesbian vampire film. Eugenio Martín, whose suspenseful murder mystery *Ipnosi* (*Hypnosis*, 1962) prefigured the Italian *giallo* films of Mario Bava and Dario Argento, also directed the cult favorite *Horror Express* (1972), starring Christopher Lee and Peter Cushing. Meanwhile, Jorge Grau followed his first horror movie, *Ceremonia sangrienta* (*The Legend of Blood*

Castle, 1973), a somber retelling of the tale of Elizabeth Bathory, with *Non si deve profanare il sonno dei morti* (*Let Sleeping Corpses Lie*, 1974), an inventive zombie film that anticipates George Romero's *Dawn of the Dead* (1978) in its use of the zombie outbreak as a vehicle for social critique (directed here against industrialism rather than consumerism). Finally, in one of the most promising genre debuts of the period, Claudio Guerín made *La campana del infierno* (*A Bell from Hell*, 1973), the unsettling story of a young man who is released from a mental hospital and returns to his hometown to take revenge on the wealthy aunt who had him committed. (Guerín's career was tragically cut short when he was killed in an accident on the last day of shooting.) Although their work has often been overlooked, each of the above directors played a crucial role in shaping classic Spanish horror cinema. The same is true of a host of actors — including Antonio Mayans, Helga Liné, Dyanik Zurakowska, Soledad Miranda, Rosanna Yanni, Maria Rohm, and Julián Ugarte — and other key personnel: screenwriters such as Santiago Moncada and Antonio Fos, cinematographers such as Raúl Artigot and Francisco Sánchez, production designers such as Gumersindo Andrés and Ramiro Gómez, makeup effects artists such as Miguel Sesé and Julián Ruiz, and special effects technicians such as Antonio Molina and Pablo Pérez. While these individuals have not received as much attention as Franco, Serrador and Naschy, they all deserve credit for the remarkable flowering of the Spanish horror film in the 1960s and 1970s.

However, by the early 1980s, the popularity of Spanish horror film started declining. The primary reason for this, ironically enough, was the death of Francisco Franco and Spain's subsequent transition to democracy. Logically, Franco's demise in 1975 — which was followed by the abolishment of state censorship in 1977 and the election of a Socialist government in 1982 — should have been a huge boon to the horror film, as its production had always been tightly regulated under his regime. Instead, Spain's liberation from fascism brought the genre to the brink of extinction, as the end of censorship proved to be a boost for sex — not horror — in the movies. This was perhaps unsurprising: strictly prohibited by the Church-backed dictatorship for decades and now suddenly permitted, cinematic sex was a novelty that filmmakers rushed to exploit. The result was a veritable flood of softcore comedies in the late 1970s that in turn gave way to a wave of hardcore pornographic films in the 1980s. As erotically charged as Spanish horror cinema was, it could not compete with the more explicit attractions of these movies. Matters worsened when the new government devoted itself to the creation of a national cinema diametrically opposed to the one promoted by Franco, implementing a system of subsidies, taxes, and quotas designed to encourage high-minded, socially conscious films while discouraging not only politically retrograde pictures, but also lowbrow genre fare like horror. Indeed, under this system — which became known as the *Miró Law* after the director Pilar Miró, who was selected to revamp state support for filmmaking — horror was branded as "non-Spanish" (Triana-Toribio, 2003: 115). The new administration also lifted longstanding restrictions on the exhibition of foreign films, allowing movies from abroad to be shown freely in Spain for the first time since the 1930s. Deprived of any kind of state support and faced with new competition from Hollywood and elsewhere, the Spanish horror film was in serious trouble. It also faced the same general challenges every other kind of Spanish cinema did during this period: the shrinking international market for European films, the declining audience for movies at home, and the ever-growing popularity of television. This perfect storm of difficulties prompted the mass exodus of many working in the genre — even stalwarts such as Jess Franco and Carlos Aured, who, like others, turned to porn to make ends meet. The classic era of Spanish horror cinema had officially come to an end.

The transitional era that succeeded it in the 1980s and 1990s saw not only a steep decline in the production of horror cinema but also the emergence of a new kind of horror movie: hip, self-aware, and often directed by young, up-and-coming filmmakers with an interest in commenting on the genre. One of the earliest and most intriguing examples of this brand of postmodern "meta-horror" is Bigas Luna's *Angustia* (*Anguish*, 1987). Perhaps best known for his outrageous arthouse melodrama *Jamón, jamón* (*Jamon Jamon*, 1992), Luna here crafts a seemingly straightforward slasher movie: when John (Michael Lerner), a shy, sensitive orderly at an ophthalmology clinic, is unfairly dismissed from his job, his overbearing mother (Zelda Rubenstein) exacts revenge by transforming him via hypnosis into an eye-gouging killer. A quarter of the way through the film, however, Luna pulls the rug out from under us, revealing that this story is in fact "just a movie" — one being watched in a theater by an audience that includes a deranged, gun-wielding fan who, inspired by the picture, intends to murder the other patrons. Deftly cutting between these two cinematic planes, *Anguish* creates a vertiginous, hall-of-mirrors effect that is multiplied if you happen to be viewing the film in a theater yourself: at one point, we watch the audience on screen being stalked by the deranged fan as *they* watch John enter a movie house and prey on spectators watching yet *another* picture. As ingenious as *Anguish* is, though, it is ultimately less a horror film than a meditation on the genre; in fact, it could be considered an anti-horror film insofar as it draws a damning causal connection between cinematic and real-life violence. This is also the case with *Tesis* (*Thesis*, 1996), the debut feature from Alejandro Amenábar, whose status as one of Spain's most exciting new auteurs was cemented with his metaphysical thriller *Abre los ojos* (*Open Your Eyes*, 1997) the following year. *Thesis* concerns a graduate student named Ángela (Ana Torrent), who, in the course of researching her dissertation on audiovisual violence, stumbles across a snuff film hidden in the archives of her university. Tense and gripping, Amenábar's film is nevertheless, like Luna's, focused on deconstructing rather than celebrating the genre: the underlying thesis of *Thesis* is that there is an innate human attraction to violent imagery, which horror filmmakers exploit to the detriment of society.

Of course, not all movies from the transitional era of Spanish horror are so critical of the genre. Álex de la Iglesia's *El día de la bestia* (*The Day of the Beast*, 1995), for example, happily revels in violent excess. Blending horror and comedy to riotous effect, it tells the story of a hapless priest (Álex Angulo) who determines from a numerological study of the Book of Revelations that the apocalypse is scheduled to begin on Christmas Day; he thus sets out to prevent the birth of the Antichrist with the help of a heavy-metal burnout (Santiago Segura) and a cynical television psychic (Armando De Razza). While the film differs radically from *Anguish* and *Thesis* in its attitude toward horror, it strongly resembles both movies in its self-consciousness and reflexivity. Borrowing the "splatstick" aesthetic pioneered by Sam Raimi, Stuart Gordon, and Peter Jackson in their early work and referencing such occult horror classics as *Rosemary's Baby* (1968), *The Exorcist* (1973), and *The Omen* (1976), *The Day of the Beast* is a paragon of postmodern pastiche and parody. Like *Anguish* and *Thesis*, it is in many ways a film about horror, rather than a horror film *per se*. Moreover, like Luna and Amenábar, De la Iglesia—who preceded *The Day of the Beast* with *Acción mutante* (*Mutant Action*, 1993), an outlandish science-fiction comedy, and followed it with *Perdita Durango* (1997), an equally bizarre Bonnie and Clyde-style road movie—did not at this point in his career demonstrate any sort of vested interest in horror. Critical of horror or not, Spanish filmmakers who came of age during the 1980s and 1990s tended to treat it as a way station rather than a home. The genre's only real loyalists were aging directors from the classic era who had managed to continue making horror movies—and they frequently seemed trapped in the past, willing (or able) only to recycle their greatest hits, as with *Faceless* (1987), Jess Franco's glossier and gorier remake of *The Awful Dr. Orlof*, or *El aullido del diablo* (*Howl of the Devil*, 1987), a nostalgia piece from Paul Naschy in which the actor shuffles through virtually every monster role he ever played.

The salvation of the Spanish horror film came at the turn of the twenty-first century, opening a new era in the history of Spanish horror cinema that is still unfolding today. This contemporary era has witnessed a massive resurgence in the popularity of horror cinema among viewers in Spain. An early sign of its renewed appeal was the phenomenal commercial success of Alejandro Amenábar's *Los otros* (*The Others*, 2001). Set in the years following World War II, the film centers on an iron-willed war widow, Grace (Nicole Kidman), struggling to raise her two children in an isolated, fog-bound house on the British isle of Jersey; her mettle is tested by the sudden arrival of unseen, possibly supernatural "intruders" who seem intent on wresting her home from her. The truth, as Grace finally discovers, is that she and her children are the ghosts haunting the house's new owners. Unlike Amenábar's *Thesis*, *The Others* demonstrates a deep respect for the genre, paying homage to masterworks of gothic cinema—particularly Jack Clayton's *The Innocents* (1961), itself an adaptation of Henry James's 1898 novella *The Turn of the Screw*. Manifest, as well, in *The Others* is a connection to the heritage of Spanish horror: while the film's twist ending may owe something to *The Sixth Sense* (1999), it also harkens back to Javier Setó's classic chiller *La llamada* (*The Sweet Sound of Death*, 1965), the tale of a young Spaniard who is thrilled when his French fiancée magically survives a horrific airplane crash, only to find out that this may not be the case. Amenábar's "old-school" genre movie was an enormous hit in Spain, ranking number one at the box office for the year and sweeping the annual Goya awards; no Spanish horror

Figure 21.2   Grace (Nicole Kidman) and her children in *The Others* (2001), a film that helped jumpstart Spain's current horror renaissance (Dimension Films). Directed by Alejandro Amenábar. Produced by Cruise/Wagner Productions, Sociedad General de Cine (SOGECINE) S.A., Las Producciones del Escorpión S.L., Dimension Films, Canal+, Lucky Red, and Miramax Films.

film had similarly captured the public's imagination during the preceding two decades (Figure 21.2).

The box office success of *The Others* helped revitalize the Spanish horror film industry. In recent years, studios in Spain have gotten back into the horror business in increasing numbers. Among the first was Filmax, a major film distributor that in 1999 launched Castelao Producciones, a production unit that almost immediately began turning out horror movies under its Fantastic Factory label (Willis, 2008). Horror has also returned to Spanish television, where Narciso Ibáñez Serrador revived his classic series *Stories to Keep You Awake* as *Películas para no dormir* (*Films to Keep You Awake*) in 2006. There has been a boom in annual horror film festivals held in Spain, adding a plethora of new venues such as the Fancine Málaga, the Cryptshow Festival, and the Horrorvisión Festival to a calendar that once only boasted the Sitges Film Festival and the San Sebastián Horror and Fantasy Film Festival. Even the work of Spanish film critics, historically hostile or indifferent to horror cinema, testifies to the genre's current cachet; the popular critic and novelist Carlos Aguilar alone has published several recent books on the horror film, including a monograph on Jess Franco (*Jess Franco, El sexo del horror*, 1999) and a weighty, two-part history of fantasy and horror movies in Spain (*Cine fantástico y de terror español*, 1999 and 2005).

The contemporary era of Spanish horror has also seen the debut of a new generation of filmmakers. Unlike their immediate predecessors, these directors have generally elected to specialize in the horror film; moreover, they have largely eschewed the irony of the transitional era in favor of the sincerity of the classic era (Willis, 2004). Foremost among them are Jaume Balagueró and Paco Plaza. Balagueró's first feature was *Los sin nombre* (*The Nameless*, 1999), the tale of a woman (Emma Vilarasau) whose daughter is apparently murdered in a ritualistic slaying. Subsequently, he directed *Darkness* (2002), in which a teenage girl (Anna Paquin) discovers that her family's new home is a portal to hell, and *Frágiles* (*Fragile*, 2005), in which a nurse (Calista Flockhart) hired to help manage the closing of an old hospital finds it is haunted by an evil spirit that will not permit the few remaining patients—all children—to leave. Balagueró's latest movie is *Mientras duermes* (*Sleep Tight*, 2011), a psychological thriller about an emotionally stunted apartment building concierge (Luis Tosar) whose only real happiness lies in secretly provoking the misery of a beautiful female tenant (Marta Etura). Paco Plaza's early features include *El segundo nombre* (*Second Name*, 2002), the story of a woman (Erica Prior) who uncovers a frightening connection between her family and a fanatical religious sect, and *Romasanta* (*Romasanta: The Werewolf Hunt*, 2004), a gloss on the legend of the "Werewolf of Allariz," Spain's first documented serial killer. In 2007, Plaza teamed up with Balagueró to make the "found-footage" zombie movie *[Rec]* (2007), which follows a television reporter who becomes trapped in a quarantined apartment building during the outbreak of a mysterious virus. Plaza also collaborated with Balagueró on a sequel, *[Rec]²* (2009), and shot a third movie in the series, *[REC]³ Génesis* (2012), on his own.

Behind Balagueró and Plaza, who stand at the forefront of contemporary Spanish horror cinema, are a host of other genre filmmakers, many of whom have only recently had their debut. A short list might include Juan Antonio Bayona, who made a big splash with his gothic ghost story *El orfanato* (*The Orphanage*, 2007); Nacho Vigalondo, whose *Los cronocrímenes* (*Timecrimes*, 2007) blends horror and science-fiction to intriguing effect; Isidro Ortiz, director of the inventive rural horror movie *Eskalofrío* (*Shiver*, 2008); Guillem Morales, whose *Los ojos de Julia* (*Julia's Eyes*, 2010) offers a fresh take on the woman-in-peril thriller; and Miguel Ángel Vivas, the filmmaker behind the harrowing home invasion horror film *Secuestrados* (*Kidnapped*, 2010). Although these directors differ—sometimes radically—from one another in terms of temperament and style, they share with one another and with Balagueró and Plaza a commitment not just to horror itself, but to a traditional mode of horror that emphasizes old-fashioned authenticity over postmodern pastiche.

One clear measure of the vitality of contemporary Spanish horror is its unprecedented success on the international stage. Beginning with *The Others*, which earned over $200 million worldwide during its theatrical run to become the highest-grossing Spanish film ever, other horror movies from Spain have racked up healthy returns at the box office, including *Darkness* (over $34 million worldwide), *[Rec]* (over $32 million), and *The Orphanage* (over $78 million). Their success has attracted the attention of Hollywood studios looking for commercially viable films from abroad to remake in English. Sony remade *[Rec]* as *Quarantine* in 2008, while forthcoming remakes of *The Orphanage* and *Timecrimes* were announced by New Line Cinema in 2007 and DreamWorks in 2011, respectively. The success of contemporary Spanish horror movies has also afforded genre directors from Spain the opportunity to work for Hollywood studios. For example, Juan Carlos Fresnadillo directed *28 Weeks Later* (2007), the much-anticipated sequel to *28 Days Later* (2002), for 20th Century Fox. Jaume Collet-Serra made *House of Wax* (2005) and *Orphan* (2009) for Warner Bros., and Gonzalo López-Gallego, made *Apollo 18* (2011) for the Weinstein Company. Even working outside Hollywood, Spanish genre directors are now able to make their own movies on a larger scale, with bigger budgets and international stars.

At the same time, Spanish horror cinema currently faces at least two existential threats. The first is that it might fall victim to its own success, leading to a potential "brain drain" (as more and more Spanish genre directors are siphoned off by Hollywood) and/or to a loss of national genre identity (as Spanish horror "goes Hollywood" in the pursuit of international box office). More than a few contemporary Spanish horror movies are already guilty of the latter, including *El arte de morir* (*The Art of Dying*, 2000), an avowed imitation of *Scream* (1996) (Lázaro-Reboll, 2008: 66–71); *H6: Diario de un asesino* (*H6: Diary of a Serial Killer*, 2005), a Spanish version of *American Psycho* (2000); *La habitación de Fermat* (*Fermat's Room*, 2007), a film heavily indebted to *Saw* (2004); and *Atrocious* (2010), a virtual remake of *The Blair Witch Project* (1999). The second existential threat faced by Spanish horror cinema is the European debt crisis triggered by the current global recession. This crisis has hit Spain particularly hard, resulting in a rapidly shrinking economy and mass unemployment, and prompting government austerity measures that have included higher taxes and drastic cuts to public spending. As a consequence, the Spanish film industry has seen its revenue drop at the same time it has seen its support from the state decline. Although horror has been one of the most robust sectors of the industry in the twenty-first century, its continued prosperity is by no means guaranteed — especially since the lion's share of government funding still available to filmmakers is earmarked for "quality" cinema (Jordan, 2011: 25). While its future is uncertain, however, its past offers hope. For from the unlikeliest of beginnings and through the darkest of times, Spanish horror cinema has developed into one of the richest and most distinctive national expressions of the genre not just in Europe, but in the world.

Patterns, Themes, and Motifs in Spanish Horror Cinema

The assertion that Spanish horror cinema exhibits certain unique characteristics that set it apart from the genre output of any other country may seem dubious at best. After all, Spanish horror is remarkably international in character, especially in regard to production. The vast majority of classic Spanish horror movies were made in partnership with companies in Italy, West Germany, France, the United Kingdom, and elsewhere in Europe. International coproductions made financial sense, as they allowed cash-strapped Spanish producers to share costs; they also afforded Spanish directors greater creative freedom, since they often involved shooting in countries where government oversight was less stringent. This practice continues unabated today, although the impetus is now more economic than political. In addition to relying on international financing, many Spanish horror filmmakers, past and present, have elected to shoot their movies in English—a tradition that dates as far back as Serrador's *The House That Screamed* (Lázaro-Reboll, 2004: 158) and remains a favored means of insuring commercial success both overseas and in Spain, where American cinema is considerably more popular than domestic fare (Jordan, 2011: 21). Another related strategy has been to feature international stars, from Christopher Lee to Nicole Kidman; indeed, with a few key exceptions, such as Paul Naschy or Belén Rueda, the lead actors in Spanish horror films tend to be foreign. Finally, it is important to note that the Spanish horror film industry itself has often been shaped by forces from abroad, both during the classic era, when many of the genre's main practitioners learned the ropes working for runaway Hollywood productions (Tohill and Tombs, 1994: 63), or more recently, as when American horror producer Brian Yuzna ran Filmax's Fantastic Factory label from 1999 to 2005 (Willis, 2008: 27). And the internationalism of Spanish horror cinema does not stop at the level of production; it is even apparent at the level of narrative and form. Spanish genre directors initially modeled their movies after British gothic movies and Italian *giallo* films; today, at least some of them take their cue from Hollywood horror, as discussed earlier. Moreover, in addition to being shot outside Spain, a great many Spanish horror movies are set outside Spain. During the Franco era, this was primarily to appease government censors, for whom the idea of a Spanish monster or horrific events occurring on Spanish soil was unacceptable (Lázaro-Reboll, 2005: 131); now it has more to do with the desire to appeal to an international audience. All of these facts problematize the notion of a "Spanish horror cinema," making it tempting to dismiss such a notion out of hand.

However, that would be a mistake, as there are a number of distinctive patterns, themes, and motifs found in Spanish horror cinema that suggest it does possess a strong national identity. One theme is that of antiauthoritarianism. In the classic era, this antiauthoritarianism was closely linked with the underground political opposition to Franco's regime and was expressed on film only allegorically, for obvious reasons. Early Spanish horror cinema is full, for example, of coded representations of the fascist state as a repressive social institution—often a boarding school or a correctional facility. This is the case in *The House That Screamed* and *99 Women* (1969), where the private girls' academy and the women's prison, respectively, become metaphors for a totalitarian political system that enforces discipline and conformity through surveillance and corporeal punishment. Classic Spanish horror movies also frequently deploy the figure of the sadistic or psychotic patriarch—the monstrous father — as a stand-in for Franco. This trope is evident as early as *The Awful Dr. Orlof*, in which the titular character commits horrific crimes in the name of restoring his daughter's beauty, and manifests itself in other mad scientist movies of the era, as well as in gothic horror films involving an ancestral curse passed from a paterfamilias to his descendants, as in *The Sadistic Baron Von Klaus* and *Frankenstein's Bloody Terror*. A related motif has the older generation representing Spain's ruling class, as in *A Bell from Hell*, where the conservative aunt cheats her unconventional nephew out of his inheritance by having him committed, or in Eugenio Martín's *Una vela para el diablo* (*It Happened at Nightmare Inn*, 1973), where two very traditional elderly innkeepers murder their young, sexually active female guests.

The antiauthoritarianism of classic Spanish horror cinema encompasses an antipathy toward religious power as well, which is not surprising given the Catholic Church's staunch support of Franco's regime. This attitude toward organized religion is apparent in the "truly anticlerical, sacrilegious tone" (Hawkins, 2000: 93) of the *Blind Dead* movies. It also clearly informs inquisition movies like *The Bloody Judge* and *Inquisición* (*Inquisition*, 1976), in which medieval church officials torture and execute accused witches, often for their own corrupt gain. The Spanish horror film's antiauthoritarian streak is prevalent in the transitional era as well, pervading pictures such as Naschy's *Latidos de pánico* (*Panic Beats*, 1983) and Martín's *Sobrenatural* (*Supernatural*, 1983), whose stories of dead patriarchs returning from the grave play on fears of the return of Francoist fascism. And it appears in contemporary movies such as Luis de la Madrid's *La monja* (*The Nun*, 2005), which concerns a group of women terrorized by the spirit of an evil nun, and *[Rec]²*, which reveals that a priest was responsible for unleashing the zombie-creating virus. Finally, it is apparent in the sympathy for the monster, the misfit, and the outcast that critics have detected in Spanish horror cinema — from Naschy's Waldemar Daninsky to the masked child, Tomás, in *The Orphanage* — which can be seen as the flipside of the genre's antiauthoritarianism.

A second key pattern in Spanish horror is the centrality of children. Since the 1960s, Spanish horror movies have been replete with heroic children, repressed children, terrorized children, ghostly children, possessed children, feral children, and even murderous children. Whatever their role, these children all have one thing in common: they have been victimized by those closest to them, a narrative trope that situates horror within the family. Typically, familial horror in Spanish cinema stems from a perversion of the parent–child relationship: rather than nurturing and protecting their young, parents often seek to betray and destroy them. In Jaume Balagueró's *The Nameless*, a girl is abducted by her father and initiated into his evil cult; similarly, in Balagueró's *Darkness*, the teenage heroine's grandfather has plotted the sacrifice of her father in order to open the portal to hell in their very home. We also find this trope in Plaza's *Second Name*, wherein the female protagonist uncovers her father's past membership in a religious sect devoted to the sacrifice of first-born children, and in Nacho Cerdà's *The Abandoned* (2006), which concerns a woman adopted from Russia who discovers that her deceased father killed her mother and has now returned from the grave to claim her life as well.

Even when parents in Spanish horror movies have their children's best interests at heart, they often inadvertently act against those interests, as in *The Others* and *The Orphanage*. Both films center on women who accidentally or in a moment of madness kill their own children, invoking, as Ann Davies (Davies, 2011: 81) writes, "the central motif of mother as monster." In these films, children clearly figure as victims, innocent casualties of their parents' wickedness, insanity, or inattention. This is even the case in Spanish horror movies where children emerge as killers. In *The House That Screamed*, for example, Luis's efforts to create the "perfect woman" out of the girls he murders are the product of his mother's overbearing possessiveness. Similarly, in *Shiver*, the deaths of the rural villagers at the hands of wild child Ángela (Blanca Suárez) are prompted by a local landowner's murder of her parents. Both movies ultimately present their killer kids in a sympathetic light, casting their homicidal tendencies as a product of parental (or adult) victimization. This is also true of the monstrous children in *Who Can Kill a Child?*, as suggested in the previous section. It is possible to read the antagonism between parents and their children in Spanish horror cinema allegorically as a conflict between the past and the future in which history itself becomes for the young "a monster to escape from, vanquish, eliminate and eventually overcome" (Acevedo-Muñoz, 2008: 215). If this is the case, though, it is by no means certain that children represent the promise that "history can still be remade and rewritten" (Acevedo-Muñoz, 2008: 215). Given how often these films' youngsters succumb to the oppressive weight of the past, it is perhaps more accurate to say that they represent Spain's fears that history has already written the present, leaving little hope for the future.

Lastly, eroticized violence is a major theme in Spanish horror cinema. During the 1960s and 1970s, eroticized violence was a hallmark of Spanish cinema in general. Marsha Kinder has shown that it was connected to a larger leftist critique:

> During the Francoist era, the depiction of violence was repressed, as was the depiction of sex, sacrilege, and politics; this repression helps explain why eroticized violence could be used so effectively by the anti-Francoist opposition to speak a political discourse, that is, to expose the legacy of brutality and torture that lay hidden beneath the surface beauty of the Fascist and neo-Catholic aesthetics. (Kinder, 1993: 138)

Although Kinder focuses on art films in her study, one could argue that the eroticized violence she describes is nowhere more apparent than in the Spanish horror movies of the time. We see it when Dr. Orlof strokes the bare breasts of one of his victims before surgically removing her face, or when Morpho paws a partially nude Wanda in *The Awful Dr. Orlof*. Jess Franco's subsequent movies are also full of such moments of erotic terror. In sex-revenge pictures such as *The Diabolical Dr. Z* and *Sie tötete in Ekstase* (*She Killed in Ecstasy*, 1971), female assassins murder their victims *in flagrante*, while scenes of sexual torture and humiliation fill S&M horror films such as *Eugenie* (*Eugenie … the Story of Her Journey into Perversion*, 1970) and *Sadomania*. Franco was by no means the only Spanish horror director who made movies that mixed sex and horror. Eroticized violence figures prominently in the films of José Ramón Larraz, especially *Vampyres*, which blurs the line between bloodletting and lovemaking, and *Los ritos sexuales del diablo* (*Black Candles*, 1982), which features orgies, rape, incest, and bestiality. We also find sexualized horror in many movies starring Paul Naschy, including José Luis Merino's *La orgía de los muertos* (*The Hanging Woman*, 1973), where the actor plays a necrophiliac gravedigger who fondles female corpses in his underground lair, and Naschy's own *Inquisition*, wherein he plays a Grand Inquisitor who takes perverse pleasure in torturing women accused of witchcraft. And while Kinder may be correct in her assertion that such eroticized violence was born out of the resistance to fascism in Spain, it outlived both Franco's regime and the classic era of Spanish horror cinema. We see it in transitional films such as Nacho Cerdà's infamous horror short *Aftermath* (1994), a clinical study of the mutilation and violation of a woman's body in a morgue, and in contemporary movies such as Adrián García Bogliano's *No moriré sola* (*I'll Never Die Alone*, 2008), a brutal rape-revenge picture set in Argentina. Like the motif of antiauthoritarianism and the pattern of familial violence surveyed above, the theme of erotic horror is a cornerstone of Spanish horror and one of the traits that makes it a unique national, as well as international, expression of the genre.

Gender and Sexuality in Spanish Horror Cinema

One of the most fascinating aspects of Spanish horror cinema is its treatment of gender and sexuality, which tends to be unconventional and even subversive. This has not been true, historically, of the genre as a whole. Where gender is concerned, horror movies frequently cater to the male gaze, casting women in the roles of fetishized sexual objects or avatars of the monstrous-feminine. Similarly, horror movies commonly cater to the straight gaze, deploying what Harry M. Benshoff (Benshoff, 1997: 2) calls "homosexual as monster" rhetoric. The lesbian vampire film, for example, has often been criticized for the way in which its scenes of objectified female vampires preying on other women work to construct "a vampire that serves only as a proscription—[one] perceived only as a transgression" (Case, 2000: 205). Perhaps surprisingly, given Spain's history as a country dominated by patriarchy and heteronormativity, where the "outlawing of any alternative didn't just make gay men and lesbians invisible, but also erased from public consciousness the plight of females who suffered from the institutionalised cult of machismo" (Stone, 2002: 184), many Spanish horror movies manage to avoid the sexism and homophobia that sometimes seem to be encoded in the genre's DNA. In fact, they frequently challenge such constructions of gender and sexuality, offering us not only female and queer characters that cut against the grain of patriarchal and heteronormative discourse, but also invite our performative identification with them.

To begin with, Spanish horror cinema often works to subvert gender norms at the level of representation. Key here is the recurring figure of the female protagonist. Women who take the lead in investigating and confronting the monsters that threaten them are remarkably prevalent in Spanish horror films. It is true, as Ann Davies (2011) points out, that in *The Orphanage* and a few other notable cases, the protagonist ultimately discovers that she herself is the monster, a narrative turn that obviously problematizes a feminist reading. More usually, though, female protagonists in Spanish horror movies struggle against male monsters aligned with the dominant patriarchal order. In many cases, the antagonist is in fact the monstrous father discussed earlier. This suggests another possible interpretation of the sadistic or psychotic patriarch in Spanish horror. While clearly functioning as an emblem of Franco's paternalistic dictatorship, especially during the classic era, the character can also be said to represent the more general threat of regressive masculinity; indeed, this would help explain his continued appearance in Spanish horror films long after the fall of fascism.

The role of the female protagonist in these films is to perform a critique of the male power structure by exposing the misogynistic brutality of the monstrous father. We see this, once again, from the very beginning of Spanish horror cinema in *The Awful Dr. Orlof*. As noted earlier, Wanda, the fiancée of the detective, plays a crucial part in solving the case. Masquerading as a potential victim, she "turns the tables and makes [Orlof] the object of her active, inquiring, investigative gaze" (Hawkins, 2000: 103). Significantly, she is not punished for "assuming the active male gaze and usurping police and patriarchal authority" (Hawkins, 2000: 103); rather, the film frames her actions as a form of gender justice. The fact that actor Diana Lorys plays both Wanda and Orlof's disfigured daughter, who, catatonic, is kept on display in a glass coffin in his laboratory, suggests that Wanda's victory over the mad scientist represents a "return of the repressed"—in this case, the reemergence of a female agency long suppressed by the dominant patriarchal order. Wanda is the first in a long line of female protagonists in Spanish horror cinema who do battle with monstrous fathers, one stretching all the way up to the heroines of contemporary genre movies such as *Darkness*, *Second Name*, and *The Abandoned*. Sometimes their antagonists are metaphorical rather than literal paternal figures—obsessive lovers, for example, or controlling mentors. Regardless of the nature of the villain, however, the female protagonist's conflict with him serves to illuminate the threat of regressive forms of Spanish masculinity. And even when the heroines in Spanish horror do not triumph, as Wanda does, over their adversaries, their defeat serves to underscore the repressiveness of patriarchal rule and the precariousness of women's place within it.

Spanish horror cinema also often works to subvert heteronormative sexualities. The character of the female protagonist is again typically involved, now joined in her struggle by a maternal monster with whom she forms a queer bond. Not surprisingly, the maternal monster is regarded as evil by the male characters, but that is not the way she is generally depicted; rather, she is presented as a "fairy godmother" whose embrace offers the protagonist a refuge from the straight world and a powerful alternative to its patriarchal and heteronormative definition of female sexuality. This is what we tend to see, for example, in the Spanish lesbian vampire film. Although critics have sometimes dismissed the subgenre as yet another instance of the "homosexual as monster" rhetoric that pervades horror cinema, Spain's lesbian vampires frequently emerge as sympathetic characters whose appeal is rooted in their transgressiveness and outsider status. In contrast, the heterosexual male representatives of "normality" — fathers, husbands, sons, and lovers — are almost always portrayed as possessive, domineering, and sadistic. Consider Vicente Aranda's *La novia ensangrentada* (*The Blood Spattered Bride*, 1972). A loose adaptation of Sheridan Le Fanu's 1872 novella *Carmilla*, it tells the story of a young newlywed named Susan (Maribel Martín) who finds that marriage is not all it is cracked up to be when her thuggish husband (Símon Andreu) begins treating her as little more than a sexual slave after they move into his isolated ancestral estate. Fortunately, her arrival awakens Mircalla Karstein (Alexandra Bastedo), an ancient vampire interred in the family crypt who seduces Susan and helps to plot her husband's demise. A "scathing critique of Spanish machismo" (Willis, 2003: 77), Aranda's film also offers "alternative views of the world, in particular relating to gender and sexuality" (Willis, 2003: 77). Indeed, it essentially posits that a lesbian relationship can be more fulfilling for women, both emotionally and sexually, than a conventional heterosexual relationship. The same basic theme is present in other Spanish lesbian vampire movies such as *Vampyres* and *Vampyros Lesbos*.

This theme also manifests itself in different subgenres. The thrust of Jess Franco's possession film *Les possédées du diable* (*Lorna … the Exorcist*, 1974) is nearly identical to that of *The Blood Spattered Bride*. It involves a teenage girl, Linda (Lina Romay), who is seduced and possessed by a maternal witch named Lorna (Pamela Stanford), despite the efforts of Linda's controlling father (Guy Delorme). Like Aranda's film, *Lorna … the Exorcist* effectively queers a popular type of horror cinema, repurposing it as a vehicle to challenge the norms governing female identity and sexuality. While rarer, there also exist Spanish horror movies that subvert normative notions of male identity and sexuality. Perhaps the best known is Eloy de la Iglesia's *La semana del asesino* (*Cannibal Man*, 1973), which concerns a slaughterhouse worker who is driven to murder a series of friends and acquaintances (including his fiancée) in part because of his inability to recognize and accept his homosexuality. His only potential salvation is his relationship with a gay neighbor, who offers him sanctuary and the opportunity to embrace his own identity. As Andrew Willis writes of the film, it does not present Marcos as "a conventionally 'evil' character" (Willis, 2005: 171); instead, "heterosexuality and the desire for sex with women are shown as restrictions that entrap him" (Willis, 2005: 172). In the end, he notes, it is the "socializing process of Spanish machismo" (Willis, 2005: 173) that is depicted as monstrous by De la Iglesia, not the queer hero. As in the lesbian vampire and possession movies, the protagonist emerges as a complex, sympathetic character, one who troubles pat notions of sexual identity, forcing us to consider the cost of denying sexual liberty — both to ourselves and to others.

Finally, however, it is important to note that the Spanish horror films discussed so far work to subvert the norms of sex and gender not only at the level of representation, but also at the level of spectatorship. For example, *The Blood Spattered Bride* encourages us to adopt a queer gaze that illuminates for us not only the possible alternatives to heterosexual desire, but also the appeal of such alternatives given the repressive nature of heteronormativity. From the beginning of the film, we are encouraged to identify with Susan's look rather than her nameless husband's: her trepidation at the sight of their marriage bed, her disgust at his incessant demands for sex, and—most importantly—her fascination with Mircalla. The two women frequently exchange lingering glances that audience members are invited to share via Aranda's use of point-of-view editing and eye-line matches, devices that suture us into the scene, affording us a queer first-person experience. Significantly, as the film progresses, these devices are never used when Susan and her husband interact; her growing alienation from him precludes the kind of intimacy that she and Mircalla enjoy. Instead, Aranda keeps our gaze aligned with that of the two women, prompting us to cheer on their efforts to be free of the strictures of the straight male world. Of course, their story cannot end happily—censorship under Franco's regime would not allow it—but the final moments of the film make clear Aranda's attitude toward the mandatory restoration of "normality." Having firmly established our identification with Susan and Mircalla, he has Susan's husband creep into the crypt where the two women sleep together and brutally murder them by firing his rifle repeatedly into their shared coffin and then slicing off their breasts and removing their hearts; he also executes his housekeeper's adolescent daughter, who reveals that she too has been bitten by Mircalla. The misogynistic and homophobic violence of this scene is so savage and extreme (and our empathy with the character who metes it out so slight) that it effectively serves to cement our alliance with the movie's queer heroines.

Spanish Art Cinema and Spanish Horror Cinema

A final facet of Spanish horror cinema to consider is its close, yet complex, relationship with Spanish art cinema. In his seminal essay on the connection between Spanish art and horror cinema, Andrew Willis (2003) demonstrates how art filmmakers working under Franco used the horror movie as a vehicle for expressing their opposition to fascism. Because the art film was subject to strict oversight by the government, which hoped to present it to the international community as evidence of Spain's progressiveness, directors committed to political resistance sought in the horror genre "a space to work that existed outside the 'art' cinema assimilated by the regime" (Willis, 2003: 75), so that they "could continue to explore contemporary social and political issues in their films" (Willis, 2003: 75) with less interference from censors. Making horror movies also allowed these directors to reach a wider viewership with their political message, since they were working in forms that "were popular with working-class audiences and therefore were not restricted to the government-sanctioned 'art house' cinemas" (Willis, 2003: 82). Willis's essay helps us understand why a group of politically committed Spanish art filmmakers — Eloy de la Iglesia, Vicente Aranda, and Claudio Guerín among them — would choose to work in the horror genre during the Franco era. It also furnishes us, however, with a rather one-sided view of the relationship between Spanish horror and art cinema, one in which art cinema emerges as a "good influence" on horror, imbuing it with a seriousness of purpose which it might otherwise have lacked; horror's effect on art cinema, meanwhile, is almost completely neglected. The fact of the matter is that horror movies have shaped art cinema in Spain in critical ways over the last half century or so. Accordingly, rather than focusing more attention on art cinema's gentrification of horror in this last section, I would like to examine the ways in which Spanish art films have been "genrified" and enriched by horror.

While the classic era of Spanish horror cinema may have been the heyday of art-influenced horror movies, it also saw the production of a number of art films that take both aesthetic and thematic inspiration from horror. Many of these films were directed by legendary auteur Luis Buñuel. To be sure, Buñuel's work included elements that could be considered horrific well before the advent of Spanish horror movies: the slashed eyeball in *Un chien andalou* (1929); the nightmarish dream sequence in *Los olvidados* (*The Young and the Damned*, 1950); or the roving disembodied hand in *El ángel exterminador* (*The Exterminating Angel*, 1962). It is interesting to note, however, that such moments appear with greater frequency and intensity in his later work, following the arrival of the horror genre in Spain. For example, in *Le charme discret de la bourgeoisie* (*The Discreet Charm of the Bourgeoisie*, 1972), there are two sequences that seem particularly indebted to Spanish horror. The first is often referred to as the *Lieutenant's Story*. Waiting for service in a tea room, three bourgeois women are joined by a young lieutenant who tells them that, as a boy, he poisoned the man he thought was his father after the ghost of his dead mother appeared to him and revealed that she and his real father, her adulterous lover, were in fact murdered by her husband. As the lieutenant relates his tale, we see it unfold in flashback. The scene relies heavily on the kind of imagery found in classic Spanish horror movies: the pale arm of the boy's mother reaching out to him from inside his bedroom armoire; the ghastly appearance of her lover, who was shot through the eye by her husband; the thunderstorm that rages outside as the two ghosts sit side-by-side on a bed silently watching the poisoned husband's death throes. Moreover, it features several motifs specific to Spanish horror cinema. Most prominent are the juxtaposition of children and violence, the theme of the monstrous father, and the focus on the plight of women in a patriarchal world.

Similar patterns are woven into the film's other prominent horror-inspired passage: the story of a police sergeant infamous for torturing prisoners who, after a violent demise, returns to the station every year in penance for his crimes. Again, Buñuel makes use of the visual trappings of Spanish horror (the suspenseful editing, the sergeant's gore-drenched ghost) while at the same time incorporating a number of its key motifs, such as the critique of authoritarianism and the notion that the present is continually haunted by the past. In both cases, borrowing aesthetically and thematically from the genre allows him to explore more deeply the dominant concern of his film (and indeed his career): the way in which the instruments of the unconscious—dreams, fantasies, desires—work to expose the facade of rationality, civility, and order erected by Western society. Buñuel was by no means the only Spanish art filmmaker who turned to horror as a means of enriching their work during this period. Víctor Erice's *El espíritu de la colmena* (*The Spirit of the Beehive*, 1973) uses a little girl's imaginary relationship with the Frankenstein monster to symbolize "a rebellion against Francoist repression and society's conformism" (De Ros, 2005: 141). Carlos Saura's *Cría cuervos* (1976) features another death-obsessed girl in a meditation on the way the sins of parents are often visited on their children.

The cross-pollination between Spanish art and horror cinema did not end with the genre's classic period. During the 1980s and 1990s, the figure of the serial killer popularized by horror movies such as *Pieces* and *Anguish* became an especially common trope in art cinema, one typically linked to the anxieties that attended Spain's shift from fascism to democracy. We see this trope in Pedro Almodóvar's *Matador* (1986), a dark comedy revolving around the twisted romance between a retired bullfighter, Diego (Nacho Martínez), and a high-powered female defense attorney, María (Assumpta Cerna), both of whom are serial killers whose lust is triggered by violence and death. By making a connection between Diego's machismo in the ring and the misogyny of his murders (he kills his female victims with his sword exactly as he might a bull), and by demonstrating the dangerous infectiousness of his bloodlust (both María and Diego's young protégé Ángel [Antonio Banderas] model themselves after him), Almodóvar expresses doubts about whether the sinister impulses that drove Franco's regime have truly been expunged from democratic Spain. The same question is raised by Luis Guridi and Santiago Aguilar in *Justino, un asesino de la tercera edad* (*Justino*, 1994), another dark comedy about a bullfighter-turned-serial killer. The murders perpetrated by Justino, a bullfighter forced into early retirement who takes revenge by continuing to practice his art on members of society, represent an "ironic staging of Spanishness" (Egea, 2008: 113) that confronts Spain's official representations of itself in the 1990s.

Easily the most disturbing art film of the period to repurpose the figure of the serial killer from Spanish horror is Agustí Villaronga's controversial *Tras el cristal* (*In a Glass Cage*, 1987). Tracing, Pasolini-like, the roots of fascism in sexual repression and violence, Villaronga tells the story of a former Nazi doctor, Klaus (Günter Meisner), who experimented on and sexually abused children in death camps during the war and is now living incognito with his family in a Spanish villa. Klaus has secretly continued to molest and murder boys while in hiding, but at the beginning of the film he tries to commit suicide, apparently in remorse for his crimes; the attempt fails, leaving him paralyzed and dependent on an iron lung. A mysterious young man, Angelo (David Sust), who has knowledge of Klaus's past subsequently appears and, blackmailing his way into the position of the ex-Nazi's nurse, begins carrying out the horrific misdeeds that Klaus is no longer willing or able to. Like *Matador* and *Justino*, *In a Glass Cage* posits a Spain in which the echoes of the past still reverberate in the present, perpetuating historical traumas and jeopardizing hope for the future. The revelation that Angelo is a former victim of Klaus's who has adopted his personality hammers home the theme of history repeating itself, as does the final scene, which shows us Angelo in the iron lung after his mentor's death, being tended to by Klaus's preadolescent daughter, whom Angelo has brainwashed. Although Villaronga's film could not be more different from the other two tonally, this theme—as well as the graphic violence associated with the serial killer movie—ties it just as closely to Spanish horror of the transitional era. In fact, there are many moments in the picture where the line between art and horror blurs, rendering one almost indistinguishable from the other and pointing the way toward a new, hybrid national cinema that might be equally indebted to both forms.

Such a cinema has effectively come to pass in the twenty-first century, which has seen Spanish art films borrowing from horror cinema more heavily than ever before. The best known example of this is undoubtedly Guillermo del Toro's *El laberinto del fauno* (*Pan's Labyrinth*, 2006), which is, to date, the most commercially successful Spanish-language film of all time. Although Del Toro is Mexican, *Pan's Labyrinth* is a Spanish coproduction shot in Spain and is deeply indebted to Spanish history and horror. Like his earlier genre-inspired art film *El espinazo del diablo* (*The Devil's Backbone*, 2001), *Pan's Labyrinth* is set in the era of the Spanish Civil War and concerns the devastating impact of that conflict on children. In it, young Ofelia (Ivana Baquero) moves to the countryside with her pregnant mother to join her new stepfather, a fascist officer committed to rooting out the last remnants of the Republican resistance. In the center of an overgrown labyrinth that sits next to the mill housing her stepfather's headquarters, she meets a magical Faun (Doug Jones) who recognizes her as an exiled fairy princess and tells her that she must perform three tasks in order to return to her underground kingdom. As the story progresses, Ofelia's two worlds—the fantastical world of the Faun and the all-too-real world of Francoist Spain—converge and finally collide with devastating consequences. Deploying horror and fantasy as its "main generic markers" (Lázaro-Reboll, 2008: 77), Del Toro's film also "connects to a long-standing Spanish cinematic tradition in which the main protagonist is a child dealing with traumatic experiences" (Lázaro-Reboll, 2008: 77–78), evoking classic art films like *The Spirit of the Beehive* and *Cría cuervos* that, as we have seen, were themselves influenced by horror. *Pan's Labyrinth* shares more with Spanish horror cinema than the theme of familial horror, however; it also adopts the genre's concern with the role of women in a patriarchal world. Indeed, its dramatic crux is Ofelia's defiance of not one but two monstrous fathers—her violent stepfather and the crafty Faun—both of whom she resists with help from her housekeeper, Mercedes (Maribel Verdú), who secretly works with the Republican rebels (Figure 21.3).

A critical focus on gender is apparent in other contemporary Spanish art-horror hybrids, such as Laura Mañá's *Palabras encadenadas* (*Killing Words*, 2003), a

Figure 21.3 Ofelia (Ivana Baquero) and the Faun (Doug Jones) in the contemporary Spanish art-horror hybrid, *Pan's Labyrinth* (2006). Directed by Guillermo del Toro. Produced by Estudios Picasso, Tequila Gang, Esperanto Filmoj, Sententia Entertainment, Telecinco, and OMM.

deconstruction of the serial killer film. Here, the figure of the serial killer becomes a vehicle not for addressing anxieties about lurking fascism in post-Franco Spain, but rather for exploring the status of gender relations and gender identity as the country moves into the twenty-first century. Mañá plays with familiar gender stereotypes, exposing them as such, but ultimately demonstrates that the patriarchal desire for authority over women—their bodies, their voices—persists in contemporary Spanish society. Pedro Almodóvar comes to a similar conclusion in his recent *La piel que habito* (*The Skin I Live In*, 2011), which tells the story of a brilliant plastic surgeon who develops an impervious, transgenetic skin that he grafts onto the body of a mysterious woman imprisoned in his home. Although the film clearly recalls *Eyes without a Face*, it also owes much to classic Spanish horror movies such as *The Awful Dr. Orlof*, particularly in its upending of gender norms: the captive female patient turns out to be a young man who raped the doctor's daughter, prompting her suicide; in revenge, the surgeon kidnaps the man and subjects him to a sex-change operation, using the experimental skin to transform him into a beautiful but deadly woman with whom he gradually falls in love. Like Del Toro and Mañá, Almodóvar blends art with horror in order to question conventional gender roles and challenge pat notions about gender identity.

The work of these directors—and that of the others discussed earlier—demonstrates that the relationship between Spanish art films and horror movies has been far from one-sided; art cinema has benefited from its association with horror at least as much as horror has benefited from its connection with art cinema. Along with its rich history, its trademark patterns, themes, and motifs, and its distinctive treatment of sex and gender, this special, symbiotic relationship is another unique facet of Spanish horror cinema. Although Spanish horror has frequently been regarded by critics as "an unacceptable part of Spanish film history" (Lázaro-Reboll, 2005: 129), it is a vibrant national tradition and a vital genre phenomenon eminently worthy of further study.

References

Acevedo-Muñoz, E.R. (2008) Horror of allegory: *The Others* and its contexts, in *Contemporary Spanish Cinema and Genre* (eds J. Beck and V.R. Ortega), Manchester University Press, Manchester, pp. 202–218.

Benshoff, H.M. (1997) *Monsters in the Closet: Homosexuality and the Horror Film*, Manchester University Press, Manchester.

Case, S. (2000) Tracking the vampire, in *The Horror Reader* (ed. K. Gelder), Routledge, London, pp. 198–209.

Davies, A. (2011) The final girl and monstrous mother of *El orfanato*, in *Spain on Screen: Developments in Contemporary Spanish Cinema* (ed. A. Davies), Palgrave, London, pp. 79–92.

De Ros, X. (2005) El espíritu de la colmena/Spirit of the beehive, in *The Cinema of Spain and Portugal* (ed. A. Mira), Wallflower, London, pp. 139–147.

Egea, J.F. (2008) *Justino, un asesino de la tercera edad*: Spanishness, dark comedy and horror, in *Contemporary Spanish Cinema and Genre* (eds J. Beck and V.R. Ortega), Manchester University Press, Manchester, pp. 107–121.

Hawkins, J. (2000) *Cutting Edge: Art-Horror and the Horrific Avant-garde*, University of Minnesota Press, Minneapolis.

Jordan, B. (2011) Audiences, film culture, public subsidies: the end of Spanish cinema? in *Spain on Screen: Developments in Contemporary Spanish Cinema* (ed. A. Davies), Palgrave, London, pp. 19–40.

Kinder, M. (1993) *Blood Cinema: The Reconstruction of National Identity in Spain*, University of California Press, Berkeley.

Lázaro-Reboll, A. (2004) Screening 'Chicho': the horror ventures of Narciso Ibáñez Serrador, in *Spanish Popular Cinema* (eds A. Lázaro-Reboll and A. Willis), Manchester University Press, Manchester, pp. 152–168.

Lázaro-Reboll, A. (2005) La noche de walpurgis/shadow of the werewolf, in *The Cinema of Spain and Portugal* (ed. A. Mira), Wallflower, London, pp. 129–136.

Lázaro-Reboll, A. (2008) 'Now playing everywhere': Spanish horror film in the marketplace, in *Contemporary Spanish Cinema and Genre* (eds J. Beck and V.R. Ortega), Manchester University Press, Manchester, pp. 65–83.

Olney, I. (2012) The whip and the body: sex, violence, and performative spectatorship in Euro-horror S&M cinema, in *Screening the Dark Side of Love: From Euro-Horror to American Cinema* (eds K. Randell and K. Ritzenhoff), Palgrave, New York, pp. 1–17.

Stone, R. (2002) *Spanish Cinema*, Longman, Essex.

Tjersland, T. (2003) Cinema of the doomed: the tragic horror of Paul Naschy, in *Fear without Frontiers: Horror Cinema across the Globe* (ed. S.J. Schneider), Flesh and Blood Press, Guilford, Surrey, England, pp. 69–80.

Tohill, C. and Tombs, P. (1994) *Immoral Tales: European Sex and Horror Movies 1956–1984*, St. Martin's Griffin, New York.

Triana-Toribio, N. (2003) *Spanish National Cinema*, Routledge, London.

Willis, A. (2003) Spanish horror and the flight from 'art' cinema, 1967–73, in *Defining Cult Movies: The Cultural Politics of Oppositional Taste* (eds M. Jancovich, A. Lázaro Reboll, J. Stringer, and A. Willis), Manchester UP, Manchester, pp. 71–83.

Willis, A. (2004) From the margins to the mainstream: trends in recent Spanish horror cinema, in *Spanish Popular Cinema* (eds A. Lázaro-Reboll and A. Willis), Manchester University Press, Manchester, pp. 237–249.

Willis, A. (2005) The Spanish horror film as subversive text: Eloy de la Iglesia's *La semana del asesino*, in *Horror International* (eds S.J. Schneider and T. Williams), Wayne State University Press, Detroit, pp. 163–179.

Willis, A. (2008) The fantastic factory: the horror genre and contemporary Spanish cinema, in *Contemporary Spanish Cinema and Genre* (eds J. Beck and V.R. Ortega), Manchester University Press, Manchester, pp. 27–43.

22

The Return of the Rural Repressed
Italian Horror and the Mezzogiorno Giallo

Xavier Mendik

Although initially dismissed for their lurid titles, explicit violence and convoluted plotting, the Italian *giallo* cycle is now widely recognized as one of the most significant horror formats of the 1970s. The cycle was often characterized by themes of alienated or foreign amateur detectives who travel to Italy, only to become inadvertently embroiled in a series of murders revolving around some aspect of unresolved sexual trauma. The resolution to these complex narratives frequently revealed not one, but multiple assailants, with a common theme of gender disassociation allowing women to be unveiled as the ultimate culprits behind these fictions. Even when the *giallo* did figure its central protagonists as Italian nationals, an element of "foreignness" was induced into a range of entries detailing a detective's journey to Italy's more "primitive" regions as part of the quest to uncover the killer's identity.

This vibrant but unconventional Italian series (most widely associated with the iconic director Dario Argento) has been the subject of a range of studies, which have evolved from journalistic defences of Argento as an auteur (popularized by the prominent film critic Alan Jones, 1996), to more formalistic studies on the *giallo*'s links to literary detective fiction traditions (Tani, 1984), before developing into detailed psychoanalytic accounts of the tortured protagonists in the film cycles that followed (Hunt, 2000; Hutchings, 2003; Mendik, 2000). This latter psychoanalytical variant of *giallo* theory has proven to be one of the most sustained modes of interpreting the cycle, with authors frequently evoking Freudian notions of the return of the repressed urges (Freud, 1991) to explain the thematic emphasis on unresolved primal trauma (which conflates violence and sexuality before an assembled viewer) underpinning many of the key entries to the cycle.

While acknowledging the significance of past primal trauma on the perverse terrain of the *giallo*, this chapter aims to expand the focus of these key accounts by considering the return of repressed material in a specific variant of the cycle, which I shall term the *Mezzogiorno giallo*. This subgenre is either partly set in the Italian South (using the motif of travel or mobility to bring outsiders into the nation's backwaters), or in a second variant, is fully represented in the rural sphere to allow for a more extended examination of the perverse and near pagan practices which reside therein. In either of these two variants, the *Mezzogiorno giallo* presents both individual maladies and sexual traumas concurrent with previous psychoanalytic readings on the format, alongside an important reading of the rural space as a zone of regional "excess," which warrants further theoretical contemplation from a specifically Italian perspective.

In making this observation, this current project follows the trajectory of recent studies on the *giallo*, which have begun to consider more fully the cycle in terms of both psychic trauma as well as the wider tensions in Italy during the 1960s and 1970s. For instance, in his brief but important overview "Playing with Genre: An Introduction to the Italian *Giallo*," Gary Needham situates the development of the cycle (from late 1920s literary product and imported novelizations) to two specific periods of cinematic activity, occurring between 1963–1964 and 1970–1975. Although the first period of *giallo* activity (strongly associated with director Mario Bava) witnessed relatively few releases identified with the trend, it remains significant for establishing not only a foundational iconography for the format (such as the use of costume to conceal the sexual identity of a killer), but also provided a firm nationalistic rationale to the emergence of the craze. For instance, commenting on the opening sequence to Mario Bava's early entry *La ragazza che sapeva troppo* (*The Girl Who Knew Too Much*, 1963), the author notes that the film introduces its heroine Nora Davis (Leticia Roman) reading a *giallo* novel on an airplane. While acknowledging the high degree of self-referentiality within the cycle, this scene also functions to highlight how the format reflected the changing socio-economic and cultural patterns in the Italy of the so-called 1960s economic miracle (Figure 22.1). As Needham notes:

> The entire scene is essentially a foundational gesture that brings together several elements all at once: the staging of the *giallo's* literary origins through *mise-en-abîme* … the foreigner coming to/being in Italy; the obsession with travel and tourism not only as a mark of the newly emerging European jet set (consider how many *gialli* begin or end in airports), but representative of Italian cinema's selling of its own "Italian-ness" through tourist hotspots … and of course fashion and style. (Needham, 2002: 2)

While Needham's comments indicate the extent to which such 1960s *gialli* clearly use tropes of travel to reflect Italy's changing status within the wider European sphere, the nation's emergent patterns of mobility and consumption are further evidenced by the author's observations on the centrality of fashion to these fictions. Indeed, Bava's later *Sei donne per l'assassino* (*Blood and Black Lace*, 1964), "situate[s] itself on the pulse" (Needham, 2002:2) of the nation's emergent clothing craze by staging its narrative action in a fashion house, where the models are being dispatched by two alternate killers (of differing genders).

Figure 22.1   A "foundational gesture" in Mario Bava's *La ragazza che sapeva troppo* (*The Girl Who Knew Too Much*, 1963): traveling heroine Nora Davis (Leticia Roman) reads a *giallo* novel on an airplane. Directed by Mario Bava. Produced by Galatea Film and Coronet s.r.l.

Although Dario Argento's 1970 debut *The Bird with the Crystal Plumage* ends, rather than begins at an airport, it confirms Needham's view that the cycle requires an analysis based on "the various associations, networks, tensions and articulations of Italian cinema's textual and industrial specificity in the post-war period" (Needham, 2002: 3). In the film, Tony Mussante plays Sam Dalmas, a frustrated American writer who witnesses the chance struggle and assault of Monica Ranieri (Eva Renzi) by an unidentified assailant in a Roman art gallery late one night. This violent act shifts Dalmas from unwilling witness trapped behind a set of glass doors by Monica's assailant, to police suspect. Remaining imprisoned on the premises when the police arrive, he has his passport confiscated by inspector Morosini (Enrico Maria Salerno), who links the incident to an ongoing series of sexual murders that have occurred against women in the city. In order to prove his innocence, Dalmas is forced to adopt the role of an amateur detective. Convinced that he can actually identify the killer, he tracks down a painting of a young woman being sexually assaulted by an unidentified assailant, which he believes is connected to the murderer's quest. This image is marked by a near-erotic component to mutilation, depicting a female victim being genitally mutilated by a concealed aggressor. Dalmas's status only shifts from suspect to victim after repeated attempts on his life and that of his girlfriend Julia (Suzy Kendall) reveal the killer to be Monica Ranieri herself. Returning to the gallery to confront the killer, Dalmas realizes that what he saw was Monica attempting to kill the unidentified man (her husband, Alberto). As a psychoanalyst explains during the film's resolution, Ranieri was in fact the girl depicted in the painting that Dalmas uncovered. Suffering a serious sexual assault as a teenager, she suppressed all memory of the event until she saw a copy of the painting in an antiques shop. On seeing the painting, Ranieri identified herself not as victim, but with the male aggressor that assaulted her, thus taking out her vengeance against women.

With its focus on a displaced American writer living in Italy, *The Bird with the Crystal Plumage* confirms the importance of transnationality to the cycle, while elevating the 1960s emphasis on fashion-houses to the more contemplative locale of the art gallery as a zone of transgression. Moreover, with its emphasis on a female killer masquerading as a male in order to replay past sexual traumas as the trigger for present transgressions, the film provided a crucial pathway between continental horror and psychoanalytic themes, to the extent that Garry Needham has argued, "The *giallo* is a paradigm case in defence of psychoanalysis. It solicits psychoanalytic interpretation and stages every Oedipal scenario literally and spectacularly" (Needham, 2002: 5). With its emphasis on a concealed scene of sexual violence, which afflicts both the killer and male amateur sleuth, Dario Argento's debut film placed the psychosexual "return of the repressed" at the center of the *giallo* narrative, providing a template that other *gialli* productions would draw on during the peak period of the cycle's production between 1970 and 1975.

However, the significance of *The Bird with the Crystal Plumage* lays not only in foregrounding perverse female aggression as a key narrative trope, but also for the way in which landscape and regionality became inculcated in the transgressions ranged across the narrative. Indeed, the key trigger for resolving the narrative quest is Sam Dalmas's journey to an unspecified rural region undertaken during the finale of the film. Here, he encounters Berto Consalvi (Mario Adorf), an itinerant artist whose pivotal painting of the unidentified woman being violated is revealed as the basis to Monica Ranieri's murderous campaign (Figure 22.2).

This fictionalized journey takes Dalmas away from the (limited but definable) security of the Italian city, to an unspecified and barbaric rural landscape that is the

Figure 22.2   Country Contacts: Sam Dalmas's Rural Encounter in *The Bird with the Crystal Plumage* (1970). Directed by Dario Argento. Produced by Central Cinema Company Film (CCC), Glazier, and Seda Spettacoli.

Figure 22.3   Rustic and Rusted: The Pre-Modernist Rural Space of *The Bird with the Crystal Plumage* (1970). Directed by Dario Argento. Produced by Central Cinema Company Film (CCC), Glazier, and Seda Spettacoli.

site of repressed knowledge, which also functions as a zone of temporal and social distinction from the metropolis. Here, the urban(e) investigator has to negotiate a barren "Other" environment, premised on its deviations from the sphere of modernist/technological advances (as evidenced in the scene where Dalmas is forced to ride in an antiquated truck to Consalvi's home in order to acquire information) (Figure 22.3).

Moreover, it is not merely technology which is retarded in the protagonist's rural encounter, but the social compact of civility itself. Not only is the interior of the artist's home defined by abject squalor (comically noted by Dalmas's expression on inspection of the premises), but his rationale for caging cats is ultimately revealed after he feeds his unwitting guest on the stewed corpses of the creatures. Indeed, even the character's sneering dismissal of Sam Dalmas as "Capitalist" at the end of their interaction indicates the depicted European inhabitant as beset by separate socio-political values, which negate their wider integration into the national *and* social body politic.

Horror Cinema and the *Mezzogiorno*

The South was one of Italy's most important banks of Otherness. The barbarous, the primitive, the violent, the irrational, the feminine, the African: these and other values, negatively connoted, were repeatedly located in the *Mezzogiorno* as foils to definitions of Italy. (Dickie, 1997: 119)

In many respects the depiction of Berto Consalvi's environment and persona from *The Bird with the Crystal Plumage* evokes a longer standing set of Southern representations, stereotypes, and mythologies, which can be traced back to the nation's alignment of the South under its uneasy incorporation into the Kingdom of Italy in the 1860s. According to John Dickie, the *Mezziogorno* or Southern rural zone has become an object of Northern intellectual, critical, and cultural concern since the late nineteenth century, where perceptions of rural life have conjoined with anthropological, sociological, and even eugenic-based studies, largely to sustain an established belief of the Italian South as "feudal, semi-civilized and even barbaric" (Dickie, 1997: 115). Indeed, citing the influence of Alfredo Niceforo's volume *L'Italia barbara contemporanea* (*Contemporary Barbarian Italy*, 1898), Dickie argues that the pseudo-scientific methodology outlined in the book (employing crime, birth, mortality, and even cranial data) initiated a template of regionalized (and indeed, racialized) distinction that continues to seep into popular culture *and* consciousness. As Dickie comments:

> Niceforo argues that Sicily, Sardinia and the Southern mainland are stagnating at an inferior level of social evolution to the northern and central provinces . . . . Italy's hopes for the future rest on its becoming a federal state, since specific forms of government are necessary to deal with the distinct characteristics of each region: government must be authoritarian in the South and liberal in the North. (Dickie, 1997: 115)

If constructions of this "imaginary South" (Dickie, 1997: 138) presume a distinct Southern body, regionally specific codes of (im)morality and localized modes of political affiliation, then these characteristics are clearly reproduced in a range of later Italian fictions including the *giallo*. Indeed, Mikel Koven's recent book-length study *La Dolce Morte: Vernacular Cinema and the Italian Giallo Film* (2006) offers a folklorist approach to the cycle, emphasizing the extent to which such narratives not only provided a mirror to the 1960s Italian economic miracle, but also facilitated a range of differing responses from those regional groups beyond the realm of such rapid industrialization. Here, these subcultural (or what Koven terms as *vernacular*) audiences reveal a resistance to both modernist modes of narration *and* the processes of modernization that accompanied the Italian economic advancement of the postwar years.

While Koven notes the *giallo's* essentially contradictory responses to the advances of modernism (through ambivalent representations of technology, mobility, and the amateur detective as a disruptive foreign influence), it is interesting to note how the South here figures as the return of the rural repressed, which displaces technocratic stimulus via immovable archaic and feudal modes of existence. This seems confirmed by historical data produced during the peak period of the *giallo's* production. For instance, Paul Ginsborg (1990), has defined the economic miracle as being of distinctly regional and "autonomous character" (Ginsborg, 1990: 216). This highly specific period of modernization concentrated on new growth industries and concurrent desire for consumer goods in the North-West and Central region, thus heightening "the already grave disequilibrium between North and South"

(Ginsborg, 1990: 216). As a consequence, regional inequality was also evidenced by marked patterns of migration between North and South during the period 1958–1963.

Arguably, the *giallo* directly responds to the geographical contradictions inherent in the economic miracle, by representing rural spaces as threatening locales that are on "the outskirts of the cities, marginalised and isolated from the modern urban experience" (Koven, 2006: 52–53). As a result, the monstrous potential contained within the motif of an amateur detective's Southern journey becomes a repeated trope within the *gialli* produced between the years 1970 and 1975, where the regional return of the repressed became associated with the eruption of prior crimes/memory traces, which subsequently infect the emancipated Northern sphere.

For instance, Argento restaged the trope of the urban detective's journey to the unspecified but uncivilized South with 1975's *Profondo rosso* (*Deep Red*), where pianist turned amateur sleuth Marcus Daly (David Hemmings) has to travel from Rome to an abandoned rural villa to unravel a (literally) repressed painting whose walled secrets reveal a murderously incestuous bond between a musical colleague and his mother. Beyond Argento's work, other key examples of this motif include Aldo Lado's *Chi l'ha vista morire?* (*Who Saw Her Die?*, 1972) and Sergio Martino's *I corpi presentano tracce di violenza carnale* (*Torso*, 1973), both of which also have significant rural inserts as part of their explorations of perversity. While the recurrence of the debased Southern journey across these titles substantiates Gary Needham's view of the regional space as a "locale of the uncanny" (Needham, 2002:5), it is interesting to note the extent to which not only its protagonists but also its landscapes are rendered libidinal.

For example, Sergio Martino's *Torso* remains a movie of two differing environments, with distinct modes of narrative impetus and audience appeal. The opening segment of the movie, which takes place in the plush Northern interiors of a University art department, is dominated by a marked drive toward character exposition (outlining how a group of female co-eds become the prey of a sexually voracious neck-tie killer). However, the closing rural sections of the movie are very much defined by grotesque/comedic and sexploitation traits with an emphasis on excess physiology. Here the heroine (played by *giallo* regular Suzy Kendall) and her surviving female friends seek refuge in a Southern holiday villa, only to find they are now subject to a new set of menaces that the environment contains. From groups of sexually coercive male villagers who constantly gaggle and gawk at the "exoticism" the young women represent, to leering comic locals reduced to hysterical displays in their presence, *Torso* presents both the landscape and its inhabitants as infantile yet sexually voracious. Importantly, not only was this reorientation of narrative toward grotesque typing and comic tradition commented on in the film's international reception, but a number of reviews also noted how the regional shift in the second part of the movie also foregrounded the role of landscape in these proceedings. For instance, *Variety* defined the "small city in the mountains" as "stunning" (*Torso*, 1974: 19), while John Duvoli's *Cinefantastique* review also concluded that the film's "Italian locations are an asset" (Duvoli, 1976: 31).

Do Not Torture the Landscape: Policies of the Picturesque

Rather than functioning as an isolated example, the regionalized foregrounding of the Southern landscape also occurs as a consistent trait within the *Mezziogorno giallo*, and this can once again be linked to the historically based tensions that the format evokes. For instance, John Dickie has identified a long-standing policy of the "picturesque" in relation to the Southern landscape, which helps to frame the region within ahistorical (and ideologically containable) parameters. In his study of popular journals such as *Illustrazione Italiana*, Dickie identifies the picturesque as present in a strategy of anaesthetizing the Southern landscape (via poetic literary prose and accompanying illustration), which serves up the South as a pastoral and nonthreatening ideal for Northern consumption:

> The word that most often encapsulates this elementary aesthetic *italianità* is "picturesque." A picturesque scene, custom or figure is foreign enough to be exotic, to belong to the poetic margin beyond a humdrum reality, and yet familiar enough to be soothingly Italian. (Dickie, 1997: 134)

These positive proclamations of landscape often stand in contrast to its depicted inhabitants, whom Dickie notes are constructed with a "crude aesthetic quality" (Dickie, 1997: 134) that nullifies the serious examination of the social or economic factors that underpin their malaise. Through this attempt to "anaesthetize social problems," the equation of the picturesque with the Southern landscape also affords "a conciliatory veil over an ugly or alien reality" (Dickie, 1997: 134).

Moreover, it is interesting to note how the Southern landscape here becomes synonymous with not only a catalogue of rural typage but also an increased aspect of polymorphous sexuality. For instance, to return to the international reception of Sergio Martino's film, it is noticeable that reviews such as *Variety*'s made a clear connection between the landscape and female sexuality, commenting that the film contained "stunning scenery and even more stunning girls" ensuring that "it should do excellently within its given market" (*Variety*, Torso, 1974: 19). These comments were echoed by other press accounts that defined the female characters "as predictably bosomy, leggy, and doe eyed" (Duvoli, 1976, 31), and highlighted the extent to which the first part of the movie was dominated by male protagonists (usually in the form of multiple suspects) with "the emphasis on heterosexual sex (intimated more than shown)." By contrast, the rural finale of the film foregrounds not heterosexual, but female sexualities, with the emphasis on "a dollop of lesbianism between the two girls" (*Variety*, Torso, 1974: 19).

Rather than just evidencing the predictable exploitation aesthetic, which aligns female sexual desire with uninhibited behaviour, the use of rural backdrops as spaces of gendered sexual exploration has a longer set of cultural values and myths once again linked with the *Mezziogorno*. Here, long-standing perceptions of the South as a zone of female dominance (sexual and matriarchal), functions via the belief that the region represents a reciprocity between the feminized and irrational. This is seen in Niceforo's conclusion that "Neapolitans, dissolute and weak by nature are a *popolo donna* (a 'feminine' people), while the Northern provinces represent a *popoli uomini* ('masculine' peoples)" (Cited in Gribaudi, 1997: 95). It is also reproduced in publications such as *Illustrazione Italiana*, which John Dickie has noted often traded on images of idealized peasant women and their location, representing an "anomalous position ... between the world of civilized progress and the spheres of either rusticity or barbarism. One of its tasks is to move the South nearer to 'us' when it is pastoral and nearer to 'them' when it is uncivilized" (Dickie, 1997: 135). The conflation between unabashed female sexuality and the rustic rural sphere is even more pronounced in those *Mezziogorno gialli* which are located centrally in the South, and detail Northern criminological investigations of past crimes committed within this archaic landscape. Key titles here include Lucio Fulci's *Non si sevizia un paperino* (*Don't Torture a Duckling*, 1972), as well as Pupi Avati's *La casa dalle finestre che ridono* (*The House with Laughing Windows*, 1976).

In the former film, detectives and journalists from Milan are drafted into the back-woods of the rural locale of Achendura, to apprehend the culprit who has been kidnapping and dispatching young boys there. From the outset, prominence is given to a range of sexually promiscuous and "mystical" females as potential suspects, including Maciara (Florinda Bolkan), whose alchemic beliefs and marginalization from extended kinship structures in the village ensure, in the words of Mikel Koven, that "She holds a liminal position within community as both insider and outsider" (Koven, 2006: 53). Maciara's near-Gothic construction is confirmed in the film's iconic opening scene, which juxtaposes the somewhat incongruous opening of a new motorway edged into the dirt track of the village, against close-up shots of the character's hands delving into the filth at the side of the viaduct in order to expose the buried foetus of a young child. From the very outset then, I would agree with Koven's observation that here the tension within the film is often regarding the vil-lagers' resistance or ambiguity toward modernity as a specific mode of "alien" North-ern advancement. Indeed, this disjuncture is also evident in Riz Ortolani's strident opening score, which mixes a jagged classical string composition with a traditional Italian folk ballad as if to signify an aural incompatibility between modernism and its macabre Other.

Rather than functioning in isolation, the pivotal role that Fulci's film attributes to female transgression extends beyond Bolkan's character, to include Patrizia (Barbara Bouchet), who is also a suspect for the child killings, due to the sexually inappropriate relations that she has with a number of young males in the movie. Indeed, she is introduced into the film attempting to seduce a clearly uncomfortable young boy, who finds her nude in front of a sunray lamp. Here, Fulci's camera alternates between Bouchet's self-confident nakedness and the pre-pubescent and poorly clothed body of the peasant child, reiterating the perverse disjuncture between them. As with Maciara, Patrizia remains another liminal female character within Achendura. Her ambivalent position is underscored by the architectural disparities associated with her status in the rural space. As we discover, Patrizia is a perennial wild child who is hiding out in the region having been arrested for drug use in Milan. Although she is associated with the accoutrements of modernism (from sports car to 1970s chic lava lamps) she derives from Southern stock, she is shunned because of her sophisticated pretensions. As the local police chief comments to Milanese investigators: "She was born here, her father made a fortune in Milan. You may have noticed that funny modern-looking type building on the way into town. Her father owns it, but he only built it for show, he hates the place." Indeed, the funny-looking building to which he refers, once again points to the disjuncture between modernist advancement and the rural space by occupying an incongruous position within a wider rural image of the picturesque.

However, while the film clearly fulfils Koven's division of the *giallo* as split between urban advancement and rural resistance, this spatial dichotomy comes to take on distinctly gendered connotations that exceed the film's disjuncture between the rational modernistic structures of (masculine) advancement/surveillance and the feminist, fleshy, irrational landscape. The female association to the landscape extends to include a psychic and libidinal dimension that utilizes the use of infantile cries to puncture the soundtrack during Maciara's frequent excavations of the soil. As we discover, although not the killer in the narrative, she (and the rest of the town folk) are responsible for the illegal concealment of the corpse of her illegitimate child years earlier, thus further conflating illicit acts with the Southern soil on which modernist advancement takes place. That landscape evokes the return of the repressed that Linda Ruth Williams (1995) has identified in her reading of John Boorman's *Deliverance* (1972), namely a rural locale that conveys "The feeling that something is in the process of being lost or buried … " (Williams, 1995: 138). For Williams, the central role that landscape has in Boorman's film is vividly demonstrated in the film's final shot, when a cadaverous hand emerges from an otherwise placid country lake as evidence of violent sexual conflict between barbaric locals and four urban males on a fishing vacation.

As with Boorman's film, the *Mezziogorno giallo* uses landscape (and its association with the female body and its irrationalities) to add an important psychic dimension into the Southern picturesque. This chimes with Williams's account of the libidinal antagonists of *Deliverance*, whom she defines as "too 'natural' to be properly human … to intimate with, and isolated by, the natural … landscape … So natural are these people that they have become unnatural … " (Williams, 1995: 139). It is further evidenced by the disenchanted Milanese police inspector who finds Maciara bludgeoned to death by the side of the new motorway after locals have wrongly assumed she is the child-killer. As he comments, "A horrible crime … bread of ignorance and superstition. We construct gleaming highways, but we are a long way from modernizing the mentality of people like this." Although the resolution of the film reveals the child killer to be the local priest Don Alberto Avallone (Marc Porel), the associations between repressed transgression and the "feminine" remain prominent by virtue of the assailant's attire and family connections. As Mikel Koven has noted:

> The ambiguity of gender with regard to the priest's cassock also points to an ambiguity of gender with regard to priests themselves. — They are born men, but cannot live "like men," from a heteronormative context of Italian masculinity and machismo. (Koven, 2006: 103)

Primal Peoples, Primal Drives

Although I would argue that the *Mezziogorno giallo* has yet to receive extended theorization in accounts of the genre, it remains significant for representing the rural space to explore wider sexual and social tensions within the national psyche. In these narratives, the conflation of unresolved psychic aberration with an "untamed" landscape facilitates a kind of return of the rural repressed, where the environment and its inhabitants come to signify a monstrous mode of expression that must remain submerged within the civilized Northern consciousness. As Gabriella Gribaudi has noted, this paradoxical strategy of revering the rural space, while condemning its protagonists has long-standing historical foundations because of which

> ... the South appeared to be a "paradise inhabited by devils." The South was a marvellous and happy land, while the inhabitants were savages. The immoral behaviour and lack of civilisation were precisely the product of the climate and the pleasant and attractive countryside which made it possible to live in a state of nature, a primitive contentment allowing only for the most extreme and basic passions. (Gribaudi, 1997: 88)

This disjuncture between a rural ideal and its aberrant inhabitants becomes more pronounced in those *gialli* set centrally in the South, as the above case-study of *Don't Torture a Duckling* indicates. Another significant example of the *Mezziogorno giallo* is Pupi Avati's *La casa dalle finestre che ridono* (aka *The House With Laughing Windows*, 1976), which uses a rural backdrop to explore startling themes of male masochism and gender ambiguity. Following the pattern of Argento's influential debut, Avati's film also employs the central image of a painting that resurrects repressed sexual urges, though here they are used to evoke scenarios of male suffering and annihilation, rather than an image of female genital distress. As indicated in psychoanalytic studies of the genre, if primal tensions remain unchecked, they perpetuate both a fatalistic pattern of compulsive repetition, as well as perverse forms of gender orientation. These are reproduced in Avati's film through a preoccupation with both transsexual and masochistic male imagery.

This pattern is demonstrated in the film's startling sepia opening montage, which depicts a partly clad and bound male being brutalized in slow motion by two unidentified figures, while his suffering is being simultaneously reproduced as a macabre painting. Echoing the often violent distortion of erotic content characteristic within the *giallo*, it seems significant that the off-screen dialogue that accompanies this sequence is coded in explicitly sexual terms. Here, the narrator discusses the punishment enacted against the depicted male body in near pornographic tone, noting that the colours of his canvas are "hot like fresh blood … the liquid flows down my arms…." This macabre variant of ejaculation is reproduced as the camera pans down the bloodied torso of the male victim during the narration. The sexualization of these scenes of primal violence is reiterated by the narrator's later comments: "Death, I can tell it's coming … Oh my God, Oh my God! I am dying, purify me," thus linking orgasmic excess to the scenes of aggression being depicted.

While many psychoanalytical studies have focused on the way in which visual content can reproduce unrepressed primal structures, Freud (1983) also examined the extent to which these infantile echoes can be recast as aural patterns, a trope reproduced by the audio recordings that come to dominate Avati's film. The voice-over narration is revealed to be that of Buono Legnani (Tonino Corazzari), a controversial and celebrated artist from a remote rural town, whose images of extreme agony sketched from models at the point of death earned him the title of "The Painter of Agonies." As we discover, the now dead artist's reputation still casts an obscene air of celebrity over the remote town, whose residents have decided to restore one of Legnani's church frescos (which depicts Saint Sebastian being attacked by two unidentified aggressors) in a bid to attract more Northern tourists. As a result, the post-credit sequence depicts art historian Stefano (Lino Capolicchio) arriving at the region, which instantly connotes the distinction between the idyllic landscape and its aberrant inhabitants that Gabriella Gribaudi has defined. Here, a gradual close-up shot of the town's pier reveals Stefano's new benefactor to be Solmi: the dwarf turned self-styled mayor who is attempting to reverse the town's fortunes. Although Solmi proudly informs his new employee that alongside the infamy of Legnani's paintings, the region is also famed for the "women, the water, and silence!", Stefano's landlady vocalizes the decay evident in the town: "The last tourist I saw was a Nazi, and that was in the 1940s!"

Beyond the figure of Solmi, it is noticeable that *The House With Laughing Windows* revels in a pantheon of physiological abnormality, which is displayed before Stefano in communal settings such as the town's (singular) restaurant, as if he were a forensics rather than an art expert. These images of the aberrant rural body very much mirror what writers such as Linda Ruth Williams have identified in studies of American backwoods texts such as *Deliverance*. Here, physiological imperfection is signified by bodily and behavioural characteristics that include "bad teeth, worn dungarees … lazy demeanour appropriate to long hot afternoons lounging on the peeling veranda—as well as their willingness to go one step further as the monstrous hillbillies of horror" (Williams, 1995: 139). Williams's comments about the essentially backward nature of the backwoods dweller's evolution also reiterate the concept of "temporal discrepancy" that Annalee Newitz has identified in the American "white-trash" horror film (Newtiz, 1997: 134). These narratives of physical and psychic regression reflect urbanite fears about the lack of development within the

untamed rural sphere, rendering the inhabitants of the countryside (and their bodies) as a source of both repulsion and fascination.

However, the monstrous nature of the *Mezziogorno giallo* even outstrips the abnor-
malities identified by writers such as Williams and Newitz, with texts such as *The
House with Laughing Windows* adding an important angle of gender ambiguity to
the return of the rural repressed. For instance, although the artist Legnani is revealed
to have perished in an act of horrific self-mutilation before the start of the narrative, his personality (and body) is kept alive by both the delirium of his murderous
audio recordings, as well as his self-portraits, which proudly hang in local digni-
taries' homes. When the restaurant owner shows one of these paintings to Stefano, to
explain the artist's limited success with women, the transgendered nature of his body
(replete with breasts and long feminine hair) becomes become startlingly apparent. Importantly, given the familial perversions that come to underpin such Italian
variants of the *Mezziogorno giallo*, the film seems to echo Williams's analysis of *Deliverance*, where:

> The rural family of cinema horror is disturbing for classically Freudian reasons: this is
> a composite monster rendered from recognizable elements of backwoods America and
> the awful suspicion that interbreeding and literal mother-fucking have shredded the
> vestiges of behavioural control … Uneasy glimpses of bodies which (we assume) wear
> the symptoms of incest push the film into difficult territory from the start. (Williams,
> 1995: 139–140)

As Williams continues, such narratives absorb horrified Northern tourists in "a sticky
genetically intensified web made by too much family" (Williams, 1995: 140).

While the proliferation of eugenic and other pseudo-scientific studies have
attempted to define, categorize (and criminalize) defective Southern American
family genes, I am interested in how this vocabulary of Otherness has been similarly
transposed into the *too much family* of the *Mezziogorno giallo*. For instance, the
familial basis to unexplained murders that occur after Legnani's death comes as
little surprise, with the finale revealing that the artist's geriatric sisters have been
mutilating male victims in a similar manner to the St. Sebastian pose that their
brother first depicted. Indeed, this conflation of carnage with creativity is verbalized
in the final moments when a fatally wounded Stefano realizes the murderous
connection between the two elderly women from the statement: "That is a lovely
wound. Legnani would make a masterpiece out of that!" The actions of these aging
matriarchs (which are in effect mirrored by the mother of the killer priest in *Don't
Torture a Duckling*) both confirm the ambivalent sexual power that these women
retain within the *Mezziogorno giallo*, while also pointing to the network of social
power they weave across their depicted communities. This is confirmed when
Stefano seeks solace from his attackers, only to have his "foreign" status confirmed
when the townsfolk ignore his pleas and refuse him entry to their homes.

These events suggest that the town effectively accepts and justifies the Legnani
family's violations, thus indicating a communal basis to the notion of *too much family*, which can also be analyzed from a specifically Italian context. Indeed, noting the

connections between Italian and American accounts of the rural Other, Gabriella Gribaudi has identified the cultural significance of the American sociologist Edward Banfield's study *The Moral Basis of a Backward Society* in relation to the ongoing debates around the Southern problem. Here, Banfield used a year-long observational study of the impoverished Italian village of Basilicata to consider the extent to which the Southern regions were becoming more disenfranchised as the result of rapid economic development. To exemplify this Southern position of regression, Banfield formulated the concept of "amoral familialism" to explain a regional rejection of the cultural and socio-political bonds associated with modernity and its advancement. Rather than a shared belief in a cohesive social body,

> the term "amoral familialism" describes a form of behaviour directed solely towards the good of the family, understood here in the more restricted sense of parents and children. It implies therefore an endemic inability to act in the common good — what is popularly called a lack of civic consciousness. It is related to societies where the fundamental unit is the nuclear family and more complex forms of social organization are absent. (Gribaudi, 1997: 107)

As Gribaudi notes, Banfield's study was initially published in 1957, receiving its Italian translation as early as 1961, precisely because the amoral familialism concept fitted so well with existing constructions of the South as dominated by the role of brigandage over that of legality, and the dominance of vendetta (between families) over the concept of the civic society. In broader cinematic terms, the visual vocabulary of amoral familialism ensures the rural return of the rural repressed in a variety of Italian cult genres from the *Mezziogorno giallo* (with its emphasis on defective female-dominated family structures), to the rogue cop series (which charts the dissolution of legality through endless vendetta and bloodletting), and even erotic genres (where Southern social mores privilege kinship-libido over morality issues).

Indeed, amoral familialism also functions within the *Mezziogorno giallo* to destabilize any moral and social institutions that do operate according to some degree of social order, as in the case of the Catholic church. Koven's analysis of the *gialli* produced during the 1970s has identified a subgenre of the cycle as dominated by killer priests, but fails to explore the significance of these representations within the traditionally religious heartland of the Italian South. As with the killer from *Don't Torture A Duckling*, the perverse cleric of Avati's film is shown to privilege ritualistic familial perversion over communal and moral duty. This subversion of the priest's role is given added dramatic weight in the shock ending of *The House With Laughing Windows* when the priest who has befriended Stefano is revealed to one of Legnani's sisters, who has been living (and accepted) in the community under the transsexual guise as a male cleric. This startling gender revelation is demonstrated when the cleric removes "his" robe to reveal a firm pair of breasts beneath, the freeze-frame ending on Stefano's shocked reaction indicating that his final fate at the hands of the return of the rural repressed remains unresolved. In many respects, the open-ending to Avati's film provides an appropriate (lack of) closure to the threat that the return of the Other evokes. Situated between the psychic disturbance of the unrepressed urge and the embodiment of an over-naturalized landscape, the freeze frame ensures that:

> this is an open text, not simply because of its inconclusiveness, its "failure" to resolve meanings, but in the way it keeps anxiously returning to its own past. Repression and remembering are intimately bound to each other across the different moments that the subject inhabits (both the characters on screen and the audience, who are invited into identification with their disruptive sense of "rewritable" reality). (Williams, 1995: 144)

What the ending to Avati's film also confirms is that rural Italian horror remains a space where social phobia and psychic disturbance meet. That *The House With Laughing Windows* remains such a startling film is attributable to the fact that its imagery draws on the long-standing and submerged fears around the monstrous nature of the Southern Italian that can be defined under the title of the *Mezzogiorno giallo*.

References

Dickie, J. (1997) Stereotypes of the Italian South, in *The New History of the Italian South: The Mezzogiorno Revisited* (eds R. Lumley and J. Morris), Exeter University Press, Exeter, pp. 114–148.

Duvoli, J. (1976) "*Torso*" (Review). *Cinefantastique*, **4** (4), 31.

Freud, S. (1983) A case of paranoia running counter to the psychoanalytic theory of disease, in *On Metapsychology* (ed. S. Freud), Penguin Books, London, pp. 148–158.

Freud, S. (1991) From the history of an infantile neurosis (The Wolf Man), in *Case Histories II* (ed. S. Freud), Penguin Books, London, pp. 227–345.

Gribaudi, G. (1997) Images of the south, in *The New History of the Italian South: The Mezzogiorno Revisited* (eds R. Lumley and J. Morris), Exeter University Press, Exeter, pp. 83–114.

Ginsborg, P. (1990) *A History of Contemporary Italy 1943–1980*, Penguin Books, London.

Hunt, L. (2000) A sadistic night at the opera: notes on the Italian horror film, in *The Horror Film Reader* (ed. K. Gelder), Routledge, London.

Hutchings, P. (2003) The Argento effect, in *Defining Cult Movies: The Cultural Politics of Oppositional Taste* (eds M. Jancovich, A.L. Reboll, J. Stringer, and A. Willis), Manchester University Press, Manchester, pp. 127–141.

Jones, A. (1996) *Mondo Argento*, Midnight Media Publishing, Cambridge.

Koven, M.J. (2006) *La Dolce Morte: Vernacular Cinema and the Italian Giallo Film*, The Scarecrow Press Inc., Lanham.

Mendik, X. (2000) *Tenebre/Tenebrae*, Flicks Books, Trowbridge.

Needham, G. (2002) Playing with genre: an introduction to the giallo. *Kinoeye: New Perspectives on European Film*, **2** (11), 1–7.

Newitz, A. (1997) White savagery and humiliation or a new racial consciousness in the media, in *White Trash: Race and Class in America* (eds M. Wray and A. Newitz), Routledge, London, pp. 131–155.

Tani, S. (1984) *The Doomed Detective: The Contribution of the Detective Novel to Postmodern American and Italian Fiction*, Southern Illinois University Press, Illinois.

"*Torso*" (1974), *Variety*, 13th November, p. 19.

Williams, L.R. (1995) *Critical Desire: Psychoanalysis and the Literary Subject*, Edward Arnold, London, pp. 125–154.

23

Recent Trends in Japanese Horror Cinema

Jay McRoy

With a rich and vital history that dates back nearly to the origins of film as a commercial medium, Japanese cinema has long been recognized not only for its stylistic diversity and visionary directors, but also for the national and global influence of its genre films. From the subtle yet emotionally devastating family dramas of Yasujirô Ozu, Mikio Naruse, and Hirokazu Kore-Eda to the kinetic samurai epics (*chanbara eiga*) of Akira Kurosawa, Kihachi Okamoto, and Hiroshi Inagaki, Japanese film continues to leave its indelible impact on filmmakers and cinephiles. One of the most popular genres to emerge in the decades following Japan's defeat in the Second World War was the horror film. This is perhaps not surprising, especially given the extent to which the horror genre's preoccupation with the uncanny and "monstrous" hybridity provides a social barometer for a myriad of cultural anxieties. Ishirô Honda's *Gojira* (1954) and the parade of giant monster films (*daikaiju eiga*) that followed in its wake [e.g., *Rodan* (1956), *Mothra* (1961)] clearly reflected national concerns over the impact of US nuclear testing along the pacific rim and evoked painful memories of the atomic destruction of Hiroshima and Nagasaki, the literal and figurative "fallout" of which is still being felt to this day. Although largely grounded in socially specific dreads, these apocalyptic cinematic spectacles also resonated with viewers beyond Japan's shores. One need only recall the deluge of Hollywood B-movies about mutated insects wreaking havoc on American towns and metropolitan centers [e.g., *Them!* (1954), *Beginning of the End* (1957)] to evidence the extent of this profound cross-cultural phenomenon.

Postwar Japanese horror cinema likewise saw the rise of the *kaidan*, or ghost story. Inspired by the Buddhist parables of the sixteenth and seventeenth centuries, and visually reminiscent of Noh theatre's popular revenge- (*shunen-mono*) and ghost- (*shura-mono*) plays, as well as Kabuki theatre's frequent depictions of supernatural

A Companion to the Horror Film, First Edition. Edited by Harry M. Benshoff.
© 2014 John Wiley & Sons, Inc. Published 2017 by John Wiley & Sons, Inc.

incursions into mortal realms, these films predominantly featured "wronged" female entities (*onryō*) returning to exact vengeance on the living. Several of Japan's most acclaimed filmmakers directed remarkable *kaidan* during the 1950s and 1960s, and these works regularly garnered major prizes at home and abroad. Kenji Mizoguchi's *Ugetsu Monogatari* (1953), for example, won the Silver Lion at the 1953 Venice Film Festival, and Kaneto Shindô's *Onibaba* (1964) won the prestigious Blue Ribbon Award from Tokyo film journalists. Perhaps most impressive was the tremendous global approbation showered on Masaki Kobayashi's *Kaidan* (1965). One of the most critically lauded motion pictures in Japanese cinema, at least in the years immediately following its release, *Kaidan* won the Kinema Jumpo Award for Best Screenplay in 1965, the Jury Special Prize at the 1965 Cannes Film Festival, and the Oscar for Best Foreign Film at the 1966 Academy Awards.

Similarly, with their roots in cultural, folkloric, and theatrical traditions largely unfamiliar to foreign audiences, Japanese horror cinema of the early 1990s offered Western horror fans the kind of novel, visually arresting texts many were seeking. Consequently, as a new wave of Japanese horror films emerged at the tail end of the 1980s and slowly found its way into Western markets, horror aficionados embraced these uncanny works as welcome alternatives to genre conventions that many saw as having become monotonous and stale. As critics such as Collette Balmain (2006), Tom Mes and Jaspar Sharp (2004), Jim Harper (2009), and McRoy (2008) have illustrated, the impact of Japanese horror films during late 1980s to early 2000s was seismic. This was due in large part to the international success of motion pictures such as Shinji Tsukamoto's *Tetsuo, the Iron Man* (1989), Hideo Nakata's *Ringu* (1998) and *Dark Water* (*Honogurai mizu no soko kara*, 2005), Takashi Miike's *Audition* (*Ôdishon*, 1999), Takashi Shimizu's *Ju-on* films (2000–2004), and Kinji Fukasaku's *Battle Royale* (*Batoru rowaiaru*, 2000), to name only a few. For audiences outside of Japan, these films' apparent originality and distinctive visual and narratological trappings galvanized a generation of horror fans desperate for alternatives to the all-too-familiar "homegrown" fare playing on the screens of suburban multiplexes and lining the shelves of corporate-owned video stores. This international dissemination of Japanese horror films, as well as the deluge of imitations and transcultural remakes that soon followed, was driven by a constellation of cultural and economic factors. These included—but were by no means limited to—the steady proliferation of Internet newsgroups and fan pages, the emergence of online merchants and torrent sites specializing in "rare" and "hard to find" works of cinema from around the globe, and the establishment of distribution companies that readily adopted sensationalist monikers such as "Tokyo Shock!" and "Asia Extreme" to market films that, while often "marginal" within their nations of origin (Shin, 2008: para. 23), nevertheless possessed a sensibility many Western horror movie fans found strangely appealing… or perhaps *appealing* because of their apparent *strangeness*.

As Chi-Yun Shin notes in his essay, "The Art of Branding," distributors of East Asian horror cinema in general, and Japanese horror cinema in particular, were quick to capitalize on the idea of the Eastern "Other" as the originator of bold new cinematic spectacles featuring uncanny, "boundary-pushing" depictions of corporeal monstrosity and/or extreme physical violence. "[T]he output of the [Asian Extreme] label," Shin writes, "and indeed the name of the label itself, invoke[s] and rel[ies] on the western audience's perception of the East as weird and wonderful, sublime and grotesque" (para. 7). Such marketing practices occasionally resulted in confusion between national cinemas (i.e., Korean horror films mistakenly perceived as works of Japanese cinema), as well as hasty generalizations regarding the significance of the films' content. Even the most cursory perusal of message boards dedicated to Asian horror cinema on popular web sites such as the *Internet Movie Database* (*IMDB*) reveals an expansive predisposition toward describing Japanese horror films as paradoxically more restrained—with a greater focus on tonality—*and* more "over-the-top," depicting violence and gore in ways that exceeded/differed drastically from representations of bodily trauma showcased in horror films dominating Western markets.

This Orientalist, and Orientalizing, tendency likewise extends to the critical discourse surrounding explorations of Japanese horror cinema by North American and European scholars. Indeed, as the popular US film critic Kent Jones reminds us, such impulses inform Western film criticism on multiple levels of sophistication and across numerous media:

> If we are completely honest with ourselves, we should admit that whenever we immerse ourselves in the contemplation of any foreign cinema, we have a vested interest in preserving its foreignness, thus keeping it untouched.... I think that all that specialized knowledge among western experts has the paradoxical effect of preserving and even enlarging said foreignness, as opposed to diffusing it. Sensitive viewers may adjust the reality-measuring they habitually bring to their own native cinema in order to accommodate a presumed or posited reality, but I think that they keep the exoticism of what they're watching carefully intact ... (2003: 46)

Jones's point regarding the challenges critics face when writing about cinema from national and cultural frameworks that differ significantly from their own is sound, and the discursive exoticization informing "J-horror's" reception and analysis in Western markets is every bit as profound as the shock/startle effects that seemingly exceed cultural differences. Many US viewers of Japanese horror cinema, for instance, may lack the knowledge necessary to decode certain socially specific meanings imbedded within a given film, but this does not mean that they will necessarily react to a work's affective style, or to an especially shocking moment, in a manner antithetical to Japanese audiences.

Dead Wet Girls with Long Black Hair

As is often the case with genre films from any culture, financially successful formulae invariably give rise to numbing uniformity as producers scramble to capitalize on the success of popular films by creating a spate of motion pictures designed to imitate the visual and narratological tropes that led spectators to distinguish the genre's offerings as "fresh" and "exciting" in the first place. It is just this phenomenon that lends this section its subtitle. As a professor of cinema studies at a modest state university in the Midwestern US, I witnessed firsthand the fervor with which the most recognizable Japanese horror films of the mid-1990s to early 2000s were met by fans and critics alike. Similarly, I observed the waning enthusiasm that subsequently greeted the parade of mediocre imitations and increasingly ineffectual Hollywood remakes. As one student who avidly embraced the initial influx of Japanese horror cinema into US theatres and video stores commented when I told him that I had been commissioned to write the very words you now read: "Oh great! So you get to what … watch even more movies [like *Ringu*] about dead wet girls with long black hair?" While this student's reply elicited a chuckle from me, if only in response to its sweeping reduction of a rich and diverse cinematic tradition to a few of its most conspicuous signifiers, it also engendered some crucial aesthetic and cultural reflection.

How, for example, should critics attempt to engage analytically with the ways in which contemporary Japanese horror cinema has transformed over the last 15–20 years? The task presents a substantial challenge, as many thriving subgenres have developed. What's more, contemporary Japanese horror cinema frequently intersects with other genres, such as "cyberpunk," "the detective film," and even "teen paranormal romance." In this way, Japanese horror cinema resembles the myriad bodies that populate not only the genre's most popular narratives, but also the radically transforming urban and suburban centers from which many of its viewers emerge. Japanese horror cinema's tendency toward graphic depictions of hybridity and mutation mirror both the tradition's multiple depictions of the fusion of the biological and the mechanical, as well as the genre's preoccupation with themes of transience, mutability, and adaptation as responses to socio-cultural and ecological change.

Following Kent Jones's insightful admonition, this essay does not pretend to erase, nor indeed does it possess the capacity to mitigate or privilege, Japanese horror cinema's "foreignness" (46). In this sense, my project in these pages is deliberately modest. Rather than endeavoring to provide anything remotely close to an exhaustive "state of the genre" assessment, an undertaking that would require an entire volume of criticism at least, this essay briefly engages with two particularly compelling developments within contemporary Japanese horror cinema. From an exploration of the emergence of a gory, hyper-stylized, and extremely popular subgenre I describe as the "mutant girl film," this study shifts its focus to a brief consideration of Kôji Shiraishi's *Grotesque* (*Gurotesuku*, 2009) as an example of a recent feature-length work of torture-horror that, building on the aesthetic and cultural paradigms advanced in the notorious *Guinea Pig* films (1985–1989), raises important questions regarding the politics of corporeal disintegration and the role of "disgust" as a response to art.

Ass Chainsaws, Breast Swords, and the Rise
of Mutant Girl Culture

In *The Japanese Cinema Encyclopedia: Horror, Fantasy, and Sci Fi Films* (1997), Thomas and Yukio Mihara Weisser deploy the phrase "dove style violence" to describe representations of interpersonal violence in which a group of young people (usually teenagers clad in high school uniforms) relentlessly abuse the perceived "weakest" member of the "flock" until he or she either dies at the hands of the bullying mob or commits suicide to escape the incessant torment. Given the conspicuous statistical upswing in suicide among young people in Japan beginning in the mid-1990s, coupled with the popularity of bullying (*ijime*)/ "dove style violence" in Japanese horror cinema, it makes sense that this motif has finally begun to receive the extensive critical attention it deserves. Dave Alexander, a staff writer for the popular international horror film magazine *Rue Morgue*, recently introduced a critical round table discussion of the recent increase in youth violence in Japan by stating that:

> [w]hether inflicting harm on adults, other minors or themselves, the country's youth are increasingly unhinged. According to government statistics, from the mid-90s to the mid-2000s, school-yard crime in the country rose 500 percent; and from 2002 to 2003, the number of children under fourteen who were processed for violent crime rose a staggering 47 percent. During this period, the suicide rate among teens and young adults also skyrocketed (a 2004 BBC article stated that in 2003, the suicide rate for those under nineteen jumped 22 percent, while primary and middle school suicides rose nearly 60 percent). (2008: 17)

Of course, bullying and suicide are by no means exclusively Japanese "issues"/"themes"/"trends"; nevertheless the numbers and demographics are certainly noteworthy. Similarly, a character suffering persecution and violence at the hands of one's peers has long been an important premise in horror cinema globally. One need only turn to such recognizable horror cinema icons as Victor Frankenstein's castigated creature and the troubled telekinetic teen Carrie White for examples of two such tortured figures. In Japanese horror cinema, the examples are increasingly plentiful. The trope informs films from Katsuya Matsumura's ultraviolent and highly controversial *All Night Long* series (1987–2009) to more notable/internationally popular works as Takashi Miike's *Visitor Q* (*Bijitâ Q*, 2001) and *Ichii the Killer* (2001), Sion Sono's *Suicide Club* (*Jisatsu sâkuru*, 2001) and *Noriko's Dinner Table* (*Noriko no shokutaku*, 2005), and Kinji Fukasaku's *Battle Royale* and *Battle Royale 2: Requiem* (2003).

As women are increasingly instrumental in influencing the country's social and political economy, it seems appropriate that this crucial shift in sex and, by extension, gender relations likewise finds expression in works of cinematic horror. The young girls in *Battle Royale*, for example, are every bit as deadly and resourceful as their male counterparts in the life-or-death "game" from which only one member of their middle-school class can emerge victorious. Similarly, Asami, the female protagonist of Noboru Iguchi's *Machine Girl* (*Kataude mashin gâru*, 2008), is a more-than-able match for not only schoolyard bullies, but also the vicious yakuza ninjas that kill those closest to her and pose an immediate and persistent threat to her life. Dressed in traditional schoolgirl attire, yet trained in the martial arts and equipped with a powerful machine gun that fits snuggly over the stump of her amputated left arm, Asami is a charming, beautiful young woman who can more than hold her own against all adversaries.

Given the extent to which these visions of sadistic violence and willful self-destruction engage with notions of social transformation and cultural change, school-aged characters seem especially appropriate choices to populate works of horror cinema. Secondary schools are, after all, primary sites of both socialization and competition, locations where young people come together to compete for social status. Furthermore, as Lindsay Nelson (2009) notes in his essay, "Ghosts of the Past, Ghosts of the Future: Monsters, Children, and Contemporary Japanese Horror Cinema," children and teens are figures invested with cultural meaning. In contemporary Japanese horror cinema, many recent cinematic depictions of *onryō* (spirits who return to take vengeance on the living) have taken the form of children, from the now iconic image of Sadako from Hideo Nakata's *Ringu*, her long black hair hanging down over her face as she slowly approaches her doomed victims, to the blue, feline-like Toshio of Takashi Shimizu's popular *Ju-on* films. Children are especially rich signifiers in that they represent a direct connection to the socio-historical consequences of a turbulent past (and present). In this sense, they are inextricably linked with not only a nostalgic yearning for "traditional" values, but also the consequences of past cultural transformations. Children and teens likewise evoke the myriad compulsions of an increasingly global "modernity" inflected by the influence of "international norms" (4). Consequently, it is not uncommon for ghostly children to emerge from technological sources such as televisual signals and the Internet. It is likewise common for filmmakers to align young people with "frequently horrific scenarios involving genetic mutation ... spirit possession, dangerous machines, and the mere earthly problems of abandonment, neglect, and bullying" (2).

Of course, as film viewers with even the most cursory understanding of the horror genre can readily attest, uncanny children and malignant teenagers have long been a staple of horror cinema across many cultures. What ultimately separates the representation of children and teenagers in recent works of Japanese horror cinema from similar depictions in comparable films from other cultures is the frequency with which this new wave of Japanese *enfant terribles* is linked with technology/machinization and hybridity. Here, too, one must look to Japan's recent past to understand its complex present, as works of "techno" and "body horror" evidence the darker components of a process of nationwide industrialization largely orchestrated as a result of, and a direct response to, western military and cultural imperialism. Horror films are vital cultural artifacts, and in the case of the motion pictures that I will explore in the paragraphs to follow, they contribute to a discourse of corporeal and cultural boundary violation that reveals biological and social bodies as flexible and permeable assemblages that disallow illusions of impregnability and reductive coherency. In other words, given their focus on notions of "biological privation, technological instrumentality, and the loss of biological control," these works closely resemble what Eugene Thacker (2002) describes as "biohorror," a fusion of "futuristic dystopia produced through science and technology" and "the violent monstrosities that manifest themselves within the human body" (112).

Among the most popular recent works of postmodern body horror to emerge from Japan are such comically exaggerated gore-fests as Noboru Iguchi's *Machine Girl* and *Robo-Geisha* (2009), Yoshiro Nishimura's *Tokyo Gore Police* (*Tôkyô zankoku keisatsu*, 2008) and *Vampire Girl vs. Frankenstein Girl* (*Kyûketsu Shôjo tai Shôjo Furanken*, 2009), and *Mutant Girl Squad* (*Sentô shôjo: Chi no takkamen densetsu*, 2010), codirected by Iguchi, Nishimura, and actor-director Tak Sakaguchi. Although the specific plot details of each of these films differ significantly, they share gruesome tropes blatantly intended to appeal to teenagers and young adults weaned on video games, cybernetics, and over-the-top martial arts extravaganzas that fetishize female warriors as both highly sexualized and extremely dangerous. The weapons wielded in these films range from knives and swords to bazookas and rocket launchers. Limbs and heads are severed with alarming regularity. Blood erupts from wounds with the force of water from geysers. Phallic appendages unexpectedly sprout forth, strange new orifices appear in biologically incongruent locations, and breasts spray corrosive acids capable of reducing bodies to bone and steaming pink tissue in a matter of seconds. However, to gain a fuller understanding of this recent trend in contemporary Japanese horror cinema, let us consider Iguchi's *Tokyo Gore Police* and the Iguchi, Nishimura, and Sakaguchi collaboration *Mutant Girl Squad* in greater detail.

When *Tokyo Gore Police* was released, it was an immediate international success with horror fans, winning "Best Asian Film" at the 2008 Fant-Asia Film Festival and playing in art-house cinemas throughout Europe and North America. Eihi Shiina (who played the deadly Asami in Takashi Miike's *Audition*) stars as Ruka, a successful officer in a privatized police force that maintains order by openly dispensing vigilante justice in the form of public executions. This for-profit paramilitary force aims to rid Tokyo (and, presumably, all of Japan) of both conventional "criminality" and entities known as *engineers*, mutated humans who possess the ability to transform wounds into deadly weapons. As the film opens, we learn that Ruka has established a solid reputation for her ability to destroy these highly adaptable "engineers." A cutter who dispassionately slashes at her own arm with a Stanley knife, Ruka possesses finely honed fighting skills and aggressive tactics that, like her penchant for self-harm, may stem largely from the trauma of seeing her father, who opposed the privatization of law enforcement, assassinated before her eyes when she was very young. As the narrative unfolds, Ruka's drive to become an "Engineer Hunter" extraordinaire soon intersects with her personal quest to bring her father's murderer to justice.

While confronting a particularly powerful engineer known as the "Key Man", who at one point "infects" her by inserting a flesh-like "key" into one of the many slash wounds on her arm, Ruka discovers that she and the monstrous "engineer" have far more in common than she could have ever imagined. The "Key Man" explains that the current Tokyo police chief murdered his father after manipulating him so that he would assassinate Ruka's father and, thus, reduce public opposition to the privatization of the police force. Furthermore, in a flurry of exposition clearly intended to explain the origin of his mutant abilities and profound psychosis, the "Key Man" reveals that his present incarnation is the result of a genetic experiment during which he modified his biological and psychological make up by injecting himself with a syringe filled with the DNA of some of the world's most notorious serial murderers. Enraged, Ruka slices the "Key Man" in half with her *kitana* and then sets out to avenge her father. Along the way she joins forces with an array of variably grotesque "engineers"—most of them young women. One of Ruka's arms transforms into a deadly, eel-like appendage with razor sharp teeth and spines, and when Ruka also loses an eye in battle, the wound generates a cybernetic upgrade. As one might expect given the narrative trajectory mapped out in the preceding sentences, *Tokyo Gore Police* concludes with a climactic battle between the "Engineer Hunter"-turned-"engineer" and the corrupt police chief.

Tokyo Gore Police immerses audiences within a world bathed in primary colors and neon hues. The characters that populate the world of the film perform in an unabashedly hyperbolic manner that marks them as overtly fictional. If these features were not enough to disallow the mode of immersion offered by more overtly representational motion pictures, then certainly the satirical "commercials" that occasionally disrupt the primary storyline posit the film as a text that does not take itself too seriously, even as it broaches some important socio-cultural terrain. One "commercial," for example, features a trio of giggling teenage girls cutting their wrists in high pop style using the new "Wrist Cutter G," a portable razor that comes in a variety of designer colors. Another advertisement touts the family bonding that can be achieved through the use of a video game called *Remote Control Exterminate*. This product, complete with a plastic controller that resembles a sword, allows the users to execute prisoners from a distance and, hence, quench their bloodlust by butchering a complete stranger from the comfort of their living rooms.

In addition, while many popular reviews fixate on *Tokyo Gore Police*'s exaggerated special effects, far too few explore how the fountains of blood and the baroque make up effects serve to heighten the work's flagrant theatricality, a visual logic that enhances the picture's sardonic cultural critique through a largely expression-istic *mise-en-scène*. By reveling in a carnivalesque atmosphere of bloody excess and images of extreme biomechanical mutation, *Tokyo Gore Police* mobilizes its dystopian elements to critique a cultural ideology that advocates rigid con-ceptions of human identity and champions disciplinary logics founded on zero tolerance laws designed to enrich those who have the economic power to define the parameters of "right" and "wrong." In this regard, *Tokyo Gore Police* recognizes the social importance of fluidity and adaptability, an approach to life that has historically allowed Japan to reconfigure itself in the face of radical socio-political transformations and ecological catastrophes. As a result, a philosophy of "'fluidity', 'viscosity', and 'connection'" (Sacchi, 2004: 232) informs much of Japanese culture's dominant social and aesthetic paradigms, allowing for a fruitful dynamism. This privileging of flexibility can be found throughout Japanese art, from the "random" architecture of Tokyo, in which "every urban rule is contorted or negated" (232), to the unruly cinematic bodies of mutant teenage girls who struggle against a mercenary disciplinary apparatus that, adorned in armor intended to evoke the warriors of a pre-Meiji feudal Japan, will not hesitate to use deadly force to maintain "order".

A similar narrative premise and ontology of corporeal transformation informs the plot of *Mutant Girl Squad*, a motion picture set in a world in which a gang of teenage girls with mutant abilities—ranging from breast swords to ass chainsaws—must fight for survival against a government bent on annihilating them (Figure 23.1). The film's central protagonist, Rin, is a 16-year-old girl who gets bullied at school

Figure 23.1 In *Mutant Girl Squad* (2010) teenage girls with transformative abilities—ranging from breast swords to ass chainsaws—must fight for survival against a hostile government. Directed by Noboru Iguchi, Yoshihiro Nishimura, and Tak Sakaguchi. Produced by Toei Video Company and Nikkatsu.

and whose mutant parents are executed in front of her. Suddenly alone and faced with a burgeoning mutation she can neither control nor understand (her fingers transform into blades), Rin finds refuge with a female gang of teenage mutants, where she learns that she belongs to a long-persecuted race known as the *Hiroku*. No longer "human," but unwilling to embrace the kind of genocidal hatred that a fraction of "humanity" feel toward the Hiroku, Rin struggles to control her new abilities, defeat a merciless general, and convince some of her fellow Hiroku that human lives have value and that love between humans and Hiroku is possible. Like *Tokyo Gore Police*, *Mutant Girl Squad* recovers physiological difference/hybridity as a potential model for personal and social identity rather than ultimately positing it as irrevocably monstrous and "other." By equating aggressive militarism with both *ijime* (bullying) and a reactionary phallocentrism (the military's attire resembles medieval armor, save for the penis-shaped guns over their noses), *Mutant Girl Squad*, like *Tokyo Gore Police*, seemingly champions a politics of hybridity and variegation over a reactionary subject position defined by apparent homogeneity and inflexible notions of gendered, national, and biological identity.

Although the films under discussion in this section are intended to lead viewers to sympathize with their mutant/mutating protagonists, claiming that the popular mutant girl genre sets forth a refreshingly progressive perspective would be problematic. One may argue, for instance, that *Tokyo Gore Police* and *Mutant Girl Squad* feature strong young female protagonists who overcome adversity and defeat predominantly male characters who not only occupy powerful cultural roles, but who also violently discriminate against those who differ from the "norm." However, such a claim risks overlooking lingering misogynist undercurrents. While deconstructing binary distinctions like human/non-human, biological/mechanical, and self/other, the conspicuously incoherent bodies on display are nevertheless clad in distinctively female attire that reinforce the very stereotypes surrounding femininity that the films' narratives ostensibly challenge. In other words, although the mutant girls in both *Tokyo Gore Police* and *Mutant Girl Squad* challenge the operant power structures within their respective—though ultimately very comparable—worlds, they do so while remaining hyper-sexualized, with the most spectacular mutations frequently linked with breasts (nipples sprout swords or spray acid) and genitalia (in *Tokyo Gore Police*, one "engineer"'s entire lower half transforms into a giant alligator-like *vagina dentata*) (Figure 23.2).

Human beings have long struggled to come to terms with the transitory nature of existence and the philosophical challenges faced by anyone who pauses to consider ideas as expansive and irreconcilable as ephemerality and finitude. In many Western cultures, anthropomorphic—and ultimately patriarchal—expressions like "mother earth," "mother nature," and "virgin territory" still function as metaphors when speaking and writing about the relationship between biological life and the vast and chaotic world it inhabits. Comparably, in several East Asian cultures (including Japan), the "transformative and fluid nature of the world is often signified through and by the female body" (Balmain, 2004: 125). It is not surprising, then, that this

Figure 23.2 In *Tokyo Gore Police* (2008) one "engineer"'s entire lower half transforms into a giant alligator-like *vagina dentata*. Directed by Yoshihiro Nishimura. Produced by Fever Dreams and Nikkatsu.

semiotic deportment finds articulation through works of popular culture, including horror cinema. Whether these motifs and the gender inequalities they reveal will mutate to the point that they vanish from our written, cognitive, and visual lexicons remains to be seen.

Japanese Torture-Horror and the Aesthetics of Disgust

In recent decades, torture-horror has steadily emerged as one of the most popular and controversial of horror cinema's numerous subgenres. As one might expect, cinematic representations of torture for torture's sake (i.e., torture not performed for the sake of extracting information) has long been a staple in works of cinematic terror. Indeed, some of cinema's most memorable "psychopaths" evoke fear in spectators not through the specific details of the physical assaults on their victims, but rather through the glee with which they execute their sadistic agendas. This is not to suggest that audiences do not experience a palpable sense of dread in response to graphic depictions of torture. Indeed, "virtually affective images of torture" frequently induce haptic responses that, in many cases, mirror the "physical agony" depicted on the screen (Powell, 2005: 84). However, as Jeremy Morris (2010) explains in "The Justification of Torture Horror," although "realistic" representations of "noninterrogational" torture effectively evoke "impressions of empathy" (52), much of the "horror" of these scenarios resides in the motivations informing the sadistic actions. In other words, the "vengeful or sadistic purposes of the torturer" exists as "a source of horror beyond the depiction of the torture itself" (44).

Japanese horror cinema has an especially rich tradition of torture-horror. Influenced by *chanbara eiga* (samurai film) and *pinku eiga* (soft-core erotic film), the scenes of rape and ritualized brutality that infuse many of these narratives reveal a mélange of aesthetic traditions and social concerns. The often deliberate and almost ceremonial evisceration of the (often eroticized) female body, for instance, recalls Japanese rituals like *hara-kiri*, "an ancient act in which female votives would offer up the 'flower' of their entrails and blood by a self-inflicted knife wound" (Hunter, 1998: 159–160); similarly, the apportioning of gender roles addresses concerns about the stability of sex- and class-based divisions of labor. It is primarily men who take on the role of torturers in these films, and it is women—and the occasional "emasculated" male—who are positioned as the recipients of phallic assaults like rape and other forms of corporeal violation.

The most notorious torture horror films in Japanese cinema are the works that comprise the much excoriated, though highly successful (in Japan) *Guinea Pig* series (Figure 23.3). Consisting of films like *Devil's Experiment* (1985) and *Flowers of Flesh*

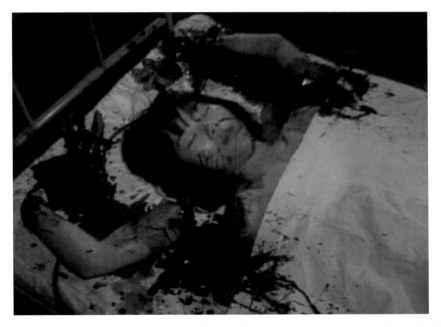

Figure 23.3   The most notorious torture horror films in Japanese cinema are the works that comprise the *Guinea Pig* series, including *Flowers of Flesh and Blood* (*Ginî piggu 2: Chiniku no hana*, 1985). Directed by Hideshi Hino. Produced by Sai Enterprise.

and Blood (1985), in which an anonymous woman is bound and systematically dismembered, the *Guinea Pig* films revel in their excessive violence and violent excess.
Like many works of body horror, these films are "obsessed with limits — with the
skin as a boundary, with the tolerance of audience expectation and desire, and with
the connection between the two, as on-screen the visceral violation provokes visceral response" (Williams, 2000: 34). Created during a time of economic prosperity
that would ultimately culminate in the devastating economic recession of the 1990s,
the *Guinea Pig* films explore the tensions that accompany a national identity/"social
body" in perceived crisis during a historical period marked by rapid and frequently
radical transformation and conspicuous instability. As remarkable exercises in special effects technology, guerilla-style editing, and gut-wrenching *mise-en-scene*, these
films merge the aesthetics of *cinema vérité* with what Mikita Brottman calls "cinema vomitif" (1997). Sadistic, contemplative, gruesome, and elegiac — the *Guinea
Pig* films, and the multiple works of torture horror that followed in their wake, bloom
their bloodiest shade of red where tradition intersects with emerging conceptions of
gender, class, and nation.

Released over 20 years after *Flowers of Flesh and Blood*, Kôji Shiraishi's
Grotesque illustrates that the aforementioned intersection remains as complex
and as challenging to negotiate as ever. Both *Flowers of Flesh and Blood* and
Grotesque feature graphic depictions of torture and dismemberment, but whereas
the nameless assailant in *Flowers of Flesh and Blood* murders his female victim with a solemn, poetic theatricality, *Grotesque*'s mad doctor is propelled by
a desire temporarily sated through violent sexual acts and genital mutilation.
Both films also met with varying degrees of censorship. In 1990, the US actor
Charlie Sheen famously mistook *Flowers of Flesh and Blood* for an actual snuff
film and subsequently alerted authorities. Two years later, a 26-year-old British
man named Christopher Berthoud was fined £600 for importing the very same
title. According to the prosecution in the Berthoud case, while *Flowers of Flesh
and Blood* was decidedly not a video-recorded document of a Japanese woman
being murdered, it was "something that is so well simulated that that is the
impression it creates" (The Christopher Berthoud Case, para. 1). Rather than
subject the jury to "the anxiety of having to watch the shocking footage" (para. 3),
Berthoud chose to accept whatever judgment the court deemed appropriate.
When Shiraishi's *Grotesque* was met with the British Board of Film Classification's open disdain in 2009, the echoes of the Berthoud case were obvious.
The board banned the film outright for its representation of "sexual sadism for
its own sake," claiming that watching the film could result in a "risk of harm"
to spectators:

> GROTESQUE … focuses, for the majority of its running time, on the sexual assault,
> humiliation and extreme torture of a man and a woman. The couple are abducted,
> bound, stripped and sexually violated. They are later subjected to amputation, eye
> gouging, castration and evisceration resulting in a gory and violent death. The film
> ends with the killer choosing his next victims. The chief pleasure on offer in viewing

GROTESQUE appears to be the spectacle of sadism (including sexual sadism) for its own sake. The work has minimal narrative or character development and presents the viewer with little more than an unrelenting and escalating scenario of humiliation, brutality and sadism. In making a decision as to whether a video work is suitable for classification, the BBFC applies the criteria set out in its Classification Guidelines.... The Guidelines set out clearly the BBFC's serious concerns about the portrayal of sexual violence, especially when such depictions might eroticise or endorse sexual assault.... After careful consideration, it was judged that to issue a certificate to GROTESQUE ... would involve risk of harm ... and the work was therefore refused a classification. ("British Board of Film Classification," para. 1)

As the British Board of Film Classification's official rejection statement points out, *Grotesque* has a very simple linear narrative structure. In contrast to *Flowers of Flesh and Blood*'s overtly "fake documentary" design, *Grotesque* never pretends to be anything other than an explicit fiction. Additionally, where *Flowers of Flesh and Blood*'s mannered ritualism invests its narrative with a femicidal tone that reveals reactionary masculinist anxieties over shifting gender roles, *Grotesque*'s depiction of torture seems arranged to foreground the erotic charge that the doctor receives from his violent actions. That said, the couple's romanticized views of gender roles and their adherence to social etiquette only exacerbates and prolongs the torture. The male captive, for instance, offers to sacrifice himself for a woman with whom he has yet to establish a lasting relationship—a behavior that apparently excites the doctor. In fact, it is the couple's adherence to social convention that provides the film with arguably its most disturbing dimension.

Of all of the physical and psychological brutalities the doctor visits on his helpless captives, no single gesture is more dispiriting or outright cruel than the torturer's continued promises to let the couple free if they provide him with the satisfaction for which he yearns. Apparently satisfied with the couple's suffering at his hands, the doctor treats their wounds and nurses them back to health. As they recover, the doctor's captives vow to formalize their relationship and support each other once they are released. Unfortunately for the young couple, their optimism is soon crushed, however, when they fall asleep only to awaken once more in the doctor's clinic/torture room. This narrative development exposes the depths of the torturer's malevolence, as it is not the infliction of pain but rather the encouragement of hope—or, the perpetuation of the notion that survival/freedom remains a distinct possibility—that stands as the most profoundly violent and inhumane of the doctor's assaults. This encouraging of hope followed by its brutal extinction finds its ultimate representation in the events surrounding the captive man's final attempt to free the woman he loves. With his intestines attached to a hook dangling from the ceiling, the man attempts to cross the floor and cut the woman free; if he can succeed, the doctor promises him, the woman will be allowed to live. The man makes it to the woman, disemboweling himself in the process, but he collapses before he can cut through the rope that binds her. The rope, the doctor reveals, was reinforced with steel and was, thus, "uncuttable" from the very start.

Grotesque's gore effects are far more evocative of the "realistic" representations of physical violence on display in the *Guinea Pig* films of the 1980s than they are of the hyper-stylized geysers of blood erupting throughout the mutant girl films explored earlier. Torture-horror films require spectators to confront images of corporeal violence simultaneously coded as "intense," "visceral," "disgusting," and "repellant." As a result, torture-horror requires that spectators come to the film with a very specific set of expectations and viewing strategies. Despite the immediate thrill or alarm provided by a horror film's visual and auditory shock/startle effects, no audience enters a motion picture theatre or purchases a DVD with the expectation that the film's contents will actually "frighten" them or cause them real harm. The images, after all, are simply two-dimensional projections arranged to create a narrative. They pose, in other words, no real immediate threat to the spectator. They can, however, *disgust* the viewer. The allure of *Grotesque*'s "repulsive"/"disgusting" images recalls Julia Kristeva's (1982) theory of abjection, specifically the role "abject"/"repugnant" images play in the process of human identity formation, or "selfing." For Kristeva, abject materials like semen, blood, feces, severed limbs, and corpses externalize the repressed understanding of our own physical corruptibility; they trouble the tenuous distinctions between interior and exterior, as well as self and other, that we invent to create the illusion of our selves as discrete and coherent beings.

In the case of torture horror films like *Grotesque*, the audience is never literally at risk and, consequently, responds by identifying with the captives' plight while "wallow[ing] in what nature commands that one reject" (Korsmeyer, 2011: 121). This wallowing in the abject or the disgusting is a somatic response, at once a visceral, haptic reaction, as well as a cognitively, psychologically, and culturally constructed response. In her recently published monograph, *Savoring Disgust: The Foul and Fair in Aesthetics*, Carolyn Korsmeyer notes that much like the Kantian "sublime," which acts as a limit point for a mode of beauty so intense that it transcends the power of our lexicons' descriptive/metaphoric function, disgust appeals to a similarly transcendent "sublate" (130). Encountering images of human corporeal disintegration forces spectators to confront the reality of their own biological identity, mortality, and finitude. The simultaneous allure and dread of images of corporeal disintegration provoke existential reflection on human vulnerability—that is, the status of human beings as transient entities that will inevitably die and decompose.

It is through this cognizance of corporeal ephemerality that a film such as Shiriashi's *Grotesque* mines similar cultural and phenomenological terrain as Nishimura's *Tokyo Gore Police* or Nishimura, Iguchi, and Sakaguchi's *Mutant Girl Squad*. The horrific torture and graphic mutilation on display in *Grotesque*, and the bio-mechanical hybridity and mutating physiologies that define the stylistic excesses of *Tokyo Gore Police* and *Mutant Girl Squad*, accomplish far more than merely illustrating anxieties surrounding cultural transformation in a historical moment in which socio-cultural disciplinary apparatuses promote nationalism and binary conceptualizations of sexual and gender identity in the face of globalism and potentially irreducible multiplicity. The hybrid and splattered bodies on display in these films foreground the transience of all life on this planet, irrespective of socially inscribed "borders" and "boundaries." Thus, regardless of the existence of specific cultural codings that may impede foreign audiences from comprehending nuances that would register immediately with Japanese spectators, the transmission of cinematic affect endures such divisions. The dread one feels at the recognition of our all-too-human bodies' inevitable corruptibility locates everyone within a larger, truly global community—the community of the dying.

References

Alexander, D. (2008) Underage rage in Japan. *Rue Morgue*, (79), 16–20.

Balmain, C. (ed.) (2004) Vengeful virgins in white: female monstrosity in Asian cinema, in *Monsters and the Monstrous: Myths and Metaphors of Enduring Evil*, Inter-Disciplinary Press, Oxford.

Balmain, C. (2006) Inside the well of loneliness: towards a definition of the Japanese horror film. *Electronic Journal of Contemporary Japanese Studies*. http://www.japanesestudies .org.uk/discussionpapers/2006/Balmain.html (accessed 2 May 2007).

"British Board of Film Classification: A Century of Cinema." http://www.bbfc.co.uk /AVV261504/ .

Brottman, M. (1997) *Offensive Films: Towards an Anthropology of Cinema Vomitif*, Greenwood Publishing Group.

Harper, J. (2009) *Flowers from Hell*, Noir Publishing, Hereford.

Hunter, J. (1998) *Eros in Hell: Sex, Blood, and Madness in Japanese Cinema*, Creation Books International, London.

Jones, K. (2003) Here and there: the films of Tsai Ming-Liang, in *Movie Mutations: The Changing Face of World Cinephilia* (eds J. Rosenbaum and A. Martin), British Film Institute, London, pp. 44–51.

Korsmeyer, C. (2011) *Savoring Disgust: The Foul and the Fair in Aesthetics*, Oxford University Press, Oxford.

Kristeva, J. (1982) *The Powers of Horror: An Essay on Abjection*, Columbia University Press, New York.

McRoy, J. (2008) *Nightmare Japan: Contemporary Japanese Horror Cinema*, Rodopi, Amsterdam.

Mes, T. and Jasper, S. (2004) *The Midnight Eye Guide to New Japanese Film*, Stone Bridge Press, Berkeley, CA.

Morris, J. (ed.) (2010) The justification of torture horror: retribution and sadism in *Saw, Hostel*, and *The Devil's Rejects*, in *The Philosophy of Horror*, The University of Kentucky Press, Lexington, pp. 42–56.

Nelson, L. (2009) Ghosts of the past, ghosts of the future: monsters, children, and contemporary Japanese horror cinema. *Cinemascope*, **Year V** (13). http://www.cinemascope.it /Issue%2013/PDF/Lindsay%20Nelson.pdf.

Powell, A. (2005) *Deleuze and the Horror Film*, Edinburgh University Press, Edinburgh.

Sacchi, L. (2004) *Tokyo: City and Architecture*, Skira Editore, Italy.

Shin, C.-Y. (2008) The art of branding: Tartan 'Asia Extreme' films. *Jump Cut: A Review of Contemporary Media*, 50. http://www.ejumpcut.org/archive/jc50.2008/TartanDist/text .html

Thacker, E. (2002) Biohorror/biotech, in *Horror* (ed. S. Hantke), Paradoxa Press, Vashon Island, WA, pp. 109–129.

"The Christopher Berthoud Case." *Beyond the Boundaries*. freespace.virgin.net/Alasdair.y /CASE.HTM.

Weisser, T. and Yukio, M. (1997) *The Japanese Cinema Encyclopedia: The Horror, Fantasy, and Sci Fi Films*, Vital Books, Miami.

Williams, L.R. (2000) The inside-out of masculinity: David Cronenberg's visceral pleasures, in *The Body's Perilous Pleasures: Dangerous Desire and Contemporary Culture* (ed. M. Aaron), Edinburgh University Press, Edinburgh, pp. 30–48.

24

South Korean Horror Cinema

Daniel Martin

The horror cinema of South Korea is understandably regarded as a "new" movement in the canon of international horror. At the turn of the millennium, in spite of a heritage of horror cinema dating back four decades, few other than the most dedicated cinephiles and fear fanatics knew anything of South Korea's genre films. Yet, South Korean horror is now regarded as one of the most globally significant, daringly original, and thematically provocative examples of the genre. The Korean horror film, in spite of its relatively recent discovery by Western audiences, really is not new. A study of Korean horror reveals a rich history of culturally specific fears played out on screen in the form of ghosts and monsters, tales of treachery, revenge, and redemption. What, then, is the South Korean horror film *about*? What are the themes of these films, and what do they reveal about the particular appeal—both local and global—of this national horror cinema? This chapter seeks to answer these questions, and establish the specificity of Korean horror without resorting to generalizations. This chapter endeavors to establish how Korean horror cinema is distinct from not just Western forms of the genre, but also from Japanese and other Asian horrors. The East Asian horror film, in spite of the claims of some marketers, is not a homogenous entity.

This chapter therefore covers the history and development of the horror film in Korea, examining influential films, filmmakers, cycles, and subgenres. The beginning of the first wave of Korean horror of the 1960s is explained, as are the earlier and even pre-cinematic origins of horror in myth and literature. The themes, preoccupations, tropes, patterns, and clichés of the genre will be dissected and discussed. This chapter lingers on key films and important moments in the development of the horror film in Korea, examining different trends and subcycles, from the "golden age" when the genre produced its first iconic, classic horror films

A Companion to the Horror Film, First Edition. Edited by Harry M. Benshoff.
© 2014 John Wiley & Sons, Inc. Published 2017 by John Wiley & Sons, Inc.

to the often-ignored period of decline in the 1980s. The genre's impressive revival in the late 1990s, leading ultimately to its international breakthrough in the 2000s is also covered. The chapter culminates with a case study of the slasher-melodrama *Bloody Reunion* (2006), a hybrid text revealing the absorption of foreign influences along with a continuation of the genre's oldest traditions. (Note: all Korean names included in this chapter are Romanized according to the best-known and most widely published spellings, and are written with the family name first, the given name second.)

Melodrama and Morality: The Origins of Korean Horror

The horror genre began in South Korea with a bolt of lightning on a stormy night, sharply punctuating a moment of adultery that would lead to psychological torture, merciless infanticide, and double suicide. The scene in question signified a shift in tone, from what had appeared to be a family melodrama to something much more sinister and gothic. The film was Kim Ki-young's *The Housemaid* (1960), widely identified as the first modern horror film in Korea, and the starting point for the country's first great cycle of horror movies (Peirse and Martin, 2013: 4). *The Housemaid* offers a searing critique of social mobility in a rapidly modernizing South Korea by examining the fate of a family who, able to afford a bigger home and the trappings of the middle class, hire a live-in maid to perform their domestic chores. The maid's jealousy and sexual frustration climax in her seduction of her employer, but desire soon becomes obsession and murderous resentment. The family's prized home becomes both a weapon and a prison. Several readings of the film note that the home's second story signifies its value and prestige (Kim, 2004; Lee and Stringer, 2012), yet the staircase itself becomes the site of violent falls; first, when the maid tumbles down the stairs, aborting her unborn child, and subsequently when the young son, believing that he has been poisoned, panics and trips down the stairs, fatally breaking his neck. However, these moments of violence are rare narrative eruptions, as the film bases its horror on the psychological and emotional torment of the adults in the house. The film's director Kim Ki-young was known as *Mr. Monster* for the way he twisted familial and societal norms in his works, yet he was also praised for his "stylistic and narrative restraint" (Kim, 2004: 241) rather than graphic depictions of violence.

Indeed, *The Housemaid* succeeds in terrifying its audiences by viewing the home as a prison, and the long-held Korean values of reputation and social standing as leverage against the family. After the maid's murder-by-deception of the young son, she threatens to expose the sordid affair unless the boy's death is covered up. Thus, the husband becomes a pawn and a plaything in his own home, powerless even to report or avenge the death of his son. In a parallel with the contemporaneous American horror, *What Ever Happened to Baby Jane?* (1962), the safety and sanctity of the home is warped, and the domestic space becomes gothic and morbid.

However, the triumph of the eponymous antagonist is temporary, even illusory. The film's narrative climaxes with an increasingly surreal double suicide, as the husband and the housemaid seal their miserable fates together. Yet at the moment of the patriarch's death, a quick cut reveals that the entire film has been a fantasy extrapolated from a newspaper article being read in the first scene. This startling and utterly unexpected conclusion only grows in absurdity when the lead actor, Kim Jin-kyu, looks directly into the camera and addresses the men in the audience, cheerfully warning them against the dangers of extramarital temptation. The film ends thus, with a chuckle and an incongruously comic music cue. *The Housemaid* therefore functions as a "warning" to families by representing the monstrous "other" as a threat from within that can be conquered not through death, as the first narrative climax suggests, but rather by restraint, as the film's true conclusion argues (Lee, 2013: 28) (Figure 24.1).

The Housemaid, though canonized as a horror film, is really better understood as a hybrid text. This period, the "golden age" of Korean cinema, when the studio system emerged and film became a major commercial and cultural force, was dominated by popular melodramas about romance and family stability (McHugh and Abelmann, 2005). More specifically, the *shinpa* film—narratives of exaggerated emotion, tragic romance, and female suffering (Paquet, 2007: 44; Choi, 2010: 9) typified this period.

Figure 24.1 Victims of destructive desire: Lee Eun-shim and Kim Jin-kyu in *The House-maid* (1960). Directed by Ki-young Kim. Produced by Hanguk Munye Yeonghwa and Kim Ki-Young Production.

The Housemaid divided critics on its release by perverting the *shinpa* film, making it gothic and homicidal; however, perhaps it is more useful to see the film as exposing the suppressed tensions and destructive potential already dormant in the genre.

The fact that the Korean horror film is derived from melodrama is significant. The emotional tone, the sense of tragedy and sadness pervading the Korean horror film, is one of its major differentiating qualities, revealing cultural specificity and playing to local sensibilities. These are horror films intended to evoke sadness as much as fear (Choi, 2010; Peirse and Martin, 2013), and the films that followed *The Housemaid*'s template would emphasize grief and suffering in even stronger terms. Hyangjin Lee (2013) identifies in the 1960s a cycle of films about wronged women seeking revenge on the deceitful, selfish, murderous men who victimized them. As more horror films were produced during this "golden age" of South Korean filmmaking, regular narrative patterns began to emerge, and the genre established consistent tropes and signifiers. Many films featured a specific type of ghost called a *wonhon*. Similar in many respects to the now-iconic Japanese virgin ghost known widely in the West since the success of Hideo Nakata's *Ringu* (1998), the Korean *wonhon* is a young woman whose death was brought about by familial treachery or sexual assault, whose spirit lingers to seek justice and punish the evildoers responsible for her murder. Thus, while many "victims" are tormented at the hands of the ghost, it is in these cases the killer who engages the sympathies of the audience, and those she kills on her quest for righteous revenge deserve their fates. These films express a specific Korean concept: *han*, best translated as a sense of agonizing grief at great injustice, of continual and undeserved suffering. *Han* is central to tales beyond the horror genre in Korea and even outside cinema, pervading literature, art, and philosophical thought. The moral code found in typical Korean horror films reflects the concept of *han* to a large extent, inviting the viewer to sympathize with the ghost, the killer, the monster, for their victims are the ones who truly deserve punishment, having committed sins and caused the suffering of innocents.

The best-known films of the *wonhon* cycle of the 1960s include *The Devil's Stairway* (Lee Man-hee, 1964), in which a doctor murders his pregnant lover to advance his medical career, only to be haunted by what he *thinks* is her ghost; *A Devilish Homicide* (Lee Yong-min, 1965), about a young wife killed by her own mother-in-law, returning through the possession of a cat and vanquished only through Buddhist prayer; and *A Public Cemetery under the Moon* (Gwon Cheol-hwi, 1967), a luridly colorful film about a murdered mother whose ghost protects her infant son from numerous attempts on his life. Hyangjin Lee argues that the *wonhon* is a symbolic reaction against patriarchy and oppression, and the threat of the "other," and further that these ghosts represent "the diverse voices of a suffering country" (2013: 33). These films continued to draw strongly from traditions in melodrama, and their themes included family relationships, generational and gender conflict, and the value of Confucianist tradition in a rapidly modernizing world.

Korean horror flourished in the 1960s, reflecting increasing trends toward the supernatural, and a greater emphasis on spectacle and special effects, while also diversifying and acknowledging foreign influence. The year 1967 saw the release of South Korea's first giant monster movies, drawn shamelessly from the Japanese *daikaiju* template established with *Godzilla* (Ishirô Honda, 1954); among these, *Yongary, Monster from the Deep* (Kim Kee-deok, 1967) is the best-known and most meaningful (Lee, 2011; Peirse and Martin, 2013). The Korean monster-horror films of the late 1960s shared many themes with the *wonhon* cycle, presenting melodramatic narratives whose themes address the repression of the unknown enemy (rather than the familiar/uncanny threat from within the family in the earlier cycle). These films also offer a more reassuring return to the status quo, yet their climaxes are not without tragedy; we feel as pained by the death of the accidentally destructive radioactive beast in *Yongary* as we do the *han* of any *wonhon*.

The end of the decade saw the release of *The Thousand Year Old Fox* (Shin Sang-ok, 1969), a horror film drawing on ancient Korean folklore of the *gumiho*, a malevolent shape-shifting nine-tailed fox, typically appearing in the form of young women, cursed to prey on humans in order to extend its life. The *gumiho* films also have a great deal in common with *wonhon* narratives, though they emphasize physical action and alarming displays of magical power more readily than the gothic ghost stories (Peirse and Byrne, 2013). The cinematic introduction of the *gumiho* demonstrates that although the Korean horror film began in the 1960s, a long heritage of pre-cinematic horror influenced the genre immensely. Tales of *gumiho*, ghosts, and revenge had been a part of Korean folklore for centuries, and early literature saw the rise of the morality tale, in which terrible crimes are met with just retribution (Hwang, 2013: 81–82). The best known of these is perhaps *The Story of Rose and Lotus*, a fable about young girls murdered by their wicked stepmother, only to return as ghosts to inform the local magistrate. This story formed the basis for one of the first Korean films to ever depict ghosts, the silent colonial-period *The Story of Janghwa and Hongryeon* (Kim Yeong-hwan, 1924), and subsequently one of the best-known South Korean horror films of the current generation: the critically acclaimed *A Tale of Two Sisters* (Kim Jee-woon, 2003). Korean horror's emergence as a cinematic genre in the 1960s, then, should be seen as a continuation of myth, folktales, and literary explorations of the same material. Yet the patterns and images established in the horror movies of the "golden age" of Korean cinema would endure and proliferate for the next fifty years. Korean horror is a cinema of *wonhon*, *gumiho*, of killers and avengers both human and monstrous; it is a cinema of secrets and revenge, of justice and tragedy, of suffering both physical and emotional.

Transformation and Terror: Korean Horror from the 1970s to the 1990s

South Korean cinema's "golden age" is generally acknowledged as covering the period from the mid-1950s until the end of the 1960s; the 1970s and 1980s are viewed as a problematic period of decline, when increased competition from foreign film led to dwindling audiences for local productions (Kim, 2004: 282; Choi, 2010: 61). The horror film was not immune to these shifts in audience taste, nor was it unaffected by larger political changes taking place in South Korea. Greater film censorship and governmental control of the media restricted the freedom of filmmakers, and in 1972 President Park Chung-hee suspended civil rights and declared a state of emergency, in response to the supposed threat posed by North Korea (Black, 2003: 187). Dissent and protests were rife, and prisoners were brutally mistreated, yet filmmakers were unable to engage with the chaos around them in any meaningful way. Instead, a cycle of "quota quickies" emerged in order to satisfy the screen quota and facilitate the distribution of the then-dominant imported foreign films (Black, 2003: 188). Little academic or critical attention is paid to films made during this period, and the horror genre experienced few deviations from, or innovations to, the commercial formula established in the 1960s. The decade saw the same themes and tropes revisited: there was another version of *The Story of Rose and Lotus* (1972s *Janghwa and Hongryeon: A Story of Two Sisters,* directed by Lee Yoo-seop), and Park Yoon-kyo's trilogy of "*han* horror films" marked continued representation of the sympathetic *wonhon* (Peirse and Martin, 2013: 13). Ironically, while explicit violence and bloodletting were often censored in horror moves of the 1970s, it was permitted — even encouraged — in several anti-Communist Korean War films made during this period, demonstrating further that violence in film was not just controlled by the government, but even used as a tool of propaganda; these "non-horror war-horror" films represent a unique aspect of the genre (Morris, 2013).

The 1980s marked a change in the political administration, and new President Chun Doo-hwan's "Three S" policy of distracting and placating an unhappy populace through the promotion of "sports, sex, and screen" led to an abundance of domestic erotic exploitation films. The horror genre saw the effects of this immediately with the instigation of a new cycle of ero-horror. In general terms, the same themes were addressed and the typical narrative patterns remained. Ko Yeong-nam's *Suddenly a Dark Night* (1981) replays *The Housemaid* with added nudity and supernatural exaggeration, and undoubtedly reflects the influence of the then-burgeoning Hollywood slasher film on Korean filmmakers (Peirse and Martin, 2013). The film, unusual in comparison to earlier Korean horror, focuses neither on the husband (imagined guilty of infidelity) or the maid (apparently in control of supernatural powers drawn from shamanistic tradition), but on the wife, who fulfills the role of the "Final Girl" as identified by Clover (1992).

Films with such lurid, explicit exploitation met audience demand for more permissive and graphic representations of sex and violence, and over these two decades of change South Korea's military dictatorships went from restricting horror to encouraging it. The horror of the 1980s shared its fortunes with mainstream melodramas of the time, as that genre too became an erotic hybrid of its former self. These films attracted audiences in the short-term, but overall failed to compete with more popular cinema from Hong Kong and Hollywood. Nonetheless, and regardless of how fallow this period is considered by historians, it is important to note that the horror film in Korea never entirely disappeared from sight. By the 1990s, when censorship was finally relaxed and a new democratically elected government allowed greater artistic expression, a wave of Hollywood-influenced melodrama-horror hybrid films emerged, exploring romance and relationships for a new generation of adults.

One example from this cycle saw filmmakers returning to the *gumiho* myth in *The Fox with Nine Tails* (Park Heon-soo, 1994). Reflecting contemporary sensibilities as much as the action-packed 1969 version, the 1990s incarnation examines the romantic and sexual dynamic between the cursed female fox-woman and her handsome lover (Peirse and Byrne, 2013). The horror of this period often imitated the popular "high-teen" genre attracting younger audiences, or explored the lives and loves of yuppies and married couples. These films enjoyed only limited success, and the cycle began to quickly wane.

Perhaps the most popular and culturally influential horror of this period is *Olgami* (Kim Seong-hong, 1997); the film has never received any official distribution in any English-speaking country, but the English-language title most commonly used in South Korea is *The Hole*, a title that is both inappropriate and inaccurate. A rare hit at a time when the industry as a whole was struggling to attract local audiences, the film combines influences from the Hollywood thriller with new exploration of some enduring social anxieties. *Olgami* portrays the increasingly tense and ultimately violent confrontations between a newlywed wife and her husband's mother. This theme has appeared in Korean horror since the genre's heyday, and the narrative of a wronged daughter-in-law seeking revenge on her cruel mother-in-law typically reveals the tensions and pressures inherent in traditional Confucian society (Oh, 2013). However, *Olgami* lacks a supernatural element and contains little bloodshed. Although *Olgami* was marketed locally as an exploitation film, its poster depicting nothing more than an apparently naked woman bound and gagged, the film is actually a psychological horror-thriller of domestic terror in the vein of *Single White Female* (Barbet Schroeder, 1992) or *Pacific Heights* (John Schlesinger, 1990). The film reveals a raft of American influences, from the thrillers named earlier to a "Hitchcockian" style (Black, 2003: 191). There is no death and rebirth-as-*wonhon*, no ghostly trickery; rather the film depicts a battle of wits as the two women vie for the affection of the man they love. The desperate daughter-in-law tries to convince her husband of his mother's wickedness, but is ultimately faced with a frantic physical struggle to survive — again, reflecting much more in common with the slasher film's "Final Girl" than with the vengeful female ghosts of Korean horror. The film certainly addresses culturally specific social pressures and familial relationships, but it lacks many of the defining qualities of classic Korean horror. *Olgami*'s success was, in effect, the last hurrah of a tired cycle. The film can be seen as marking a split between the old guard of dwindling erotic/romantic horror of the 1980s and 1990s, and an unexpected new wave of Korean horror that would reinvigorate the domestic market and achieve unprecedented international visibility.

Revival of the Dead: New Korean Horror

The release of Park Ki-hyung's *Whispering Corridors* in 1998 marked a turning point for the horror film industry in Korea (Black, 2003; Hendrix, 2004; Choi, 2010; Peirse and Martin, 2013). The film proved popular and original enough to give birth to a new subcycle of Korean horror that would reignite critical and creative interest in the genre and see the first boom in the popularity and profitability of horror since its instigation in the early 1960s. Just as Wes Craven's *Scream* (1996) revived Hollywood horror by bringing a younger audience to the genre, *Whispering Corridors* accomplished the same thing in Korea, striking a chord with local teenaged cinemagoers. So began the high school horror subgenre.

Whispering Corridors shifts the focus of gothic horror from the domestic space to high school and the social sphere of teenagers. While *The Housemaid* and *Olgami* had penetrated cultural anxieties by depicting the horror of the home and the dangers posed by familial/sexual rivalries, *Whispering Corridors* instead exaggerates the pressures of high school and the menace of teachers. The film offers a new presentation of old material, restaging the familiar *wonhon* narrative in a new context: the pitiful ghost of a schoolgirl, ostracized and abused by her morally repugnant teachers, returns from the dead to exact ghostly revenge. As is typical of films of this type, her victims are presented as deserving of their punishment, and the ghost is a figure of tragic identification for the protagonist and the audience.

Whispering Corridors speaks to its audience in a powerful way. Jinhee Choi has argued that the film foregrounds a girls' sensibility and reflects the social concerns of a younger audience more than the previous generation's horror by focusing on "friendship, not kinship" (2010: 129). As others have noted, the film's themes reveal the intense competitiveness and exhausting hardships experienced by high school students in contemporary Korea; the film attracted a "national furore" when the national teachers' association tried to have it banned and teenaged audiences responded by flocking to cinemas in huge numbers (Black, 2003: 193). *Whispering Corridors* thus balances cultural specificity and universal appeal. Like the popular

Japanese melodrama-horror *Battle Royale* (Kinji Fukasaku, 2000), the Korean film addresses the educational experience through violent symbolism.

This period saw the emergence of "New Korean Cinema" more broadly, just as the flurry of imitative films followed in the wake of *Whispering Corridors* set the template for new Korean horror films. These horror films refocused on a younger audience through their consistent depiction of younger characters, and honored old traditions while updating the genre. What, then, are the defining qualities of the contemporary Korean horror film? How is it at once old and new, different and familiar? What are the themes and tropes that identify this cycle, and speak to the cultural specificity of this national horror cinema?

Revenge. The majority of Korean horror films, old and new, hinge on an act (or multiple acts) of revenge. The *wonhon*, as discussed earlier, seeks revenge and justice. This marks a key difference from the template established by Hollywood horror films, especially those of the slasher cycle of the 1970s and 1980s. The villains of the American slasher film — Michael Myers, Freddy Krueger, Jason Voorhees — are all seeking revenge in some form, but they slay the innocent to express a merciless vengeance. They take revenge on "people" in an abstract sense, killing to express their evil desires (though they are not always without tragic motivation). The ghosts and killers of Korean horror, meanwhile, choose their victims carefully, logically, enacting an "appropriate" revenge, upholding a world order in which crimes against morality are punished. *Whispering Corridors* accomplished this by thoroughly demonizing the teachers who fall victim to the ghost, showing their abuses (physical, psychological, sexual) before depicting their deaths.

Flashbacks. The contemporary Korean horror film is about the past; history, secrets, and buried crimes are exhumed and live again. There have been almost no horror films made in Korea since 2000 that do not feature at least one flashback sequence. Narrative development is inexorably tied to twists and revelations. This emphasis on the past reinforces the notion that crimes will not go unpunished, and those poor victims who suffer unfairly will not remain unavenged. A series of flashbacks in *Phone* (Ahn Byung-ki, 2002) climax with a dead body pulling itself from a secret burial in a wall; a *wonhon* in *Face* (Yoo Sang-gon, 2004) haunts the protagonist, a facial-reconstruction police consultant, until he agrees to sculpt her face, thus literally bringing her visage back into physical being. Flashback sequences reveal illicit affairs, treachery, rape, torture and murder, unearthing secrets in the past of the characters, or even from generations ago: *The Red Shoes* (Kim Yong-gyoon, 2005) includes flashbacks to Korea's colonial past in order to explain its vengeful ghost.

Outcasts. *Whispering Corridors* and the films that followed, especially those set in high schools or focusing exclusively on teenagers, include characters best identified by the Korean word *wanggda*, meaning "outcast" (Hendrix, 2004: 46; Black, 2003: 196). Although reminiscent of the way that the families shown in classic Korean horror would depict an ostracized or rejected member of the family unit—the daughter-in-law, or perhaps the maid—the *wanggda* of contemporary Korean horror is the ultimate figure of tragic sympathy, excluded from the social group for reasons beyond their control. Typically female, the *wanggda* is victimized based on perceptions that she does not fit in, because of her social class, her family background, or any number of superficial offenses against hegemony. Tied in obvious ways to the concept of *han*, the *wanggda*'s suffering typically leads to death, ghostly reincarnation, and revenge.

Religion and Superstition. The outcast girl of *Whispering Corridors* (the *wanggda*-turned-*wonhon*) was despised by her teachers and feared by her peers because her mother was a shaman priestess (a *mudang*), linking the abuse of the character to a rejection of Korea's premodern past. Shamanism is one of the country's oldest religious traditions, and it was increasingly marginalized and ruralized with the rapid development of the twentieth century. Recent Korean horror films often deal with religion and superstition, from problematic depictions that equate shamanism with a refusal to adapt to modern conventions and the customs of the majority, to several recent films dealing with Christianity/Catholicism in South Korea, from *Possessed* (Lee Yong-joo, 2009) to *Thirst* (Park Chan-wook, 2009).

Sexual Innocence. One of the key factors distinguishing the new Korean horror film from its immediate predecessor of the 1980s and 1990s is the re-sanitization of sexual content. The erotic excesses that were introduced in the 1980s have been wiped away to accommodate the juvenilization of the genre. In order to make these films more appropriate and relatable for a teen audience, sexual content is virtually nonexistent, as the narratives moved away from exploring the psycho-sexual dynamics of married couples to the friendships and shared hardships of younger people. The contemporary Korean horror film rarely concerns romance in any meaningful way, and the sex and nudity that is often seen as stereotypical of the Hollywood teen-camp slasher film is nowhere to be found.

Sadness. It bears repeating, even briefly, that the contemporary Korean horror film is derived from melodrama and aims to make its audience cry as much as it wants them to scream. The monsters of these films elicit not fear, or disgust, but rather quiet sympathy (Choi, 2010: 136). There is no triumph over evil at the climax of *Whispering Corridors*, only the sad conclusion to a misfortunate ghost's bloody quest for peace and justice. The Japanese horror film *Dark Water* (Hideo Nakata, 2002) and the American classic *Carrie* (Brian De Palma, 1976) express the potential sadness and sympathy of the horror film in a similar way, but it is in the Korean horror film's consistent and enduring turn to melodrama, from the "golden age" through the contemporary period, that signifies its unique appeal and identity.

The contemporary Korean horror film continues to diversify, and the post-*Whispering Corridors* period saw several important developments. The high school horror film remained a popular subgenre, achieving its most recent success with *Death Bell* (Yoon Hong-seung, 2008) and its sequel (2010). Indeed, the trend toward horror sequels was only established after the success of *Whispering Corridors* grew to a five-film franchise with the sequels *Memento Mori* (1999), *Wishing Stairs*

(2003), *Voice* (2005), and *Blood Pledge* (2009). The extension of the high school horror film into sequels, imitations, and new inspirations led to some new territory for the genre. *Memento Mori* is noteworthy for being one of the few and first Korean films — of any genre — to tackle homosexuality. The lesbian romance at the heart of that film exists only in the past, and is depicted only through flashback, adding a typically tragic dimension to the relationship. In fact, some of the first representations of homosexual love in Korean cinema used the device of a ghost taking possession of the living to resolve its earthly desires: though not a horror film, *Bungee Jumping of Their Own* (Kim Dae-seung, 2001) depicts cross-gender reincarnation as a major complication (but not a barrier) to true love (Grossman and Lee, 2005). These youth-focused films of ghosts and revenge have therefore become one of the most potent outlets for discussion of some of South Korea's most controversial social issues.

Global Korean Horror

The high school horror subgenre has dominated but not defined the contemporary horror film in Korea. The success of *Whispering Corridors* undoubtedly started a trend and set a new pattern, but horror films made over the last decade in Korea extend far beyond the troubles of teenagers. Old stories have been retold, and iconic monsters revisited. One trend of the recent cycle has been a reinvestment in the brief *daikaiju*/giant creature subgenre of the golden age. Director Shim Hyung-rae twice tried to breathe new life into 1967s *Yonggary, Monster from the Deep* with the brash remake *Yonggary* (1999), re-released with improved special effects just two years later, as *2001 Yonggary: Yonggary vs Cyker*. This new version of the giant monster movie blatantly targeted the international market (and even received a home video release in the United States as *Reptilian*), as did its spiritual sequel by the same director, *Dragon Wars* (2007). Both films feature an almost entirely American cast and English-language dialogue. The latter film, though drawing on Korean mythology (the fearsome snake-like dragon creature called an *imoogi*), almost entirely disguises its national identity, and is better regarded as a blockbuster in the vein of Hollywood's *Godzilla* (Roland Emmerich, 1998) than a genuine horror film. Surely the best known of the new monster movies is Bong Joon-ho's *The Host* (2006), a profound genre-defying film that received wide international distribution. Though these films are vastly different in terms of quality and theme, in concert they represent a basic fear of the past, of the unknown, of invasion by a foreign monster: all appropriate themes, given the global ambitions of these films.

Indeed, the contemporary Korean horror film has flourished, in part, by assimilating foreign influences and developing even greater hybridity. Recent horror has added to traditional local menaces such as the *wonhon* and the *gumiho* by incorporating zombies, vampires, and werewolves. These hybrid films, born of a fusion of Western and Korean influences, are also typically generically mixed, functioning not primarily as horror films, but as comedies, melodramas, and even war films. A recent example is *A Werewolf Boy* (Jo Seong-hee, 2012), a smash hit (achieving over seven million local admissions) beauty-and-the-beast tale of the impossible love between a sickly girl and the feral boy she discovers and educates. The film's only moment of horror passes swiftly, like a brief dream: in it, the eponymous young man transforms into a werewolf and fatally savages the throat of his love rival. Likewise, the first vampire film of the contemporary period, *Vampire Cop Ricky* (Lee Si-myong, 2006), is a farcical crime comedy with none of the gothic atmosphere typical of Western films of this type. Along similar lines, the first depiction of zombies—in the iconic Western sense of the concept—in recent Korean film is a war-horror film set on an army base, *The Guard Post* (Kong Soo-chang, 2007). The film draws on military tensions rather than fears of the unknown. These films demonstrate both cultural specificity and the adoption of foreign tropes—a sense of global hybridity that has also defined Korean horror on an international level.

The recognition of Korean horror on the global stage occurred with a burst of excitement and curiosity; this was not a gradual process, but rather the "discovery" of a handful of films and filmmakers who led the way for wider exposure for the genre. While the international achievements of Korean horror films are impressive, it must be acknowledged that their distribution and exposure in the West was part of a wider cycle of cult cinema from East Asia. Korean horror found its audience along with a new wave of Japanese horror spearheaded by Hideo Nakata and Takashi Miike and the renaissance of the Hong Kong "bullet ballet" action film. Korean horror has, ultimately, achieved a distinct identity in the international market, but its initial steps toward global recognition were as part of the nationally indistinct "Asia Extreme" brand concept. The Asia Extreme brand was the invention of British distributors Tartan Films. After the unprecedented critical and cult audience success of the gothic Japanese horror *Ringu* on its UK release, Tartan Films acquired the rights to *Audition* (Takashi Miike, 1999) and *Battle Royale*, and then expanded their catalogue to include other Asian action films and horror, including the Hong Kong/Thai coproduction *The Eye* (The Pang Brothers, 2002), and eventually several South Korean films. Seeking to draw these generically and nationally disparate films together under a single brand, in order to capitalize on a perceived trend for more violent/thrilling/terrifying/arousing East Asian cinema, Tartan Films established "Asia Extreme" as its niche label (Shin, 2009; Dew, 2007). The brand proved successful in attracting controversy and ticket/DVD sales, and at the peak of its success expanded to include a US-based distribution wing.

Asia Extreme selected is acquisitions and created its marketing materials on a blatantly Orientalist basis, falling back on inviting stereotypes of the Far East as exotic, erotic, permissive, sexually deviant, and morally alien. It promoted sex and violence in its releases, and sought controversy wherever possible. Under these circumstances, the brand promoted the work of two Korean directors in particular—Park

Chan-wook and Kim Ki-duk—taking advantage of their film festival hype to promote their most high-profile releases. Kim Ki-duk's first moment in the spotlight came when *The Isle* (2000), a slow-paced psychological drama featuring startling scenes of physical and sexual mutilation, triggered controversy at a number of international film festivals. Members of the audience were reportedly vomiting and passing out, and the hype surrounding the film's apparently transgressive content created intense anticipation. Park Chan-wook, meanwhile, is surely best known for *Oldboy* (2003), his operatic revenge thriller that also broke taboos with its depictions of incest. *Oldboy* arrived in the United States and the United Kingdom after a spectacular reception at the 2004 Cannes International Film Festival at which it won the Grand Prix and reduced jury member Quentin Tarantino to tears (Lee, 2008). These were the first "extreme" Korean genre films to achieve significant visibility in the United States and the United Kingdom, yet it must be acknowledged that in spite of their violent content and dark tone, these are arguably *not* horror films. Indeed, this is precisely one of the problematic aspects of the Asia Extreme brand: by discarding existing generic categories in favor of creating a new concept of "extreme" cinema as a unifying concept, it blurs boundaries and slows the recognition of "real" Korean horror.

However, two films released under the Asia Extreme brand, *A Tale of Two Sisters* (Kim Jee-woon, 2003) and *Phone* (Ahn Byung-ki, 2002), arguably do reflect the greatest achievements and cultural specificity of contemporary Korean horror. Ahn Byung-ki is a rarity in the Korean film industry: an *auteur* director with a devotion to the horror genre. Typically in Korea, debut directors are given horror movies to direct as a proving ground before moving on to work with greater freedom in other genres. However, Ahn has directed only horror films, and has achieved success both at home and abroad by calculating the factors that will give his films appeal to both markets. Ahn in fact regards his own work as "Asian horror" rather than Korean horror, following the trends that brought Korean horror to the West as part of the homogenous "Asia Extreme" wave (Martin, 2013). His films typically combine the cultural sensibilities common to Korean horror with the tropes of a variety of Asian and even American horror films, from exploitative slasher films to restrained gothic horror. *Phone* can thus be read as a typical entry in the grand tradition of *wonhon* films, but also as an example of the then-new (and highly popular) cycle of East Asian techno-horrors instigated by the videotape terror of *Ringu*. Ahn's approach to the genre, and his attentive sense of trends in the international reception of East Asian cinema, reflects an increasing trend toward the globalization of Korean horror.

Kim Jee-woon, meanwhile, is known (and admired) for "playing" with genre, working in a variety of styles over an interesting career; at his best, he is praised for bringing something original to familiar genre films. His two horror films represent opposite ends of the spectrum: one is a masterpiece of restraint and suggestion, the other is visually explicit and highly gory. The former, *A Tale of Two Sisters*, has justifiably attracted the attention of critics and academics for its delicate, beautiful aesthetics and its sophisticated sense of psychological horror.

It is a film with universal appeal to fans of gothic horror, yet the film also reflects a great deal of cultural specificity and can clearly be tied to the traditions and tropes of typical Korean horror: it adapts a Korean tale filmed several times before, focuses on female bonds and the innocence of youth, involves trauma relived and revealed through flashbacks, victimization, and sadness. On the other hand, Kim's 2010 film *I Saw the Devil* (2010) is a response to the post-*Oldboy* global trend for revenge narratives and an answer to the appetite for even greater "extreme" Korean horror. The film reveals a cynical desire to please an international audience; in the version of the film submitted to the Korean censors, it was deemed unsuitable for domestic release because of its problematic violence. *I Saw the Devil*, like so many classic and contemporary Korean horror films, is concerned with revenge: a grieving husband systematically tracks and tortures the man who murdered (and beheaded) his wife. However, unlike virtually every other Korean horror film, sympathy is short for the avenger, as he becomes just as monstrous as the criminal he seeks to punish. The level of violence and abuse in the film reaches heights never before seen in Korea: the avenging "hero" severs the tendons of his prey with a scalpel, rips open another man's jaw with his bare hands, and finally decapitates his enemy in front of the man's son and mother. The film also includes a truly reprehensible rape scene in which the victim begins to enjoy the assault.

I Saw the Devil had little success with domestic audiences, but predictably achieved wide international distribution. It is just one film in an emerging subcycle of Korean horror films designed for the global (i.e., Western) market created by the Asia Extreme boom. Another such film is *Missing* (Kim Seong-hong, 2009), a film seemingly inspired by the American "torture porn" cycle in general and *Captivity* (Roland Joffé, 2007) in particular. *Missing* breaks almost every rule of the contemporary Korean horror cycle, and would be unrecognizable as Korean if not for its geographic and linguistic signifiers: the tone is one of disgust (or perhaps arousal) at the spectacle of sexual torture, not sadness; there are no flashbacks, and no long-buried secrets revealed; there is no reincarnation or revenge for the first woman murdered by her psychopathic abuser; no sense of *han*. The film instead is a simplistic tale of kidnap, torture, and rape, as a vicious middle-aged man abducts a nubile young woman, abuses her at length, kills her and grinds up her corpse, only to subsequently kidnap her inquiring sister and (attempt) the cycle again; he meets his death in the same grinder at the hands of the vengeful sister only after the meaningless deaths of several ancillary characters.

The domestic fortunes of the contemporary Korean horror film have been inconsistent, from box-office highs in the wake of *Whispering Corridors* to concerning declines more recently. The international market has proven a valuable source of exposure and appreciation for horror filmmakers in Korea, and the majority of the films made specifically for foreign audiences have been artistically disappointing. However, several films made with a more moderate sense of international ambition, combining local sensibilities with attempts to satisfy global tastes, have proven to be more satisfactory.

The Best of Both Worlds: *Bloody Reunion* (2006)

Bloody Reunion (Im Dae-woong, 2006) is exemplary of this new trend for hybrid horror in Korea; the film reflects Korean traditions and foreign influences, and has both domestic significance and an international profile. The film combines the revenge-of-the-outcast high school horror narrative with the explicitly violent "torture porn" subgenre, appealing to an international market through its unusually graphic violence and appropriation of slasher film tropes, yet reflecting the core values and style of contemporary Korean horror. *Bloody Reunion* achieved note-worthy success on its domestic release, attracting almost half-a-million admissions during what was generally a relatively difficult period for horror in Korea. The film was then acquired by Tartan Films and released in the United States on their Asia Extreme DVD label in 2007, where it joined a handful of other Korean horror films in the consumer market.

Bloody Reunion begins with the discovery of apparently horrific multiple murders, and the story unfolds in extended flashback, as a survivor of the massacre recounts for a sympathetic detective the events leading to the crime. A twist later in the film will reveal that this flashback is the invention of a guilty party: borrowing liberally from *The Usual Suspects* (Bryan Singer, 1995), the version of events we see is pre-sented to deceive both the detective in the film and the viewer-as-detective. The flashback begins with a disparate group of 20 somethings gathering for a reunion of sorts: their now-retired high school teacher is gravely ill, and they are assembling at her rural home to pay their respects and comfort her on the annual "Teacher's Day" (a long-standing Korean tradition). As the former students reunite with each other and their teacher, the polite façade begins to fade, revealing brewing tensions and resentments. Each student, it transpires, has a particular grudge against the teacher; each was abused by her in some way. One young man, a promising athlete in high school, had his future career ruined when the teacher forced him to overwork and permanently damage his knee as punishment for some trivial offence. Two of the stu-dents are now engaged to be married, yet both remember how they were humiliated by their teacher because of their lower class and relative poverty. Now a beautiful woman, one student reveals she became addicted to cosmetic surgery after being relentlessly teased by the teacher for being obese. Another was socially crippled after an incident in which the strictness of the teacher caused him to defecate in his pants in view of the entire class. Even the teacher's favorite former student appears haunted by memories of inappropriate affection that imply sexual abuse.

The traumatic suffering of these innocent students, now psychologically damaged adults, reflects the central theme of the high school horror cycle: the intense pressures and abuses of the educational system in Korea. Each student is wracked with *han*, and their pasts continue to haunt them. Their resentment toward their former teacher creates not only tension, but contradiction: in the traditional order of a Confucian society, teachers are in one of the most respected and admirable positions, to be adored with filial loyalty. Tensions rise, and the former students vent their grievances to an apparently oblivious teacher; she recalls none of the abuses that haunt these young adults. One by one, as night falls, the characters are abducted by a mysterious masked assailant (implied to be the teacher's own child, himself a deformed outcast) and tortured to death, presumably as punishment for their verbal rebukes of their former teacher. The graphic nature of these scenes of torture and murder make this film unlike most of the restrained, gothic horrors of the high school cycle. The mobile camerawork and speedy close-ups capture the bloodied bodies of the victims in tight detail. The first victim, the first of the students to speak out against the teacher, is repeatedly slashed with a razorblade, then strapped to a chair and forced to swallow shards of sharp metal, fatally wounding his throat. The second victim, abducted to the same room, has her eyes stapled open (an apparently lethal procedure) as punishment for failing to "see" when her teacher needed help earlier in the day. The other students are killed in similar manner. Only one of the former students, a kindly young woman called Mija, is apparently genuinely loving to the teacher, having no traumatic resentments at all. It is Mija, thus, who survives the ordeal, along with her ailing and weakened teacher.

However, the film's twist reveals a very different truth: the story depicted in flashback, recounted by Mija, is a fiction created to cover her crimes. Following Mija's escape from the hospital and abduction of the teacher, a final flashback reveals the truth of the crime: Mija (whose true name is Jungwon, a character depicted in the fraudulent flashback as male, and the most quiet and traumatized of the former students) is the true killer, having murdered all the other students by poisoning them. The abuses suffered by the other students—insulted for being poor, humiliated for being overweight, permanently injured in the course of a harsh punishment, ostracized after publicly soiling themself—were *all* experienced by Mija/Jungwon. The other students, far from growing up to become resentful and psychologically damaged, were successful in their fields (a star athlete, a prosperous CEO) and genuinely adoring of their former teacher. It was only Jungwon who grew up with resentment, with *han*, and sought revenge.

The film's "Final Girl" is thus actually its killer, and she represents the ultimate outcast. In the original/false version of events, the traumas are shared, and the students all suffered equally; yet solidarity is a comfort typically unavailable to the pitiful *wanggda* of Korean horror, and thus the "true" flashback restores this narrative convention, heaping the suffering onto a single poor soul. She believes that if not for the terrible treatment of her teacher, she could have equaled the achievements of her peers. The killer here is highly sympathetic, and her personal suffering extensive. Her desire for revenge is understandable, yet she chooses her victims with the manic jealousy of an evil slasher villain. Unlike most Korean horror films, her

Figure 24.2   The face of horror is sadness, not cruelty. Seo Yeong-hee in *Bloody Reunion* (*To Sir with Love*, 2006). Directed by Dae-wung Lim. Produced by Fineworks, and U Zone Films.

quest for vengeance creates more innocent victims, it does not avenge them; justice does not prevail, instead the film gives us a vicious cycle of repaying thoughtless cruelty with the same. The ambiguous climax depicts the apparent suicide of Jungwon/Mija, and the possibility that the guilt-ridden and regretful teacher also took her own life; the predominant tone of the film's final moments is, undoubtedly, sadness (Figure 24.2).

Bloody Reunion thus grafts the violent excesses of torture horror and the narrative/moral structure of the slasher film onto the contemporary Korean high school horror film, resulting in a film appealing to both markets and reflecting a high degree of hybridity and artistic integrity. Even in departing from convention in several significant ways, the film is recognizably and specifically Korean. In "undoing" the entire narrative with its final twist, *Bloody Reunion* recalls the French horror film *Switchblade Romance* (aka *High Tension/Haute Tension*, Alexandre Aja, 2003). The film's marketing department, further, tried to emulate the poster for the Australian horror film *Wolf Creek* (Greg McLean, 2005). It is fair, then, to say that the film reflects more than a melding of American and Korean horror; rather, it demonstrates an awareness of (and a desire to join) a newly forming canon of global horror.

Conclusion: The Future of Korean Horror

The Korean horror film, after five decades of development, refinement, decline, and resurgence, is still best characterized as a hybrid cinema. The sadness, the emotion, the emphasis on suffering and salvation—all reflect the melodramatic properties of the genre. The Korean melo-horror is thus a (culturally) specific type of horror film, demonstrating commonalities with a raft of other national horror cinemas but ultimately establishing its own identity, regardless of international influence. Indeed, in spite of the newness of the trend for globalized Korean horror, it is, as argued above, not just recently that the genre has demonstrated foreign influences. As the international audience continues to demonstrate a desire for "extreme" Korean cult and horror cinema, the genre continues to demonstrate a fixation on recurring themes, concepts and plots while leaving considerable room for variation and experimentation within this flexible formula. The Korean horror film, though now global, is still recognizable, more than fifty years after that fateful stormy night in *The Housemaid*.

References

Black, A. (2003) Coming of age: the South Korean horror film, in *Fear Without Frontiers: Horror Cinema Across the Globe* (ed. S.J. Schneider), FAB Press, Godalming, pp. 185–203.

Choi, J. (2010) *The South Korean Film Renaissance: Local Hitmakers, Global Provocateurs*, Wesleyan University Press, Middletown, CT.

Clover, C.J. (1992) *Men, Women and Chain Saws: Gender in the Modern Horror Film*, Princeton University Press, Princeton, NJ.

Dew, O. (2007) 'Asia Extreme': Japanese cinema and British hype. *New Cinemas*, **5** (1), 53–73.

Grossman, A. and Lee, J. (2005) *Memento Mori* and other ghostly sexualities, in *New Korean Cinema* (eds C.Y. Shin and J. Stringer), Edinburgh University Press, Edinburgh, pp. 180–192.

Hendrix, G. (2004) Back with a vengeance: the psychic delirium at the dark heart of K-horror. *Film Comment*, **40** (6), 46–47.

Hwang, Y.M. (2013) Heritage of horrors: reclaiming the female ghost in *Shadows in the Palace*, in *Korean Horror Cinema* (eds A. Peirse and D. Martin), Edinburgh University Press, Edinburgh, pp. 73–86.

Kim, K.H. (2004) *The Remasculinization of Korean Cinema*, Duke University Press, Durham, NC.

Lee, N.J.Y. (2008) Salute to Mr. Vengeance! The making of transnational auteur Park Chan-wook, in *East Asian Cinemas: Exploring Transnational Connections on Film* (eds L. Hunt and W.F. Leung), London and New York, I.B. Tauris, pp. 203–219.

Lee, N.J.Y. (2011) Localized globalization and a monster national: *The Host* and the South Korean film industry. *Cinema Journal*, **50** (3), 45–61.

Lee, H. (2013) Family, death and the *wonhon* in four films of the 1960s, in *Korean Horror Cinema* (eds A. Peirse and D. Martin), Edinburgh University Press, Edinburgh, pp. 23–34.

Lee, N.J.Y. and Stringer, J. (2012) Remake, repeat, revive: Kim Ki-young's housemaid trilogies, in *Film Trilogies: New Critical Approaches* (eds C. Perkins and C. Verevis), Basingstoke, Palgrave Macmillan, pp. 145–163.

Martin, D. (2013) Between the local and the global: 'Asian horror' in Ahn Byung-ki's *Phone* and *Bunshinsaba*, in *Korean Horror Cinema* (eds A. Peirse and D. Martin), Edinburgh University Press, Edinburgh, pp. 145–157.

McHugh, K. and Abelmann, N. (eds) (2005) *South Korean Golden Age Melodrama: Gender, Genre and National Cinema*, Wayne State University Press, Detroit, MN.

Morris, M. (2013) War horror and anti-Communism: from *Piagol* to *Rainy Days*, in *Korean Horror Cinema* (eds A. Peirse and D. Martin), Edinburgh University Press, Edinburgh, pp. 48–59.

Oh, E. (2013) *Mother's Grudge* and *Woman's Wail*: the monster-mother and Korean horror film, in *Korean Horror Cinema* (eds A. Peirse and D. Martin), Edinburgh University Press, Edinburgh, pp. 60–70.

Paquet, D. (2007) *Christmas in August* and Korean melodrama, in *Seoul Searching: Culture and Identity in Contemporary Korean Cinema* (ed. F.K. Gateward), State University of New York, Albany, NY, pp. 37–54.

Peirse, A. and Byrne, J. (2013) Creepy liver-eating fox-ladies: *The Thousand Year Old Fox* and Korea's *gumiho*, in *Korean Horror Cinema* (eds A. Peirse and D. Martin), Edinburgh University Press, Edinburgh, pp. 35–47.

Peirse, A. and Martin, D. (2013) Introduction, in *Korean Horror Cinema* (eds A. Peirse and D. Martin), Edinburgh University Press, Edinburgh, pp. 1–20.

Shin, C.Y. (2009) The art of branding: Tartan "Asia Extreme" films, in *Horror to the Extreme: Changing Boundaries in Asian Cinema* (eds J. Choi and M. Wada-Marciano), Hong Kong University Press, Hong Kong, pp. 85–100.

25

Sisterhood of Terror

The Monstrous Feminine of Southeast Asian Horror Cinema

Andrew Hock Soon Ng

Southeast Asia is home to a host of supernatural creatures, many of whom are remnants of a history before the region's incorporation of the various belief systems that have today become the official religions of the countries located there. Before Buddhism exerted its influence on Myanmar (then Burma) and Thailand (then Siam) in the thirteenth century, and before the advent of Hinduism (fourteenth century) and Islam (fifteenth century) in the Malay Archipelago, the people of Southeast Asia practiced diverse forms of animistic beliefs and folk magic characterized by a profound respect for the natural world, and the guardian-spirits that inhabit it. Even with the arrival of these religions, which resulted in the eventual marginalization of these animistic worldviews (often through mechanisms of state disavowal), such beliefs remain a stubbornly integral part of the region to this day, although many have undergone recalibrations in order to adapt to the context of contemporary ideologies and modernity. Belief in a multitude of otherworldly monsters is a primary example of the persistence of a premodern past within the modern, one that various nation states' religious orders and modernization projects are only able to exorcise to a point, beyond which they must negotiate with uncomfortably. These negotiations often occur in the states' deployment of these monsters to reinforce the supremacy of the status quo.

One of the more potent avenues for specific (re)negotiations is popular media, especially films. In the twenty-first century, horror films in Southeast Asia have witnessed an aesthetic reinvigoration due in part to the success of Japanese and Korean horror cinema on the international scene, and in part (in some countries) to the loosening of governmental restrictions placed on the genre. Once a staple of low-budget productions, which often also functioned as thinly disguised soft-porn, the horror genre in Southeast Asia has undergone a radical transformation to

A Companion to the Horror Film, First Edition. Edited by Harry M. Benshoff.
© 2014 John Wiley & Sons, Inc. Published 2017 by John Wiley & Sons, Inc.

become respectable works of art reflecting the region's cinematic developments. Horror films are effectively encouraged by film industries, with sponsorships from government bodies, and direction by highly acclaimed filmmakers. Aided by the latest cinematographic technologies, and with careful attention to details in order to create a sense of local verisimilitude, these films also draw on abiding local myths about supernatural beings, refashioning them for contemporary ideological ends.

It is notable that as much as these monsters predate these nations' histories, they are also the products of current ideological agendas. As signifiers, these monsters are clearly anachronistic: originating in the premodern and encompassing specific meanings associated to the past, they are realigned to specific national pursuits in the present, resulting in the acquisition of new significations that give them a distinctively modern (and even globalized) flavor. Theorists of teratology have frequently reminded us that monsters are embodiments of culture and thus do "cultural work" (Cohen, 1996: 4). Monsters can either be created to articulate particular political, social, and/or economic anxieties (such as those in the Anglo-American Gothic tradition) or be recalled, as in Southeast Asian horror films, to address contemporary ideological distresses within a given nation. What is especially interesting is the fact that even when they are resurrected and "coerced" into serving official agendas, they rarely lose their distinguishing premodern configurations, and indirectly compromise the very mechanisms used to coerce them. To put it differently, while these monsters are deployed by the status quo to reinforce certain religio-nationalist objectives, they invariably surpass their prescribed roles, effectively placing the functions they are meant to serve under erasure.

If films serve as a thermometer that measures the cultural temperature of particular historical moments, then horror, I argue, is an especially potent one. As Brigid Cherry observes:

> It is often the ideological imperative of the narrative of a film that gives it meaning in a historical or cultural context: the point of analysis here is to ask what the film has to say about the world it reflects. This is important because … the horror genre seems to be a form that is easily adaptable at addressing a range of ideological issues. Horror films invariably reflect the social and political anxieties of the cultural moment. (Cherry, 2009: 210)

These anxieties are often experienced at the level of the national unconscious, and thus difficult to express. Horror films can foreground what is otherwise unspoken or unspeakable, often by carefully camouflaging these issues in exaggerated symbols to escape censorship. But while horror films "reflect the social and political anxieties of the cultural moment," their reliance on a variety of monstrosities as principle narrative catalysts also frequently render them ambiguous in terms of what these films say. As mentioned, monsters may do cultural work, but precisely what this entails is at best, unclear, and at worse, subversive. For instance, they may be evoked to remind the audience of the nation's pagan and premodern past, thus requiring repression as part of the nation's progress toward enlightenment by a "true" religion and modernity. However, the fact that audiences often neither remember, nor place much emphasis on, the denouement of these narratives—focusing on the creatures' formidable presence instead—suggests that it is what these monsters signify, rather than their subservience to the narratives' overarching ideologies, that most enthralls the audience's imagination.

Another example of how Southeast Asian horror films negotiate with cultural anxieties is through their representation of women. In a region noted for its strict adherence to gender hierarchies that plot women as secondary and inferior to men—a structure further reinforced by various religious and cultural traditions—its horror films have proven refreshingly dissident in their subtle redrawing of gender boundaries. Women, when transformed into or aligned with monsters, discover a new and empowered sense of self otherwise denied them. Unlike their Western counterparts, who must usually be eliminated to bring about narrative closure, Southeast Asian monstrous females' triumph is often instrumental in restoring order and effecting narrative closure. This directly aligns the audiences' sympathy with her, and not her "victims." But this narrative strategy is never straightforward. On the surface, horror films will usually reinstate the legitimacy of the status quo, but on closer reading, they sometimes reveal an oppositional stance that questions its logic.

In this essay, I focus on films featuring a specific female creature known throughout the region. Known as Nang Nak in Thailand, Tiyanak in The Philippines, Kuntilanak (or Matianak) in Indonesia, and Pontianak in Malaysia, she is believed to be the revenant of a woman who has died during childbirth (in most traditions, usually the firstborn), and subsequently lingers to prey on the living (Ng, 2008). In some variations, she assumes the guise of a beautiful woman to lure unsuspecting (male) victims, and may be subdued by embedding a nail behind her neck, rendering her powerless and subservient. The popularity of this creature throughout Southeast Asia cannot be overemphasized: she not only is a staple of the horror genre of Malaysia, Thailand, and Indonesia, but plays a significant role in their cinematic histories as well. My discussion will focus specifically on *Nang Nak* (Thailand, dir. Nonzee Nimibutr, 1999), the series of Pontianak films from Malaysia culminating in *Pontianak Harum Sundal Malam* (*Pontianak of the Tuber Rose*, Malaysia, dir. Shuhaimi Baba, 2004), and *Kuntilanak* (Indonesia, dir. Rizal Mantovani, 2006). While the representation of women is my main concern, this dimension cannot be isolated from other related ideologies such as religion, modernity, and nationalism, since they construct, inform, and uphold regional codes of gender and sexuality. As such, my analysis of women in Southeast Asian horror will touch upon the socio-cultural contexts from which these films emerge, and within which they ambivalently operate.

Nang Nak (1999): The Paradox of Thai Femininity

Nang Nak (1999) is widely acknowledged to be a turning point in Thailand's film industry. While conscientiously made to emulate art-film (*sakon*), and carefully publicized to instruct the local audience of the film's equal worth to the finest Western productions, the narrative is also explicitly Thai in its unmistakable historical references, its emphasis on (alleged) values associated with Thai culture, and its adherence to Buddhist principles. However, despite the film's claim to represent Thainess unambiguously, its being aimed at a global market suggests that some degree of repackaging of Thainess is inevitable. *Nang Nak* is the director's attempt to redesign a popular, local ghost myth into "national history" (Ingawanij, 2007: 188) that has the power to evoke a Thailand uncontaminated by Western influence and modernization, and to provoke a sense of exceptionalism that uniquely identifies the nation and its people to the world.

Nonzee Nimibutr's refashioning of the Nang Nak legend has received both local and international acclaim, but what Nang Nak signifies for contemporary Thailand remains an intriguing paradox. To clarify this point, I must first underscore a feature of this monstrous feminine that is particular to the Thai culture. Unlike her sisters in neighboring countries, Nang Nak is not a creature *any* woman who dies during childbirth could potentially become, but allegedly an actual nineteenth-century historical figure renowned for her unparalleled devotion to her husband, which even death cannot undo. According to legend, Nak perished during childbirth when her husband was away in battle, but she refused to relinquish her dutiful wife's role, and used her supernatural powers to remain with her husband on his return, who remained oblivious to the circumstance until the village abbot alerted him. This tale of a wife's unflinching and undying loyalty ennobles Nak for posterity as the model Thai woman *par excellence*, in short, a national icon.

And yet, it is her embodiment of this model of perfection that compromises her national belonging as well. In a country where Buddhism is the dominant religion and belief system, Nak's devotion to her husband is clearly incompatible with a fundamental Buddhist tenet: that desire is suffering and ties us to the wheel of life, or, *samsāra* (the constant cycle of rebirths); desire must be overcome in order for a Buddhist to achieve enlightenment (*mokhsa*). That Nak chooses to cling to the living evinces a persistent craving, a "sin" that is further compounded her deployment of deception to keep her husband innocent of the fact. And to further indemnify her unnatural status, Nak shows no qualms in killing anyone who threatens to interrupt the monadic fantasy she has created for her family (Figure 25.1).

Nak clearly occupies a paradoxical position within contemporary Thailand. Nak reflects "a kind of cultural heritage" (Fuhrmann, 2009: 225) but she is also the embodiment of "the truths of impermanence and of the futility of desire" (222). In Buddhism, sexual craving constitutes the most potent, and therefore most dangerous form of attachment, because its consequence is the perpetuation of *samsāra*. Sexual desire "ties humans to their earthly body, to the circle of rebirths, and inscribes them in a long line of ancestors and descendants" (Gowans, 2003: 44). It is a "poison" that "pollute[s] and maintain[s] human existence" that Buddhists must avoid (45). Although Buddhism essentially does not give preference to one gender above another, its primary goal to relinquish all cravings tacitly presents women as inferior. As conduits of rebirth, women's bodies inevitably serve as metonymical signifiers of suffering, and their carnal inclination is a potential source of temptation for men.

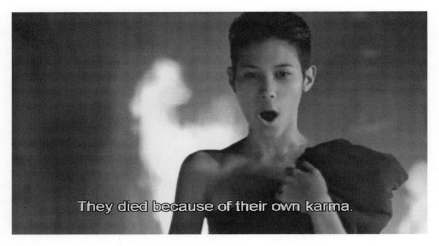

Figure 25.1   Nang Nak justifying her murder of the villagers who wanted to destroy her. *Nang-Nak* (1999). Directed by Nonzee Nimibutr. Produced by Tai Entertainment.

Nang Nak increasingly emphasizes this point as the narrative develops, placing the Thainess of Nak's womanhood under *erasure* in order to accentuate its Buddhist message. Nang Nak becomes recalcitrant and willful (Knee, 2005: 148), characteristics often associated with the sensuous woman, and as the text implies, uses her sexuality to keep her husband Mak under illusion. From the point of Mak's returns, Nak, who has thus far exemplified the loyal wife longingly awaiting her husband's homecoming, is now transformed into an eroticized succubus that satiates her victim with bodily pleasures. Much of the film's *mise-en-scène* depicting them together is underscored by the erotic. Their scanty clothing may be attributed to the warm climate and their poverty, but their bodily proximity throughout the text suggests more than mere intimacy.

Despite this, however, Nak's signifier as the model Thai woman is never altogether effaced. She continues to demonstrate unfailing commitment to her husband, and makes every effort to ensure his happiness and contentment. In one especially moving scene, Mak suddenly awakens before dawn to find Nak in the process of preparing rice for breakfast; when he gently reprimands her, she responds that she must redouble her wifely efforts in anticipation of a time when she will no longer be able to tend to him.[1] Her words reveal that she is fully cognizant of the ephemeral condition of their time together, lending them a deeper pathos. Nak's paradoxical qualities clearly confound any neat attempt at labeling her duplicitous, as Buddhism (especially of the Theravada tradition, to which Thailand subscribes) invariably would. Her devotion to Mak cannot be attributed to mere deviousness, for it also genuinely expresses her love. This, in turn, directly compromises the (Buddhist) audience's identification with Nak, ambiguously shifting it between sympathy for her plight, and disquiet over her stubborn craving and wanton extermination of the innocent.

Figure 25.2 The renowned Abbot Somdej attempting to reason with Nang Nak. *Nang-Nak* (1999). Directed by Nonzee Nimibutr. Produced by Tai Entertainment.

The story reaches its climax with the arrival of the monk Somdej To to subdue Nang Nak, after various attempts have proven altogether unsuccessful.[2] The scene depicting the confrontation between monk and ghost, witnessed by Mak and the villagers, is replete with Buddhist symbology (Figure 25.2). While the prominent abbot is an obvious one, this scene also shows Nak in her true state—a decaying corpse which transforms into a beautiful woman—and thus directly referencing the Theravadian Buddhist soteriology that links female sexuality and death (Fuhrmann, 2009: 226), by juxtaposing the fleeting nature of desire and the inevitability of all fleshly cravings. This scene also invites the audience to both recall and vicariously participate in the Buddhist practice of *asuba kammatthān*—"meditating on corpses or images of corpses"—a practice aimed at "break[ing] the causality of desire-attachment-suffering" via a "protracted visual encounter with death" (232).

What is exchanged between the monk and Nang Nak is not for the witnesses' (including the audience's) hearing, but the result is a resolution that will, unsurprisingly, reinforce the supremacy of Buddhism. Nak is made to realize the impossibility of her pursuit, and submits to the monk's reasoning to relinquish her attachment to her husband and to this world. After a tearful farewell, she returns to a corpse. Somdej proceeds to extract a small bone fragment from her skull into which he inscribes Nak's spirit, which he will later install in his temple to commemorate her for posterity as testimony to her purity and nobility. Adam Knee interprets this as a reflection of Nang Nak's integral place within Thailand's cultural heritage which, although incompatible with Buddhist worldview, cannot be "erased" but only "contained" by the latter (Knee, 2005: 146). This reading, however, reveals an incomplete understanding of Buddhism. That Nang Nak is eventually "contained" is correct, but this is not, as Knee asserts, the result of a compromise arrived at by the monk after failing to eliminate her. The virtue most exalted in Buddhism is compassion, and no

Figure 25.3   Agreeing to renounce this life, Nang Nak returns to the earth from which she came. *Nang-Nak* (1999). Directed by Nonzee Nimibutr. Produced by Tai Entertainment.

creature, however evil, is beyond the pale of the Buddha's compassion. When reading *Nang Nak* in this context, it is evident that the monk's decision is precisely in accordance with his religious conviction. In demonstrating compassion, the monk helps reinscribe Nak back into the dominant order so that she can have a place within it and therefore attain peace (Figure 25.3).

Yet, the film's reification of Buddhism's supremacy remains somewhat equivocal. As Fuhrmann postulates, *Nang Nak*, like many Thai ghost films, actually refuses the closure prescribed by the Buddhist truth that death signifies impermanence and the futility of attachment. Instead, these films refashion loss into a "domain of fantasy" (Fuhrmann, 2009: 233) where death actually reinforces desire by reminding the viewer of what must be forsaken when one dies. In the case of *Nang Nak*, I would suspect that rather than inoculating viewers against desire, the film actually encourages them to treasure their significant others more, not less; as Nak tells us, a time will come when they will no longer be here for us. Moreover, while Buddhism may succeed in containing the creature and thereby restoring order, it is only because Nang Nak consents to the abbot's reasoning. Resolution is arrived at due to *her independent decision* to relinquish attachment, and not because of coercion or fear. One could argue that this further reinforces the supremacy of the faith, since even a dangerous, otherworldly creature cannot deny its noble truths. But this reading fails to appreciate the fact that narrative closure is reached through negotiation between two parties who view each other as equals and with respect. Unlike the Brahmin priest who attempts to forcefully subjugate Nang Nak earlier in the film, the monk deploys reason and compassion to convince Nak that he is a friend who only wants to show her the error of her ways. Nak is won over not by a superior power, but by the monk's sincerity and goodness.

Significantly, in choosing finally to leave this world, Nak indirectly also helps her husband attain transcendence to become the most exalted of men in Buddhist cosmogony: a monk. In this way, while she may fail in one respect to embody true Buddhist womanhood—the "mother who nurtures the religion by bearing sons who will one day enter the Sangha [the Buddhist order]" (Keyes, 1984: 233)—when understood in the context of her submission to the abbot's advice, she not only emulates, but actually surpasses this embodiment. In leaving him, Nak ironically gives Mak life ("nurture") again, prompting his entry into the Sangha. As a monk, Mak becomes her metaphorical "provision" to the order—one that exceeds "regular" provision of sustenance, since he will represent her offering to the religion *every day until his death*. Such narrative cues make it apparent that while the authority of the dominant order may be undeniable, what it signifies can also be read against itself, rendering its ideological coordinates unclear and in need of continuous reassessment. Buddhism's cause, as *Nang Nak* insinuates, can sometimes be abetted even by beings the religion deems aberrant: this then begs the question of whether Buddhism's dominant presence in Thailand is ultimately also the result of its constant compromises with other systems of belief that are entrenched, albeit peripherally, within the social fabric of the country.

The *Pontianak* Films of Malaysia: Pre-Oedipal Pleasures of a National Ego

In *Nang Nak*, the religious theme clearly defines the trajectory of the narrative. As a result, the film also reifies, although equivocally, Thai nationalism, since Buddhism and Thainess are intricately intertwined. A similarly twinned ideology also operates in Malaysia, where its official religion, Islam, extends into almost every aspect of the country's political, social, and economic agendas. The Constitution of Malaya (established in 1957, the year Malaya gained independence from British rule[3]), while recognizing the legitimacy of other faiths, also identifies Islam as the religion of the Malays, the ethnic group that forms the majority of the country's population. Accordingly, this same constitution makes it compulsory that a Malay must *de facto* be Muslim. As such, in Malaysia, "religion (read Islam) [becomes] the ethnic identifier (read Malayness) for the Malays" (Aziz and Shamsul, 2004: 351). The Constitution, moreover, also establishes that the head of the government *must* be a Malay, which, by logical extension, will inevitably make the teachings of Islam the fundamental principles by which the government is guided. And while Malaysia is not adverse to differing (especially Western) ideologies, the government, through various state apparatuses, nevertheless monitors them in order to expurgate elements that can potentially threaten, compromise, or undermine Islam. Hence, while Western films and books are freely available throughout the country, those with explicit content incompatible with Islamic teachings (nudity, homosexuality, extreme violence, etc.) are either banned or heavily censored. In the case of home-grown Malay popular culture, it must be inflected with Islamic signifiers and uphold government policies, whether implicitly or otherwise; any local cultural product that fails in this count will be denied recognition by the government, and disallowed from public consumption.[4]

In view of the country's restrictive regulations that stringently prescribe the forms and contents to which Malay popular culture must subscribe, it is perhaps unsurprising that horror films have been unofficially banned in Malaysia for three decades, beginning 1974.[5] This year is significant as it coincided with the period of aggressive Islamization undertaken by the ruling party (Barisan Nasional, or the National Front) to prevent the oppositional ultra-Islamic party, PAS (Pan-Malaysian Islamic Party) from securing majority votes. While the obvious reason for the ban on horror films was that they depicted belief systems and practices that Islam disallows, the more clandestine one is the fact that these alternative belief systems are often strangely attractive and could potentially reignite the cultural unconscious of the land's distant past before Islam. As Benedict Anderson notes, there are "genealogies older than those of the nations over which they are now perched" (Anderson, 1983: 94); from this vantage point, what is repressed, as Freud famously tells us, always threatens to return.

Curiously, the Pontianak films of Malaysia (there are 12 altogether) seem to reflect uncannily the condition of a nation-as-ego coming into being. The relationship between these films and the dominant ideology can be read against a psychoanalytic framework that suggests the country's uneasy but persistent ties to its premodern past, even as it increasingly embraces Islam and modernity. If the birth of this nation is read as an Oedipal story, then modernity and Islam would be the twin-father-figures after which this newborn must fashion itself, while the Pontianak is the premodern, maternal other that must be rejected, but which continues to haunt the nation with a sense of loss. Lest this reading is construed as farfetched, I want to draw attention to the fact that 1957 was not only the year Malaysia became independent and made Islam the official religion, but it also marked the production of the country's first two Pontianak films, *Pontianak* and *Dendam Pontianak* (*The Pontianak's Revenge*, both directed by B. N. Rao and now lost). When understood from a Freudian perspective, what seem like coincidental events are actually pieces to a story of a nation's symbolic experience of a traumatic parturition. The establishment of an ego (Malaysia) necessitates the installation of a disciplining father-figure/Superego (heavily inflected with patriarchy) to help it separate from and finally reject all its pre-Oedipal (maternal) desires. But, as Freud tells us, the ego can never fully accomplish this, but will continue to accommodate these desires, albeit repressed. In producing the first two Pontianak films the year it gained independence, Malaysia-as-ego reified its unrelenting desire for the maternal other even as it acceded to the superiority of the paternal self. For unlike the Pontianak of traditional folklore, which paints the creature as singularly menacing and virulent, the Pontianak in the first five film versions is also a *loving mother* cursed into becoming a Pontianak, but who nevertheless retains her human goodness and, more importantly, her parental links with her child.[6]

This filmic departure from folklore is significant from a psychoanalytic perspective because it potentially reflects the nation's ambivalence with regards to *both* its ties with the premodern and its embrace of Islam and modernity. In all of the first five films, the Pontianak is a hideous and unnatural creature, clearly premodern; however, she can also transform into a beautiful woman and is consistently an affectionate mother — an attribute especially sought-after in the womenfolk of any nation, particularly a recently established one. This second set of characteristics (coupled with the fact that these films largely unfold from the Pontianak's focal point) might cancel out the first, allowing her a place in the national imaginary despite her incompatibility with existing official ideologies. Notably, the Pontianak must remain distanced from her child but still sustain a strong parental bond, metaphorically reflecting the nation-as-ego's attachment to its maternal other that may be repressed but never completely abandoned.

Yet, like any maturing ego, Malaysia sought to increasingly iterate its subjective position by concomitantly strengthening its identification with its father-figure(s) and further repressing its maternal other. In developing a self-identity and seeking international recognition as a viable trade partner, Malaysia accentuated its regulating ideology (modern Islam) and relegated any irreconcilable elements (premodern, anti-Islamic) to the margins. Once again, the Pontianak films are intriguingly reflective of this shifting circumstance. The sixth and seventh versions of the film, made in the 1960s, no longer emulate the earlier ones. In both *Pontianak Gua Musang* (*Pontianak of the Civet Cave*, 1964; dir. B. N. Rao) and *Pusaka Pontianak* (*The Pontianak's Heritage*, 1965; dir. Ramón A. Estella), not only is the Pontianak deprived of its motherly affection, she is not even present. Instead she is evoked merely as a symbol of feminine diabolism: the creature is a ruse used by the films' villainesses to serve their avaricious ends. Tellingly, the wicked woman in *Pusaka Pontianak* actually declares (as she dies engulfed in flames) that she *is* the Pontianak, thus metonymically aligning the monster with a woman who contravenes the ideological imperatives of the nation's Symbolic order. Unsurprisingly as well, both women are also childless and adulterous. The Pontianak films of the 1960s clearly evince a role reversal on many levels, all of which emphasizes the incompatibility of this creature with the status quo. This premodern creature, now recast as symbol, on one level signifies women who are un-Islamic and refuse to assist the nation's pursuit of progress, and on another, becomes consigned to the realm of superstition in order to fool those lacking in faith or modern, rational thinking. The 1974 installment, *Pontianak* (dir. Roger Sutton), is a decidedly poor affair: badly made and unintentionally comical, it seems like a parody of the original films and thus further indemnifies the Pontianak as a creature not to be taken seriously.

Even so, Sutton's version will mark the eclipse not only of the Pontianak films, but the horror genre in Malaysia in general. Despite the creature's gradual demonization and/or relegation to the laughable, she had remained a cinematic icon for the Malaysian audience 20 years after independence. For a country aggressively trying to revitalize Islam and augment modernity as agendas of nation-building, the Pontianak's popularity, along with that of other monstrous manifestations in Malaysian horror, is an indicator that suggests an unrelenting fascination with anti-Islamic, premodern ideologies and the desire to engage, if only vicariously, with them. For this reason, as I am inclined to suspect, the unofficial ban was established to disallow the local production of horror films. Throughout the administration of Mahathir Mohamad, the country's fourth and most charismatic Prime Minister, Islamic ideology (reinforced with an emphasis on "Asian Values") became steadily mapped onto the nation's socio-cultural fabric, giving almost no room for any competing ideologies to root, much less develop. During this period, while Malaysia became an economic powerhouse (until the 1997 Asian Financial Crisis), its art and popular culture suffered a significant setback. Under the direction of this powerful Superego, who deployed various state apparatuses as mechanisms of coercion or surveillance, the nation-as-ego was compelled to exert more repression of desires prohibited by the status quo. And since art and popular culture often serve as subtle avenues to vex the official, they must be regulated with greater severity. The vagueness of the country's Sedition Act (1948) and the Internal Security Act (1960) are especially ominous, because any aspect of socio-cultural life that the symbolic order deems threatening can be easily removed by evoking these Acts.

The arts and cultural scene would be revived when Mahathir left office in 2003. Almost immediately, the horror genre returned with a new Pontianak film, *Pontianak Harum Sundal Malam* (or *Pontianak HSM*, 2004). The moment the exacting father-figure that had personified Malaysian Islam and modernity (Mahathir is widely regarded as the Father of Modern Malaysia) was no more, the nation-as-ego relaxed its guard and allowed the repressed to return.[7] Moreover, since the forward-looking modern Malay in Mahathir's discourse, although never explicit, is always gendered male (Thompson, 2003: 428), the return of this premodern, female monster at the wake of his administration's end is strikingly reminiscent of the Freudian family romance. *Pontianak HMS*, directed by Shuhaimi Baba, a filmmaker well-known for her controversial, feminist-slanted films, is possibly the best Pontianak film to date, having won awards at local and international festivals. It resurrects many of the earlier Pontianak films' characteristics, and takes itself very seriously, paying close heed to character development and narrative subtlety. For example, the relationship between mother (Pontianak) and daughter (human) is imbued with qualities reminiscent of ghostly possession and the gothic double (the same actor plays both roles)—a tropes not found in any previous version. Through the dynamics of this familial bond played out against a backdrop inhabited by morally depraved and symbolically castrated men, *Pontianak HMS* can be read as a subtle criticism of the nation's dominant discourses.

Kuntilanak (2006): Disconcerting Women

If Malaysian popular culture has significantly refashioned the creature's myth to suit its ideological ends, the Indonesian 2006 film version has completely redesigned it to the point of negating all references to tradition. Entitled *Kuntilanak*, the film deprives the creature of some of her most basic characteristics — including her origin and the method of her subjugation — and recharges the myth with unrelated elements that serve to reify its embedded messages about gender and nation. More problematic, as I will discuss later, is the fact that these elements are obviously drawn from the Western slasher film. This deprives *Kuntilanak* of its cultural distinctiveness, for even its Indonesian features become directly compromised by this heavy borrowing. Briefly, the story revolves around Sam, who recently moved to a student hostel after suffering her stepfather's molestation. The building is located beside a graveyard overlooked by an ancient tree, which, according to rumors, is purportedly the abode of a Kuntilanak. While Sam is skeptical, her boyfriend Agung is apprehensive. Soon after, several students turn up dead. When Agung himself mysteriously disappears, Sam finally learns that a Kuntilanak is behind these horrific incidents, and *that she is the creature's source*. Somehow related to the monster by blood, Sam is able to summon it with a chant to punish whoever disconcerts her; however, because the chant also puts her in a trance, she is unconscious of her action. In the end, braving into a forbidden room located in the hostel, Sam rescues Agung and confronts the Kuntilanak. Using scattered memories of a recurring dream (depicted in the film's opening scene), she succeeds in defeating the creature by destroying the portals it uses to gain entrance into the human world.

To a point, *Kuntilanak* exemplifies the observation that women in Indonesian films often occupy the role of the "dependent" or the "sinful" (in Heider, 1991: 116; see also Sen, 1994). Their bodies are either domesticated to reflect their "subsidiary roles" (Sen, 1994: 135) or figured as sexual weapons that culminate in self-destruction. Despite the prominence of female characters and the power they wield, *Kuntilanak* necessarily begs the question that Sen raises in her rebuttal of Heider's criticism against her summary of women in Indonesian films: "We need to ask, then, when the woman is represented as powerful or vocal, to what effect, and in whose interest is this strength mobilized in the text?" (Sen, 1994: 135). Tacit as its message may be, the film can be read as recognizing the dangers animistic beliefs pose to a nation-state that embraces Islam and modernity as its dominant ideologies. Like the Pontianak films of Malaysia, *Kuntilanak* superimposes the premodern onto the female body, suggesting women's entrenched association with the past, thus requiring their constant monitoring by patriarchal forces. Unlike Malaysia however, which sets up various state apparatuses to ensure that its popular culture strictly tows the ideological line or face censorship, in Indonesia popular culture is not subjected to any such interference by the state.[8] Hence, if its popular culture indeed reflects the regulating directives of the status quo, it is because, in an acutely Foucauldian sense, it has internalized the mechanism of censorship itself. I see such self-censorship at work in *Kuntilanak* when it deliberately divests the creature of its familiar characteristics, and recasts it instead as a monster of matrilineal will-to-power and female vanity. This shift incriminates and punishes "powerful or vocal" women for their supposed desire to supplant the symbolic order and/or for their overt focus on individualism expressed as sexual independence.

A strategy the film employs to encourage such an interpretation is its reframing of the *ibu* (mother) ideal familiar to and extolled by Indonesian society. According to Anke Niehof, this term is not merely a "polite form of address for women of all ages, whether they are actually mothers or not," but is used as a title of respect for women whose responsibility is to safeguard the "prestige of the family and the [community] as a whole, not only by observing the correct etiquette and maintaining the network of social and kinship relations, but also by acquiring the material means necessary for keeping up the desired lifestyle" (Niehof, 1998: 245). The concept was established as a homage to Raden Ajeng Kartini, a Javanese princess who perished fighting the Dutch in 1904, and who has since been commemorated as the "mother" of Indonesia (although she was only 25 at her death). *Ibu* has also been a catalyst for feminist sentiments in both Indonesia's history and popular culture, and parallels what Nang Nak means in Thailand: "the role model for the modern, yet very Indonesian woman" (Heider, 1991: 75). In Indonesian film, this matronly figure is usually middle-aged, "always dressed in elegant Indonesian attire," with a face that is "[prototypical] of Indonesian feminine beauty" (76). Although her role is often minor, "at a certain moment [it] is crucial. She intervenes, offers good advice, and is important as an agent who restores order" (76).

In *Kuntilanak* however, the *ibu* figure fails to uphold these ideals, but is instead turned against itself to manifest female transgressiveness. Certainly, the scene that introduces the *ibu* character (known only as Madame) is constructed to suggest her compliance with the matronly image outlined in Heider's observation. She is clearly upper class, middle-aged, elegantly attired, and prototypically beautiful according to Indonesian standards; she is invited by the hostel's warden after a second death has occurred to help resolve the situation. This plot point however, serves to deceive an audience familiar with the *ibu's* usual meaning and function: to provide "good advice" and restore order. Her initial meeting with Sam also carries a decidedly ambiguous tone when she tells Sam to stop wasting time on a useless "human" like Agung. Madame is actually a member of a secret sisterhood connected by blood with the Kuntilanak, and her desire is to resuscitate this sisterhood after its base was burned down (and rebuilt since as the student hostel where Sam now resides). Clearly, her function is not to reinstate order, but to perpetuate chaos and death.

While the narrative succeeds in suggesting the outmodedness of the *ibu* ideal for contemporary Indonesian women[9] (by evoking this image and then subverting it), it is less successful in terms of *representing* this image: it is not clear if Madame is meant to reflect this ideal for purposes of irony, or merely a caricature that parodies the ideal. Throughout the film, she is dressed in clothes reminiscent of the 1970s; garishly made-up, she speaks in a deadpan, highly affected manner, which makes her rather comical and ridiculous. Clearly, her representation is meant to serve as a foil to Sam, an ordinary-looking and shy girl who is nevertheless intelligent and assertive. Despite this, it is clear as the narrative develops that Madame is a potently dangerous woman: her transgressive nature is not expressed in sexual terms, but in her desire to reestablish the secret sisterhood. In this way, the *ibu* is metonymically aligned with the other "bad" women in the narrative in two ways: first, all desire the power of the gaze, which directly threatens the specular rights that belong only to men. Second, both modes of femininity compromise the rigid socio-cultural codes that govern gender roles and identities in a country pursuing modernism: the overtly-sexualized woman because she is unacceptable to Islam, and the traditional *ibu* figure because she is clearly outdated and no longer relevant. Both are monstrosities different only in degree, whose deaths merely serve to literalize their aberration.

That the film rejects both the traditional female role model and the ultramodern, assertive woman is, I argue, in part to align it with the nation's ideological propensities, and in part due to the influence of Western horror. Unlike *Nang Nak* and the series of Malaysian films featuring the Pontianak, *Kuntilanak* has no clear reference at all to the original legend other than the fact that the film's title recalls a creature familiar to the region. More blatantly is the way in which *Kuntilanak* replicates two distinct conventions borrowed from Western slasher films: the "Final Girl" motif, and the certainty of textual punishment (usually violent death) to any young women who flaunt their sexuality. Throughout the film, women (and one young man) who openly display their libido are killed soon after. Unsurprisingly, these characters are also duplicitous and treacherous, thus further justifying their fate. Instead of emulating qualities such as passivity and subservience, they manifest (sexual) agency and wrest the power to look away from men. These individuals, in Linda Williams's view, dare to look, but in doing so, they become metaphorically conjoined with the monster even as they are its victims. According to Williams, the gaze performed by a woman in horror film narratives

> can only function to entrap her within [the] patriarchal structure of seeing . . . . In other words, her look [...] becomes a form of not seeing anything more than the castration she so exclusively represents for the male. If this were so, then what the woman "sees" would only be the mutilations of her own body displaced onto that of the monster. (Williams, 1996: 22)

In *Kuntilanak*, the monster is shaped curiously like the mangled bodies of its victims, underlining an unholy relationship between the creature and the assertive women. For the latter, it is as if their assault against men's ocular prerogatives has transfigured their bodies into the very thing that will penalize their gaze, and thus "shift[s] the iconic center of the spectacle away from the woman to the monster" (18).

Perhaps unsurprisingly then, the film's most potent symbol is that of the mirror. The monster, when summoned, enters the human realm through one of the hostel's three antique mirrors. Because it is a symbol that signifies the two apparent dangers women traditionally pose to men (the desire for beauty and the desire to look), and because it serves as a gateway for the creature, the mirror fittingly captures in figurative terms the distorted image of young women who display overt sexuality and egocentric pursuits that undermine the ideological parameters prescribed by the state. In *Kuntilanak*, what the mirror shows is not merely "an ocular reflection that acts as a sign" (La Belle, 1988: 11) (i.e., of female vanity and individualism), but an image that has the capacity to exceed its "mimetic fidelity" and *act on its own* in terrifyingly unimaginable ways.

The film's other obvious loan from Western slasher films is the "Final Girl." This role is satisfied by Sam, who curiously also infuses the narrative with a degree of ambiguity with regard to what she signifies. On the one hand, the final girl can be appreciated as a narrative means to realign the film back to the "national culture" (Heider, 1991: 13). On the other hand, however, this motif can equally be read as subverting precisely such an aim. Both Heider and Sen refrain from devoting much discussion to horror in their book-length studies of Indonesian cinema; if they had (especially Sen), they may have recognized that this genre *almost always* affords a counter-narrative, even while patently conforming to the one prescribed by the Symbolic order. In *Kuntilanak*, there are telling cues to suggest that the narrative incriminations against the *ibu* image and the individualistic women are not as straightforward as they seem. On the surface, Sam's character may serve as a foil to them, but careful reading will also reveal that she will figuratively consolidate them in the end as well.

As the final girl, Sam is tasked to restore order and facilitate narrative closure by destroying the Kuntilanak *via* wrecking the mirrors from which it emerges. Arguably, her actions suggest her subordination to, and therefore the film's reinforcement of, the Symbolic system. Sam, in other words, is the father's perfect daughter, for even though she wields the power of the archaic (m)other, she not only willingly relinquishes it, but uses it against the latter, upholding the status quo. But as a final girl who will look into the face of terror and survive in order to destroy the very embodiment of that terror itself (Clover, 1992: 35), Sam [whose name already suggests gender indistinctness (40)] already deprives the male of his prerogative as savior and hero—a prerogative from which Indonesian films almost never digress. Qualities commonly associated with men that the final girl must also exemplify, such as "smartness," "gravity," and "competence in […] practical matters" (35) are all evident in Sam. And unlike her hostel mates, Sam remains "sexually reluctant" and thus ensures her safety from the Kuntilanak (35). But it is possible to read this reluctance also as Sam's way of safeguarding her *difference* from her peers, and therefore, her *affiliation* with the monster. Sam may have initially rejected Madame's invitation to join the secret sisterhood, but as the narrative concludes, there are clear hints that she might do so after all. Sam's powers are obviously greater than the older woman's, and the damages she caused to the mirrors are not beyond repair. The strongest hint is provided in the scene just before the end credits, where recently discharged Agung drops by the hostel for a visit, only to encounter Sam in the midst of chanting again, this time consciously. While this may be nothing more than the conventional strategy deployed by horror films to indicate a potential sequel, it also undermines the simplistic view that the film necessarily buttresses the dominant ideology. Instead, it renders the answer to Sen's question—"in whose interest is this strength mobilized in the text?"—fundamentally hazy.

Conclusion: Vexing the Modern

Commenting on Thailand's modernizing impulse, Alan Klima once argued that the country mobilizes this through what he calls "the neoliberal economy of history":

> This grain ... concerns the economics of memory and forgetting in historical consciousness and visual culture. It is ultimately an economics of storytelling, the narrative economy by which the past is left behind and exchanged for the present, and the present is left behind and exchanged for the future, where each may go its separate ways ... with no strings attached. (Klima, 2002: 12–13)

Klima's observation, in my view, is equally relevant to the rest of Southeast Asia, where the impetus to modernize and achieve a competitive edge in the global market, while retaining cultural exclusivity, has resulted in "an economics of memory and forgetting" rehearsed largely through its visual culture. In this chapter, I have demonstrated how such an economics is performed via the deployment of a widely known horror story that focuses on a particular creature. In all the narratives discussed, what is evident is the extent to which this story has been altered to suit contemporary ideological purposes, resulting in some aspects of the region's past becoming "left behind and exchanged for" present purposes, and auguring the possibility that this story may undergo further recalibration in the future. *Nang Nak* may allegedly remain true to the original myth, while *Kuntilanak* clearly disavows any links to it, but both share one thing in common: a significant degree of repackaging in order to align themselves to national objectives, while simultaneously pitching themselves as authentic representations of their nations' distinctive identities. Yet, as I have insisted throughout my discussion, horror films never comply unproblematically with such ideological goals. Any project to coerce horror into serving the status quo is already compromised from the start, for the "noncontemporaneous" nature of the genre (Lim, 2001: 294) — where the past perpetually haunts the present and obstructs the future from arriving — already insinuates its subversive potential to undermine the Symbolic order.

Notes

1. Nak explicitly uses the term *pronibat*, literally meaning "to take care of," which also implies the unquestioning services an inferior individual (i.e., wife, servant, subject) must pay to her superior (husband, master, monarch).
2. Somdej To was one of Thailand's most widely recognized historical monks. He served under King Mongkut (Rama IV). In fact, *Nang Nak* is set in 1868, significant in Thai history as marking the end of the reign of King Mongkut, Siam's greatest monarch.
3. Malaya changed its name to Malaysia in 1965. I will use Malaysia henceforth in the essay.
4. This directive is not required of non-Malay popular media, as long as it does not violate the country's Sedition Act (1948), which, among others, expressively forbids criticism

against the special privileges enjoyed by the Malays, and the supremacy of official religion and national language.

5. I use the term *unofficial* for two reasons: (i) there was never any overt declaration by the government; (ii) it seems to target only local productions, since Western horror films continued to make their rounds in the nation's cinemas during this period.

6. Since the first two Pontianak films are now lost, and the fifth one, *Pontianak Kembali* (*The Return of the Pontianak*, 1958; dir. Ramón A. Estella) remains elusive (it still exists, but I have been unable to locate it), I am only conjecturing what their narratives may be like based on the third one, *Sumpah Pontianak* (*The Curse of the Pontianak*, 1958; dir. B. N. Rao). The first four *pontianak* films purportedly form a tetralogy.

7. This does not however suggest that there was a total relaxation of regulations targeting Malay popular culture. While Baba was granted the license to make a horror film, she had to abide by a set of strict rules prescribed by the Malaysian National Film Development (Perbadanan Kemajuan Filem Nasional Malaysia, or FINAS) board including: no scenes of excessive horror; no depiction of the creature rising from the grave; a clear moral lesson at the end of the story; no undermining of Islam in any way.

8. This is partly due to the fact that while Indonesia may be the country with the largest Muslim population in the world, it is "neither a secular nor an Islamic state" but a compromise of the two. See Hosen for a discussion (2005).

9. The framework of this image was developed from "tradition, Islam, and state ideology" (Niehof, 1998: 253). The *ibu* is therefore incompatible with contemporary Indonesian women, who desire a more varied and dynamic role-model who can help them chart and "[control] their own destinies" in an increasingly globalized age (254).

References

Anderson, B. (1983) *Imagined Communities: Reflections on the Origin and Spread of Nationalism*, Verso, New York.

Aziz, A. and Shamsul, A.B. (2004) The religious, the plural, the secular and the modern: a brief critical survey on Islam in Malaysia. *Inter-Asia Cultural Studies*, **5** (4), 341–356.

Cherry, B. (2009) *Horror*, Routledge, London/New York.

Clover, C. (1992) *Men, Women and Chainsaws: Gender in the Modern Horror Film*, Princeton University Press, Princeton.

Cohen, J.J. (1996) Monster culture (seven theses), in *Monster Theory: Reading Culture* (ed. J.J. Cohen), University of Minnesota Press, London/Minneapolis, pp. 3–25.

Fuhrmann, A. (2009) *Nang Nak*—ghost wife: desire, embodiment, and Buddhist Melancholia in a contemporary Thai ghost film. *Discourse*, **31** (3), 220–247.

Gowans, C.W. (2003) *Philosophy of the Buddha*, Routledge, London/New York.

Heider, K.G. (1991) *Indonesian Cinema: National Culture on Screen*, Hawaii University Press, Hawaii.

Hosen, N. (2005) Religion and the Indonesian constitution: a recent debate. *Journal of Southeast Asian Studies*, **36** (3), 419–440.

Ingawanij, M.A. (2007) *Nang Nak*: Thai bourgeois heritage cinema. *Inter-Asia Cultural Studies*, **8** (2), 180–193.

Keyes, C.F. (1984) Mother or mistress but never a monk: Buddhist notions of female gender in rural Thailand. *American Ethnologist*, **11** (2), 223–241.

Klima, A. (2002) *The Funeral Casino: Meditation, Massacre and Exchange with the Dead in Thailand*, Princeton University Press, Princeton/Oxford.

Knee, A. (2005) Thailand haunted: the power of the past in the contemporary Thai horror film, in *Horror International* (eds S.J. Schneider and T. Williams), Wayne State University Press, Detroit, pp. 141–159.

La Belle, J. (1988) *Herself Beheld: The Literature of the Looking Glass*, Cornell University Press, Ithaca/London.

Lim, B.C. (2001) Spectral times: the ghost film as historical allegory. *Positions*, **9** (12), 287–329.

Ng, A. (2008) "Death and the Maiden": the Pontianak as excess in Malay popular culture, in *Draculas, Vampires and Other Undead Forms: Essays on Gender, Race and Culture* (eds C. Picart and J.E. Browning), Scarecrow Press, Lanham, pp. 167–185.

Niehof, A. (1998) The changing lives of Indonesian women: contained emancipation under pressure. *Bijdragen tot de Taal—Land-en Volkenkunde*, **154** (2), 236–258.

Sen, K. (1994) *Indonesian Cinema: Framing the New Order*, Zed Books Ltd., London/New Jersey.

Thompson, E.C. (2003) Malay male migrants: negotiating contested identities in Malaysia. *American Ethnologist*, **30** (3), 418–438.

Williams, L. (1996) When the woman looks (originally pub. 1983), in *The Dread of Difference: Gender and the Horror Film* (ed. B.K. Grant), University of Texas Press, Austin, pp. 15–34.

Part V

Selected Archetypes, Hybrids, and Crossovers

26

Vampires and Transnational Horror

Dale Hudson

If vampires were once figures of occasional horror, they have become figures of everyday horror. The term *vampire* is used to describe both controversial heads of state such as Nicolae Ceausescu and Joseph Stalin, who drained the "lifeblood" of countries, and celebrities such as Marilyn Monroe and Michael Jackson, whose bodies "shifted shape" in extraordinary ways. Jean Painlevé's *Le Vampire* (France 1947) infused science documentary with surrealist art and film, intercutting images of vampire bats with scenes from F. W. Murnau's *Nosferatu* (Germany 1922), which itself included live-action shots of carnivorous polyps, Venus flytraps, and vampire bats. In *Laviamoci il cervello/Let's Have a Brainwash* (Italy-France 1962), a middle-class father finds his son Ricky masquerading as a pistol-toting villain. After incorrect guesses about his costume—Billy the Kid, Dracula, Nembo Kid (an Italian derivative of Superman)—Ricky declares, "Sono Pasolini!" ("I am Pasolini!"), later displaying paper vampire fangs. Vampires move from the realm of the extraordinary to one of utter banality after classical Hollywood's "monster mashes" of the 1940s. By the 1970s, vampires are commodified as products for children such as Count Chocula breakfast cereal (1971) and the muppet Count Von Count, debuting in 1972 on *Sesame Street* (USA 1969–present), who transformed the folkloric vampire's compulsion to count into an educational activity. Still, vampires retained their power to frighten. Jiří Barta's *Poslední lup/The Last Theft* (Czechoslovakia 1987) makes a frightful account of the power of greed and corruption in eastern Europe.

Vampires in these domestic horrors are ultimately local manifestations of vampires in transnational horrors. The figure of the vampire actually emerges from colonial exchanges. Beginning in the seventeenth century, appropriations of eastern European folklore by western European poets, dramatists, and novelists

A Companion to the Horror Film, First Edition. Edited by Harry M. Benshoff.
© 2014 John Wiley & Sons, Inc. Published 2017 by John Wiley & Sons, Inc.

produced characters such as Count Dracula and Countess Carmilla Karnstein. The vampire's sensationalized and eroticized difference required brave vampire hunters — invariably patriotic, straight, white men — to issue nationalist, masculinist, and heterosexist punishments (usually death) on the unruly bodies of vampires. Subsequent writers and filmmakers reconfigured vampires according to "empire-writes-back" and "queering" veins of resistance, opposition, and challenge. They often appropriated vampires in ambivalent and indifferent ways that nonetheless still reject the "self-evident" priority of what was called "the West" to recognize contemporary economic and military power structures, as well as historical ones. In the animated *Vampiros en la Habana/Vampires in Havana* (Cuba 1987; dir. Juan Padrón), for example, vampirism represents US and European colonialism. Vampires infect and contaminate the imagination beyond the confines of Hollywood and Europe, becoming apt figures for conveying "rumors" in colonial East Africa about the theft of African blood by European colonizers (White, 2000). Even today, vampirism appears in headlines in various contexts. An *India Today* cover story describes "Pakistan's Vampire Plans for Khalistan" (14 November 2011). A story in *Newsweek* reports: "It was inevitable in the rapidly shrinking world of global entertainment, Hollywood was destined to discover Hong Kong. Can a vampire resist fresh blood?" (19 February 1996: 66). Hong Kong was already well aware of such foreign intentions. In *Goeng si ji sang/Doctor Vampire* (1991; dir. Jamie Luk), an English vampire enslaves women to feed on the blood of men, which he then drinks from their bodies. Intoxicated by the blood of a visitor from Hong Kong, he declares "the blood is like your Chinese ginseng" in a self-conscious commentary on the reanimation of Hollywood through an influx of Hong Kong fight choreographers. By contrast, vampirism in Abdelkrim Bahloul's *Un Vampire au paradis/A Vampire in Paradise* (France 1992) serves as a trope to expose and critique racism against French Maghrébis in France and Algeria. Vampires appear almost indiscriminately, as horror emerges transnationally within different moments of globalization.

For film studies, vampires trouble what might seem fairly stable notions of "nation" and "genre" by not conforming to the field's frameworks for analysis and interpretation. David Pirie once lamented the near exhaustion and possible extinction of a vampire film genre (1972: 173). His anxieties remained unabated despite a proliferation of vampire films in East Asia, Latin America, Southeast Asia, and Europe, if not in his native England. Assumptions persist in proclamations that "the modern vampire has gone global" with "mobility beyond the borders of America" (Abbott, 2007: 215). However, cinematic vampires had "gone global" at least three decades earlier when both the character and the name "Dracula" entered the public domain. Vampire films have been produced in Argentina, Australia, Brazil, Canada, China, Cuba, Europe, Hong Kong, India, Japan, Lebanon, México, New Zealand, Nigeria, Pakistan, the Philippines, Russia, South Africa, South Korea, Turkey, the United States, and elsewhere. Hollywood vampire films can be contextualized in relation to the colonial ties of Hollywood filmmaking in Europe, México, and the Philippines (Hudson, under review).

Although Bram Stoker's *Dracula* (1897) has been analyzed according to postcolonial theory (Valente, 2002), book-length studies on vampire films are often indifferent to the postcolonial condition as part of the transnational horror of vampirism. Early critical evaluations of vampire films focused primarily on their relationship to anglophone literature, often debating "Englishness" in the context of the British film industry. Other studies deploy theoretical paradigms from psychoanalysis, structural anthropology, cultural anthropology, and Marxism. Interventions through cultural, feminist, gender, and queer studies (Gelder, 1994; Auerbach, 1995) have destabilized some of these earlier universalizing approaches, yet general cultural histories continue to work from assumptions that vampire films are a subgenre of horror, tracing movements from "Old World" to "New World" sensibilities, for example, or from misogynist to post-feminist themes, particularly in regard to the *Twilight* franchise (USA 2008–2012). These studies do not explore vampirism in relation to colonialism or even the "cultural imperialism" of Hollywood's unfair advantage in free-trade agreements, nor do they consistently integrate textual analysis with attention to the political economies of film. Conventional critical frameworks might not be sufficiently capacious to include particular types of film. As a transnational body of texts, vampire films prompt film studies to consider historiographic paradigms more complicated than the nationally or culturally discrete spaces of "national cinemas" or "world cinema," critical paradigms more complicated than the hierarchical spaces of "auteur" and "trash" cinemas, and theoretical paradigms more complicated than those proposed by the often eurocentric spaces of "film theory." More flexible or self-reflexive frameworks offer possibilities for future research, not only on vampire films, but for film in general.

Shifting Critical Paradigms

Vampire films suggest transnational frameworks for formulating film histories according to nuanced multiplicities rather than linear developmental narratives for national cinemas or jigsaw puzzles of world cinema that exclude Hollywood to affirm its self-promotion as universal. Film history offers possibilities for critical inquiries into the relationship between academic discourse and political economy; however, in Shohini Chaudhuri's words, film studies "has yet to address properly the extent to which current critical coverage manifests the inequities of global film distribution" (2005: 4). Anglophone scholarship emphasizes English-language films as though these films were more numerous and important than films shot in other languages. Some scholarship addresses this imbalance. Anne Ciecko suggests: "It is clearly time to redraw the map of world cinema and put Asia in the center" (2005: 6). Indeed, Asia has produced more films and exhibited them to larger audiences than

Hollywood and Europe combined for as long as anyone can remember. By situating "vampire films" from Hong Kong, Lahore, and Mumbai at the center of its analysis, this chapter explores what can be gained by not prioritizing the European subcontinent as equivalent to the rest of Asia and by not universalizing the particular of Hollywood.

Transnational vampire films deterritorialize film theory by pointing to ways that theorization is contingent on selected objects of study. Classical film theory of Arnheim, Balász, Bazin, Delluc, Eisenstein, Kuleshov, Kracauer, and Pudovkin is based almost entirely on Hollywood or European features. Much of the film theory that emerged during the 1970s to pose ideological critiques of it is bound to a canon that is only slightly more inclusive. As scholars of what was called "third world" or "nonwestern" cinema argued during the 1980s, film theory based exclusively on the framing and editing structures of Hollywood/European filmmaking can be counterproductive in the face of aesthetics and conventions that were developed millennia before the technologies of vision were invented by Daguerre, Edison, and the Lumières. Cinematic modes of representation and audience address are complex and transnational, requiring acceptance that other modes might be at play even when the technologies appear the same. Mustafa El-Akkad's *Al Rissala/The Message* (Libya-Lebanon-Kuwait-Morocco-UK 1977), for example, places the camera in the position of the Prophet Mohammed, thereby avoiding his direct representation without Brechtian alienation or avant-garde disruption of the illusory "fourth wall," in the process displacing the (Judeo-Christian European) film theorist as a privileged decoder of meaning (Shohat, 2006: 86–91). Similarly, theorizations about the voice in cinema consider the complex relationships between visual and auditory images, drawing their examples largely from classical Hollywood and French cinemas, but rarely considering ways that dubbed voices function in places where dubbing has been a standard practice, such as India, Italy, and Hong Kong.

Comparable to ways that national and world cinemas were dominant models for organizing global film history, categories of genre and authorship continue to dominate film criticism and theory. Transnational vampire films direct questions away from such industrially defined spaces. Among the strengths of genre theory is its development of a critical vocabulary for analyses of codes and conventions that depart from the demands of realism's cultural and photographic verisimilitude, while rejecting the priority of "original" expression over social engagement and critique. Among the weaknesses of genre theory are its occasional foreclosures to other questions precisely due to the persuasiveness of genre as an organizational category. If vampires carry associations of impurity and contamination, then transnational vampire films carry associations of "generic impurity and contamination." Rather than give evidence of the film's inferior quality, vampire films refocus attention on other criteria. They share affinities with certain East Asian and South Asian films discussed below, as well as US film exhibition during the 1910s when nickelodeons included a "mixed" program of comedies, dramas, actualities, and trick films.

Vampires unsettle national and generic assumptions that often pass themselves as self-evident, unremarkable, and inevitable. Universal Pictures, for example, has been historicized according its "horror cycles" and "movie monsters." While genre films tend to play on repetition and variation of audiovisual codes and narrative conventions, the discursive strategies of Universal's vampire films defy strict categorization as horror, drawing on conventions from comedy (slapstick interludes) and modes of audience address from melodrama (nondiegetic music and sound effects). The long-running television series *Buffy the Vampire Slayer* (USA 1997–2003; cr. Joss Whedon) extends this "mixed-genre" structure by self-consciously violating television codes. Mostly shot in conventional medium close-ups with long shots for martial arts, special episodes adopt whimsical modes, such as musical in "Once More with Feeling" (6.7) and home video in "Storyteller" (7.16). In "Spiral" (5.20), Buffy and her Scooby Gang travel in a large recreational vehicle that comes under attack by medieval European warriors, rendered as multicultural with a token African American actor. Although the multiracial horde includes no Native Americans, the scene reproduces the narrative device in Westerns of "bloodthirsty Indians" attacking stagecoaches with "innocent" white colonizers, much like Francis Ford Coppola's "John Ford Western finale" to *Bram Stoker's Dracula* (USA 1992). If colonial discourse invented the "vanishing race" to suggest that indigenous nations would naturally become extinct, then this episode of *Buffy* accepts that Native America has effectively been "vanished," surviving only in empty references to irrational villains in Hollywood Westerns. Even the most nationalist of domestic horrors can reveal complex transnational histories.

Vampire films have been largely dismissed as cultural curiosities and are infrequently examined in introductory textbooks. They are usually understood to constitute local manifestations of an international (rather than transnational) genre with little to say about any place in particular. While Hollywood Westerns were legitimized as heroic (masculinist/heterosexist) national objects, vampire films were marginalized as lowly (non-national) "body genres" that may be potentially feminist. Although vampire films are sometimes recuperated in discourses of "bad," "trash," "drive-in," or "grind-house" cinema, these frameworks often invert preexisting evaluative criteria. They may be attentive to the pleasures that such films afford, but they examine disproportionately the pleasures of derision that produce a sense of aesthetic or intellectual superiority. Critical frameworks developed via non-Hollywood/European films can yield new understandings. For example, vampires migrate into South Asian *masalas* (literally, "spice mixes") and East Asian *wuxia pans* (loosely, martial-arts fantasies). Although marketed as "horror," horror is not the dominant mode in these films. The films dedicate higher production values to fight scenes and song-and-dance sequences than to horror, which is undercut by self-conscious rubber masks and plastic fangs. Horror becomes one among many spices to "add to the mix," to borrow an expression from Bollywood (Hindi-language industry in Mumbai), Kollywood (Tamil-language industry in Kodambakkam, Chennai), and Tollywood (Telugu-language industry in Hyderabad). They typically feature mainstream stars unlike Hollywood/European vampire films that generally featured typecast horror stars such as Lon Chaney Jr., Peter Cushing, Boris Karloff, Christopher Lee, Béla Lugosi, Vincent Price, and Barbara Steele. Looking at critical approaches to *masalas* and *wuxia pans* offers ways to rethink vampire films in less nationally and generically prescriptive ways.

Rethinking Vampire Films as Transnational Horror

Classical Hollywood's first vampire film was shot in multi-language versions as *Dracula* (1931; dir. Tod Browning) and *Drácula* (1931; dir. George Melford). Hungarian-born Béla Lugosi and Spanish-born Carlos Villarías can both be considered Hollywood's first transnational vampire "movie stars" of the sound era. Historians debate whether the films borrowed from earlier European films such as *Drakula halála/The Death of Dracula* (Hungary 1921; dir. Károly Lajthay), or, more likely, *Nosferatu*, but the films are transnational in the ways that Hollywood itself was. Among the crew were Bohemian cinematographer Karl Freund and Mexican director Enrique Tovar Ávalos as an "accent coach." Another immigrant, Paul Kohner from Austria-Hungary, produced both films. Although the story involves the vampire's immigration to London, the films' production describes the emerging transnationalism of Los Angeles as fascism drove emigration from Europe. As Catherine Portuges (1998: 46, 58) argues: "Revitalized by the contributions of so many refugees from the East," particularly Jews seeking exile, "Hollywood cinema of the 1930s and 1940s can scarcely be called unqualifiedly 'American'." Although the English-language *Dracula* is sometimes called "American" (Skal, 1990: 221), the Spanish-language *Drácula* mixed so many Latin American and Peninsular idioms and dialects that the film might scarcely be called unqualifiedly "Spanish."

Classical Hollywood was transnational in its own way, but the film market after the Second World War was defined by an internationalism that mirrored the remapping and redivision of empires into nation-states. A golden era of "foreign film" emerged, even within Hollywood's highly protected "home market" of Canada and the United States, and transnational vampire films are part of that history. Germán Robles's sexually charged performance of the vampire Conde Duval in Cinematográfica's *El vampiro/The Vampire* and *El ataúd del vampiro/The Vampire's Coffin* (both México 1957; dir. Fernando Méndez) anticipated Christopher Lee's articulate and physically imposing performance of the vampire Count Dracula in Hammer Films' *Horror of Dracula* (UK 1958; dir. Terence Fisher). Other Mexican vampire films of the period — such as Federico Curiel's *La maldición de Nostradamus/The Curse of Nostradamus* (1961) and Miguel Morayta's *El vampiro sangriento/The Bloody Vampire* (1962) — succeeded in frightening audiences where Hollywood's *Drácula* had failed three decades earlier. If "the Latin American audience laughed Hollywood's know-nothing portrayals of them off the screen, finding it impossible to take such misinformed images seriously" (Shohat and Stam 1994: 182), then Hollywood found its revenge on the Mexican industry through derision: US film producer K. Gordon Murray reedited, rescripted, and dubbed Mexican horror films so as to appear technically inferior to Hollywood, thus suitable for early-morning and late-night television broadcast (Hudson, under review). Belittled by middle-class audiences in México as "churros" (after the inexpensive fried pastry), *luche libre* (professional wrestling) films with vampires as stand-ins for "rudos" (antagonists to the heroic "técnicos") such as *El Santo en El tesoro de Drácula/Santo in "The Treasure of Dracula"* (1969; dir. René Cardona) and *El Santo y Blue Demon contra Drácula y el Hombre Lobo/Santo & Blue Demon Vs. Dracula & The Wolfman* (1972; dir. Miguel M. Delgado) fared even worse. With the dubbing of *El Santo contra las mujeres vampiro* (1962; dir. Alfonso Corona Blake) into *Samson Versus the Vampire Women*, the Mexican middle class itself became fodder for racist stereotypes in a *Mystery Science Theater 3000* lampoon aired in March 1995.

International exhibition is defined by transcultural translations on both the side of production and the side of distribution or exhibition. For example, the first Philippine sound horror film *Ang aswang* (1932; prod. George Musser), based on a folkloric female creature that transforms into a flying fiend at night, was given the English-language title *The Vampire* (Tombs, 1998: 48). *Terror is a Man* (1959; dir. Eddie Romero and Geraldo de Leon), however, created an international market for Philippine horror. *Beast of the Yellow Night* (Philippines-USA 1971; dir. Eddie Romero) became an example of the "crass commercialism that characterized the competition among the numerous independent production companies," reflecting competing demands for international and national audiences (Mundo, 1999: 42). US-based Hemisphere Pictures purchased *Kulay dugo ang gabi/Blood is the Color of Night* and *Ibulong mo sa hangin/Whisper to the Wind* by director Gerardo de Leon, which it dubbed, reedited, and renamed as *The Blood Drinkers* and *Creatures of Evil* in 1966. Another US distribution company, Independent-International Pictures Corp., retitled them as *The Vampire People* and *Curse of the Vampires* in 1971. Although these films reached ever-widening audiences as "cheap drive-in cinema" for non-Philippine audiences, recent films such as the Sundance hit *Aswang* (USA 1994; dir. Wrye Martin and Barry Poltermann), subversive black-and-white *Aswan ng QC/Vampire of Quezon City* (2006; dir. Khavn Delacruz), disturbing *Patient X* (2009; dir. Yam Laranas), and box-office hit *Ang darling kong aswang/My Wife the Monster* (2009; dir. Tony Y. Reyes) are relatively ignored for not conforming to foreign expectations of "bad" or "cheesy" horror from the Philippines.

With the physical destruction of the Second World War and the structural readjustments of the European Recovery Program, European film industries turned to export markets for survival against Hollywood's unfair advantage in their home markets. Italian producers recognized the potential of horror, distributed in multiple language versions, edited for different markets, and starring internationally recognizable horror stars such as Christopher Lee in *Tempi duri per i vampiri/Uncle Was a Vampire* (Italy-France 1959; dir. Pio Angeletti and Steno). Released even earlier, *I vampiri* (1956; dir. Riccardo Freda and Mario Bava) is a suspenseful thriller about a series of "vampire murders" in Paris. After decades of censorship, Italian film-makers mixed horror and eroticism in *L'amante del vampiro/The Vampire and the Ballerina* (1960; dir. Renato Polselli) and *L'ultima preda del vampiro/The Playgirls and the Vampire* (1960; dir. Piero Regnoli). Like Mexican vampire films, Italian ones brought new complexity to familiar narrative formulas and cinematic devices. For example, *La maschera del demonio/The Mask of Satan* (Italy-West Germany 1960; dir. Mario Bava) opens with a slow 360° pan, revealing the crypt of the vampire Princess Asa. Deep-focus and high-angle shots reveal the depth of sets seeped in shadows. Considered cheap effects in Hollywood by the 1960s, zooms are used expressively. Financed through official coproduction agreements with France or informal pre-sales agreements with Hollywood, other Italian vampire films such as *Et mourir de plaisir/Blood and Roses* (France-Italy 1960; dir. Roger Vadim) emphasized the vampire's sexuality. Others featured world-class bodybuilders as vampire hunters, as in *Maciste contro il vampiro/Goliath and the Vampires* (1961; dir. Giacomo Gentilomo) and *Ercole al centro della terra/Hercules at the Center of the Earth* (1961; dir. Mario Bava).

Throughout western Europe, filmmakers used the vampire's sexuality and violence to critique oppressive political structures. Beginning with *Le Viol du vampire/The Rape of the Vampire* (France 1968), Jean Rollin's surrealist-inspired vampire films challenged European social norms, even as they sometimes reproduced colonial norms. Harry Kümel's *Le Rouge aux lèvres/Daughters of Darkness* (Belgium-Italy-France-West Germany 1971), Werner Herzog's *Nosferatu: Phantom der Nacht/Nosferatu: Phantom of the Night* (West Germany-France 1979), and Alain Robbe-Grillet's *La Belle Captive* (France 1983) experiment with critical possibilities. Spanish filmmakers—often in exile—also used overt sexuality and violence to challenge the oppressive Franco dictatorship in films such as Jesús Franco's *El Conde Drácula/Bram Stoker's Count Dracula* (Spain-West Germany-Italy-UK 1969) and Vicente Aranda's *La novia ensangrentada/The Blood-spattered Bride* (Spain 1972). Shot on location in Turkey, Franco's *Las Vampiras/Vampyros Lesbos* (Spain-West Germany 1970) centers its narrative on international tourist resorts and vampire celebrity. Soledad Miranda's performance of Dracula's heiress, Countess Nadine Carody, parodies Lugosi's performance of Count Dracula. She sunbathes, swims, and drinks wine. Long pans of the iconic Ayasofya (aka Hagia Sophia) establish the setting as Istanbul, yet Turkey is reduced to scenery for narratives involving non-Turkish characters. Turkey's presence takes the place of Spain's absence. *Drakula Istanbul'da/Drakula in Istanbul* (Turkey 1953; dir. Mehmet Muhtar) provides a counterpoint by evoking the historical relationship of Vlad Tepes to Turkey.

During the 1950s, Japan produced more films than Mumbai and almost four times more than Los Angeles, including Nakagawa Nobuo's *Kyûketsuki-ga* (1956) and *Onna kyûketsuki* (1959), marketed abroad as vampire films under the titles *Vampire Moth* and *The Lady Vampire*. Best known outside Japan for *Gojira/Godzilla* (1954; dir. Honda Ishiro), Toho Studios produced a trilogy of "vampire films" directed by Yamamoto Michio: *Chi o suu ningyo/Blood Thirsty Doll* aka *Night of the Vampire* (1970), *Noroi no yakata: Chi o suu me/Blood Thirsty Eyes* aka *Lake of Dracula* (1971), and *Chi o suu bara/Blood Thirsty Rose* aka *Evil of Dracula* (1974). Japanese cinema has reinvented vampires as its own, particularly through *manga* in animated films such as *Kyûketsuki Hunter D/Vampire Hunter D* (1985; dir. Toyoo Ashida) and series such as *Kyûketsuki Miyu/Vampire Princess Miyu* (1988; dir. Toshiki Hirano) and *Vanpaia naito/Vampire Knight* (2008; dir. Kristi Reed and Kiyoko Sayama), as well as live-action films like *Kyûketsu Shôjo tai Shôjo Furanken/Vampire Girl vs. Frankenstein Girl* (2009; dir. Yoshihiro Nishimura and Naoyuki Tomomatsu).

The narrative of the third Toho film incorporates earlier efforts to appropriate conventions from vampire films into different cultural contexts, particularly in its English-language subtitled version. A young schoolmaster, Professor Shiraki, takes employment at a girls' school, where he learns about the local "vampire legend" of "a white man who turned on his god" after his ship wrecked near a fishing village. The villagers tortured him until he renounced Christianity, converted to their religion, and spat on the cross. He developed a thirst for blood, murdering a teenaged girl then crying over her corpse until it returns to life. Disguising themselves under new identities, the vampire and resurrected corpse live together for the next two centuries. He assumes his current identity as the principal by ripping the face from a Japanese man and placing it over his own European face. The trope of the severed face as mask inverts certain practices by European/Hollywood companies to produce "exotic-looking" vampire films in East Asia, Latin America, Middle East, North Africa, South Asia, and Southeast Asia by putting a "new face" on old characters. In the Hammer Films and Shaw Brothers coproduction *The Legend of the Seven Golden Vampires* (UK-Hong Kong 1974; dir. Roy Ward Baker), for example, the vampire hunter Professor van Helsing travels to China to defeat Count Dracula, who has colonized the body of Kah, the high priest of the seven golden vampires. Hammer allegedly later announced its intention to produce *Kali: Devil Bride of Dracula* in India. The conflation of Kali and the vampire is potentially insulting to Hindus. "Kali is, as opposed to the vampire, an affirmative principle," explains Arok Bhaula; "she is a part of the sacred ritual of creation, destruction, and renewal of the world" (1990: 5). Also mischaracterized as "Indian vampires," *vetalas* are folkloric figures that animate corpses in charnel grounds, appearing ubiquitously as in the recent animated *Vikram & Betal* (India 2006; dir. Aman Khan). Like Japanese filmmakers, Indian ones also appropriate European vampires into filmic contexts other than horror.

Foreign Dances and Rubber Masks: *Zinda Laash* (1967) and *Bandh Darwaza* (1989)

Mumbai produces films, colloquially called *masalas* (Ganti, 2004: 139), with some of the most internationally recognizable stars in the world from Raj Kapoor and Nargis to Shahrukh Khan and Kajol, and, of course, BBC "star of the millennium" Amitabh Bachchan. Preferences among South Asian audiences for *masala* films dates to the 1930s, providing "a kind of 'natural protection' against foreign film domination of the Indian market long before India gained political independence in 1947" by offering "the seductive appeal of modernity with a reaffirmation of conservative, socially oppressive values" (Binford, 1986: 145). In them, narrative coherence, psychological complexity, and visual authenticity are less important than stars, music, visual spectacle, stylized emotion, and theatrical melodrama. Films emphasize and audiences value *how* things happen rather than *what* happens. Rosie Thomas argues that the form's "ordered succession of modes of affect (*rasa*) by means of highly stylized devices," derived in part from Sanskrit aesthetics, facilitates their commercial appeal "across wide linguistic and cultural divides," not only in South Asia but in many regions where the films are the dominant cinema (1985: 130). Similarly, Lalitha Gopalan has theorized the *masala*'s "interruptions" (2002), while Ravi Vasudevan has explored its use of iconic framing, *darshan* (auspicious viewing), and tableaux shots (2010). *Masalas* reject Aristotelian unities of time, space, and action that were used in Hollywood and Europe to transform cinema from fairground attraction to middle-class entertainment. South Asian audiences have historically found such unities simplistic in their mode of address and unimaginative in terms of narrative. Vampires appear in all grades of South Asian films from A-grade prestige pictures to B-grade lower-budget productions and C-grade "quickies." The most well-known are *Zinda Laash/The Living Corpse* (Pakistan 1967; dir. Khwaja Sarfraz), an A-grade Lollywood film, and *Bandh Darwaza/The Closed Door* (India 1989; dir. Tulsi and Shyam Ramsay), a C-grade Bollywood film.

Credited as an adaptation of Stoker's novel, *Zinda Laash* appropriates the narrative of Hammer's *Horror of Dracula*, making a typical South Asian *mahal* (palace) appear exotic through high key-lighting, emphasizing shadows. It appropriates the device of repeated stabbing from *Psycho* (USA 1960; dir. Alfred Hitchcock) to destroy the *bad-rooh* (evil spirit). Like *Diwana/Madman* (1964; dir. Zahur Raja), Pakistan's first horror film, *Zinda Laash* mixes horror into the *masala* format (Gazdar 1997). An opening inter-title frames the film's moral universe: "It is inevitable that every mortal shall taste death. Only God has dominion over life and death. There is no power in the world, neither good nor evil, that can challenge that dominion. Our film tells the story of a famous professor who with the best intentions tried to conquer death through scientific experiment." In the film, Professor Tabani's discovery of an elixir of life results in his monstrosity. Found unconscious on the floor by his female assistant, Tabani awakens with bloody nostrils. Later, eyes agog and fangs bared, he leers over her neck as the image fades to black, followed a woman's scream. When Dr. Aqil arrives to investigate a series of murders, Tabani admits that he is responsible for the "hauntings." Actor Rehan's performance of Tabani, particularly his dramatic entrance in which he descends a stairwell with purposeful, confident movements, cape fluttering behind him, recalls Christopher Lee's performance of Count Dracula. Set design and use of high-angle shots to show the size of the sets in relation to the actors also recalls *Horror of Dracula*. Other settings highlight upper middle-class family life in Lahore.

In *Zinda Laash*, European melodies played with South Asian instrumentation become an auditory representation of cultural hybridity that is at once a legacy of modern colonialism and a reworking of colonial modernity, conveying broader themes of transnational horror developed through song-and-dance more than a *bad-rooh* visualized and performed like Count Dracula. Lyrics celebrate the intoxication of youth and love, and caution against their inherent dangers. Tabani's assistant (Nasreen) performs the film's first dance to seduce Dr. Aqil. Her white robe suggests Count Dracula's three wives in Universal's *Dracula* and *Drácula* that like other Hollywood films implicitly reproduced stigmatizations of Muslims as having "harems," thus evidencing "the inferiority of the polygamous Islamic world" (Shohat and Stam, 1994: 156). Unlike the precision of classical *Kathak* performed by actors such as Meena Kumari and Vaijayanti Mala, classical *Bharat Natyam* by Hema Malini and Rekha, or the purposeful mixture of classical dance with cabaret and cha-cha by the legendary Helen, Nasreen's movements are purposefully awkward, certainly not South Asian and almost un-human (Figure 26.1). Images of her "exotic" European bat-like movements and inelegant facial expressions,

Figure 26.1 Nasreen performs the exoticism of Europe with awkward bat-like movements and inelegant facial expressions in *Zinda Laash* (*Dracula in Pakistan*, 1967). Directed by Khwaja Sarfraz. Produced by Screen Enterprise and Bari Studios.

Dr. Aqil's puzzled reaction, and birds of prey painted on the walls position Aqil as the victim of the *bad-rooh*.

Zinda Laash's song-and-dance sequences deploy editing patterns that resist universalizing codifications of film theory derived from Hollywood cinema, such as "visual pleasure" and "the male gaze." For example, at the Golden Crown nightclub, the nautch girl (an anglicized version of *nach* or "dance") Cham Cham performs upbeat dances. While men chatter and sing during her dance, the camera cuts to close-up reaction shots of women. Frontal shots of Cham Cham, particularly ones masked to a vertical frame, emphasize her address to the film's audience. In other scenes, music and other sounds convey mood, both empathetically and anempathetically, according to melodrama's retrospective logic of "too late." Unaware that her fiancé Dr. Aqil is dead, Shabnam sings and dances with her friends along the shoreline. Long shots capture the choreography, and close-ups capture the women's smiling faces and play of light on their shimmering *salwar-kameez* (pants-shirts). Levity is undercut when Shabnam runs through a forest and Tabani attacks her, even as the upbeat music continues; such extended instrumental sequences emphasize affect over plot. Similarly, immediately following the violence of the opening credit sequence, Dr. Aqil's car drives to the carefree tune of "La Cucaracha." In the final scenes, music from Gioachino Rossini's *Il barbiere di Siviglia* accompanies self-conscious Foley effects in a fight scene that continues far longer than would be narratively necessary.

Before recently, Bollywood "horror" *masalas* were produced mainly for village audiences. F. U. Ramsay, his sons, and grandson were "considered kings of the genre" after the success of *Do Gaz Zameen Ke Neeche/What Lies Beneath* (1975; dir. Tulsi Ramsay). However, the success of more recent films such as *Bhoot/Ghost* (2003; dir. Ram Gopal Varma) "rescued the B-movie genre from its C-grade theatrical screening" and "made the industry sit up and take notice" (*India Today* 23 June 2003): "Gone are the rubber masks, chopped hands and large, thinly clad women that were so favoured by the Ramseys." Films such as *Bhoot, Darna Mana Hai* (2003; dir. Prawaal Raman), and *Haunted 3D* (2011; dir. Vikram Bhatt) employ high production values, A-list actors, and limit song-and-dance sequences to end credits or ancillary music videos. *Bandh Darwaza* might be considered a transitional film (though not in Vasudevan's sense) since it includes stars in stock roles, such as Aruna Irani as Mahua, a devotee to the *shaitan* (demon) in an "evil female" role, and Johnny Lever as Gopi in a dark-skinned, "male buffoon" role. Its playback singers—Alisha Chinoi, Anuradha Paudwal, Sadhana Sargam, and Suresh Wadka—are well-known for their work in A-grade films. Like *Zinda Laash*, the film conveys a sense of alternative modernities whose participants are "not naïve" and "not unaware of its Western origins, its colonial designs, its capitalist logic, and its global reach" (Gaonkar, 2001: 3). The film's 18-min, pre-credit sequence establishes *Bandh Darwaza*'s site of horror as a *kali pahari* (black mountain), where the *shaitan* Neola has awakened. Just as Christopher Lee's Count Dracula towers over his assassins, Neola dwarfs humans, particularly in terms of his enormous head ("rubber mask") with its prominent veins, red eyes, and white fangs. Rapid shot/counter-shots and canted angles charge visual images with multiple layers of meaning. In the pre-credit sequence, the *thakur* (landowner) Pratap and his wife Lajjo pray to Siva for the blessing of a child. The *darshanic* exchange between iconic shots of Siva and supplicant Lajjo convey the obedience required of a "good" wife like Sita to Rama in the *Ramayana*. The narrative is thus typical of epic family melodramas. Pratap does not impregnate Lajjo, so his aunt pressures him to find another wife. Lajjo enters into a bargain with Mahua, according to which she must give her child, if female, to the *shaitan*. When Lajjo enters the *kali pahari*, Neola cuts his finger and marks a *kumkum* in blood on her forehead, as a husband does to his wife in cinnabar. Animalized noises suggest rape, as Neola's body descends on hers. Refusing to give her baby Kaamya to the *kali pahari*, Lajjo is poisoned. Pratap retrieves their daughter, but Neola prophesizes that she will return.

The film's main narrative concerns a love triangle: Kumar loves Sapna but is loved by Kaamya. Neola offers sexual liberation to Kaamya, which she cannot express outside the *kali pahari*. Kumar refuses her sexual advances. Sapna expresses her desire for Kumar through the more conventional means of a "wet sari" dance, an on-screen substitute for kissing or sex, whereas Kaamya rolls on the ground and wantonly beckons Kumar. In Neola's attack on Kaamya, he lays the length of his body over hers and bites her neck (Figure 26.2). As in Hollywood, European, Philippine, and Latin American vampire films, religion and patriarchy save women

Figure 26.2 Patriarchal horrors: Aruna Irani and all the *shaitan's* men surround the sexually awakened *thakur's* daughter in *Bandh Darwaza* (1989). Directed by Shyam Ramsay and Tulsi Ramsay. Produced by Ramsay Productions.

from uncontained sexuality. Unlike the vampire, which is easily repelled by the Christian cross, Neola recoils at the sight of a crucifix, an open Qur'an, and a staff topped by an Om. Hinduism restrains him best, allowing the male protagonists to destroy his "effigy," a large winged statue. The film ends with a voice-over, relating that "good" has triumphed over "evil." Like the Hammer films, *Bandh Darwaza* and other Ramsay films contain unruly female sexuality with patriarchal religion. The films titillate with suggestiveness of "the bits" (frames removed by censors) without challenging dominant power structures.

Plastic Teeth and Pyrotechnics: *Mr. Vampire* (1985)

Combining aspects of a Hammer vampire film with the figure of the *jiangshi* or *goeng si* (stiff corpse) from Chinese literature, along with aspects of Chinese opera and Japanese *chanbara* (swordfight) films, *Gwai ckui gwai/Encounter of the Spooky Kind* (1980; dir. Sammo Hung Kam-bo) and *Yan haak yan/The Dead and the Deadly* (1982; dir. Ma Wu) established the conventions for the *goeng si* in Hong Kong *wuxia pan* (martial arts fantasies). Much like the Ramsays in Mumbai, producers in Hong Kong appropriate fangs and bloodlust from vampire films to add an "exotic" European quality to the *goeng si*, which was even promoted as a "hopping vampire" to anglophone audiences in Hong Kong. The films, however, are not atypical of the *wuxia pan*, which moves between kinetic fight choreography, slapstick comedy, impossible romance, supernatural monsters, and occasional song-and-dance with internationally recognized stars. In *Sin lui yau wan/A Chinese Ghost Story* (1987; dir. Ching Siu-tung), Cantopop and art-house star Leslie Cheung plays the role of a tax collector, which involves only acting, whereas actor-director Ma Wu sings and dances before "busting" ghosts as the character role of the Taoist Swordsman. Like commercial films from Bollywood, Hollywood, and Nollywood (colloquial name for film industries in Nigeria and Ghana) these films are generally socially conservative. In most *goeng si* films, the *sifu* (master or teacher) destroys the *goeng si* and cures its victims with musical cues and small pyrotechnics for *fashu* (magic). The most spectacular fight scene comes at the close of the films that are primarily concerned with the relationship between the *sifu* and his disciple; the *goeng si* serves mostly as a situation for comedic conflict (Ho, 1989: 29). In later films such as *The Era of Vampires/Tsui Hark's Vampire Hunters* (Hong Kong-Japan-Netherlands 2002; dir. Wellson Chin), comedy disappears, transforming the *goeng si* film much as *Wo hu zang long/Crouching Tiger, Hidden Dragon* (USA-China-Hong Kong-Taiwan 2000; dir. Ang Lee) transformed the *wuxia pan*: "Hollywoodizing" it with higher production values and simplifying a complex hybrid form to a single "genre."

Produced by companies such as Bo Ho Film Company Ltd. and Golden Harvest Company Ltd., earlier *goeng si* films adopt strategies of costume drama. The *sifu* typically wears a yellow Taoist robe in the fight sequences. The physical strength and movement of his body is endowed with the "ability to protect positive social values," which "transforms his victory against evil into a reaffirmation of the system's legitimacy" (Giukin, 2001: 58). The *goeng si* is often dressed in a Mandarin robe, figured as an ancestor whose soul must be put to rest to ensure the family's prosperity and well-being. *Goeng si* films situate horror within the comedy of human relations, often a playful rivalry between two male characters over a *sifu*'s attention or beautiful woman's affection. Arms and legs may demonstrate physical strength, agility, and balance in martial-arts sequences, but vulnerable groins and butts attest to bodily weakness, injury, or displeasure. For example, in *Geung shut ga chuk/Mr. Vampire 2* (1986; dir. Ricky Lau Koon-wai), a snake crawls up the trouser leg of a male character. The male character squirms and screams until the snake exits through the man's unzipped fly. Female characters avert their gazes, but male characters yank on the snake, suggesting both homoerotic fantasies and homophobic anxieties alike.

In *Geung si sin sang/Mr. Vampire* (1985; dir. Ricky Lau Koon-wai), Lam Ching-ying plays the *sifu* Kou, a character that prefigures his role as "one-eyebrow priest" in later films. *Mr. Vampire* opens with Man Chor, one of Kou's two students, providing "dinner" to eight *goeng si* "clients." The spooky setting is enhanced with prominent use of blue lighting, accented with rays of white lighting through open doors and windows, as well as cracks in the shutters. High- and low-angle shots enlarge the studio to structure the scene's power dynamics. Man Chor notices movement in a coffin. A skull peeks out and bites him, and then a *goeng si* runs out. Man Chor frightens the *goeng si* with a *feng-shui* mirror, only to learn that the *goeng si* is Chou (another of Kou's assistants) in disguise. Chou's plastic fangs drop from his mouth, and a musical prompt confirms the scene's slapstick comedy (Figure 26.3). Unfortunately, the chaos has caused magical talismans to detach from

Figure 26.3 Revealing plastic vampire fangs in *Geung si sin sang* (*Mr. Vampire*, 1985). Directed by Ricky Lau Koon-wai. Produced by Bo Ho Film Company Ltd., Golden Harvest Company, and Toho-Towa.

the actual *goeng sis*. Kou and the other *sifu* restore order with martial arts and *fashu*. The older *sifu* leads the *goeng sis* away with a bell in a practice called *corpse driving*. Man Chor and Chou's non-mastery drives much of the film's horror-comedy.

Set in Republican China, the plot begins with Yam hiring Kou to supervise the relocation of his father's corpse. He invites Kou to discuss the transaction over English tea. Afraid he will fumble this foreign custom, Kou brings his disciple Man Chor to "do things first." Yam's daughter Ting-ting, who has returned from school abroad, recognizes their discomfort and plays a joke at their expense. Later, she is betrayed by her cosmopolitanism when she is mistaken for a prostitute, introducing the film's thematic exploration of the perils of foreign contamination. Bad *feng shui* becomes another symptom of association with foreigners. Following bad advice, Yam has his father's corpse buried vertically in what Man Chor calls a "foreign" practice, causing the Yam family's prosperity to decline. As a businessman with European contacts, Yam himself evokes the historical legacies of British control over Chinese ports following the Opium War.

Kou and his assistants notice something awry with Yam's father's corpse. Owing to a lack of air, the corpse is turning into a *goeng si*. They prepare a mixture of cock's blood, sticky rice, and black ink. Chou and Man Chor pull strings, dipped in the mixture, tightly across the coffin, leaving a grid that locks the coffin. Under the full moon, the grid glows. A hand creeps out of the coffin like Béla Lugosi's exploratory movements in *Dracula*. Once it touches the lines, it recoils. The *goeng si* then bursts out of the coffin, killing two lambs and Yam. Police captain Wai informs onlookers that Yam has been shot. Kou notes that fingernails punctured Yam's neck, but Wai has him arrested as a suspect. Although Kou and Chou affix a talisman on the forehead of Yam's corpse, Wai dislodges it. Since *goeng sis* are blind, they locate victims by sensing breathing patterns of inhalation and exhalation. Eventually, Kou and Man Chor trip Yam's corpse, stab it with a wooden sword, and light it on fire.

Meanwhile, Yam's father's corpse returns to Yam's house, where Man Chor and Ting-ting hide. Man Chor sustains injuries. His body will stiffen and lose feeling, making him a *goeng si* in two days. He must remain in perpetual movement. Chou is sent to buy sticky rice to extract the poison. Duped by a greedy merchant with a mix of regular and sticky rice, Man Chor stiffens, growing long fingernails and elongated fangs; meanwhile, Chou is seduced by the ghost Jade. Kou learns that one assistant is "poisoned" and another is "haunted." Inside a cave, the heavily bloated *goeng si* rests with rats crawling over his head and body. After an extended martial-arts sequence, the elder *sifu* returns with his eight clients. He commands them against the *goeng si*, who knocks them down like dominoes. Eventually, the *goeng si* is captured and burned. Fight sequences are filmed in long shots to display the choreography, often enhanced with accelerated motion to convey supernatural powers or with slow motion to dramatize movement. Close-ups and medium close-ups capture specific kicks and punches, as well as reactions. Conventions of Hollywood/European horror function like Chou's plastic vampire fangs: an exotic foreign element that heightens the spectacle of martial arts and reinforces socially conservative themes.

Conclusion: Vampirism, Transnationism, and the Political Economies of Horror

Generic "infection" and national "contamination" within vampire films reveal globalization's uneven and unequal transnational histories and processes. Although international copyright has been one of Hollywood's main weapons to dominate foreign markets, other industries freely appropriate its narratives. As sequels to *Mr. Vampire* were released, they appropriated Hollywood plots while pointing to political issues in transnational China. *Mr. Vampire 2* reworks the narrative of *E.T. the Extra-Terrestrial* (USA 1982; dir. Steven Spielberg) in relation to ethnically Chinese refugees from Viet Nam. *The Romance of the Vampires* (1994; dir. Ricky Lau Koon-wai) reworks *Pretty Woman* (USA 1990; dir. Garry Marshall) as a Category III (violence and erotica) film; *Geung shut yee sang/Doctor Vampire* appropriates details from *Vampire's Kiss* (USA 1989; dir. Robert Bierman) and *Fright Night Part II* (USA 1988; dir. Tommy Lee Wallace). *Fei chow woh gwing/Crazy Safari* (1991; dir. Billy Chan) adapts *The Gods Must Be Crazy* (Botswana-South Africa 1980; dir. Jamie Uys) and opens with a London auction-house sale of a "Chinese mummy," including an educational documentary on differences between Chinese and European vampires. Comparably, *As Sete vampiras/The Seven Vampires* (Brazil 1986; dir. Ivan Cardoso) adapts *Little Shop of Horrors* (USA 1986; dir. Frank Oz). While film producers in places with stronger economies appropriate freely, film producers in places with weaker economies often cannot exercise such power.

Everyday horrors now include the shifting terrains of globalized economies under transnationalism. Vampires appear in films produced in places where Hollywood shoots runaway productions to bypass US trade unions. *Pure Blood* (South Africa 2002; dir. Ken Kaplan), *Eternity* (South Africa 2010; dir. Christopher Lee Dos Santos), and the crowd-funded "first Afrikaner vampire film" *Bloedsuiers* (South Africa, in production; dir. Jon Day) appropriate codes and conventions from runaway Hollywood films such as *From Dusk till Dawn 2: Texas Blood Money* (USA 1999; dir. Scott Spiegel) and *From Dusk Till Dawn 3: The Hangman's Daughter* (USA 2000; dir. P.J. Pesce) that use the South African veldt as a stand-in for the Mexican American borderlands. The renaissance of theatrical 3-D includes *Underworld: Awakening* (USA 2012; dir. Måns Mårlin and Björn Stein), the most recent film in Hollywood's *Underworld* franchise (2003–2012) whose transnational (runaway) production extends from British Columbia to Hungary. Transnational vampires respond to neoliberal economics and free-trade zones. Dual-language conversations in Guillermo del Toro's *La invención de Cronos/Cronos* (México-USA 1992) acknowledge transnational histories that escape many US critics acculturated to Mexican films dubbed to seem infantile. *Vampires: The Turning* (USA 2005; dir. Marty Weiss), the third film in a trilogy launched by *Vampires* (USA 1998; dir. John Carpenter), is largely indifferent to legacies of US military presence in Southeast Asia despite its setting in Bangkok. *Vampire Hunter D* (1985) and *Blood: The Last Vampire/Rasuto buraddo* (Hong Kong-Japan-France-Argentina 2009; dir. Chris

Nahon) engage this history. *Atlal/Le dernier homme* (France-Lebanon 2008; dir. Ghassan Salhab) situates vampires in the postcolonial context of a recent civil war; and *Armageddon King* and *Armageddon King 2* (Nigeria 2003; dir. Ralph Nwadike), in one of contemporary Lagos.

More frequently, vampires appear as part of everyday horrors in less recognizable violent ways. The popularity of young-adult novels has propelled vampires into globalized public culture with the *Twilight* franchise and *The Vampire Diaries* (USA 2009 – present; cr. Kevin Williamson and Julie Plec), spinning rumors that a Philippine television channel had purchased the rights to produce *Takipsilim* ("twilight") with the leading roles played by Shaina Magdayao and Rayver Cruz — and inspiring the serial *Pyaar Kii Ye Ek Kahaani/This One Love Story* (India 2010 – 2011; pr. Ekta Kapoor) and, indirectly, Sahara One's horror series *Haunted Nights* (India 2012 – present; cr. Vikram Bhatt). Previously, vampires appeared in soap operas such as *Dark Shadows* (USA 1966 – 1971; cr. Dan Curtis) and in *telenovelas* such as *O Beijo do Vampiro/The Kiss of the Vampire* (Brazil 2002 – 2003; cr. Antônio Calmon) and *Gabriel* (USA 2008; cr. Agustin and Raul Alarcon Jr.). New series and *telenovelas* appear every year, including *The Originals* (USA 2013 – present; cr. Julie Plec) and *Chica vampiro* (Colombia 2013; dir. Toni Navia). Vampires are adapted for art-house cinema with commercial appeal, such as *Låt den rätte komma in/Let the Right One In* (Sweden 2008; dir. Tomas Alfredson), *Bakjwi/Thirst* (South Korea 2009; dir. Park Chan-wook), and *Kyûketsu Shôjo tai Shôjo Furanken/Vampire Girl vs. Frankenstein Girl* (Japan 2009; dir. Yoshihiro Nishimura and Naoyuki Tomomatsu). The vampire appears in a segment of *Paris, je t'aime/Paris, I Love You* (France-Lichtenstein 2006) and in recent releases such as *Vampires* (Belgium 2010; dir. Vincent Lannoo), *Wir sind die Nacht/We Are the Night* (Germany 2010; dir. Dennis Gansel), *The Moth Diaries* (Canada-Ireland 2011; dir. Mary Harron), *Byzantium* (UK-USA-Ireland 2012; dir. Neil Jordan), and *Only Lovers Left Alive* (USA-UK 2013; dir. Jim Jarmusch). Nordic vampires in *Frostbiten/Frostbitten* (Sweden-Russia 2006; dir. Anders Banke) and *Vampyrer/Not Like Others* (Sweden 2009; dir. Peter Pontikis) suggest moments of self-reflection on European racism. *Frostbitten* examines Swedish complicity with Nazis by tracing vampirism's infection to a voluntary unit in the S.S. army. Vampires are "stuck in the past." *Nochnoy dozar/Night Watch* (Russia 2004; dir. Timur Bekmambetov) and *Dnevnoy dozor/Day Watch* (Russia 2006; dir. Timur Bekmambetov) explore the corruption of post-Soviet Russia as a battle between "light" and "darkness," suggesting that "evil" does not need to be supernatural. Humans have cursed other humans.

A few films have even addressed the transnational character of the vampire directly. Guy Maddin's *Dracula: Pages from a Virgin's Diary* (Canada 2002) films the Royal Winnipeg Ballet's production of Mark Godden's ballet *Dracula* through the distorting lens of German expressionist cinema to highlight connections between xenophobia and petty male jealousies in the ritualized murder of the wealthy and seductive immigrant, Count Dracula, performed by Chinese dancer Zhang Wei Qiang. *Trouble every day* (France-Germany-Japan 2001; dir. Claire Denis) is a very loose adaptation of Le Fanu's *Carmilla* (1872), linking vampirism with biomedical research conducted by a transnational pharmaceutical corporation in colonial Guyana. *Daybreakers* (Australia-USA 2009; dir. Spierig Brothers) makes a similar critique. Whether they are considered art films, science fiction, comedy, romance, or horror is less relevant than the ways that filmmakers use the figure of the vampire to complicate assumptions about the ever-increasingly transnational basis of experiences and histories. As a transnational category, vampire films offer different ways to formulate questions asked of cinema than ones premised on knowledge that divides the world into discrete nation-states or film into genres. In so doing, they ask us to rethink some of the familiar conventions of thinking that have largely shaped twentieth-century film scholarship.

References

Abbott, S. (2007) *Celluloid Vampires: Life after Death in the Modern World*, Texas, Austin.

Auerbach, N. (1995) *Our Vampires, Ourselves*, Chicago, Chicago.

Bhaula, A. (1990) *Politics of Atrocity: The Vampire Tale as a Nightmare History of England in the Nineteenth Century*, Sterling, New Delhi.

Binford, M.R. (1986) The two cinemas of India, in *Film and Politics in the Third World* (ed. J.D.H. Downing), Praeger, New York, pp. 145–166.

Chaudhuri, S. (2005) *Contemporary World Cinema: Europe, Middle East, East Asia, South Asia*, Edinburgh, Edinburgh.

Ciecko, A.T. (ed.) (2005) *Contemporary Asian Cinema*, Berg, Oxford.

Ganti, T. (2004) *Bollywood: A Guidebook to Popular Hindi Cinema*, Routledge, London.

Gaonkar, D.P. (2001) On alternative modernities, in *Alternative Modernities* (ed. D.P. Gaonkar), Durham, Duke, pp. 1–23.

Gazdar, M. (1997) *Pakistan Cinema, 1947–1997*, Oxford, Karachi.

Gelder, K. (1994) *Reading the Vampire*, Routledge, London.

Giukin, L. (2001) Boy-girls: gender, body, and popular culture in Hong Kong action movies, in *Ladies and Gentlemen, Boy and Girls: Gender in Film at the End of the Twentieth Century* (ed. M. Pomerance), SUNY, Albany, pp. 55–69.

Gopalan, L. (2002) *Cinema of Interruptions: Action Genres in Contemporary Indian Cinemas*, BFI, London.

Ho, N. (1989) Abracadaver: cross-cultural influences in Hong Kong vampire movies, in *Phantoms of the Hong Kong Cinema* (ed. C. Li), HKIFF/Urban Council, Hong Kong, pp. 24–35.

Hudson, D. (under review) *Blood, Bodies, and Borders: Figuring Immigration and Globalization through Transnational Hollywood's Vampires*.

del Mundo, C. Jr., (1999) Philippine cinema: an historical overview. *Asian Cinema*, **10** (2), 29–66.

Pirie, D. (1972) *A Heritage of Horror: The English Gothic Cinema, 1946–1972*, Paul Hamlyn, London.

Portuges, C. (1998) Accenting L.A.: Central Europeans in Diasporan Hollywood in the 1940s, in *Borders, Exiles, Diasporas* (eds E. Barkan and M. Denise Shelton), Stanford, Stanford, pp. 46–57.

Shohat, E. (2006) *Taboo Memories, Diasporic Voices*, Duke, Durham.

Shohat, E. and Stam, R. (1994) *Unthinking Eurocentrism: Multiculturalism and the Media*, Routledge, London.

Skal, D. J. (1990) *Hollywood Gothic: The Tangled Web of Dracula from Novel to Stage to Screen*, Norton, New York.

Thomas, R. (1985) Indian cinema: pleasure and popularity: an introduction. *Screen*, **26** (3–4), 116–131.

Tombs, P. (1998) *Mondo Macabro: Weird & Wonderful Cinema from around the World*, St. Martin's Griffin, New York.

Valente, J. (2002) *Dracula's Crypt: Bram Stoker, Irishness, and the Question of Blood*, Illinois, Urbana.

Vasudevan, R. (2010) *The Melodramatic Public: Film Form and Spectatorship in Indian Cinema*, Permanent Black, Ranikher.

White, L. (2000) *Speaking with Vampires: Rumor and History in Colonial Africa*, California, Berkeley.

27

Trash Horror and the Cult of the Bad Film

I. Q. Hunter

"Trash horror" verges, to some extent, on tautology. Horror films are often seen as intrinsically trash in the sense of being disreputable, offensively taboo-breaking, and at the lowest end of popular culture. But trash in this context is not meant as a flippantly dismissive value judgement on an entire genre. Rather it denotes an unpretentious mode of disposable filmmaking that cuts across horror: namely the exploitation movie. Neatly summed up thus by the horror director and "Godfather of Gore" Herschell Gordon Lewis, "An exploitation film is a motion picture in which the elements of plot and acting become subordinate to elements that can be promoted" (Lewis in Curry, 1999: 13). Such low-budget, sensationally advertised independent films have, since the 1920s in the United States, catered to niche audiences by promising outrageous material unavailable or forbidden in mainstream cinema. Exploitation also covers sex films, violent thrillers, and pseudo-documentaries, but horror (or SF-tinged horror) has remained one of its exemplary modes, from the drive-in "creature features" of the 1950s, to 1980s gore and slasher films, to contemporary straight-to-DVD and video on demand "mockbusters" such as *Snakes on a Train* (2006) and *Mega Piranha* (2010). While many of these are "bad" films, their intention is never, exactly, to be "good." Their chief aim is the extra-aesthetic one of exploiting, as quickly and cheaply as possible, certain audiences' desire for transgressive spectacle. It is true that mainstream critical opinion now regards some exploitation horror films once despised as worthless trash, such as *Night of the Living Dead* (1968), as "good" rising to "classic." Indeed, this positive reevaluation of trash, continuously revising what is meant by good and bad, has always been an important engine of film culture (Hunter, 2013a: 15–26). Other exploitation horror films, however, have generated a lasting "cult" reputation among an impassioned minority of

A Companion to the Horror Film, First Edition. Edited by Harry M. Benshoff.
© 2014 John Wiley & Sons, Inc. Published 2017 by John Wiley & Sons, Inc.

enthusiasts precisely for their spectacular and comprehensive "badness," whose appreciation requires a camp sensibility attuned to the alluring counter-merits of trash cinema.

This chapter looks at "bad" horror films that have attracted significant cult followings, typified by passionate advocacy and intense repeat viewing. Although exploitation generally is a cult field, fans have singled out these films for their compelling difference, unpredictability, and comic surrealism. As the author of one guide to bad films writes, "We, the lovers of bad movies, dig through piles of trash, looking for those shining gems of pure cinematic magic. We prefer that quest over the blandness and uniformity of the 'good movie' and its adherence to standards determined by convention and critical fiat" (Miller, 2010: xiii). This chapter is not, therefore, about mainstream horror regarded as appalling by either critics or fans; the focus is strictly on exploitation films which, to cultists, can appear so beguilingly distant from the conventions of mainstream cinema as to represent an alternative universe of cinematic practice, an exotic far shore of incompetence and tastelessness.

Horror as Comedy

"The bad film" is of course an unstable artifact of critical reception that can apply to all levels of cinema, from art films to exploitation. Serious film study tends to shy away from evaluation and so the notion of the "bad film" as a quasi-generic category may seem altogether too flimsy and subjective. For that reason it is most usefully understood as a discursive construct invoked and mobilized by cult audiences who cherish the "worst" films and the distinctive pleasures made possible by their transcendent "badness." This chimes with a more general reevaluation in film culture of trash and bad taste as privileged entry points into the cultural id, seething with society's unconscious repressions.

The term *cult*—yet another slippery discursive construct—is itself ambiguous nowadays. Arguably this category has lost much of its coherence since the flourishing of "midnight movies" in the 1970s, when a canon first emerged mostly of weird and overlooked cult films, then shown in repertory cinemas rather than, as now, invariably consumed on DVD or enjoyed via live-tweeting. Nevertheless, cult films still tend to share certain "brand" characteristics, though they are defined by their audiences' enthusiasm and emotional investment rather than by stable textual markers. Roughly speaking, cult films are marginal, orphaned failures that may well be "bad" in their flouting of stylistic norms and mainstream sensibilities, and are typically transgressive in subject matter, notably in relation to violence, sexuality, and gender representation. Umberto Eco's celebrated definition of a cult film, which he applied to *Casablanca* (1942)—not, *pace* Eco, usually regarded as a bad or even mediocre film — was that it had a ramshackle quality, was quotable and intertextual, and was easily disintegrated in the memory:

> I think that in order to transform a work into a cult object one must be able to break, dislocate, unhinge it so that one can remember only parts of it, irrespective of their original relationship with the whole … A movie … must be already ramshackle, rickety, unhinged in itself. (1987: 198)

Such qualities are more easily identified with bad films than with mainstream commercial hits such as *Casablanca*, for it is the aesthetic liabilities of a cult film that make it so especially different and appealing: "It must live on, and because of, its glorious ricketiness" (Eco, 1987: 198).

Not surprisingly, the bad film, supremely ramshackle and rickety, is now a recognized and large category of cult. On the one hand, there are big-budget mainstream follies, such as *Boom* (1968) and *Showgirls* (1997), whose melodramatic excesses have earned them numerous camp followers. On the other, there are the majority of cult bad films — low-budget movies that, with rare exceptions such as *The Room* (2003), are exploitation horror and science fiction films whose Golden Age was from the 1950s to 1970s. Horror and science fiction, already only loosely moored to realism, have perhaps the greatest potential to become entirely and comically unhinged or "so bad they're good."

The cult of the bad is at once a deliberate reveling in low culture and bad taste, and intermittently a serious and even political assault on the canon by cinephiles. The cult of bad films, which took off in the 1970s, initially focused on American movies and continues in endless delight and *schadenfreude* at cinema's waste of its possibilities. But it really began with the Surrealists, who forged the abiding connection between trash and the unconscious and pioneered the belief that the lowest, "worst," and most unrespectable forms of cinema could be sublime (Hawkins, 2000: 37–38; Hoberman, 1999: 146–147). During the hey-day of the midnight movie, bad films such as the campy anti-drug exploitation movie *Reefer Madness* (1936) were celebrated ironically for their naivety and unhip values. As camp and cult sensibilities filtered through into culture, programmatic, deliberately bad trash films, such as Russ Meyer's *Beyond the Valley of the Dolls* (1970) and John Waters's *Pink Flamingos* (1972) were produced specifically for the cult crowd. The consolidation and commercialization of the category of the bad film can be dated to 1978 and the Medved brothers' book *The Fifty Worst Movies of All Time*, which cobbled together a makeshift canon of bad films, centering on horror and science fiction films of the 1950s and 1960s. For the Medveds these films were not only wastes of money but vulgar or, worse, pretentious offences against classical Hollywood. Along with their subsequent *Golden Turkey Awards* books (1980, 1986), the Medveds popularized the cult of *auteurs maudits* such as Phil Tucker [*Robot Monster* (1953)] and

Edward D. Wood, Jr., whose *Plan Nine from Outer Space* (1959) they crowned the worst film of all time. Books subsequently inspired by the Medveds offered consumer guides to bad films as they became available on video and DVD (for instance, Margulies and Rebello, 1993). The cult of the bad film peaked in 1981 with the inaugural Golden Raspberry Awards (The Razzies), which handed out the year's worst achievements in cinema. The canon was further promoted in a compilation film, *It Came from Hollywood* (1982); a Channel 4 series in the United Kingdom, *The Worst of Hollywood* (1983), presented by Michael Medved, which included such Turkeys as *Plan Nine from Outer Space* and *They Saved Hitler's Brain* (1969); and the American TV show *Mystery Science Theater 3000* (1988–1999), in which the silhouetted robot hosts commented sarcastically on screenings mostly of sub-B movies of the 1950s and 1960s.

It is not hard to see the straightforward and even mass appeal of low-budget horror films that stumble from oddness into surrealism because of their appalling special effects and inability to sustain a believable diegesis. At the more professional end of cult bad cinema, *Night of the Lepus* (1972), for example, delights cultists because its ridiculous premise about Arizona overrun by giant mutant rabbits is approached with complete seriousness and no hint of self-parody. The special effects are not in fact entirely contemptible, given the limited options available before CGI (computer generated imagery), but they fail pathetically to render the genial mammals as a plausible threat. Although give-away process shots of rabbits are avoided, rabbits and humans never interact on screen — apart from a few shots of rabbits filmed in close up with humans far off in the background — and there is consequently little sense of scale and none at all of genuine leporine terror. The "herd of killer rabbits" is presented largely by close ups of eyes and teeth, slow motion shots of real rabbits lolloping through miniature sets, and during attacks on humans brief glimpses of people dressed in furry costumes. Even so, it is not these rudimentary special effects so much as the very concept of bunny apocalypse that is truly bizarre and mind-stretchingly Pythonesque (Figure 27.1).

Frequently, a film's cult is augmented and burnished by outlandish rumors and stray facts about its production, circulated among fans as subcultural capital and meticulously gathered in lengthy blog and Wikipedia entries. Enjoyment of *Night of the Lepus* is much enhanced, for instance, by knowing that the shots of gore-splattered rabbits were achieved by smearing their little muzzles with ketchup. This snapping up of trifling back-stories is a crucial feature of cult appreciation and applies equally to "good" films with arrestingly chaotic production histories [*Apocalypse Now* (1979), *Fitzcarraldo* (1982)] as to films with eccentric auteurs, such as Ed Wood, whose intriguing biography [his transvestism, e.g., bravely foregrounded in his first effort, *Glen or Glenda* (1953)] and anecdotes about his films' traumatic manufacture feed back into and energize his cult.

Convention among trash film scholars makes a distinction between merely bad films, such as *Night of the Lepus*, *The Swarm* (1978) and *Battlefield Earth* (2000), and "Badfilm," often written as one word. *Badfilm* refers chiefly to ultra-low-budget exploitation movies with irresistible pulp titles such as *The Mole People* (1956),

Figure 27.1 Truly bizarre and mind-stretchingly Pythonesque: the killer bunnies in *Night of the Lepus* (1972). Directed by William F. Claxton. Produced by A.C. Lyles Productions.

The Killer Shrews (1959), and *They Saved Hitler's Brain*, whose badness is not, as it were, ontologically separable. They are what J. Hoberman called *objectively bad films* (1999: 147). Their badness is not a mere summary of critical disapproval but denotes a complete abrogation of the minimal standards of filmmaking, generally caused by a catastrophically unsympathetic production context. Badfilm is perhaps the purest kind of trash cinema, disconnected even from the conveyor-belt professionalism of hack filmmaking or the highest profile fiascos of mainstream Hollywood [*The Conqueror* (1956), *Batman & Robin* (1997), *Gigli* (2003)]. The badness of Badfilm is taken to be naive and unintentional, unlike the deviant amateurism of George Kuchar, Jack Smith, and other underground filmmakers, or the strategic comic badness of recent straight to video and DVD studios such as The Asylum, for whom trashiness is a style of homage designed to brand such films as *Mega Shark vs. Giant Octopus* (2009) as cult ready-mades. Pleasure is in fact, for devotees, diminished with Badfilms if there is a suspicion that a film is actually meant to be bad or camp.

Take for example a truly canonical Badfilm such as *Manos: The Hands of Fate* (1966). This amateurish horror movie, which according to legend and Wikipedia was made for a bet, was propelled into cult status in 1993 when it featured on *Mystery Science Theater 3000* (Ross, 2005). It was directed by, written by, produced by, and starred Harold P. Warren, an El Paso fertilizer salesman. A family headed by Mike (Warren) finds itself at a rundown house on the edge of the desert, where a caretaker, Torgo (John Reynolds), runs it on behalf of "The Master," who is some kind of vampire and a priest of Manos (a "God of primal darkness"), and who sports enormous red "hands of fate" on his cloak. Torgo awakes The Master from his underground chamber, which he shares with six bickering wives kept bound to pillars. Torgo's punishment for coveting Mike's wife Margaret (Diane Mahree) is to have his face massaged by the wives and one of his hands burned off, whereupon he abruptly disappears from the plot. Manos then hypnotizes the family and the film ends with Margaret and her daughter Debbie becoming his dormant wives and Mike taking over from Torgo as caretaker.

For a horror movie, this set up is actually quite serviceable, combining as it does the vintage "old dark house" scenario and the encounter with an alternative family that would become a key device of 1970s rural "family horror" such as *The Last House on the Left* (1972) and *The Texas Chain Saw Massacre* (1974). It is Warren's untutored style of stag-film like primitivism and "rule-breaking" that set the film apart and earned it a reputation as one of the worst films ever made — that is, dubbed dialogue, narrative padding, and non-sequiturs (Torgo spends a good deal of the first part of the film pointlessly lugging bags back and forth to the family's car), stilted acting with interminable pauses between lines, poor continuity and evident day-for-night shooting, hiccupping jump cuts, glimpses of the clapper board, unmotivated out-of-focus shots, and all the other staples of bona fide Badfilm-making. Like Ed Wood's films *Manos* is virtually a home movie and its cult fascination derives not from its qualities as a horror movie but from its mysterious intentions and peculiarly complete failure to look anything like a conventional Hollywood film, features all now detailed at exhaustive length on online forums and, of course, Wikipedia.

One's cult appreciation of a film that is otherwise, to a sober and disinterested viewer, perfectly unwatchable expands with knowledge of its backstory, whose symptomatic interest, as a time capsule and all but unmediated record of its production, dwarfs any possible value of the film itself. For example, Reynolds, who plays Torgo, killed himself at only 25 just before the film's release, and it is easy to take his agitated nervous performance as evidence of his troubled state of mind. Some of the film's bewilderments are explicable only by pursuing extra-textual information; the cult experience of this enigmatic film is not circumscribed by merely watching it but spills over into researching its production, filling in narrative gaps, and solving numerous diegetic mysteries. Torgo, for instance, stumbles about in consequence of his massively protruding knees, which apparently indicates that he is a satyr, but the point is never actually explained in the film. At the same time, the film's (or rather its director's) erotic compulsions seem haplessly exposed by a guileless absorption in the staging of erotic scenarios. The multiple wives, fetishistically clad in what look like sheer nighties over tight undergarments, spend much of the plot engaged in long cat-fights; and at the end Debbie, who is around eight-years-old, is inducted as one of the Master's concubines — a queasy touch not so much deliberately pedophiliac as simply not consciously registered and thought through. The film is readable, as more competent and guarded films are not, as an unmediated projection of the stolid-looking director's fantasies of sexual plenitude and transgression. The supremely patriarchal Master is a proto-Anton LaVey or Charles Manson, and the film's tortured harping on sexual expression — for further example, the sheriff endlessly stopping a couple necking in a car — makes it a barely disguised day-for-night dream of middle aged male control over beautiful young women. The exploitation film, which sometimes openly canalizes a personal fetish (Russ Meyer's for breasts, Wood's for angora sweaters), is transformed into a feverish message from the director's tormented unconscious.

Cultists revel in such a mixture of unbidden visual delights, erotic frissons, and subversive access to hidden ideas and perverse motivations. Horror films are often seen as closer to unconscious springs of fantasy and peculiarly apt to express them in coded and haphazard form. Bad horror films, which appear under minimal creative control, enable conditions for a kind of automatic filmmaking or at any rate can be gratefully appropriated as such for the style of excessive overinterpretation that cultists and academic fans value, revel in, and competitively share. Even so, a film as appalling as *Manos* is made bearable only by a determined entry into a zone of cult tolerance, such as the shared ordeal and collective hilarity of a stoned midnight movie. The film's hypnotic dullness might thereby acquire an uncanny quality, which transforms its absolute failure as a horror film — it is not remotely frightening — into an inadvertent triumph of counter-cinema.

Needless to say, this is not how one usually watches films. Cult can itself be seen as involving a bad or errant form of film-watching: "Ritual repeat-viewing is regarded as childish, boring, compulsive, but not tasteful" (Mathijs and Sexton, 2011: 18). Cult viewing in a midnight movie screening, for example, can be noisy, collaborative, theatrical, performative, and disintegrative of the film, an occasion for bad behavior and the competitive exchange of subcultural capital more important than the film itself. A parallel text cobbled together by cultists may be more entertaining than the film, as when fans of *The Rocky Horror Picture Show* (1975) augmented the film in the 1970s with an alternative script of shouted-out comments, or when tweets of derogatory witticisms accompanied the premiere broadcast of *Sharknado* (2013) on the SyFy Channel. Before the wide domestic availability of these films, cultists took pleasure in their rarity, which lent them an auratic quality. They could be seen only at one-off screenings at a place of pilgrimage or on dubbed copies of collectable videos, of which an uncut copy might be a Holy Grail. In fact, cult viewing practices, which evolve along with technology, do not necessarily imply watching the film whole. Choice snippets of films such as *Manos* can be shared to recall cult moments of photogenic excess or strangeness. Online cult practices these days also usurp the film with the production of an alternative text in the form of a fan mash-up of favorite clips and images. Watching bad films, usually against the grain of the director's legible intentions, is in short a delinquent viewing practice, valuable both for its exciting immediacy and for the rare pleasure of belonging to an exclusive community of those with similar dissident tastes and esoteric knowledge.

In a crowded market defined by mediocrity, the absolute badness of *Manos* is as rare and precious as superlative excellence. Such immaculate anti-achievements can see their notoriety turned years after their release to commercial benefit, lending bad films more "legs" than many quickly forgotten run-of-the-mill films. Horror films such as *Manos*, *Troll 2* (1990) (as it happens, neither a sequel nor featuring trolls) and *Birdemic: Shock and Terror* (2008), which would otherwise be lost in

Figure 27.2   "Word of mouse" helped turn the truly terrible *Birdemic: Shock and Terror* (2010) into a cult hit. Directed by James Nguyen. Produced by Moviehead Pictures.

straight-to-DVD hell, have achieved a considerable cult following, not only through midnight movie screenings and self-promotion but also via "word of mouse" on the Internet (on the cult of *Troll 2*, see Olney 2013: 70–82). *Birdemic*, an homage to Hitchcock's *The Birds* (1963) self-financed for about $10,000 and one of the most notable recent cult Badfilms, is remarkable for its extraordinarily poor special effects, which counter and parody the pristine digital realism of contemporary science fiction blockbusters (Figure 27.2). The attacking eagles and vultures are represented by feebly animated gifs and sprites, and, in a delightfully insane touch, have been mutated by global warming so that they spit acid and explode on contact. The film's status is as "Outsider Art," a work of beguiling naivety whose unwitting perpetrator, James Nguyen, seems oblivious to the "rules" of filmmaking:

> At their best—which is to say, at their fascinating worst—movies like *Birdemic* can be surprisingly rich experiences. They don't merely afford us a groan at their wooden acting or a laugh at their crude charms: They drop us into a murky vortex of authorial intent, sabotage some of our most basic notions about character and narrative, and remind us of film's power to disturb, disorient, and discombobulate us. (Weiner, 2010)

The comedy derives from the gap between intention and achievement, along with a sense of pathos at the filmmaker's delusion. Significantly, *Birdemic* is packaged on Severin Films's DVD specifically as a bad film for cult appreciation, and includes a director and cast commentary to furnish the cultist's background knowledge of its curious production history. The commercialization of cult, now a brand, ensured that there is now a sequel, *Birdemic 2: The Resurrection* (2013), whose "success" would need to replicate the "failure" of its predecessor and evince the same essential authentic sincerity.

This highlights one of the problems with lionizing bad films. It is true that with distance and revised critical priorities, even the worst film can be made to seem good by specifically focused political criteria. Wood's *Glen or Glenda*, for example, can be re-read as a work of delirious queer radicalism, made possible only by its obscurity and incoherence. Thinking makes it so, for, of course, "good" and "bad" are products of discursive play rather than fixed qualities attaching to films. It is true that no one, you might think, in their right mind would argue that *Birdemic* is a good film, even though its eco-sensitivity and seeming encephalogram of its director's warped unconscious make it more compelling than many studio productions. Yet such qualitative judgements are static, unambitious, and incurious—conservative, in fact, and not very reflexive about the "obviousness" of the film's badness, which, to a receptive cultist, is a Godardian deconstruction of the received conventions of ordinary cinema and an act of creative incompetence.

One sees this in the "petulant philistinism," as J. Hoberman described it (1999: 151), of the Medveds and their inclusion in *Fifty Worst Films* of Antonioni's *Zabriskie Point* (1970), Eisenstein's *Ivan the Terrible* (1944), and Dennis Hopper's *The Last Movie* (1971) as well as *Myra Breckinridge* (1970) and *Robot Monster*; and *The Omen* (1976), which, for all its gory set-piece decapitations, is a perfectly well-made mainstream horror movie. Although promulgating cult tastes, the Medveds were effectively anticult figures, since many of the films they despised were precisely the type that cultists in the 1970s were lionizing. Their books were a backlash against the counterculture and an assertion of the unchallengeable limits of good taste, at a period of reaction to the New Hollywood's challenge to the well-made family film and blurring of distinctions between the mainstream, avant-garde, and exploitation. As a result the Medveds' books, while full of valuable primary information, take remarkably little pleasure in films that (for them) are mostly objects of contempt and symptoms of cultural decadence. Indeed, the "so bad, it's good" kind of response even among cultists can itself be dismayingly normative. As Richard McCulloch notes of *The Room*, fans of "so bad it's good" (SOBIG) films are self-reflexively conformist when watching the films at cult screenings:

> "Fans" derive great pleasure from their ironic/comic reading of the film, but these readings must subsequently be justified and legitimated by the reactions of others. In some respects, then, "so bad it's good" appreciation is only concerned with cultural capital to the extent that it can be used to enhance one's social capital. Where cult fans distinguish themselves in part by distancing themselves from the "mainstream" … SOBIG "fans" tend to mobilise their tastes primarily as a way of building their pre-existing social networks. (McCulloch, 2011)

Watching bad films can in fact be a paradoxically reassuring experience. The cultist may not only feel a sense of superiority over the film and the deluded filmmaker—especially pleasurable given the glamor and wealth attaching to cinema—but also over other cinemagoers and fans, who—much as devotees of high art may despise the masses—lack the contextual knowledge and learned tactics of irony to "get" the film in the fan-approved way.

This is not, it should be stressed, entirely the case with the cult of the bad film, either as part of the midnight movie phenomenon or in cult appreciation since. A crucial, and arguably the most valuable, aspect of cult-viewing practices has been to draw on auteurism and to mobilize terms such as surreal (as with Jean Rollin or Joe D'Amato) and *transgressive* to reframe bad filmmaking as art or self-expression, aggressively reversing critical frameworks to elevate over conventional standards the badness of what Jeffrey Sconce has called *paracinema*:

> Paracinematic taste involves a reading strategy that renders the bad into the sublime, the deviant into the defamiliarised, and in so doing, calls attention to the aesthetic aberrance and stylistic variety evident but routinely dismissed in the many subgenres of trash cinema. (Sconce, 2010: 119)

A key reading strategy of some cultists has been to confound high and low and value their simultaneity, so as to break down cultural boundaries, which have never been very clear, between art cinema and body genres in the ways they have been distributed, received, and consumed by fans (Hawkins, 2000). Badness, according to the idiosyncratic or oppositional aesthetic criteria of cult fans of paracinema, is a legitimate mode of alternative film production rather than simply a failure to stick to the rules and imitate Hollywood. Bad films can have a revelatory usefulness in showing the rote mechanics of filmmaking and in demystifying its art and industry (Sconce, 2003). This recognizes too that bad (or "mad") films and filmmakers can stray into areas out of bounds to more controlled imaginations and be properly appreciated only according to quirky taste criteria: "anti-masterpieces break the rules with such exhilaration as to expand our definition of what a movie can be" (Hoberman, 1999: 150). There is an idiosyncrasy in perfectly achieved badness that raises the genuinely incompetent auteur above the mainstream hack, as well as a sense that the trashiness of these films latches onto an essential trashiness about cinema itself. This approach is taken by Tim Burton's biopic *Ed Wood* (1994), in which Wood is presented not as a failure but rather as a heroic Wellesian rebel against the system on the grounds that "Ed Wood had a vision: blurred, grotesque and cross-eyed, but a vision nonetheless" (Warren, 1986: 155). Wood, like other celebrated masters in the pantheon of bad film, such as the pioneer of feminist exploitation Doris Wishman or the contemporary adapter of video games, Uwe Boll, has all the passion and energy of the true artist and absolutely none of the talent. Yet their films and minus-capability of style imply lone wolf auteurism and the radical tunnel vision weirdness of *art brut*, where personal expression is shadowed by delusion and autistic obsession lacking all self-awareness. This conferring on them of the status as naive primitivists suggests their films have access to the unconscious through the enforced evasion of cultural conventions, even though in truth most Badfilms are less often attempts at personal expression than botched efforts to imitate commercial formulae.

This cult reframing, with its own abstruse oppositional criteria parallels and parodies the comprehensive elite reframing of art by modernism, which downgraded craft and enabled ephemera, detritus, and the nonaesthetic (urinals, graffiti, bricks, unmade beds) to be recontextualized as high art. Much of the history of the transition from modernism to postmodernism hinges on the inclusion of trash into high art, and the same goes for cultists attentively reviewing worthless films:

> This so-bad-they're-good reason to champion bad films asserts that watching these films as valueless trash offers a form of phenomenal experience that is transgressive: it lifts the viewer out of the dreary normalness of everyday life … [C]elebrating badness alters everyday life as it elevates ordinariness and banality to a level where it can be actively enjoyed. (Mathijs and Sexton, 2011: 38)

Hence the films' badness can be viewed positively, sometimes with a degree of irony or contrarianism, as an assault on notions of good film-making, absence of quality offering a space for other cinephile pleasures to flourish.

Abject Horror

Badness has other, more troubling implications as well. To certain types of horror, as with pornography, there clings a sense of moral as well as aesthetic calamity, for the emotions, fantasies, ideologies, and pleasures they promote might also be described as "bad." The horror genre itself is often felt to be a bad object in cinema, in need of redemption by style, comedy, or by keeping the horror off screen (a favourite claim of people who, one suspects, do not really like or approve of horror films). A horror film may indeed not only be bad, which suggests a disinterested judgement merely of aesthetic failure, but ethically suspect, dangerous, or *evil*. To see or possess a "video nasty" may be a criminal offense. Horror fans are a suspect minority, construed as made horrifying rather than horrified by the films. As Andrew Tudor has said, "a taste for horror is a taste for something seemingly abnormal, and is therefore deemed to require special attention" (1997: 446).

Bad horror films such as *Manos* or *Birdemic* convert horror into accidental comedy. The badness detracts from the generic effect, for the films are *failed* horror and often relatively innocuous as well as ineffective. Another sort of trash-horror, however, aims precisely at a horrific affect, even if cultists may convert shock, dulled by repetition and extra-textual knowledge of the film's production (special effects, for instance), into intellectual distance. Certain especially toxic and soiling horror films, very low-budget, gratuitously gory or "sick" and in extreme bad taste, break the boundaries of entertainment and art and may be considered Other even by genre fans.

Horror's cultural location as trash, as the Other or unconscious of mainstream cinema, has become one of its most valuable assets to cultists. This line is pushed by Mikita Brottman in relation to what she calls "Offensive Film":

> The unprofessional production values, clumsy narratives, and hastily conceived structure of such films, as well as their wide commercial appeal, give them the same kind of

value that free association has in psychoanalysis, making them important vehicles for helping us to understand the bodily nightmares of the culture that gives rise to them. (Brottman, 2005: 13)

Such films share the technical shortcomings or outright indifference to style of the Badfilm, but their badness is equally defined by grossness. Rather than incompetent, they set out to be sick, offensive, and disgusting exercises in bad taste, and their status as ultimate bad objects in cinema is a mark of their success, which is closer to the deliberate transgressions of underground cinema (Figure 27.3).

A key, indeed trend-setting film here is Herschell Gordon Lewis's *Blood Feast* (1963). It is an exploitation film in a wider sense that developed from the 1950s, when the term *exploitation* loosened to mean simply inexpensive sensational films, notably science fiction and horror films aimed at teenagers such as *I Was a Teenage Were-wolf* (1957). *Blood Feast* was a genuinely new kind of film, an outright gore film in color. Lewis had made "nudie cuties" with David Friedman such as *Boin-n-g* (1963) before turning to horror. *Blood Feast* was made for $24,000 in either four, six, or nine days, depending on which fan-source you believe. The rudimentary plot concerns Fuad Ramses (Mal Arnold), an Egyptian chef in Miami who murders and plans to cannibalize beautiful young women in homage to the cult of Ishtar. The film is constructed around a handful of gory set-pieces—a leg chopped off, brain removed, tongue cut out—but, unlike the rabbits in *Night of the Lepus*, the special effects here are fairly vivid and convincing and have a degree of grubby and unsettling realism.

Figure 27.3   Grubby and unsettling realism in Herschell Gordon Lewis's *Blood Feast* (1963). Directed by Herschell Gordon Lewis. Produced by Friedman-Lewis Productions.

The film ends with Fuad ground up in a garbage truck, a handy metaphor for the film itself: "he died a fitting end, just like the garbage he was." The plot, with its sacrifices to ancient Gods, is echoed by *Manos*, which with it shares a voyeuristic interest in the sexuality of the younger generation. *Blood Feast*'s primitive aesthetic was one of unabashed gawking, and it cared little for verisimilitude except in the raw documentary sense of *showing*; only the gore is believable, while the acting never rises above stilted amateurism. Although Curry, in his biography of Lewis, calls it "intentionally plotless and near mindless" but "skilfully directed" (1999: 53), Danny Peary calls it "one of the most inept pictures of all time" and goes on to detail "how awful *every* scene is" (1983: 27).

After *Blood Feast* Lewis made numerous horror films, including two more in his "Blood Trilogy" — *Two Thousand Maniacs!* (1964) and *Color Me Blood Red* (1965) — before retiring to make a reputation in direct sales. The cult of Lewis caught on in the 1980s with the release of his films on video (*Blood Feast* was listed as one of the forbidden "video nasties" in Britain in the early 1980s) and accelerated by the support of John Waters (1991: 192), who cited Lewis and Russ Meyer as the "two greatest masters in film history." Lewis was interviewed in influential books on trash such as *Incredibly Strange Films*, which did more sympathetically for paracinema in the 1980s what the Medveds did for bad films in the 1970s (Vale and Juno, 1986: 18–35, 175–176). The cult of Lewis later led him to return to filmmaking with *Blood Feast 2: All U Can Eat* (2002). Lurid anecdotes about the production of *Blood Feast* were engagingly recounted by Lewis in interviews, including stories about the hopeless acting of Connie Mason (the 1963 Playmate of the Year) and the half million "barf bags" distributed to cinemagoers to accompany such scenes as this:

> We needed a girl with a big mouth. Astrid came to the room in the motel and here she was going to be in show business. We stuffed the sheep's tongue in her mouth, put in the cranberry juice, our special stage blood, gelatine, and the other goodies and pulled the tongue and her head lolled to one side and she gagged. It worked out very nicely. (quoted in Waters, 1991: 206)

Such anecdotes are subcultural catnip to the cultist, who, unlike the appalled original audience that made it a hit at 1960s drive-ins, is in a superior position of camp distanciation, appreciating the film *as* exploitation and enjoying the imagined discomfort of other, "ordinary" audiences at the film's politically incorrect offensiveness.

Unlike, say, the films of Dario Argento or Ruggero Deodato, Lewis's are less easily reevaluated as "good," not least because the legend of Lewis is his complete cynicism toward the films, and the outright commercialism of his approach in the tradition of the exploitation or "carny" showman. Lewis has an altogether different persona from Wood or the director of *Birdemic*. Far from an innocent or marginal crazed auteur, he is more a slyly knowing businessman in the mold of Roger Corman, a heroic all-American huckster — "no Ed Woodian naïf, but a sour profiteer, a bookkeeper, a cinematic accountant on the lookout for a quick buck" (Grossman, 2004). Like Whitman's poetry, Lewis has often said, *Blood Feast* may not be very good but it was unquestionably the first. To argue that the film is good, in the sense of aesthetically achieved or polished, would detract from its attraction as a work of vibrant ineptitude, which by-passes aesthetic criteria in favor of visceral impact and raw shock. In this case the cult audience is in on the director's joke rather than he and the film being the butt of the audience's humor — that is, Grossman's high camp appreciation, in an online fan-piece, of *Blood Feast*, "whose ridiculous nadirs of execution meld, trancelike, with sublime heights of fearless intent, creating a synthesis so indescribable as to make the belletrist balk" (2004). Lewis's combination of gore and bad taste became a model for programmatic trash that set out to become cult films through bad taste, compensating for their low-budgets by engaging self-selecting audiences with their knowing trashiness, turning viewers into participants rather than pleasurably scandalized onlookers. This turns *Blood Feast* also into a comedy, which Peary finds disturbing:

> Because the film was done tongue in cheek, it's hard to say how much of the humor was intentional.... I can understand those people who enjoy *Blood Feast* for its camp value. I only question those who thrill to the no-holds-barred-violence. (1983: 27)

Blood Feast, from this point of view, is bad in the sense of morally reprehensible. Although time has lent it a camp quality, emphasized in its repackaging over the years as a cynically innovative exercise in deliberate bad taste, it has become in many ways even less acceptable than in the pre-politically correct 1960s. The film's single-minded focus on dismembering beautiful young women makes it an arguably unembarrassed and unedited version of what horror is *really* about — the disgusting and pornographic spectacle of female death. This, naturally, must be disavowed in cult responses to it.

As Mathijs and Sexton remark, a film like *Blood Feast* belongs to "various subdivisions of the horror genre that stubbornly refuse to be recognized as 'just another form of horror'" (2011: 107). A useful example of this style of horror is *The Incredible Torture Show* [*Bloodsucking Freaks*] (1976), a sick comedy written and directed by Joel M. Reed. It is about Sardu (Seamus O'Brien) and his midget assistant Ralphus (Luis De Jesus) who run an S&M theatre, Theatre of the Macabre, in New York, with a sideline selling slave women to a Middle Eastern dealer; the women are kept in a cage in a basement and fed raw meat. Meanwhile on stage, bound naked girls are subjected to what the theatre audience wrongly takes for Grand Guignol special effects, such as an eye-gouging and darts thrown at a target painted on buttocks. In one scene a surgeon (Ernie Pysher) sucks a woman's brains out through a drill hole. In another a woman holds the rope of a guillotine in her mouth and is decapitated when she screams from a caning; Ralphus then uses her head for a blow job. These set-pieces, gruesome but jokily staged, gained the film its cult notoriety. *Bloodsucking Freaks* borrows elements from Lewis's *The Wizard of Gore* (1970) and Corman's *Little Shop of Horrors* (1960) in playing with ideas about art as horror—"It is not SM, it is art," Sardu insists—and this saving element of self-reflexivity enables cultists to read the film as an intense, even intellectual statement about exploitation, the voyeurism of audiences, and the instability of art and trash. "Exploitation films," as Martin Barker notes, "… by dint of their very limitations as films create terrains of intensified reflection. The 'doubling' of arousal and reflection, of excitement and horror, will never be comprehensible to nervous critics" (Barker, 2013: 235). An appeal to self-reflexivity in horror, so that postmodern double-coding enables cultists to interpret trash as art, is a mark of cult appropriation of otherwise trashy horror—for example, *Peeping Tom* (1960), *Cannibal Holocaust* (1980), and *Henry: Portrait of a Serial Killer* (1986). This gives the more extreme films a connection with the modernist avant-garde, with the films of the Vienna Actionists, for example, and with a truly fearsome movie such as Stan Brakhage's presentation of autopsy footage, *The Act of Seeing with One's Own Eyes* (1971).

Bloodsucking Freaks, though, is exceptionally unpleasant in its deliberate extremity (it was picketed by Women Against Pornography), and to some extent resists reevaluation as more than staged sadism. Rather than technical incompetence—the tortures in fact are "done" quite well—the film's cult derives from its excessive moral hazard as a pseudo-moralizing exercise in extreme bad taste that is in the end perfectly indefensible. Other cult examples are the Japanese "Guinea Pig" films of the 1980s, including *Devil's Experiment* (1985) and *Flowers of Flesh and Blood* (1985), stripped down short pseudo-snuff films for the video market that depict, in the first, the torture of a woman kidnapped by three men and, in the second, a woman butchered by a man in samurai costume. Recent horror films in this gross out mode have tended to be either critic-baiting exercises in shock, such as *The Human Centipede (First Sequence)* (2009), or deliberately bad cult comedies such as *One-Eyed Monster* (2008), which features the porn star Ron Jeremy and the titular killer penis. A more confrontational kind of horror is represented by *Slaughtered Vomit Dolls* (2006). This straight-to-DVD underground film mixes what the director, Lucifer Valentine, calls *vomit porn* (fetishized footage of vomiting) with set piece murders in the nonlinear story of a drug-addicted stripper (Ameara Lavey) and a Satanist who kills four women and a man, all of it presented in a joltingly fast-edited montage that fuses avant-garde film and a punk DIY (do-it-yourself) aesthetic. These entertainments, like *Grotesque* (2009) or *Murder Set Pieces* (2004), are for radically specialist tastes, much like "shock sites" such as Bestgore.com, and do not pretend to inhabit the usual aesthetic criteria beyond those shared by aficionados of the extreme and marginally illegal.

How can we conceptualize these films and their various invitations to cult viewing, from the innovative exploitation of *Blood Feast* to the literally nauseating trash of *Slaughtered Vomit Dolls*? It is easy enough to pathologize and demonize viewers of cult horror. As with pornography, the first question asked by the unsympathetic critic tends to be why, unless sick or morally adrift, should anyone want to watch these films at all? The most useful account based on audience research is Martin Barker's, where he explores how for fans of exploitation cinema, "every extreme feature is *simultaneously bad and thereby good*" (Barker, 2013: 221). "Good" is what it does to you, the degree of extremity and outrage it may occasion, or the cancellation of such ineffective descriptors in favor of rising levels of experience, arousal, and intensity that distance one from the ordinary tedium of real life. This relates to another way of thinking about horror as a body genre.

> The ultimate aim of offensive films is the arousal of strong emotions in the lower body—nausea, weakness, faintness, and a loosening of bowel and bladder control—normally by way of graphic scenes featuring the by-products of bodily detritus: vomit, excrement, viscera, brain tissue, and so on. (Brottman, 2005: 9)

Rather than simply suggest technical failure, this suggests a phenomenology of bad film, which cuts through subjective reactions and militates against aesthetic reevaluation. This would relate the films to the *abject* as Julia Kristeva defined it (1982). The films enable us to rehearse in mediated safety our reactions, both fascinated and repulsed to the point of nausea, to that which threatens our identity—especially shit, vomit, blood, semen, and other substances that break the boundaries of the body and cause the loss of distinction between self and the Other, of which a chief symbol is the corpse. The abject threatens a breakdown in meaning through the traumatic experience of encountering something liminal and outside the social and cultural order. This breakdown may in fact be enhanced by the sheer badness of the films, as if their insult to aesthetic categories completes their disassociation from normal viewing experiences (Hunter, 2013b). Although cult-horror films may be grossly off-putting, they can also be seen, paradoxically, as a kind of security (or comfort) blanket—transitional objects that enable rehearsal of emotional and physical responses to the abject. Extreme gore films, said to be especially popular among young men, may be ways of mediating the world, as well as rejecting the (feminized) mainstream. But they also demonstrate an ability to survive extreme screen experiences—including that of extreme badness—outside the usual comfort zones. Exposing oneself to dangerous extremity is itself both challenging and sublime, allowing for "self-reflexive modes of performative reception in the negotiation of the phenomenal experience of moments of abjection, impurity, and grotesquerie" (Mathijs and Sexton, 2011: 106). Cultists' ritual return to the scene of the abject is a way, both masterful and masochistic, of coping with threatening images and experiences and domesticating them through compulsive repetition.

This is, of course, speculative and rather too sweeping. But it touches, I think, on why bad films, both aesthetically incompetent and morally suspect ones, can be genuinely disconcerting, for they enable entry into imaginative worlds where the usual criteria no longer seem to apply. The worst films are culturally dislocating but they can leave you, paradoxically, wonderfully alive in the shaken and repulsed body and the befuddled but energized mind.

References

Barker, M. (2013) Embracing rape: understanding the attractions of exploitation movies, in *Controversial Images: Media Representations on the Edge* (eds F. Attwood, V. Campbell, I.Q. Hunter, and S. Lockyer), Palgrave Macmillan, London and New York.

Brottman, M. (2005) *Offensive Films*, Vanderbilt University Press, Nashville.

Curry, C.W. and Curry, J.W. (1999) *A Taste of Blood: The Films of Herschell Gordon Lewis*, Creation Books, Manchester.

Eco, U. (1987) *Travels in Hyperreality* (Trans. William Weaver), Picador, London.

Grossman, A. (2004) *Blood Feast* revisited, or H.G. Lewis, keeper of the key to all erotic mystery. *Bright Lights Film Journal*, **44** (May). http://brightlightsfilm.com/44/feast.php#.UeQYc0GTiSo (accessed 15 July 2013).

Hawkins, J. (2000) *Cutting Edge: Art-Horror and the Horrific Avant-Garde*, University of Minnesota Press, Minneapolis.

Hoberman, J. (1999) Bad movies, in *Movies* (ed. G. Adair), Penguin, London, p. 1999.

Hunter, I.Q. (2013a) *British Trash Cinema*, British Film Institute, London.

Hunter, I.Q. (2013b) My my, how did I resist you?, in *Mamma Mia! Exploring the Movie Phenomenon* (eds L. Fitzgerald and M. Williams), I B Tauris, London and New York, pp. 154–170.

Kristeva, J. (1982) *Powers of Horror: An Essay in Abjection* (Trans. Leon S. Roudiez), Columbia University Press, New York.

Margulies, E. and Rebello, S. (1993) *Bad Movies We Love*, Marion Boyars, New York and London.

Mathijs, E. and Sexton, J. (2011) *Cult Cinema*, Wiley-Blackwell, Chichester.

McCulloch, R. (2011) "Most people bring their own spoons": *The Room*'s participatory audiences as comedy mediators. *Participations*, **8** (2). http://www.participations.org/Volume%208/Issue%202/2d%20McCulloch.pdf (accessed October 9 2012).

Medved, H. and Medved, M. (1980) *The Golden Turkey Awards: The Worst Achievements in Hollywood History*, Angus & Robertson, London.

Medved, H. and Medved, M. (1986) *Son of Golden Turkey Awards*, Angus & Robertson, London.

Medved, H., Medved, M., and Dreyfuss, R. (1978) *The Fifty Worst Movies of All Time (And How They Got That Way)*, Angus & Robertson, London.

Miller, S. (2010) *150 Movies You Should Die Before You See*, Adams, Avon, MA.

Olney, I. (2013) *Euro Horror: Classic European Horror Cinema in Contemporary American Culture*, Indiana University Press, Bloomington.

Peary, D. (1983) *Cult Movies 2: 50 More of the Classics, the Sleepers, the Weird, and the Wonderful*, Delta, New York.

Ross, D. (2005) The Worst Movie ever Made: The Long, Strange Journey of *Manos: The Hands of Fate*. *Entertainment Weekly* (June 6), http://www.ew.com/ew/article/0,,1068572,00.html (accessed 15 July 2013).

Sconce, J. (2003) Esper the renunciator: teaching "bad" movies to good students, in *Defining Cult Movies: The Cultural Politics of Oppositional Taste* (eds M. Jancovich, A.L. Reboll, J. Stringer, and A. Willis), Manchester University Press, Manchester, pp. 14–34.

Sconce, J. (2010) 'Trashing' the academy: taste, excess and an emerging politics of cinematic style, in *Horror Zone: The Cultural Experience of Contemporary Horror Cinema* (ed. I. Conrich), I.B. Tauris, London and New York, pp. 103–122.

Tudor, A. (1997) Why horror? The peculiar pleasures of a popular genre. *Cultural Studies*,
    11 (3), 443–463.

Vale, V. and Juno, A. (eds) (1986) *Re/Search #10: Incredibly Strange Films*, Re/Search, San
    Francisco.

Warren, B. (1986) *Keep Watching the Skies*, vol. 2, McFarland, Jefferson, NC.

Waters, J. (1991) *Shock Value: A Tasteful Book about Bad Taste*, Fourth Estate, London.

Weiner, J. (2010) The Worst Movies ever Made. *Birdemic*, *The Room*, and what Makes
    a Horrible Film Great. *Slate* (April 6), http://www.slate.com/articles/arts/culturebox
    /2010/04/the_worst_movies_ever_made.html (accessed 7 June 2013).

28

"Moody Three"
Revisiting Ken Russell's The Devils

Joan Hawkins

British director Ken Russell (1927–2011) remains a vexed figure in the history of European Art Cinema. Despite a prolific career spanning almost six decades (1958–2009) and engaging virtually every important media platform (film, television, video, Internet), he receives scant notice in *The Encyclopedia of European Cinema* (Vincendeau, 1995): one longish paragraph (370) as opposed to the full column received by Italian producer Angelo Rizzoli (362). And the paragraph itself immediately foregrounds Russell as a problem. "The excess and 'bad taste' of Russell's later work is in sharp contrast to the 'good taste' of his work in the early 1960s," *The Encyclopedia* notes. "His bad taste ought to be a relief from the proprieties of a cinema of restraint, but ends up being rather wearying" (370).

The image of Russell as a failed director, as someone who somehow lost his way in the thicket of cinematic taste, carries over to his postmortem reviews as well. Virtually every obituary highlighted his "controversial" status. For *The Guardian's* Derek Malcolm, Russell was a romantic, "a talented boy who never quite grew up" (2011: 2). *The New York Times* called him "a polarizing figure who delighted in breaching the limits of propriety and cinematic good taste" (Lim, 2011: 1). *The Los Angeles Times* obituary approvingly quoted Peter Rainer, who dubbed Russell's fantasies "luridly sexual" (McLellan, 2011: 1). And *The Telegraph* found Russell so distasteful that it enclosed even the most innocuously positive adjectives in quotation marks. "The director," Murray Wardrop wrote, " … was praised today as an 'innovative' director, who made a 'unique' contribution to British film-making" (2011: 1).

If Russell remains a vexed presence in mainstream art film culture, he has remained an equally problematic figure in the arena of art horror. The very things that trouble mainstream critics — mixing high and low culture, visual excess, breaching the limits of propriety and good taste, flamboyant style, lurid psycho-sexual

A Companion to the Horror Film, First Edition. Edited by Harry M. Benshoff.
© 2014 John Wiley & Sons, Inc. Published 2017 by John Wiley & Sons, Inc.

fantasies—are the very things that define art horror as a category (one has only to think of Dario Argento, Alfred Hitchcock, Michael Powell, and Georges Franju). So I was surprised to find so little mention of him in art-horror references. He does receive an entry in Kim Newman's *BFI Companion to Horror* (1996: 281) and his 1971 film *The Devils* is listed in *The Encyclopedia of Horror Cinema* (Hardy, Milne, and Willemen, 1986: 232). But most works on European Art Horror and Eurotrash mention him only in passing, citing his film *The Devils* as one of the trends leading to nunsploitation and possession films, but giving little discussion of the film itself (Nakahara, 2004: 127–128; Olney, 2013: 175). And I omitted him from my own discussion of art horror and taste politics in *Cutting Edge* (2000), an omission I hope to remedy now.

What I plan to do in this chapter is give a brief overview of Russell's career and recurring themes, situate his work within the broader context of "tonality" in cinema, and argue for further consideration of *The Devils* (1971) as an important art-horror text. What is at stake here is not merely Russell's art-horror reputation but a certain theoretical lacuna in the field of horror studies. That is, I believe that Russell has been a difficult director to discuss, appreciate, and recuperate precisely because we have no theoretical vocabulary to describe the challenging, frequently antihumanist tone of his films. And it is precisely tone and taste politics of his films that make him such an important, "polarizing" director.

Russell Overview

Ken Russell began his cinema career making films about artists for the BBC (British Broadcasting Corporation). He quickly distinguished himself by radically changing the conventional television art-bio formula to include actors and improvised scenes, and by inserting what can only be called a certain *Russellian tone* into previously standard television fare. In 1970, he made *Dance of the Seven Veils*, "a comic strip in 7 episodes on the life of Richard Strauss 1864–1949" for the BBC *Omnibus* program. The film begins with "Also Sprach Zarathustra" playing over a cave scene that features not only prehistoric man but also a group of self-flagellating monks and nuns; a kind of paean to both Stanley Kubrick's *2001: A Space Odyssey* (1968) and Luis Buñuel's Surrealist masterpiece *L'âge d'or* (1930). In that sense it prefigures much of Russell's later work; its depiction of a Fascist Strauss was so controversial that it was broadcast with a warning to the audience. This work at the BBC was the beginning of a lifelong fascination with artists and with the artist biopic.

Russell's first commercial film success came with the 1969 adaptation of D.H. Lawrence's *Women in Love*. Playing up the homoerotic aspects of the novel, the film became famous for a nude fireside wrestling scene between Alan Bates and Oliver Reed, and for its frank depiction of female sexual desire. Despite some unpleasantness with the censors (for full frontal male nudity), the film won an

Oscar nomination for Russell, and as Derek Malcolm notes, "made him a director to be reckoned with" (2011: 3). A stream of movies quickly followed: *The Music Lovers* (1970) about the composer Tchaikovsky, *The Devils*, *The Boyfriend* (1971), *Savage Messiah* (1972) about sculptor Henri Gaudier Brzeska, *Mahler* (1974), and *Tommy* (1975), Russell's film version of The Who's rock opera. This phase of the director's career culminated in *Lisztomania* (1975), about composer Franz Liszt. The title refers to "Liszt Fever," the frenzy that used to overtake fans during the nineteenth-century composer's concerts. Russell brilliantly links nineteenth-century fan frenzy to twentieth-century rock-concert hysteria through the casting of The Who's Roger Daltrey in the starring role. The film devotes a great deal of time to Liszt's friendship with fellow composer Richard Wagner—depicted here as a Nazi.

The fascist theme running through so much of Russell's work of this era (*Dance of the Seven Veils*, *Mahler*, *Lisztomania*, and to some degree, *The Devils*) links him to an already established art cinema trend. But whereas films such as *The Conformist* (Bernardo Bertolucci, 1970), *The Damned* (Luchino Visconti, 1969), and even the café-sequence in Jean-Luc Godard's *Masculin-Féminin* (1966) treat fascism as a deadly serious philosophical and political commitment, Russell consistently plays with the pop, media aspects of the Third Reich. His Fascist scenes were often offensive to critics and viewers, not only because they suggested that beloved musical figures (Strauss, Wagner, Mahler, Liszt) were linked in some way to Germany's brutal totalitarian regime, but also because they depicted Fascism itself as a kind of circus—a mania if you will—that engaged sexual fantasy and mimicked pop-rock fan hysteria. This was not the banality of evil so skillfully evoked by Hannah Arendt (1977), but the wilding, stupidity, glitter, and carelessness of it.

Russell's fascination with the artistic process and with individual artists continued throughout the 1970s and 1980s with *Valentino* (1977) and *Gothic* (1986). *Altered States* (1980), a Hollywood film, was a techno-horror take on the Jekyll and Hyde story, and marked his move into genre filmmaking. In 1984, he made *Crimes of Passion*, a thriller starring Kathleen Turner as the prostitute China Blue. In 1988, Russell made a low-budget horror-comedy for Vestron, based on Bram Stoker's last (and some would say his least) novel, *The Lair of the White Worm*, starring a very young Hugh Grant.

Russell continued to work until his death in 2011. He adapted *Lady Chatterley's Lover* (*Lady Chatterley*, 1993) for British television and directed several TV documentaries and features. He directed, *Whore* (1991), a melodrama about a prostitute, as well as several operas; he made the strangely conventional video for Elton John's "Nikita" (1985). Later in his career, he organized small video productions such as *The Fall of the Louse of Usher: A Gothic Tale for the 21ˢᵗ Century* (2002), acted, and joined the cast of *Celebrity Big Brother* (2007); he left the show voluntarily after 1 week, due to an altercation with another "star."

Thematic and Formal Concerns

As this brief overview shows, Russell revisited the same themes throughout his career. From his earliest days at the BBC, he continually returned to impressionistic artist biopics, and he remained fascinated by disturbed genius and by the artistic process. Like many people of his generation, he never quite got over World War II. Born in 1927, he would have been 12 years old when England declared war on Germany in 1939. And Fascism—both its horror and its spectacular appeal continued to fascinate him. At the same time, he felt an almost Proustian need to remind his audience—romantic about great musicians—that many German artists of a certain period *had* to be complicit with the Reich if they wished to work, to survive. Resisters, in Russell's view, left Germany or went underground. The ones who stayed? Whose careers thrived? Well there was no way in the immediate postwar era to recuperate people as "good" Germans or as apolitical; nor did Russell have any wish to do so. Furthermore, the Reich had not arisen out of a vacuum. As the beginning of *Dance of the Seven Veils* makes clear, Russell was keenly aware of the degree to which a certain Fascist groundwork had been laid by late nineteenth- and early twentieth-century high German culture. Indeed, by *all* high culture. Hence, the reference to Nietzsche in the choice of music; "Also sprach Zarathustra" is a work named for one of Nietzsche's philosophical tracts (Nietzsche, 2006).

Hysteria—in the colloquial sense of uncontrollable emotional excess—was a source of perennial fascination for the director. And he explored just about every form it could take—out and out madness, Lisztomania, the religious frenzy of supposedly possessed nuns, the equal religious mania of the Church Fathers who felt driven to exorcize them, sexual obsession, nymphomania, Fascist thralldom, and, always, the lure of pop culture. And one aspect of Russell's work that frequently nagged critics and audiences alike was his absolute refusal to draw distinctions based on the end goal of excessive behavior. Fascists in Russell's films can become as silly as rock-fans, and rock performers can become as grotesque as Hitler. Excess in the service of a perceived good is just as dangerous—perhaps more so—than the dark, drug-fueled excesses of someone like Lord Byron (who, in *Gothic*, wittingly calls up a monster drawn from the ids of everyone staying at the Villa Diodati). Furthermore, our quotidian desire to idolize, to create stars, is inextricably linked in Russell's universe to the Nietzschean desire for a Superman, for a Führer. We are all potential Nazis, he seems to say, and there is no redemption or release for any of us.

This is dark, heavy stuff; and perhaps if Russell had treated his sacred cows with the sobriety of an Oliver Stone, his films would have been more legible, more accessible to the critical establishment. Even the controversial *Natural Born Killers* (1994), which was written by Quentin Tarantino and remains more a Tarantino vehicle than a typical Oliver Stone flick, leaves viewers no doubt about the director's sympathies; it still functions as an essentially humanist text. But Russell's films are not legible in that way; they don't teach you how to read them the way that *Natural Born Killers* does. They are excessive, flamboyant, and, frequently, very funny. *Anything* can happen at any time, and for that very reason, it becomes hard to master reading strategies and patterns. Furthermore, unlike the critics who read Russell as essentially a Romantic director (Malcolm, 2011; Williams, 2007), I believe he has the same relationship to art cinema and art horror that William S. Burroughs has to "Beat" literature. A non-humanist outlier, he throws the rest of the field into sharp relief through his very difference.

Tone and Distinction

As Chris Dumas has noted, the key to Ken Russell is tone. And, as Douglas Pye reminds us, tone is

> among the most slippery of all critical concepts, difficult to define and almost always open to question … matters of tone are pervasive and inescapable. In all its varying forms and at many levels of a film, it is one of the central ways in which a film can signal *how we are to take what we see and hear*; it points both to our relationship to the film and to the film's relationship to its material and its conventions. (2000: 12)

In a word, tone is nebulous. Perhaps for that very reason, it has gone largely under-theorized and under-discussed in Film Studies. As a category it differs from mode (suspense, horror, comedy), which can always be linked back to genre and which maps nicely onto formal elements (editing, mise-en-scène, sound) that are always tangible in cinema. And I would argue that it also differs from mood, which maps onto specific *kinds* of aesthetics, like camp.

If tone as a concept is "difficult to define and always open to question," tone in Russell's films is almost impossible to pin down. There is a kind of distance that seems to hold us at arm's length and which subverts the usual ways in which we enter a film and lose ourselves in a story. Even a Hollywood vehicle such as *Crimes of Passion* makes easy identification virtually impossible. We never know why a successful business woman feels driven to transform into the prostitute China Blue night after night. In fact, knowing why—the film seems to suggest—is beside the point. And while the plot here is easier to follow than the plots of many other Russell films, important sections remain totally opaque. For example, we never know the exact nature of the group setting that begins and ends *Crimes*. The performative nature of it is highlighted, so it scans as a theatrical piece that pits women against men in a kind of snarling psychodrama and which permits each gender to say appalling things about the Other. But where it takes place and whether it is a dream or a staged performance or a therapy session is never clear.

Even more difficult, there is a constant slide between humor, irony, and over-the-top representation that makes it hard to get one's bearings. Going back to *Crimes of Passion*, Anthony Perkins is laughably overdone as the murderous

Reverend. Even when he forces his way into China Blue's apartment and may well succeed in killing her, it is difficult to take him seriously. This leaves viewers wondering what we are to make of what we are seeing, and can lead untutored viewers to feel that both their "relationship to the film" and the "film's relationship to its material" are entirely unstable, unreliable and unknowable.

As Chris Dumas writes in a passage worth quoting at length, in terms of [Russell's] tone, a crucial scene occurs in *The Devils* when the King visits the bedeviled church: is this slapstick or tragedy, social commentary or pornography, subtlety or exploitation?

> Distinctions like these collapse at key moments in Russell's work, especially in the string of exploding masterpieces that begins with *Dance of the Seven Veils* and ends with *Lisztomania*. Tonally, we are past the limits of horror as well as the limits of comedy; we are in that place in De Sade that Pasolini did not understand, i.e. the rape trial of the Three Stooges, *a place where humanism and art are no longer compatible*. Certainly one could read *The Devils*, for example, as a plea for a more inclusive Church or as a mournful depiction of Man's Inhumanity To Man, but to do so would be to ignore what makes Russell different from a humanist like, say, Renoir. This is a vision of life on Earth in which redemption, in any form, is a completely delusional proposition, and therefore that anyone who strives for redemption is contemptible—which is why the only character in *The Devils* who seems vaguely reasonable is Baron De Laubarde-mont, since he has no illusions. Is this fascism? Perhaps. But unlike Peckinpah—whom Pauline Kael correctly identified as a fascist filmmaker—Russell has no illusions either. Fascism, after all, thrives on delusions of redemption; it requires them. (2013: 1. Emphasis mine)

As Dumas indicates here, tone is often defined by what it is not and by what is unnameable (he links it to specific directors and specific moments in films). That is, it defies easy categorization. But more importantly, certain tonalities thwart our ability to make clean distinctions between good and bad taste, high and low culture, the ironic/comedic and the serious. And it is precisely this kind of hybridity-in-culture that has so troubled Russell's critics. Viewers of Russell's films often find themselves "beyond the limits" of recognizable categories, unsure of how to read the film they are watching. For critics who dislike Russell, anxiety about tone is often displaced onto a criticism of specific tropes and modalities—"camp imagery," "gross exploitation," and "virulent contempt of women." I say "displaced" because other, easier-to-read directors, who use camp imagery and exploitation, and who are nastier to women than Russell is (Dario Argento, for example) are not dismissed in quite the same way (Hardy, Milne, and Willement, 1986: 226). Even critics who *like* Russell's films describe the director himself as a strangely alien character, as someone who seemingly comes from another era. Derek Malcolm calls him "one of the last of the great British romantics" (2011: 2); the title of Kevin Flanagan's book on Russell dubs him "England's last mannerist" (2009).

The problem is not just that Russell's tone is confusing, or thwarts what Pierre Bourdieu calls "distinction" (1984). The most troubling aspect of Russell's work is that his tone is so often antihumanist. He depicts a world where, as Dumas writes, "humanism and art are no longer compatible." This is a world recognizable to people trained in a certain kind of literary theory and history. But since moving away from continental theory in the 1990s, Film Studies has not really developed an adequate vocabulary for addressing the antihumanist tendencies in certain art, avant-garde, and horror cinema. Some scholars have begun to redress this critical absence in Film Studies (Hallam, 2011; King, 2012), but a great deal of work remains to be done on what might be called the *Niezchean, Sadean,* and *Bataillean* elements in film. This is particularly true in the arena of art horror, where the monster so frequently functions to show us (literally "monstrare" — to teach, demonstrate) these dark, Sadean, antihumanist strains in ourselves and in our so-called culture.

There is not enough space here to do a complete analysis of all Russell's art-horror films. And Russell's films demand elaborated readings, not only because they are so complex but also because they — like Godard's films — function as metacritical essays. So what follows is a discussion of his most controversial film, *The Devils,* that will, I hope point up Russell's importance as an art-horror director, and his contribution to the larger field of horror cinema itself.

The Devils (1971)

Many critics — myself included — consider this film to be Russell's masterpiece. Based on Aldous Huxley's non-fiction novel *The Devils of Loudun* (1952) and John Whiting's play *The Devils* (1961), the film treats a documented historical case of supposed demonic possession, which ended in a witchcraft trial in Loudun, France. Father Urbain Grandier was burned at the stake in 1634 for alleged sexual and metaphysical crimes against a group of Ursuline nuns; in short, for witchcraft. He went to the stake protesting his innocence and refusing to confess.

As Chris Dumas notes earlier, the film *can* be read in rather conventional ways. In fact, the editing supports a straightforward political interpretation. *The Devils* opens with a theatrical pageant, celebrating the coronation of Louis XIII as King of France. At the pageant's end, Cardinal Richelieu, who barely stifled his yawns throughout the show, has a hurried conversation with His Holy Highness. Richelieu says that Louis's interpretation of the Birth of Venus symbolized for him the possible birth of "a new France, where Church and State are one." "Amen," the King replies. To which Richelieu adds, "and may the Protestant be driven from the land." The film then cuts to a close-up of a skeleton mounted on a wheel and a long line of imprisoned Protestants is an illustration of just how cruelly the Church plans to accomplish the routing of the Huguenots.

This is followed by another cut, to the funeral of Geoges de Sainte-Marthes, Governor of Loudun, who has died of the Plague. As Father Urbain Grandier (Oliver Reed) lays the body of Saint-Marthes to rest, he hails the end of the Religious Wars, praising Loudun for its moderation and for its ability to achieve détente between Catholic and Protestant factions. Nearby, in the cloistered Ursuline convent a group of nuns form a human pyramid trying to reach the uppermost grated convent window, in order to get a better look at the much esteemed Grandier. As the lucky nun at the top of the pyramid exclaims at Grandier's beauty, some townswomen walk by the convent, loudly heralding his sexual prowess. "Grandier could have me anywhere," one exclaims, "even on the Holy Altar itself." This scene is interrupted by the arrival of Sister Jeanne des Anges (Vanessa Redgrave) in the cloister room. Initially, she appears solely as the voice of religious authority, chastising the Sisters for their athletic attempts to peek out at the world. But once she dispatches them back to the duties of the convent, the humpbacked Prioress locks herself in a small secluded cell, where she too writhes at the thought of the comely Grandier and pleads with God to remove her hump.

This opening sequence introduces the three stories that the film continues to interweave throughout. The first plotline is blatantly political. Richelieu's desire to consolidate a united, Catholic France under Louis, means that walled towns such as Loudun must be brought into the nationalist fold. For Richelieu, this means destroying the fortifications and self-governance of Provincial towns. It also means the religious persecution of all Protestants and the destruction of "Huguenot strongholds." Grandier, who succeeds Sainte-Marthes as the temporary Governor of Loudun, is committed to keeping Loudun's walls intact, to preserving its right to self-rule and to maintaining its commitment to religious tolerance. He has also called undue attention to himself and to Loudun by writing a tract critical of Richelieu's political ambitions. Incensed, the Cardinal becomes obsessed with bringing both Grandier and Loudun to heel; he sends the Baron de Laubardemont (Dudley Sutton) to do just that.

The second major plotline involves the transformation of Grandier from profligate priest to martyr. Shortly after the scenes described earlier, in which nuns and townswomen alike seem smitten with the priest, we see Grandier giving a "Latin lesson" to a naked girl mounted on top of him. When Phillipe (Georgina Hale) tells him at the end of the lesson that she is pregnant, he informs her that she must bear the cross that God has inflicted on her, tell her father the truth, and allow M. Trincant (her father) to find a good man for her to marry. As for himself, well, he can do nothing. Subsequent scenes lead us to believe that this is not the first time Grandier has impregnated a young girl and that he also has a long history of consorting "with whores." As he tells his assistant Father Mignon later in the film, he uses worldly things — ambition, lust, women — as weapons against himself because he has "a great need to be united with God." If this strategy seems disingenuous to contemporary viewers, it also seems to be failing Grandier as well. When we meet him, the priest is in danger of losing his faith altogether. And then he meets Madeleine De Brou (Gemma Jones), a pious woman whose simplicity genuinely moves him. Breaking the Catholic vow of priestly celibacy, he marries her in a secret ceremony. Through his love for her, he believes he can, at long last, come to God.

The third plotline is that of Sister Jeanne and the Ursuline nuns. Driven by a kind of sexual hysteria, they begin confessing to erotic feelings, which they attribute to nocturnal Satanic visitations. When it becomes clear that the man inspiring these erotic dreams is Father Grandier, Laubardemont seizes on the nuns' fantasies as the means to destroy both Grandier and the city. He declares the nuns to be possessed and orders Father Mignon to bring in a professional exorcist, Father Barré (Michael Gothard). Barré conducts exorcism after exorcism, whipping the nuns into a truly sexual frenzy. Repeatedly denounced by women whom he has never seen, Grandier is arrested, tried, and tortured. Refusing to confess, he is burned at the stake. At the moment when the execution fire is lit, Laubardemont gives the order for the walls surrounding Loudun to be blasted. Grandier's last words to the crowd, are "look at your city ... If you would remain free men, fight."

At its most basic, this is a story of political, religious, and sexual scandal; the story of an unlikely hero destroyed by his own vanity, ambition, and weakness; and of corrupt institutions that use literal witch hunts to achieve cynical political goals. Because of Russell's particular approach to the material, *The Devils* was censored twice, first by the British Board of Film Censors and then again by Warner Brothers Studio, the American Company that had provided much of the funding for the film. Even in its expurgated state, the film received an "X" rating both in Britain and the United States and was banned outright in several countries. For many years it was unavailable on the legal commercial home video market. In 2012, a complete restored version of the film was finally released by the British Film Institute and a special 2-disc DVD set is now available for purchase. As of this writing, however, no legal commercial American version of the restored film exists, so some of the scenes described later may not be available to all viewers. [For a complete discussion of the censorship history, see Crouse, 2012 and *The Devils*, the booklet accompanying the BFI DVD. (BFI, British Film Institute)]

Unlike traditional horror films, *The Devils* does not encourage viewers to accept the story of witchcraft and deviltry. In fact, Russell includes four scenes designed to show that there is no demonic possession, that the horror here is located in the marriage of Church and State, not in the supernatural realm. Shortly after Father Barré is summoned, a group of nuns is taken to the forest, penned, and corralled. They are told that their attempts to protect Sister Jeanne from the exigencies of exorcism amount to treason and that they will be executed unless they confess to being possessed by the same demon that disturbs the Prioress. "You may save yourselves," Laubardemont and Barré tell them. "You will scream. You will blaspheme. You will not be responsible for your actions. Denounce your devilish master, Grandier." The next scene shows the nuns tearing off their clothes and masturbating in the Church.

The second scene occurs after the exorcisms have become a great public spectacle and the nuns themselves something of a tourist attraction. The "Duc de Condé" (actually the King) arrives at the Church, bearing a relic taken from the "King's own altar," a phial of the Divine Blood of Our Lord Jesus Christ. Father Barré assures him that the proximity of such a relic will immediately—even if only temporarily—drive the devils from the nuns' bodies. And to be sure, as soon as Barré approaches the nuns with the box supposedly containing the relic, the Sisters scream and are still. At this point the King opens the box and reveals that it is empty. "What kind of trick have you played on us?" Barré demands. "What kind of trick are *you* playing on *us*?" replies the King before leaving. Subsequent scenes show a nun threatened into signing a confession, in which she claims that Grandier has bewitched her. And when Sister Jeanne tries to commit suicide later in the film and confesses that she has wronged an innocent man, Barré dismisses the truth as still further evidence that Sister Jeanne is possessed by Grandier's Devil.

So this is not a supernatural horror movie in the same way that *The Exorcist* (William Friedkin, 1973) is. We do not hear the Devil's voice here or watch him take possession of an unwilling body. And we are never expected to accept the supernatural truth of what is happening onscreen; in fact we are actively discouraged from doing so. But we *are* supposed to believe that the townspeople depicted onscreen believe these manifestations. In that sense the film operates in the kind of subdued horror register that the sci-fi horror classic *The Last Man on Earth* (Ubaldo Ragona and Sydney Salkow, 1964) and Todd Haynes's art film *Safe* (1995) do; we are not actively scared but we are uneasy and queasy in a way that exceeds the usual conventions of non-generic drama (Cinquemani, 2002). And we understand that what we are witnessing *is* a horror show for the diegetic characters onscreen. "The whole world is dying of panicky fright," reads the title card that opens Todd Haynes's *Poison* (1991), another subdued horror masterpiece. That could certainly be the tagline for *The Devils* as well. While Russell takes pains to show us that the supposed demonic possession troubling the nuns is orchestrated by the political institutions of Church and State, he also insists that we take seriously a world view in which demonic possession might seem plausible, a routine occurrence. This is the world as described by Michel Foucault in *Madness and Civilization* (1965), the world before the medicalized model of insanity (or of repression) became possible. It is a world in which people literally *saw* things differently.

In the film this translates into a stunning mise-en-scène. Although the film was shot using color stock, the palette is largely black and white. This makes for stark contrasts, with few subtle gradations and fewer grey tones. It is a literalization of the Manichaean worldview, which divides all things into binaries of absolute evil and absolute goodness, pure black and pure white. At the same time, Russell wanted us to be aware that for the people of Loudun themselves, this stark world view was modern. He decided against shooting on location, because he did not want Loudun to be represented by antiquated grey, ivy-covered walls. He wanted it to look new, as it would have looked then. So he commissioned art director Derek Jarman to build a dazzling white set. It does look new, but in key scenes it also looks very much like a set, in which you can see painted backdrops. This contributes to an overall theatricality, which will be discussed at greater length later. For now, suffice it to say that theatrical aspects of the set mitigate against the naturalistic reading that the editing encourages: it complicates the tone (Figure 28.1).

As mentioned earlier, the editing supports a straightforward political interpretation of the story. And it is masterful; there is not one excess shot in the entire film. The montage, too, is highly effective. Graphic matches, matches on action, eyeline matches, and associative editing maximize the links between Church and State, and contrast Grandier with the corruption around him. This is most evident in the

Figure 28.1 Father Grandier (Oliver Reed) featured against one of Derek Jarman's stark black-and-white cityscapes. *The Devils* (1971). Directed by Ken Russell. Produced by Russo Productions.

infamous Rape of Christ sequence which was originally cut from the film, and has only recently been restored to the BFI version. Here, scenes of Grandier returning from a visit to the King, a royal summons protecting Loudun in his pocket, is intercut with the nuns' wild frenzy back in the town. Most compelling are the scenes of Grandier saying Mass, a mark of his newfound pastoral spirituality. As he blesses bread for Communion, we cut to an image of a nun spitting out the purgative that had been forced into her mouth. The scene continues in this way. Idyllic moments showing Grandier praying alone in nature are intercut with a veritable orgy, as nuns masturbate, kiss one another, spew liquid, and rip off their clothes in Loudun.

Hell, Jean-Paul Sartre once famously wrote is "other people" (1947: 92, translation mine); horror in *The Devils* is located both in other people and in the institutions that govern them. Affective horror is located in the body genre moments of the film — the more punishing moments of the exorcisms and "the question ordinary and extraordinary" that the Church puts to Grandier, his torture at the hands of the Holy Fathers. Here we hear the bone splinter and see gaping wounds, even as the torture scenes are shortened and somewhat modified from the original director's cut. Some of the truly grisly, gory, and gross effects (e.g., feces on Sister Jeanne's legs after an exorcism) were cut at the behest of the British Board of Film Censors, and as far as I can tell, were not completely restored to the new BFI print. Still, enough remains to shock people who are not used to body genre films.

Horrifying, too, is the behavior of the Church Fathers and of the townspeople who ultimately turn against Grandier and gather to celebrate his execution. The scenes of Father Barré blessing and praying over the instruments of torture provide an additional subversive moment in a film that is already highly critical of the seventeenth-century French Catholic Church. And the scene in which M. Trincant holds Phillipe's baby, so that he — too — can see Grandier's execution, provides the same kind of biting Freudian commentary on the family that Robin Wood claims for American slasher films (1978). "Watch, Bastard. See how your mother's honor was avenged," he says. Another friend chimes in. "Lucky little bastard. It's not everyday Baby sees Daddy burned to death."

The Devils' Tone

But as Dumas notes, to read the film solely in terms of its editing and its more conventional message is to "ignore what makes Russell different from a humanist like, say, Renoir." It is also to ignore the distinctive elements that make *The Devils* seem offensive even to horror scholars such as Phil Hardy, Tom Milne, and Paul Willemen (1986: 232). The reading I have so far given of the film's narrative elements is decidedly complicated by the mise-en-scène and by its tone. That is, while everything I have said in my analysis thus far is true, the attentive viewer does not quite know how she is to react to any of the elements I have mentioned.

As noted earlier, the film begins with a theatrical pageant. The new King of France, Louis XIII, wearing glitter makeup, a gold cape, pasties, and a g-string re-enacts the Birth of Venus as part of his coronation ceremony (Figure 28.2). This immediately sets him up as something of a fop, someone who will be easily dominated by the politically minded Richelieu. But it also sets up a theatrical motif that recurs throughout the movie and distances us from any easy naturalistic read. The stage set of the

Figure 28.2   Artifice and theatricality: King Louis XIII opens the film with his recreation of Botticelli's *The Birth of Venus*. *The Devils* (1971). Directed by Ken Russell. Produced by Russo Productions.

pageant itself works against traditional modes of viewing. The first things we see are moving cardboard cut-out waves, meant to represent the sea. The effect is in keeping with the technologies of seventeenth-century theater, but it immediately plunges the contemporary viewer into a world of play-acting and works against usual processes of suture.

This disarming, Brechtian effect, comes up again during the funeral of Saint Marthes. The previous governor of Loudun has died of plague and we see piles of bodies surrounding the funereal scene. These piles of bodies recur throughout the film. They are moved in wheelbarrows, blessed, tossed into ditches and burned, but it is important that the film does not appear to treat either the bodies or the plague with any kind of gravitas. Instead, a *danse macabre* air hangs over the proceedings. The two men most responsible for transporting the bodies joke and provide a running sight gag through their physical comedy and the strange head-gear they wear. In addition, the presence of the plague seems to have unleashed a general theatrical atmosphere throughout the town. Well before the frenzied orgy sequences provoked by exorcisms, the nuns in the Ursuline convent act out scenes — the marriage of Grandier to Madeleine De Brou, for example — complete with props and costumes. In fact, it is their repeated theatrical representations of the priest's reputed sexual prowess that inflames Sister Jeanne's erotic fantasies about him. But to us, it looks very much like the kind of drama you might see in a particularly hysteric middle school.

In the town as well, people act out various moments of Grandier's lecherous life, and these mummeries form the backdrop of Grandier's trial, his torture, and his execution. In part, these displays are meant to show, within the diegesis itself, the carnival atmosphere that did historically accompany public executions. But their obvious theatricality has an apposite effect for viewers of the film. For us, it represents something of the "rupture between things and words, between things and the ideas and signs that are their representation," which Antonin Artaud identifies as the "confusion" that is "the sign" of modernity (1958: 7). And it is important that here theatre has none of the salvific, purgative possibilities that Artaud attributes to it. It is a diversion, for player and spectator alike. Something meant to distance oneself and one's audiences from the horror of everyday life, it is not meant to be naturalistic or to stand in for a readily identifiable Artaudian ritual. It is bawdy, body humor: a Punch and Judy show with living actors.

If the set theatre pieces set an odd tone, an even stranger tone is introduced through the theatrical costume and makeup that bleeds over into action marked as "real." As mentioned earlier, the men responsible for removing bodies of people felled by the plague wear exaggerated head gear — one has a kind of snorkel, the other elaborate goggles — that give them the strange clownish air of Beckett protagonists. Other characters routinely appear in white face, for reasons that are never explained. Phillipe, for example, wears whiteface and Harlequin makeup the first time we see her, mounted on Grandier. She wears a less exaggerated version of this same makeup

Figure 28.3   Exaggerated white make up also calls attention to the notion of performance, especially when Phillipe (Georgina Hale) has sex with Grandier. *The Devils* (1971). Directed by Ken Russell. Produced by Russo Productions.

in the final execution scenes. Crowd scenes—even the most mundane ones—contain people wearing white face, and—occasionally—people dressed to resemble skeletons. The court scenes contain white-faced onlookers made up as mimes. This is a much more marked theatrical effect than the powdered faces and cosmetics of other characters, the nobles who come to visit the convent, for example, who are simply made up in the manner of the times (Figure 28.3).

Further, the acting style of the protagonists within the "real" story emphasizes the theatricality of the characters themselves. These are men who, for the most part, are keenly aware of the roles they are expected to play. And it is for that very reason that we never know how sincerely we are to take them. Michael Gothard gives a completely and at times laughably exaggerated performance as the fanatical exorcist, Father Barré. But even Oliver Reed's Father Grandier seems oddly theatrical and freakish in his heroic stance. Surrounded by clownish, declaiming priests and hysterical nuns, Grandier seems less admirable than deluded himself. This really does seem to be part of Reed's portrayal, as he dramatically intones lines in a manner that allows us to *see* the performance. In speaking of Reed's execution of the part, Russell told Richard Crouse (2012: 9):

> It's a rather unique performance insofar as he really pulled out all the stops. I had a special working relationship with him. It was quite simple but very effective. He called me Jesus.
>
> He'd say, "What do you want, Jesus?" and I would say, "Give me Moody One." Moody One was one of the simplest instructions that I could give him. Moody Two was a little more important and Moody Three was "do anything you like." … [Moody Three] could be extremely dangerous.

Crouse followed by asking Russell if Reed's unpredictability is what made him a great actor. "Great actor?" Russell replied. "I never said he was a great actor. No, he was a terrible actor" (2012: 9). And it was precisely because he believed Reed to be a terrible actor, that is, someone who would always overact and show the theatrical work, that Russell cast him in the key role. Russell did not want the priest to seem like a hero in any believably natural way. To put it another way, he *wanted* his hero to look like an actor overplaying his part.

As Dumas notes, "the only character in *The Devils* who seems vaguely reasonable is Baron De Laubardemont, since he has no illusions." That is, he is the one character who is driven by his own ambition and political goals, not by any vision he has of himself as a hero, or a Saint, or a creator of Unified France. For that very reason, perhaps, Dudley Sutton, the actor who portrays him, gives one of the few naturalistic performances in the film. The other naturalistic performances are provided, interestingly enough, by Vanessa Redgrave as the hysterical Sister Jeanne and Gemma Jones as the simple Madeleine.

If the acting style lends the film a certain über-theatrical feel, so too at times does the set and art design. The exorcisms themselves are, as Dumas noted earlier, hard to read, since we truly cannot tell if this is "slapstick or tragedy, social commentary or pornography, subtlety or exploitation." What makes it even harder is that the instruments themselves seem to occupy so many registers. A favored seventeenth-century method for driving out devils was the administration of outsized enemas, "a quart of holy water" as Aldous Huxley tells us. And even in real life the instruments needed to administer such a quantity of liquid, Huxley writes, were theatrical, "the huge brass syringe of Molièresque farce" (1952: 113). Wielded here by the medical mummers mentioned earlier, the instruments seem even more preposterously stagey. But their effects are real enough. Sister Jeanne is exhausted and bleeding by the time they are done with her, and it is in this state that she first gives Grandier's name to Father Barré. It is farce turned to torture and, thus, very difficult to parse.

The set too veers from naturalistic to theatrical depending on the scene. When we first see the walls of the town, they seem stunningly "real." This is during the funeral scene for Saint Marthes, the scene when we first also see Grandier. Introduced to us by way of extreme low angle shot, a black garbed figure on top of a dazzlingly white wall, Grandier certainly looks like the kind of man that could set religious hearts thumping. But later in the film when Phillipe's father confronts Grandier against those same walls, they look every inch a stage set. There is even decorative writing over one of the porticoes, suggestive more of an avant-garde stage production than of commerce. And, as though this were not enough to introduce a level of staginess, Grandier defends himself against M. Trincant's swordplay with a stuffed crocodile that he plucks from a trash heap. The fact that this scene features one of the key "moral" speeches of the film makes it all the harder to read. How seriously are we supposed to take this?

The theatricality of the mise-en-scène, which extends to key performances, operates here as a Brechtian distancing effect, guaranteeing that viewers will be more intellectually interested in the film than emotionally moved by it. In that sense, it is not a humanist film. In fact, it can be called an *antihumanist film* since part of what it dramatizes is the ways in which people can be manipulated — via emotion as well as overt threat — into believing anything and doing the most horrific things. And herein lies the real horror. Russell himself has said that he was not moved to make the film by any of the humanist and humanitarian arguments that Huxley makes in his wonderful book. Rather it was one stark image, given by Huxley, that for Russell became the core of the film, the center around which everything else would revolve. In publicly exorcising Sister Jeanne, Huxley wrote, "Barré had treated her to an experience that was the equivalent, more or less, of a rape in a public lavatory" (1952: 115). That image, the rape of a nun in a public lavatory, was the image around which Russell orchestrated the rest of the film, even the sound. The composer Peter Maxwell Davis has talked about the way that image influenced the sound of the film. Everything had to sound "as if it were taking place in a public toilet," he commented in the documentary *Hell on Earth* (Paul Joyce, 2002). "Everything sounds louder than it is because it resonates back at you."

In *Cutting Edge* (2000), I argued that art horror emblematizes a particular hybrid cultural mode that Fredric Jameson identifies in *Signatures of the Visible* (1992). Art horror films invite us to "read high and mass culture as objectively related and dialectically interdependent phenomena, as twin and inseparable forms of the fission of aesthetic production under capitalism" (1992: 14). Nowhere is this clearer than in the art horror of Ken Russell. Here latrine references mingle with tableaux meant to resemble Renaissance paintings. And for Russell, it is clear that this layering and weaving of cultural categories is deliberate and intentional. In *Hell on Earth*, the documentary that accompanies *The Devils* in the BFI DVD set, various *Devils'* actors and Mark Kermode (the person largely credited with enabling the film's restoration) praise Russell for his supreme visual style, his intelligence, and his use of high culture. "Don't forget kitsch," Russell bellows. "There's a bit of kitsch as well."

Actually more than just a bit, as I hope the earlier discussion of tone makes clear. And in *The Devils*, elements of high art and kitsch (low culture) really do exist in a kind of mash-up. That is, you cannot simply remove the film's "low," bawdy, and/or kitschy elements without damaging the overall warp and weft of the total film itself. Tim Lucas makes that abundantly clear in his excellent pre-restoration essay on the film's censorship, "Cutting the Hell out of the Devils" (1996). And I think it is intrinsic to the film's meaning that this cultural confusion — slapstick *and* tragedy, social commentary *and* pornography, subtlety *and* exploitation — was an endemic part of the original historical event itself. As I hope I have shown, *The Devils* is a dense, rich text that not only rewards multiple viewings but *needs* to be seen more than once. For this alone, it is an important art-horror film. Given the way it both enlarges the vocabulary of art horror — indeed of art cinema itself — highlights tonality, and demands that we look at the humanist expectations we bring to film texts, it deserves a stronger place in the art horror canon than it currently occupies.

References

Arendt, H. (1977) *Eichmann in Jerusalem: A Report on the Banality of Evil*, Penguin Books, New York.

Artaud, A. (1958) *The Theatre and Its Double* (trans. Mary Caroline Richards), Grove Press, New York.

Bourdieu, P. (1984) *Distinction: A Social Critique of the Judgement of Taste* (trans. Richard Nice), Harvard University Press, Cambridge Massachusetts.

Cinquemani, S. (2002). "Safe". *Slant Magazine*. http://www.slantmagazine.com/film/review /safe/288 (accessed 22 July 2013).

Crouse, R. (2012) *Raising Hell: Ken Russell and the Unmaking of the Devils*, ECW Press, Toronto, Canada.

Dumas, C. (2013) "Meditations on *Lisztomania*," unpublished MS. Quoted by permission of author.

Flanagan, K. (ed.) (2009) *Ken Russell: Re-viewing England's Last Mannerist*, Scarecrow Press, Lanham, Toronto, Plymouth UK.

Foucault, M. (1965) *Madness and Civilization* (trans. Richard Howard), Pantheon, New York.

Hallam, L. (2011) *Screening the Marquis de Sade: Pleasure, Pain and the Transgressive Body in Film*, McFarland, North Carolina.

Hardy, P., Tom, M., and Paul, W. (1986) *The Encyclopedia of Horror Movies*, Harper and Row, New York.

Hawkins, J. (2000) *Cutting Edge: Art Horror and the Horrific Avant-garde*, University of Minnesota Press, Minneapolis and London.

Huxley, A. (1952) *The Devils of Loudun*, Carroll and Graf Publishers, New York.

Jameson, F. (1992) *Signatures of the Visible*, Routledge, New York.

King, C.S. (2012) *Washed in Blood: Male Sacrifice, Trauma and the Cinema*, Rutgers University Press, New Brunswick, NJ and London.

Lim, D. (2011). Ken Russell, Director Fond of Provocation, Dies at 84. *New York Times* (Nov 29). http://www.nytimes.com/2011/11/29/arts/ken-russell-controversial-director -dies-at-84.html?_r=0&pagewanted=print (accessed 24 June 2013).

Lucas, T. (1996) Cutting the hell out of the devils. *Video Watchdog*, **35**, 36–51.

Malcolm, D. (2011). Ken Russell Obituary. *The Guardian* (Nov 28). http://www.guardian .co.uk/film/2011/nov/28/ken-russell (accessed 24 June 2013).

McLellan, D. (2011). Filmmaker with a Flair for Fantasy and Flamboyance. *Los Angeles Times* (Nov 29). http://www.latimes.com/obituaries/la-me-ken-russell-20111129,0,6146567 .story#axzz2wz0jzKuL (accessed 24 June 2013).

Nakahara, T. (2004) Barred nuns: Italian nunsploitation films, in *Alternative Europe: Eurotrash and Exploitation Cinema since 1945* (eds E. Mathijs and X. Mendik), Wallflower Press, London and New York, pp. 124–133.

Newman, K. (1996) *The BFI Companion to Horror*, Cassell and London, British Film Institute, London.

Nietzsche, F. (2006) *Thus Spoke Zarathustra: a book for all and none* (trans. Adrian Del Caro), Cambridge University Press, Cambridge, New York.

Olney, I. (2013) *Euro Horror: classic European horror cinema in contemporary American culture*, Indiana University Press, Bloomington and Indianapolis.

Pye, D. (2000) Movies and point of view. *Movie*, **36**, 2–34.

Sartre, J.-P. (1947) *Huis Clos: suivi de Les Mouches*, Éditions Gallimard., Paris.

Vincendeau, G. (ed.) (1995) *Encyclopedia of European Cinema*, British Film Institute, Great Britain.

Wardrop, M. (2011). Ken Russell Dies Aged 84. *The Telegraph* (Nov 28). http://www.telegraph .co.uk/culture/film/film-news/8919984/Ken-Russell-dies-aged-84.html (accessed 24 June 2013).

Whiting, J. (1961) *The Devils*, Hill and Wang, New York.

Williams, L.R. (2007). Ken Russell: Sweet Swell of Excess. *Sight and Sound*. http://old .bfi.org.uk/sightandsound/feature/49385 (accessed 25 June 13), pp. 1–4.

Wood, R. (1978) Return of the repressed. *Film Comment*, **14** (4), 25–32.

29

Horror's Otherness and Ethnographic Surrealism

The Case of The Shout

Adam Lowenstein

Surrealism and the horror film share a long history of mutual admiration and reciprocal influence, but thus far, connections between the two have been relegated to specialized, rather minor mentions in the scholarly literature. Neither are most critical accounts of surrealism particularly interested in the horror film nor are most critical accounts of the horror film very concerned with surrealism. For example, Robin Wood's landmark "An Introduction to the American Horror Film" (1979) devotes only a short paragraph to the topic as a way of legitimating horror's intellectual value, particularly regarding the psychoanalytic theory he applies to the genre:

> It is worth noting here that one group of intellectuals did take American horror movies very seriously indeed: the writers, painters, and filmmakers of the Surrealist movement. Luis Buñuel numbers *The Beast With Five Fingers* (1946) among his favorite films and paid homage to it in *The Exterminating Angel* (1962); and Georges Franju, an heir of the Surrealists, numbers *The Fly* (1958) among *his*. The association is highly significant, given the commitment of the Surrealists to Freud, the unconscious, dreams, and the overthrow of repression. (Wood, 2004: 117)

Wood deserves praise for noting the horror-surrealism relationship, but he neglects to mention or misconstrues enough details to make the relationship seem less significant than it actually is. For example, the surrealist affection for horror did not limit itself to American films, even though Jean Ferry's appreciation of *King Kong* (1933) is one of the great examples of surrealist film criticism (Ferry, 2000); think also of André Breton and Georges Bataille's shared admiration for *Nosferatu* (1922) and the widespread surrealist fascination with Louis Feuillade's horror-inflected crime serials *Fantômas* (1913), *Les Vampires* (1915), and *Judex* (1917). Buñuel may

A Companion to the Horror Film, First Edition. Edited by Harry M. Benshoff.
© 2014 John Wiley & Sons, Inc. Published 2017 by John Wiley & Sons, Inc.

or may not have enjoyed *The Beast With Five Fingers*, but more pertinent is the fact that he made an important uncredited contribution to its production during his sojourn in Hollywood—he wrote a sequence in which the disembodied hand of the film's title becomes alive, an image he had already begun to explore in his surrealist masterwork *Un Chien andalou* (1929) (De la Colina and Turrent, 1992: 45). Buñuel's collaborator on *Un Chien andalou*, Salvador Dalí, went on to work with no less of a horror innovator than Alfred Hitchcock, on *Spellbound* (1945). Hitchcock's own brand of horror owes something to surrealism, as he himself admitted (Hitchcock, 1995: 142) and as *Psycho* (1960) in particular makes plain. Franju may have liked *The Fly*, but his own syntheses of horror and surrealism in *Blood of the Beasts* (1949) and *Eyes Without a Face* (1960) remain unparalleled cinematic achievements (Lowenstein, 2005: 17–54) that Wood was certainly aware of (Wood, 1973) but chooses not to cite here. Finally, although it is true that Freud exercised a powerful influence on the surrealists [and whose own essay "The Uncanny" (1919) also functions as an incisive piece of literary criticism on horror], Freudian and surrealist conceptions of the unconscious, dreams, and repression are often so at odds that it is no wonder the famous meeting between Freud and Breton in 1921 resulted in nothing more than mutual disappointment (Rabaté, 2002: 60–61).

I have gone on at some length concerning Wood's account of the horror-surrealism relationship for several reasons. First, the influence of Wood's "An Introduction to the American Horror Film" on the scholarly study of horror cannot be over-estimated, but even so it is noteworthy how few critics have followed up on his stated connections between surrealism and horror. Second, Wood's formulations of how horror film's monsters must be understood in relation to social and political otherness will become a central focus later in this chapter, while the horror film I will examine, Jerzy Skolimowski's *The Shout* (1978), is contemporaneous with "An Introduction to the American Horror Film" but does not appear in it. Third, the crossroads of surrealism and horror were already more crowded and complex than Wood recognized at the time, but it has become even more so in the years since his publication. Horror-associated directors as varied as Dario Argento, David Cronenberg, Marina de Van, Michael Haneke, David Lynch, Takashi Miike, Gaspar Noé, Roman Polanski, Arturo Ripstein, and Jan Svankmajer (to name a prominent few) have made major contributions to the horror-surrealism imaginary, no matter what their stated loyalty toward or distance from the original surrealists may be. I believe Skolimowski belongs on this list as well. Fourth, Wood's statement, however brief and incomplete, ranks as elaborate when compared with most scholarship on surrealism, which tends to marginalize surrealist cinema in general and ignore especially surrealist cinematic investments in horror [a major exception is Ado Kyrou, whose foundational *Le Surréalisme au cinéma* (1953) still remains unavailable in English]. For example, Michael Richardson's *Surrealism and Cinema* (2006) is already relatively unusual for its emphasis on film within the surrealist orbit, as opposed to painting or literature (for other notable exceptions see Harper and Stone, 2007; Kuenzli, 1996; Williams, 1992). But Richardson dismisses the possibility of directors such as Cronenberg and Lynch having any relevance for surrealism (Richardson, 2006: 173n3, 72–73) and insists that surrealism's original investments in popular culture in general (never mind horror in particular) are no longer possible today (Richardson, 2006: 26, 72).

In this chapter, I will argue that surrealism and the horror film deserve more detailed consideration as intersecting discourses, particularly around what the anthropologist and historian James Clifford calls "ethnographic surrealism." For Clifford, ethnographic surrealism is born of the historical moment in interwar France when surrealism and ethnography developed in close proximity, often overlapping in surprising ways that remain productive for us today because they illuminate "a crucial modern orientation toward cultural order" (Clifford, 1988: 117). Rather than enforce clear boundaries between self and other, familiar and strange, domestic and exotic, ethnographic surrealism endeavors to locate the other in the self, the strange in the familiar, the exotic in the domestic. In this way, ethnographic surrealism challenges our basic assumptions about the nature of cultural order and the politics of its representation.

How does the horror film, a key form for visualizing otherness from the beginnings of cinema to the present, contradict, support, or transform surrealism's desire to change our very habits of perception? How does surrealism oppose, embrace, or complicate the horror film's desire to terrify, to project fear onto otherness? By pursuing these questions, I want to show how the horror film can advance our knowledge of cinematic surrealism in general and ethnographic surrealism in particular. At the same time, I maintain that we can learn important things about the nature of the horror film through ethnographic surrealism. Although I will focus on a single, remarkably ambitious horror film that exists in the borderlands between art cinema and genre cinema, I believe my analysis provides a guide for alternative interpretations of more canonical examples of the horror film. Furthermore, recent research suggests that the line often used to separate conventional, genre-based horror from unconventional, art-based horror is a thin or entirely illusory one the more carefully we examine film history (Hawkins, 2000; Lowenstein, 2005). The other is a constant presence in horror, and my larger argument here is that we have often simplified or misunderstood how otherness functions in the genre. By turning to the conjuncture between horror and ethnographic surrealism, I hope to offer a new vantage point on horror's use of otherness.

The Shout, a British film directed by the celebrated Polish auteur Jerzy Skolimowski and based on a short story by Robert Graves, tells a horror story embedded within an ethnographic framework. Charles Crossley (Alan Bates), a white British man who claims to have spent the last two decades living among Aborigines in the Australian outback, enters the world of the troubled English couple Anthony Fielding (John Hurt) and Rachel Fielding (Susannah York). Crossley seduces and terrorizes the Fieldings with his Aborigine-derived otherness, including a "terror shout" that kills all living things within its radius. Many scholarly accounts of the horror film, including Wood's, critique the genre for its tendency to code its threatening monsters as inseparable from the social or political other. But in *The Shout*, Crossley's relation to Aborigines is constructed as unreliable—the product of fantasy and desire on the part of the Fieldings, or Crossley himself, or perhaps even the audience as they struggle to make meaning from a deliberately fragmented narrative. Skolimowski, a one-time student of ethnography and a longtime veteran of transnational filmmaking (Mazierska, 2010), turns to the methods of ethnographic surrealism in ways that refigure our understanding of the horror film, surrealism, and how the two imagine the ethnographic others haunting the shadowy territory between them.

The Otherness of Horror

Wood offers a remarkably influential formulation of otherness in the horror film that I have described and critiqued elsewhere (Lowenstein, 2012) in ways that I will now quickly summarize. The other, according to Wood, is "what bourgeois ideology cannot recognize or accept but must deal with" through rejection, annihilation, or assimilation (2004: 111). Examples include women, the proletariat, foreign cultures, racial or ethnic minorities, homosexuals, alternative political ideologies, and children (2004: 111–113). For Wood, these others enter the American horror film as monsters that threaten American society's investments in monogamous, heterosexual, bourgeois, patriarchal capitalism ("bourgeois ideology" or "normality" for short). Here Wood arrives at his well-known "basic formula" for the horror film: "normality is threatened by the Monster" (2004: 117). The flexibility and utility of this formula offsets its obviousness and simplicity, according to Wood. The formula's three variables (normality, monstrosity, and the relationship between them) offer the means to categorize horror films as politically "progressive" or "reactionary" (2004: 133). Progressive horror films challenge conventional distinctions between normality and monstrosity by generating ambivalence between the two—through a sympathetic monster, for instance, or a doubling between the forces of normality and monstrosity. Reactionary horror films consolidate the status quo divisions between normality and monstrosity by squelching any possible ambivalence—most often through aligning the monster with such complete negativity that normality's oppressions are rationalized and reinforced. For Wood, progressive horror films such as *The Texas Chain Saw Massacre* (1974) or the work of George A. Romero achieve "the force of authentic art," while reactionary horror films such as *The Omen* (1976) or the work of Cronenberg do not (2004: 133).

The strength of Wood's model is that it allows the horror film to be read in social terms, but its weakness is the rigidity with which the social realm and its cinematic representation are imagined. The model's reductive equation between progressive politics and authentic art, on the one hand, and reactionary politics and inauthentic art, on the other, is finally too inflexible, moralistic, and bound to conventional notions of narrative-driven meaning to accommodate how horror films navigate art and politics as matters of sight and sound as well as story. Note, for example, how Wood's judgments of progressive and reactionary often lean heavily on narrative analysis for their primary criteria, highlighting especially the narrative endpoints of the films: "the 'happy ending,' (when it exists) typically signifying the restoration of repression" (2004: 113). What escapes Wood is the possibility of cinematic significance in registers other than those dominated by narrative or its close associate, psychologized characterization. In other words, Wood tends to ascribe "realistic" rather than "surrealistic" meaning to the horror films he analyzes. As a result, his sense of horror's others is restricted to the terms of realist representation, not surrealist suggestion.

In order to recognize how *The Shout* ultimately resists Wood's understanding of otherness in the horror film, I would first like to apply his terms to the film. To do so, one would need to align the Fieldings with normality, Crossley with monstrosity, and the relationship between them as a reactionary one; by the end of the film, Crossley is dead and the Aboriginal magic he bewitched Anthony and Rachel with dispelled. When *The Shout* concludes, nothing would seem to remain of Crossley's otherness, his challenge to the bourgeois, heterosexual, patriarchal, capitalist world represented by the Fieldings. Added fuel for a Wood-style analysis of *The Shout* would include its trafficking in precisely the sort of psychoanalytic theory that Wood considers essential for describing the horror film's "true subject" as "the struggle for recognition of all that our civilization represses or oppresses: its reemergence dramatized, as in our nightmares, as an object of horror, a matter for terror" (2004: 113). Crossley is monstrous not just as an ethnographic other, through his connection to Aborigines, but as a psychoanalytic other — he is diagnosed as mad and imprisoned in an asylum, but he also haunts the dreams of Anthony and Rachel. What's more, his apparently heterosexual masculinity carries enough queer connotations, perhaps in an allusion to the author Graves's closeted homosexuality — showcasing his nude body for Anthony, flirtatiously nudging the foot of a character also named Robert Graves [Tim Curry, fresh from his transsexual turn in *The Rocky Horror Picture Show* (1975)] — to qualify Crossley as other for his sexuality as well.

At the levels of narrative and realism, this all seems true and *The Shout* fits quite comfortably within Wood's critical apparatus. But at the levels of image and sound and surrealism, *The Shout* refuses to conform to the interpretations stated above. Crossley's status as monstrous other in the ethnographic, psychoanalytic, and sexual sense depends on our belief in him as a character whose psychology, history, and actions are, however bizarre, recognizable as realistic within the diegetic universe of the film. They are not. In fact, Skolimowski takes great pains to remind us that they are not.

There are at least two Crossleys in the film. One appears in the film's opening and closing frame story, set during a cricket match held at an asylum in North Devon where the inmates and villagers mix in ways that make them difficult to distinguish. Here, Crossley is a mild-mannered inmate who offers to tell Graves, the visiting friend of the asylum's chief medical officer (Robert Stephens), a story while he and Graves score the match. The second Crossley appears within this story, which constitutes the majority of the film. Here, Crossley is an imposing, powerful stranger who upends the lives of the Fieldings through his mastery of Aboriginal magic, vanquished only when Anthony discovers the stone that houses his soul and smashes it to pieces. The first, weaker Crossley of the frame story thus comes into being when the second, stronger Crossley is made impotent—he is arrested and taken from the Fieldings's house to the asylum. But as Crossley himself insists (at least according to the chief medical officer), his soul is split into four fragments, not two, presumably corresponding to the four pieces of the broken stone (although we do not see a clear image of these four stone fragments at any point). In addition, Crossley prefaces his story by telling Graves that his tale is very much true but does not correspond to typical notions of veracity (he changes the "sequence of events" and varies "the climaxes a little" in each telling in order to "keep it alive"). He also admits that he deliberately lards his stories with flamboyantly symbolic imagery to please the chief medical officer (fathers, snakes, apple pies).

So to think of Crossley as a single, realistically psychologized character who fulfills the role of the monstrous other is simply not adequate to the way he has been presented in the film. Rather than calling him a person or even a monster, it is far more accurate to say that Crossley attracts a number of forces, desires, and dreams that may at times belong to him but at other times belong to those surrounding him. His is not the single, rational subjectivity of psychologized realism, but the dispersed, irrational subject-as-object common to surrealism. "I believe in the future resolution of these two states, dream and reality, which are seemingly so contradictory, into a kind of absolute reality, a *surreality*, if one may so speak," writes Breton in his "Manifesto of Surrealism" (1994 [1924]: 14). Crossley materializes precisely at this intersection of dream and reality, so he cannot be said to be any more or less "real" than the objects through which he manifests his power (a bone, a stone, a shoe buckle, an English tailcoat). Even his most fearsome quality, the shout that kills, is ultimately immaterial. It cannot be seen or measured or proven or reproduced but only heard, felt, sensed. The effects of his shout are real (corpses of animals and humans attest to this), but its essence is surreal—pulsating between dream and reality. The same can be said for Crossley himself, as his introduction in the film testifies.

The first time we see Crossley, we can recognize him only as a presence, not a character with a name, a history, or even an identifiable face. *The Shout* begins with a flash-forward to its ending, as Rachel races to the asylum in search of someone she only speaks of as "he." She is directed to a well-appointed dining room, where three of the long tables have been partially cleared of their plates and silverware to make room for corpses covered by the fresh white tablecloths. She uncovers two of the faces without pausing—she clearly has not found what she is looking for, although we will be able to identify them later as the chief medical officer and one of the other

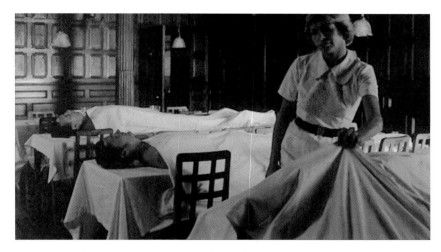

Figure 29.1 Rachel uncovers the corpse of Charles Crossley. *The Shout* (1978). Directed by Jerzy Skolimowski. Produced by Recorded Picture Company (RPC), The Rank Organisation, Jeremy Thomas Productions, National Film Trustee Company, and National Film Finance Corporation (NFFC).

inmates playing in the cricket match—but when she moves to reveal the third, a whipping wind overwhelms the soundtrack (Figure 29.1). When Crossley's face is uncovered, the image immediately dissolves and we are transported, via the sound bridge of the wind, to a desert landscape with a single, hazy human figure wandering among the sand dunes. As this figure draws closer to the foreground of the frame, we can see him more clearly: an Aborigine wearing a dark blue English tailcoat, carrying a bone he has unearthed from the sand pointed menacingly at the camera—at us. The atmosphere of threat is enhanced by the ominous electronic score composed by Tony Banks and Mike Rutherford (of the British rock band Genesis) that mixes with the sound of the wind in this scene.

But before we can learn anything more about this man, we are overcome by sound once more. Only this time, the wind of the desert gives way to the mechanical drone of an engine, as another sound bridge overlays the cut from the Aborigine to reveal the source of the noise: a white man on a motorcycle speeds down a country road and soon overtakes a car with two occupants. The motorcycle driver's face is obscured by goggles, but the woman driving the car who exchanges a look of recognition with him when he passes is Rachel, with the man we will come to know as Anthony seated beside her (does she wish she could jump into the motorcycle's empty sidecar? Or is she relieved not to be there?). We, too, have a nagging sense that we know this man on the motorcycle, for he wears a sport jacket of the same dark blue color as the Aborigine's tailcoat and a cricket uniform beneath it as white as the tablecloths covering the corpses in the film's first scene. This man, we will soon learn but already sense, is Crossley.

Skolimowski's introduction of Crossley makes meticulous use of sound and image to implant questions that compete with answers about who or what he is. On the one hand, he seems familiar: the colors he wears match him visually with the mysterious figures we have seen in the film's first two scenes, while Rachel's look toward him (which he seems to return, although the goggles and the encounter's brevity make this moment of recognition rather uncertain) indicates that he is known. On the other hand, he is unfamiliar: he has no name, no face we can easily see, no way of connecting him explicitly with the Aborigine or the corpse. But we do have the film's title to direct us toward sound as a form of identification, and this force called *Crossley* registers in these opening scenes as an aural presence at least as much as a visual one. The sound bridge transition from the dining room to the sand dunes, and then from the sand dunes to the roadway, is prominent and unusual enough to draw attention to itself. Perhaps we are not sure of what Crossley looks like, but we do have a notion of what he sounds like: loud, sudden, unexpected, jarring. Yet even these sound signatures are themselves split and ambiguous. The first sound bridge (wind) arises from the natural world; the second (engine) comes from the world of modern, man-made technology. To which world does Crossley belong?

Even with plenty of additional information about Crossley at our disposal by the time the film concludes, that question is no easier to answer at the end of *The Shout* than at the beginning. What Skolimowski has done so masterfully in the film's opening scenes he deepens as the film continues: generating a cumulative experience for the spectator that instructs us how relying on our eyes and ears in the conventional, rational sense will not allow us to unlock this film's meaning. Instead, Skolimowski encourages us to follow our sensory impressions rather than our need to make sense of what we see and hear. In other words, he encourages us to inhabit that shadowland between dream and reality where surrealism lives. The very contradictions that Crossley embodies—familiar/unfamiliar, natural/artificial, ancient/modern, black/white, even alive/dead—are surrealist signposts insofar as they blur distinctions between subject and object, dream and reality. Crossley's initial incarnation, as a corpse on a dining room table, evokes one of surrealism's favorite phrases, Lautréamont's definition of beauty: "the fortuitous encounter on a dissecting table of a sewing machine and an umbrella." Crossley's body appears ready for dissection in its shrouded, medicalized presentation, but the incongruous setting of the dining room also suggests that this body is a meal awaiting con-sumption. The doubleness creates a disorienting, vertiginous sensation, where we know where we are yet cannot feel the ground beneath our feet, and is symptomatic of the surrealist "spark," that surprising, often shocking connection between two disparate images or levels of reality. Crossley belongs nowhere—his place of origin is neither the asylum nor the desert—but he simultaneously matters everywhere, in

Figure 29.2 Crossley conjures the Aborigine, or vice versa. *The Shout* (1978). Directed by Jerzy Skolimowski. Produced by Recorded Picture Company (RPC), The Rank Organisation, Jeremy Thomas Productions, National Film Trustee Company, and National Film Finance Corporation (NFFC).

that Rachel looks for him or toward him at the asylum, on the roadway, and, in the film's next section, in the desert as well.

The Shout returns to the desert once Crossley begins narrating his tale to Graves. As Crossley asks Graves, "Have you ever wandered the sand dunes?" his words fade away and are replaced, in a superimposition enabled by a slow dissolve, with an image of the Aborigine from the earlier sequence, again wandering in the desert (Figure 29.2). The Aborigine, due to the dissolve, appears to spring quite literally from Crossley's forehead—a figment of his imagination, perhaps? No, as it turns out. Or at least this figment does not belong to his imagination alone. The Aborigine is soon shown to emerge also from a dream shared by Anthony and Rachel. They are sleeping in the very sand dunes we have seen the Aborigine traversing (so have we always been in North Devon, rather than the Australian outback?), but when they awake, the Aborigine is nowhere to be found. They each describe him in terms that match the images we have seen and cause him to rematerialize briefly as a visual flashback to the dream, but they do not pause to comment on the strangeness of the dream or the even more unusual fact that the dream was shared between them. They are chilled, literally and figuratively, by the experience of the dream and seem eager to shake its influence. When Rachel finds the bone buried in the sand that she and Anthony saw the Aborigine carrying in their dream, she reburies it hastily. This bone is familiar to us not only as the bone carried by the Aborigine, but also as the same bone that falls out of Crossley's jacket as he begins to narrate his tale to Graves. Crossley, like Rachel, attempts to hide it, but Graves has seen it and so have we. The bone is the object that cues us to how dream and reality are not separate dimensions here — the bone is concrete for Crossley and Graves in the film's frame story, for Rachel in Crossley's narrated tale, and for the Aborigine in sequences that float between dream, memory, and imagination. But the only way the bone can exist on all of these planes at once is through a distribution of dream and reality that makes standard demarcations of what is real and what is unreal fall away. In the same spirit, Crossley is objectively real in terms of being a man spoken about and with by Graves and the chief medical officer (men of science both), but subjectively unreal — his presence as the Aborigine that doubles for him appears only in relation to dreams and visions that are as unforgettable as they are impossible to verify. Indeed, we will never see the Aborigine again during the remainder of *The Shout*, causing us to wonder by the film's end whether we ever really "saw" him at all.

In all of these ways, Crossley fails to function as a monstrous other in Wood's sense. Crossley's surreal presence in the film, his location between dream/reality and Aborigine/English, immunizes him against the entire normality/monstrosity dichotomy and its conflations of fear with social otherness. Crossley is not subject to repression or oppression as Wood has it because he is ultimately neither real nor unreal, psychologically or socially. His indeterminacy is not about a monster lying in wait for the sake of suspense, or a monster whose actuality or artificiality remains unclear for the sake of narrative structure, or even a monster whose patently fantastic or "primitive" nature encourages an allegorical social interpretation. Instead, Crossley's otherness is inseparable from our own modes of perception, our own habits of ordering our sensory impressions according to dream/reality and Western self/non-Western other categories. In other words, he is the embodiment of those tensions that constitute ethnographic surrealism.

The Otherness of Ethnographic Surrealism

Clifford's account of ethnographic surrealism emphasizes its ability to forge a path between science and art, to denaturalize both ethnography's drive toward empirical, classificatory science and surrealism's drive toward a romantic cult of the artist as transgressive genius (1988: 147). At the height of ethnographic surrealism's influence, in France during the interwar years, ethnography and surrealism informed each other in profound ways that would be much more difficult to maintain once surrealism's identity as "art" and ethnography's identity as "science" became more fully entrenched (Clifford, 1988: 134). The promise of ethnographic surrealism is its insistence on questioning what counts as cultural value and cultural order once the anchoring notions of self and other are unmoored, so that the self, so often hidden or obscured in ethnographic analysis, becomes at least as much an object of research as the ethnographic others under anthropological examination. The risk of ethnographic surrealism is its sometimes queasily close proximity to orientalism and racism, as well as the danger of dispensing too quickly with crucial specifics of historical and cultural difference when unleashing the decentering heat of juxtaposition and collage. Clifford admits that his conception of ethnographic surrealism is a "utopian construct" in that it merges productively forms of science and art that much more often than not remain separate or come together in more troubling, unproductive ways, but I agree with his conviction that excavating ethnographic surrealism is not merely an archival project — it matters enormously as "a statement at once about past and future possibilities for cultural analysis" (1988: 119).

Although Clifford explores a host of guises for ethnographic surrealism — literature, museum collections, academic research, avant-garde journals, ad hoc intellectual collectives, organized expeditions to foreign countries — film surfaces only at the vanishing point of his chapter. The film he mentions as an example of ethnographic surrealism, the celebrated documentary *Trobriand Cricket: An Ingenious Response to Colonialism* (1975) that chronicles how Trobriand Islanders in Papua New Guinea adapt and transform traditional English cricket for their own purposes, shares striking affinities with *The Shout*. These affinities suggest that connecting cinema and ethnographic surrealism is a project that has really only just begun, despite pioneering efforts by a number of film scholars (Griffiths, 2002; Rony, 1996; Russell, 1999) and the flowering of visual anthropology as a field in its own right (MacDougall, 1998; Taylor, 1994).

The Shout, like *Trobriand Cricket*, presents a game associated with Englishness, whiteness, and colonialism in a manner that makes it strange, that recasts our assumptions of known and unknown, self and other. Not only does the cricket match in *The Shout* take place at an asylum with inmates as players, it also transpires in a meadow where cows have already laid their claim (the immaculately attired players and bystanders must slip and slide through shit), the scoring is entrusted to a man who seems to practice Aboriginal magic, and the match ends in destruction and death most likely wrought by that magic (a violent thunderstorm masks Crossley's shout so that the ensuing deaths are probably attributed to a lightning strike). Clearly, we are far from the traditional decorum of English cricket. Yet those traditions remain strong as an organizing visual presence, from the whiteness of the uniforms to the equipment and procedures of the game itself. Skolimowski's goal is not to make cricket unrecognizable, but to defamiliarize it enough so that "we" who "know" the game meld with "they" who "do not" (the insane, the Aboriginal).

The cricket match is already a central conceit in Graves's 1924 short story, but it is not outlandish to imagine the ethnographic surrealist impulses behind *Trobriand Cricket* influencing *The Shout*, whether directly or indirectly. Skolimowski studied ethnography himself earlier in his life while at school in his native Poland (Mazierska, 2010: 175), but when he made *The Shout* he was living and working as a Polish exile, in an England whose alienness provides crucial inspiration for some of his most important films, including *Deep End* (1971) and *Moonlighting* (1982). In addition, Jeremy Thomas, the producer of *The Shout*, had just come off producing the Australian film *Mad Dog Morgan* (1976), so Australia (the country of origin for *Trobriand Cricket*) was likely not just an abstract idea on set. Skolimowski was also doubtlessly aware of his fellow Pole Bronislaw Malinowski, the famed anthropologist who conducted groundbreaking fieldwork on the Trobriand Islands as well as in Australia (among other locales).

The eyes and ears of an outsider are fundamental to *The Shout*'s structure, so that even those situations, settings, and activities associated with normality or even banality — work, couplehood, meals, the countryside, cricket — return to us as uncanny. I have already described how the film's opening scenes use sound to unsettle our sense of how much we can trust or even understand what we see, and the cricket match is treated similarly. Voices are subtly detached from the bodies of those speaking, sound perspective is inconsistent (sometimes we hear as if almost inside the head of a player who mutters to himself, at other times the sounds of the match are conveyed more evenly), noises that are electronic and nondiegetic abruptly override those that are diegetic only to disappear just as suddenly. The result: when the Aboriginal bone drops from Crossley's jacket, it is not so much an entirely disruptive moment as a consistently incongruous one. The sights and sounds of the "familiar" cricket match have become at least as unfamiliar to us as this image of the "other," especially since this is not the first time we have glimpsed the bone. The appearance of an Aboriginal ritual object alongside the ritual objects of English cricket has the effect, in Skolimowski's hands, of ethnographic surrealism's doubled disorientation — we see the strange in the familiar, the familiar in the strange (Clifford, 1988: 121). "The surrealist moment in ethnography," Clifford writes, "is that moment in which the possibility of comparison exists in unmediated tension with sheer incongruity" (1988: 146). In such a moment, there is no attempt to "explain away those elements in the foreign culture that render the investigator's culture newly incomprehensible" (1988: 147). I believe this moment in *The Shout*, like so many others in the film, captures this provocative power of ethnographic surrealism.

Another important example of ethnographic surrealism in the film occurs when Anthony and Crossley's methods of creating extraordinary sound are juxtaposed. Anthony is a musician who spends much of his time generating and recording otherworldly sounds in his home studio by amplifying and distorting "natural" noises through modern technological means. Marbles colliding in a metal pan, a violin bow drawn across a ruptured sardine tin, a drag on a cigarette — all of these sounds, among others, get warped electronically by Anthony to exaggerate their most discordant aspects. So by the time we hear Crossley's shout, we are accustomed to experiencing sound as a force subject to unsettling manipulation. But what Anthony toys with through machines, Crossley accomplishes with his own body to much more dire effect. Still, the obvious equation of Anthony with the technologically modern (the Western, scientific "us") and Crossley with the physically primitive (the non-Western, magical "other") proves as impossible to maintain here as it did in the film's opening scenes. For Crossley's shout is the film's technical centerpiece, a spectacular showcase for state-of-the-art Dolby sound experimentation achievable only through precisely those sorts of devices that populate Anthony's studio. As Skolimowski describes it, "the human voice is fortified on forty or more tracks by all the things that came into my mind that might be helpful, the Niagara Falls, the launching of a Moon rocket, everything. But over the top is the real human voice of a man shouting like hell" (Skolimowski, quoted in Mazierska, 2010: 161). In the tenor of ethnographic surrealism, Anthony and Crossley sound more like twins than opposites.

But we do not simply hear the similarity between Anthony and Crossley—we feel it. Anthony's studio-produced sounds grate on our ears almost as dramatically as Crossley's gut-wrenching shout overpowers us; in both cases, the impact is visceral. Anthony and Crossley may look like opposites, almost to the point of parody (Skolimowski makes brilliant use of the wildly contrasting physiques of John Hurt and Alan Bates), but the effect their sounds make on us cause them to feel like brothers. This feeling is a form of viewer participation in the film irreducible to sight or sound alone. According to Clifford, a dominant mode of ethnographic surrealism is "a prevailing attitude of ironic participant observation among the hierarchies and meanings of collective life" (1988: 130). There is plenty of irony on hand in *The Shout*, most notably with regard to Christianity, a belief system ridiculed by Crossley philosophically and by Anthony through his blasphemous actions (he uses his post as guest organist at the local church to conduct an extramarital affair). Christianity clearly holds no moral or practical superiority to Aboriginal beliefs in *The Shout*, so we are invited to reflect on religious faith as a matter of ironic relativism. But what I want to focus on now in Clifford's formulation is participant observation. By playing out self/other distinctions along the axis of sensory impressions rather than strictly narrative meaning, the film encourages us to feel our way through it when our habit is to think. *The Shout* asks us to participate in its constructions of self/other, to feel those constructions the way we feel Crossley's shout in the pit of our stomach.

Skolimowski invites viewer participation at the level of feeling in a variety of ways, but one important strategy I have touched on already but wish to elaborate is training spectators to process image and sound unconventionally. For example, Anthony's studio decorations include reproductions on paper of disturbing paintings by Francis Bacon, the well-known Irish-British artist often referred to as a modern surrealist. The first one of these we see, "Paralytic Child Walking on All Fours (from Muybridge)" (1961), is not simply presented to us as a symbol of Anthony's alienated, conflicted soul, but as an image we must look *through* as much as we look *at*. The painting appears to breathe as it flutters against the speaker it is posted on, in time to the vibrations produced by Anthony's sound experiments. A lesson for the viewer along the lines of, "This image is not static, it is alive, available for transformation and incorporation," begins to emerge through this simultaneously visual, aural, and tactile treatment. This lesson develops further when Anthony's dog appears in the studio soon after, as if the painting's haunting humanoid figure that appears dog-like by walking on hands and feet were taking on material form. This impression is heightened when Anthony announces the dog's name: Buzz. Is Buzz an extension of the painting as image, with his visual resemblance to Bacon's half-human, half-dog figure? Or is he a manifestation of the painting as sound, with his name that mimics the noise that causes the painting to tremble (literalized further when Anthony rubs his microphone directly on Buzz's fur, making buzz out of Buzz)?

Rather than answer these questions, Skolimowski expands their range by modulating the connotations of Bacon's painting throughout the film. One side of "Paralytic Child" depicts a window with two panes of glass, an image foreshadowed earlier in the film when Anthony and Rachel encounter their own reflections in a large mirror that two men carry across their path as they walk through town. This image of their doubleness is itself doubled by the shots Skolimowski places on either side of it: Anthony's lover looking down from an open window split into multiple panes of glass; the lover's husband peering out from behind a window similarly divided. So the visual associations with splitting so central to Bacon's painting (human/dog; upper window pane/lower window pane) have been anticipated earlier in the film and continue to radiate outward later. When Crossley enters the Fieldings's house, he rests in a spare room that contains a tall, narrow window much like the one in "Paralytic Child." This particular window has been removed from its mounting and set aside for repair, as one of its panes is shattered.

The shattered pane reminds us of a feat Crossley just performed at the dinner table: breaking a wine glass through sound vibrations made using a separate glass. Yet another instance of glass breaking occurs soon after, when a frustrated Anthony sends a piece of firewood sailing through a nearby window pane; the accident creates a damaged window similar to the one we have already seen in Crossley's room. Again, these chains of related images and sounds (shots of windows and broken glass are legion in this film) trouble routine attempts to set them in temporal, narrative, or even allusive order. What is more primary, the painting or the mirror and the windows that resemble it? Are all of the examples of broken glass separate or one and the same, variations on a single event unstuck in time and place? Is the film imitating the painting or recovering its cinematic origins? After all, as Bacon's subtitle points out, this painting began as a form of film—the proto-cinematic pioneer Eadweard Muybridge's "Infantile Paralysis, Child Walking on Hands and Feet" (1887), a series of photographic plates that record the locomotion of a disabled child.

The painting continues to metamorphose later in the film, when Rachel, under the spell of Crossley's magic, traipses nude through the spare room and pauses while crouching beside the broken window pane. The image switches momentarily from color to black and white, completing a striking materialization of the chief visual elements in Bacon's painting (which is in color in its original form, but reproduced in black and white in Anthony's studio) as well as in Muybridge's photographic plates. Is painting possessing film here, or vice versa? Is this an image of Rachel's actions or Anthony's imagination of her actions? Is Rachel under the influence of Crossley's magic or is she responding to Anthony's split loyalties, captured so hauntingly in Bacon's painting through divided visual structures? Or is she somewhere outside and above the two men, as it seems in the film's beginning and end when she appears to hold more knowledge about her relationship with each of them than either do on their own? Again, Skolimowski does not want us to answer these questions as much as he wishes for us to hold them in tension, forcing us to challenge our habits of making meaning. In the face of such a challenge, our instinct to pin down Crossley's identity as monstrous other crumbles and the invitation to inhabit the stance of ethnographic surrealism's participant observer coalesces.

In fact, Crossley himself is both participant and observer when it comes to the other. He seems to be the other when he employs Aboriginal magic to dark purposes as if it were his own, but he also reveals that this expertise is the result of many years spent observing the Aborigines in the Australian outback. So Crossley is at least as much an ethnographer as a monster. This point is underlined when he relates an anecdote from his outback experience to Anthony. Crossley describes witnessing an Aboriginal chief magician, a "genuinely terrifying figure" dressed in an English tailcoat, slice open his skin with a stone and shed it "like a snake" in order to bring rain during a long drought. Anthony is aghast, and not just due to the horror of what Crossley describes. It seems Crossley's ethnography matches Anthony and Rachel's shared dream of the Aborigine in the dunes. The vision is both dream and ethnography—it is ethnographic surrealism.

Crossley also tells the Fieldings that he took an Aboriginal wife while living in the outback, but killed all of the children he fathered with her. He explains that this is the lawful right of every parent in Aboriginal society, and that he chose to exercise this right because he knew he would eventually leave and the children would have nothing in his absence. Rachel is more visibly upset by this story than Anthony, but not for the reasons we might assume. She mentions that she and Anthony have been unable to have children, a topic that Anthony is eager to avoid. The conflict over childlessness between Anthony and Rachel surfaces again later, but this time in images rather than words. When Crossley leaves Rachel temporarily, Anthony scoops up in a white towel the bone he has left behind like a toothbrush in the bathroom and throws it out the window. When he rises to cover himself after he and Rachel caress each other in the bath (the closest thing the Fieldings have to a love scene), the bloodstain left by the bone on the towel is apparent to both of them. "It's probably Crossley's," Anthony says. "I don't know why you let him bother you so much," Rachel replies.

The arresting image of the white linen stained with blood spins both of their statements back toward the earlier discussion of infanticide and childlessness. Crossley has brought them together again, metaphorically encouraging the re-consummation of a relationship that has languished in infidelity and childlessness, but he has also left the taint of death on them. The Fieldings's lovemaking is interrupted by news from the vicar that Harry the shepherd has died. We know that Harry's death was caused by Crossley's shout, and that his shout was in turn caused by Anthony's insistence that he demonstrate it for him—an insistence rooted in Rachel's flirtation with Crossley, which pushes Anthony toward an attempt to diminish him, to prove his stories false. So Harry, a mentally disabled innocent whom Anthony addressed earlier in the film in the tone one uses with a child (emphasizing Harry's kinship with Bacon and

Muybridge's paralytic child), is dead through the collaboration of Anthony, Crossley, and Rachel.

Crossley has made the Fieldings killers as well as lovers; in the surrealist logic of associated images, their relationship partakes of the lifeblood of Crossley's energy as an exotic other, as well as the spilled blood of Crossley's most heinous, othering crimes. Perhaps this is why the film ends with Rachel's ambiguous expression of relief as well as loss when uncovering Crossley's corpse. She finds a string tied around his neck that holds her shoe buckle, that personal possession he has used to exert his magic on her. She takes back the buckle, indicating the end of Crossley's power over her and the resumption of her own individual agency (further underlined by Anthony's complete absence). But then she stays beside Crossley's body and looks at him with a mixture of puzzlement and affection, suggesting that their relationship is still unfolding and that we are returning with her, as if in a loop, to the film's beginning. She will then have another opportunity to confront, and we along with her, the surreal self/otherness of Charles Crossley in all of its allure and horror.

References

Breton, A. (1994) Manifesto of surrealism, in *Manifestoes of Surrealism* (trans. R. Seaver and H.R. Lane), University of Michigan Press, Ann Arbor, pp. 1–47.

Clifford, J. (1988) On ethnographic surrealism, in *The Predicament of Culture: Twentieth-Century Ethnography, Literature, and Art*, Harvard University Press, Cambridge, MA, pp. 117–151.

De la Colina, J. and Turrent, T.P. (1992) *Objects of Desire: Conversations with Luis Buñuel* (ed. and trans. P. Lenti), Marsilio Publishers, New York.

Ferry, J. (2000) Concerning *King Kong*, in *The Shadow and Its Shadow: Surrealist Writings on the Cinema* (ed. and trans. P. Hammond), 3rd edn, City Lights, San Francisco, CA, pp. 161–165.

Griffiths, A. (2002) *Wondrous Difference: Cinema, Anthropology, and Turn-of-the-Century Visual Culture*, Columbia University Press, New York.

Harper, G. and Stone, R. (eds) (2007) *The Unsilvered Screen: Surrealism on Film*, Wallflower Press, London.

Hawkins, J. (2000) *Cutting Edge: Art-Horror and the Horrific Avant-Garde*, University of Minnesota Press, Minneapolis.

Hitchcock, A. (1995) Why I am afraid of the dark, in *Hitchcock on Hitchcock* (ed. S. Gottlieb), University of California Press, Berkeley, pp. 142–145.

Kuenzli, R.E. (ed.) (1996) *Dada and Surrealist Film*, MIT Press, Cambridge, MA.

Kyrou, A. (1953) *Le Surréalisme au cinéma*, Arcanes, Paris.

Lowenstein, A. (2005) *Shocking Representation: Historical Trauma, National Cinema, and the Modern Horror Film*, Columbia University Press, New York.

Lowenstein, A. (2012) A reintroduction to the American horror film, in *The Wiley-Blackwell History of American Film*, vol. 4 (eds C. Lucia, R. Grundmann, and A. Simon), Wiley-Blackwell, Oxford, pp. 154–176.

MacDougall, D. (1998) *Transcultural Cinema*, Princeton University Press, Princeton, NJ.

Mazierska, E. (2010) *Jerzy Skolimowski: The Cinema of a Nonconformist*, Berghahn Books, New York.

Rabaté, J.-M. (2002) Loving Freud madly: surrealism between hysterical and paranoid modernism. *Journal of Modern Literature*, **25** (3–4), 58–74.

Richardson, M. (2006) *Surrealism and Cinema*, Berg, Oxford.

Rony, F.T. (1996) *The Third Eye: Race, Cinema, and Ethnographic Spectacle*, Duke University Press, Durham, NC.

Russell, C. (1999) *Experimental Ethnography: The Work of Film in the Age of Video*, Duke University Press, Durham, NC.

Taylor, L. (ed.) (1994) *Visualizing Theory: Selected Essays from V.A.R., 1990–1994*, Routledge, New York.

Williams, L. (1992) *Figures of Desire: A Theory and Analysis of Surrealist Film*, University of California Press, Berkeley.

Wood, R. (1973) Terrible buildings: the world of Georges Franju. *Film Comment*, **9** (6), 43–46.

Wood, R. (2004) An introduction to the American horror film, in *Planks of Reason: Essays on the Horror Film*, rev. edn (eds B.K. Grant and C. Sharrett), Scarecrow Press, Lanham, MD, pp. 107–141.

30

The Documentary Impulse and Reel/Real Horror

Caroline Joan S. Picart

The theoretical foundations of this chapter find their moorings in prior projects. For example, in *Frames of Evil: The Holocaust as Horror in American Film* (2006), David Frank and I discussed the cross-fertilizations that have evolved binding Holocaust films, usually shot in a documentary or docu-dramatic mode, and horror films, usually visually coded as drawing from the Gothic tradition. Such cross-fertilizations force us to confront whose point of view we adopt as we view these films. "Realistic" documentary modes actually draw from "fictional" Gothic modes, which themselves have a complex relationship with the real. Yet the appropriation of fictional Gothic modes into factual documentary or docu-dramatic modes are acceptable or convincing as "true" only if these cinematic footnotes masquerade as partaking of the look of the "real." The issue of representation — of juxtaposing factual (documentary) modes of narration with fictional (horror) modes of narration — immediately brings to the fore the question of how we locate ourselves, as consumers of these films, which allude to and imaginatively recreate, a very real historical trauma such as the Holocaust.

What updates that line of inquiry is an explosion of books and films that link violence, images of "monstrosity," and Gothic modes of narration and visualization in American popular culture, academia, and even public policy. As Mark Edmundson notes:

> Gothic conventions have slipped over into ostensibly nonfictional realms. Gothic is alive not just in Stephen King's novels and Quentin Tarantino's films, but in the media renderings of the O.J. Simpson case in our political discourse, in modes of therapy, on TV news, on talk shows like *Oprah*, in our discussions of AIDS and of the environment. American culture at large has become suffused with Gothic assumptions, with Gothic characters and plots. (1997: xii)

A Companion to the Horror Film, First Edition. Edited by Harry M. Benshoff.
© 2014 John Wiley & Sons, Inc. Published 2017 by John Wiley & Sons, Inc.

Ultimately, this chapter is rooted in a larger and ongoing project, which critically interrogates contemporary visualizations of the Gothic and the monstrous in film and media (Picart and Browning, 2012). The ongoing fascination with evil, as simultaneously repellant and irresistibly attractive, both in the Hollywood film, criminological case studies, popular culture, and even public policy, points to the emergence of "Gothic criminology," with its focus on themes such as blood lust, compulsion, godlike vengeance, and power and domination. Rather than assuming that film and the media tell us little about the reality of criminological phenomena, "Gothic criminology"—a concept derived from Stanford Lyman (1990) and developed in various contemporary applications (Picart and Greek, 2007)—explores how critical academic and aesthetic accounts of deviant behavior intersect with public policy in complex, non-reductive ways. Gothic criminology gestures toward an account that moves in between the realms of Gothic fiction and film (which entertains its horrified and fascinated readers with unreal horrors attendant on a realistically/cogently imagined fictional world), and factual cases (e.g., of terrorists, stalkers, serial murderers, rogue cops) framed in Gothic terms. Such considerations are essential to plotting the social construction of evil and where it resides within modernity (Picart and Greek, 2007).

It is this edge, between reel horror and real horror, as evidenced in the cross-fertilizations between documentary modes of narration, art-horror, and real horrors that this chapter explores. Ultimately, the chapter is not moralizing about "proper" modes of production or consumption, but the complex modalities of horror as they intersect with and break free of the documentary impulse. There are two ways this chapter analyzes the relationship between the documentary impulse and horror film techniques. The first deals with the attempt to render seamless or invisible the use of horror-framing techniques in order to render an apparently historical account more "real." The second deals with an attempt to use unresolved incongruity to leverage the anxieties of juxtaposing a reel frame with a "real" narrative. Both cinematic attempts I explore, interestingly enough, were done by an auteur whose cinematic reputation was first cemented by his commercial success in the horror and science fiction-fantasy genres: Steven Spielberg.

Hiding the Horror by Simulating the Look of the "Real"[1]

Schindler's List (1993) has simultaneously been praised as forging "a searingly illuminating portrait of the human heart, mankind at its most depraved and most noble" (Byrge, 1993), and of being "a cartoon in which an Aryan superhero outwits the forces of evil while stereotyped Jews provide the local color" (Koplin, 1994). David Denby (1993) gives it the accolade of being an epic "made in a style of austere realism—flat, angry and hardheaded—that is utterly unlike anything Spielberg has attempted before," while Leon Wieseltier (1994) lambastes it as "hale and self-regarding," robustly trumpeting a "complete absence of humility before its subject matter." Of more serious import are claims, made by the Jerusalem correspondent of the (London) *Times*, that survivors found the portrayal of Oscar Schindler "unrecognizable" and its story "nothing like what really occurred," and that not a single survivor was consulted in making the film (Jenkins, 1994). Those who praise the movie do make legitimate points about its impact, while the movie's critics rightly point to its limitations.

In filming *Schindler's List*, Spielberg used the traditional conventions of the classic Hollywood horror film, turning to an intimately familiar narrative of good and evil, one in which he was well practiced. Film scholars have grouped Steven Spielberg with Brian De Palma, Wes Craven, Tobe Hooper, and other directors of horror films (Carroll, 1990: 3). Indeed, Spielberg's embrace of the horror genre began at an early age as he cast one of his sisters in a science-fiction-horror film called *Firelight* (1964) (Reed and Cunneff, 1999). In many ways, *Schindler's List*'s narrative functions like a classic horror film, particularly given its portrayal of the Nazi perpetrator and Jewish victim, with its portrayal of suffering borrowed from sadomasochistic horror conventions (Rothberg, 2000; Brenner, 2000). The perpetrator/victim binary established in the movie is problematic, not because the Nazis were not the perpetrators and the Jews were not the victims; rather, the issue hinges on the fact that the binary becomes a simplistic rendering of both perpetrators and victims. Key moments illustrating this dynamic in Spielberg's apparently historical cinematic rendering of the Holocaust are the shower scene at Auschwitz, and the seduction-turned-torture of Helen Hirsch (Embeth Davidtz) by Amon Goeth (Ralph Fiennes), discussed later.

Nevertheless, there are other scenes that also illustrate the problematics of Spielberg's use of Hollywood conventions in visualizing the events of the Holocaust. For example, the use of color to differentiate the movements of 4-year-old Genia (Olivia Dąbrowska) from the chaos going on around her during the liquidation of the Krakow ghetto illustrates Spielberg's hallmark use of children as symbols of innocence and absolute good within the modes of fantasy and melodrama, as in his top-grossing *E.T. the Extra-Terrestrial* (1982). The scene is shot subjectively — that is, from Schindler's (and his mistress's) point of view, as they look down from the hill. Narratively, the scene is shot to convey the message that "Schindler thought that if a child such as she perished who would be the only witness to the crime, and he decided to assume the role (of witness) and also to save as many Jews as he could for the future" (Palowski, 1998: 101). Though Mila Page, one of the Schindler Jews, attests that the girl in the red coat did exist (Palowski, 1998: 101), there is no evidence that Schindler's "turning point" occurred particularly during this period, or that the murder of the little girl was what pushed him into accepting his role as the protector of "his" Jews.

Another scene in the film conflates two different events into one in order to "enhance the dramatic action" (Palowski, 1998: 108). This scene, in which Schindler is presented with a birthday cake by his Jews, combines two historical incidents: Niusia Karakulska's presentation of a birthday cake to Schindler when she was a child, and Schindler's passionate kissing of a young Jewish woman in celebration of the opening of his factory in Kraków. Schindler actually did spend a few days in the Gestapo prison at Pomorska Street as a result of the second incident, for having violated the prohibitions of the law of racial purity (Palowski, 1998: 118). What is important to note is less the conflation of the two events than the reasoning behind the changes: "[Spielberg] needs a passionate kiss to enhance the dramatic action, but an actor should not kiss an underage girl on the mouth because the audience may perceive it as an act of molesting, which has complicated the reception of more than one American film" (Palowski, 1998: 118–119). Dramatic impact (here correlated with sexual titillation) and audience appeal trump historical accuracy within a film that markets itself as a historical document.

The film's two pivotal "shower scenes"—the first at Auschwitz-Birkenau and the second Goeth's seduction-torture of the sweating Helen, who has the "shower victim" look—illustrate the attempt to integrate horror techniques of narration as seamlessly into the historical documentation as possible. It is important to note that these two scenes were not part of Steven Zaillian's original screenplay (1990), and therefore must have been inserted due to Steven Spielberg's reworking, or at least endorsement, of these changes. There is a significant convergence, in the use of both film techniques and thematic elements, between the famous shower scene in Alfred Hitchcock's psychological thriller *Psycho* (1960) and *Schindler's List*. An analysis of these particular scenes leads to a reflection on how this attempt at "visualizing the unvisualizable" eventually falls back on a recall of familiar imagery cemented in public memory by the force of popular culture and conventions of classic Hollywood cinema. In fact, Rajeev Syal and Cherry Norton (1998) claim a direct "influence" by *Psycho* on Steven Spielberg.

Well before *Schindler's List*, Hitchcock's *Psycho* established now iconic cinematic patterns of depicting contemporary horror, effectively establishing a template of contemporary horror locating evil in the "real" and ordinary, a representation mimicked in *Schindler's List*. In attempting to work through the Holocaust, Spielberg and his crew made it clear that "authenticity," and not simply verisimilitude, was the goal. Spielberg declared to his cast that "we're not making a film, we're making a document" (quoted in Schickel, 1993: 75–76), one with which Spielberg intended to "scare" the audience (quoted in Richardson, 2000: 168). Yet the film also draws upon the conventions of documentary realism. The bulk of *Schindler's List* was shot in black and white, the "colors of reality" for Spielberg (Richardson, 2000). As Lisa Grunwald reports, the actual lens Spielberg chose for *Schindler's List* was attached to a camera that originally shot black-and-white film. According to Spielberg, "Shooting in black-and-white gives everything a sloppy urgency … which is what real life is" (quoted in Grunwald, 1993: 54). Anna Sheppard, who was in charge of preparing 17,000 costumes, was able to rent 1000 striped prisoners' uniforms in Poland but she had to dye them gray to make them credibly filthy. She explains: "I ruined what I rented, but it was unavoidable … Spielberg wants his film to have as close to a documentary look as possible" (quoted in Grunwald, 1993: 54, 58).

Both *Psycho* and *Schindler's List* use peepholes as prisms through which the audience witnesses murder. In *Psycho* the peephole is complex. Hitchcock's camera includes shots of the viewer–voyeur (who is himself a victim) and the victim (who had earlier preyed on an unsuspecting but unsympathetically boastful man: Cassidy, the "overgrown child who has not mastered—or cared to master—the rules of middle class social intercourse" (Sterritt, 1999: 103). In contrast, the camera in *Schindler's List* does not consider the role of the viewer–voyeur, or the complexities of the victim–victimizer relationship. Instead, it enters the gas chambers through the peephole by visualizing the terror of naked women, using soft core pornographic effects. That the peepholes in both movies are used in such different manners reveals much about their views of how evil is best represented. Hitchcock's camera captures the literal gaze of Norman Bates as his eyeball fills the screen. The peephole refracts his vision to conflate the audience and Norman Bates. In *Schindler's List*, the audience is separated by the peephole, and is not acknowledged as a direct participant; it masquerades as a "neutral" or documentary gaze. Indeed, Hitchcock himself actively dissected the politics of the gaze in *Psycho*: at the beginning of Truffaut's interview on *Psycho*, Hitchcock commented on how the long zoom opening into a dark window, which establishes the locale as "Phoenix, 2:43 PM," penetrates that dark space to reveal Marion and Sam as erotically involved, thus situating the viewer as a "Peeping Tom" (Hitchcock, quoted in Gough-Yates, 1972: 27).

In contrast, Embeth Davidtz (who played the attractive Jewish woman Helen, the object of Amon Goeth's desire and cruelty in *Schindler's List*), reflected on a parallel experience of nudity before the camera. She was in one of the scenes in which naked bodies teem, reduced to livestock: nude, her head shaved. "It's not like a love scene where you disrobe and there's something in the moment. Here I'm standing there like a plucked chicken, nothing but skin and bone. That is to say, stripped of human dignity" (quoted in Schickel, 1993: 76). Kevin Gough-Yates brilliantly points out that the aesthetic of *Psycho*'s shower scene evokes images of the prototypical victim of the Holocaust gas chamber. "When [Marion] is savagely murdered in the shower, her hair has become flattened by the water and she looks as though her head has been shaved. The shower sequence relates to the whole social guilt of mass murder and the propensity to pretend it does not exist" (Gough-Yates, 1972: 30).

Similarly, Sara Horowitz remarks how the aesthetics of *Schindler's List*'s shower scene simulates the camera technique used and mood conveyed in the shower scene at a Nazi brothel in Zybneck Brynuch's ... *and The Fifth Horseman is Fear* (1965).

> In Brynuch's shower scene, a group of Jewish women prepare themselves to "service" soldiers in a Nazi brothel where the film's male protagonist comes to find his sister. The camera lingers on the faces and bodies of the women. Slow, fluid, and softly lit, the scene is markedly different from the rest of the film in mood, tone and lighting. Moreover, its depiction is superfluous to the development of the film's plot. Indeed, after the film's completion, the shower scene was inserted at the insistence of the producer Carlo Ponti, in hopes of making the film more marketable. (1997: 129)

Both the contents of the scene and the circumstances of its production reveal it as yet another instance of the eroticization of the female Holocaust victim.

Gary Weissman echoes similar observations regarding how scenes of violence alternate with images of women viewed as beautiful objects. In relation to *Schindler's List*'s "shower scene," he writes:

> The sequence treats the viewers' uncertainty as to whether or not these women will be gassed as part of an extended drama involving two kinds of voyeurism, or pleasure taken in illicit seeing. One concerns sex, the other atrocity; both raise the question of how much will be shown. Helen provides the answer to one of these questions in a shot which shows the women in the undressing room at Auschwitz-Birkenau. Centered on screen and dramatically lit, she stands out while the other women frame her. Whereas these other women, half-hidden in shadow, slowly remove their dresses and long undergarments, Helen pulls her dress and slip over her head in one smooth, continuous motion, revealing a three-quarter view of her naked body. The erotic image is so inconsistent with the narrative that viewers may disregard what they see. (2004: 178)

In *Schindler's List*'s shower scene, the freneticism characteristic of the latter part of *Psycho*'s shower scene is conveyed by the camera's rapid cuts and tracking shots as it follows the women into the showers' darkened interior; yet as they stare at the showerheads, the camera pace appears to slow down and the mood intensifies, heightening an atmosphere of tense anticipation.

Further reminiscent of *Psycho*, the Auschwitz-Birkenau shower scene in *Schindler's List* details the shaving, disrobing, and frightened huddling together of mostly young women, seen through a round glass opening, resembling a peephole. These shots, which culminate in scenes of water pouring out of the shower heads, resemble the frames characteristic of Hitchcock's *Psycho*, where Norman Bates, whose gaze alternates with that of the audience's, voyeuristically enjoys the sight of his victim's undressing and nude indulgence in the pleasures of a shower. Noting a similar pattern in *Schindler's List*, Omer Bartov writes:

> [I]t seems that Spielberg, possibly unconsciously, catered to Hollywood's tradition of providing sexual distraction to the viewers. Most troubling of all, of course, is the shower scene, since that mass of attractive, frightened, naked women, finally relieved from their anxiety by jets of water rather than gas, would be more appropriate to a soft-porn sadomasochistic film than its context … (1996: 49)

Spielberg, in *Schindler's List*, simulates this series of shots in a manner that appears to reverse the order of *Psycho*, rather than directly replicate that sequence. Nevertheless, even this time, the camera hovers from the side, rather than directly below the showerhead, still maintaining the position of the voyeur.

Despite the allusions to *Psycho*'s psychologically complex Norman Bates and Fiennes' masterful performance, it becomes increasingly clear that Amon Goeth, unlike Norman Bates, is psychologically two-dimensional at best. Ultimately, Spielberg's portrait of Goeth renders him inscrutably, perhaps even congenitally or genetically evil, and therefore, thoroughly and monstrously other. As Quentin Curtis (1994: 18) remarks: "Though Fiennes gives a compellingly detailed psychological portrait, Spielberg hints that Goeth's evil may be *innate* [italics mine]." Goeth, who appears overly cathected to guns and is similarly addicted to alcohol and sex, emerges as a powerful instantiation of this second, hyper-masculinized shadow. Like Anthony Perkins, Ralph Fiennes, despite his gaining weight in order to play the part of the debauched hedonist, displays a boyish attractiveness, and has been described by J. Hoberman as "a dead-eyed, baby-faced Caligula" (1994: 65). Yet unlike Perkins's Bates — whom the audience learns not only to care about, but also to identify with, at least until the moment of revelation of the killer's identity — Goeth's humanness is displayed mainly through his excesses, which render him a fascinating figure, though one difficult to identify with, much like Hannibal Lecter in *Silence of the Lambs* (1991). In fact, Spielberg himself seemed aware of the possible parallelism, which he tried to obscure: "[I] had Fiennes play many of his scenes 'behind dull, drink-shrouded eyes, because I don't want him to become the Hannibal Lecter of the Holocaust genre'" (quoted in Richardson, 2000: 163).

The resonances binding Goeth to the compellingly repulsive figure of the cult psychopath have not gone unnoticed by critics. Ken Jacobs, in a collective interview conducted by J. Hoberman (1994) remarks, "What's bothering some of us is that this is a trendy movie — it's sexy psychopath season — about a kind of Jekyll and Hyde character split between two major male characters." The seduction-turned-torture scene features Goeth's clumsy attempt to confess his feelings to a silent and immobilized Helen, and ultimately culminates in his brutal beating of her. Once again, the catharsis of violence substitutes for repressed sexual desire, and establishes his active hyper-masculinity against her passive hyper-femininity, though it is clear that Goeth is depicted as being in the reactive position. As Philip Koplin (1994) notes, Helen's depiction reifies the all-too-common view that Jewish women "possess a passive sex magic that beguiles and imperils Aryan virtue."

It is clear that the narrative space Helen Hirsch occupies converges with the dangerous and endangered space Marion Crane occupies in *Psycho*. Her sexually charged and imperiled body becomes the backdrop against which the story of Goeth's insanity is told. The fact that Helen, in that crucial basement and second implied shower scene just happens to be wearing skimpy white underclothing that reveals, rather than hides, her figure, is no less significant than the fact that Goeth, long before this scene, has been established as an irrational and pathological cipher. Helen's physical and emotional vulnerability are heightened through shots that show her body glistening, wet, through the sheer fabric, whose whiteness against the dark backdrop, is emphasized. It is not clear why her body is wet — it could be that she was taking a shower when Goeth surprised her (because her hair is also damp and clings to her face) — but it could also be that fear has caused her to perspire excessively (Figure 30.1). Yet if it is perspiration, it is not depicted as an animal secretion but as an aphrodisiac-like sweat that simulates the exertions of sexual excitement; her heavy breathing as her breast heaves with fear does little to dispel the eroticized

Figure 30.1   The second "shower scene" in *Schindler's List* (1993): Helen's skimpy wet attire and heavy breathing creates an eroticized amalgam of courtship and stalking. Directed by Steven Spielberg. Produced by Universal Pictures and Amblin Entertainment.

atmosphere of this strange amalgam of courtship and stalking. Sara Horowitz concurs with these observations on the not-too-subtle politics of the gaze in this particular scene:

> As Goeth catches sight of her and she fills the camera's gaze, Helen is clothed in an inexplicably wet shift which clings to her breasts. The audience thus anticipates in Goeth's erotic gaze. Like Goeth, the viewer is meant to desire Helen's body, visually sexualized by the wet clothing. As Goeth's desire resolves in a physical beating, the audience participates in a voyeurism which encompasses both sex and brutality, with the victimized Jewish woman as its object. (1997: 127–128)

Weissman's analysis of the film (2004: 157) provides some important production history that supports the claims of this chapter even more vividly. He asserts that Thomas Keneally's novel is perhaps more notable for its omissions, rather than its exaggerations, which are magnified in the film. Helena Sternlicht was Goeth's house-maid at his villa by the Plaszow camp; she shared a room in the villa's basement with another house servant named Helena Hirsch. Keneally consulted with Hirsch, but Sternlicht, because she was approached at the time she was mourning her husband's death, declined to be interviewed. Consequently, Sternlicht was effaced from the novel as well as the film, whereas "Helen" Hirsch figures prominently in both:

> Spielberg's film goes further than the novel in depicting Hirsch as Goeth's solitary maid, creating a special relationship between the Commandant and the Jewess...

> The film … fabricates an overtly sexual relationship between Goeth and Helen, eroticizing his violent treatment of her … As Horowitz points out, this scene, having no basis in the historical record, is beholden to a tradition of depicting eroticized female victims in films and novels on the Holocaust, such as *The Night Porter* (1974) and *Sophie's Choice*. (Weissman, 2004: 157)

It is hardly surprising that Helen remains silent as Goeth indulges in his monologue, which begins as an apparent attempt to reach out to the young woman, and ends in his cruel verbal and physical abuse of her as subhuman vermin. Any sympathy that might have been elicited by Goeth's clumsy attempt to come to terms with his forbidden desire is instantly shredded. He again emerges as the prototypic Nazi male: inhumanly exploitative, devoid of genuine compassion, incapable of apprehending moral issues. Through such narrative techniques of eroticization and distance, the audience is allowed to share Goeth's sadistic and pornographic gaze, and yet is allowed to deny this affinity by depicting Goeth as Purely Monstrous. *Schindler's List* invites the viewer to take on a "murderous gaze" of violent and eroticized images under the guise of a supposedly "documentary" look (Rothman, 1998: 251).

Leveraging the Anxieties of the Documentary Impulse through Dark Humor

I now move on to a second attempt by Spielberg to conjoin the documentary impulse with horror, but this time also employing, to some extent, *dark* humor (by which I do not mean, simplistically, the "funny" or "laughable"). To truncate the theoretical core of my reflections on the complex conjunctions binding horror, the documentary impulse, and humor (broadly construed), I draw analogically from Noël Carroll's explorations into the nature of the monstrous in relation to humor. However, I transform those insights in relation to Spielberg's film because his version resists cathartic release and instead compounds incongruity and tension, drawing the look of realism to an extreme that refuses the usual narrative resolutions characteristic of the classic Hollywood style, which Spielberg expertly wielded in *Schindler's List*. In contrast, it is significant that though *Munich* (2005) was nominated for five Academy Awards, it did not win a single Academy Award.

I begin with an analysis of the structure of what constitutes the "monstrous" because the subject of *Munich* — terrorists (and their evolving mirror-images, counter-terrorists — constitute probably the most gripping contemporary iteration of a type of Gothic criminological creature, straddling both horror and the real/reel, with a close affinity to serial killers (Picart and Greek, 2007: 256–288). In his book *Philosophy of Horror*, Carroll observes that monsters, the quintessential embodiments of horror, "are beings or creatures that specialize in formlessness, incompleteness, categorical interstitiality, and categorical contradictoriness … Horrific monsters often involve the mixture of what is normally distinct" (1990: 32–33). In a more recent piece, Carroll turns to affinities binding humor and horror as conventionally configured antitheses to beauty (2000: 37–56). He notes that both horror and humor, broadly and structurally construed, root themselves in the terrain of the "ugly" (2000: 39), for example, the not-beautiful clown and not-quite-human monster, and in category violations for creatures of horror (e.g., simultaneously alive and dead; animate and inanimate; human and animal), and conceptual incongruity for humor. In addition, Carroll's comments on the unseen political effects of seemingly value-free aesthetic pronouncements are instructive:

> If beauty—the perfect realization of the concept of the human—rhetorically implies goodness, ugliness and category violation encourage the suspicion of evil and moral defectiveness. Where beauty can be used to valorize, horror and humor can be used to dehumanize and vilify … (2000: 53)

Though Carroll is right to point out the similarities and differences between humor and horror based on category violation and its political import (the alienation of the other), Carroll makes essentially the same assumption that Zakiya Hanafi does in *The Monster in the Machine*. She repeatedly characterizes the monster by negation—"A monster is whatever we are *not*" (2000: viii).

While I applaud these analyses as highly insightful, they constitute only a partial explanation of monstrosity (and the nature of horror as a film genre). This characterization of the monster as a "not-I" would explain the fear and suspicion with which monsters have been increasingly treated as their sacred origins have been sundered, but it does not adequately explain why there is a continuing fascination with, and ambivalent admiration of, monsters. Hanafi herself observes in her Afterword: "Our favorite contemporary monster of all—the extraterrestrial—always arrives in a spaceship born from a superior technology. More often than not, we envy their superior advancement. Perhaps the truth is that we all secretly yearn to be aliens" (2000: 218). Thus, monsters are the liminal point of *not only* what we are *not*, but also what we *are*; they reveal and conceal not only what we *fear* but also what we *hope for*; and allow us imaginatively to excavate the depths of not only who we *could be* in relation to nature and divinity, but also who we *are* in relation to the daemons that lurk within. This insight is crucial, as I shall show, particularly in a film like *Munich*, where the heroic figure seems but a hair's breadth away from the villains he hunts.

In cinema and literature, both humor and horror have progressive and regressive political tendencies. Humor and horror destabilize and problematize only to fall back, many times, but not all the time, on some iteration of a conventional "ending." There is something similar to this dynamic in *Munich*, but in it, "closure" is never fully achieved, and the tension built by sustained and multiple layers of incongruity never gets diffused through laughter. The emphasis on plural hybridity that is characteristic of the portraiture of monsters is crucial to my analysis of how horror is configured in relation to humor. To explain this, I adopt some aspects of Arthur Koestler's notion of "bisociation"—a condition, Koestler explains, that compels us to interpret the situation in "two self-consistent but incompatible frames of reference at the same time; it makes us function simultaneously on two different wave-lengths" (1978: 112–113). The tension caused by bisociation can be potentially purged either through laughter, scientific fusion, or through artistic confrontation (Koestler, 1978: 129).

What I explore below is how bisociation, as well as an uneasy and complex tension between the "monstrous" and the "all too human" constitute the fulcrum on which the darkly humorous, the tragic, and the horrifying converge. *Munich* explores those uneasy tensions in relation to a traumatic and real historical event: the massacre of 11 Israeli athletes by Palestinian terrorists in the 1972 Munich Olympics. Yet the movie is less about the killings and more about Israel's retaliatory response, and the age-old question regarding whether the morals and politics of "an eye for an eye" ever works. Nevertheless, from the start, the bisociation of "documentary" and "arty" formal properties make the issue of what "looks" authentic paramount. Indeed, the film—partly because of political anxieties (Goldberg, 2012: 1; AbuKhalil, 2012: 1) and partly because it depicts shadowy incidents with some basis in actual historical events—constantly attempts to deflect how closely it depicts "reality" even while reinforcing the look of the real. The film begins with an enormous title card that declares the film to be "Inspired by True Events," a strategic move that Howe described as a gesture of "dazzling ambiguity" (2006: 1).

For example, the issue of "genre" was crucial to marketing the film. For Kathleen Kennedy, Spielberg's longtime friend and producing partner—allegedly the one who persisted in overcoming Spielberg's qualms on approaching this topic (Schickel, 2005: 3)—"[T]his [was] clearly a thriller from a movie-making standpoint" (3). Kennedy declared that they were "not making a documentary" (3). Nevertheless, Kennedy and Spielberg seemed to arrive at the compromise term, *historical fiction* to describe their project (3), and Spielberg seemed particularly concerned that *Munich* not become cast in the same class as Clint Eastwood's *Dirty Harry* and Charles Bronson's *Death Wish* action-revenge films (Levy, 2012: 2). Spielberg stressed that the "fictional" part lay largely in the "interpersonal relationships of the five members of the ex-Mossad team" (Schickel, 2005: 3). Spielberg explained the use of the explanatory/defensive use of the title placard by saying: "I was very careful … to start the movie by saying 'Inspired by real events' [sic], because until the secret files are opened up nobody will really know actually who did what" (3). The film's press notes give an even more detailed account of how the filmmakers created a complex rhetorical dance both officially disavowing and yet emphatically reinforcing the film's connection to "real" historical events.

> In the press notes, the filmmakers claim that though neither Israeli government, nor the Mossad, had ever acknowledged the existence of such hit squads, several books and documentaries, utilizing inside sources, have since provided details of how the team carried out its goals. They cite two Israeli generals, who have publicly confirmed that the target assassination squads did exist: General Aharon Yariv in a 1993 documentary, and General Zvi Zamar in a 2001 interview for *60 Minutes*. (Levy, 2012: 2)

Spielberg's film focuses on a small Israeli killing team: five men, more or less ordinary, tasked with hunting and destroying the Palestinian Black September planners of the Munich massacre across Europe and the Middle East in the fall and winter of that year. As Stephen Hunter observes, Spielberg's killers

> still kill the old-fashioned way, by bomb and gun, and almost always they're close enough to see the blood in lakes on the dirty floors, or the limbs hanging as if meat-hooked to the ceiling after the detonation. It's not pretty, it's not Hollywood, it has the scabrous dirty feel of reality.... And the killers, being human themselves and not bull-goose loonies, get sick and tired of it. (2005: 1)

The screenplay for *Munich* (credited to Tony Kushner and Eric Roth) draws much of its material from a book by George Jonas (1984) called *Vengeance: The True Story of an Israeli Counter-Terrorist Team*, though many doubts have been raised about its authenticity. Other books, such as Aaron J. Klein's *Striking Back: The 1972 Munich Olympics Massacre and Israel's Deadly Response* (2005) tell differing accounts of these events. Jonas ascribes the Israeli action to one team; Klein suggests a much wider operation with teams combining and recombining as circumstances warranted over the months. Nevertheless, both books agree: Israeli assassins went hunting and hunted hard—and that forms the narrative nucleus of the film. Kushner, prizewinning author of *Angels in America*, allegedly worked on the 300-page first draft with Spielberg for a year, and the two agreed on the following arrangement: according to Spielberg "You [Kushner] speak the words, and I'll provide the pictures" (Schickel, 2005: 3). Kushner was allegedly on the set for the shooting of the film 90% of the time, which is unusual for a screenwriter (3). Kennedy verified that "[w]hen something was more action driven, Steven would take the lead ... and when something was more dialogue driven, Tony would take the lead" (3). For Spielberg, collaborating with Kushner was "as close as I've ever come to directing a play" (3).

Perhaps the most arresting sequence in the movie is its beginning, with its meshing of the realms of the documentary and the fictional in a McLuhanite frenzy.

Actual news clips featuring Jim McKay, Peter Jennings, and others are used during a 15-min prologue. Yet the documentary footage does not remain "naked," as Manohla Dargis notes:

> With its art-directed verisimilitude and promiscuous use of archival material (Jim McKay makes a cameo appearance in the film, as does the voice of Peter Jennings), *Munich* is one of those Hollywood fictions that seem to befuddle those who miss the nuance in the words "inspired by real events." (2005: 1)

In addition, Eleanor Ringel Gillespie points out:

> The picture revisits the unspeakable incident repeatedly, sometimes as actual news footage, other times as reenactments of what may have gone on inside the athletes' rooms or on the airport runway where everything fell apart. In one bit of virtuoso film-making, Spielberg films a terrorist in a ski mask heading out to the balcony and then cuts to the infamous real-life image of him out there, machine gun in hand. (2005: 2)

Yet despite the film's reliance on the "look" of the "real," the film's multiple hybridities (docu-drama, action thriller) result in uneasy and humorous tensions, some of which are more "forgivable" than others. Indeed, there is evidence that Kushner's use of a "dry, allusive, sometimes bleakly comic language" (Schickel, 2005: 3) was what set the tone, and the eventual graphic look, of the film (3). Nevertheless, Dargis (2005: 2), partly tongue in cheek, notes:

> Despite the brief pop-cultural dissonance brought on by the sight of the Incredible Hulk, whom Mr. Bana played in the 2003 blockbuster, sharing the screen with the new James Bond (Mr. Craig) and HBO's Julius Caesar (Mr. Hinds), the actors quickly make these character types their own.

Dargis continues:

> *Munich* is as much a meditation on ethics as a political thriller, but it takes nothing away from the film to say that the most adrenaline-spiked part of this genre hybrid involves getaway cars, false papers and the sight of the future Israeli Prime Minister, Ehud Barak, who pops up during a mission in Lebanon, mowing down terrorists while dressed in a woman's wig and high heels. (2005: 1)

Anthony Lane picks up the more pernicious aspects of humor in relation to stereotyping when he notes:

> *Munich* is a fidgety, international affair, and the cultural clichés come direct from your travel agent: Eiffel Tower for Paris, bicycles for Holland, and feast-laden tables for Israelis, wherever they are—plus a running gag about getting a receipt for expenses, which, to my taste, seemed moldy with prejudice. Spielberg is plainly nervous about the impulse behind this scene, which is why he tosses in wisecracks, further flashbacks to Munich, soft chats between Avner and his mother, and anything else he can, so as to honor and legitimize a series of state-approved kills. (2005: 2)

Indeed, there are many bisociative juxtapositions in the film that could be justified as "arty," which are ethically problematic: for example, the juxtaposition of Avner's brutal copulation with his wife as the Israeli athletes are violently murdered; the erotic aestheticization of the vicious murder of the Dutch femme fatale, whose naked breasts heave as she tries to breathe with a hole in her chest; the dreamy and bucolic settings against which deadly negotiations with a French godfather are made (Figure 30.2). Nevertheless, perhaps the most serious denunciation of the film's connection to history seems to be one of omission. As Tunzelmann observes:

> It's incongruous in this context [of allegedly attempting a careful narrative "balance"] that Spielberg leaves out the most famous blunder [of the Israeli Mossad]. On 21 July 1973, Israeli gunmen shot and killed a Moroccan waiter called Ahmed Bouchiki in Lillehammer, Norway. They had mistaken him for Black September mastermind Ali Hassan Salameh … In Jonas's book, the Lillehammer affair is attributed not to Aviv but to a different cell. Perhaps that is the reason it isn't here. Also, the film is already half an hour too long … (2012: 3)

Figure 30.2   Ethically problematic? The erotic aestheticization of the Dutch femme fatale's vicious murder in *Munich* (2005). Directed by Steven Spielberg. Produced by DreamWorks SKG, Universal Pictures, Amblin Entertainment, The Kennedy/Marshall Company, Barry Mendel Productions, Alliance Atlantis Communications, and Peninsula Films.

In many ways, *Munich* is the most un-Spielberg-ian of Spielberg films. It avoids the usual saccharine and sentimentalist endings characteristic of his other works, such as *Schindler's List* and *The Color Purple* (1985). The film ends with what appears to be an insight replete with Kafka-esque-like touches, juxtaposing the horror-banality of serial murder in the name of a political cause with the banality-horror of accounting for receipts to finance this activity. As Murphy observes: "In the film's powerful conclusion, Avner meets Ephraim in Brooklyn. Avner fruitlessly asks for evidence that the men he killed were involved in planning Munich, bringing full circle the theme of accountability set up earlier in the film by a Mossad accountant repetitively asking Avner to save his receipts" (Murphy, 2006: 3).

Tellingly, in an interview with Roger Ebert, Spielberg claimed that *Munich* says, ultimately, "I don't have an answer" (quoted in Reich, 2006: 1). That assessment is in line with Kushner's declaration that he "never like[s] to draw lessons for people … It's not an essay; it's an art" (quoted Schickel, 2005: 3). In the end, *Munich*'s Avner becomes a self-imposed, bitter exile. At one point, when two young Israeli soldiers express admiration for what he has done, he recoils in horror. However, it is worth noting that this dark, existential theme is one Spielberg did not sound in *Saving Private Ryan* (1998). In that film, he argued quite the opposite: kill them until they're all gone. The last shot of *Munich*—which returns to a ghostly vision of the Twin Towers during the 1970s, alongside Avner's being alone (his invitation of "breaking bread" with him and his family refused by a fellow Israeli citizen)—does not offer the moral security Spielberg's earlier films did. In some senses, *Munich* seems to have learned essential lessons from Roman Polanski's *The Pianist* (2002), not only formally but also thematically. Indeed, the stark blue light that infuses much of *The Pianist* increasingly becomes a piercingly cold and gray light in *Munich*. *Munich* is not so much about a hero, as much as an ordinary man with simple convictions and loyalties: to serve his country and to provide for his family. Those

Figure 30.3 In our post 9/11 world, the final shot of the Twin Towers in *Munich* (2005) suggests moral insecurity rather than certainty. Directed by Steven Spielberg. Produced by DreamWorks SKG, Universal Pictures, Amblin Entertainment, The Kennedy/Marshall Company, Barry Mendel Productions, Alliance Atlantis Communications, and Peninsula Films.

certainties, in a manner resembling Kakfa's novels, are violently sundered as the movie proceeds (Figure 30.3).

To close this section, Palmer, quoting Morreall (1983), distilled out three types of theories connecting the structure of incongruity with humor and laughter. These are: (i) where humor springs from a sense of superiority over the target of the joke; (ii) where humor is a result of the sensation of psychological relief; and (iii) where humor "derives from the perception of incongruity in what is laughed at" (Palmer, 1994: 94). The third theory perhaps approximates the dynamic of Spielberg's *Munich*, with the exception that save for occasional nervous and temporary titters characteristic of gallows humor, the film is unrelenting in its exposure of these incongruous juxtapositions; no catharsis or resolution occurs. In some ways, this is hardly surprising, as comic relief becomes possible only with distance, with the deactivation of a perceived threat (Palmer 100). And that is not currently possible, with either the situation in the Middle East, or the enduring traumatic memory of 9/11, unlike, to some extent, the history of the Shoah.

Conclusion

This chapter has attempted to show how Spielberg's use of documentary film techniques involves a dialectic between real historical events and reel-world events (cinematic depictions that move across fact and fiction). In *Schindler's List*, Spielberg's appropriation of horror-derived techniques of narration, specifically from *Psycho*, serves to cement the "real" look of his supposed historical documentary, despite the numerous instances of poetic license he took in creating the film. The stock horror characters of psychopathic Monster and hyper-feminized and helpless victim became reinterpreted as the "real" characters of Amon Goeth and

Helena Hirsch. The use of black and white film (with the exceptions previously noted) was unabashedly marketed as "the look of the real." The "shower scenes" of the Schindler women's near brush with death is shot in a manner that mimes *Psycho*'s shower scene but reverses its narrative to become not a story of near-horror, but ultimately, one of redemption. Helena's brutal victimization by Goeth in the basement scene clearly features the revolving, stalking gaze characteristic of serial killer films, in which the audience partakes of the killer's voyeuristic gaze. Yet, despite the prolific use of nondocumentary techniques to tell the story of a real historical event, Spielberg conceals these fictional techniques of cinematic storytelling to make the look of the "real" even more "authentic."

In contrast, in *Munich*, Spielberg's hybrid use of the documentary format reveals a restlessness with standard cinematic devices of storytelling to depict a real event. Yet despite Spielberg's consistent reliance on the "look" of the "real" (though this time in a muted color), the film's multiple hybridities in genre (docu-drama, action thriller) results in uneasy and darkly humorous tensions. Again, the eroticization of violence occurs in this film, as in the juxtaposition between Avner's violent love-making and the Israeli athletes as they are viciously murdered, and the graphic aestheticization of the Dutch femme fatale' vicious murder, during which the audience participates in her killer's gaze. But unlike *Schindler's List*, there is no attempt to hide the restlessness—the heart of darkness—that lies at the center of the movie. *Munich*'s bisociative use of unrelenting incongruity, with varying degrees of darkness and attempts at ironic distance, probably shaped by Kushner's script, does much more to make the audience aware of the complex relationships binding the real and the reel.

Note

1. Adapted from: Caroline Joan S. Picart and David Frank, *Frames of Evil: The Holocaust as Horror in American Film*. Carbondale, IL: Southern Illinois University Press, 2006.

References

AbuKhalil, A. (2012) "Munich": The Humanization of Israeli Killers, and the Dehumanization of Palestinian Civilians, http://www.revisionisthistory.org/steinsaltz.html (accessed 11 March 2014).

Bartov, O. (1996) Ordinary monsters. *New Republic*, **214**, 32–38.

Brenner, D. (2000) Working through the holocaust blockbuster: 'Schindler's List' and Hitler's willing executioners, globally and locally. *Germanic Review*, **75**, 296–316.

Byrge, B. (1993) Schindler's List. *Hollywood Reporter* (Dec 6), p. 6.

Carroll, N. (1990) *Philosophy of Horror, or Paradoxes of the Heart*, Routledge, New York, NY.

Carroll, N. (2000) Ethnicity, race, and monstrosity: the rhetorics of horror and humor, in *Beauty Matters* (ed. P.G. Brand), Indiana University Press, Bloomington, IN.

Curtis, Q. (1994) Lest We Forget. *Independent on Sunday* (Feb 13) (London), p. 18.

Dargis, M. (2005) An Action Film about the need to Talk. *The New York Times* (Dec 23), http://www.nytimes.com/2005/12/23/movies/23muni.html?ex=1166850000&en =813ac1e98b64d79d&ei=5083&partner=ROTTEN_TOMATOES& excamp=mkt:5083 (accessed 19 October 2012).

Denby, D. (1993) Unlikely Hero. *New Yorker* (Dec 13), p. 82.

Edmundson, M. (1997) *Nightmare on Main Street: Angels, Sadomasochism and the Culture of the Gothic*, Harvard University Press, Cambridge, MA.

Gillespie, E.R. (2005) Murder Takes its Toll in 'Munich'. *Atlanta Journal Constitution* (Dec 23).

Goldberg, M. (2012) Profoundly flattering to Israel. Revisionisthistory.org, http://www .revisionisthistory.org/steinsaltz.html (accessed 12 March 2014).

Gough-Yates, K. (1972) Private madness and public lunacy. *Films and Filming*, **18**, pp. 27, 30.

Grunwald, L. (1993) Steven Spielberg Gets Real. *Life* (Dec), pp. 54, 58.

Hanafi, Z. (2000) *The Monster in the Machine: Magic, Medicine and the Marvelous in the Time of the Scientific Revolution*, Duke University Press, Durham, NC.

Hoberman, J. (1994) Myth, Movie, Memory. *Village Voice* (Mar 29), pp. 24–31.

Horowitz, S. (1997) But is it good for the Jews? Spielberg's Schindler and the aesthetics of atrocity, in *Spielberg's Holocaust: Critical Perspectives on 'Schindler's List'* (ed. Y. Loshitzsky), Indiana University Press, Bloomington, IN.

Howe, S. (2006) 'Munich': Spielberg's Failure. *Open Democracy* (Jan), http://www .opendemocracy.net/arts-Film/munich_3216.jsp (accessed 12 March 2014).

Hunter, S. (2005) Spielberg's 'Munich': The Circle of Death. *The Washington Post* (Dec), http:// www.washingtonpost.com/wp-dyn/content/article/2005/12/22/AR2005122202142 .html (accessed 19 October 2012).

Jenkins, S. (1994) Stories that Get in the Way of Facts. *Times* (Mar 12) (London).

Koestler, A. (1978) *Janus: A Summing Up*, Hutchinson, London.

Koplin, P. (1994) Why is this Film (No) Different from any Other Film? *Santa Barbara Independent* (Mar 24).

Lane, A. (2005) The Other. *New Yorker* (Dec 19), http://www.newyorker.com/critics/cinema /articles/051226crci_cinema (accessed 19 October 2012).

Levy, E. (2012) Munich: Spielberg's hot-button movie. Emmanuellevy.com, http://www .emanuellevy.com/comment/munich-spielbergs-hot-button-movie-6/ (accessed 12 March 2014).

Lyman, S. (1990) Rereading Robert E. Park: toward a gothic perspective on capitalism and imperialism, in *Explorations: The Age of Enlightenment* (ed. M.W. Duquesnay), University of Southwestern Louisiana Foundation, Lafayette, LA.

Morreall, J. (1983) *Taking Laughter Seriously*, SUNY Press, New York.

Munich (2005) Universal Studios. http://www.universalstudiosentertainment.com/munich/ (accessed 12 March 2014).

Murphy, M.C. (2006) 'Munich': Spielberg's Thrilling Crisis of Conscience. *The Electronic Intifada* (Jan 14), http://electronicintifada.net/content/munich-spielbergs-thrilling -crisis-conscience/5833 (accessed 12 March 2014).

Palmer, J. (1994) *Taking Humour Seriously*, Routledge, New York.

Palowski, F. (1998) *The Making of 'Schindler's List'* (trans. A. Ware and R.G. Ware), Birch Lane, Secaucus, NJ.

Picart, C.J. and Browning, J. (2012) *Speaking of Monsters: A Teratological Anthology*, Palgrave Macmillan, New York, NY.

Picart, C.J. and Frank, D.A. (2006) *Frames of Evil: The Holocaust as Horror in American Film*, Southern Illinois University Press, Carbondale, IL.

Picart, C.J. and Greek, C. (2007) *Monsters in and Among Us: Towards a Gothic Criminology*, Fairleigh Dickinson University Press, Madison NJ.

Reed, J.D. and Cunneff, T. (1999) Steven Spielberg. *People* (Mar 15), pp. 138–141.

Reich, W. (2006) Something's Missing in Spielberg's 'Munich.' *Washington Post* (Jan 1), http://www .washingtonpost.com/wp-dyn/content/article/2005/12/30/AR2005123001581.html (accessed 12 March 2014).

Richardson, J.H. (2000) Steven's choice, in *Steven Spielberg: Interviews* (eds L.D. Friedman and B. Notbohm), University of Mississippi Press, Jackson, MS.

Rothberg, M. (2000) *Traumatic Realism: The Demands of Holocaust Representation*, University of Minnesota Press, Minneapolis, MN.

Rothman, W. (1998) The filmmaker as hunter: Robert Flaherty's 'Nanook of the North', in *Documenting the Documentary: Close Readings of Documentary Film and Video* (eds B.K. Grant and J. Sloniowski), Wayne State University Press, Detroit, MI.

Schickel, R. (1993) Heart of Darkness. *Time* (Dec 13), pp. 75–76.

Schickel, R. (2005) Spielberg Takes on Terror. *Time* (Dec 4), http://www.time.com/time /magazine/article/0,9171,1137679,00.html (accessed 12 March 2014).

Sterritt, D. (1999) *The Films of Alfred Hitchcock*, Cambridge University Press, New York, NY.

Syal, R. and Norton, C. (1998) Cut! How Hitchcock Took Knife to 'Psycho'. *The Sunday Times* (Oct 6) (London).

Tunzelmann, A.V. (2012) Spielberg's Munich: Earnestly Searching for Truths that Refuse to be Found. *The Guardian* (Mar 15), http://www.guardian.co.uk/film/2012/mar/15 /reel-history-spielberg-munich (accessed 12 March 2014).

Weissman, G. (2004) *Fantasies of Witnessing: Postwar Efforts to Experience the Holocaust*, Cornell University Press, Ithaca, NY.

Wieseltier, L. (1994) Close Encounters of the Nazi Kind. *New Republic* (Jan 24), p. 42.

Zaillian, S. (1990) '*Schindler's List*', A Screenplay Based on the Novel by Thomas Keneally. Academy of Motion Picture Arts and Sciences Script Collection.

Index

A Companion to the Horror Film, First Edition. Edited by Harry M. Benshoff.
© 2014 John Wiley & Sons, Inc. Published 2017 by John Wiley & Sons, Inc.